Ethics and the Good Life

ETHICS AND THE GOOD LIFE

A Text with Readings

Brad Art

Westfield State College

Wadsworth Publishing Company
Belmont, California ∗ *A Division of Wadsworth, Inc.*

Philosophy Editor: *Kenneth King*
Editorial Assistant: *Kristina Pappas*
Production: *Merrill Peterson, Matrix Productions*
Print Buyer: *Karen Hunt*
Permissions Editor: *Jeanne Bosschart*
Copy Editor: *Victoria Nelson*
Cover Design: *Harry Voigt*
Cover Illustration: *Ambrogio Lorenzetti.* The Effects of Good Government. *Detail of the City Scene. Siena, Palazzo Pubblico, Scala/Art Resource, NY.*
Compositor: *Graphic Composition*
Printer: *Arcata Graphics/Fairfield*

1 2 3 4 5 6 7 8 9 10—98 97 96 95 94

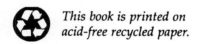

This book is printed on
acid-free recycled paper.

Library of Congress Cataloging-in-Publication Data

Art, Brad.
    Ethics and the good life: a text with readings / Brad Art.
        p. cm.
    Includes bibliographical references and index.
    ISBN 0-534-17653-4
    1. Ethics. I. Title.
    [BJ1012.A695 1993b]
    170—dc20
                                                    93-6669
                                                    CIP

To another of no finer making,
Gloria

Contents

2. What Is Morality?

3. What About Belief in God?

4. Isn't Everyone Different?   85

5. What If I Do Whatever I Want?   112

Part Two   *Philosophers Answer the Questions*

Introduction

6. *Authority and Freedom: A Discussion with the Grand Inquisitor*

7. *Freedom and Self Control: A Discussion with Epictetus*

8. The Greatest Good for the Greatest Number: The Philosophy of John Stuart Mill

9. Absolute Moral Values and Reason: A Conversation with Immanuel Kant

10. Existentialist Ethics: Jean-Paul Sartre's Ideas on Being Free   253

Part Three   *Does Morality Answer the Questions?*

Introduction   292

11. Is Life Meaningful or Absurd?: The Wisdom of Solomon and Sisyphus   295

12. How Can We Relate with Other People?: A Talk with Martin Buber   322

13. What Is the Best Life?
The Virtuous Sage of Spinoza and Lao Tsu   343

Part Four   *Moral Questions*

Introduction   370

14. Sexual Morality   374

Preface

What is the best life? How can I live it? These two questions are fundamental in each person's life. How we answer them defines who we are. Of course, there are spells when we ignore them. "Real" life has a way of distracting us from our philosophical wonderings. But when we return to these questions, we recognize that all other concerns pale in comparison. No matter how successful, or popular, or accepted, or wealthy a person may become, the questions of the best life are more important. We all want to know how to live, and to live well. *Ethics and the Good Life* explores a variety of philosophical theories that reply to these fundamental questions.

Objectives

Ethics and the Good Life has three main objectives. It teaches students (1) how and why the questions and answers of philosophers matter to them, (2) how to read original philosophical texts critically and sympathetically, and (3) how to think carefully about living well.

An Accessible Writing Style

One problem in teaching ethics is engaging students in thinking critically about morality and the best life. *Ethics and the Good Life* brings the issues to students in their own terms, and in a context they understand. Although each chapter introduces sophisticated concepts, the presentation is free of technical philosophical jargon. For example, Kierkegaard's aesthete, A, embraces metaphysical and epistemic assumptions radically different from those our students and other moralists make.

Yet his definitions of the self, other people, and freedom that lead him to despair are discussed without using language that might intimidate or confuse the student.

Another problem is that students often have difficulty reading and understanding sustained arguments. Philosophers write to present ideas for consideration and to remedy philosophical problems. Philosophical writings, however, are difficult to understand. They can overwhelm students. This is especially true when an argument is developed in a book-length work and written by a philosopher in philosophical language. For example, Kant's *Groundwork of the Metaphysics of Morals* is an important work in ethics, and should be examined in ethics courses, but it is difficult for the novice to understand. To remedy this problem, *Ethics and the Good Life* "recreates" philosophers. Without sacrificing rigor, the student discusses the position presented with the actual "living" philosopher. Led by Art's comments and questions, readers learn to critically evaluate the philosopher's own words and arguments, but in manageable "bites." To bring the point "home" to students, the philosophers' points are interpreted and evaluated as they are discussed, then are summarized at the end of each chapter. By introducing questions and concepts in approachable language and manageable segments, this book makes the works of philosophers understandable and compelling. It equips students to read and appreciate original works in philosophy and related disciplines.

Ethics and the Good Life encourages students to *do* philosophy, not merely to learn about it. For example, Dostoevski's Grand Inquisitor directly challenges students' belief in their freedom to select their careers, friends, and interests. It requires a good deal of thinking to counter the Inquisitor's claim that people are merely frightened sheep.

The book also encourages students to make intellectual leaps on their own. As the questions are refined and more precisely expressed, the discussion urges students to connect ideas and to synthesize positions. Epictetus' reply to the Stranger's caprice is that freedom is self-mastery. Kant's reliance on reason to guarantee autonomy is also a response to the hedonist's passionate abandon. Students are encouraged to make these connections and to see the synthesis of Epictetus and Kant proposed by Sartre.

Organization

The material has been organized to allow flexibility in the classroom. It is organized around the central questions in the first two chapters: What is morality? and What is the point of living the moral life? The instructor should feel free to skip around after Chapter 2. The chapters within Part Two are written without reference to earlier discussions within that part; each chapter can stand alone. The present order of readings has served me well, but I encourage you to experiment with thematic or historical organization.

Ethics and the Good Life differs in two ways from my text, *What Is the Best Life?* First, it includes a reading following each chapter in Parts Two and Three. I have two motivations for including the readings in Parts Two and Three. (1) The dialogues within the text are designed to give students the skills necessary to profitably read philosophy. Including readings further promotes these skills and allows students to benefit from reading original sources. (2) Students can see alterations in themes within philosophy and the persistent development of these ideas. Kant's insistence on reason is corroborated by Rawls's use of the veil of ignorance. Buber's sometimes enigmatic urgings toward relating are clarified by Hume's description of "social sympathy." Socrates' own words in the *Apology* effectively exemplify the dignity, freedom, and responsibility urged by Sartre in the accompanying chapter text.

Ethics and the Good Life also contains a set of readings in applied moral issues. Part Four brings to the student contemporary readings on sexual morality, abortion, discrimination and preferential treatment, capital punishment, and animals and the environment. I find it effective to mix applied issues and moral theory. Not only does this mixing provide a change of pace for students, it also helps them develop their considered judgments on current issues. Studying contemporary thinkers' analyses further demonstrates to students the importance of understanding moral theory. Each chapter in Part Four also stands on its own.

Coverage

Ethics and the Good Life is more than an analysis of traditional moral philosophy. Although it incorporates a discussion of Kant and Mill, the book challenges morality as merely one way of living and compares morality with other visions of living. The discussion of four varieties of freedoms in the chapter on Epictetus is an example of this ongoing comparison.

As a challenge to the moral life, the book offers not only Plato's ring of Gyges, but also Kierkegaard's and Camus' aesthetes. It entertains authoritarian morality in the person of Dostoevski's Grand Inquisitor. It rebuffs mindless obedience in the dialogues with Epictetus and Sartre and in the readings of Socrates' *Apology* and Mill's *On Liberty*.

The discussions of the aesthete, hedonist, and moralist lead to the questions in Part Three. What is the point of living? Are there better ways of relating to other people than those offered by the moral life? The final chapters discuss the interconnection of morality, psychology, and metaphysical and epistemic commitments in formulating the best life. Spinoza and Lao Tsu outline the conclusions of our book-long journey. Reading selections from Aristotle's *Nicomachean Ethics* helps students to envision that an integration of emotions and intellect is necessary to produce the virtuous life.

Ethics and the Good Life encourages students to cull the most desirable features of each vision of living and to create their own answer to the question of the best life. Its range covers Western religion in the examples of the Ten Commandments, the Golden Rule, and Ecclesiastes; utilitarianism as formulated by Mill; deontology through Kant; and existentialism in Sartre, Kierkegaard, and Camus. It also includes the Eastern tradition as represented by Lao Tsu and Gautama Buddha. We are challenged to rethink the meaning of our lives in the discussions with Solomon and Sisyphus and in the reading by James. Finally, the tentative conclusions of earlier discussions lead to Buber's philosophical anthropology. All of this culminates in a synthesis of perspectives—the theory of the virtuous life presented by Spinoza, Lao Tsu, and Aristotle.

Dialogue Style

The dialogue style of *Ethics and the Good Life* engages the reader in the discussion of the questions of moral philosophy. Dialogue gets students involved enough to learn what they value, why they hold their values, and whether or not their values are reasonable. The book also places student concerns and the theories of philosophers into a common context and language. The discussion of suicide and the meaning of living are just as important to our students as they were to Solomon and Sisyphus. So students learn from themselves and from the philosophers, too.

The dialogue format encourages us to enter into the human discussion about morality and the best life. We become active participants when we realize that the other participants, great philosophers all, are also tentatively going through the questions. Dialogue allows each "resurrected" philosopher to reply to students' objections. Mill's utilitarianism, for example, is not so easily misunderstood or dismissed when the philosopher himself participates in the discussion. In this way students learn that legitimate criticism can be demanding, rewarding, and constructive.

Finally, dialogue allows a place for humor in learning philosophy. The book's relaxed, sometimes irreverent approach to the questions prevents it from taking itself too seriously. *Ethics and the Good Life* is fun to read.

Acknowledgments

My students continually contribute to my learning. I want to thank each one of them, past, present, and future. Most of the ideas that appear in this book are theirs. I want to express appreciation to the reviewers: Hilquias B. Cavalcanti, Nashville State Technical Institute; Robin S. Dillon, Lehigh University; Kevin Galvin, East Los Angeles College; James W. Gustafson, Northern Essex Community College; John Kultgen, University of Missouri–Columbia; J. E. Magruder, Stephen F. Austin State University; Levonne Nelson, Fullerton College; Robert Nielsen, D'Youville College; Robert Sessions, Kirkwood Community College; and Eugene C. Sorenson, Rochester Community College. Their critical comments and encouragement came at just the right times. Thanks, too, to my son, Adam, and to my colleague, Gerry Tetrault, for their suggestions on improving earlier drafts, and to Susan Hirsh for undertaking so much of the photocopying work for me. The expert staff at Wadsworth who helped produce this book was a pleasure to work with. In particular I want to thank Hal Humphrey, Peggy Meehan, Jeanne Bosschart, and

Kristina Pappas. Merrill Peterson has been a continuing aid in my writing projects and deserves special praise. And to my friend, Ken King, the "ogre" editor, a special thanks. I hope more editors take the risk to publish textbooks that make philosophy the vital and intense study it can and should be. Thanks, Fred, for everything. Everyone should have such a wonderful teddybear. Finally, thank you, Katrina and David Robert Art, for being my little excellences.

Introduction

I know you don't want to read a long introduction. I don't blame you. Introductions are usually worthless. But before you turn the page, let me tell you a couple of things you need to know.

Learning

We are going to explore your basic beliefs and values. I hope that we will be able to discover *what* you believe, *what* values you hold, *why* you believe and hold them, and whether or not your beliefs and values are *reasonable* to believe.

Learning is an activity. Learning is not simply believing what you want to believe, nor is it uncritically accepting your beliefs. It means being able to state your beliefs and values and to make a reasonable case for them. It means subjecting your thought to critical and careful analysis. Participate! Subject your beliefs and values to critical appraisal. By the end of our discussions, I hope you'll know what you are thinking and why you are thinking it. And that's just the point of learning.

Patience

To succeed in finding the best life, it's important that you believe that I am from Jupiter. Why? If you imagine that I have recently come to earth from the far side of Jupiter, you won't assume that we agree on beliefs and values. Assume that I have the ability to reason just like you do. But on Jupiter, at least on the far side, we don't have morality and religion. I don't understand these ways of living. Imagine that I am a kind of Jupiterian scientist. I have come here to study you. So bear with me in our discussion. If I ask questions that seem to you to have obvious answers, please be patient. Patience is a virtue.

And don't be offended by my comments. I am not accustomed to the earth beliefs appropriate to these topics. Besides, philosophy asks questions about our most
basic beliefs. Most of what we believe is so obvious to us that we never even consciously think about it. Philosophy asks questions, almost like a small child asks
questions. You know when a kid asks why? Then you answer, and the kid asks why
to that, too. The questioning goes on until you feel like—well you get the idea.
Philosophy asks about three "whys" beyond where most children stop. So be patient. How else are we going to learn?

Of course, you have a right to your own view. But having a right to your belief
is not the same as being right. Our quest is to find the best life, not to assert rights.
I'll respect your ideas. (Okay, I'll tolerate them.) Together, we're going to question
a whole range of beliefs and values. Just keep in mind that questions are not always
attacks. Questions and disagreements can aid learning.

Criticism can be Seductive

Criticism can be seductive. I knew that would catch your attention. It's true, too.
Criticism is an exciting, often seductive, and powerful activity. It's tempting to believe that you have the truth. It makes criticizing other people's beliefs safe. Safe,
but boring. You aren't going to learn much that way. What is really exciting is to
analyze your own values and beliefs critically.

Don't panic if your values are challenged or even changed in the course of our
conversation. It's always acceptable to return to your earlier values. And just think,
in the process you may learn why you hold the values you hold.

Dialogue

All worthwhile learning happens *between*—between you and another person, between you and another object or idea, between you and you. First, you and I will
discuss morality and religion. After several chapters, the dialogue will switch parties. This book is a dialogue between you and each philosopher we encounter.

The Philosopher Resurrection Machine

That's right, you and I will actually get to talk to long-dead, certified big shot,
important philosophers. I have invented a device that allows me to resurrect these
great thinkers. We'll get to ask them any questions we want. I could put this on
television (PBS, no doubt) and make a fortune. But I'm reserving the experience
for you. So sit back and enjoy reading the book. I'll see you in just a few pages.

Part One

Do We Need Morality?

Introduction

I Can Read Minds

I can read minds. Yes, it's true. I am a mind reader. No, really, it's true. Actually, I can't do it all the time, though I am getting better at mind reading. So far I have been able to read my own mind with some accuracy. Let me see if I can read your mind. You have serious doubts about my truthfulness. No, no, about my sanity. See, I read your mind.

As we look at morality, think. I'll read your mind and reply to your ideas. Get involved in our discussion. As I ask my questions, think of your reply. Because of my astonishing mind-reading ability, you are actually able to participate in the writing of this part of the book. It's true! Every page in this part is blank until you turn to it. Then, as you open to the page, your ideas appear as if by magic. If you don't believe any of this, just play along. I hope the discussions reflect your interests and concerns. We all want to know what the best life is.

What to Expect

We're going to cover a lot in our initial discussions. We're going to ask: What is morality? and: What is the point of living a moral life? We're also going to talk about your belief in God. Since so many people get their moral values from religion, it's important to discuss religion and God.

If that isn't enough to keep us busy, we are also going to challenge morality. Many people think that moral values are different for different people, or different societies. We're all tempted to believe that now and then. Of course, if moral values are different for different people, then we can't morally judge anyone else. At least, we can't judge anyone in a morally meaningful way.

One way to get into this problem of different values is to examine what counts as truth. We'll look at ways of understanding moral truth. Another way to resolve this problem is to find out what human nature is. If we can say what makes us uniquely human, we might be able to show that people are not as different as some people believe. If we are all basically the same, then the best life will be basically the same for all of us.

Yes, I know what you're thinking: "But everyone is different. What makes one person happy doesn't make another person happy. We're all different." (How's that for mind reading?) You may be right; I don't know. That is just the sort of idea we're going to look into.

Besides moral values, God, and human nature, we're going to ask questions about society, and freedom, and pleasure. Finally, we're going to see whether the best life is doing whatever you want. That's my choice, but then, I'm a mind reader from Jupiter.

1   What Is the Point of Morality?

Idleness is Immoral

Recently I was lying outside. Sun shining in the cloudless blue sky, gentle breeze blowing. . . . you get the picture. I was doing nothing. Two acquaintances came up and interrupted me.

Smith and Jones asked if they could talk to me. Their names aren't really Smith and Jones. I'm just using these names to protect them from being recognized. Smith is the boring one. Jones is the serious one. Sometimes it's impossible to tell them apart.

"What are you doing?" asked Smith.

"Nothing," I replied.

"Just soaking up some rays, huh? Trying to get a head start on your tan?"

I shook my head. "Just nothing."

"Well, that's not possible," interrupted Jones. "You must be doing something. You are either resting, or relaxing, or thinking, or daydreaming, or some other activity. You can't be doing nothing." Jones is such a pain, but I knew if I said that, he might be offended.

"Jones, you're such a pain. Go away."

"No, really, what are you doing? Doing nothing is immoral."

"Immoral, huh? Well actually, I was just thinking 'deep' and 'significant' thoughts," I said. Actually, I *was* doing nothing, and if I may say so, I was doing nothing very well. There are times when I am able to do nothing near perfectly.

"Ah, just as I thought," interjected Smith, sounding just like Jones. "No one ever does 'nothing.' Every human action has a goal. All people have goals. For example, everyone wants happiness! That's just the way we are. It's our human nature. It's what makes you a human being. Being idle is boring and meaningless. Don't you agree?"

"No."

"Well, we don't have to talk about human nature or happiness right now. It's up to you."

"I don't want to talk about human nature, happiness, or anything else." And I didn't, either. I would rather lie here happily than talk about being happy. "Can't you see that I was doing nothing? And I was doing it quite well. Far from being meaningless, idleness is the opposite of boredom and work. So why are you two bothering me?"

"You're an interesting person," replied Smith, obviously attempting to manipulate me to their way of thinking. Who knows, perhaps they were trying to "save" me from myself.

I don't mind when people manipulate me. Going one way is no different than going another way, as long as it's the way I want to go anyway. But now they had broken my nearly unbreakable concentration . . . hmm . . . how can I get rid of them?

"What do you two want? Tell me what you want, and then go away," I said.

What's the Best Life?

Jones asked, "What do you think is the best life?"

"What do you mean?" I responded decisively.

"What is the best life? What else could it mean? What do you want out of life?"

Pleasure: Wine, (Wo)men, and Song.   "For me the best life involves pleasure. Wine, women, and song! That's what I think is the best life," I answered smartly, hoping they'd go away now. I wanted to go back to doing nothing.

"Which one?" Jones asked, obviously setting some kind of trap for me. He's clever. Most likely he was out to confuse, and finally to judge, me.

Throwing the question back at them, I said, "What do you mean, which one? Do I have to choose among wine, women, and song?"

"That's not what I'm asking. Which woman?"

He's a devious one, and so moral! He's trying to guide the discussion to morality. He knows I've been steadily seeing one woman ever since she and I were married. It ran through my mind that I could answer, "What do you mean?" but on first try that didn't work very well.

"What do you mean?" I answered. I've always found that a good defense is to ask a question. The problem is that I'm not good at making up questions.

"If the best life involves a woman, it must be your wife you are referring to," said Jones. "So it's just as I thought, you do endorse the sanctity of marriage."

"Actually, I was not referring to my wife. When you asked me what I thought was the best life, I had pleasure in mind." (Not that my wife isn't a . . . well, never mind.)

"So you believe that pleasure is the best life?"

"Absolutely! What else could it be? Some is good, more is better."

The Moral Life.   "Some of us think that the moral and religious life constitutes the best life," said Smith with a look of assurance and certainty. Doesn't that look drive you crazy?

"Okay, I'll bite. Why should I give up pleasure to live morally? What is the point of the moral life?"

"Some people think that living for the pleasure of the moment makes the best life. Those of us who know better, however, know that the life of adherence to moral and religious law is far better than pleasure seeking."

Pretty smug, but then I've come to expect that from people who have answers. But how can she be so sure?

"That is not what I'm asking, Smith," I said. "What is the point of morality? What do I get out of being moral?"

"I could tell you that, but one cannot express such a complex theoretical justification in one brief statement."

"Huh?" I said with genuine sincerity.

"You cannot expect me to express all the subtleties of the moral life in one brief statement," she answered. Oddly enough, I don't think she was being evasive.

What's the Point of Morality?

"I don't want to know *all* about morality. When I ask, 'What is the point of morality?' I'm not asking for a long-winded lecture. I think that living for pleasure is all that life offers. Life has no other point. If you don't agree, tell me why. And don't take forever. Long answers bore me. What is the point of morality?"

"All right. You probably won't understand this," she said looking aside to Jones for approval. (Have you ever noticed how impossible it is to distinguish moral people? Smith and Jones and all other moral people are so boringly alike.)

"Are you listening to me, Art?"

"What did you say?"

"Morality gives us a standard to live by. Without morality there would be chaos. People would do whatever they wanted! We'd have anarchy! If it weren't for morality and religion, the world would be a dangerous place to live. People would hurt each other. Without some moral code, and the law, we would have anarchy! People would kill each other. They would steal." (I don't know whether or not Smith and Jones are correct, but they sure are certain!)

"Is that all?" I just love to make fun of serious, good people.

"Is that all?" she said, outraged (and inraged as well, I suspect). "No, actually, that is not all that morality and religion do for us," she said, regaining her composure.

"You know, Smith, when you're passionate you're very engaging," I said in my best Bogie impersonation.

"That's sexist and trite," said Jones, feeling threatened.

"It can't be both. Sexism is not trite, and I wasn't making a sexual comment. She's very engaging and very alive only when she is angry. The same applies to you. Your jealousy and anger make you more alive. That's as close as you moral people get to being alive. Passion is what life is all about!"

"Morality also gives us security and acceptance. You would become an outcast," added Jones, evidently missing the point.

"It's just wrong to kill." Smith provided the proper input statement. "It's just wrong to harm other people. One should 'do unto others. . . .' Following the moral and religious truths is what gives us human dignity. It's what makes our lives meaningful and worthy."

"If you kill someone, you will be punished!" added Jones with real concern and genuine alarm.

Whoa!   "Whoa!" (In philosophy that's a technical term meaning "whoa!") "Slow down, you two. I'm not interested in killing anyone right now. Let me give you an example. I just stole this 39-cent pen," I said, taking a cheap yellow pen out of the pocket of my jeans. I steal only the fine-points. "Why is that such a big deal? If all we're worried about is getting caught, then we can stop worrying. Did you know that only one-half of 1 percent of the crimes committed in this country cause their perpetrators to see even a day of jail time? (I made that up, but it turns out it's true.) So why not try to get away with it?"

"Who do you think you are? Trying to get away with more than you deserve! Other people work hard for their pens!" said Jones angrily.

"It's the principle involved," said Smith. "You can't go around stealing just because you want to steal."

The Point of Morality

Here they go in stereo. "Okay, okay. I can see you're serious about morality and religion. Let's look more closely at each of your reasons. To be honest (and I rarely am), I don't understand morality." I think I am quite generous. I could have shown them the other 39-cent pen I stole, but I refrained.

When I asked, "What *is* the point of morality?" Jones and Smith had a lot to say. Let's list their claims. First, we need morality because we need a standard to live by. Second, we need morality so that society will not crumble. Morality helps us avoid social chaos and anarchy. Morality also gives people security and acceptance within their society. That's a third point. Let me see. Fourth, morality gives people human dignity. It makes their lives meaningful and worthy.

Smith also claimed that it is just wrong to kill people. I'm not sure what she had in mind there. She probably meant that it's just wrong to kill. Hmm, what else could she mean? Oh, yes, she may mean that if you kill someone, you will be caught and punished. So part of the point of morality is to help us avoid punishment. Is that all there is to morality?

Enter the Reader! Yes, You!

"Art, we are supposed to be moral so that our society remains stable. Morality guarantees that chaos and anarchy do not ruin our lives."

Who thought that? Oh, who let *you* into the conversation?

"I bought this book and I have a right to think whatever I want!"

All right, since you bought the book, you're in. From now on, I'll put your ideas in quotes, okay? By the way, be careful, I can read minds.

"Sure."

I heard that thought. You don't sound convinced. Why is this format so strange to you? Every author writes to a reader. I just don't want to talk at you without giving you your chance to reply. Besides, I like you because you bought this book. Now, as I was asking, what do you—yes, you, my reader—get out of morality?

Promises, Responsibilities, Duties, and Other Four-Letter Words. "Art, I've just told you. Morality and religion keep society from becoming chaotic."

Have you looked around?

"Yes, society is pretty crazy, but it would be much worse if morality and religion didn't exist."

Is this what motivates a person to live morally? Social stability? Why bother with it? What makes morality so important?

"Morality derives its authority from the past. That's where its strength and importance come from. That is what promises, obligations, duties, responsibilities, and contracts are all about. They tie down the future. They make the future more predictable."

That's why moral people get involved in promises, obligations, duties, responsibilities, and the acceptance of the rights of others?

"That's the primary reason, yes."

How can responsibilities and rights and duties and obligations and promises *not* be burdens? Who would ever knowingly accept these burdens? What's in it for me?

"Well, those qualities seem like burdens to someone like *you,* but they are needed. Respecting the rights of others is easy because people are people just like us. We all belong to the same society. Respecting others is just the right way to live. Do unto others! If you don't want someone to harm you, then don't hurt anyone else."

Respecting others? An interesting idea.

"Come off it, Art. In your conversation with Smith and Jones, you admitted that you are married. You even wear a wedding ring."

So? (I wonder how you know that.)

"So! You made a sacred vow to your wife. You promised her that you would remain faithful. That you would continue to love her till death do you part. You make promises, don't deny it."

I don't know about sacred vows. That sounds pretty serious. All I "promised" my wife is that I will stay with her until something better comes along. No one has a right to make lifelong promises. You want a person to come with a lifetime warranty. That doesn't allow for change.

"Sure. And what if your wife feels the same way? You can't be serious!"

I'm not being serious, but I am telling you how it is. What kind of person would I be if I wished an inferior life on someone I love?

"What do you mean?"

If someone better comes along, and if I love my wife, wouldn't I want her to live the better life?

"Now you're just being evasive. You believe that no one better will come along for your wife. That's why you're saying all this."

Well, as a matter of fact, my wife and I do match up well. Sometimes we match perfectly. But what's the alternative? Should my wife and I stay together because some legal document says we should stay together?

"Yes."

A license that we bought where people buy hunting and fishing licenses! You place a value in that?

Love and Duty.   "But you admit you love your wife."

I admit it readily, if you call that an admission.

"Then you stay with your wife because you love her. That was just my point. You made a promise."

Not at all. I love my wife, and that's that. But love is a very different reason to stay with someone than a contract. Loveless people sign and respect contracts. Corporations enter contracts. Maybe if more people loved and fewer people married, the world would be a happier place. There would sure be fewer hurt feelings.

"That's outrageous! What about your children?"

What about them?

"You have a responsibility to your children. You brought them into this world, so they are yours; they are your responsibility."

Can I kill them?

"What are you talking about?"

If they're mine, I should be able to do whatever I want with them.

"No, look, this is crazy. All I mean is that you have a promise, an obligation, to care for them. That's what a responsible parent does."

I'd just as soon not use that kind of language.

"What kind of language?"

Responsibilities, promises, obligations, duties, rights, those words. They bother me.

"But you must feel some responsibility toward your children. When your youngest one cries, don't you pick him up?"

Sure. I pick him up, at least most of the time. Sometimes he's crying to get his own way. Generally, he hates naps. But if you're asking me, do I pick him up because I feel a responsibility, then the answer is "no!"

"I don't understand. You admit you pick him up."

Sure.

"I'm not quite understanding you. I don't see the difference. You and I both pick up the baby. So how are our approaches different?"

The difference is in our motives. You pick up the crying baby because you are obeying a moral rule. I pick up the crying baby because if I don't pick him up, I'll be bothered. I'll get no peace of mind if I let him cry on needlessly.

"You're bothered by your conscience. That's what you're really saying."

No way. I pick up the little guy because I love him. It hurts me to hear him cry. I don't pick him up because of a sense of responsibility, or because of guilt! Every little kid in the world can tell the difference. Kids are neat that way. They know sincerity when they feel it. So take your sense of responsibility; keep it. What bothers me is not doing whatever I want. I want to pick up the crying baby. If I don't pick him up—

"Call it what you will, but it's guilt. I've caught you on this one."

Maybe I can make the difference clearer this way. You obey moral rules. I know what I want to do. It's the difference between obedience and feelings. We'll have to talk about this later.

"Why don't we return to our question about the point of morality?"

Where did we go astray?

"We were discussing promises, duties, responsibilities, that kind of thing. It all boils down to the idea that 'one should do unto others.' If you don't want someone to harm you, then don't hurt anyone else."

My, you have a menacing way of thinking. But I am not disagreeing with you. I just don't understand. Maybe I don't know what morality is.

"Now you've shown yourself, Art. Of course you don't know what morality is. If you knew, you wouldn't be asking these questions." ("Is it too late to return this book?" you are thinking.)

Beyond protection from chaos and anarchy, what else is morality good for?

Society's Limits vs. Doing Whatever You Want

"Smith and Jones were right. Morality controls us. Without morality, people would do whatever they wanted."

Excuse me, but what's wrong with that?

"What's wrong with that? If people did whatever they wanted, they would kill and steal and do other hurtful things. The world is a dangerous place even with morality. Without morality (and religion), the world would be unimaginable!"

There we finally agree. Without morality and religion, the world would be unimaginably free and happy. What's wrong with people doing whatever they want? That's freedom, isn't it?

"Oh, you're a word twister! We certainly do not agree. I meant that the world would be unimaginably worse than it is now. Dangerous beyond belief."

Or so you imagine.

"Stop being flippant. This is a serious issue."

What about freedom? What's so wrong with letting people do whatever they want?

"Freedom is fine as long as we don't abuse it."

You mean I can do whatever I want, just as long as society approves? I can do whatever I want, within limits?

"That's not the way I'd put it, but yes. There must be restraints. People cannot be allowed to do whatever they want, at least not without limits."

And society sets the limits of what I can do?

"Exactly."

If I follow society's rules—or limits, as you call them—I'll be okay? I'll be allowed to remain within the society, within the flock?

"Yes. Though your allusion to people as a flock is not accurate."

Sorry, isn't that what your priests, ministers, and rabbis call you, their flock? Isn't that a dominant idea of the Judeo-Christian religions? So morality and religion want people to be sheep? Baa! baa!

"That's not it at all! People need to be restrained. The evidence is all around you. You can't walk down any city street at night without worrying you will be robbed, or worse."

Agreed. Why blame all the problems on a lack of morality?

"Because only immoral people would mug and rape and kill, that's why!"

Morality, Immorality, and Being Neither

Oh, now I see the source of our confusion, at least of my confusion. I see morality and immorality as basically the same.

"Nothing could be further from the truth. How could you even say such a thing!"

Moral and immoral people recognize the same rules and laws, don't they? It's just that moral people basically stay within the rules. Immoral people break the rules. Either way, the rules are acknowledged.

"That's stupid. That's all the difference in the world."

Not quite. Let me give you an analogy. A couple of years ago, I was talking with several people about religion. They were going after each other on the most trivial points. Had the messiah come? What was the true sabbath day, the last day of the week, Saturday, or the first day, Sunday? I listened for quite a while, about forty-five minutes.

"What's your point?"

Then I asked why they believed there was a God. The people who were just at each other's throats turned on me. Suddenly they were united.

"What does this have to do with moral and immoral people?"

Only that the religious people were speaking the same language. Moral and immoral people are also speaking the same language. Each side understands what counts as morally significant. Each recognizes that morality demands obedience.

"What alternative could there be to morality and immorality?"

I'm not sure what we should call it, but nonmorality sounds catchy. Nonmoral people, like me, do not know what morality or immorality are about. We just do what we want.

"Whatever you call it, you are encouraging people to break the moral and legal laws. That's terrible."

Not at all. I am not advocating or encouraging anything. I'm just saying that I should do what I want; I should do what is pleasurable.

"That's all?"

That's all. Why are you so surprised? That's all I've been saying right along.

"No, that is not all. And I am not surprised; I'm disgusted. Being immoral is wrong. You may not call your actions immoral, but if they are not moral, they are immoral."

Why do you say that? Look, if I do whatever I want, I am not deliberately or knowingly following or breaking any rules or laws. I am just doing what I want. The moral person obeys the rules. That I understand.

"Right. But the immoral person goes against the laws and the moral rules."

Yes. And when the immoral person has committed a terrible immoral act, then what?

"What do you mean?"

What does the immoral person do? He or she hides. Immoral people try to get away with it! Right?

"Yes, they try to get away with it because they fear punishment. They know they have done something wrong. Most of the time they get good lawyers to defend them. They try to get off on legal technicalities."

By technicality, you mean they try to seek protection within the law, right? What's wrong with that?

"They use the law."

Just like a law-abiding person? Look, the point is that immoral people recognize that their actions are wrong. They either try to get away with it, or find excuses, or find some other way out. Nonmoral people don't bother with any of that. For example, I just do what I want.

"Let me see if I follow you. There is a difference between moral and immoral people, and between them and nonmoral people. But if that's true, then you are far worse than immoral people."

How so? I don't see myself as better or as worse. I am just doing what I want.

"You are worse because you are out of control and unpredictable. Immoral people have a sense of right and wrong, good and bad. You don't know the difference, do you?"

As a matter of fact, you've been reading my mind! (You should write a book!) No, I do not know the difference between right and wrong, or between good and bad.

Avoiding Guilt

"Do you ever feel guilty when you do something wrong?"

How could I? Nothing I do is wrong, so I never feel guilty. If I can't distinguish right from wrong, good from bad, how am I to feel guilt?

"You've never felt guilty about anything? Never? I can't believe that. Most of my life is based on avoiding that feeling. Really, I don't believe you."

I really don't feel guilt. (This is not a lie.) I'll make you a promise. By the time you're done reading this book, you won't feel guilt, either. Would you like that?

"That would be great, but I don't believe it's possible."

We'll see.

"Still, you are much worse than the immoral person. Immoral people feel guilt. They do not always act immorally. But you, who do not feel guilt, you can do whatever you want."

Just what I've been saying all along. Great, isn't it?

"Aren't you afraid you'll get caught?"

What If You Knew You Wouldn't Get Caught?

Ah, dear reader! (See how close we've gotten.) So that's your problem? Are you afraid of getting caught? There's a way around that.

"No, that is not my problem. . . . but how can one not get caught?"

I am glad you asked. There is a special ring. The ring gives you immunity from ever being caught.

"How could a ring do that?"

Plato has a story of such a ring, the Ring of Gyges, he calls it. The ring makes people invisible. Then they can do whatever they want.

"Are you telling me that you have Plato's mythical Ring of Gyges? You are crazy."

Actually, I do not have the Ring of Gyges. The ring I have is the ring from Tolkien's *The Hobbit* and *The Lord of the Rings*. I have Frodo Baggins's ring.

"Who? Look, this is supposed to be a serious discussion on the nature of morality, not a stage for Art's nutty imagination."

Imagine that I do have such a ring, a ring that makes its wearer invisible.

"What's your point?"

If I had the ring, would you want to borrow it?

"I would *not* want a ring like that."

Why not? What would you do with it? Think about it for a moment. You could do anything you wanted and no one would be able to catch you.

"I wouldn't want the ring because I'm not sure I could withstand the temptation to use it."

Of course you'd use it! What's the point of having it if you don't use it? Would you use it for immoral purposes? For pleasure?

"Both. Pleasures are usually immoral, and vice versa. Anyway, I wouldn't take the ring. Someone might get hurt."

Repression, anyone?

"What do you mean?"

Maybe we could build in a safeguard so that no one would get hurt. Would you use the ring to get some money? Or you could take an air trip, free. You could go anywhere in the world, free. That wouldn't hurt anyone. You could "borrow" a red Ferrari! What about it? Do you want the ring?

Immorality Is Tempting. "Okay, you've made your point. Being immoral is tempting. That's why we have to obey the moral rules even when we don't understand them. We have to live in society, you know. Nothing would get done if we're immoral."

Why do you think something has to get done? And why do you assume that having the ring will lead to immoral behavior? You could do good with the ring. No one's stopping you. You just assume that we're all basically immoral. Do you assume that's part of human nature?

"Well, no, I'm not assuming that. I'm just assuming that we are all subject to temptation. I still say if everyone were immoral, nothing would get done."

Living Forever.   Interesting. Look, what if you found out that you were going to live forever?

"That's impossible. Besides, who would want to age forever? Would you get older?"

What if you aged one day every 500,000 years? And your health stayed good. Would you have any reason to be moral? All the things you want to do would get done, eventually. Would you change your lifestyle?

"I'm not sure. I guess I would. Would any of my friends and family live on with me?"

We can make the example work any way you'd like. So, sure, family and friends age just as you do. Is there any pressing reason to struggle and to sacrifice, to work and to slave, and to follow duties and obligations? Wouldn't you calm down and live a more leisurely, pleasant life?

"Yes, I suppose so. I wouldn't feel the pressure that time imposes on me. I would have a lot more time to spend doing what I want."

Great. But isn't this your life now, only with different expectations of how long people live? You don't live forever, but seventy to ninety years is a long time, a lifetime.

Dying Soon.   Now let me alter the example slightly. What if you found out that you were going to die in exactly six months?

"No medical opinion can be that accurate."

For the sake of my example, say you found out that you have an incurable ailment, the kind of disease characters in soap operas get all the time. You will live exactly six months, then your contract is not renewed. During that time you will feel healthy, then wham! you die. Would you change the way you presently live?

"You call this example a slight change from living forever?"

Would you change the way you presently live? Would you give up your goals?

"Yes, I would change how I live. I'd quit school. I'd quit my job. I think I'd travel."

Come on. You wouldn't do those terrible immoral deeds that you moral people dream about?

"No, I wouldn't. Do you mean, would I kill anyone? No, I wouldn't kill."

Too bad. There are probably a few people who ought to be killed. That wasn't what I had in mind, though.

"Which immoral deeds do you mean?"

Whichever ones you're thinking. You wouldn't steal? Or sleep with your neighbor? You wouldn't lie? Even if you knew you could not be punished? Living for six months and living forever give you immunity from punishment. You wouldn't act immorally?

"I guess I'm confused. I'm not sure what I would do."

Good. Then I'm doing my job. You can't learn anything as long as you have answers. What confuses you?

What Do You Really Want Out of Life?

"First, I told you that living morally is worthwhile for its own sake. And you asked me why that was true."

And you said that morality allows us to accomplish goals.

"I said that nothing could get done if we were immoral."

Right. Then I gave the example of living forever.

"Why did you ask that?"

To see just how committed you are to achieving your goals because you want to achieve them. But even more, to see how important your goals are to your life. And what you would do if you didn't feel the constant pressure to accomplish.

"So you want to know how I would spend my leisure time?"

Yes. What do you really want to do? Living forever, you could do whatever you want.

"I see. Both of your examples are trying to trick me into telling you what I really want."

Bingo! What do you really want? Set aside all the obligations you've learned. What do you really want out of life?

"I still want to accomplish my goals. But now you've changed my mind somewhat. What if I live for only six months? Most of my goals would be unreachable. But wait. I'm lost. How did we get here? And where are we?"

Moral Repression.   We are back to my original question. What is the point of morality? If I'm tempted to do whatever I want, why shouldn't I follow my wants? So far, morality sounds like a lot of repression.

"What do you mean by repression? You said that already. You keep using the word, but you haven't said what you mean."

Repression is just a fancy way of saying that being moral is the pits. When I want to do something that is immoral, I'm supposed to "bury" the want. That's repression. That's crazy.

"There's nothing crazy about it. We need to control ourselves. Without control, people could not live together in a society. The only way to avoid chaos is for everyone to contain his passions and antisocial wants."

Yes, so you say, but why should I be moral? Or let me put it a different way. I

want society to be perfectly stable and predictable. I like living among moral robots. (Another lie.) My question is not about everyone's being moral. I want to
know why *I* should be moral.

"Who do you think you are?"

Time out. Smith and Jones already played that number with me. But it doesn't
work.

"And why not, Mr. Special Case?"

It doesn't work because it assumes that I am moral. And I'm not, happily.

"Well, you should be, you—"

Back to name calling? Frustrated? Telling a pleasure seeker that she should be
moral is like arguing the fine points of etiquette with a hungry lion as she is about
to eat you. I want to know why I should be moral. Your moral indignation is not a
compelling reason. I think you need to show me a nonmoral reason to live morally.

"Why do I have to do that?"

A nonmoral reason appeals to moral and nonmoral people alike.

"What kind of reasons are you looking for?"

Show me that the moral life is more desirable than other ways of living.

"If you think you're so right, Art, can you show me what's wrong with the moral
life?"

I've already argued that morality is imposed on people and that even you would
live very differently if you were immune to morality.

"I'm not persuaded by those arguments."

Eternal Recurrence.   Then here's another example. Maybe this one will bring
you over to the right way of living—pleasure!

"Doubtful, Art. I am perfectly happy living by the rules of morality. They give
me a lot more than you can evidently imagine."

We'll see. Imagine that you must live your entire existence—no, better, you must
live for eternity doing just what you have been doing for the past twenty-four
hours. Would you be willing to live that way?

"The past day would repeat over and over again, forever? This is ridiculous."

Maybe, but would you live this way? Think about it. Think about all the responsibilities, and goals, and promises, and duties, and pressures you have had to fulfill
in the past twenty-four hours.

"So?"

Think how little pleasure you have while you're fulfilling your moral duties.
Look at all the opportunities for enjoyment you've sacrificed. Come on, take the
example seriously just for a moment.

"Would I be willing to live exactly the way I have lived for the last day? Could
we stretch it out to the last week?"

What difference would that make?

"I had a good weekend. I really enjoyed myself, so I'd like to include that."

I think you're getting the point. The time frame doesn't matter as much as the
point of the example.

"Which is what?"

Moral people put up with a lot of stress and forfeit a lot of pleasure. Imagine spending an eternity living with the pressures of exam week or income tax filing!

"I see the point, but you have to face reality. We have to do those things. Besides, they don't take that much time. And the rewards are worth it."

You already admitted that you would quit school and your job if you knew you were going to die soon. Why not quit school and your job and enjoy your life?

"I don't know what keeps you on the ground! Be realistic. No one that I know can just quit everything and live the way you want."

Why do you bother with school?

"Because I want to get a good-paying job."

I think the point of the eternal repeat idea is that most people do what they have to do, but they don't really enjoy it. Even you say that you are in school so that you can get a better job. You moral people worry so much about the results of your actions and your plans that you don't enjoy what you're doing now.

"School isn't so bad. There are lots of courses I really enjoy, especially courses in my major. You make it sound like all of school is a terrible torture. It isn't, you know."

Well, at least we're making headway. You do some things you enjoy!

"Of course I do. Everyone does. You use extreme examples to prove your points, and that forces me to say things I don't feel comfortable saying."

Comfort is hardly the test of truth, but I see your point. I think there is some merit in isolating our intuitions by using extreme examples. Since this bothers you, however, let me give you a more realistic example.

"Okay, and could we keep the example in the realm of reality? Life can't be all pleasure and no struggle or pain. Life just isn't like that."

The Pleasure Button.   Oh? Then you'll be happy to hear this. I am the regional distributer for a miraculous invention, the pleasure button. With this button you can eliminate unpleasant experiences. All you have to do is press the pleasure button and you feel a surge of pleasure. Goodbye, pain and worries; hello, pleasure!

"What are you talking about? There is no such button."

Ah, but there is. It was invented by some researchers at a major medical school. Its primary use is to alleviate the pain for people who suffer from migraine headaches and from certain types of cancer. Evidently the pain is so great that the only effective chemical painkillers also kill the patient. I guess the dose has to be so strong that the patient can't survive it.

"Even if there is such a device, you can't use it for people who don't suffer from that kind of pain."

Why not? By the way, the Food and Drug Administration doesn't need to hear about this. I have been granted distribution rights. Because I like you, I am willing to sell you our best model for only $29.95. Just think what a pleasure-filled life you can have.

"What about the side effects? You haven't mentioned how addictive your device is."

Addictive? That's its best feature. There's no physical addiction, unlike drugs.

See, the pleasure button works on a simple principle. An electrode is planted into the pleasure center of your brain.

"Wait a minute, that sounds dangerous! I'm not having anyone put wires in my brain."

Cool down. The electrode isn't even the width of a hair. I have been assured that because of the location of the pleasure center, the procedure is absolutely safe and effective. I'm thinking about franchising implantations at better department stores across the country.

"Art, this idea is nuts."

If the department store franchising fails, I'm willing to farm out the work to hardware stores, but they aren't my first choice.

"That's not what I think is nuts. It's nuts, too, but your whole example is crazy. No one is going to let somebody put an electrode into his brain and then have control over when he feels pleasure."

Oh, I agree. The control of the pleasure button is completely in the hands of the person who buys the product. Once the electrode is implanted, I give a hand-held button to the person. It looks a lot like a garage door opener. Whenever the person wants to feel pleasure, she just pushes the button. It turns out that the pleasure center overrides the pain center. You never have to feel pain again.

"There must be a drawback. This thing can't be as simple as you say."

There are a few bugs in the system. For example, sometimes when a plane flies overhead the person below feels a surge of pleasure. It's a problem with overlapping frequencies or something, but we're working on it. And then there's the garage door opener problem. If you're going by someone's house and you push the button, their garage door may open.

"Stop right here! I'm not concerned about garage doors and planes flying overhead."

So you'll buy one? $24.95 plus tax.

"No, I will not buy one. I don't want someone else controlling what I feel. What happens when someone else pushes his button?"

Good question. Each pleasure button is set on a different frequency. I suppose we could market two buttons for couples who want to feel pleasure at the same time. Hmm, let me work on that marketing strategy.

"Art, my concern is not with marketing strategy. My concern is with self-control and with progress. People who have this pleasure button of yours will stop working. If everyone has a pleasure button, progress will come to a halt. Civilization will crumble."

Sure, but we won't care. If the fall of civilization bothers you, just push the button. By the way, did I mention that the pleasure button comes in two models? One model is powered by a nine-volt battery.

"There's a problem. If people have the pleasure button, they'll stop working. How are they going to eat? How are they going to be able to afford to pay for their food, or house, or even the batteries they need? Answer that one."

Well, the answer to the first two questions is easy. When you get hungry or cold, just push the button. Pleasure.

"People will die! They'll stop working, and they'll starve to death or freeze to death."

But they'll die with a smile on their faces. You do raise an important issue, though. How will they provide themselves with the batteries they need? People will be like drug addicts, committing crimes in order to get their batteries. That's what worries you, isn't it?

. . . Well, if you won't answer, I'll assume that's your problem. The battery situation is resolved by buying the advanced model. It's operated by a solar cell and has a battery backup for cloudy days. Great, huh? It can be yours for only $34.95.

"I don't want it. I'd rather deal with some of the struggles of life and feel I've accomplished something. What you offer is pleasure, but there aren't any emotions or friendships to get through this device."

You can make friends by giving them a pleasure button.

"I'm serious. As much as your pleasure button sounds appealing, there is more to life than pleasure!"

Like what?

"Like work, and progress, and meaningful activity. Like friendships and love and trust. There's such a thing as dignity. Your pleasure button gives people pleasure, but where would their sense of belonging come from?"

Why would anyone care about all of this stuff? Once you feel supreme pleasure, the rest is just worthless. Did you know that whenever the pleasure center is directly activated, the person feels as much pleasure as his body can generate. Truly, it don't get any better than this. So what about it? May I take your order now?

"No."

What Does the Moral Life Have to Offer?

What does the moral life have to offer that makes it more desirable than a life of pleasure?

Security and Acceptance.   "What you're asking isn't that easy to define, but let me try. You should be moral because if you are not moral, you will be rejected."

By whom?

"By us. By everyone. By society. Society provides security for its members. I think that means that we owe something to society. I guess you don't see it that way."

Nope.

"Within this organized, safe society you get the benefits. But you get the benefits only if you are an accepted member. If you act immorally, you'll become an outcast. No one will love or trust or befriend you. People won't care about you."

So what?

"Don't you want to be accepted? If you don't live a moral life, you'll never feel accepted by others. You'll never feel the sense of community that moral people feel.

You'll never understand that you are one person in the long history of the human race. Morality gives us a sense of our place in the unfolding history of humanity."

I'm getting dizzy from the excitement!

Commerce, Creativity, and Continuity.

"Make fun all you want, but morality gives us the chance to cooperate with others. It allows us to have give-and-take relationships with each other."

Give and take? It sounds like a business transaction. I'd like to deposit this in checking and take that from savings, thank you.

"It is a little like commerce. Take promises. Promises allow people to count on each other. Morality also lets us be creative."

How so?

"Seeing ourselves in the context of history gives us a sense of the importance of the past and the future. Knowing that other humans will follow, we are motivated to create. Just look how creative people have been throughout history. Art, music, architecture. Why, civilization itself is a product of the ability of people to see themselves in the context of a continuing humanity."

Baa. Baa.

"What? Are you starting that again!"

You readers sound like sheep. Baa. I ask why I should be moral, why anyone should be moral. All you tell me is that morality makes me part of the flock. Morality makes society safe for me! Morality lets me be accepted! Morality keeps me from being punished! Or so you snivel. You are a bunch of frightened sheep. You want to be one continuous, homogenized flock! Even offering you the ring frightened you. Look how you responded. You wanted the ring. And you were afraid to use it.

"That's not true, Art! I was thinking of using it."

How would you use it?

Don't Hurt Anyone.

"I would use the ring in lots of ways. Just as long as I didn't hurt anyone, then using the ring would be fine."

So, you're willing to steal money?

"As long as it doesn't hurt anyone, sure."

Wimp! You aren't really serious. What about all the times you do hurt someone?

"When's that? I don't knowingly hurt people. Maybe you do, but I don't."

You hurt people all the time. Every time you compete, you hurt people. Competition is designed to have a lot of losers. That's why people like it. Do you think losers like losing?

"Competition is different. People enter competitions knowing they might lose. It's part of the game. No one has to enter the competition."

Pretty good rationalization, but it doesn't work. If you are reading this book for a course, you are probably using the course to fulfill a general education requirement. If your school is like any other I've seen, the seats in those courses are limited. So, by being in this course, you are depriving someone else of this seat.

"Big deal. The space goes to whoever gets there first. It's a fair lottery. I'm not hurting anyone by being here ("except perhaps myself," you realize!). There's a difference between inconveniencing, bothering, and hurting. Being here isn't hurting anyone else."

Fair enough. Does any of this noble thinking apply outside the classroom? Aren't we unfairly hurting others by using most of the world's raw materials, and energy, and food? But wait. Let's not get into that issue. I don't care. You do.

"You really don't care about the plight of others, do you?"

Why Should I Care About Others?   Why should I care about others? (You knew I was going to say that.)

"You just should care about others. They're people. They have feelings. That's why you should care."

I admit that they and you are people, and that you may have feelings, but so what? I don't feel your feelings, so why should I care?

"Art, you are the most self-centered egomaniac I ever came across. How can you be this way?"

Just good luck, I guess. Look, I have a hobby. I mug old people on the weekends. (It's an example! Don't get bent out of shape.) Is there anything wrong with that?

"Anything wrong! Of course, there's something wrong with that!"

What's wrong with mugging old people on the weekend? Is it the weekend part that bothers you? I could change the day if it offends you.

"It's not the day; it's you. Mugging old people is wrong. It's disgusting!"

There is a difference between wrong and disgusting, isn't there? If you want to hear it, I have a disgusting example involving—

"Spare me. Mugging old people is wrong. Period."

Why?

"Look, Art, how would you like it if people mugged you?"

I'm not old.

"If you were old, would you want people to mug you?"

No.

"Then why do you mug them?"

I've told you, because I'm not them. I don't see why I should give up a perfectly enjoyable hobby just because it bothers a few old people.

"This is amazing. Here's a guy writing a book on ethics and he doesn't have the faintest idea why it's wrong to harm others."

Why *is* it wrong to harm old people?

"Why don't you pick on someone your own age? Why don't you try to bully people who are bigger than you?"

That's silly. I pick on old people because I don't run any risk that way. I'm not into getting hurt, you know. This hobby is not as simple as you might imagine. For example, you have to be careful. Old men often carry canes. You know what the curved end is for? After I knock them down, they try to snag my foot as I leave. Sneaky! Or those darn aluminum walkers! One woman threw one of those at me.

"Good for her!"

Luckily she missed. What do you mean, good for her? I thought you were against people hurting each other.

"Unbelievable! Let's get off this topic. I don't think we're likely to resolve anything."

What Is Morality?

I didn't say that. I think you've just explained the basis of morality to me.

"I did?"

Being One Among Many Equals.   Sure. It's probably so obvious to you that you missed it. I just got it, though. Morality is seeing yourself as one person among many equals. That's why you objected when I gave the example of hurting older people. Morality demands that we view them as equals in some sense. I'm not sure what that sense is, but have I gotten it right?

"Yes, I think so. Morality is opposed to just being selfish and self-centered. It's seeing others as important, as equals, just like you said. Yes, that's at least part of morality."

So your idea that morality gives us a sense of security and belonging is really a partial definition of morality. Interesting. To be moral is to avoid being selfish and self-centered. It means to be more objective?

"Yes, good. Objective and impartial. Now that you understand it, morality sounds pretty appealing, doesn't it?"

I didn't say that. I still don't understand why I should be moral. I understand that it means treating others as "equals," but I don't see why I should bother. Why should I give up my hobby? Even if I continue to mug old people, society will remain stable and fairly secure. People will accept me.

"How can you say that? Who is going to accept you if you mug old people?"

Everyone will accept me. I'm aware of your moral bias against hurting old people. Knowing that, I won't tell anyone about my hobby. I can do whatever I want. For example, I can hurt old people and still get the most out of society. I can embezzle money from my employer. As long as I can get away with it, I'm safe and accepted.

"So, you intend to take a free ride?"

Sure, why not? Why shouldn't I try to get away with it? Isn't that how everyone lives anyway?

Human Dignity.   "There's more to morality than you've realized. There are more reasons to be moral. Being moral gives dignity to us as human beings. It puts us above the animals. It puts us into the entirely human realm of civilization. Being moral makes us better people."

I don't get it.

"Human dignity. It's what makes us human."

I thought my parents made me human.

"Wrong. To be human is to progress, to grow, to reason, to get along with others in a human society. It's to set and accomplish goals."

Are you saying that people like me are not human? That's pretty harsh.

"Dignity is what allows us to sacrifice ourselves for the greater good. It's what allows us to be fulfilled."

I'd just as soon wallow in my lusts, thank you.

Meaning and Worth.   "But if you wallow in your lusts, as you call it, your life will be pointless. Don't you want your life to have meaning? Don't you want people to value you? Don't you want to accomplish anything? Life would be meaningless without morality."

Now you've hit on something that has always fascinated me. Every time I'm really enjoying my pleasure, people ask me if it's meaningful. Why is it that only when I'm wallowing in my passions does the question of meaning come up? It doesn't come up when I appear to be working. It doesn't even come up when I appear to be suffering. (I never suffer, but it's a good example.) Comments about meaning come up only when I'm enjoying myself. Why?

"You really do lead a shallow life."

Shallow, huh? What makes a life meaningful? I don't think there is a meaning of life. I think this idea of life having a meaning is just a distraction. It's a way of controlling people. Baa!

"Part of the meaning of life is to fit into the order of the universe, into God's plan. Sometimes that involves suffering, but it's worth it. That's what gives life meaning."

And if there is no God, then is your life meaningless?

"No God! Of course there is a God!"

We'll discuss God later. (Just look at the table of contents.) But I don't see how being an insignificant part of an infinite universe gives meaning to anyone's life. So what if you're needed for the great machine of the universe?

"But the universe runs according to God's plan."

Even if there is a God, and even if the universe runs by God's plan, so what? How can the life of an infinitely small cog be meaningful? The point of the "plan" isn't even yours! No, sorry to say it, but the only meaning is in enjoying one's pleasures in the moment. Or do you see an alternative?

"Well—"

If you don't have an answer, I do. The question of meaning comes up because experiencing momentary pleasure and passion competes with being moral. Morality can't permit people to enjoy themselves.

Contentment.   "Now you've gone too far. I enjoy myself, and I'm moral."

How do you enjoy yourself? Do you throw yourself into the passion of the moment? Do you lose your ability to reason? Are you overwhelmed by the ecstasy of the occasion?

"I do enjoy myself, don't mistake that. The moral life is a life of higher, more cultivated pleasures."

So now you're a field that has to be cultivated? What do you mean by higher pleasure? What special kind of pleasure does morality offer?

"The moral life gives me a sense of peace and contentment. I'm happy living the moral life."

Which is it? Are you happy, or peaceful and contented?

"There's no difference."

Of course there's a difference. I can see we're going to have to figure out what happiness is. (Another chapter? On Happiness.) I know one thing, though. Peace and contentment are not happiness. The word *peace* reminds me of "rest in peace." That's for tombstones, not for people. And contented is what farmers want their cows to be. Contentment isn't for people! Can't you ever just let go?

Consequences.   "Of course not. That kind of abandon always leads to trouble, to undesirable consequences."

So? Are you telling me that what comes after your pleasure matters more to you than the pleasure? What has morality led you to? This is madness.

"No, this is morality. It does matter what happens in the future. Whether you like it or not, your actions do have consequences."

So?

"It is our responsibility to consider those consequences. We can't just isolate our actions from what they bring."

Why not? I do it all the time. In fact, if I think about the past or the future, my immediate experiences aren't as intense. Distractions, you know.

"You are the most irresponsible person I've ever run across. Moral people look to the consequences of their actions."

The action itself has no value apart from what it brings?

"We judge whether or not our actions are right in themselves, and we judge them according to their consequences. Some actions are simply wrong no matter what the consequences. And some actions are simply right. And sometimes consequences are important to consider, too."

Recap: Definition of Morality.   This strikes me as confused thinking.

"But you must admit, Art, that I've taught you quite a lot about morality. Morality involves consequences, and judgments, and seeing others as equals. It puts a person into the human community. It gives the person a sense of connection with other people. Not just with people who live in different parts of the world, but with people of the past and people who will live in the future. Morality is an impartial, objective view of others."

It concerns punishment and security?

"Yes. Morality and religion also give us direction in our lives. They prevent harm to others, and they help humanity progress and prosper. That's why you should be moral."

Interesting. The way you describe morality, it is not merely a set of rules I must obey.

"Exactly. Morality also involves a whole way of thinking and living."

You actually think of other people as being a lot like you are.

"Yes, as moral equals. As people with plans, wants, rights, duties, and all the rest. People may not be equal in skills or talents or wealth or knowledge or any other characteristic, but they are equal morally. Each person is important no matter what his background or what her use to society."

And let me see if I've got this right. I'm supposed to be moral because it promises contentment and some kind of meaningful life?

Do You Have Any Objections?

"That's right, yes. Now that you understand morality, do you have any objections?"

Absolutely! It sounds painfully safe and boring and confining!

"Safe? Boring? Confining? You are hopeless, Art. I think you've misunderstood. I've tried my best to explain the point of morality. I don't know what else to say to you."

Morality and religion create a sense of guilt, a conscience, and then promise to soothe your conscience. What's this? What a marketing scheme! I give you a conscience, and then I claim to be the only store in town with the product that will pacify your guilt? I tell you that you have sinned and that only I have the remedy. And the beauty is that the overhead is so low. All I have to do is tell you everything is okay.

"You're so cynical. Morality serves us very well, thank you. It serves us whether or not you approve of it."

Spoken like an open-minded person.

Why Not Experience the Moment?   "Okay, let me ask you, Art, what's so great about your intense, momentary experiences? Why should anyone live for the moment?"

In the moment, not *for* the moment.

"What's the difference? For the moment, in the moment? Neither is morally acceptable."

Living for the moment sounds like a life seeking nothing but pleasure. The pleasure of the moment. Living in the moment is to open up to what there is in the here and now.

"I don't see the difference. All I see is that you want to avoid responsibility and consequences."

It's a great difference, but let's put off that discussion for a later time. The difference between living and being alive is more to the point right now.

"What do you mean?"

See, I knew you wouldn't get it. You're so moral.

"What's the difference?"

Being moral commits you to looking to the past and to the future, right? Living in the moment means that you concentrate on the here and now.

"Brilliant. So what does that distinction give us?"

Do Moral People Exist?   You're too impatient (which proves my point, I think cleverly to myself). If you live morally, then you need to prove that you exist.

"That's the big question?"

How do I know that I exist? With morality, I know that I exist because I am connected to others by an elaborate web of social conventions.

"Yes, morality makes you feel an historical connection with people who have already lived. Morality also lets you communicate and relate to people alive now."

And the desire to create and to accomplish shows that you moral people care about people in the future. Do I have that right?

"Yes, morality does all that for us. It does even more. Morality also gives your life a sense of meaning."

I remember what you said. You fit into the universe, into a God's great plan. That sense of your "importance" also lets you know that you exist. You assume that you must exist for the plan to go on.

"This is pretty persuasive evidence for morality."

It isn't evidence at all. What it shows is that you and everyone else want to exist, and to know you exist.

"Kind of like 'I think, therefore I exist'? I am moral, therefore I exist."

Kind of. I think morality is looking for some way of proving you exist.

"Obviously I exist. Why should morality have to prove that?"

Because from the moral viewpoint, you aren't really sure that you do exist. Intellectually you're certain, but experientially there's doubt. All your elaborate "evidence" for morality shows that you need to "justify" your existence. See, the problem is that morally speaking, you don't exist in the present. Morality doesn't have much of a present. The past and future distract you from your present experience.

"Why do you say that?"

Subjective Time and Objective Time, or Having the Time of Your Life.   All of the moral person's attention is directed toward the past and the future. Come on, admit it, you think that the present moment lasts the tick of the clock.

"Well, sure, what else is there?"

Exactly! Think about it. There are hours when time moves very quickly.

"Like when I'm having fun with my friends."

And there are hours when time d-r-a-g-s.

"Like when I'm reading this book?"

Cheap shot. But right again. So we all know that time is not always the same.

"But the clock doesn't change. It runs the same no matter how or what I'm doing."

Right, there's objective time, the clock, and there's subjective time. The clock's objective time is morality! What a terrible invention, the clock. Without it you would never be late. You would never have to rush. You would be able to experience the moment for all it's worth. You'd live forever.

"So you're saying that moral people don't experience as intensely as nonmoral people. And this is because we are distracted by the past and the future?"

Yes, for you the past and the future are indefinitely long. You even talk about eternity running into the past and into the future. But that leaves out the eternity of the present moment. And without the eternity of the present moment, you have to make up all of this historical connectedness and meaningfulness and creativeness stuff. You're alive, but you aren't living, at least not when you're being a moral person. You're alive, but you don't exist as an *experiencing* person.

"But I do experience the moment sometimes. I know what subjective time is. Reading this book has shown me how long an hour can be."

That's because you are not completely moral. The nonmoral part of you can understand what I'm saying. See, if you were completely and thoroughly moral, through and through (shudder), then you would experience the moment always as the tick of the clock. Time would be uniform. And you would never be tempted by the pleasures in the moment.

"Why?"

Because the pleasures in the moment would be quickly over. Their intensity would be dulled with the passing moment. The genuinely moral person is never tempted. The past and the future, and all the connectedness and meaning, let genuinely moral people know that they exist. But they aren't living!

"I still don't quite get your point."

Morally Speaking, You Don't Exist.   If your immediate experience doesn't let you know that you exist, that you're living, then you need all the other mumbo-jumbo (another technical philosophy term). Fully moral people don't feel the present moment, so they need an elaborate system of beliefs to verify that they exist. But they don't feel passion or emotion or sensual pleasure. Those are limited to the present. Think of an example of a completely moral person. He's always dead, bloodless, and nice. Nice is like lukewarm mush. Don't be nice, live!

"Who is an example of a genuinely moral person? Do you have some saint in mind?"

Actually, the Vulcan side of Mr. Spock is the example that comes to mind. Sarek, his father, is even more moral. Always acting on duty. Unemotional. Big deal. When you live morally, passions are unavailable to you.

"And who is the nonmoral person? Kirk?"

Not bad. At least he is aware of his senses. Living in the present moment guarantees that you're living, that you exist. And it's not some intellectual knowledge. It's not some "I think, therefore I exist" stuff. That's for the intellect. What moral people really want is a guarantee that they exist. Nonmoral people have that guarantee at every moment of their experience.

"How so?"

Whenever you're feeling intense pleasure, or intense pain, you don't wonder whether or not you're real and living. You *know.* You know, not intellectually, but you know with your gut. (Sometimes this is called affective knowledge.) Physically and emotionally, you know. And you can't be mistaken. Unfortunately, you moral people don't allow yourselves the kinds of pleasures I have in mind. But you are allowed to suffer pain. When you're in pain you know it, and you know you exist. Although you spiritualize pain too much.

"Spiritualize?"

Yes, you look for its meaning. Pain has no meaning; it just hurts.

Relativism

"I have to think about all this. Do you have any other problems with morality?"

Just one more. From what we've said, the content of the moral/religious values doesn't matter. You have argued for the benefits of morality, but I don't see why morality isn't relative to each society.

"Relative? What do you mean?"

Why can't each society pick its own values? Why can't each person? Each religion has its own doctrine and values. Each political system has its own values. So values depend on the surroundings. When in Rome, do as the Romans do.

"I'm not comfortable with this. Are you saying that morality and religion are arbitrary?"

Not the point of view of morality and religion. Not the form. Morality is always objective and impartial. The changeable, arbitrary part is the content, the values themselves. Morality and religion are socially desirable, but the values themselves don't matter. You get all the stability and security and social connection you want. That comes from accepting the authority of morality and religion. The values themselves don't matter. One value is as good as another. Isn't that what you've told me?

"Of course not! Morality isn't relative. There are moral truths!"

Look back to the opening of this discussion. I was asked what is the best life. I suggested pleasure. You (and Smith and Jones) argued for morality. Well, now I wonder about that. At least pleasure is not relative or uncertain in the way that good and bad are relative and uncertain. When I feel pleasure, I know it. I can distinguish pleasure and pain. (Except in the case of tickles!)

"There are moral and religious truths."

Sure, mine.

"Which religious doctrine do you follow?"

Oh, I didn't mean mine, I meant "mine." Is that perfectly confusing?

"Almost. What are you saying?"

Whenever the question comes up about moral and religious truths, people always say that their own religion and their own morality is correct. Mine. It's always "mine." It gets pretty tiresome. I'd like to know what makes one moral or religious truth true and another moral or religious truth false.

"Except that it's 'mine'?"

Exactly.

"There are values that transcend moral and religious differences. Maybe we can use the common values."

Can you tell me what these are? Can you show that any moral and religious truths are really true?

"That won't be an easy thing to show, but it can be done."

Then why don't we get a clearer picture of morality by looking at some examples of morality? From there we may be able to select the most desirable values. (I'm still betting on living in the moment.)

Summary of Discussion

In our opening conversation we question the point of morality. One contender against the moral life is the pleasure-seeking life. Though pleasure recommends itself, morality calls for further motivation. Why bother being moral? To live morally means to submit to society's limits. It means to submit to responsibilities and duties. Living morally means one does not do whatever one wants.

Why do people accept the burdens of morality? There are many reasons. People fear chaos, uncertainty, and guilt. They want security, acceptance, and protection. Morality makes us feel part of the human community—past, present, and future. It instructs us not to hurt other people and even to care about the welfare of others.

What is morality? Our first answer to this question is that morality is a special point of view. The moral point of view is that each of us is one person among many equals. Morality gives us dignity, meaning, and a sense of worth. Finally, morality makes us look to the past and to the future: for example, a promise made yesterday must be kept tomorrow. Consequences matter to moral people.

There are several objections to the moral way of living. Morality limits our actions. We don't get to do what we want. Just think what we would do if we knew we could get away with it! The pleasure button is certainly appealing. The moral life distracts us from experiencing the moment we actually live in. Finally, moral values appear to be relative to the society or the person. Different societies and different people appear to support different moral values.

Discussion Highlights

I. There are two answers to the question: What is the best life?
  1. The pleasure-seeking life
  2. The moral life
II. The point of morality is to guarantee:
  1. The prevention of chaos by promoting a stable society
  2. Protection for each member of society
  3. A secure world
  4. Respect for human dignity
  5. Acceptance
  6. The avoidance of punishment and guilt
III. Morality offers important social gains:
  1. Security and acceptance
  2. Commerce, creativity, and social continuity
  3. Prevention of harm
IV. What is the moral point of view?
  1. Being one person among many equals
  2. Acknowledging human dignity

  3. Viewing life as meaningful and worthy
  4. Offering guarantees of contentment
  5. Concern with the results of one's actions
V. Objections to morality
  1. Repression of wants, desires, and pleasures
  2. Alteration and distortion of one's sense of time
  3. Distortion of one's sense of self
  4. Values are relative to time, place, society, and person

Questions for Thought/Paper Topics

1. Would you buy the pleasure button? Why or why not? Keep in mind that any guilt you might feel can easily be relieved by one push of the button.
2. Some people believe that living morally gives life meaning. What does this mean? Do you agree with this assessment?
3. Why do you keep your promises? How do you justify the times you fail to keep your promises?
4. Everything that enriches us renders our neighbors relatively poorer. If morality involves not hurting other people, how can we justify the amount of material wealth we enjoy in North America?
5. Is there any evidence that moral values are relative to specific cultures? Is there morality that underlies culturally different "moralities"?
6. Is contentment happiness? Can you distinguish the contentment of a satisfied animal and the happiness of a person?
7. Putting aside the rules, why shouldn't you hurt other people?

For Further Reading

There are any number of books encouraging you to be moral. There are a few that question the moral enterprise. It would be worth your time to look at Plato's *Republic* (Hackett, 1973), especially book II, where he discusses ways to avoid getting caught. Another critic of morality is Friedrich Nietzsche. Nietzsche's *The Gay Science* (Random House, 1974) and *On The Genealogy of Morals* (Vintage, 1989) are both provocative, though somewhat difficult, readings. A very readable book by Raymond Smullyan, *The Tao Is Silent* (Harper & Row, 1977) is wonderfully entertaining and insightful.

2   What Is Morality?

In our last conversation I asked, "What's the point of morality?" You said that I (and, presumably, you) should be moral. You said that morality strengthens society and makes it stable. It gives us a sense of belonging. Morality makes life meaningful. It gives us human dignity. Moral guidelines let us control our passions so that we can act reasonably and responsibly. At the same time, morality also gives inner peace. It preserves humanity. Morality organizes the world. Does that capture the highlights of your thinking?

"What you don't understand is that morality satisfies our important wants. Morality is what makes each of us an individual, a person different from everyone else. In the religious context, moral values bring us closer to being the ideal person. They show us how to live in the image of God."

I'm not denying any of this. Now I realize I asked the wrong question. Since I don't know what morality is, I can't say what it does, or how well it accomplishes its goal. How can we say anything about morality until we've figured out what it is?

"Isn't that what we did in our last conversation?"

Not really. You explained the point of morality. Now I want to know *what* morality is. Before we can judge whether or not morality does what you say it does, we need to know what it is. You have to help me identify morality.

"How can we figure out what it is? How do you suggest we proceed? It seems obvious what morality is. I guess I'm still not following you."

What if I asked you: What is the point of owning a dog? What would you say?

"I don't know. Something like: a dog protects your home, and offers companionship, and plays with your children, and takes walks with you. Is that what you have in mind?"

Yes, good. Now for a person from the far side of Jupiter to understand your claim about the point of owning a dog, you would have to explain what a dog is. Right? Then anyone not familiar with dogs could watch what dogs do and find out that you are correct.

"And the way we define *dog* is by showing examples of dogs."

By Jove, he's got it!

What Are Some Examples of Morality?

"Once we have examples of dogs, we can come to a definition, right?"

Right. Can we do this with morality? What are examples of morality? What are some examples of moral systems, of moral rules?

"Are these the same?"

I don't know, but we can get an idea of the moral point of view by starting with any of them.

"What do you mean by the 'moral point of view'?"

You judge people by moral standards. I don't yet see why I should give up my pleasures and adopt the moral way of living. I guess I'm contrasting living for pleasure and living morally, though that may not exactly capture the distinction I want.

"I don't quite follow you."

Okay, how about this? Sometimes you feel like doing one action, but you know it's wrong to do it. You feel like stealing something, but you know it's wrong. I want to know why the moral way is better than stealing the object. I want to know why I should not always just give in to my temptations. So I want to know what in the moral point of view is correct, and how you know it. I want to know which moral values, and roles, and rules, and systems are correct. I'm not even sure how many varieties of moral "things" there are.

"Okay, but how will this help you?"

If we find some clear examples of moral values, we can come up with common, defining features of the moral point of view. Then we'll be in a position to find out if morality is worth the effort.

"Worth the effort?"

Sure. Being moral means I have to give up a lot. Every time I'm locked into a pleasurable moment (like when I'm doing nothing to perfection), someone interrupts. People ask me whether or not my momentary pleasure is worthwhile, or meaningful, or (can I say it?) productive. If I'm going to be worthwhile and meaningful and productive, I still want to know what I get for it. I know what I lose!

"What do you think you lose?"

I lose pleasure and a sense of freedom.

"I think you're hopeless, but let me try to answer your question. There are a number of approaches to morality. In the end, I am confident that they'll all reduce to the same insight. But if you want examples, I can think of some moral and religious rules. The Ten Commandments and the Golden Rule are perfect examples of morality."

Any others?

"Why would you need any others? These two work well enough for me."

Humor me. If we only look at two examples, this book won't be as thrilling as my publisher wants. Your silence would hurt me. You would be acting in an immoral way by failing to do unto others (me). You would also be in error for not following the Ten Commandments. Remember the one that says, "Help Art whenever he needs it"?

"I don't remember that one, but I can think of other ways of describing the moral point of view. Even you might understand these."

Excellent.

Everyone Has a Conscience. "Everyone has a conscience."

Everyone is conscious?

"No, a conscience. *Conscious* means awake or alert. Conscience is very different. Everyone has an intuition of what is right and what is wrong."

You're not going to tell me you hear voices or that you talk to yourself! A little angel and a little devil argue on your shoulders?

"No, a conscience needn't be that kind of experience. It's more of a feeling. You just feel strange when you are about to do something wrong. You know it's wrong, and you feel odd about it."

When you say *you*, you mean you, not me. (I just put this in to show just how confused I am.)

"What? I mean anyone, everyone. Everyone has a conscience that tells them right from wrong. Whether or not people follow their conscience is a different matter. Like you said before, even immoral people try to get away with their immoral actions. They conceal their actions, but in their minds they know they're wrong."

I don't have a conscience.

"I knew you were going to say that, Art. But that isn't a good enough objection. If you're interested in the moral point of view, then having a conscience is part of being moral."

Fair enough. But saying that people have consciences doesn't tell me enough.

"What else do you need to know?"

Well, for one, what is the point of a conscience?

"Conscience is your intuition about what is right and wrong. When you think about doing something wrong, your conscience lets you know that it's wrong. And before you say it, Art, no, people do not always follow their conscience. And after the action they feel guilty."

Okay. Still I have a problem with conscience. Conscience doesn't tell me what is moral and immoral. Conscience only tells me that I think something is immoral.

"What's the difference? If something is immoral to you, then it's immoral."

I don't think you want to go that far, especially when you're talking to me. What I find moral may not be acceptable to you or to anyone else.

"You know what I mean."

Actually, I don't know what you mean. My objection to conscience is that people have different values locked in their consciences. I guess I'd say that conscience is the way a person checks her own moral values. But that doesn't mean the values are correct.

"I think I see what you mean. It's possible for people to have consciences that hold the wrong values. Some people may even feel guilty when they are tempted to do what we would consider right."

That's it! Now I don't deny the usefulness of consciences, but I do doubt that consciences are reliable guides to finding moral values.

Social Roles.   "There are other examples of morality, too. There are social roles that a person must follow."

Social roles?

"By social roles, I mean there are responsibilities."

Stop right there! This is my book. I won't allow that kind of talk in my presence.

"What talk?"

Responsibilities, duties, obligations. Next you're probably going to bring up rights and promises.

"As I was saying, there are social roles we must play. For example, I am a student. I am expected to learn something from my courses and instructors. I may be required to take tests, or write papers, or read difficult texts. As a student I have those responsibilities."

I shudder every time you use those words. Are there other kinds of roles that people have? And please leave out the R-word.

"Other kinds? Yes, of course. People have a whole range of roles: personal, natural, professional, social. The point is that each of these roles requires something of the person. I call the requirements *responsibilities.*"

Keep going. You're on a roll (get it, a roll/role?). So far we have more examples of morality than I imagined possible. Are there any more versions? We might as well get them all listed. Then we'll compare them to see what morality is all about.

The Law.   "The law is a kind of moral system, I guess. Laws are at least based on moral and religious rules. It's illegal to kill, to steal, to lie in court."

Would those actions be wrong if it weren't for the religious rules? Isn't there supposed to be a separation of church and state?

"Sure, though I don't think that's what the separation means. From my point of view, we should follow the law for the benefit of everyone. There would be chaos if no one followed the law. I remember what you pulled on Smith and Jones, and that won't work on me. Keep your cheap stolen pen in your pocket. Most people benefit from having everyone follow the laws. Whether you like it or not, you and I live in a democratic society where the majority's good must be included."

The Most Good for the Most People.   So "the greatest good for the greatest number" is what you are proposing?

"Yes, something like that. I know you're going to try to poke holes in the idea, but I think something like this is at the heart of morality. Maybe I can say this even stronger and avoid your criticism."

Me? Criticism?

"Don't interrupt. Everyone who lives in our society has to follow the laws. We have agreed to follow them. That's what it means to be a member of this society."

I don't recall being asked to endorse any of the laws. I don't even know most of the laws.

"If you don't like the laws, you can leave. But as long as you stay in our society, you are required to follow them."

And if I don't follow all of your laws?

A Social Contract.   "You'll be punished. But that's beside the point. You should follow the laws because you live here. Whether or not you agree with the laws, you are bound by a kind of unspoken contract with everyone else in society. We follow the laws, so you have to follow them, too."

A social contract? Hmm. I need to think about this one. Are there any other examples or explanations of morality? I hesitate to ask, but can you think of any others?

Tradition and Spiritual Needs.   "There are just a couple more. I'm not sure of these, but I'll try them. I think tradition sometimes tells us what is right and what is wrong. I think this might be part of the other categories; I'm not sure. And the other one I just thought of is this: when someone's real needs are satisfied, that might be part of morality, too. I'm not sure. I mean, if an action satisfies someone's spiritual needs, that might be part of morality."

I don't know about these, either, but there's no loss in trying a few ideas, even if they don't work. Before we go on, could you go back to the one about your social contract?

"What about it?"

Aren't there some laws that are just wrong? Don't we want to be able to say that? After all, laws change all the time. New laws are added, old laws are taken off the books. Legal interpretations change.

"I guess so. What's your point?"

Well, you based your contract idea on the idea that democracy requires that the greatest good for the greatest number be taken into account. But if we want to be able to criticize some laws, we have to say that there are times when the greatest number of people may not be our sole concern.

"I don't quite follow."

Aren't there some actions or attitudes that are just wrong? No matter what the majority thinks or how much it benefits, some actions are wrong? I guess what I'm asking is, are there absolutes in morality?

Moral Rules Are Absolute

"Of course, at least some moral rules are absolute. But beyond following the absolutes, one should do what benefits society. The Ten Commandments are ten examples of absolutes. I didn't add absolutes because of the commandments. I'm willing to examine absolutes separately if you want. Do you have any other examples of the moral point of view?"

Who made you the author of this book? I'm the one who asks the questions.

You're supposed to answer. As a matter of fact, though, I do have one suggestion. Egoism.

"What's egoism?"

I should always act in my own self-interest.

"You're outrageous. That's being selfish. That isn't being moral at all!"

Examples of Morality

It was just an idea. I'll give it up if you insist. I did give you all your examples, though. Let me list them. Then we'll look at them one by one throughout the book.

1. Ten Commandments
2. Golden Rule
3. Conscience or intuition
4. Social and natural roles
5. Laws
6. Greatest good for the most people
7. Social contract
8. Real needs fulfillment
9. Tradition
10. Absolutism
11. Egoism

"Hey, I didn't agree to egoism!"

Egoism is an alternative to moral and religious values. I doubt that morality is a desirable way to live.

"Your doubts are not enough to persuade me, Art."

Okay, that's fair enough. Why don't we take up a fuller discussion of egoism later in Chapter 5?

"All right."

What Makes a Principle a Moral Principle?

I still don't get it. What makes a principle a moral principle? What is it about the moral point of view that distinguishes it from other ways of approaching problems?

"That's a good question, Art."

Does that mean you don't have an answer?

"No, it means you have finally asked a worthwhile question. I think it's a good idea to look closely and critically to see what the formal features of morality are."

I'm not following you.

"You have been asking me for examples of the moral point of view. In fact, you have been doing this without much regard for precision. So I have been giving you examples of morality off the top of my head."

Did that hurt your head?

"Corny, Art. What I'm suggesting now is that we both look at the formal features of morality. Where do we begin? Do we look for common qualities from the examples we have just stated?"

That's one way, and I think we should use it as a check. But since you aren't happy with my lack of precision, I have another suggestion. Let's see which types of reasoning compete with moral reasoning.

"What are you talking about?"

The moral point of view is only one way of approaching problems. It's one way of defining situations and solving issues.

"What other ways are there? Give me an example."

Well, before I give you an example, let me spell out what I have in mind. You are pretty entrenched in the moral and religious point of view. That's why you so obstinately rejected egoism.

"Yes, it's objectionable to me."

Okay, now I'm suggesting that there are other alternatives to morality. For example, there is economic reasoning, and military reasoning, and . . .

"Oh, I understand. Are you saying that with each practical situation in life, there are different ways of approaching the problem to find the solution?"

Exactly. Take a military person, a general. In deciding on combat strategy, a general's first objective is to win the engagement. He knows that lives will be lost. People will be intentionally wounded and killed. That's part of warfare. What he is concerned with, however, is defeating the enemy.

"It's not that simple, Art. Generals consider the morality of their actions. They don't just wipe out whole cities because the enemy has troops there."

Tell that to Hiroshima and Dresden. During World War II the Allies destroyed cities just to demoralize the enemy. Similar strikes have been made in every conflict, from Vietnam to Panama to Iraq to whatever comes next.

"What would you expect a general to do? Generals have to fight in order to win."

Though I might disagree, I'm not disagreeing with you now. The point is that generals think in terms of military practice and military goals.

"Even if I grant that generals think in terms of military goals, that does not mean they're immoral. Their decisions are still made with morality in mind. It's just that war is an extreme situation."

Generals think in moral terms? How so?

"There are rules to war, moral rules. Certain weapons, like chemical and biological weapons, are deemed too horrible and inhumane to be used. Prisoners of war are supposed to be given certain protections. I know what you're going to say. None of this ever happens, but you're wrong. Even in war, people try to behave as morally as the situation allows."

As the situation allows. That's just the point. Since the general has a military goal, he is bound to act in the militarily correct ways. He may have moral concerns. I'm not saying all generals are immoral.

"Then what are you saying?"

Only that military reasoning, and military goals, are a separate type of practical reasoning.

"I'm confused. What do you mean by practical reasoning?"

Practical reasoning applies to the real world. As opposed to theoretical reasoning, like math and physics.

"Math and physics apply to the real world."

Of course they do. I didn't mean to imply that they were a waste of time. Let me see, how can I explain this? Math is theoretical in that a mathematician doesn't need to use her experience to do math properly. In fact, math is primarily a discipline of the mind. Physics is also theoretical. I know physicists run experiments and make observations. In that way science is dependent on experience. But one can do theoretical physics. For example, physicists talk about moving objects where friction is not a factor. They know that the real world doesn't happen that way. Or they theorize about subatomic particals that may not exist. Then they look for evidence to confirm or deny their guess.

"I think I see what you mean. Math and physics are applied all the time, but the principles are theoretical, at least at first."

Close enough. Now the same does not apply to morality, or to military and economic reasoning. The aims of these approaches is practical. The moral philosopher aims to discover the good course of action. The military strategist aims to win battles. The economist or business-minded person desires to maximize profits.

"Still, there's lots of theory involved in each of these. All you seem to mean by practical reasoning is when people apply the theories in practice."

Okay, I'll accept that. I didn't mean for us to get bogged down with the distinction between practical and theoretical reasoning anyway. All I want to distinguish is that there are different types of practical reasoning. The military general has goals that are different from the goals of the moral person. And the businessperson has goals different from those of either the moralist or the militarist.

Moral Reasoning Is Overriding.   "The goals are not as separate as you insist. I've already gotten you to admit that generals also consider moral variables. If you're unconvinced, I have another example."

By all means, tell me.

"Say a general can take either of two courses of action. Both alternatives will give him the same military result. Both involve the same losses to his troops. The only difference is that the first strategy involves destroying hospitals that house infants and small children. The second strategy avoids the hospitals, so no innocent infants will be killed."

Oh, I see. You're saying that when all things are equal from a military point of view—

"Right, the general will opt for the strategy that harms fewest innocent people. And I don't think this applies only when all things are militarily equal. I believe generals are more moral than you seem to credit them."

Maybe so. Does this apply to businesspeople, too?

"Certainly. I know we all hear about the businesspeople who trample everyone to make their money. But most businesspeople are moral. Sure, they want to make money. That's what they're there for. But most businesspeople are pretty honest. They don't intentionally make products that will harm their customers. I know you're going to have a cynical reply to this."

No, actually I think you have a good point. I admit that it's easy to fall into the attitude that all businesspeople are greedy, that all doctors are greedy, that all politicians are . . .

"Greedy?"

Actually that wasn't the word that came to mind, but never mind. I agree with your main point. And I think you point out an interesting feature of moral reasoning.

"Which is what?"

Moral objectives override military and business objectives. Moral principles are more important than the principles of the other types of practical reasoning. Your two examples show that. We're actually making headway.

"Yes, I think moral concerns do override the other practical concerns we've discussed. People condemn generals, businesspeople, and politicians if the generals, businesspeople, or politicians act immorally. And people condemn these public figures even when the military or business or political success is gained. Sometimes that condemnation does not happen right away. People seem to get carried away with winning wars and all. But later, when their emotions calm down, people expect a certain level of moral decency."

I find myself forced to agree with you. (See, I can agree with you, and if you're ever right again, I may agree again.)

"So where do we go from here? Are there other formal characteristics of the moral point of view?"

Let's go back to examining the examples of moral principles, or whatever we're calling them. Let's see—from our examples what else is unique about morality? Where should we begin?

The Ten Commandments is a Perfect Example

"The Ten Commandments and the Golden Rule are perfect examples of morality."

You sound more and more like Smith and Jones. Okay, let's look at the Ten Commandments. To be fair, can we look at the nonreligious rules?

"What do you mean, the 'nonreligious' ones? They're all religious. They are God's commandments."

I didn't mean to offend you. If you look at the table of contents, you'll see that we get to discuss God. For now I'm suggesting we look at the commandments as purely moral rules.

"What makes you think you can distinguish moral and religious rules so easily?"

For your sake, I'll admit that the distinction is artificial. Can't we just look at the commandments that don't refer to God? Don't be so defensive.

"All right. Do not kill, or steal, or bear false witness. Honor your parents. Do not covet your neighbor's donkey or his wife."

My neighbors don't have donkeys!

"Do not covet *anything* of your neighbor's. And you are not allowed to commit adultery with your neighbor's wife."

Is that all? I'm not attracted to my neighbor's wife. By the way, can my neighbor's wife commit adultery with me? Or does the rule go in only one direction?

"The rules apply to everyone. The Ten Commandments is an excellent example of morality. Each commandment is absolute; there are no exceptions. And each commandment stands on its own. Together the Ten Commandments describes the best life. So what do you have to say?"

Which Is Your Favorite Commandment? Which is your favorite commandment?

"You're not allowed to have favorites. They all apply with equal seriousness. No exceptions, so don't look for any."

But I don't know how to apply the rules. For example, if I must either kill or steal, which do I do?

"Killing is the more serious offense."

How can you say that?

"In our society killing is the more grievous crime."

I grant that. But the commandments do not say that! Or, for example, if I am tempted to abide by the wishes of my parents, and they ask me to kill, should I kill?

"When would parents ever ask such an immoral thing of their child? That's ridiculous! You're just making light of the Ten Commandments. You're probably an atheist as well as immoral."

Name calling aside, what if my parents ask me to kill someone? Many parents instill in their children the need to defend the country. That involves killing. What if I do not want to kill in time of war?

"Now you turn out to be a coward as well. It's right to defend one's country. It's self-defense."

Excuse me, but we're getting sidetracked. What if my parents' wishes conflict with one or more of the commandments? Do I honor my parents, or do I break the other rule? Don't you see? It's not the commandments I see as deficient, it's that there are no priority rules.

Priority Rules. "What do you mean by priority rules?"

There are no rules to tell me which commandments are relatively more important than the others. You say they are all absolutes. What I don't understand is how to act when I can't follow two rules, yet both apply. How am I to decide in cases of conflict? For example, imagine a society where the Ten Commandments are fully and completely followed. Imagine that in this society the prohibition on killing is ranked as less significant than the rule to honor one's parents. Maybe stealing is next, then adultery, and so on. Just reverse the order that we put on the Ten Commandments. Wouldn't this society be very different from the one we live in? Could you imagine that "dishonoring" one's parents could be a capital offense!

"And that killing would be no more serious than how we treat dishonoring our parents. I see what you mean. Why can't we place our own priority rules on the Ten Commandments? The priorities are given by common sense anyway."

It takes only common sense to correct the commandments? So your God lacked common sense when he created them? And we are going to fix God's mistake?

"That kind of talk is offensive. No wonder you can't understand morality."

Again, you're getting off track. It's morality we're examining. Since we don't understand morality yet, it's inappropriate to label me either moral or immoral. My personal beliefs, however, have nothing to do with our investigation. You wanted to place priority rules on the Ten Commandments.

"But you insisted on priority rules!"

Excuse me? I asked about the need for priority rules. I don't see the point of morality or the Ten Commandments. It's you who are offering priority rules.

"The reason I offer priority rules is to clean up the commandments."

I think it's a good idea. However, common sense is not going to help you here. The people of my imaginary culture would have very different common-sense ideas about their priorities. Common sense is created by your moral values. The values come first. So you can't justify your values by referring to common sense.

"Explain that."

Imagine our example. Imagine yourself living in a culture like traditional Japan only a couple of centuries ago. There dishonoring one's parents required one to commit ritual suicide. Is that the common sense you have in mind?

"Of course it isn't! What you say is correct, I guess. But if you are correct, can we ever find any morality? Can we find any way of justifying our values?"

Don't give up so easily, my friend. We haven't thrown out the Ten Commandments. Even if we do toss all the commandments, the Ten Commandments is only one set of moral rules. People have been working on developing a firm and unshakeable moral system for quite a long time. Look, you've helped me understand that if moral rules are to be useful, they need to be set in some kind of hierarchy. They need to be given with priorities mapped out. More important rules need to be placed above less important ones. That's a good start. Can I ask another question that's been on my mind?

"Go ahead."

Theories of Action/Theories of Character.   To what do the commandments apply?

"To people. What else?"

I'm sorry. We people from the far side of Jupiter are sometimes not very clear. Let me give you an example. Let's look at the Ten Commandments again. How about the one about honoring your parents? What does that mean?

"Everyone knows what that means! Honor your parents. Listen to what they tell you."

Is our interpretation the same as it would be in the Japan of our example? The Japan of the recent past? We just said that there a child was bound to commit ritual suicide if he disgraced his parents. Is that what we mean by honoring our parents?

"That's too strong! All the commandment means is that we have to listen to them and make up our own minds. You may not have to follow their advice, but you should listen."

So we can rephrase the rule: One should tolerate the opinion of one's parents, then do what one wants anyway?

"No! You know what it means! It means *do* what your parents want while you live in their house. Once you're out of their house, you can do what you want."

Ah, so Eddie Haskell, the guy on *Leave It to Beaver,* is the most moral guy around. "Yes, Mrs. Cleaver. My, don't you look nice today. I was just telling young Theodore that committing murder is morally unacceptable." Morality is not how you think or feel, it's what you do?

"Now you're just being intentionally stupid. Of course, morality is not just a question of how one acts. Morality applies to how one lives. Eddie Haskell is not moral; he's acting. For example, a person in a movie or play is not being courageous, he's just acting."

Good distinction. (I knew this distinction was coming. I read the heading at the top of this section.)

"So now we think that morality does not apply to actions alone. Morality applies to character. And whenever there is more than one moral rule, we need to define our priorities."

We're making great progress! What else can we say about morality?

A Religious Anxiety. "I've already given two examples of the moral point of view. The Ten Commandments may not work exactly as I'd hoped. That's why we have the Golden Rule. With the Golden Rule there is no need for priority rules. And before you ask, let me tell you. The Golden Rule applies absolutely, and to all situations, *and* to one's character."

Don't be so defensive. We're only taking a casual look at morality. I sense that there is something underlying your anxiety. Could there be an unconscious idea or implicit premise? Could a cherished belief be threatened?

"There's no secret, if that's what you mean. The reason I'm upset is because God gave us the Ten Commandments and the Golden Rule. If we attack these rules, I'm afraid you will take that as a proof that God does not exist. I think that you don't believe in any values!"

Well, to answer your first worry, I don't see what God or gods have to do with our discussion. After all, if there is a best way to live, why think we need a God or gods to discover it? And to answer the second concern, I do think there is a best way to live. I'm no nihilist! I've already told you. I think living for pleasure is the best way to live.

"You're being evasive. Do you believe in God or don't you?"

Whether or not a God exists is just not important.

"Not important! Of course it's important. Without God, life would be pointless. There would be no meaning in life. People would run wild. They would . . ."

I don't see why you interpret my questions as attacks. Besides, you're beginning to repeat yourself. Your insistence on the need for God sounds like your insistence on the need for morality. Since it is so important to you, later we'll discuss and read about God's contribution to finding the best life. But you have to promise me that we will first discuss our original two questions. I still want to know the point of morality. And I want to hear more about examples of the moral point of view.

"Okay, but don't you see, morality and religion are interconnected. God is the point of morality. God has given us two wonderful examples of moral rules. That's what I have been trying to tell you."

I do not agree that morality depends on gods, either your God or ancient, nearly forgotten gods. But let's take one issue at a time. So far, this discussion has been pretty chaotic. Let's focus on examples of morality. I need to get clearer on the idea of morality.

The Golden Rule: Do Unto Others

"The Golden Rule works for me."

I don't know what "works for me" means. That's what we're asking. What does the Golden Rule say?

"The Golden Rule is: 'Do unto others as you would have them do unto you.' That's clear, isn't it?"

I suppose so. Well, actually it's not clear to me. Why would I want to impose my weird wants on someone else?

"That's not what the Golden Rule says. You're playing word games. I certainly do not want to play word games."

The Golden Rule says that if I want something done to me, then I should do it unto others? If I want others to lie to me, or to break their promises, or to be mean to me, I should lie to them, or break promises made to them, or be mean to them. Right?

"That's ridiculous! No one wants someone else to lie to them, or to break promises made to them, or to be mean to them. You're using stupid examples. If you don't want people to lie, or break promises, or be mean to you, you should not lie, or break promises, or be mean to them. That's what the Golden Rule says."

The Golden Rule Inverted: Do Not Do Unto Others. My, it's difficult to keep you "on track." We were discussing the Golden Rule. Now you've given me a new rule.

"No, I haven't."

Sure you have. The new rule you've just stated is: "Do not do unto others as you would not have them do unto you."

"What's the difference? The double negative gives us a positive. The statements are equivalent. Everyone knows that."

Actually, everyone does not know that. There is a guy in Idaho who does not know it. And there is a woman in Mexico City who isn't sure. . . .

"Cut it out. You know it, and that's all that counts."

I do not know it. If I 'do not do unto others,' I am not committed to acting at all. To fulfill this rule, all I need is to refrain from doing anything. A guy in a coma becomes the perfectly moral person. He does not do anything at all. It follows that if he does not do anything at all, he surely does not do anything unto others that he does not want done unto himself. Don't you agree?

"Okay."

The "do not" rule (from which we probably get the word "doughnut"?) asks for nothing more than passivity (which may be why people prefer sitting when they eat their doughnuts). The "do not" rule doesn't ask us to commit ourselves to anything. It requires only that we omit certain unwanted actions. Perhaps it requires that we do not harm each other. I don't know.

"Yes. That's just what it requires. We should never knowingly harm others."

Maybe, but the Golden Rule requires us to be more active and assertive. Do unto others tells us to *do* something. My confusion is I don't understand what it is I am asked to do.

Treat Others As You Want to Be Treated.   "I see the distinction. What the Golden Rule tells you is that you should treat others as you want to be treated."

So again, let me ask my question. What if I am not like you? What if my wants are strange to you? Should I impose my wants on others? If I am a racist, I might believe that if I were a member of the "other" race, then I should be treated badly. If I am a consistent racist, I have just justified treating others in ways undesirable to them.

"That's crazy. The Golden Rule doesn't justify that! The racist was just using religion as an excuse for his own prejudices."

I remember hearing a story about a Nazi who believed that if he were a Jew, he would want to be exterminated. So he killed Jews. All the while he believed he was abiding by the Golden Rule.

"That's crazy. The Golden Rule certainly doesn't justify that!"

The interesting part of the story is that there came a time when he found out that he had Jewish blood in his veins. One of his grandparents had been a Jew. He marched into a concentration camp and asked to be put to death. That story is not common, I grant you. But he was not the only fanatic to do something like that. Wasn't he following the Golden Rule? He did unto others just as he would (and did) have done unto himself.

"That's not what the rule means."

Doesn't the Golden Rule assume that our wants are pretty much the same? And that is clearly not true. What does the Golden Rule mean, if it doesn't mean what it says?

Do For Others So They Will Do For You.   "No, no. The Golden Rule does not assume we have the same wants. It's more general than that. You should treat people respectfully, with kindness. If you're riding a bus and you see a tired older woman or man standing, you should give up your seat."

Why?

"Because what goes around comes around. Because you're young and probably nearing your stop. Because you would want others to do that for you. If you give up your seat, chances are someone will do the same for you someday."

Sort of an investment? I give up my seat to this older woman, and someday when I'm an older woman, some guy will give me his seat?!

"Not exactly. Obviously, you're getting caught up in the words. The spirit of the Golden Rule is what I'm explaining. Sure, no one is going to keep track of who gives up his seat and who doesn't give it up. But if you give up your seat on the bus, others will see your example. You could be influencing people. As the idea catches on, you could benefit from it."

But I have to give up my seat? Look, in all honesty, I don't see the connection. No one is going to give up a seat for me just because I gave up my seat. As far as setting an example goes, I'd say that is pretty unlikely. I do all sorts of things, and no one has decided to copy my lead. Unfortunate, but true. People do not copy my actions. No one takes me as a role model, though I can't figure out why.

"You should still give up your seat."

I'm not denying that. All I'm saying is that your motives are wrong. If I expect to be rewarded directly, by getting a seat next time I ride the bus, I'm going to be disappointed. If I give up my seat to set an example, then I'm fooling myself. People don't model themselves after me. So I'll just keep my seat. Besides, what you're suggesting sounds like deferred greed.

Treat Others As They Would Have You Treat Them. "I agree with you. You aren't supposed to follow the Golden Rule for a reward on earth. I guess the best way to explain the Golden Rule is to say that you are supposed to treat others as they would have you treat them."

That's not what it says. It does not say, "Do unto others as they would have you do unto them." Even if the Golden Rule were rewritten to say that, our problem would still be there. Why should I do what other people want? What if their wants are weird or strange, or—shall I say it?—immoral? Remember the Nazi who discovered he was Jewish? Should I exterminate him just because he wants me to murder him?

"Of course not. I see what you mean. Still, I think the idea behind the Golden Rule is right. Don't you agree with the sentiment?"

That depends. What is the sentiment behind the Golden Rule?

Treat Others Well: Don't Harm Them. "I think the Golden Rule means to treat other people well. It means to treat them with kindness and respect, to be nice to them. It means to do what they want when it does not harm them."

So now I have to concern myself with what others want, and whether or not it will harm them? That requires a great deal of calculation on my part. Now I really am confused about how to interpret the Golden Rule.

"What confuses you?"

It first sounded like the Golden Rule meant I should do things to people. Then

...t I should be passive toward people. Then we thought ... as I would want to be treated. Pressing on through my ...ed that the reason for the rule was expediency. I am supposed ... that I could get a reward. Putting aside greed as unacceptable, ...at the Golden Rule meant that I should treat others as they would ... treat them. Finally, the Golden Rule means that I should treat others ... at least not cause them unnecessary harm. Of course I'm confused. To avoid ...oming even more muddled, let's put aside interpretation for a while. My real objection to the Golden Rule is more practical. I don't understand how to use it. I don't understand how to apply the Golden Rule.

How Can I Apply the Golden Rule? "I admit that a rule loses credibility if it is difficult or impossible to apply, but I don't see how this is a problem for the Golden Rule. The beauty of the Golden Rule is that it's easy to apply."

This past summer I was wandering along the street. I came to an ice cream store and decided I wanted an ice cream cone. As I went into the store, I saw a cute little kid. He must have been around three or four years old. He was standing outside the store, staring in. Now I thought to myself, "Self, I'm going to apply the Golden Rule. How do I do that? Let's see. Do unto others. . . . If I were a little kid, and it was a hot day, I would want someone to give me an ice cream cone. If I were a little kid, I would want a chocolate ice cream cone. That's not a weird want." In fact, as I looked at the kid looking into the store, I could see he wanted a cone. So I bought a chocolate ice cream cone for myself and one for him.

"That was the right action. You made the child happy, and you gave yourself a good feeling at the same time. I applaud your action."

Thank you. I admit I did not feel any good feelings, but I was interested in trying out the Golden Rule, at least once in my life.

"Still, you did the right thing. I'll bet the child was delighted. And without realizing it, your action encouraged him to act that way toward others."

I don't know about that. What happened was interesting, though. The little kid took the cone. As he walked down the street, he began eating the ice cream. The next thing I knew, he had fallen, and was shaking violently. He evidently had some sort of allergy to chocolate, or he was diabetic or something. Anyway, he died. So much for the Golden Rule.

"You made that up!"

So what. The point still stands. I did unto another. . . . But did I do what was right? The little kid's parents were none too thrilled with me. (I bet I lost their votes for sainthood.) Or am I wrong? I should do unto others even if it kills them?

"No, of course not. But, you fool, what you incorrectly calculated was what the child really wanted. He did not want to die! You misapplied the Golden Rule."

Just my point. On one level, I applied the rule properly. You even agreed. I gave the kid an ice cream cone because I would have wanted one in similar circumstances. It was even chocolate, just as I would want. On a more "abstract" level, however, I misapplied the Golden Rule. I should have realized that I would not want someone to give me something that would poison me, so I should have given the little tike a different flavor? Or no ice cream at all? Come on. How could I know how to apply the principle?

What the Golden Rule Really Means. "The Golden Rule is not meant to be taken literally."

Where does it say that?

"Don't interrupt. The Golden Rule is meant to point to a certain attitude of respect for others."

Then why doesn't the rule say, "Respect others"? I can agree to that. We've just written a better rule.

"That's what it means. And we have not written a better rule. The Golden Rule is a commandment from God."

One comment and you've just raised several provocative points. First, the Golden Rule requires that we respect others. Second, the Golden Rule gets its authority, its validity, from God. And third, God gives out Golden Rules to humans. You are asserting quite a lot there. Let's take each issue in order.

The Golden Rule Means We Must Respect Others? "Okay, I'll go along."

If the Golden Rule requires us to respect others, it should be stated that way. Then we wouldn't have had to go through all of our earlier discussion. But I don't see how this interpretation helps. Eddie Haskell is again elevated to sainthood. He *shows* respect to the point of making everyone want to run from the room.

"I've caught you on this one. We agreed earlier that our theory would be a theory applied to character. It is not merely actions that concern us."

With all the calculation that is necessary to apply the Golden Rule, how can I be expected to incorporate the Golden Rule into my character? How can I be expected to act spontaneously on such a complicated rule? Aren't we back to a theory of action?

"No. Calculation can also become a part of one's character. For example, a mathematician or a scientist calculates. These people see problems and immediately reason them out. It's just part of their point of view on the world. It's part of their character. It can become automatic for them, even second nature. So calculation can become part of someone's character. It's not only actions that we're interested in."

Excellent! Your point is well taken. So respecting others is where it's at. But I don't know what that means. Should I respect people who do not deserve respect? Should I respect others in the ways they find appropriate, or in my own way?

"You should respect others, period."

I thought the Golden Rule is an explanation of how we are to respect others, not just a prescription to respect others. Tell you what. Let's tentatively agree that we ought to respect others, whatever that means. My question is, why? Why should I respect others?

The Golden Rule Gets Its Authority From God. "What do you mean, why? We should respect others, and follow all of God's other rules, because they are given to us by God. That's why!"

Are the rules of morality prior to the gods, or are the gods prior to morality? Take a look at Plato's dialogue *Euthyphro*. Socrates asks Euthyphro which comes first, the moral laws or the gods' approval of the laws.

"Explain the difference."

Socrates wants to know whether the gods approve of the moral law because it is right, or whether the moral law is right because the gods approve of it. Have I made this obscure?

"Yes, you have. Can you give me an example?"

Certainly. Better yet, you give me an example. Tell me an action that you find morally blameworthy?

"That's easy—it's wrong to kill."

To kill anything? I just killed and ate a stalk of broccoli last night. It was delicious. You aren't going to call me a murderer, are you?

"Don't be so picky. It's wrong to murder. It's morally wrong to kill innocent people. Forget the broccoli. Do you see some problem with the rule that it is wrong to kill innocent people?"

Which Came First, Good or God?

I'm not sure why I should agree with that principle, but let's get to our present point. Is killing wrong because it is morally wrong, or is it morally wrong because God says it's wrong?

"What's the difference? God says it's morally wrong and it's morally wrong."

The difference is substantial. If morality stands on its own, we don't need God to support morality. It changes our way of understanding morality.

"I don't follow."

If morality stands on its own, in a sense it's above God. Or better, morality is independent of God and only discovered by God. Would that be acceptable—God discovers morality?

"That might be okay."

Well, if God can discover morality, maybe humans can, too. Morality becomes a part of knowledge, accessible to gods and to people. If you grant that, then we don't need God, at least as far as morality is concerned. Murder would be wrong whether or not God recognized it as wrong.

"Why is that important?"

What If God Asks Us to Murder?   If morality is independent of God, then if God asks us to murder, we can legitimately say no.

"My God would never ask that we murder innocent people."

What if God asked you to kill for him?

"Why would God do that?"

You don't get to ask why. God tells you to kill, to kill someone you love. Would you do it?

"God would never ask that."

God asked that of Abraham. God asked old Abe to kill his kid.

"That was just a test to see if Abraham had faith. God didn't let Abraham kill Isaac. He supplied a ram for sacrifice instead."

Abe couldn't have known that it was only a test. If he had known it was a test, it wouldn't have been a test at all. It would have been easy to pass. Even I could pass that test. "Go kill your son, Art," bellows a deep, resonant voice. "I'm on my way. Gotta get one of those stone knives. Oops, better not tell my wife. It's only a test anyway."

"What's your point?"

Can We Separate the Moral Rules and God?   The point is that your God has asked someone to murder an innocent person. Your resistance to the question itself shows that you believe that murder is wrong, even if God commands it. Let me put it a different way. Suppose God came down and told you, and all of us, that he changed his mind. "Those rules I gave you? Never mind. I've got a new set."

"God wouldn't do that! Besides, how would I know it was God?"

It's your God; I don't know how It identifies Itself. No, wait, I've got it. God comes down, shows His American Express platinum card. Don't leave home without it! It says "GOD" on it. And this God guy says, "Forget the old rules. Do whatever you want." What do you do? And don't try to slip out of the question. God already intervened once, with Abraham and Isaac. He's shown he can change his mind. That's what miracles are about. Your God decides that the standard laws of nature shouldn't apply. God raises the dead, or parts the sea, or lands a guy in the belly of a fish, or turns a woman to salt.

"I don't know how to answer."

Would you want people to continue on the moral path?

"Yes, of course."

Then that is what we need to look at. Forget God. We don't need to discuss God in relation to morality. We've just discovered that morality is independent of God. Morality can be known without God. After all, surely you do not want to say that only people who believe in your God are moral people. There are people all over the world who live moral lives. Hindus, Buddhists, Shintoists, Moslems, even a few atheists. They don't believe in your God.

"You've made your point. At least, I'll think about it more. You seem to be right, but I'm not sure why I feel uncomfortable with the conclusion."

Comfort is hardly an appropriate criterion for truth. But I'm willing to leave this part of the discussion. We can return to it when you're ready. The reason you feel uncomfortable is because you still want there to be a God. We'll pick up on this theme in the next chapter. Until then, let's assume that morality is not necessarily bound to God.

"Okay, but you promise to get back to a discussion of God and religion."

By now you should know. All you have to do is check the table of contents. What was our next example of the moral point of view?

Conscience and Intuition

"Conscience and intuition were next. We all know that it is wrong to hurt other people. That's what the Ten Commandments and the Golden Rule are all about. The way we know this is by our conscience."

Conscience?

"Conscience allows all people to know about morality. Their religious training and beliefs sharpen their consciences. Believing in religion improves their understanding of morality. But everyone on earth has a conscience. Everyone except you, of course."

You mean I'm the only one without a clear idea of what morality is? The rest of you know what morality is and you follow it? What a shame.

"I don't appreciate your sarcasm. Everyone knows that killing is wrong. Stealing and lying are wrong. Even if you don't know it, others know."

You're right, I don't know. And not everyone else knows, either. At least lots of people act as if they don't know that it's wrong to kill or to steal or to lie. In times of war, entire countries seem to forget these "obvious" rules. What happens, just a massive outbreak of amnesia? Oops, we forgot, killing and stealing and lying are wrong?

"Times of war, times of self-defense are different. The rules have to be understood within their proper context. Killing is wrong, but people have a right to protect their lives and their property."

So the moral rules apply only when they are convenient? Did the Ten Commandments have a footnote that I missed?

"You have to be realistic. Common sense tells you that you can't expect people to just stand there and let their country be overrun. People have to be able to defend themselves. They have to be able to arm themselves for defense."

In cases of war, people do not lose their consciences, they are just forgetting to listen to them?

"Not exactly. It's wrong to kill innocent people. Aggressors are not innocent. Even when it comes to aggressive people, there are rules in war."

Cruelty and the Absurdity of Morality.   Okay, I see. Of course, usually each side is aggressive, though neither sees itself this way. Just how strong is conscience?

"That is a problem. Some people follow their consciences better than others. That doesn't diminish the fact that consciences tell people the difference between right and wrong."

Why Do People Disagree About Values?   Good point. But if conscience tells us the difference between right and wrong, why do people disagree about values?

"You mean moral questions like business ethics, or abortion, or suicide and mercy killing?"

Actually, I didn't have those in mind, but they are excellent examples. I had something cruder in mind. Some people think it is okay to kill healthy, unarmed civilians.

"You mean like when we bomb cities in time of war?"

Okay, but I can make the example even cruder. In "peacetime" people have been known to brutalize their own countrymen. Remember our example about the Nazi who worked all day putting victims to death? There was no war going on. The victims posed no threat. The Nazis worked their shift, then went home to their families. Can you imagine that? "So how was your day, Daddy?" "Fine, my little one. There were a few of those darn folks who resisted, but I got them into the ovens."

"You have the most disgusting examples."

True, it's a gift. The point is that this example is not isolated. People are cruel to other people. Corporate executives put workers and consumers at risk. That's one way to get higher profits. Are their consciences defective? Do their consciences give them the wrong values? Or do we have to admit that consciences are unreliable? Keep in mind, these people think they are doing the right thing. No doubt, there are people acting in cruel ways right now. What does this say for your conscience theory?

"Different intuitions about right and wrong do weaken the idea of universal conscience. And the evidence of cruelty is difficult to deny. I guess I'd just have to say that these people know they are doing wrong. They are just deceiving themselves and others."

That may be, my friend. But then there isn't much left of your conscience theory.

"Why do you say that?"

If conscience is so easily overturned, or if intuitions can vary so widely, what good is the theory for defining right and wrong? Or even worse, if we are so susceptible to being self-deceptive, how do we know when we are following the right and avoiding the wrong?

Conscience Is a Reflection of Society's Values.   "Still, there is something true about conscience. I know I have one and I follow it as best I can. Art, you've been pretty quiet. What do you have to say about conscience? It's easy for you just to ask questions and attack my views. I'd like to hear what you have to say."

As you can tell from the heading, I think conscience is just a reflection of society's values. We learn our values within our society. We learn them when we are children. Values are internalized like so many other things we learn as children. Think about it. The language you speak you learn as a child. If you learn a certain grammar, your "language conscience" tells you which "rules" to follow. Ain't I learnin' ya good?

"So if different societies have different values, they create different consciences?"

I think so.

"Do you have any other objections to conscience?"

Almost No One Knows Why It's Wrong to Kill.   My objection to conscience is that it doesn't explain how or why an action or motive is wrong. Let me ask you, what's wrong with killing babies?

"You've got to be kidding. Why would anyone want to do something that horrible?"

I don't know. Maybe as an artistic expression. No, forget that. That would be for some reason. Is it wrong to kill babies just to kill them? Not for religious reasons, not for preservation of the mother or of society. Tell me what's wrong with it?

"Oh, I get it. You're trying to trick me into making some statement about babies. Then you'll apply it to fetuses and the abortion issue."

That would be devious and manipulative and clever. Had I thought of it, I would have done it. But it's not my idea. If you can't say what's so terrible about killing innocent babies, then why shouldn't people be allowed to do it?

"How would you like to be killed?"

I'm not a baby.

"When does it become wrong to kill a baby? If it's okay to kill babies, where does it stop?"

You don't know what's wrong with killing babies, do you? Don't be ashamed, almost no one knows. Everyone knows *that* it is wrong, but not *why* it's wrong.

"This is too much. How can you advocate killing innocent babies?"

Have you seen what they do in their diapers? Innocent, indeed! But I am not advocating anything. I am asking a question. To be honest, I don't think this is a question that comes up in real life. Very few people are ever seriously tempted to kill babies. I picked this extreme example thinking if we could make headway on one moral value, the others might become easier to handle.

"But why such a strange example?"

Strange? The technique of taking extremes is not so unusual. In science, there is talk about vacuums and of the movement of rolling objects where friction is neglected. All this is to help get an understanding of basic principles and laws.

"But that's different. Neglecting friction is not the same as killing babies."

Duh, it isn't? Of course it isn't. But the technique of reasoning is the same. By the way, don't minimize friction. If you take a 50-mile bicycle ride and return to your original starting point, all you have done is overcome friction. I'll bet you'll be pretty tired.

"I'm not sure I can say why killing babies is wrong. It just is wrong. Maybe our other examples of morality can help. We should look to see if these help explain why killing babies is wrong."

Other Examples of Morality

What else did we say we would talk about?

"Let's see, we thought of several other ways of approaching morality. We said there are social and natural roles."

And the greatest good for the most people might indicate what is right to do.

"I suggested that there is a contract between each person and society. The law is kind of a contract among members of society. The law is based on morality."

Yes, and you also suggested that morality might be based on something like our genuine, natural, or spiritual needs.

"Right, and then there is a question about moral absolutes. Are moral values absolute, or are they different for different people and different societies? I think that about covers it."

Don't forget egoism, my favorite.

"And egoism. Why don't we start with that one and get it out of the way?"

Let's Finish This Chapter With Egoism

You read my every thought! Okay, let's finish this discussion with egoism. We can take up the other examples later.

"So what do you mean by egoism?"

All I mean by egoism is, well, ego is the self. Egoism is a kind of self-ism.

"You mean selfishness?"

Not exactly. My principle is that I should always act in my own self-interest. If doing something benefits me, then I have a reason to do it. I don't see why I should bother to be moral.

"That's selfish! What about everyone else?"

Of course! That's a great suggestion. Everyone should act in my self-interest. If some act benefits me, then it ought to be done. I and everyone else ought to do it, if (and only if) it benefits me. Thanks for the revision.

Individual Ethical Egoism.   "That's a challenge to morality! Surely not everyone is going to follow that rule! But that isn't what I mean. What I mean is, are you willing to have everyone act on your principle, 'I ought always to act in my own self-interest. If doing some act benefits me, then I have a reason to do it'?"

You mean you're requiring everyone to be selfish and egocentric. What kind of person are you?

"Ah, so you're not willing to make your individual egoism apply to everyone! That's just what I thought. You are not willing to have everyone act entirely as you suggest. If you can't want everyone to do it, then what makes you so special? If your principle is not open to everyone, then it isn't a moral principle."

If everyone acted selfishly, then I'd be a fool not to act that way. Why should I be the only one not acting selfishly? But to answer your more serious question, no, I don't want to have everyone act exclusively for his or her own benefit. I want everyone to act for my benefit. Why? Because I'm me, not them. Simple.

"That will never happen. People aren't so foolish. You may go about acting immorally. That's up to you. But while you are acting like an egoist, the rest of us are going to be moral."

That's not as perfect as everyone acting for my benefit, but it's almost as good. You should all be good, boring, moral people, and I'll act for my own benefit.

Free-Rider Egoism.   "Now you're taking a free ride, and I object to that. It isn't fair for one person to take advantage of everyone else. That's not what morality is about."

There you go, assuming what you need to prove.

"What do you mean?"

You're assuming that morality is correct. That's why you object to my free ride.

"I object because the only legitimate principle of action is one where everyone can follow it."

Just my point. You are assuming what you need to prove.

"You are not some special creature who should be given more than anyone else."

Universal Egoism.   Okay, so everyone ought to pursue his or her own benefit.

"What you suggest, Art, will cause people to separate. Each person will be off chasing his or her own goals and benefit. Then what? No, this will end badly. This is not morality at all."

But it was your suggestion that we make universal the egoist principle. Are you changing your mind? If so, fine. I'm willing to have all of you be moral people, and I alone will pursue my benefit. Unless, of course, you all want to contribute to my self-interest.

"Forget it. I reject the free ride, and individual egoism, and even universal egoism. But I have a question for you. By self-interest, do you mean momentary pleasures, or long-term benefits, or enlightened interests?"

Yes.

"Which?"

I guess I hadn't thought about this.

"There is a trap laid with each option, Art. If you go for momentary pleasure, you may be sacrificing a greater pleasure later. If you pursue long-term benefits, you become too distracted to appreciate the present."

I'm really not sure what you mean by "enlightened" interests. But look, I'm getting tired. Why don't we wrap up this discussion and pursue the loose ends in our next conversations? For example, when we discuss *The Stranger,* we can get into the strengths and shortcomings of living for short-term sensual pleasures. The idea of enlightened self-interest will no doubt come up in several contexts.

So What Have We Learned?
Formal Features of Morality

"So what have we learned?"

Absolutely nothing. No, no, I'm kidding. We have learned a few things. In looking at examples of the moral point of view, we have found a number of desirable features to any moral theory. The moral point of view is different from other approaches to living. We've learned that any set of principles that we are going to live by, and call morality, must have special features. For example, with the Golden Rule we found that a principle should be able to be easily and clearly applied. We agreed that a rule should be as comprehensive as possible. It should apply to as many "moral decisions" as possible. That's one of the strengths of the Golden Rule. With the Big Ten (Ten Commandments), we found that any set of laws must have rules for ordering them, priority rules. Otherwise we don't know what to do in cases of conflicting laws. Oh yes, and we're talking about a way of life, not just rules of behavior. The person is supposed to *be* moral, not just act that way.

"Yes, we have also sorted out formal features that are required before a point of view is properly called morality. I just realized that I have been assuming several of these formal features. When I object to your selfishness and egoism, I am really demanding that moral guidelines be universal, that they apply to everyone equally. You can't just leave blanks in a moral rule and then write in your name. You can't expect that everyone is going to follow that sort of rule. That wouldn't be impartial enough."

So impartiality is a necessary feature of a moral rule. The rules or principles have to be stated in general terms?

"Right. And they must be open to everyone in another sense. Your egoism bothers me because you can't make it public."

What do you mean?

"You can't state your principles without automatically defeating them. That's not true of moral principles. If I want people to be honest, and not steal or kill or lie or commit adultery . . ."

This sounds familiar.

"Don't interrupt. If I don't want people to do these things, I can and should tell everyone. I can make my moral values public. The more successful I am, the more they will be followed."

I'm quivering with excitement.

"Admitting your point of view lets people guard against you."

Military strategy and business strategy are in the same position.

"That's one way they differ from morality. Finally, moral principles should be considered more important than all other types of rules. That's what makes them so important. That's what gives meaning to a person's life. The moral principles we live by are the most important rules. No matter how strongly someone is tempted by economic gain or military victory, moral considerations come first. Over profit, over other goals, certainly over pleasures. We are all equals when it comes to morality. That's a good definition. The moral point of view is: Each of us is one among many equals. That applies to everyone."

Summary of Discussion

In an effort to discover what makes a point of view a moral point of view, we look to possible examples of morality. People use several methods to judge their actions. Conscience, social roles, and legal restrictions direct people's decisions. What creates the greatest good for the greatest number has an affect on our decisions. There is an unwritten contract that people recognize in society; this contract promises rights and protections as long as each of us abides by it. Two prominent examples of the moral point of view are the Ten Commandments and the Golden Rule.

We can abstract from these examples some of the features that help us identify moral principles. Moral reasons have priority over other kinds of reasons, such as economic reasons, military reasons, and business reasons. Like any other set of reasons, morality requires priorities set out for us. In cases of conflict, then, which commandment should I follow?

The Golden Rule promises to reveal the defining moral insight. The Rule itself, however, is open to interpretation and is too vague for us to apply with confidence. Implicit in the Ten Commandments and the Golden Rule is the Judeo-Christian assumption of the existence of a God. God upholds the principles and gives us confidence in their worth. However, good is independent of gods, and we are again left to discover a source of confidence in our values.

Some people think that the fundamental moral insight is gained through intuition or conscience. There are difficulties with these approaches. All types of cruelties and indignities have been heaped on people and "justified" by intuition and conscience. The fact that we cannot easily agree on the moral insight suggests there is no uniform moral intuition. Conscience is merely a reflection of society's values. Why do I say this? Because almost no one knows why it's wrong to violate any particular moral rule.

Egoism mounts a compelling challenge to the moral life. Why shouldn't I take a free ride in society? Why shouldn't I take advantage of other people? The point of asking these questions is that each of us is tempted to think of our own desires first. The moral life must motivate us to be moral.

Discussion Highlights

I. Examples of morality
   1. The Golden Rule
   2. The Ten Commandments
   3. Inverse of the Golden Rule
   4. Conscience
   5. Social and natural roles
   6. The greatest good for the greatest number
   7. Social contract
   8. Fulfillment of real or spiritual needs
   9. Traditional rules
   10. Absolutes
II. Formal features of morality. Moral reasons must
   1. be overriding of other types of reasons
   2. be universally applicable
   3. be general
   4. be impartial
   5. be public
   6. view each person as one among many equals
   7. be comprehensive, ordered, and relatively easily applied

Questions for Thought/Paper Topics

1. Which versions of the moral point of view do you think best capture the essence of morality? Can you defend this perspective?
2. Do you think everyone has a conscience? Except for a psychopath, can you imagine anyone without a conscience? Here's one! See if you can find any evidence that either Jesus, Moses, or Gautama (Buddha) had a conscience.
3. If you believe we have a social contract between members of our society, how binding is the contract? What should each member of society be willing to give up to maintain the health of the society? If a person is wrongly convicted of a crime, should that person be willing to accept punishment for a crime he or she did not commit?
4. Can you interpret the Golden Rule and make sense of it? How much do you have to stretch the literal meaning to accomplish a sensible principle?
5. Which is your favorite commandment? Why? Do you have any right to have your opinion?
6. Egoism must be appealing. What's stopping you from adopting the egoistic attitude? (Careful, don't tell everyone; that would ruin your position.)
7. Which strikes you as more important, actions or character? Give reasons for your answer. (How well do you know Eddie Haskell?)

For Further Reading

One unique story that depicts a moral character is Robert Bolt's play *A Man for All Seasons*, also made into an impressive movie. Many rules and principles incorporate the moral point of view; look at the Ten Commandments and the Golden Rule for tight packages. A contemporary source that discusses the defining features of morality is John Rawls's *A Theory of Justice* (Harvard, 1971). Two parts of Rawls's discussion are particularly appropriate: "Some Remarks about Moral Theory" (chap. 1, #9) and "The Formal Constraints of the Concept of Right" (chap. 3, #23).

One pointed critique of the moral point of view is Friedrich Nietzsche's *On the Genealogy of Morals* (Vintage, 1989). Come to think of it, Nietzsche's book *Twilight of the Idols* (Penguin, 1968) is also a hard-hitting attack on moral living. It's worth reading, too.

3   **What About Belief in God?**

"Moral and religious rules should be followed because they are God's will. It's all a matter of faith. We are supposed to follow God's rules. These reveal God's plan for us on earth. Besides, it is our duty to follow God's will. That's what gives morality a purpose. That's the point of morality. That's what it means for morality to work. Now do you agree?"

No, I don't agree. Why do you think there is a God?

God Does Exist

"There just is a God. God exists!"

How do you know?

"I believe for lots of reasons. I believe because the belief in God has a long history, nearly four thousand years. I believe because the universe must have had a beginning. Even your scientists can't explain what caused the 'Big Bang.' I believe in God because without Him the world would be chaotic. I believe in God because the world is an orderly place. I don't mean socially and politically orderly; evil people keep the world from being orderly in that way. But the entire universe is organized. If the earth were tilted just two degrees farther away from the sun, plant life on the planet could not survive. Do you want more reasons?"

Sure, if you've got more.

"I believe in God because without Him life would be meaningless. Everything speaks for God, and nothing against Him. I believe in God. Can you show me that there is no God? I certainly doubt it."

Wow! Ask a simple question and get a flood for an answer. And what emotion! I had no idea there were so many reasons for God to exist. You'd think with all these reasons that It must exist.

"God does exist. I've just given you the reasoning that leads to the belief in God."

Let's look at each reason.

The Majority Believes in God

"Belief in God is important to me, and to most people."

There I have to correct you. Most people do not believe in your God. China and India are sizeable countries, and they do not believe in the Judeo-Christian God. Even if most people did agree with you, that would not make God exist. Truth isn't democratic. And belief in something doesn't cause the thing to exist. Right? Even if everyone believed in Santa Claus, he would not exist. Have I offended you? You did know that Santa Claus is mythical, didn't you?

"My, you're an arrogant one. If most people believe in God, you don't think that means something?"

Of course, it *means* something, though what it means isn't clear to me. My point is simpler. Your ancestors and mine probably believed that the earth was flat. They thought it was shaped like a pancake. That was the common belief only a few centuries ago. Except for a few "crazies," the vast majority of Europeans believed that the earth was flat. Did that make the earth flat?

"Of course not. But that's different. The earth is a concrete thing. God isn't that sort of thing."

Still, everyone or nearly everyone believed the earth was flat. That did not make the earth flat. And then people began to speculate, and in increasing numbers they believed that the earth was more of a globe. Did the earth become more and more globelike with their changing views? Or did the shape of the earth change suddenly when 50 percent plus one person finally believed?

"No, the earth's shape doesn't depend on people's beliefs. That's certain. But like I said, God's existence is different."

Different? Does God's existence depend on people's beliefs? Just for a moment, imagine if reality depended on human beliefs. Imagine what life would have been like. Fifty percent of the people believe the earth is flat. The other half believe it is a sphere. Then, in 1412, along comes a guy named Wally. He's the kind who can never make up his mind. He believes the earth is flat, then a sphere, then flat. . . . The changing shape would make bicycle riding hazardous.

"You've made your point. Truth is not a matter of agreement. By the way, there were no bicycles in the fifteenth century." (Ah, you're finally getting a sense of humor.)

Actually, truth probably is a matter of agreement. I really don't know. I was not speaking to the question of truth. I am more concerned with what's real than with what's true. By the way, it's too bad those people didn't have bicycles. They're really fun to ride, especially whenever Wally believes that the earth is flat.

Belief in God Has a Long Tradition

"I keep telling you, but you keep ignoring me."

Did you say something?

"God is not a concrete thing. Your argument works well enough on a concrete thing like the earth or a table. But it does not work on God. God is different."

Very well. Let's look into your other reasons for God's existence. If we have to, we can come back to the point that God's reality is not the same as the earth's reality. By the way—

"I already know your odd sense of humor. The earth is not concrete; it is grass and trees and lava and rocks, etc. Right?"

Very promising. One reason you gave for belief in God is because there is a long tradition of belief.

"That's right. Monotheism goes back to the time of Abraham, Isaac, Jacob, and Joseph. For thousands of years people have dedicated their lives to that belief. And listen, before we go on, I want to tell you something. I have noticed how you refer to God as 'It.' I resent that. You could show more respect for our beliefs, you know."

Fair enough. Though I'm not comfortable calling an idea Him, I'll try to remember to keep your God's name from being used in vain. As far as your assertion that the belief in your God goes back to perhaps 2000 B.C.E., I do not see how this has any bearing on our discussion.

"It shows that people have believed for a long time. Could they all have been wrong?"

Sure, they all could have been mistaken. What we are trying to establish is whether or not they were mistaken. Just because a belief is old, it does not follow that it is true. We accept very little of the other old beliefs that Abraham and friends shared. We do not accept their physics, or chemistry, or belief in actual human sacrifice. Do we?

"But those are not the beliefs we are examining. We are asking about their belief in God. I am saying that this one belief is true."

Very well. But then we are going to have to use a different standard of truth. Truth is not established by age any more than it is established by majority vote. Given your point of view, you should be a Shintoist.

"What is a Shintoist?"

Shintoism is one of the dominant religions of Japan. Its roots go far back into the prehistory of Japan. If age makes a belief true, Shintoism may be just what you are looking for.

"Look, you've misunderstood. It is not all old beliefs, only the belief in God that I'm urging you to accept."

Then we can abandon your earlier claim. Tradition itself does not validate a belief. Old beliefs are not necessarily true beliefs.

The Universe Had to Have a Beginning

"That may be true, but the universe had to have a beginning. Even your 'Big Bang' theorists can't answer *how* the universe came into being. God is the only plausible answer."

You're going too fast for me! Why do you think the universe had to have a beginning?

"Everything has to have a beginning. That's just the way things are. No one would disagree with that! Or do you have a problem understanding a claim as simple and as obvious as that?"

Duh. Perhaps you're right, I don't know. Let me ask a couple of questions first. Does the universe have an end? Can you imagine a time when the universe will not exist? Or do you think that the universe will go on for eternity?

"I'm not sure which way to answer. I guess it could end, but I think the universe will go on existing for eternity. If that's God's will."

Wills aside, your principle is that all things have a beginning. All things may not have an end. Right?

"Right. I guess so."

You do have a point. When I look around, everything I see seems to have a beginning. Or so I think. I mean, I've never seen a mountain or an ocean begin, but I suppose they do. There is evidence for that.

"Yes, that's my point."

But when I look around, I also see that everything has an end. Your hypothesis is only that everything has a beginning. That's odd.

"What's so odd about that?"

The way you came to the belief that all things must have a beginning was from your observations. But when you also observe that all things have an end, you do not carry through. You do not speculate that all things end. That's what's odd.

"Well, I'm not sure what to say to that, but I still believe that all things have a beginning. Including the universe. And God created the universe. He created it out of nothing."

Glory be! (I would have written "hallelujah!" but I don't know how to spell it.) And what or who created God? And please, don't say Mr. and Ms. God. And their parents, and their parents. . . .

"God is, was, and always shall be. God has no beginning and no end."

That's neat, but it doesn't work. You claim that everything must have a beginning. Then God must have a beginning.

"Everything does have a beginning, everything but God!"

If you can say that, then why not say that everything has a beginning but the entire universe? Don't you see, you haven't made any headway. By thine own claims hast thou entangled thyself.

"Stop mocking religion."

I assure you, I am not mocking religion, at least not right now. I'm mocking you, but only a little. Look, as far as I am concerned, everything does not have to have a beginning or an end. Experience tells us that *within* the universe everything has a beginning. It doesn't follow that the universe itself must have a beginning. As far as ends go, I haven't died yet. And I'm not sure that I will. Frankly, I haven't decided yet. So the only conclusion we can safely make is that the universe or God may be without beginning.

"So you agree with me!"

Not at all. All I am saying is that your idea goes no further in proving God's existence than in proving its nonexistence. Translation? It proves neither. Your original principle that everything must have a beginning is mistaken.

The Universe is Ordered by God

"Now you're talking gibberish, Art. Even if the universe didn't have to have a beginning, you certainly cannot deny that it is orderly. Who do you suppose ordered the universe? It couldn't have been chance! It had to be God."

Orderly? You call this orderly?

"Not society. Society may not be orderly. That's our fault. God gives humans free will. It's up to us to use it wisely."

I don't believe there is any free will. And I don't mean that society is disorderly. It is, I guess. What I mean is that the universe is disorderly. And becoming more disorderly every moment. At least that's what physicists tell us. The Second Law of Thermodynamics—they call it entropy.

"That doesn't make sense. There is order everywhere you look. Day follows night. The seasons are orderly. The stars in the sky are orderly. Little electrons race around the atom's nucleus in orderly fashion. Oaks spring from acorns. And so on. The universe is like an immense, finely tuned watch mechanism."

One of those electronic digital jobs? Or the old windup?

"You know what I mean."

Our Minds Impose Order on Nature.   I certainly do not want to deny that there is an apparent order in the universe. But I wonder if it is no more than apparent. Maybe it has more to do with our minds than with the natural environment.

"This is the craziest thing you've suggested so far. Do you deny that there is an order to the seasons?"

Well, no—and yes. Actually, I do deny it. For example, have you ever experienced a "summer" day in late winter? I presently live in the northeast. Occasionally we see winter day temperatures reach 70 degrees. Pretty summerlike! I lived in North Dakota for a year. There the temperatures went from 50 degrees to -25 degrees in a week's time. A rather sudden autumn?

"What's your point?"

I think we often experience winter as winter because that's what we expect to experience. Each day's temperature is taken in the context of the proper—that is, the expected—season. So we talk about unusually warm winter days and cool summer days. Spring and fall are hopelessly confusing.

"And I suppose oaks do not spring from acorns? This is ridiculous."

I don't deny some apparent uniformity in nature. I am simply saying that the universe may not be as regular as we experience it to be.

"I'm not going to let you get by with this one. Do you have any reason to believe this? Or are you merely speculating? Is this just more of your 'it could be' stuff?"

I have two responses. First, who made you the author of this book? I'm supposed to be the one who asks the difficult questions. That's the power of author-ship. I can rig the discussion any way I want.

"Not this time. You have to answer the question. Do you have any evidence to support your contention that our minds impose order on a disorderly universe?"

Your ability to argue is improving. (I am desperately hoping that the editor of this book removes your more telling arguments.)

"Well, I'm waiting."

An Experiment With Fire.   Okay. Here's an experiment you can try. Tonight go into your room. Light a candle and turn on some music. Now turn out the lights, except for the candle. Sit in front of it and concentrate on the flame's movement.

"Is this some kind of sixties hippie ritual? Are you going to advocate drug use, too?"

Now look who is mocking whom! (Nice grammar, huh? I hope you're learnin' good from my example.) I am not a throwback to the sixties. And I do not advocate drug use. I do not use drugs. More to the point, oh ye of many repressions, drug use would throw off my experiment.

"Okay. So I concentrate on the flame. Now what?"

What you will find is that the flame dances to the music.

"No way."

It does. The flame will begin to dance to the music. Slowly at first. As your concentration gets better, the dancing will quickly occur. The flame's motion will conform to the rhythm of the music.

"The movement of air caused by the speakers is what causes the flame to move."

That's plausible. So try this. Put on your headphones. That way, no air vibrations will reach the flame. Unless, of course, your candles also wear headphones.

"Still, there may be movement we cannot detect."

Fair enough. Ask some friends to join you. Smith and Jones are likely candidates. Tell each one to concentrate on the flame. Same dance to the same song? Of course. Now have each person put on his or her headphones. Have them play different styles of music. Each person will see the flame dance to the beat of his or her music.

"Even though each is listening to different rhythms?"

Exactamundo. That shows that at least some of the order we see in nature is imposed by us.

"This sounds pretty farfetched. Even if it works, there may be a cause we are overlooking."

An Experiment With Children.   I read once that people used to think that children were just small adults. They believed that kids were just as responsible for their actions as adults. That's probably what allowed them to put kids to work in factories and in mines. Not that I oppose abusing children in the name of profit.

"When was this belief around?"

For some people it is probably current today. But the period I heard about was in Europe in the early part of the seventeenth century.

"Why are you telling me this? Where is this going?"

As it turns out, the microscope was invented, or at least came into use, in Holland at about this time. For the first time scientists looked at fertilized human embryos. And guess what they saw?

"Fertilized human embryos. What else?"

They saw little people, completely formed and dressed.

"No way."

It's true. Little bearded men with walking sticks. Little women with aprons. Sounds culturally determined to me! And no, I do not know how they explained how babies are born without clothes.

"These people were obviously demented."

Not at all. They saw what they were looking for. In every other respect they were good scientists, just trapped in their way of thinking. Just as we are, at least until we realize that we are trapped. Do you want another example?

"No, your examples are weird enough. Let me think about this."

Experience is Colored by Beliefs

Experience is colored by beliefs. That's all I am saying. When you see something, you see with the beliefs and concepts and expectations that you carry with you. When people are hungry enough, things start looking like food. When we are thirsty enough, things start looking like water.

"So you are talking about mirages on the desert?"

Good example. I hadn't thought of that.

"But mirages happen in cases of extreme thirst."

Near-Death Experiences.   True, but the extreme shows us a lot about the "normal." Did you ever hear about "near-death" experiences?

"Interesting that *you* should bring that up. I was going to use that as further proof of God's existence."

Beat you to it! What happens in near-death experiences?

"The person dies and has the experience of a long dark tunnel. At the end of the tunnel is a bright light. If the person goes into the tunnel, she hears Jesus calling in a soothing voice. Some people have gone far enough into the tunnel to actually see Him."

Right, and how do we explain such experiences?

"I believe that this is further proof that God loves us."

Of course you do. But do you really think that is what it *proves*? Aren't you wishing it proves that?

"What do you mean?"

Do you really think that people from other cultures experience what Christians experience?

"I never thought of that. I think they have 'near-death' experiences. Why wouldn't they?"

They do have similar experiences. After all, we humans are physiologically similar enough to expect that. But do you really think that a good Hindu or Buddhist (or Jew or Moslem, for that matter) sees Jesus at the end of the tunnel? Don't you think the Christian's interpretation is slanted?

"Slanted? Maybe. But maybe what it shows is that God loves all of his creatures and reveals Himself in the form of His son, Jesus. God may choose the time of death to reveal Himself to us, no matter what religion we grew up believing."

Na na, my religion's better than your religion! Is that what you're saying? Don't answer. I'm not sure I can deal with such multicultural awareness and sensitivity right now.

"You don't have to resort to sarcasm. I didn't mean to sound so biased. But what is wrong with my interpretation?"

Plenty. Here's the difficulty that's relevant to what we are discussing. How would a good Buddhist or Hindu recognize your God? These people may have never heard of your Jesus. He's not such a significant person worldwide. How would they know it was Him?

"Their descriptions would sound like descriptions of Jesus."

Right. We have this videotape from the year C.E. 30. There's Jesus and his buddies, the dirty dozen.

"There you go, mocking religion again!"

I didn't mean any harm. Look, Jesus had how many apostles? Twelve, a dozen. And as far as I know there is no mention of taking showers. Hence, a dirty dozen. But I withdraw my offensive language. I'm sorry.

"Thank you."

Where is the tape of Jesus and the dirty dozen? Do we have any accurate picture of them? Without an accurate i.d., how can we say who is at the end of the tunnel? It could be Buddha, or Moses, or Siva, or Vishnu, or Uncle Charlie. Or it could be tied to the "dying" person's wants and beliefs and fears.

"What do you mean?"

It's pretty clear, isn't it? Here we have a person going through some pretty unusual and serious physiological changes. The guy is "dying." I don't know much about the chemistry of the brain, but I can imagine some powerful chemicals being released. The person sees a light at the end of a tunnel. Hallucination caused by the release of drugs natural to the brain during trauma could do that. Just being choked on the sides of the throat causes people to see tunnels with lights at the end.

"No way!"

Sure, it's true. If the oxygen to your brain is cut off, you will experience a narrowing of your visual field. Blackness starts at the periphery and closes in. What you can see becomes brighter. Finally, you will hear a tingling in your ears. It sounds like music, but the beat is usually off, so on a scale of 1 to 100, I never give it more than a 42.

"That doesn't account for Jesus calling from heaven."

No, the calling is part of the person's wish to be comforted. The calling from the particular deity is a result of one's training.

There Are Atheists in Foxholes, and Buddhists and Hindus, Too. "Maybe, but you'll never find an atheist in a foxhole."

Clichés aside, sometimes you will. I was very ill once. (This sad story is truly true.) I had a ruptured appendix. Thinking it was the flu and being reluctant to seek medical care, I waited three days.

"That's pretty serious."

By the time I got to the hospital for treatment, my temperature was at a life-threatening 106.8 degrees. They were frying eggs on my chest. (That may be an exaggeration.)

"What happened?"

They packed me in ice, brought down my temperature, and operated.

"So you were okay. You were not close enough to death to have a 'near-death' experience."

I grant that. But I was told that I would probably not survive the surgery. (I assured the surgeon that my health insurance would still pay. He was relieved.) Lying there, believing I was going to die, I thought of a number of things. Your God and religion were not among them. So, you see, some foxholes do have atheists in them.

"Maybe so, but then you're the exception."

There are lots of examples of similar experiences. People from nonbelieving heritages are not going to pray to gods. They wouldn't think of doing that any more than you believers would think of praying to gods of other traditions. So there are atheists in foxholes, and Buddhists and Hindus and Christians and Jews, too!

Atheist or Believer, It Just Doesn't Matter

"But atheists aren't any more sincere or honest than believers."

I grant that, too. Look, most of the atheists I know are only atheists in that they do not believe in God. It's an intellectual thing with them. Most people I know say they believe in God, but it's just a belief. They don't know. It's the same with atheists. People are just too lazy and too intellectual about their beliefs. Besides, it doesn't matter.

"Doesn't matter!"

Of course not. The only reason we give people religion and a belief in gods is to keep them controlled. This even applies to atheists.

"How could that be?"

Atheists are people who look at religion and think, "How could there be a god? Maybe there isn't one." Not finding sufficient evidence or reason to believe, they say, "There isn't one." That's all. They just don't believe in God.

"That's all!"

Sure. But the brilliant thing about religion is that it doesn't matter. Religion still keeps control. It's difficult enough for people raised in our culture to break with their parents and peers. Everything you learn as a kid insists that there is a God. Parents, teachers, many public buildings, even money ("in God we trust") promote the belief. Breaking free from those influences is an emotional affair.

"Then how can you say it doesn't matter?"

It doesn't matter, because religion gets its way. Religion tries to control you. If you are a good atheist, you have probably exhausted yourself emotionally just breaking away from the beliefs of loved ones. That's where you were right in what you said just a while ago.

God Exists as a Psychological Truth. "What did I say that you agree with?"

You argued for God's existence by claiming that there was a long tradition of belief and that most people believe in God. You were on to a good intuition there.

"So I wasn't so far off."

Not at all. What you showed were two interesting psychological truths that apply to our society.

"Psychological truths?"

Right. You correctly showed the psychological reasons for why so many people believe in God, and why so few are able to be atheists. Breaking from a longstanding tradition, including the beliefs of your parents, grandparents, aunts, uncles, etc., is emotionally trying. That was your first point. Then you correctly added that most people believe in God.

"But you denied that claim. Remember all the Buddhists and Hindus?"

Exactly. But now I'm taking your claim as a psychological statement, not as a statement about ultimate reality. Nearly everyone you know is a believer. That's a pretty compelling (psychological) reason to believe in God. Especially for a moral person.

"Why do you say that? 'For a moral person'?"

We already decided that moral people seek stability and security. What is more destabilizing and insecure than going against an important and old and widely held belief? Nothing. Belief in God satisfies the need to belong, the need for community. So, you were right. I was wrong.

Why Doesn't It Matter? "But why doesn't it matter if someone is an atheist?"

Oh, right. Back to my earlier idea. It doesn't matter because it takes so much out of a person to break from society. Psychologically speaking, atheists are doing pretty well just to break free on this one isolated belief in God's existence. What remains in them is all their social awareness. All their moral values are still there. They still do not kill or steal or pillage, at least no more than believers do.

"So it doesn't matter? The results are the same, at least in terms of action. But aren't they different in terms of how they live their lives? Aren't they a different sort of person?"

Atheist or believer? If it's merely a difference in one belief, I don't see how it matters.

"I don't agree. What more is there than one's belief?"

I think there is more. But why don't we return to our original plan in this discussion? Later we can talk about what more there is to living.

God Answers the Unanswerable Questions

"Where does this leave us? I admit, we've talked a great deal, but what have we been able to conclude?"

We know that some arguments for God's existence are faulty. We know that the universe does not have to have a first cause—namely, God. And we've learned that the universe may not be as orderly as we suspected. But more helpful are your insights into what we've called the psychological causes of belief. Do you have any other reasons to believe?

"Yes, I've just thought of another reason. God answers the unanswerable questions."

Surely you don't mean that literally. How could anyone answer what is not answerable?

"Now *you* are being overly serious, Art. What I mean is that God provides answers to questions that science cannot answer. I had thought that God gave security and structure to the universe."

And now?

"Now I see that the questions about security, order, chaos, and a first cause are not so important."

I've been holding back on you. I am willing to admit that your arguments make a kind of logical sense, but they don't work.

"I agree now that they are problematic, but why do you say they don't work? That's strong language from a person who sounds like he does not believe in truth."

I have listened to the arguments. I am a fairly reasonable person, and there are others who are far more reasonable than I. After hearing the arguments for God's existence, I am unconvinced. And I don't think that is because I have a closed mind. I think people believe first, and then they find reasons for belief. The reasons we have examined fit that category. Even as we rejected your earlier proofs of God's existence, you didn't lose your belief, did you?

"No, I didn't."

I think that's because we haven't really touched on the real reasons for belief in God. I think those reasons are difficult to find and to articulate.

"Perhaps, but what do you think of my most recent idea?"

What do you have in mind? What sort of questions does your God answer?

God Gives Meaning to Life and to Death

"God answers questions about life and death, about pain. God gives suffering a point. God brings meaning and purpose to living and to dying. Without God, this life would be pointless and meaningless."

I agree. This life is pointless and meaningless, cosmically speaking. There is no meaning of life.

"You agree! I am not saying that at all, and I suspect you know that. You're avoiding the issue. I'm quite serious about this."

Sorry. I've grown accustomed to mocking you. It's great fun, but I'll refrain for a time. How does belief in God avert suffering and pain?

"Belief in God does not avert suffering. I never said that."

Then God averts suffering?

"No, God does not avert suffering. He could if He wanted, but there are reasons for suffering."

So far, I don't like this God. It can prevent suffering, but It doesn't want to? Why not?

"One reason God allows suffering is because of original sin."

Stop there. Look, I want this book to have a worldwide market. If you bring in your provincial religious doctrines, my market will shrink.

"Who cares about your market?"

I do. And God may care, too. Since God isn't averting suffering, It has time to care along with me. And I *am* making fun of you, but only a little.

"If I can't use the doctrine of my religion, how am I to answer your questions?"

Actually, it's not the doctrine of your religion, or of any religion, I object to. I want to avoid the details, unless you can show me one thing.

"What's that?"

Can you show me what the standard is for religious truth? Can you show me that your religion is correct and some other religion is incorrect?

"I see what you mean. I'm committed to my religious perspective, but not everyone is. Can I reserve the right to challenge you later with specifics?"

God Allows Suffering

Fair enough. Where were we? Oh, yes. Your God allows people to suffer. It allows good people to suffer at least as much as bad people. Why? And why would you pray to such a god?

"God does allow some suffering. In His infinite mercy, however, He also averts suffering. God is a loving God."

Are you telling me that God does avert some suffering?

"Of course. God prevents the suffering of the faithful. That is, God prevents some of their suffering. God protects us!"

How does God decide who to protect and who to let suffer?

"The answer to that is understandable to God alone."

Try anyway. Is there any pattern you've detected? Is there any way I can avoid suffering?

"Oh, I see what you mean. God looks with grace on the faithful. He answers our prayers. But you have to know how to pray, and you can't fake your faith."

Heaven forbid! Let me see if I've got this. God alleviates the pain and suffering of the truly faithful? God answers their prayers?

"Not always, but usually. You see, sometimes God has a greater reason to let you suffer than to save you from suffering. It's sometimes thought of as a test. If you maintain your faith, then you get the richest rewards in heaven."

Surely there were some believers among the 12 million people who died in Nazi concentration camps. And what about Cambodia more recently? There are lots of examples of people who must have had faith and who must have prayed to be protected. What about them?

"Like I said, God's understanding transcends human knowledge. He has a plan. Those people were sacrificed, but they are rewarded in heaven. Don't assume, though, that all those people had the right kind of faith."

The right kind of faith?

"Right. Faith is a special kind of belief. Faith has to be childlike in its innocence. I remember when I was a child, I wanted this one bicycle. Every time we went to the toy store, I'd go over and see whether or not it had been sold. And every night I prayed I would get that bike. Finally, my birthday came around, and I got the bike."

I'm moved. Are you telling me this is an example of childlike innocence? You wanted a bicycle for yourself, and that's a prayer God would answer? But this immense and powerful deity would refuse to answer the pleas of starving Ethiopian and Eritrean children! God! What a guy!

"Obviously, you don't understand."

Obviously.

How Can We Know That God Answers Prayers?

"Sometimes God answers prayers, and sometimes He has a greater plan in mind. I'm trying to explain that to you. Some suffering is necessary. God doesn't like it, but it's necessary."

If God doesn't like suffering, why can't It figure out a better plan? But I have a better question. How can we know that God answers prayers?

"We see prayers answered all the time. Miracles occur even today."

But how do we know the prayers are being answered? These miracles might be just events that occur. The event may coincidentally fit someone's prayer.

"That's not very likely. How could you explain my bicycle example?"

What's the test?

"What do you mean?"

Some prayers are answered; some are not answered.

"All prayers are heard and answered. Just not always in the way or when the person wants."

Then how do you know they are being answered at all? Look, what would falsify this idea of yours? You have a bunch of prayers. Some are answered in the way and when you want. Others are answered, but not in the way or when you want. So every prayer is answered, whether or not it's answered in the way or when you want.

"Right."

But that allows too much. What could show that this hypothesis is correct or incorrect? It's an empty belief. It doesn't explain how things happen, or why or when they happen. There is no sense of justice revealed in this plan. There isn't any sense of proportion, either. Your God lets innocent infants be tortured and killed. Yet It contents itself with giving you a bicycle or a "B" on a spelling test in the third grade!

Why Bother with Prayer?   "You haven't understood. God's ways are beyond human understanding."

No amount or quality of prayer will change God's will. Isn't that really what you're saying? You can pray or not pray. It all comes down to the same thing. This God of yours will do as It wants. So why bother with prayer?

"Prayer makes me feel closer to God."

Isn't this closeness just your way of humanizing nature?

"What do you mean?"

You assume that there is a God, or many gods. You pray to It or them. All this is just an attempt to make sense out of a universe that doesn't show any concern for you. The universe isn't just. It doesn't respond to human needs in any noticeable way. So you manufacture a God and a phone line to God—prayer.

"How can you say that?"

Nothing changes when you pray. If your prayer is answered, you're content with your little belief. If your prayer is not answered, you say your God had something else in mind. All you have accomplished with this belief is to make yourself feel more in control. You know the Big Guy who runs the store.

Morality Works When We Follow God's Plan.   "It's all a matter of faith. We are supposed to follow God's rules. These reveal God's plan for us on earth."

Just on earth? When people go to other planets or moons . . .

"Stop being irreverent. You know what I mean."

This is great. We're back to where we started this discussion. You said that moral and religious rules should be followed because they are God's will. You said it is our duty to follow God's will. That's what gives morality a purpose. That's the point of morality.

"Now do you agree?"

Why We Want to Believe

You have already told me why people want to believe in God. In our Western society most people do believe in God. It's indisputable that the belief has a long tradition. Putting aside these democratic and historical inclinations, I want to ask whether or not there are reasons to believe in God.

"We considered that the universe had to have a beginning and that it is organized and orderly. We also want someone to answer the questions that appear unanswerable. Of course, we also questioned the soundness of these reasons."

You also suggested that order and security are part of our most deeply held wishes. That is exactly the insight Freud examines. Experience itself might be "colored" by these wishes.

"Yes, when we looked at the example of near-death experiences, we closed in on one of the deeper anxieties that people suffer, the fear of death. People fear death, and pain, and insecurity."

I suspect that these fears make it difficult for believers to understand how others might disagree with them. How could anyone stand alone and face the fear of death, or meaninglessness, or suffering! We desire to know that there is a reason for suffering, and for death. We want someone to give purpose to our mundane lives. We want to believe that there is a God answering our prayers.

"It is reassuring to believe that our religious beliefs lead us to living morally praiseworthy lives. This life is part of God's great, but secret, plan. That's what many religious people believe, and it's comforting to agree with them."

Put Yourself in the Right Frame of Mind

Sigmund Freud challenges just these ideas.

"Who is he?"

Freud was the founder of psychoanalysis. His ideas on the method of therapy, on the existence of an unconscious element of the mind, are very much a part of the way we think. Freud also has some interesting ideas about religion and society.

"Like what?"

He questions what motivates religious belief. To put yourself in the right frame of mind, as we examine civilization and religion imagine you are a being from outer space. You have come to earth to see how earth creatures live and what they believe. You are an intergalactic social scientist. What do you see in the behavior and beliefs of humans in the Western world? What I'm asking is that you remove yourself from your religious and social beliefs. Pretend that you have never heard of these practices. Freud's analysis is aimed at figuring out not what we think religion is about, but what it actually is about.

What Is the Value of Religious Ideas?

Freud asks: What is the value of religious ideas? The question arises in the context of our civilized lives. Each of us has a hostility to civilization.

"Why? What causes the hostility?"

Our anger is produced by instinct renunciation.

"What does that mean?"

Society doesn't let us satisfy our deepest wants. We can't do whatever we want, whenever we want. No matter how pressing the need or desire, we cannot act in certain ways because society will not allow it.

"That's just why we have rules and laws. The role of morality, law, and religion is to show us where the boundaries lie. Some experiences are denied us. They are immoral, illegal, or sacrilegious."

Bad, bad!

"Joke all you want, but that keeps this society running. Do you have any better way of organizing society?"

One way to avoid this effect of civilization is to do whatever you want. Don't surrender your instincts to society, live them!

"That's pretty stupid. If everyone did whatever he wanted, soon we'd all be dead."

Freud argues the same way. He says it would be shortsighted to abolish civilization and return to a "state of nature" where each person is out for himself or herself. We started civilization to defend ourselves against nature. Since nature has not yet been completely subdued and rendered harmless, we need to stay together.

"Just my point. Nature presents a real danger to us. Nature is our real antagonist. Compared to nature, we are weak and helpless. We are defenseless to stand against the overbearing power of nature."

You and Freud sound alike. He says that the terrors in living in the vast universe must be silenced. We cannot be happy under such conditions.

"Right, and civilization offers us this protection. Working together in an orderly way, we are able to subdue nature just enough to draw some of its riches. Through work, we get food and raw materials for housing and other comforts."

To quiet our deeper fears, to make them manageable, we humanize nature. Although we are still defenseless against it, a humanized nature can be appeased, bribed, or otherwise influenced.

"What do you mean by humanizing nature?"

We imagine nature to be something like us. We go so far as to believe that humans have been created in a form similar to the "human" nature god. God stands over nature. Unlike mute nature, however, God, the controller of nature, can be appeased, bribed, or otherwise influenced.

"Prayers and sacrifices are made in an effort to relate to God, and therefore to prevent nature and death from permanently and arbitrarily harming us. Promises are made to show our sincerity to God."

You bribe God into doing what you want or, more often, to prevent what you fear.

"I'm not comfortable with the way you describe it."

God relieves each of us of the need to defend ourselves against nature. Each of us is equally represented by civilization. Each of us is protected by God. People seek God's protection collectively.

What's the Harm?

"What is the harm of believing, anyway? Sure, there are no logical reasons to believe, but that is just what faith is, belief without evidence. What's the harm?"

The harm in believing without evidence or reason is that doubting but still believing breaks our intellect. Why go without the ordinary guarantees that we require in everyday living? No one would buy a used car without first having a genuine guarantee of its reliability. "Trust me" just would not convince us. Surely it is dangerous to believe without evidence or from a perceived sense of historical momentum.

"It's more than that. Belief is based on the confidence that our ancestors knew what they were doing."

Just because people once believed that earth was flat is no reason to believe it now. Or, more important, imagine that you believe the stork brings babies. That's how babies come to be; the stork brings them. Wouldn't that be a dangerous belief? One could imagine engaging in all sorts of behavior ignorant of the consequences. The harm of ignorance is potentially very great. The history of ignorance has proven that.

People Will Keep Believing Anyway.   "People will continue to believe in God no matter what Freud writes and no matter what Art says."

You're probably right. That's an interesting and important point. But I don't think it is a reasonable objection to anything Freud has stated.

"It shows how intense the inner force is that holds people to religious beliefs."

To what do they owe this power?

"What do you mean?"

If religious teachings are not the results of ordinary experience, or of thinking, what is their source?

Mystical and Ecstatic Experiences

"It could be mystical or ecstatic experience. My inner experience proves that God exists."

But your experience is not evidence to me. My inner experience could be correct, or it could be nuts. ("Nuts" is yet another technical term in philosophy.)

"Why do you say that?"

The inner experience and interpretation of one person are not convincing to anyone else. Just think how boring it is to listen to people telling you about their dreams.

"What does this have to do with anything?"

Maybe dreams reveal inner truths, or unconscious desires and questions, I don't know. What I do know is that people get really involved in retelling their dreams. Almost no one else cares to hear it. What appears vital and dramatic to the dreamer is uninteresting to the listener.

"What does that prove?"

This example doesn't prove anything, except that intense inner experiences do not always relate to anyone but the person who has the experience.

Invisible Green Goblins

Here, let me give you an example. My own intense experience reveals to me the existence of invisible green goblins.

"What?"

That's right. I have experienced invisible green goblins.

"How can they be invisible and green?"

It's one of their many amazing talents. No doubt you're convinced of their existence.

"No way."

Why not? I have experienced them. Why isn't that good enough for you? As a matter of fact, one is sitting on my lap right now. He's helping me write this section of the discussion. You're still stuck on the apparent contradiction between being invisible and green. I can resolve that. It's one of the mysteries! Every religion has its own mystery. The goblins have their own mystery.

"This is unbelievable."

I sense that you are still unmoved by my assertions.

"How about evidence? If you can ask for evidence for God's existence, then I can demand evidence for your goblin."

Invisible green goblins, thank you. I can give evidence for their existence. The evidence is not direct, though if you believe in them their existence becomes obvious to you.

"If I believed in them, I'd be as crazy as you are."

Okay, here's some evidence. You know when you wash your clothes and then throw them into the dryer? Every once in a while you lose a sock, right? Where do you think it went? The goblins take them. They eat them. If you're skeptical, try to explain where the sock goes.

"It's trapped in the dryer."

Do you realize how large dryers would have to be in order to capture and consume all the socks that are lost in the life of a dryer? Besides, many people do not use dryers. Their socks are "lost" in the washer. Pretty suspicious, I think. By the way, have you ever noticed that the next sock you lose is never from the broken pair? The goblins always steal one from a complete pair.

"Why do they do that?"

I don't know why. They just do. They don't think like we do. They have a plan for the world that we can't fully understand. So now you believe in goblins, right?

"Of course not."

If you don't believe, you must show where the socks go. And don't try to explain your way out of it by claiming again that the washers and dryers eat them. Who is going to believe that washers and dryers eat clothes? That's absurd. The goblins are also the ones who hide your car keys, but never mind.

"I'm not convinced."

Neither my intense experience of invisible green goblins nor my remarkably sound evidence convinces you? That's just the point. No person should feel compelled to believe without evidence that is available to that person. And secondary evidence, signs of the existence of something, are not completely reliable. Just like you just denied my explanation of the loss of socks, so too all "tracks" are suspect.

"What do you mean by tracks?"

Since only a very few "elect" people ever get to bear "inner" witness, it is wrong for the majority to have the interpretation of those experiences imposed on them. Imagine a world where you were required to serve my fantasy goblins.

"That would be weird."

The imposition is wrong unless you, too, experience the goblins. By the way, if that starts happening, write to me in care of Wadsworth Publishing Co. I have a psychiatrist friend who could use the business.

What Are These Ideas in Light of Psychology?

Freud asks: "What are these (religious) ideas in light of psychology? What is their real worth?"

"What does he mean by these questions? Is he just an atheist?"

Freud is not denying the existence of God. He was an atheist, but he is not trying to convince anyone to be an atheist.

"Then why did he write this stuff? What does he want?"

Freud wants us to look at a most practical question. Why do we think that our God is the way we imagine him to be?

"Because that's what we learned growing up. And because people who have experienced God describe Him that way. God's personality is described by religious teachings."

Yes, but we found difficulties verifying those beliefs. Why should we believe that God is the way he is described?

"You are trying to convince me that God does not exist."

Assume that God does exist. That doesn't change Freud's point. How would we know what It is like?

"I'm not sure. If you close off our traditional way of knowing God, there is no way of knowing what He is like. The Bible is the primary source of our knowledge of God. What else is there?"

Illusions.   Freud has a controversial explanation of religious beliefs about God, the father figure. He speculates that religious teachings are illusions.

"Illusions?"

I told you it's controversial! But before you slam the book closed, it isn't as terrible as it seems. Freud says that illusions are not necessarily false. Illusions are not necessarily errors or mistakes.

"How could an illusion be true?"

You might believe in something based solely on your wish that it be true. And it may turn out that it is true. You may believe and hope that someday you will be picked to undertake some great and noble task. And it may turn out that that will happen. Not all wishes are impossible.

"I suppose not. Why call religious beliefs illusions?"

What makes a belief an illusion is that our wishes play an important part in the belief.

"Our illusions are tied to our wishes?"

Yes. The most basic and widespread illusions are derived from the most basic human wishes. Illusions may be true, or they may be false. A belief is an illusion when wish fulfillment is a prominent factor in our motivation to believe it. We believe something because we want to believe.

"For example?"

We believe our local sports team can win the championship because we want them to win. It's a harmless illusion that keeps us interested in the team's performance.

"I think this is just cheering on the home team. There's no illusion involved. But maybe I'm still not clear on this. Could you give me a better example?"

I Am Irresistible to All Women!   I am irresistible to all women. You've just read it twice; why is it so hard to believe? I swear it's true. Let me explain. I have discovered that all women are irresistibly drawn to me. Of course, some are not fully conscious of the attraction, but it's clearly there. Whenever I am near a woman, she acts just like I expect.

"And how is that?"

Basically women fall into two categories. Some stay at a discreet distance, loving me from afar; others come over to me. Those who stay at a distance tend to resist my charms by pretending to ignore me.

"Come off it, Art!"

Really. I see them walk by me and they act as though I don't exist. It's incredible to me that they are able to pretend so convincingly. My friends don't even notice when they are with me. But I see all these beautiful and attractive women walking by, longing to be near me but resisting with every fiber of their being. You have to admire their self-discipline.

"Sure, and what about the other group?"

A very few of the women I see actually come up to me. Usually it's because I unconsciously turn on the charm and they can't resist. I don't even know I'm doing it, but it works.

"What happens when you 'turn on the charm'?"

The woman walks up to me. Invariably, as she approaches she is overwhelmed by my presence. But she has already committed herself.

"What does she say to let you know about her attraction?"

She tells me to drop dead, or to get off the face of the earth, or some other similar sentiment.

"And you think this shows that the woman is attracted to you? You are pathetic!"

Don't you see, women are embarrassed by their loss of control. Their only way of protecting themselves from my obvious good looks and appeal is to push me away. They pretend that I am obnoxious. Of course, I know better.

"Have you sought professional help for this? I think you should, because you are not at all in touch with reality."

Illusions Fulfill Our Wishes.   Exactly, and that's why this is an example of an illusion. My own desires and wishes motivate me to interpret the facts in a way that is not necessarily false, but certainly unlikely. All women might be attracted to me. Sometimes when a person is uncomfortable with his or her attraction to another person, he or she may be embarrassed. He may even insult the attractive person.

"So?"

So my belief that all women are attracted to me *may* be true.

"Not likely."

Or my belief may be false. We could reconstruct the example to make it more plausible. What if I told you that one woman is attracted to me, but she is too shy to show her feelings? That might be plausible. What if she went out of her way to be near me but always acted in a shy way?

"Well, that's more reasonable, and more likely to be true."

The plot thickens, right? In this case my illusion could be true. What makes it an illusion is the part my wishes play. Believing it corresponds to my own wish to have this one woman notice me.

"Yes, I see what you mean. A belief may be true or may be likely to be true, but that doesn't make it any less of an illusion."

The Oldest, Strongest Wishes.   In either case, it is my own desires and wishes that cloud my judgment. That's Freud's point. Whether or not there is a God is not Freud's interest.

"Then what is his point?"

How we understand God is his concern. Do we put a "face" on God, a "face" that is motivated by our own wishes? Freud suggests that by understanding illusions we can understand the "face" we put on God and the strength of our religious beliefs.

"Be more specific."

The content of our religious beliefs about God relies on our experience with our parents. By analogy, God is a big parent in the sky.

"Oh, I see. Freud thinks that we choose a parent figure because it's familiar. What's wrong with seeing God that way?"

There's nothing wrong with it, not exactly. It's revealing, though, to see how people describe their God, and what convenient images they choose to describe God.

"Maybe. What else does Freud think about the belief in God?"

The strength of our religious beliefs about God lies in the strength of the wishes that motivate us.

"What do you mean?"

People believe strongly because they need to believe strongly. Other people who do not believe strongly do not have the same fears and desires, so they do not need to believe strongly.

"Are you saying that whenever our wishes play a motivating role in our beliefs, we are reluctant to give up the beliefs? Like your belief that all women are attracted to you?"

Exactly. I want to believe that all women are attracted to me. My desire to believe this is very strong. Therefore—

"Therefore, you are reluctant to give up the belief even when the evidence is against you."

Right. Freud suggests that the fulfillment of the oldest, strongest, and most urgent wishes of humankind can be found in the "face" of God. God is just what we need Him to be, not because we have any reliable evidence that He is this way, but because we need Him to be this way.

"What oldest, strongest, and most urgent wishes do we have?"

We experience terrifying helplessness when we face the immensity of the universe or when we contemplate our own deaths as annihilation.

"It is difficult to imagine that someday I won't exist."

Our need is for protection against our helplessness, against insignificance, against death.

"What face do we put on God? What could make death less terrifying?"

The benevolent rule of God the father figure allays our fears of death. God promises an afterlife if we follow his rules. God is like most parents.

"Yes, but that's just our way of describing God."

God also fulfills our desires for justice. He ensures a moral world order. If evil people flourish while they are on earth, they will pay all the more in the next life. Finally, our despair is solved by the Father. God promises that there is a point to the entire universe, to human suffering, and to death. What makes the belief so appealing?

"Our deepest desires? I know that is what Freud thinks. But does that mean that all religious beliefs are illusions?"

Religious Illusions.   Yes, according to Freud all religious doctrines are illusions. Religious doctrines are based on the fundamental wishes of humanity. Religions admit that their beliefs are not susceptible to direct, objective proof. And look how strenuously the beliefs are held. With an (almost) irrational fervor, just as all illusions are held.

"Religious people often cite how pervasive religious belief is. Can you and Freud explain how almost nowhere on earth can we find societies where religion is not practiced? Even though the local gods are not like our God, people believe they exist. The widespread existence of religious belief shows that there must be a God."

Or so it is asserted. Freud thinks it is the people who are similar. Therefore their beliefs are going to be similar.

"How can that explain why we find religious societies everywhere? How can you explain why God seems to be everywhere?"

The belief in gods is everywhere because people are similar, not necessarily because God is everywhere. People have parents, and they have fears. Because these similarities are (nearly) universal conditions, we should not be surprised that people formulate similar illusions to deal with their situations.

Does God Exist?

"Does God exist?"

Actually, Freud is not concerned with the truth value of statements for or against God's existence. It would be wonderful if a God created the world, a benevolent providence, a moral world order, and an eternal life after this life.

"It is possible that this idea is true."

It is striking, however, that all these beliefs are exactly what we most wish to be true. Whether or not God exists, the belief in God is an illusion.

"Then God may exist? Is it okay to believe?"

To go beyond that uncomfortable claim, we need to hear much more about God and we need to receive much more evidence. The only reasonable approach is to suspend belief in God until we have irrefutable evidence that God exists. Given our tendency to create illusion, we need to guard ourselves by leaning the other way.

Religious Assertions Cannot Be Refuted By Reason

"Religious assertions cannot be refuted by reason. Religious belief is beyond reason."

Freud has a simple answer to this. "Ignorance is ignorance." No reasonable person would believe even an insignificant claim based on such "feeble grounds." The amount of emotional and physical energy required of the religious person certainly makes religious belief far from insignificant. No, belief under these circumstances is only pretending to believe. People need to learn to accept reality.

"But the portrait of God that is found in the Bible is reassuring. God gives us an ideal to strive toward."

What sort of ideal?

"God is just and loving and merciful. That is the way people ought to act toward each other. Don't you agree?"

That God is this way, or that people ought to act this way toward others?

"Well, both. They're the same."

No, I don't agree that they are the same. Maybe people should be this way, I don't know. That is worth looking into. But your God is not this way.

"How can you say that?"

Look at the stories in your own book! A being who destroys virtually all the sentient life on earth is not very loving, and not obviously just.

"What are you talking about?"

The Noah's ark story. Your God is the greatest mass murderer in the history of humanity. God murdered everyone but Noah and his family. "Oops! I didn't realize they couldn't breathe under water."

"The other people were living sinful lives. They were evil. We said that God disapproved of murdering innocent people. Those people were not innocent. They deserved to die."

Very sensitive of you. But there must have been pregnant women back then. What with all the sinning going on, someone must have been pregnant. And others must have just borne their children. Were these fetuses and babies evil? What sense of love and justice are we using?

"I'll admit those cases are difficult to answer. Perhaps God was punishing them for the original sin of Adam and Eve."

Lame. I can see the headlines now. "God kills children because of the sins of their great-great-great-great-great-great-great-great . . . grandparents." Does this make any sense? Does this sound like justice or love? I am going to murder my children and destroy their toys, because their grandparents screwed up!

"Okay, forget original sin. I can see you don't appreciate the theological significance. All of us are sinners. We are all subject to temptation. God punished that."

But newborn babies and fetuses? Look, being tempted is one thing; giving in to temptation (one of my goals in life) is something very different. But let's assume your analysis is correct. Why would your silly God save Noah and his gang? Aren't they susceptible to temptation? They probably gave in to temptation, too, at least more than fetuses and newborn infants.

"God knew that these newborns would sin when they became older."

Goodbye, free will! Your God punishes people in advance? Very efficient. A little confusing, though. "Gee, Mommy, why did God kill poor (pure) cousin Charlie? He was just born." "Charles died because God knew he would sin someday." What kind of message is this to give to a child? What kind of loving justice is that? Your God lets some people sin big time all their lives, and they live long lives. Then he turns around and slaughters newborns who ain't never done nothin' to nobody.

"The Lord has His reasons."

I don't doubt it. Put my objections aside. Let's get us back on track.

How Does This Apply to Our Discussion of Moral Values?

"How does this apply to our discussion of moral values?"

Belief in God supports morality. God gives authority to morality. That's what you said when we started this discussion. I think you are correct.

"Then belief in God is desirable."

I don't agree. But I don't think it matters very much. If a person's belief in God is an illusion, then all we will be able to extract from the belief is the person's wishes. When we try to extract values to live by, we will get nothing but the person's own values.

"What's wrong with this?"

Well, first, to have each person's illusions and deepest desires reflected in our values hardly gives any authority to morality. Why should anyone else live according to my desires?

"Because that just takes us back to egoism?"

Yes.

"And second?"

What have we gained? The idea of a God is to do away with relativism, right? If there is one God, then there is only one set of values. But if belief in God is merely based on illusions, and people's illusions can vary, then we are left with relativism.

"What if everyone's basic desires are the same? Then we would have a constant set of values."

Good move. Yes, if everyone's desires were the same, then we might extract a common set of values. There are problems with that approach.

"Such as?"

It isn't clear to me that everyone has the same basic desires.

"We could adopt the majority's desires."

No, truth and goodness are not a matter of majority rule. That won't work. But there is a more serious problem with basing morality on people's most basic desires. It's always open that we could find our desires undesirable.

"Come again? How's that?"

Just because a desire is natural, it doesn't follow that we want to make it into a moral value. The two categories are separate.

What's Left to Believe?

"What's left to believe?"

I'm glad you asked that. That's where our next talk will begin.

Summary of Discussion

There are a number of reasons people use to explain their belief in God. The majority of people we know believes in God. The belief in God has a long tradition in our civilization. Another reason is that the universe had to have a beginning, and it is orderly. Then there is the testimony of people who have had "near-death" experiences.

God also answers the "unanswerable" questions that we face. God gives meaning to life and to death. Although God allows people to suffer, it is for a greater purpose. God also answers people's prayers. Of course, the answers they receive are not always what people want. God works for the betterment of the entire universe. Tragedy is, therefore, actually merely a misunderstood good.

What is interesting about all these reasons is that they appeal to our wants and needs. But they do not speak to evidence. Of course, there are problems with these reasons. God's existence is not so easily proven. In fact, none of these reasons would convince a reasonable person. Proof of that is that no believer would lose faith if one or more of these reasons were successfully dismissed. We need to look further.

When we look at the value of religious ideas, we see that religion is responsible for many of the accomplishments of civilization. Yet we also see that religion as an institution has had a numbing effect on our ability to think. When we examine other religions, we are struck by their quaintness. We are able to see these belief systems as intellectual curiosities. Why would anyone believe in invisible green goblins?

Freud helps us by asking, "What are these (religious) ideas in light of psychology?" His conclusions are dramatic. The belief in God is a psychological truth, but that does not make it a truth of reality. Freud argues that religious beliefs are illusions. Though that does not mean they are false, Freud suggests that the source of our beliefs in the father-figure god are merely projections of our own wants. The religious illusions are illusions because they fulfill our oldest and strongest wishes. With religious beliefs we continue the child's need to receive protection from the parents, especially from the father.

Does God exist? In the context of our search for moral values and for the best life, the answer does not matter. Even if there is a God, it is our task to figure out whether or not our values are sound. So we are left with our original question. What is the best life?

Discussion Highlights

I. God exists
   1. The majority believes in God.
   2. The religious beliefs of our culture have a long tradition.
   3. The universe had to have a beginning.
   4. The universe is orderly.
   5. Near-death experiences prove that God exists.
II. God provides for us
   1. God answers "unanswerable" questions.
   2. God gives purpose to our lives and our deaths.
   3. God only allows suffering because it fits the grand plan.
   4. God answers the prayers of the faithful.
III. God is merely a psychological truth
   1. Invisible green goblins don't exist just because I believe they exist.
   2. God is an illusion.
      a. Belief in God depends on our wishes and desires.
      b. Our oldest, strongest wishes determine our belief in God.
IV. The relation between God and values is confusing
   1. God's existence does matter in this context.
   2. Each of us is left with the task of discovering the best life.

Questions for Thought/Paper Topics

1. People used to believe in Zeus and all the gods on Mount Olympus. Do you think their reasons were so different from the reasons of today's believers? If the reasons and the commitment are similar, why don't people believe in Zeus now?
2. How do Freud's ideas about illusions affect one's belief in a God? Can you respond to Freud?
3. If you don't believe in invisible green goblins (you a-goblinist!), explain why. What does happen to the socks lost in the dryers?
4. Can you reasonably support with arguments any one of the reasons favoring God's existence? (Use the library to help you find support.)
5. If there is no God, must morality vanish? Why?
6. If God appeared to you, presented the platinum American Express Card, "G-O-D," and said, "Don't leave home without it," would you do whatever

it told you to do? If God ordered it, would you murder your mother? (Remember, your mother receives your answer to this question.)

7. Is there any type of faith that does not require a suspension of one's critical abilities? Don't give up too quickly.

For Further Reading

It's no surprise that a great deal has been written about the existence of God and the nature of religious values. I suggest you look at Sigmund Freud's *The Future of an Illusion* (Norton, 1961). Another interesting conversation is Plato's *Euthyphro,* where Socrates discusses the concept of piety and the role that the gods play in defining morality. Bertrand Russell has a well-written book, *Why I Am Not a Christian* (Simon & Schuster, 1967). A fascinating discussion of faith is presented by Søren Kierkegaard in *Fear and Trembling* (Penguin, 1986). It's difficult reading, but well worth the trouble once you figure out what he is doing.

4   Isn't Everyone Different?

What's Left to Believe?

"I'm troubled by our last three conversations."

Pity.

"No, really. Several times you said there is no God."

Actually, I agree with Freud. God is an illusion. Whether or not God exists is irrelevant to finding out which life is best.

"What?"

We do not need God in order to find out how to live the best life. Because the "face" of God is influenced by our wishes, we could never figure out what God wants. So, even if God does exist—

"If there is no God, then anything goes."

And it's not my fault. Dostoevski, the Russian novelist, wrote, "If there is no God, then everything is permitted." Are you a Russian novelist, too?

"Be serious for just one moment."

Why does the nonexistence of God bother you? Didn't we decide that good and evil are independent of God? An action is good not because God approves of it. It is good *and* God (possibly) approves of it.

"I know what we concluded. I agree it makes sense, but I'm left feeling pretty shaken. You've just destroyed some important beliefs of mine. You shouldn't be allowed to do that. Some people can't take that, you know. They might get upset with you."

Are you going to offer me a glass of hemlock?

"I don't get it."

Hemlock? The reasoning we used to find out that good and evil are independent of God(s) was used by Socrates. Remember, he urged Euthyphro to see it just as we have. The next thing poor Socrates knew, he was on trial, found guilty of atheism and corrupting the youth.

"Euthyphro took him to court?"

No, actually Socrates was already charged. But his conversation with Euthyphro was much like the ones that got him into trouble. Sometimes asking these questions can be pretty frightening. Socrates was asked to drink hemlock. Great taste, but hard to digest. Poison!

How Can We Choose Our Moral Values?

"Where does this leave us? If God does not exist, how can we find out which values are true? Every moral system we look at will have something wrong with it. Even if we could fix them, there are too many to choose from, and I don't know how to choose. How can we figure out what is good and what is evil? All that's left is to say that morality is relative to each person."

Relative?

"Everyone's values are different, and there's no way to choose between them."

We could always use the method of historical preference. Force.

"No, that won't do. We want to know that our values, our way of life, is correct. There's no way of coming to answers to the questions you're asking."

Slow down, we've just started. People have been working on these questions for a long time.

"That's just the point. No one has come up with a morality that works. Every time we come up with one idea about morality, another problem gets in the way. No, I think that morality is different for different people. What you think is right is up to you. And what I think is right is up to me. There's no way to resolve the problem. You were right and I was wrong. You can do whatever you want."

Please note the time and date of this admission.

Doing Philosophy

"Seriously, where can we go from here? I'm confused. Doesn't your book on ethics end here?"

Confused? Good. If you think you already know everything about morality, how can you learn anything?

"But this is frustrating. Every idea I come up with, you shoot down."

Shoot down? Not really. I think we're just realizing that stating our ideas isn't easy. Nothing we've said has been wrong, yet. At least, I don't think so. I think we need to bring these ideas together carefully. Be patient. Patience is a virtue. Besides, we've only started.

"So where are we?"

Last time we asked for examples and for explanations of morality. We looked at several. We started with the Ten Commandments and the Golden Rule.

"Those didn't last long. Though I'm still not sure what happened. I don't feel comfortable rejecting such time-honored principles."

Good, because we didn't reject them. We just found reason to ask what they really mean and why we should follow them. We'll come back to each example and try to keep its strengths and avoid its weaknesses. My idea is that we can avoid the problems but take what we want from each example of morality.

"When does that happen? So far, all we've done is destroy them."

One cannot fill a vessel that is already full. Be patient. (I sound very Eastern, don't I? It's because I'm having a cup of tea right now.) Even Plato, one of the all-time superstars in philosophy, believed that you can't learn until you know what you do not know. Perplexity is what he wanted.

"Perplexity?"

Yeah, I think it's some kind of plastic used to cover tables.

"It isn't perplexity, it's frustration!"

What Plato had in mind was that learning can't happen if the person believes she already knows all the answers. To learn, you have to be involved and active. You have to realize that you may not have much supporting your beliefs and values. I think you have to be emotional to learn. *You're* certainly emotional.

Is There Agreement On Values?

"So?"

So besides the Ten Commandments and the Golden Rule, we discussed conscience.

"Yes, and we thought of several other ways of explaining morality. We didn't get to these in any detail, but you promised that we will later. Now I don't see why we should bother. What's the point?"

What systems are left?

"There were social and natural roles, and doing the most good for the most people. And I suggested that there is a contract between each person and society. Then there is the law as an example of morality."

Yes, and you also suggested that morality might be based on something like our genuine, natural and spiritual needs.

"Right, and then there is the question of absolutes. Are moral values absolute or are they different for different people and different societies? I think that about covers it. And I think that's just the position I am denying. There are no absolutes."

Don't forget egoism, my favorite.

"And egoism. Don't you see, that's just the point. With all these competing ways of understanding morality, none seems to be right."

But we haven't even examined them in detail.

"I know, but everywhere I look there are different moral values. There doesn't seem to be any agreement on values. People in our own society disagree about abortion, about business practices, about weapons and war, even about the importance of education."

(Dis)Agreements in Form and Content.   Sure, there are apparent disagreements. But one thing you have to admit is that the different groups agree enough to offer moral reasons to one another. That at least shows some common ground.

"What do you mean?"

Some disagreements are disagreements in content; some disagreements are disagreements in form.

"I don't understand."

The groups argue with each other. And their arguments apparently make sense to the other group.

"But they never agree. How can you say their arguments make sense to the other side?"

They speak the same language. Listen to them. For example, in the case of abortion. Each of the sides takes a stand. Then they argue with the other side.

"But they will never agree."

But the arguments are important. Each group appeals to the basic moral intuitions of the opponent. They try to show that moral values common to both sides lead to one conclusion on abortion, theirs. Each side does this.

"Of course. But they still will never agree."

That's because they argue with each other. Each side believes it knows the truth, but each side refuses to listen to the other's opinions. Arguments of this kind do that to people.

"Arguments of what kind? What kinds of arguments are there?"

Well, there's arguing in the sense of closing one's mind and just fighting. It's always pointless to argue that way. Then there's arguing with a critical but open mind. Philosophy is supposed to be this kind of arguing. We listen to each other, then carefully analyze what is said so that we genuinely understand. Then we draw conclusions. Some of the best arguments of this kind have people changing their views, if only slightly. And, of course, sometimes people just cannot agree.

"I'm still not quite following you. If the arguers can't agree, where is the common ground you see? Why don't you think these moral disagreements are real?"

On one level the disagreement is real. On the emotional level the people who argue get high blood pressure, and go red in the face. It's actually fun to watch them. On a more interesting level, they do agree.

"How so?"

Not long ago, I heard several people arguing about the rights of abortion. Back and forth they argued. Red faces, loud voices. I started to laugh. Mistake. They asked what was so funny. I wanted to say that they were in basic agreement, but I knew they'd take off my head.

"What did you say?"

I told them that we should let the fetuses reach maturity and be born. It was a waste to sacrifice a fetus or a newborn infant.

"So, you are opposed to abortion?"

I told them that a newborn baby should be cared for and well treated. That way, they can be put to work in mines and factories by the time they're five years old.

"That's terrible."

No, really. If the babies aren't well fed, they won't have the stamina for a good day's work. Why should adults have to take risks when unwanted children can do all the dangerous and demeaning work for us?

"How can you say that!"

Just their response. (You should read Swift's "A Modest Proposal.") See, I wasn't talking the same language. My reason for keeping fetuses alive was not moral. Both sides came down hard on me. They realized that they had more agreement than disagreement. They all agreed that raising babies to do dangerous work is wrong. (I'll bet they don't know why.) Their disagreement was over when a fetus becomes a baby. There are other disagreements in the abortion question, but they all come to the same thing. Moral people argue about these issues. People who aren't moral just ask you to pass the salt.

Disagreement on Content.   "Even if that made me feel better (and it doesn't), there is evidence of real moral disagreement. Different subcultures within our country have different values. And before you interrupt me, there are even greater differences between different cultures and countries. Bigger differences still between different times in history. Once people thought that slavery was acceptable. Now we don't believe that. People's gods change. Once no one believed in God. They believed in all sorts of other gods. There is just no agreement. Even in our own time, one religion tells people to love their enemies. Another tells them to kill nonbelievers. Or in one country it's okay to eat meat; in another place it's a terrible thing to do. It's frustrating!"

I can see that you're genuinely upset. But I don't understand what all the fuss is about. Why should agreement on values matter that much? We did agree on several defining features of morality. You know, each system is impartial, general, public, consistent, comprehensive, ordered, and final. Remember?

"That's just the form. What about the content? If we can't agree on values, that puts all our values in jeopardy. How are we to know that one set of values is true and another is not true? It means we have to accept all values as equally plausible. I don't know about you, but I feel uncomfortable doing that. Still, it seems like the only option left."

Tolerance and Acceptance.   Wait a minute. There are at least two problems here. First, you want to know what makes a moral principle true. For some reason you think you need agreement in establishing truth. Second, you are confusing tolerance and acceptance. Let's assume the worst, at least from your point of view. Let's assume that there is no moral truth. (In fact, there is no moral truth.) And let's also assume that you see a variety of apparently conflicting moral values out there. There are a number of viable contenders seeking your support.

"I do see different moral values out there, and I don't know how to sort them out."

Fine. But just because you see different values doesn't mean that you have to adopt all of them. You may find a way of deciding between and among them.

"But how can I do that? We are assuming that there is no moral truth. How can I decide among competing moral principles?"

That is the first and more important question, I agree. All I'm saying is that even if we do not determine which moral system is most true, we still don't have to accept all values as equally desirable. Look, cultural diversity is interesting whether it's in values or in customs. You don't have to become a Buddhist or a Shintoist or a Christian just because you see Buddhists, Shintoists, and Christians around. Appreciate the differences.

How Can We Decide Which Value Is True?

"I guess you're right. But what about moral truth? How can we decide which principle is true? Without agreement, we are stuck without truth."

I wish I had some clever piece of Eastern wisdom to offer. Wait, here's one. The cackling flock does not determine the leader's path of flight.

"What are you talking about? Who said that and what does it mean?"

I don't know what it means, but I said it, just now.

"Do you have anything helpful to say?"

Yes, well—no. Maybe? I think you're confused by apparent disagreements. Sometimes disagreements are not what they appear to be. And I think you have a pretty problematic idea of what makes a statement true.

Apparent Cultural Disagreements. "What do you mean, disagreements aren't what they appear to be? A disagreement is a disagreement."

Well, there are disagreements and then there are disagreements. Some disagreements are merely disagreements in words. I say the wall is blue and you say it is cyan. Cyan is a shade of blue, so we haven't really disagreed.

"But that isn't a big deal."

It is when the labels start applying to people. Judgments can be a big deal. Recently I was talking to some philosophy teachers who were upset with one of their colleagues, another teacher. His approach to problems was different than theirs.

"Wouldn't you expect diversity? Isn't that what philosophy is all about? At least that's what I'm getting from our talks."

Get real. Philosophers form rigid "camps" just like every other insecure group. Anyway, these teachers challenged my approach. Attacking me let them politely and indirectly (safely) attack their colleague.

"What did they say about you?"

They resorted to name calling. They called me a nihilist.

"A what?"

They were upset because there is no God, and they blamed it on me. (Maybe I should write an exam to go with this book. T or F There is no God and it's not Brad Art's fault.) They assumed that because there is no God, there is no guarantee for morality.

"That's just my problem. How did you answer?"

Actually, it is not your problem. You have not blamed anything on me. Well, at least not for the past several pages. You see, in a certain sense I am a nihilist. In a certain sense. If what they mean by nihilist is that values cannot be guaranteed by the gods, then I am guilty as charged. But a nihilist is more than that. To say that there are no values and that there's no way of guaranteeing values is much stronger.

"Are you that kind of nihilist? That's kind of what people mean by relativist, isn't it?"

That's what you fear about relativism. You (and they) fear that if we cannot find the true values, then there are no legitimate values. But that's not true.

Take Responsibility For Your Values. "What alternative is there?"

We can take responsibility for our values. We can admit that there are many values out there. We can also work to discover what the point is for having values in the first place. But look, let's get back to the original point.

"Which is?"

Those philosophy teachers feared a loss of all values. When I did not appear to agree with their strategy (God), they labeled me an atheist and a nihilist. They were shortsighted. They cut themselves off from other ways of approaching their questions. Where we agreed is that we are looking for one way by which to live.

"You still haven't given an answer. How can I take responsibility for values? First, I need to know how to choose them. If you think there is one best way, tell me. What is it?"

I'll tell you what. Let's work carefully through your "trouble." By the end of the book, I promise we'll have a desirable way of living.

"But you confuse me all the time. You don't keep your promises. Why should I believe you?"

What's to lose? Trust me. (Translation: Right now, I have no idea.)

Disagreements Over Basic Beliefs.   "There are more troubling disagreements. What about the disagreements between cultures? In India people would rather starve than eat cows. Cows are sacred in India. Here most people eat meat. How can you reconcile these differences?"

Cultural differences are sometimes real, but I don't think that is such a big deal. Take your example. We don't really disagree with the Hindus on what should and should not be eaten. Would you eat the body of another person?

"I hope not!"

That's all the Hindus are against.

"Then why don't they eat cows?"

Reincarnation. Hindus believe in the reincarnation of the spirit. People and animals are born and reborn in an almost endless cycle of births and deaths. The cow is sacred because it holds the reincarnated spirit of another person or of someone about to become a person.

"But that's ridiculous."

Spoken like a tolerant person! The disagreement you have with the Hindus is on the level of basic beliefs.

"Basic beliefs?"

The beliefs that form a background to your daily life. We have all sorts of background beliefs. I think of philosophy as discovering and questioning these basic beliefs. Most disagreements occur either because of language (cyan and blue), or because of factual disagreements, or because of different basic beliefs.

"But isn't it hopeless? How can we decide which basic beliefs are true? Aren't we back to the same problem? There are so many value systems and so many basic beliefs. How can we decide among them?"

I don't think we'll have to choose at all. The best life will just emerge. I think you're too hung up on what's true and not on what's real.

There's an Exception to Every Rule.   "There's an exception to every rule."

Huh?

"You heard me. What bothers me about so many value systems isn't that we have trouble understanding each other, or that we have different basic beliefs, or that I feel compelled to accept any of them. What bothers me most is—"

I know—that there's an exception to every rule.

"Right, there is an exception to every rule. It's wrong to kill, but self-defense is okay. Or it's okay for the state to kill a criminal. At least some people believe in capital punishment. You can find examples that show that every rule has an exception."

Except that one.

"Which one?"

That there is an exception to every rule. That rule (that there is an exception to every rule) doesn't have any exceptions.

"That's just a cheap trick, and you know it."

Okay, okay. You're right. (Actually I don't think it is a cheap trick.) I'm not so sure rules do have exceptions. Maybe it's because of the way we state the rules. For example, we can restate the rule against killing. One should never kill a fellow citizen or a welcomed foreigner. That's really what the law is all about.

"Why do you say that?"

If you fly off to some foreign country where we have no diplomatic relations—

"You mean, where they hate us and we hate them?"

Close enough. If you go there and you kill their head of state or their chief military officer, our country is not going to press charges when you return. (To help make this point, please fill in the name of our most current "enemy.")

"They'd probably throw a parade for me."

Right. So our country doesn't object to killing. It all depends on whom you kill. Oops, let me add one more provision. We tend to frown on people being killed on our soil. Messy. And we aren't thrilled if you kill a foreign person, even on their soil.

"If we have diplomatic relations with them. If we like them."

Now you've got the idea.

"But what about capital punishment?"

It's basically the same idea. When people commit certain crimes, we remove certain rights. If you get caught driving while drunk or drugged, you can lose your driver's license.

"Felonies result in prison terms and the loss of the right to vote in national elections, I think."

So, by the same reasoning, we strip a "cold-blooded murderer" of citizenship rights. You moral people deem the offense so great that you repeal the agreement to protect the murderer.

"You mean, the social contract no longer applies?"

That's one way of putting it. The long and short of it is that the murderer loses immunity from being killed. The state can do as it wishes. No murder of a citizen or of a "covered" alien occurs.

"I still think there are going to be moral and legal rules that you can't sneak out of. I can't think of one right now, but I'm sure there must be some."

Maybe we should do away with moral rules altogether.

"You can't do that!"

All I meant was that we could do away with moral rules and replace them with, ta da—understanding! No, no, forget that. It might be a good idea.

"I have no idea what you're talking about, or where this is going. What I want to know is, which values are true? Which moral values work?"

Agreement Is Not Truth

You seem to think that agreement is truth. But that's unlikely. Here, look at this example. Not long ago, people believed that the earth was flat. Your ancestors, and mine, believed that. Was the earth flat?

"Of course not."

But most people believed that. So truth is not merely agreement. And I'll take it even farther. Even if everyone believed that the earth was flat, it wasn't.

"I've already agreed to that."

So the majority does not decide on what's true.

"Okay. Where does this leave us? I don't think you're trying to make progress on this question. Because I don't think you have an answer to this one, do you?"

I'm wounded by your attack on my integrity. But let me try a bit harder.

"You're stalling."

Types of Truth

Okay, what are some examples of truths?

"To avoid another one of your long-winded discussions, I can give you different types of truths. There are mathematical truths, $1 + 1 = 2$, and the Pythagorean theorem. And there are scientific truths, the law of gravity, the shape of the earth. There are personal truths. I feel pain or pleasure. I see a chair over there. There's other knowledge, too. A lot of what we know is based on what people tell us. Historical knowledge, and when you were born and who your parents are. All that is based on what people tell you."

You really do cut right to it. Let's see what each type of truth is.

Mathematical Truths Are True by Agreement.   "Let's start with mathematical knowledge."

Mathematical truths are true by agreement. That is, some knowledge is just agreement. Math is one set of those truths.

"But you just showed me that isn't true! The earth's shape doesn't change with changing belief."

I lied. Look, truth is not as simple as you want it to be. There are different types of truth.

"That statement brings us right back to relativism. I want to know which truth is better, which truth is true?"

Look at your first example, math. Mathematical knowledge is agreement. Mathematics is by definition internally consistent and self-contained.

"What does that mean?"

Once you know the meaning of the symbols, the rest becomes obvious through practice. That's why once you learn a mathematical truth, it isn't difficult to figure it out again. You have arrived at the agreed-on answer, by the agreed-on method.

"Language seems to be that way, too. Words mean what we want them to mean. For example, the word *red* means red to English-speaking people. But *rouge* means red to the French. Is that what you have in mind?"

I hadn't thought of that example. It's more complicated than mine, but yes, that's the kind of distinction I'm going for. The other revealing thing about mathematical knowledge is that it doesn't make any sense to doubt it.

"I'm not following you."

Well, say someone says that $1 + 1$ does not equal 2. Would that put the statement $1 + 1 = 2$ into question?

"Of course not. Everyone knows that $1 + 1 = 2$."

So when someone denies or contests the truth, what do you do?

"I'd say the person didn't know how to add."

Exactly. Either the person is a child who hasn't yet learned to add, or the person may speak another language and merely be caught up in a language difficulty. Either way—

"I get it. Either way, math can't be doubted. It can't be doubted in the sense that it doesn't make sense to doubt it. Doubt shows that there is something 'wrong' with the doubter. Math is true by agreement. So some knowledge *is* true by agreement. Does this apply to morality? If it does, we can't reject relativism. We'll have to admit that different cultures have different values."

And that there's no way of resolving differences. Except by force.

Is Moral Truth Like Mathematical Truth? "Is moral truth like mathematical truth?"

Unfortunately, and no offense, mathematical knowledge doesn't tell us anything about the outside world. When we're looking for moral truth, math just won't do as a model. Morality is about the world, not about symbols.

"But the absolutist wouldn't agree with you."

Why do you say that?

"What kind of author are you, anyway? You're supposed to know this stuff, not me."

Right, but why wouldn't the absolutist agree?

"At least some absolutists wouldn't agree. For example, if you believe that moral values and principles can be reached only through reason, then you wouldn't reject the mathematical model. Do you follow?"

Not exactly.

"Say you believe that reason can give you your moral principles. Reason isn't about this world any more than math is. Reason applies to the world when we want it to apply. So does math, when we want it to apply. But reason takes us into another realm, the realm of the objective."

Hold on for a minute. Are we traveling into a space-time warp or something? (Hum the theme to any space adventure movie.)

"You're losing it, Art. Look, the absolutist might claim that morality is basically objective, and impartial. We agreed to this in our earlier talk. Well, what makes someone objective and impartial? Reason. And the beauty of the idea is that everyone has the same reason."

Everyone doesn't reason the same way. Some people are better at it than others. And don't mention names.

"But see, everyone does reason the same way. Just like everyone does math the same way. Sure, some people are better at math than others. But that's just ability and practice. The math itself doesn't change. That's the strength of math. And it's the same with reason."

Logic doesn't depend on the person's personality?

"Right. Personality and emotions aren't impartial like logic. They're not morally relevant."

This is clever. If I understand your idea, moral knowledge may be like mathematical knowledge. Both are objective and impartial. But is moral truth true by definition of the symbols used? That's the part that confuses me.

"Morality isn't exactly true because of the symbols, but math isn't really that way, either. It's not the symbols; it's what they stand for. If you understand the ideas that the symbols stand for, then you are doing math. The same goes for morality. If you use reason, you can arrive at the moral truth."

Ha, got you.

"What are you talking about?"

I don't want to disagree with your idea about moral absolutism. When we get farther into the book, we'll examine a theory by a guy named Kant. Your idea is similar to his. (You might want to look at it now.)

"How have you gotten me?"

Your idea doesn't apply to relativism. The original point was that math truths are true by agreement. I guess you've shown that isn't quite accurate. Still, my original point stands. Your view of math isn't a good analogy for morality.

"But my absolutist version of morality corresponds to math."

It does, and it is nonrelativist. So the problem we were trying to avoid can be solved by your absolutist strategy. If moral truth is like mathematical truth, then relativism isn't true. And we have no problems.

"And what makes you think you got me?"

So I "exaggerated." I felt like arguing and not listening. We've also agreed to look more closely at Kant as a representative of your "reasoned" absolutist approach. I think what you've offered gives a powerful way of avoiding relativism. You have given a good reason to adopt a theory like Kant's absolutism.

The Scientific Method Lets Us Trust Scientific Claims.   "So where's the problem? Why hasn't this chapter ended?"

What if morality can't be discovered through reason? There's one problem with the reasoned approach. It seems to deny that in a moral dispute both sides can be using reason properly.

"That might be a problem."

What if morality is more like my example of the belief in the shape of the earth?

"We might need another model of truth?"

My thinking exactly. Scientific knowledge is not found through reason alone. A scientist has to make observations. That's how we discovered that the earth is not flat. It's also how we discover that 1 + 1 does not equal 2.

"What are you talking about? 1 + 1 does equal 2. We just showed that math truths are true by agreement and that it doesn't make sense to doubt them."

Oh, I'm not doubting that 1 + 1 = 2, at least in math. I'm just saying that 1 + 1 does not equal 2 in a real-world example, or in science.

"I suppose one apple and one apple does not equal two apples?"

Sure it does. But one gallon of liquid and one gallon of liquid does not equal two gallons of liquid. Not always, anyway. Take a gallon of water and add a gallon of antifreeze. You won't get two gallons. In fact, you get noticeably less than two gallons. I say we sue mathematicians everywhere for this gross deception.

"You idiot. The reason there is less than two gallons is because of the chemical bonding that occurs between water and antifreeze molecules."

Likely story. You're in with the mathematicians. But doesn't my point still stand? 1 + 1 does not equal 2. In math it does, in science it doesn't.

"Maybe so. Your examples are strange. What does make a scientific claim true?"

I think the scientific method lets us trust scientific claims. If, after making an observation, I make a claim about reality, you should be able to make the same observation. Science is based on reproducible observations. That's what makes it objective. No single person's feelings are allowed to cloud the observation.

"The scientific technique guarantees objectivity and accuracy?"

In theory, yes.

"Why do you say 'in theory'? What's wrong with this approach?"

Since our concern is whether or not moral truths are relative, the scientific approach does not guarantee Truth. It only guarantees *t*ruth.

"You're becoming more and more obscure."

All I mean is that science has its own truths. But we're interested in Truth. Truth with a capital *T* is *the* truth. The truth apart from the possibility of error. The other truth, with a small *t,* is truth relative to any one scientific theory.

Scientific Truths Are Relative Truths.   "But that isn't how science operates. Scientific information is either true or it isn't true."

Not quite. Scientific observations are theory laden.

"What?"

Impressed you, didn't I? Science is biased by the assumptions it makes. Different scientific theories use different assumptions. They all use similar techniques; that's what makes them science. But they make different assumptions.

"For example?"

For example, say you've got two scientists making observations. One speculates that the earth is perfectly flat. The other's theory is that the earth is a perfect sphere.

"Obviously, the first is mistaken and the second is correct."

Well, that depends on all sorts of other beliefs. For example, what if they both believe that there are demons and serpents and sea monsters? What if they both trust their senses? They see a ship leave port. Just as it gets to the open sea, it sinks.

"The ship doesn't sink. It goes beyond the horizon, beyond where they can see it. The curve of the earth makes it appear to sink."

Horizon is a concept they can't have. That would prejudice their observations. That assumes a spherical earth. All they know is that the ship goes down. When the ship does not return, they presume it is lost to the ocean gods or to sea serpents. Isn't that a reasonable conclusion?

Is Moral Truth Like Scientific Truth?　"Are you suggesting that moral truth is like scientific truth? Are you saying that moral truth is relative to our other beliefs?"

Actually, I'm being careful not to say anything. But no, I don't think that scientific truths are like moral truths. I think moral truths are much more fundamental than scientific truths. Science frequently unearths new data. Discoveries bring new scientific information.

"And moral truths?"

Morality doesn't unearth new data or make new moral information. Morality doesn't change nearly as rapidly as science does. For example, virtually no one takes ancient physics seriously as a practical science for today. Right? How many physicists today believe that the primary "stuff" of the universe is air, or water, or earth, or fire?

"So?"

So we give up scientific truths pretty readily. (I've exaggerated, but only a little.) But we still respect the moral insights of the ancient world. Think about it. If you met Moses and Aristotle, Jesus and Gautama (the Buddha), Abraham and Plato, you'd probably be fascinated by the similarity of their discussion of morality and the spiritual life to our own talk.

"Of course!"

But you'd laugh (respectfully) if they discussed the "latest" scientific beliefs of their day.

"Scientific truths change more readily than moral insights."

I think so. It's that way partly because science depends on the senses. Scientific truth is a hostage to data. We are compelled to reassess old theories and to explain new data in science. Science goes even beyond the senses. And we aren't comfortable with that. Remember how we tested math? Does it make sense to doubt scientific facts or theories?

"Yes, of course. In fact, that's what a good scientist does. She tries to invalidate the accepted theories. If that fails, then she tries to extend, or to simplify, the theory."

Science lacks the certainty of math. It's the nature of scientific truth to be tentative. Science is supposed to challenge itself.

"Science is relative?"

I guess you could say that, but the real point is that it doesn't bother anyone.

"But it bothers me if morality is relative."

Why? You live most of your life accepting scientific truths as True. Why doesn't it bother you that science is changeable?

"I guess I never thought of science as that changeable. Maybe it's because science progresses. The 'relativism' of science brings new and better truths. But morality isn't that way. I don't see how one moral theory improves on another."

Does Morality Work?

First off, science does not progress. Read some history of science. There's lots of evidence that science changes, but progress is difficult to establish. After all, what does it mean to say that science progresses?

"It works."

That's one idea of progress. Look, let's not get into a discussion of scientific progress. What we want to know is, when morality changes, does it progress? What counts as moral progress?

"Why not say that morality progresses when it works?"

What does that mean? What does it mean for morality to work?

"If it helps you get along in society, then your moral values have worked."

So if you live in a disgusting, vicious society where people do all sorts of cruel and mean things, your morality would be cruel and mean and disgusting? That's the only way of living that would fit into that kind of society. How else could you "get along"?

"You know that isn't what I mean. Morality is supposed to make you a better person."

Then what does it mean for a moral system to work? I think we're onto an important question. If we can decide what morality is for, we might be able to resolve your—

"Perplexity?"

Yeah.

"I'm not sure what the ultimate aim of morality is."

Human Nature

Then let's put aside morality and relativism for a while. I think the problem of relativism comes up because we believe that people differ. Therefore, their values differ. So we need to figure out what makes people human.

"What do you mean? People are people. That's pretty easy."

Sure, but what is it that makes us human and not tables or dogs? I think we have to figure this out. If we know what makes us uniquely human, maybe we can discover the best way to live. After all, creating a best way of life for cattle is not the same as for people. Right?

"Right. Cows aren't as complex or as interesting as people. They don't require much to be happy. So what makes us human? That's what you want to know?"

Yup.

What Difference Does It Make?

"But what difference does it make whether or not we can define humans?"

I'm just trying to make sense of your idea that the best life is filling one's needs and playing one's natural roles.

"What does human nature have to do with that?"

If we can define what makes us human, we can determine which of our wants are real and which are artificial. Doesn't that strategy make sense?

"Artificial wants? What do you mean?"

Some wants are socially and culturally determined. Those are artificial. Other wants are more natural to us.

"But I still feel artificial wants. I don't think I can tell the difference just by feeling them. But I think I see what you mean."

So my strategy is acceptable, at least for now?

The Abilities to Think and to Feel

"Okay. One thing that makes us human is that we can think and feel."

That's two activities, not one.

"Whatever. We are intelligent in a way that animals cannot be. We reason, whereas animals count on instinct."

I don't understand.

"We can evaluate problems and find solutions. We humans can figure out how to get water. Animals just instinctively need water. They don't reason about it. Of course, now that I think about it, we don't reason about being thirsty, either. We get thirsty, then we figure out how to satisfy our thirst. Never mind, I changed my mind."

So where does that leave us? We can't reason?

"No, we can still reason in ways that animals can't reason. We are able to evaluate problems and to create solutions. And we have feelings."

Animals experience emotions, don't they?

"Yes, they probably do. But they don't have the same emotions as people have."

How do you know? How could anyone ever know what an animal feels? Even if we could know, the question is: Do animals experience emotions? And the answer is?

"Okay, yes they do. But they can't reason."

I don't know about that. I admit they act on instinct much of the time, but they do reason, too. Chimpanzees have been known to carry their old even to the point of sacrificing the younger, stronger monkeys. They carry and protect the old. That way the group is able to find food and water in time of famine or drought.

"How do they do that?"

The older chimps remember where food and water are from the last famine or drought. They reason that this crisis is similar to the past crisis. Pretty good, huh?

"That doesn't seem to be the same as human reason. Chimps can't do math or philosophy."

Neither can infants or very small children! Then again, maybe infants and small children aren't human.

"Don't be stupid. The point is humans reason in ways that animals cannot reason. We're better at it than animals."

So we confer the status of "human" based on how well one reasons! There's a danger lurking here.

"That's not what I'm saying. If you allow a normal infant or child to develop, it will be able to reason in ways that animals can never reason. They'll be able to do math and science, for example."

Computers Can't Think.   Like a good computer?

"Not at all. Computers only do what we tell them to do. They only know what we put into them. They need people to program them."

How are people any different? Don't we take kids and put them into school? What do they do there? They are taught, sometimes by teachers and sometimes by computers.

"Still, people are unique. No two people are exactly identical. Computers don't have unique personalities."

Our uniqueness probably comes from having different experiences from others. I suppose if two computers had different experiences, they would develop differently.

"This is crazy. Computers can't think. They can only calculate; they can't create."

Artificial intelligence.

"Are you insulting me?"

Heaven forbid! Artificial intelligence studies ways to make computers that think. The idea is to make computers that are able to learn from their mistakes, to plan strategies based on the rules of the game, etc. I heard about a computer that was taught to play chess.

"I agree, computers have incredible memories. That's all the chess-playing machine is doing. It plays chess by searching its memory for the right moves."

Not quite. Since there are an indeterminate number of possible moves in chess, relying on memory won't work. The programmers had to give the machine a knowledge of the rules of the game. It started out losing, but it got better and better. Now it can beat experienced players.

Computers Can't Feel.   "But computers can't feel."

Actually, sensors can be placed on computers to allow them to recognize heat, light, sound, and other experiences. They're pretty sophisticated.

"But those are sensors telling them that the light is on. They can't feel heat or light. They know there's a change of light or temperature, but that isn't feeling. They don't have any internal sensation."

Eyes pick up light, convert it into electrical impulses, and send them to the brain. You're just prejudiced. Why are you prejudiced against things that aren't like you? Just because a computer is plastic and wire? And we are muscle, hair, fat, and liquids? Is that it, you don't approve of beings that aren't liquidy?

Computers Depend on People.   "That's not what I'm saying. Computers aren't human, that's all. They can't reproduce. They depend on people."

Animals reproduce, but you don't call them human, either. You're fickle.

"I still say, computers can't feel and they don't reproduce."

But they do reproduce. From the little I know about computers, I understand that this "generation" of computer is being used to design the next generation. Neat, huh? And you can imagine that computer robots can be taught to assemble the new generation.

"They can't maintain themselves. They need people to fix them when they break. And they can be turned on and off. You can't do that with people."

One idea at a time. Maybe computers can't maintain themselves, but they can diagnose their problems. "Excuse me, Mr. Jones, but I seem to have a malfunctioning LD 2995 chip."

"But they need Jones to replace the chip."

Have you ever heard of medical people? We need people to maintain us, too. I don't see much difference there. As for turning them on and off, we can turn people off. Bang, you're dead.

"But we can't turn them back on. That's a big difference."

It sounds like computers have the edge there. They can think faster, remember better, diagnose their problems, and be resurrected. My vote goes for the computer.

"Feelings, what about feelings?"

I suppose you could program a computer to say, "Hurray!" when it wins a chess game.

"But that would only be programmed. It wouldn't feel the excitement."

I don't know about that. I really don't know. I'm not sure how we could ever know that about anyone or anything. What else makes us human?

Computers Don't Care.   "This may sound a bit morbid, but we know that we are going to die. Computers don't have that knowledge, and neither do animals."

Hmm, I think you're right. Although computers don't have to worry about it. They can be resurrected. It's a holy ritual.

"Oh, stop it. Computers don't care. They don't have a personality. They don't care whether or not they live—I mean, continue."

That's an interesting point. People do care!

"I suppose we could program a computer to want to live, but people have that naturally. Wait. I just realized. Some animals do know when they are going to die. Elephants have graveyards. The older elephants wander to the graveyards when they are about to die."

I wouldn't have thought of that. But we can still say that people want to continue living, and computers don't care. Unless they're programmed to care.

"No, Art, we can't say even that. People commit suicide. Heroes sacrifice themselves. At least some people are not afraid of dying. And besides, animals also try to stay alive. That's why it's so dangerous to corner them."

So what makes us human?

Humans Communicate Through Speech

"I've thought of two more traits humans possess. We can communicate through speech, through language, and we know the difference between right and wrong."

Can't animals communicate with each other?

"Yes, but not through speech."

Dolphins and even dogs seem to understand when we talk to them. In fact, they're smarter than we are. I've heard of dolphins who understand us, but I've never heard of a human who understands dolphin. Or dog, for that matter.

"Dogs and cats and other animals are conditioned to understand. They don't really understand language. They understand the tone of voice, not words."

Everyone is "conditioned" when it comes to language. Babies have to be taught the language they learn. Think what it'd be like if that weren't true. Could you imagine a baby being born to an English-speaking family and not knowing English? Instead it speaks some Tibetan dialect. Wow, if it were born here, its parents would freak.

"People understand what their pets are saying. When the dog stands by the refrigerator and barks, it's hungry. It waits for the owner or someone to come and feed it."

So animals condition us? Rover thinks, "Now how am I going to train this human?" Can you imagine poor Rover when you're away and another human has to be broken in? "Roof, roof, the refrigerator, you fool. Don't you people understand anything?"

"Now that I think about it, I have heard that monkeys and gorillas can learn some form of sign language. So I guess they can at least mimic communication."

Yes, I've heard of that. In one case I heard that a gorilla made up a new hand sign. It combined two or three hand signs to say something.

Humans Distinguish Right and Wrong

"Okay, so animals can communicate. They don't know right from wrong, though. I mean, the only way they know something is wrong is if they are trained that way."

Just like—

"People? I guess so."

Sure, right and wrong aren't innate.

"No, of course not. We talked about that. And values differ from culture to culture, and time to time. Relativism, that's where our discussion started. So what do you think makes us human?"

Family Resemblance

Dunno! Maybe everything we've said is what makes us human. If you have enough of these traits, you're human. Some people call it a family resemblance. Little Johnny may have features that combine both sides of the family. He looks like his maternal grandmother in the nose, sort of. If you look at large families, you can see a resemblance, even though two of the children don't share any features.

"But that still leaves babies out of our calculation. The human traits we've picked are not reflected in infants."

Big loss! Do you know what they do in their diapers?

"Seriously. Do babies feel and express emotions, and reason, and communicate, and know that they will die? Do they evaluate problems and create solutions? I guess they do some of these activities, but no better than some animals. And they don't know right from wrong until we teach them. Still, they are human. Maybe what makes us human is that we have human parents."

How do you know? If we can't determine what makes someone human, how can we know that her parents are human?

"We all know what humans are. We may not be able to define the concept, but we know examples of humans. Just like when we looked at examples of morality. From the examples, we found common features. Remember?"

Gee, you're learning. Still, I don't think it's because someone's parents are human. We all call people human, even when we haven't met their parents.

Genetics and Being Human

"That's not what I mean. We don't have to know their parents, or their parents' parents. Proving that someone is human would go on forever. What I mean is that being human is a genetic trait. If you examine someone's genes, you can determine whether or not the person is human. What do you think of that? Science—in this case, biology—has decided for us."

But people were human before we ever thought about genetic codes and other biological jargon. Besides that, your idea puts the cart before the horse. Biologists looked at humans and then found out what unique biological trait they had.

"What's wrong with doing that?"

Nothing, except that it automatically limits humans to a certain group of animals with similar ancestry. From what we were discussing earlier, I thought we were being more open. You gave features like being able to feel emotions and being able to think or reason. Those traits opened the field to a more interesting range of beings.

"But it's humans we are trying to define, not intelligent, caring antelopes. What other kinds of creatures do you want to make human? And don't say computers."

Good point. I guess what I had in mind was not so much a physical description of humans. I think your point is a very good one. Biologically, we are human because of our parents, because of our genetic code. That is one sense of the notion of being human. It's a description.

"What else is there other than the descriptive sense?"

The Moral Sense of "Human"

I'm not sure what to call it, but when we call someone human we give that person special status.

"You mean there is a moral sense of the word *human*? I didn't think you liked morality, Art! I think I've caught you in a contradiction."

I'm not sure it has to be a moral sense. I don't think you have to give people rights or duties or obligations, at least not just because they are human. And I certainly don't think you have to do unto them and all of that other stuff we talked about.

"Nonetheless, you are granting special status to humans. You're moral after all."

I resent that. (Somehow you've turned the tables on me!) I am willing to treat lots of creatures like you treat humans. Computers, for one. Can you imagine how the last political elections would have gone if computers got to vote? See, what I have in mind is to find out what makes us special. Imagine—

"Not another one of your extreme examples."

No, no, this one is likely to happen. Imagine that more beings from the far side of Jupiter come down to visit. Not all of them are as human looking as I am. (I am too!) How can we determine they are human?

"In the moral sense?"

In the special sense we are discussing, whatever you call it.

Greed

"To be human is to always want more. Humans are never satisfied with what they have. You know, like when someone starts a job. The person wants to do well. Then, after a while, you want to advance. At first, all you want is a promotion. But each promotion satisfies you only for a short time. Then you want to move ahead. People always want a bigger house, a better car, a vacation to a more exotic place. That's what makes us human. And it's probably innate. You can even see it in young children. They always want what they see."

So what makes us human is that we are greedy? How uplifting!

"Yes, we are innately greedy. Go on—'But what about?' I'm sure you don't agree. Go on, 'What about'—

What about what?

"You always have an objection or an example that doesn't fit my definitions. So—"

What About Unselfish People? Okay, but what about people who help others? Are they greedy or selfish? What do they get out of it?

"They get a sense of satisfaction from doing the right thing. They feel good about themselves. You probably never felt that, but we call it self-esteem."

Self-esteem? Interesting concept. But I don't understand. You help an old person cross the street so that you'll feel good about yourself. Did the old person want to cross the street, or are you forcing her?

"Of course I don't force people across the street. But when I help them, I feel good about it."

Why?

"Because they need help, and they have feelings."

So you help them because they need the help?

"Of course, you nitwit."

But how is this selfish? You get something out of it. But you are helping the other person. Which is your primary motive, to help or to feel good?

"To help. If I do it just to feel good about myself, then the feeling doesn't happen. The good feeling is a kind of by-product of doing the right thing."

Because otherwise your motive would be selfish? See, here's where I don't get it. You help people because they need help. Then you feel good about yourself. The ideas of selfish and selfless become confused. Your action is primarily directed at helping the other person. It's only secondarily self-oriented.

"I see what you mean. Still, people are often very selfish and greedy. Maybe it's because of socialization, because of moral training, that we overcome our innate selfishness."

Maybe.

Greed and Private Property. "But?"

Well, only one small "but." The whole idea of greed assumes that we understand the notion of private property. That's pretty complicated stuff. I can't honestly say I fully understand private property. How could an infant know about this idea?

"What does private property have to do with it?"

Imagine living in an environment where there is more than enough of everything to go around. When you're hungry, you just reach up and pick a ripe fruit. In this kind of place would there be greed?

"What if I didn't want to work? All I do all day is lie around. When it's mealtime, I see you eating and I want your fruit. What prevents me from taking it?"

Nothing. Except that there's no reason to take anything. If you take "my" fruit, I just lean back and take another piece. There's plenty.

"Yes, I see your point, but that doesn't change my mind. People are innately greedy and selfish. All your example shows is that we can imagine a place where people don't have to be greedy. But just bring in a shortage of something. Then you'll see how fast they change. Besides, our society isn't like your fantasy. Here there isn't enough to go around. Only people on welfare get to take without working for it. The rest of us have to work."

I'm not sure I see the connection. I'll give you your first point. We do live in a society where shortages occur. We'll get back to this in a moment. But your complaint about welfare strikes me as strange.

"Strange? How so? Those people get a lot from the system, but what do they have to do for it? Nothing. I'd love to have a free ride like that."

The ride isn't quite free. But think about it. You are getting a similar "free ride." You're a college student. (I use the term loosely.) If you are going to a private school, there are lots of people who donate money so that the school can operate. Your tuition money probably doesn't pay for what you get. And if you're attending a public, state, or community college, it's taxes that pay much of your way. You're a welfare recipient, though probably not a poor one.

"But someday I'll return the favor. I'll donate money to education and I'll pay my share of the taxes that go to public schools."

Perhaps. But that's the idea of any decent welfare system, to get people back into the flow of society.

"But those people stay on welfare for generations. They don't work."

Sometimes we blame people for "taking advantage of the system." That's odd. When we take advantage of the system, it's okay. We expect our rights. When a really rich person takes advantage of the system, we admire him. But when some poor guy gets almost enough to live on, we scream and yell. If you're assuming everyone is innately greedy, why blame only the poor person for showing it?

"Let me think about this one. I want to add laziness to my definition of human nature. We are instinctively lazy and prejudiced. Everyone is lazy, prejudiced, selfish, and greedy. That's why we need morality. If we didn't have morality, society would never progress."

Cynicism

Progress?

"Yes, progress. We can do things now that people only imagined before. Our technology gives us longer lives and better weapons for protection."

I don't agree that we are more advanced than other societies. Maybe we are more technologically advanced in some ways, but—

"But nothing. Would you want to live anywhere else?"

My country's better than your country, na na! Is that what you're saying?

"Well, isn't it? We are more secure and better fed."

Yes, that may be true. Why do you have such a cynical view of people?

"Cynical?"

Yes, negative.

"I know what 'cynical' means."

Look at your definition of humans. You seem to be saying that humans are weak, vicious, selfish, and destructive. Is that what you see in people?

"It's hard to deny that we are not that way. Look how destructive people have been. Maybe a way of distinguishing people and animals is that only people destroy and dehumanize each other."

Dehumanize?

"Yes, only humans treat other people as though they were worthless."

I won't deny that you humans are occasionally cruel.

"And then we rationalize our actions. We treat our actions as though they were appropriate. We go all out to justify what we know is wrong."

I've seen some of that, too. But it doesn't mean that people are like this by nature.

"Oh?"

Creative and Inventive

People can be cruel and selfish and destructive, but they are also kind and giving and creative. (This is a switch, me arguing for the good in people.)

"What are you saying? That we aren't selfish and cruel and destructive?"

I don't see any evidence that people are this way by nature. People also enjoy beauty and humor. They even overcome their learned prejudices with some effort.

"Then you don't think people are very accurately reflected in their actions?"

Gee, I don't know. All I'm saying is that your cynical view is more a sign of frustration than anything else. Just because we cannot easily define human nature doesn't mean we have to be unjustly harsh on humanity.

Religion

"Fair enough, Art. I say what distinguishes us as humans is that we have religion."

So atheists aren't human?

"No, they are just misguided. But humans are the only species that asks religious questions, that believes in souls and spirits and psyches. Maybe that's what makes us human, that we ask religious questions."

What do you mean by religious questions?

"We care about spiritual things. We want to be comfortable and well fed and safe. But we also want more."

Humans do not live by bread alone? Is that it?

"Something like that, yes. We believe in souls. What makes a person human, and not a machine, is that people have souls. Machines don't have souls."

I haven't ever seen a soul. Have you?

"You want concrete proof that souls exist, and there just isn't any. Just because you can't see them doesn't mean they don't exist."

I don't want cement proof. Remember, I believe in invisible green goblins. You can't see them, either.

"I'm not going to get into that discussion again. Lots of people believe in souls. That's what makes us human."

Hmm.

"What are you doing?"

I'm looking into my shirt. I'm looking for my soul. I'm also wondering why my soul picked this body?

"You can make fun of my idea all you want, but people have souls."

I doubt that we'll resolve this. What else about religion defines us as humans?

Humans Have Free Will

"Because we have souls, we are free. We have free will. We can choose any way we want. That's what makes us human."

Interesting idea. Why does this have to be tied to religion?

"It doesn't. People are human because we are free."

And animals and computers—

"Animals act on instinct, and computers don't choose. They react to programming. I know what you're going to say. People are programmed, too. Yes, we are. Only we can go beyond our programming. We can even choose to ignore our programming. Machines can't do that!"

Maybe our programming is more diverse and more sophisticated. Maybe our learning is more random than a computer's programming.

"You can say maybe all you want, Art. But I say people have free will."

What is an unfree will?

"Don't distract me with your little puns, or whatever you call them. People are free. We are also spiritual in another sense I just thought of."

Compassion

Compassion?

"So you can read! Yes, people can feel compassion toward one another. Computers can't do that. And I doubt that animals feel that kind of emotion. So what makes us human is some of what we have already talked about, but clearly what makes us human is that we have free will and compassion."

Can I choose not to feel compassion? Or am I unfree when it comes to compassion?

"Now you're just playing word games. There's a place for that, I guess, but not now. You don't deal very well with people, do you?"

Relating to Other People

Actually, I do get along well with other people. I usually just do whatever they want, and they're content. But that's another story. I think your final comments have solved our problem.

"Which comments?"

I think compassion is too limited, but you're on the right track. People relate to other people in special ways. Compassion is one of them.

"And the special ways we relate to other people is what makes us human?"

Yeah. What do ya think?

"Well, humans do relate to each other in ways that machines and animals can't communicate. That does seem true."

Right. When you said that people feel, and communicate, and care, that was on the right track. People don't always relate to other people in the special ways reserved for humans, of course.

"But only humans can relate to others in those special ways. Now all we have to do is figure out what those ways are."

Why don't we leave that to the philosophers who take up Part II and Part III? I think we can learn a lot from them. Whatever the final answer is, I think you have hit on a very important point. The best life has to include relating to other people.

"Do we know what makes us human now?"

Not exactly, but I think our talk has made us sensitive to the right things to look for in each upcoming theory. I think we deserve an extra 250 brownie points for our work here.

"What do brownie points give you?"

An infinite number of brownie points gives nothing, but they're still always good to have. Just in case you need them.

Summary of Discussion

Isn't everyone different? Don't we all have different values? Relativism is the observation that values vary from person to person, society to society, and over historical times. From this variation in values, relativism concludes that values are not stable and unchanging. What is right for one person (or society) may not be right for another person (or society).

We are left with the question: "Which values are true?" Some disagreements are only apparent and can be resolved. The problem is that many other disagreements are disagreements over basic beliefs and values. The relativist uses genuine disagreements as evidence that values are not absolute.

There are at least two replies to the relativist. First, the relativist assumes that agreement is truth. This assumption is not safe to make. Nearly every European once believed that the earth was flat, yet we know that the earth's shape did not depend on their agreement. Reality is separate from human belief. So agreement is not truth. Disagreement, therefore, does not entail falsity. Because you and I disagree does not mean that we are both mistaken.

Second, as in morality, in the sciences we also find disagreement. We do not say, however, that science is relative just because of disagreements. Science is a method that receives and uses tentative truths as a part of its project. Progress can be made only by recognizing that we do not have the entire, absolute truth. However, science can still work toward the Truth.

Relativism has an appeal because we believe people differ. Therefore, their values differ. That may be true, but it is equally apparent that we share some qualities that make us human.

What constitutes human nature? Humans think, feel, communicate through speech, and distinguish right from wrong. Computers can function in these ways, too. Humans have human genes and other biological similarities. Our question, however, is not directed at physical resemblance, but at a moral sense of the term *human*.

Humans may be greedy by nature. There is a problem, though, in determining whether greed is naturally or culturally determined. Other less cynical aspects may also be part of human nature. Humans are creative and inventive. They concern themselves with religious questions. They may exercise free will. But if we do exercise free will, then the question of a human nature may be irrelevant. Free will may negate the impact of human nature. Compassion and other ways of relating to other people is another way of defining what makes us human. How we relate to each other may be what makes us human. There may be no human nature as such, only a human way of relating to our reality.

Discussion Highlights

I. Relativism
   1. Values vary between people, societies, historical times.
   2. Values are not stable and unchanging.
II. Disagreements
   1. There are disagreements in form and on content.
   2. Cultural disagreements can be misunderstandings.
   3. They may also be disagreements over basic beliefs.
III. Types of truth
   1. Mathematical truths are true by agreement.
   2. Scientific truths are "guaranteed" by the scientific method.
IV. Human nature
   1. People can think.
   2. People can feel emotions and sensations.
   3. People can communicate through speech.
   4. People can distinguish right and wrong.
   5. People have similar physical and genetic structures.
   6. People may be greedy by nature.
   7. People are naturally creative and inventive.
   8. They can be concerned with religious questions.
   9. People enjoy free will.

10. They feel compassion, sympathy, and like emotions.
11. Humans are distinguished in their way of relating to each other and to reality.

Questions For Thought/Paper Topics

1. An ancient Chinese philosopher, Chuang Tsu, once wrote that he dreamed that he was a butterfly. He flew about happily, enjoying the life of the butterfly, never asking who he was. Then he awoke and found out that he was a man. Did Chuang Tsu dream he was a butterfly, or did the butterfly dream he was Chuang Tsu? Which reality is true?
2. Do disagreements between cultures imply that there is no truth? What method is used to resolve differences in the sciences? Can you think of a similar method for resolving moral differences?
3. Moral people tell me that they want conformity to the moral rules and that they value individual differences. Assume both can be true simultaneously. How would that work?
4. What are the essential features that make us human? Try to keep in mind that we are looking for more than a biological/physical distinction.
5. Do computers think? If you think they can't think, describe what humans do that computers fail to do. (Then construct a computer that can think in the ways you describe.)
6. Do humans have free will? How free is that will? In light of all we know about enforced conformity brought about by socialization, advertising, education, and so on, how much room is there for free will?
7. Do you humans relate to each other in special ways? Can we use this to define what makes us human?

For Further Reading

There is a very readable little book by Bertrand Russell, *The Problems of Philosophy* (Oxford, 1959). Russell clearly discusses a series of questions in philosophy, including knowledge. Another book on the topic of relativism and knowledge is Ludwig Wittgenstein's *On Certainty* (Harper & Row, 1972). It presents a picture of one way of understanding what counts as knowledge. John Ladd edited an anthology called *Ethical Relativism* (Wadsworth, 1971) containing several worthwhile articles. Another place to look for a discussion of human nature and relativity in values is the works of Chinese philosophers, Lao Tsu and Chuang Tsu.

5　What If I Do Whatever I Want?

I KNOW WHAT you're thinking. "Art has tried to convince us of this already. And we have shown him that doing whatever one wants is dangerous to society and to each of us. If each of us did whatever he wanted, we would have chaos!" That's what you're thinking, isn't it?

Okay, I concede your point. Doing whatever I want could lead to the breakdown of society as we know it. After all, I am quite the influential trendsetter! People do whatever I do. Everywhere I go, people watch my every move.

"Actually, what I was thinking is that I'm tired of these talks where you have the upper hand. Why don't you pick on someone else in this chapter? I'll sit back and watch—or read, as the case may be. That's what I was thinking."

Fair enough. Let's pick your average, fanatical moralist to carry on the conversation.

"No fair. Pick a moralist who is reasonable. Anyone can knock down a straw man, Art."

Straw man?

"A straw man is someone who is set up to be knocked down. You know, an easy target that doesn't fight back. Make your moralist believable and intelligent."

I'll try. This should be challenging. Okay, for this chapter imagine that I am locked in semimortal, intellectual combat with an intelligent moralist. Now let me get back to the discussion. Doing whatever I want could lead to the breakdown of society as we know it. After all, I am quite the influential—

MORALIST: All right, you've made your point. Fortunately for us, Art, you are not an influence on people. Our point is still true, however. Our point is more of a theoretical one than a practical one. What if everyone, or nearly everyone, did whatever she wanted?

ART: Then I would be a fool to be the only one following moral rules.

MORALIST: Seriously, what if each person did whatever she wanted?

ART: Then everyone would be happy! (I can probably stop with the 'Art,' 'Moralist' designations, now, huh?)

Material in this chapter taken from Søren Kierkegaard, *Either/Or* (Princeton: Princeton University Press, 1944, 1959). David F. Swenson & Lillian Marvin Swenson translation.

"No, no, there would be chaos. No one would go to work. Nothing would get done. You wouldn't be able to do what you want, because there would be no police to protect you. Soon everyone would starve. Who would grow the food?"

Maybe you're right, but I think it's unreasonable to automatically exclude living for the moment. Pleasure is desirable, right? What is wrong with a life in pursuit of pleasure? All I want is that we look at one example of a character who does whatever he wants. If the life is unappealing even after our quick look, I promise I won't raise the issue again. What could the harm be, just one little look? We might even discover features of this life that are appealing to us.

"Art, you are confusing two distinct positions. A person could pursue pleasure—or any goal, for that matter—yet not live for the present moment. Someone might carefully plan out a long-term strategy to get more and more pleasure, or to succeed at any other goal. That's one option. The other option is a person who lives for whatever comes along in the momentary present. This person may not seek pleasure. Which option are you suggesting?"

How about both options? What I mean is, I think I misstated my idea. It's too late to change the title of this chapter, isn't it? Oh, well.

Life is Meaningless

"What is your idea?"

Life is meaningless. And since life is meaningless, I might as well do whatever I want.

"So now we have finally come to it! You don't believe in anything!"

That's not quite true. I believe in lots of things. Tables and chairs, people and bears. It rhymes, did you notice?

"But you don't believe in anything you can't see, anything intangible."

I am cut to the quick. Ouch! Of course I believe in some things that I can't see. The far side of the moon is out of my sight. Sure, there are pictures from some of our spacecraft, but I would believe in the existence of the far side of the moon without that kind of proof.

"That's not what I mean. You're being stupid intentionally, just to avoid the issue."

I am not being stupid intentionally. I'm naturally like this. (Ooh, I think you tricked me there.) I believe in other things that I can't see. Like you, I have other sense organs. I believe in odors, for example.

"That's not the point. Do you believe in anything you cannot physically touch, taste, smell, see, or hear? That's what I want to know. Does your reality stop at the limit of your senses?"

Hmm. (*Hmm* indicates that I'm pondering your question, even though I'm not.) Yes, I've found something intangible that I believe in—pleasure.

"But that's still physical, or at least caused by physical sensations!"

Not true. Some of my pleasures are mental.

"Like what? You aren't going to tell us that you enjoy thinking, are you?"

Sometimes I imagine a really great physical pleasure, and—

"Enough of this! (You really were thinking this, weren't you?) This is getting us nowhere."

That's just the point. You think there's somewhere to go. But one way of occupying my time is just about the same as any other way. That's because there's no meaning to life. Every action and event is just about the same as every other action or event. So "wasting" my time discussing this with you is no worse than any other occupation.

"This is ridiculous."

It may be mistaken, but it's not ridiculous. Just assume for a few minutes that there is no meaning to life. What follows from that?

"I don't know. What?"

Don't resist so much. We'll have a chance later in the book to examine the question of the meaning of life. It comes in the third part of the book. There's even a piece from your Bible in that part. So for now, just assume that life is meaningless. Let's see how terrible such a life would be.

"I can't just assume that life is meaningless!"

Joe and the Ants.   Then let me give you an analogy. There is a species of tree ant that has exactly fifty generations each spring-summer season. If the warm seasons last longer than usual, then each generation lives a little longer.

"How do they know how long the summer will last?"

How do I know? I'm not an ant. So these little bugs produce exactly fifty generations per year.

"Where is this example going?"

Wait, this gets better. The first and last generations hatch from their tiny eggs with wings. The forty-eight generations between the first and last are wingless. The first generation flies from the trees to the ground. Exactly forty-eight wingless generations spend their little ant lives on the ground. Then the fiftieth generation sprouts wings and flies back into the trees, where the eggs are planted to wait for the next spring.

"Amazing! What does this have to do with our question?"

What if someone comes along and steps on one of the little ants? I'm sure it happens, though unintentionally. What would be the significance of an ant's death? The generations would continue. The other ants of his generation would live out their precious few days. The fiftieth generation would sprout wings, fly to the trees, and lay their eggs. Next spring, more ants hatch. What significance does any one ant have?

"Nice story; now explain the analogy. Put it in human terms."

What significance does any one person's life have? The generations continue. What's the difference between a person's life and an ant's life?

"For one, the lives of humans are longer than the lives of the ants."

But in light of eternity, a few decades is insignificant.

"Their friends and families will miss them. Some of them will make contributions to their societies."

So what? There was a man who lived 8,237 years ago in Mesopotamia. His name was Joe. He had friends and a family. He made contributions to his society. A couple of his inventions even made life easier for people. Then along came someone who stepped on Joe. Do his friends and family and society matter? Undoubtedly they missed Joe. But they're long dead themselves. Does Joe's life matter any more than the ant who was crushed? Fifty generations or fifty seasons later, and the poor bug is forgotten.

"Joe probably felt that his life was meaningful. The ant didn't think its life was meaningful or anything else."

I agree. Joe the Mesopotamian may have thought his life was meaningful, but Joe's life had no more meaning than the ant's life.

"His family and friends thought so, too."

But we don't even remember Joe. Joe may have participated in great battles or great debates, but we have no record of it. Nor did his society have any apparent effect on ours. Neither he nor his family nor his friends nor his society has left a trace of itself. Joe's very existence is insignificant now. Just like the ant's life.

"You're depressing."

Come on, Smile.   Come on, smile. This is a happy thought. I recognize that Joe's life, and the ant's life, amount to the same thing—nothing. In the grand scheme of things, there is no grand scheme. But rather than getting depressed over this, drop your illusions. Realize that life is futile. It doesn't matter how you live. Moral people and religious people, conservative people and liberal people, all people die. In the space of the time between birth and death, there are no limits. There is only boredom. So live for the moment.

"What kind of life would that be?"

The Stranger

One character who lives life by doing whatever he wants is the main character in the novel *The Stranger,* by Albert Camus. You may have read the book, but if you haven't read it let me describe this character. By the way, he's one of my heroes.

The Stranger is not your ordinary pleasure seeker. He tries to avoid boredom. That's his defining feature. He finds it futile to try to alter the world, so he alters himself. He gives up goals and ambition and lives as much for the moment as he can manage. He never consciously sets out his strategy, but the way he does this is genuinely ingenious. He lives almost completely in the moment. For him, the object in front of him receives his complete attention. He does not see a larger meaning in life than what is presented by the momentary experience. Quite calmly, he tells the reader, "All that counts is the present and the concrete."

The Stranger does not connect the past, the present, and the future. He reaffirms this point of view near the end of the book. He says he has "always been absorbed in the present moment, or the immediate future."

"So what if a character in a novel says some crazy things! He's just weird."

The Stranger's point of view is not as foreign to us as it is uncomfortable. We are supposed to respect the past and look to the future. That's what morality is all about. Look at promises. I promised you something yesterday that I must guarantee to perform tomorrow. Morality ties the past me to the present and future me.

"You make it sound like they are different. The past me, the present me, and the future me are all me!"

The Stranger is immune to this kind of thinking. He does what he wants, as he wants to do it. He's spontaneous! Most of us live this way, too, only we reserve the weekends for our spontaneous acts.

Spontaneous. (Read this in a deep, resonant voice.) "Hello there. Do you have any plans for the weekend?" (Now read this in your own voice.) "Sure do. I plan to be spontaneous this weekend. Well, at least for part of the weekend."

We schedule our spontaneity! "Yes, I'll be doing the laundry from 2:15 to 4:30, then I'll be able to be spontaneous until 7:30." Sounds pretty stupid, huh? But that's as close as most people get to understanding the Stranger. He lives the way we would all like to live, if it weren't for responsibilities. Aaah!

"How is it possible to live for the moment? There *are* responsibilities, and promises, and obligations. And I feel guilty if I don't keep my promises and all the rest."

Good question. Let me give an analogy.

Concentrates Like a Work of Art. I bet you think I'm going to make some silly pun about art and Art. Well, wrong. A work of art can help us understand how someone like the Stranger looks at everyday experience. Imagine a painting. No, not that one; nothing abstract. Imagine a "regular" painting. You know, one that portrays a street scene or something like that. A painting or a photograph is a frozen moment. Now look at the object of the picture. The object is in the foreground. The rest of the world is in the background. In a really good painting the artist uses the background to draw the viewer's eye to the object of the picture.

"So?"

That's how the Stranger views the world. Whatever object is in front of him engages him. All the rest of the world is insignificant background. Whether he is smoking a cigarette, or making "love" with Marie, or eating eggs from a pan, or hearing the slam of a door, or spending an entire Sunday afternoon watching the street scene below his balcony, each experience is significant for the Stranger. Each is in the present; each is concrete. There is nothing abstract about his perspective.

Avoids the Evils of Morality. The Stranger lives as though reality is a painting. Everything is in the experience. Nothing else counts for him. This attitude lets him experience fully whatever is in front of him. Neither rules nor roles, nor guilt nor shame distract him from experiencing the moment. Living as he lives, the Stranger is able to avoid all the evils of morality.

"Are you saying that he is a moral person? That he avoids evil?"

No way. He avoids the evils of morality itself. He avoids the boredom, the anxieties of indecision and responsibility, the goals, the pressures, and the illusion of meaning. He completely avoids choices and the regrets that accompany all choices. He avoids all the distracting parts of morality. Being spontaneous and concentrated on what stands before him, he is free.

Avoids Boredom. "This sounds really boring. How can anyone live such a boring life? What's so interesting about eating fried eggs from a pan or watching people walk by on the street? The way you describe him, he's too passive, too submissive, and far too much oriented toward his senses. Doesn't this guy have any friends?"

One question at a time. Is he bored? Why are you wondering about that? I admit, most people would be bored with his life. But that's because most people are goal oriented. They think that what they do in life really matters. The Stranger is never bored. He is never bored because he is able to throw himself completely into his experience. He is never distracted by things he is supposed to do, or by conscience. He is completely spontaneous. He never has to think about what he's doing. His surroundings and his inner desires determine his actions. I think I have found my hero.

"Our lives are more significant than merely spending our days watching the street scene below our balcony or smoking cigarettes. Our lives aren't spent in meaningless inactivity."

The Anxiety of Indecision. Significant, huh? Meaningful? Perhaps most people would be bored with the Stranger's existence. But that's because they probably have an inflated sense of their own importance. What the Stranger accomplishes is really incredible. His way of life lets him avoid the anxiety of indecision.

"What is that?"

I think the reason so many people want a moral code is to avoid the indecision that comes with freedom. The Stranger avoids indecision by being passive and letting events take their own course. And, of course, he realizes that life is meaningless, so it doesn't matter what happens.

"How does freedom bring indecision? It's freedom that allows us to decide for ourselves what we want and how to get it."

Does it really seem that way to you? Think of the last decision you freely made. If it was a difficult decision, I'll bet you didn't feel free. Choice brings anxiety and indecision. I'll bet you anguished over the decision. What's the point? What's the difference? Just be spontaneous.

"It's not that easy. You underestimate the importance of our choices. How I choose affects my whole life."

This is another point where I disagree with you. Your choice does little but cause you anxiety. You and almost everyone else are under the illusion that you can affect the outside world with your choices. But there is virtually nothing that you can control. Try it. Pick a job or a potential friend and then see if you can just walk into the position you've chosen.

"Well, of course you can't just pick a job and just show up. They have to hire you. And the same goes for a new friend."

They have to hire you, too?

"No, friendship grows between two people. You can't just decide that the person over there is going to be your friend. The other person has to want to be your friend, too."

So why decide? If the other person wants to befriend you, let her. If an employer wants to hire you, let her. Why decide at all? One friend is as good as another; one job is as good as another. And look at all the anxiety you avoid.

"This is crazy. I should just sit back and let people come to me with friendship and with jobs? The real world doesn't work like that, Art. You've been sitting too long in a dark corner of your basement."

Nobody Wants to Make Choices.   Live like the Stranger. Avoid decisions and the sense of indecision will disappear. Don't you feel most free after you've decided? Isn't the time of indecision that comes before choice really anxious and uncomfortable?

"It is uncomfortable making important choices."

Exactly. That's why so many people look for someone else to choose for them.

"What do you mean?"

Look how many times people seek advice. They ask friends for advice. They read books and ask experts. They turn to their morality and religion. Nobody wants to make choices.

"This is going too far. I would never give up my right to choose. That's what living in a free country is all about."

Oh, I agree. People want to have the right to make their own choices. They just don't want to make the choices. Because there is so much anxiety involved in the decision process. But of course, all that is avoidable. Give up choice and you avoid indecision.

"I don't want someone else making my choices for me. That's what totalitarian countries are all about."

You don't want people making choices for you, and yet you seek advice? You follow the law, and moral rules, and religious commandments, and yet you don't want other people making your choices?

"But I freely choose who to get advice from, and which society and religion I adopt, and whether or not I want to be moral."

Even assuming this is true (and of course it isn't true), you still seek these people and institutions in order to avoid the anxiety of indecision associated with choices. Look at it this way: Don't you feel better after the choice is made?

"Yes, but that's because the problem or issue has been solved."

Right, or another way of saying that is that once the decision has been made, you don't suffer any longer from the anxiety of indecision. See, we agree. There's another reason why you seek advice from people and moral and religious rules.

"Why is that?"

Anxiety of Responsibility.   To avoid the anxiety of responsibility. That's why you ask other people what they would do.

"We ask other people's advice to get a better picture of the options. Other people may see things differently than we do. For example, because they aren't as involved in the situation, they can take a more objective look at the circumstances."

You're not going to believe this, but people sometimes come to me for advice.

"What do you do?"

I use my magic quarter. I make heads one option and tails the other option. And I make the person promise to abide by the flip of the coin.

"This can't be. People come to you for your opinion and you pull out a coin? What kind of friend are you?"

Probably a good one, although as often as not I hardly know the person seeking my advice. I know that the person asking my opinion doesn't want my opinion.

"Then why does he ask you?"

To hear his own choice. But since he wants to avoid responsibility for the choice, he asks me. I guess in his mind he thinks that if things don't go well, it's Art's fault. I know this thought is probably unconscious, but I think that's what's going on. I used to have people blame me for my bad advice, at least before I began using my magic quarter.

"How does a quarter help? I'd think you were just making fun of me, and that you weren't taking my problem seriously."

Right on both counts. I am making fun of the person, for taking himself so seriously. And I am not taking his decision seriously. He's already done that. Here's what happens with the magic quarter. Before I pull out the magic quarter, I let the person talk about the options available to him. It's interesting that there are almost always only two options. I guess the person has gotten that far himself. Anyway, after the options are explained, I make the person promise to abide by the decision of the coin. Then I flip it into the air, catch it in one hand, and turn it onto the back of my other hand.

"Then what? No one could possibly take this seriously."

As a good moral person who has just made a promise to respect the coin? I beg your pardon! With the coin hidden by my hand, I look intently at the person. Obviously he wants to know what the coin has decided. Look how easily he has displaced his right to choose.

"And?"

And I ask him which side he hoped for when the coin was in the air. Which did he want, heads or tails? Now that his fate rests with the coin on the back of my hand, he can tell me. People always tell me.

"And I suppose you crush them by lying about what the coin says."

Actually, I sneak a peek at the coin and confirm that it turned up just the way he wanted it. You can't believe the relief on people's faces. They get to do what they want, and I have resolved their anxieties of indecision and responsibility.

"But the person already knew what he wanted even before he went to see you!"

Sure. How many people would come to me who wanted to hear that they should make the moral choice? No one who knows me would do that, right? People always go to the person who will tell them what they want to hear.

What Makes Living for the Moment Desirable?

"So you are arguing that living for pleasure is the only way to live? And you think this because you believe people want to avoid boredom and the anxieties involved in choosing?"

Yes, the anxieties of indecision and responsibility are heavy burdens to bear.

"Okay, just so I get clear on this. You also think that it is advisable to see life as meaningless."

Right. If life is meaningless, then you don't have to ever wonder what you missed by choosing one way instead of the other way. You avoid regrets; you avoid responsibility; you avoid guilt.

"These are the primary reasons for adopting the 'live for pleasure' attitude?"

These reasons and the fact that once you realize that one action is as good as another, then you can be spontaneous. You can be free!

"Anything else?"

More Pleasure.   How much more can there be? Yes, there is something else. If you live the carefree, spontaneous way, you get more pleasure.

"How do you figure that? What pleasures are available to you that are not open to moral people?"

If you don't have to worry about moral and religious rules, or guilt, then you can do whatever brings you pleasure.

"What if I like the pleasures offered by morality and religion? What if I feel comfortable with those pleasures and don't want to participate in your sordid pleasures?"

If you don't want to experience nonmoral pleasures, fine. But I doubt this is true. I've seen you moral-religious people tempted by forbidden pleasures. If the pleasures weren't tempting, they wouldn't be forbidden by your way of life. Come on, what's so bad about lust and greed, gluttony and laziness, and all the rest?

"Look, Art, some of the passions you refer to are tempting. Part of the reason is because we are only human, with human bodies. Morality requires strength and discipline. Those kinds of pleasures are intense, more intense than more acceptable pleasures."

Ah, yes, that's just the point. People like me feel pleasures more intensely. Since there are no external obligations and no moral prohibitions to distract us, our pleasures are more intense. And because we never choose, and let things happen, we are never distracted by regrets, either.

"Your pleasures are meaningless, Art. They are superficial and pointless. That's why you think life is meaningless, because your pleasures are meaningless."

It's funny, but nearly every time I get caught up in one of my passions, some moral person like you tells me that my actions are meaningless. So what? They're not supposed to be meaningful; they're supposed to be pleasurable.

What Makes Living for the Pleasure of the Moment Undesirable?

"You have had your say, Art. I've listened carefully. Now it's the moralists' turn. I have several criticisms of your proposed life. First, the life you describe is unrealistic. Second, your life is not as pleasure filled as you think. There are many pleasures you cannot experience. Your life lacks emotions. Third, your outlook cuts you off from other people. It makes you lonely and alone. Fourth, you have no values, therefore you have no strong sense of self or self-esteem. Do you want to hear more?"

Okay.

"Fifth, you claim to be free, but you misunderstand freedom. And because of all this, sixth, you are irredeemably depressed."

Depressed? Why do you say that?

The Life is Unrealistic. "I don't mean you personally. I don't know you. To make living for the moment sound appealing, you chose a character like the Stranger. That sort of person doesn't exist. He's a character in a novel. He's an idiot! No one lives like that. He's an extreme. The character from Kierkegaard's *Either/Or* is much more believable. If we take a close look at him, we'll find all the elements of the point of view you attribute to the Stranger. The only difference is that the character A is intelligent enough to be depressed by his life."

Why do you say that?

"Not so fast, Art. I'm onto your strategy. Whenever you get in trouble and your ideas start to fail, you distract me by asking questions. You try to change the subject. Not this time! I've read a lot in this book about doing your own thing, or whatever you call it—"

Living in the present moment.

"Whatever! I want to say something about each of my criticisms. Then you can ask all your questions and defend your position as much as you want."

I appear to have no choice. You've taken charge of my book.

"Good. Then first, the life you depict is unrealistic."

It Is Not So Pleasure Filled. What else?

"Your life is also not as pleasure filled as you think. Yes, you do not have the distractions that we moral people have. But you also lack the purely moral pleasures found in emotions."

Like what?

"You cannot experience any of the emotions and pleasures associated with joy. What I mean by joy is the experience of pleasure for the good fortune of someone close to you. There probably aren't enough words to label these feelings, but they're real."

You feel something pleasant when someone else feels pleasure?

"Absolutely. When someone close to me—"

Standing next to you?

"When someone emotionally close to me does well, or wins a contest, or has a special event, I feel pleasure. I feel joy. Unfortunately for you, you cannot feel this. You are so wrapped up in your own pleasures that you think you're the only person on earth. You probably don't realize that other people have hopes and dreams, fears and things they are shy about."

I never really thought about it.

It Cuts You Off from Other People.   "The nonmoral life you describe is pathetic. Not only can't you experience the pleasure of joys, but you can't even understand that other people are real just like you. You are lonely because you think you are the only person on earth who has wants and needs. You are so self-centered that you think only you feel pleasure.

Self-centered? How should I be centered? Being self-centered is the only way to get pleasure.

It Misses the Moral Continuities.   "That's part of your problem. With pleasure as your goal, you miss out on the moral continuities."

Absolutely. The what?

"The moral continuities. You can't imagine the pleasures and the sense of security that moral people feel. Moral people see themselves as part of the human race."

I'm human!

"Yes, you are, Art, but you don't see yourself as part of the long line of human tradition and history. With your self-centered attitude of living for pleasure, you miss out on a sense of heritage."

Big deal. The people you refer to are long dead. What can I get from them?

"You could get a sense of who you are and how you fit into the human race. Respecting people who lived in the past could help you learn from them. Many of their rules and insights help moral people to live better and more meaningful lives."

So?

"Seeing yourself as part of the long line of humans gives meaning to your life. People start projects, and we carry them through. People of the past made sacrifices so that we would have a better life. We need to realize that and to respect them."

Is that all there is to your moral continuity?

"No, there's more. Feeling respect for the people of the past is what I call historical continuity. Feeling connected to the people living now in the present is also important. You see, moral people feel akin to living, breathing people, and not merely because they bring us pleasure."

You took the words right out of my mouth.

Communication and Community.   "Feeling connected to people in the present sets the stage for communication and community. Before you can say, 'Huh?' I'll tell you what that means. Moral people are able to communicate with other people. We see others as real, as feeling, as worthy. That sense of other people lets us form genuine communities."

I've lived in lots of cities.

"There's a difference. Living in a city does not mean you live with a sense of community. People who live around other people often feel very lonely. Having a sense of community is having a sense of connection."

Okay, moralist, now I have to respect a bunch of dead people and feel some deep affection for my neighbors. Is that it?

"Not quite! It's not a matter of affection. It's a matter of being human, and recognizing the worth in others because they are human, too. For moral people, the feeling goes beyond one's neighbors. You may have noticed that moral people are charitable to others whom they will never see. Now do you see why?"

I suppose so, at least I think I see the point. You're saying that only moral people develop relationships of the sort you describe.

"Yes. How could someone who lives for pleasure recognize the worth of other people? How could someone who believes that life is meaningless ever feel connected to people of the past and the future? You're so focused on the moment that you lose sight of people."

Creativity.   Hold on. You moral people want me to think about people who aren't even born yet? Why should I?

"The ability to think of yourself as part of the unbroken line of humanity allows you to be creative. Without seeing the people of the present and the future as part of yourself, there would be no reason to create anything."

But I might stumble on some invention or paint a picture or something. Why can't I do that without being moral?

"You can invent and paint all you like, but what would be the point? Inventing, painting, writing, and all the other perfectly human activities are ways of communicating with other people. It's our way of relating to others. When you're distracted by your pleasure seeking, you cannot relate to other people in a significant way. When you're distracted by your despair over the meaninglessness of your life, you are out of touch with other people. Only moral people enjoy the pleasures and securities of the moral continuities. We feel the continuous chain of humanity, and we feel secure because of it."

Wow! What else am I supposed to be missing?

It Is Empty of Love, Trust, and Friendship.   "You are unable to have relationships of love, trust, and friendship. Because of your inability to relate with others, you fail to receive the joys of intimacy."

How so?

"Just look at your example of the Stranger. You said that he got as much pleasure from eating fried eggs from a pan as watching the street scene from his balcony, right?"

Yes, that's right. Because he doesn't discriminate among experiences, each pleasure is as good as any other pleasure. That is meant as a strength of his lifestyle.

"No doubt it is meant that way, but look what follows. You also said that these pleasures were comparable to smoking a cigarette or making 'love' to Marie. Don't you see? He is so caught up in his pleasures that he cannot love Marie. He can't be intimate with her."

They make love.

"But they don't love, at least he doesn't. Sex is not love. Sex is physically intimate, but it's not emotionally intimate."

Yes, but it's still pleasurable.

"The moral person has both the physical and the emotional experience. You think our moral obligations distract us from feeling sensual pleasures. Did you ever think that the distraction is an emotional experience that is far more pleasant? Emotional intimacy enhances pleasurable experience."

What do you want me to say? Duh.

It Lacks Values and a Self. "I'm sorry to have to tell you all this, but the life you advocate is not very attractive. Your perspective also lacks any real sense of a self."

How do you mean?

"Because you concentrate as completely as you can on the present, you can't attach your own past and future to yourself. I know you intend for this to be another strength, but it isn't. You can't have a unified, integrated character."

Huh?

"If you take seriously the extreme character that you draw, then you could not live a coherent life."

What do you mean, "a coherent life"?

"If each of your experiences is really separate, really discrete from every other experience, then your life would be completely disjointed. There'd be no unifying theme to you. I guess we'd have to say that you would not have a character at all."

Is that bad?

"Yes. You would not have an enduring sense of your own self. You would not have any sense that you are connected to your own past and future. You would achieve intensity in your experience, but you would sacrifice your own sense of being a real person."

You mean of being a moral person, don't you?

"No, not at all. Really living for the moment in the extreme would cut you off from any sense of your self. It would cut you off from other people. How can I say this better? If you really lived with this attitude, you would live for a million intense moments, but each moment would be separate and distinct. You'd live a million lives but never know it. The more I think about it, the more I see this life as impossible. We couldn't even carry on conversations because you wouldn't be the same person from day to day."

Now who's taking the extreme view? I didn't say that this life has to be a mindless life without any memory. You're taking it too far.

It Misunderstands Freedom. "Your character mistakes being spontaneous with being free."

But he acts without having to think about his actions, their moral worth, meaningfulness, etc.

"That is true, there is an immediacy in his actions. Just because his reasoning is not used, though, it does not follow that he is free. Look at your own example of the Stranger. As you describe this fictional character, he acts according to his surroundings."

What do you mean?

"If Marie shows up, he desires her. If Marie does not visit, then he smokes a cigarette or looks out at the street scene below. His own desires are unimportant. He desires whatever comes along."

That's the beauty of the lifestyle! He never faces frustration. He desires whatever comes along. That way he always gets what he wants. Who could be freer than that? The Stranger does what he wants.

"But his wants conform to the situation. He has no control over what will happen. He is thoroughly passive and apathetic. He doesn't *do* anything. He just waits for events to occur around him."

What's wrong with that?

"A person is not free when his actions are determined only by natural contingencies."

Huh?

"There isn't anything free in letting one's desires be determined for one."

Huh?

"You say that the Stranger does whatever he wants. The problem is, his wants are not up to him. We might say that he does what he wants, but he does not necessarily want what he wants."

Sure he does. He wants Marie, and cigarettes, and fried eggs. He wants all of that stuff.

"Only because he has learned to acquiesce, to be passive. What would happen if events should present him with no desirable option? What would he do?

"Hmm. One time, while in prison, he asks for a cigarette. The guard tells him he can't have one; that's why it's called punishment.

"What does the character do?"

He gets used to going without cigarettes. Perfectly practical, if you ask me.

"He is not in control of himself. His surroundings control him. By the way, why is he in prison?"

He murdered an Arab.

"What! Why did he do that?"

It was a very hot day. The sun was beating down on him, and he wanted to get to the cool water across the beach.

"How would that lead to killing someone?"

There was an Arab lying on the beach in his way. The story is more complicated than that, but the Stranger ends up killing a person because the sun was in his eyes.

"How can you call this person free? It is just as I have been saying. He is out of control. His surroundings, the sun, act on him."

Perhaps.

"He sounds like a child in a candy store. That sounds like a pleasant analogy, but it isn't meant to be. This lifestyle you propose involves more frustration than you admit. Imagine the child for a moment. She wants whatever she sees. No sooner does she put her hand into one jar than she sees another jar filled with candies. She is led from jar to jar, never really getting the candy she wants. Your life of pleasure is not as pleasure filled as you think. At least moral people, with all of our rules, are disciplined enough to enjoy what we get."

It Is Irredeemably Depressing.   I've heard enough about freedom. Why do you say that my character is depressed?

"Irredeemably depressed; look at the heading. The best way to show what I mean is to look at another example."

Kierkegaard has one?

Kierkegaard's A

"Yes, in *Either/Or* Søren Kierkegaard creates a character much to our point. I think his character, named A, is believable. He's depressing, and I think he's terribly misguided, but looking at him will help me show you what is wrong with living for the moment."

Okay, you describe him as you see him. This should be great, watching you distort this poor guy's life.

Lonely and Sad.   "First, A lives in a world about which he cannot care. He has lost all of what he calls his illusions about living. He says that he is melancholic because of his sense of extreme isolation. These are just the criticisms I was making about your character. No one desires a life that leads to constant sadness and loneliness."

How do you figure that A is this way?

"A tells us. Just look at what he writes. He says, 'I do not care at all. . . . My melancholy is the most faithful mistress.' Not only that, he feels alone. He is disoriented: 'What if everything in the world were a misunderstanding, what if laughter were really tears?'"

So?

Powerless.   "He is keenly aware of his own powerlessness in the face of what he sees as an absurd, futile reality."

Where do you get that?

"He says that he feels 'the way a chessman must, when the opponent says of it, That piece cannot be moved.' This guy believes that the world is out to get him. Look where he writes that 'the doors of fortune do not open inward, so that by storming them one can force them open; but they open outward, and therefore nothing can be done.'"

Sure, it's easy when you use the book.

"There's more. He's a lot like you, Art. Look what he writes about the future. 'What drives me forward is a consistency which lies behind me. This life is topsy-turvy and terrible, not to be endured.' He makes life sound like it has to be mindless and habitual."

Yeah, so? What else is there?

"Talk about resigned to being depressed! He says that 'life has become a bitter drink to me, and yet I must take it like medicine, slowly, drop by drop.' Except to see how ridiculous this lifestyle is, why even bother reading this?"

I didn't read it, you did. A really bothers you. Is it because he is so nonmoral?

Cynical. "Just reading a few pages of this is disheartening. I feel sorry for A. Look what else he writes! He describes 'a busy man of affairs,' a businessperson, right? Then he describes how 'a tile from the roof falls down and strikes him dead.' What do you think this bizarre person has to say about this tragedy?"

What? (These brief responses of mine are only included to make you think that I'm listening, and that I care.)

"He laughs heartily. That's what he says, that he laughs when a good, hard-working person dies accidentally. He thinks life is absurd. But that's not the worst of it. This guy is cosmically nuts!"

Oh?

" 'No one ever comes back from the dead, no one ever enters the world without weeping.' "

It's hard to disagree, so far.

Depressing. " 'No one is asked when he wishes to enter life, no one is asked when he wishes to leave.' Come on, you don't find that depressing?"

But it sounds true. Is that what's bothering you? I don't remember being asked about when and where I wanted to be born. And unless you're lucky enough to be able to afford to put a death contract on yourself or commit suicide, you don't get to decide when you will die.

"You're just as crazy as Kierkegaard's A!"

I was only pulling your leg; didn't you feel it? Even suicide victims don't have the control they appear to have. They are people driven by outside influences. There isn't much control there, either.

"I can't believe you agree with this depressing stuff."

Depressing? How is it depressing? A is just telling us the way real life is. If you find that depressing, it isn't A's fault.

Empty and Meaningless. "This guy is hypersensitive! Every glance, every event is magnified. Everyday living depresses him and makes him lonely. His strongest complaint is that our society lacks passion. Where has this person been hiding? Our age is passionate. The world is changing at an incredible rate. Maybe his life is passionless. Maybe he's depressed and bored. Great life!"

But what difference do the changes make, anyway?

"He says that 'life is so empty and meaningless.' He asks, 'Why do we not finish it at once, why do we not stay and step down into the grave with him [the deceased], and draw lots to see who shall happen to be the last unhappy living being to throw the last three spadefuls of earth over the last of the dead?' "

Well, if life is empty and meaningless, then I guess the rest does follow.

"But life isn't empty and meaningless! And just because we are going to die doesn't mean that living is a waste of time. That's what I think this guy believes, that living is a complete waste."

Hmm. (See, you think I'm bothering to follow the conversation.) Does he say anything about the valued goals in living?

"Yes, he does, but he is overly cynical. He says that he came to realize that 'the meaning of life was to secure a livelihood, and that its goal was to attain a high position; that love's rich dream was marriage to an heiress; that friendship's blessing was help in financial difficulties; that wisdom was what the majority assumed it to be,' and on and on. Can you believe it!

Of course, I believe it. He's stumbled onto the secret of the good life.

"Both of you are hopeless. I suppose you also agree with him when he writes that one is 'better to take things as they come, and make no fuss?' Of course you agree with that, too."

Yup. Why try to accomplish anything? What's the point? It's better to enjoy life.

"That's just the point. A doesn't enjoy life. He believes life is wretched and miserable."

And tedious?

Pessimistic.   "And terribly tedious. He's the ultimate pessimist."

Why do you say that?

"Read the ecstatic lecture! Whether you marry or do not marry, you will regret it. Whatever you do or do not do, you will regret it. Laugh or weep at the world's follies, believe or disbelieve a woman, hang yourself or do not hang yourself; in each case whatever you do you will regret it."

A Wants to Be Moral.   Okay, what's your point? You have gone on and on about this A fellow, so what is your criticism?

"Don't you see, I've been criticizing him right along. He's depressed, lonely, pessimistic, and bored. This is no way to live life. A shows the weaknesses in the life you are bragging about. You think living as if life has no meaning is enjoyable. The writings of A disprove that.

"A's greatest 'hope' is never to have been born. Can you imagine that? Barring this aborted wish, he seeks neither pleasure nor intensity. I think he realizes how unfulfilling pleasure and intensity are. What he finally wants is a moral life."

Why do you say that?

"A seeks 'a constancy that could withstand every trial, an enthusiasm that endured everything, a faith that could remove mountains, a thought that could unite the finite and the infinite.' "

How is this morality?

"Do you see yourself in Kierkegaard's A?"

Constancy.   I haven't thought about it, but yes, I guess I do. Why?

"Then like A, you see yourself caught between a safe but dull life and an insecure but spontaneous and exciting life. Because your life does not allow you to shape your own character or to act on your surroundings, you yearn for constancy. You yearn for constancy in your surroundings because you have no constancy in your self. You yearn for an enthusiasm that could endure anything because you cannot maintain your self."

Why would I do that?

"Because your way of life doesn't allow endurance or constancy, and yet it depends on them."

How does it depend on constancy?

"If some pleasure is good, more is better, right? My picture of you was too extreme before. No one could actually live for the moment, not really. So here you are with a sense of your self but without a way of stabilizing your self. You have no moral rules, or duties, or continuities to help you. All you have is the lust for pleasure."

And that's not enough?

Faith (Control). "And that's not enough. You yearn for faith that could remove mountains."

Interpret that for me. I want to move mountains?

"You want to remove obstacles. See, your lifestyle does not let you actively alter the world. Remember, you have to let pleasures come to you. Your seductions have to be passive. The thrill of having the pleasure come to you is vital."

What's wrong with that?

Regrets and Choices. "You fear choice. That's what the *Either/Or* is about. Whichever you choose, you will regret. You are easily disturbed by the decisions of everyday living. Decisions like choosing a career, jobs, housing, promises—those kinds of decisions."

Why would these choices bother me?

"You have no values. You value only what presents itself to you. But having no values means that each moment requires you to choose."

So what? People like me who live for pleasure just take whatever comes along.

"True, except that you aren't quite as passive as you want me to believe. You have wants. In fact, that's your real problem. You have conflicting wants. That's why everyday choices drive you out of your mind. You have no values to help you. Choosing between contrary desires paralyzes you, Art. For you, choice involves regret. To choose one experience means that the other possible experience will go unrealized."

Can't I set up priorities?

Either/Or. "That sounds too rigid for your lifestyle. Setting up priorities to avoid choice leads to boredom and lack of engagement. That's just what you objected to in the moral life. So either you choose and suffer from indecision and regret, or you do not choose, in which case you fail to resolve the conflict you feel between your desires. Or, to avoid conflicting desires, you set up priorities. But this strategy brings responsibilities and boredom. You're trapped."

How could I feel moral responsibility? All I would be doing is choosing which experiences *I* prefer over other experiences. Where's the obligation in that?

"To be sure, you won't feel moral obligation. But a similar feeling takes hold of you. Your own priorities would act like external standards."

But it's what I want!

Priorities

"Not exactly. Each time you act on one of your priorities, you knowingly eliminate a desire. The priorities don't make the conflicting desires go away. Priorities just help you avoid complete frustration and regret. Your priorities make you responsible to yourself and to your plans. Wouldn't you feel badly if you gave up a greater pleasure for a lesser pleasure?"

Absolutes

Yes. I guess I see your point. What was the final yearning you said I had?

"Well, Kierkegaard's A also wants a thought that could unite the finite and the infinite."

I don't remember ever yearning for anything like that. Mostly, I don't think I understand what that means.

"At the heart of your lifestyle is the need for a fixed point upon which to base your life."

That's the constancy.

"Right. You and A search for absolutes in a world where you can find only relative truths and changing values. You interpret your surroundings and other people as an ever-reeling chaos. That's why you cannot consciously commit yourself to laws. You seek excitement in chaos because chaos is all you see."

This is getting a little over my head.

"Then sit up straighter! Only kidding."

Affirming Your Own Reality

What is the bottom line on all of this analysis and criticism?

"Finally, and most importantly, what you really want is some way to affirm your own reality."

Huh? (Yes, we're back to that.)

"It's what moral people are trying to do, too. We affirm our sense of self, and our sense of being alive by relating to other people, by having goals and projects and all the rest. You and A are cut off from this. So you try to feel real by having intense experiences."

Hmm, at least when I am having an intense experience I know that I'm alive.

"Sure, that's why some people, even moral people, sometimes 'live on the edge.' Exhilarating feelings, adrenaline rushing, that does make you feel alive. But those experiences are limited. The moral life offers a more stable, constant, and predictable way of being alive in the way we are discussing it."

And what is the finite and the infinite?

"I think that is the desire to feel at home in the universe. It's to feel like you're a part of it all. The finite is you, and the infinite is the universe, or God. Wanting to unite with the infinite is the—"

Yearning?

"The yearning to feel connected with other people and with whatever else is real. And it reflects the hope of having a stable set of values by which to live."

The Best Life

Is living for the moment a complete waste, then?

"What you want is the same as what moral people want. In fact, the reason your lifestyle looks so appealing is because there is a lot to be said for being able to concentrate on the present experience."

I see so many moral people so distracted by their obligations that they aren't aware of what is right in front of them.

"Agreed. And seeking pleasure is also appealing. I guess we'd have to agree that both lives are desirable, only morality offers more of what we want."

Yearn for?

"On the more important level. Both you and moralists are asking the same questions when it really comes down to it."

Wow!

Summary of Discussion

Assuming that life is meaningless and all our actions are futile gestures signifying nothing lasting, life becomes a pleasure-seeking adventure. One example of living for the moment is captured in Camus's character, the Stranger. The Stranger lacks the attitude and mindset of morality. He sees himself as a spectator of life, but without any moral consciousness. He is incapable of seeing anything from another person's point of view, incapable of feeling guilt, and completely happy when his body is not suffering discomfort.

Because he recognizes no moral restrictions, the Stranger is spontaneous. He avoids boredom by living in the moment, interacting with whatever presents itself to him. He never makes choices. Therefore, he avoids the anxieties of indecision and responsibility. What he receives from this strategy in living is pleasure.

Unfortunately, there are some problems living in a straightforward, simplistic pursuit of pleasure. The Stranger's life is unrealistic and not as pleasure filled as first appearances promise. Although the Stranger avoids the repressive influences of morality, he cuts himself off from other people. He misses the moral continuities. He communicates superficially and has no sense of community. Nor is he able to be creative. Creativity assumes that one thinks beyond the present moment. The Stranger's life is empty of love, friendship, and trust. He lacks an enduring sense of self and misunderstands freedom as caprice. Worst of all, his pleasure-seeking life is depressing.

Kierkegaard's A is another attempt at living in the moment. Unfortunately, A is lonely and sad. He feels powerless, and therefore he has developed a cynical, depressed attitude toward living. For him, life is something to be gotten through. Living is empty and meaningless, and he is pessimistic about nearly every aspect of it.

In his moaning, however, A does reveal important aspects of morality. A wants what morality promises. He wants constancy and control. He wants to avoid decisions and the regrets that are so often brought on by choices. Finally, neither the Stranger nor A is able to affirm his own reality. For as much as it promises, living for the moment is not the best life.

Discussion Highlights

    I. The Stranger
        1. Is spontaneous
        2. Avoids the "evils" of morality
          a. boredom
          b. anxieties of responsibility and indecision
    II. Living for the moment is undesirable
        1. It is unrealistic.
        2. It is not as pleasure filled as promised.
        3. It cuts one off from relating to other people.
        4. It misses the moral continuities
          a. of communication
          b. of community
          c. of creativity
        5. It is empty of love, trust, and friendship.
        6. It lacks values and an enduring sense of self.
        7. It misunderstands freedom as caprice.
        8. It is depressing.
   III. Kierkegaard's A is
        1. Lonely and sad.
        2. He feels powerless.
        3. He feels cynical and depressed.
        4. He believes life is empty and meaningless.
        5. A wants
          a. constancy
          b. control
          c. avoidance of choices and regrets

Questions for Thought/Paper Topics

1. Is the Stranger's spontaneity appealing? How can we incorporate his freedom into our construction of the best life?

2. I suggested that Joe the Mesopotamian's life is meaningless. Do you agree? Explore the question of whether or not life is meaningful.

3. Can one compromise and lead a moral life that has spontaneous moments of concentrated pleasure? Or does this amount to scheduling one's spontaneous moments?

4. Is freedom doing whatever one wants? If that is freedom, isn't the Stranger free? Is his freedom desirable?

5. A is cynical, depressed, and lonely. We might attribute this to his belief that life is empty and meaningless. If a person believes that life is meaningless, why can't he or she be carefree, spontaneous, and joyful?

6. Is it a fair trade to give up the pleasure of the moment for constancy, security, control, and relief from responsibility? Is that the tradeoff that moral people make?

7. How can a person avoid choices and decisions? Is it possible to live a nonmoral life without decisions? What would direct such a person's actions?

For Further Reading

It's odd to recommend books to read on doing whatever *you* want, but here goes. Albert Camus' *The Stranger* (Vintage, 1989) is certainly worth reading. Another source is Søren Kierkegaard's *Either/Or* (Princeton, 1987). Kierkegaard skillfully draws the character A from the opening pages. There are other analytic expressions of this character type, one of which is David Gauthier's *Morality and Rational Self-Interest* (Prentice-Hall, 1970). Finally, there is a persuasive book written by Ayn Rand, *The Virtue of Selfishness* (New American Library, 1964). Be particularly critical when you read this one.

Part Two

Philosophers Answer the Questions

Introduction

IN PART ONE we struggled with several questions. No doubt you are uneasy with our inconclusive discussion. That's okay. So far the aim has been to introduce the questions that relate to morality and the best life. Part Two presents the answers that philosophers offer to our questions.

Not surprisingly, philosophers do not take a uniform position on the nature of morality or the best life. Nor do philosophers respond to our questions in the order that the questions come to us. What Part Two offers are selections from philosophers who hold differing points of view. You will find some of them in agreement with your intuitions. Others will sound plausible enough, but you will not fully agree with all of them.

Part Two gives us a chance to question these philosophers. Through the use of my own invention, the philosopher resurrection machine, we get to actually speak to long-dead philosophers. Most of what you will read comes directly from them. Of course, it's best to read their entire works, but resurrecting them gives us the chance to ask questions. If you do want to read more, look at the end of each chapter for the best sources. Ah, here's one of our philosophers now. I'd like to introduce you to John Stuart Mill, a nineteenth-century British philosopher.

Mr. Mill, welcome. It's generous of you to join us. I have a number of questions for you.

"That should wait for our complete discussion in Chapter 8, Art."

Then why are you here now?

The V-8 Principle!

"There is one condition before any of us enters into a discussion with you. You have to follow the V-8 principle."

What's that?

"People often read a philosophical work and make criticisms of the author's ideas."

And they don't bother to be clear about the ideas?

"That's one problem. They do not bother to understand the philosopher fully.

They just disagree with what they too quickly judge is the philosopher's position. That is not what I was going to say, however. One type of criticism is caused by an inadequate reading. Another type of criticism comes from an unsympathetic reading."

I don't follow you.

"Imagine that you are in a classroom during a discussion. Everyone has read the assigned reading with care. In the course of evaluating the ideas critically, someone raises an objection to the philosopher's ideas."

What's wrong with that? Isn't that the point? Aren't we supposed to find out where the theory goes wrong?

"My, you are impatient, Art. Yes, of course, criticism is important. An adequate objection is praiseworthy. But you also need to imagine how the philosopher would respond. Be sympathetic to the philosopher's point of view and construct an argument in defense of the position."

Why would I do that? I thought the idea was to show where the philosopher is wrong.

"The aim is to reach the truth. If you are genuinely interested in the nature of morality and in finding the best life, then a sympathetic understanding of other views is essential. Even if the philosopher is only partially correct, understanding the correct point or the correct strategy is important. If the philosopher is completely incorrect—and that I find unlikely—there is still much to be gained from understanding. One gains from carefully rejecting incorrect ideas. One's own thinking becomes clearer; the truth becomes livelier in one's own mind."

Okay, you've made your point. So what is the V-8 principle?

"When the student or teacher has made an objection to the philosopher's ideas, imagine how the philosopher would respond. Surely you don't believe that we philosophers would merely sit in the back of the room, listen to the objection, place our palm on our forehead, and say 'Gee, I could have had a V-8!' We would have a response. It is up to you to construct a plausible response for us."

Fair enough. In Part Two you philosophers will have your say. First, we will ask questions to become clearer on the ideas. Then we will evaluate the theory critically. Where we detect a problem with the theory, we'll try to find a response consistent with your position. Does that satisfy you?

"Yes, that's fine. That satisfies the V-8 principle. I will speak with you shortly. Goodbye for now."

A Road Map

That was easy enough, wasn't it? All that's left for this introduction is to draw a road map of ideas for you to follow. What's a road map of ideas? In the first part of the book we mentioned quite a few possible ways of understanding the moral plan of living. I think it would be helpful to point out where your comments lead, just in case you want to pursue one more than another.

If you think that authority, intuition, law, and social roles reveal our moral principles to us, then Chapter 6 is for you. The discussion with the Grand Inquisitor puts religious morality, authority, and social roles in a pretty cynical light. Don't despair.

Being free is also one of our desires. I think Kierkegaard's character A and Camus's Stranger demonstrate that. An interesting sense of freedom is discussed in Chapter 7, in which Epictetus creates a whole attitude toward living by emphasizing his special brand of freedom. (Freedom also serves as the foundation for the existentialist plan of life Sartre offers in Chapter 10.)

Remember democracy? One way we considered defining right action was in terms of the greatest good for the greatest number. Lo and behold, Chapter 8 is an explanation and defense of that view. John Stuart Mill also agrees with you when you argue that not all pleasures are equally worthy. It's important reading, especially if you already lean in that direction.

Chapter 9 discusses the absolutist position on moral values. This doctrine states that no matter what the circumstances or consequences, some actions are right to perform and other actions are wrong to perform. Immanuel Kant advocates this view. He argues for a fixed set of moral laws, in principle like the legal laws we encounter in society. So if you want to find a haven from relativism or from determining moral right by reflecting on the good of the greatest number, Chapter 9 may be to your liking. At least with moral absolutes you don't have to struggle with uncertainty and dangerous moral calculations.

Sartre defends subjectivism, but avoids your disdain for egoism, in Chapter 10. For him, relativism is not the issue; the best life is a life lived authentically and freely. Sartre argues that individual differences in people are desirable, but he does not threaten the social stability offered by morality. I think you'll like his way of putting his ideas.

I know religion and God play a dominant role in people's moral education. Chapters 11 and 12 address religious faith in a most positive way. So if you are interested in the religious aspect of living, look there.

If I can make one suggestion: Please read each chapter with an open mind. Only after you have examined the view that each thinker takes can you make an informed, balanced, and intelligent decision about your own position. Learning all these points of view will also help you understand what someone else believes. Agreement is not as important as understanding, so read each chapter. I hope you enjoy the conversations.

6 Authority and Freedom: A Discussion with the Grand Inquisitor

Morality Makes Us Free

"Morality works, Art. It makes us free."

Free? What do you mean?

"Morality helps us choose our own values. By picking the correct values, we are free and happy. That's what makes morality such a great way of life. Morality helps us choose our values. That's its purpose."

Do we really want to be free?

"Of course we do. Why do you even ask? Being free is the most important aspect of human life."

Humans can never be free. They are weak, vicious, worthless, and rebellious. How can rebels be happy?

"Art, that is outrageous! Where did you ever get an idea like that?"

The Grand Inquisitor

From my friend, the Grand Inquisitor.

"Who?"

There's a nice little story, "The Grand Inquisitor on the Nature of Man." It's one chapter in a novel, *The Brothers Karamazov,* by a Russian writer, Fyodor Dostoevski. It takes a provocative view of human nature and freedom. So for now, let's abandon our regular format. Let me sum up some of the highlights of "The Grand Inquisitor." Of course, reading it is much better than letting me retell the story.

The story opens with the coming of Christ. But this is not *the* Coming, just a visit to see how everyone is doing. It is the time of the Spanish Inquisition during

Material in this chapter taken from Fyodor Dostoevski, *The Grand Inquisitor,* (New York: Bobbs-Merrill/Macmillan, 1948). Constance Garnett translation.

the fifteenth century. Jesus visits Seville, Spain. Everything is going fine in Seville. The Grand Inquisitor, a cardinal in the Christian Church, is in the process of cleansing the earth of undesirables. He burns heretics to the "greater glory of God."

Jesus enters the town unannounced, and as it turns out uninvited. People recognize Him and flock around. He performs a couple of miracles for the masses. He brings sight to an old man who was blind from birth, then He raises a dead child from her "slumber." The people, who already know who He is, are even more convinced by these feats. But the second miracle is also viewed from afar by guess who? Right, the Grand Inquisitor. The ninety-year-old cardinal sends his guard to arrest the intruder.

With the arrest the people back away, of course. If someone is arrested, the person is assumed to be guilty. (See how little we've changed?) The Inquisitor has Him taken to the prison. In the darkness of night the old cardinal visits Him. This is where it gets fascinating.

"Does the Inquisitor know who He is?"

The Inquisitor asks Him if it is He. But when no answer comes, the Inquisitor realizes that He has no right to say anything. Jesus has no right to add any new rules to the sayings of old.

"What does the Inquisitor do with Him?"

The Inquisitor explains what religion (and morality) are all about. He confesses his conviction to the divine person. In the morning the Inquisitor says that he will burn Him at the stake. And, says the Inquisitor, with a sign from him, the people will help in the burning. That's the essence of the story, but the Inquisitor goes on to explain in detail.

People Want to be Free

"What was the point of arresting Him?"

Look what Jesus offers humanity! He offers freedom!

"What's wrong with that? People want to be free."

No, people can never be free. It took centuries for us to realize what a terrible gift freedom is.

"Us? Who is us?"

The Grand Inquisitor and I, the Church, all of organized religion. We have done more for people than Jesus could do. For the Church, in the person of its Inquisitor, has taken freedom from the people.

"How could that be? Why would you do that?"

The Church has not taken away freedom from the people; it has accepted it. People do not want to be free. People want to be happy.

"Can't people be free and happy?"

No. That is the remarkable insight of the Church. Freedom brings too many responsibilities and anxieties. Happiness is not for rebels. Once people willingly give up their rebelliousness, their desire for freedom, then they can be happy. He was warned.

Three Temptations in the Desert

"Warned?"

The warnings came from the spirit who tempted Jesus in the desert.

"The Devil!"

The wise and dread spirit tempted Him with three temptations.

"What is the significance of the warnings, of the temptations, as you call them?"

The three temptations tell us the nature of humans. Jesus exaggerates the human potential. Surely, some few people can live freely, but the vast majority of people cannot cope with freedom. They are too weak.

"Too weak?"

Stones into Bread. Yes, too weak. The first temptation is to turn stones into bread. Jesus rejected the offer, saying that we do not live by bread alone. We prefer heavenly bread to earthly bread.

"But what that means is that people need more than just animal comforts. Security (bread) is worthless if it costs people their freedom."

That is Jesus' response. Of course, now we know differently. Now we know better. Give them bread. Give them security and material prosperity, and people willingly give up their freedom. Think about it. What would people rather have, freedom and starvation or security and food? We offer the latter. The flock of unruly humans obediently and gratefully follows us.

"They fear you!"

They fear us, yes. They love us and they fear us. After all, we have the power to remove their security.

"But it's the people who give you the bread in the first place. All we have to do is refuse to give it to you. All your power comes from us, the people. You must know that."

Absolutely. But I also know that it is your freedom that you most want to rid yourselves of. So I accept your bread and redistribute it. More important, I accept your freedom and with it your anxiety and responsibility.

Anxiety of Indecision. "What anxiety?"

People approach freedom with dread. It is awful to be free. Freedom creates anxieties. First, there's the anxiety of indecision.

"What's that?"

Almost no one wants to decide on one's own.

"I make decisions and I don't feel any anxiety or dread. I think you are just exaggerating or imagining."

Moral and religious people do not make decisions.

"I make decisions all the time. And so do other people. We decide where we live, where we go to school, where we work, what occupation we pursue, whom we marry, whether or not we marry, and all the rest."

And how do you make those decisions? You decide based on what we tell you is important.

"We?"

The other religious leaders and I. We belong to a group called Religion, Inc. We orchestrate your lives for you. You get to make small decisions. We make the *big* decisions. Actually, we don't decide anything. We teach you which choices are available and which are unavailable.

"That's no big deal. Anyone can picture the options. If that's all you do, you have no control over me."

Oh, that's not all we do. We do one more little thing. We tell you what is good and what is evil. In doing that, we give you your wants. Some wants are acceptable, some are "dangerously" immoral, and some are unthinkable. The wants that are acceptable include most of the standard choices in life.

"You make our lives sound like selling cars."

Well, they are. Some people choose the family and career model. Some people want the luxury option. The wants that are acceptable include education (without any knowledge of good and evil), and job, and family, and hobbies.

"What about the immoral wants? How can you deal with those? If I want to break free from your control, all I have to do is break your rules. Then what do you do?"

Relieving Your Conscience.   We forgive you.

"What do you mean, you forgive me?"

Just that. The religious leaders and I know that you are weak of flesh and of mind. We know that you lack nobility and self-control.

"What do you mean?"

To put it in religious language, we know you are sinners. The second and more powerful part of our appeal is that we relieve your conscience. It is part of the plan that you break the rules. We forgive you. It does not make any difference if you follow or break the rules. Either way, we have you aware of the rules and of our authority. So we do not care whether you are moral or immoral.

"This is outrageous. How can I be free?"

You don't want freedom. You merely think you do. We've given you that want. And we supply the satisfaction.

So I Am Free?

"So I am free?"

We let you make decisions, just as long as we determine how you make them. The only truly free person is the one who is able to hold unthinkable values.

"Unthinkable values?"

The values that one creates oneself. But such values are for the very few! We sacrifice those people in order to protect you.

"Protect?"

From becoming aware of the option of genuine freedom and the terror that realization invokes in you. We seek to make you feel secure. We realize, however, that you sheep do not live for security only.

"Right, Jesus said that. Man does not live by bread alone. So you do agree with Him?"

No, Jesus misunderstood humans. You also want meaning in your lives. We give your insignificant lives meaning by telling you that you fit into the 'Grand Scheme,' or into society, or into the flow of history. You want goals and structure and security. We give you a stable, unchanging, secure way of living. The moral and religious values may change some, but moral thinking stays stable.

"Moral thinking?"

That everyone is morally equal. That objectivity is important in deciding questions. Impartiality. Rights, duties, responsibilities. All that. That is moral thinking. We instill in you a concern for consequences! And then you ask us to judge you. Judgment is a significant part of morality and religion.

"Without judgment, you and the leaders of religion lose control."

And you lose your security and comfort.

"But I still think that I am free. I do decide what course of study I want, and what career I want, and who I will marry. Those are pretty big decisions. You can't deny it."

I do not agree at all.

"You don't think it's important whom I love and marry and what kind of work I do?"

Not only do I not see these as important decisions, but I don't see them as decisions at all. The other religious leaders and I determine whom you love and marry and which career you pursue. For example, you will marry someone close to your own age, in roughly your same socioeconomic class (maybe a little above your present status). You will most likely marry someone of the opposite sex, of the same nationality, of the same (or of an acceptable) race, of roughly the same religious denomination. We even determine which physical traits are attractive. In some centuries being thin is attractive; in some centuries being heavy is a sign of prosperity.

"But we marry a person because we love that person."

In your century and in your part of the world, yes. But that isn't universally true. In other places, and in other times in your society, we had people marry by arrangement. In fact, we're considering going back to that.

"No way. Why would you do that?"

The rise in the divorce rate bothers people. Another one of those insecurities, no doubt. If we arrange marriages, the divorce rate will drop.

"This is crazy. People pick their own mates."

Which man or woman you marry is of no concern to us. All we're interested in is that you acknowledge the guidelines and our authority. So marry or don't marry. We'll sanctify all of it. And when you marry and the little lambs start coming, we'll make sure to teach them all our values and obedience as well. Don't you see, the ideas of marriage, of love, of having children—all this happens by virtue of our wish!

Conscience

"Let's get back to the idea of conscience."

Giving you bread is a start, but you want more. You want an authority to take care of your conscience. Nothing is worse than a guilty conscience. Guilt is one of the devices we install to get you to do what we want.

"You mean 'instill.' You instill people with a sense of right and wrong, good and evil. Saying *install* makes it sound like brainwashing."

After we install guilt, you are ours. We know you will break the rules. Some of the rules are so burdensome that it's too difficult for anyone to follow them. Just thinking about committing some sins is itself sinful.

"So?"

Guilt. It's guilt, don't you see! You carry our authority with you. It's like carrying around an emotional club. Whenever you think about committing a sin, bang! you hit yourself right on the head. A great invention, the guilty conscience.

"But you said you forgive every sin."

We forgive you. Forgiving you your transgressions is what it's all about. That's the second great insight. Nothing is more seductive for humans than their freedom of conscience, but nothing is a greater cause of suffering. There is no greater burden.

"I still don't understand the first temptation."

The first temptation of Jesus was to take away your freedom and to give you security and the modest happiness you are capable of living. In refusing the first temptation, Jesus cast away a lot.

"What did He throw away?"

In the place of rigid, ancient law, humans must hereafter with free hearts decide for themselves what is good and what is evil. How could we live with the dreadful burden of free choice?

"How?"

Miracles

The second temptation addresses this question in a most impressive way.

"In what way could anything that the Devil offers be impressive?"

Devil? I don't know about any devil. The "dread spirit" may be human nature, but take it for whatever you wish. The second temptation is the desire for miracles. Jesus is asked to throw Himself from the Temple pinnacle.

"Why would He do that?"

To prove that He is the messiah. The angels are supposed to catch Him before He hits the ground. It is a way for Jesus (and everyone else) to see whether or not He is the messiah. In a sense it is to test Jesus' faith that God will protect Him. What happens?

"Jesus refuses to jump."

Why? Why would He not just prove who He is?

"He does not want to tempt God and show that His faith has to be proven."

I believe He had a healthy respect for gravity. Jesus fails again.

"Fails? He has faith in God."

His faith is not the question. Where He fails is in his overestimation of humanity.

"Jesus wants people to believe from the heart. He does not want people to follow Him because of the miracles He performs. How is that a failure? That seems to be a very noble success. Jesus wants people to feel Him in their hearts. He wants people to love Him and to understand His message."

Yes. What He got is a flock of sheep who cannot know or love or understand. Only the very few, the strong ones, can know and understand. Ironically, the few who can carry their own conscience, and who can create their own values, really do not need Jesus. But for the vast majority, the tens of hundreds of millions, would a few miracles have hurt?

"Are you disagreeing with what He offered? Certainly freedom and knowledge are desirable. What greater gift can He give than freedom? What greater demonstration of concern and love?"

We Care For the Weak, Too!

If, for the sake of the bread of Heaven, thousands and tens of thousands shall follow Him, what is to become of the millions and tens of thousands of millions of creatures who will not have the strength to forego the earthly bread for the sake of the heavenly? No, we care for the weak, too.

"Are you saying that Jesus made a mistake? He was showing respect for humanity."

By showing humans so much respect, He ceases to feel for humankind. Respecting us less, He would have asked less of us. That would have been more like love, for our burden would have been lighter. Why not let the vast rabble believe in the only way they can believe?

"What way is that?"

With blind faith. People want miracles. Even more than a God, people want the miraculous. They want miracles, mystery, and authority. Jesus should feel more for humans. He should care more. His overestimation places humanity at a disadvantage that it cannot overcome by itself. Jesus respects humans too much and loves too little. With more love He would have brought an easier burden to shoulder.

Universal Unity

"But you're working for Satan!"

Not exactly. We members of Religion, Inc. realize that the 'wise and dread spirit' is correct in its assessment of human potential.

"I can't listen to this!"

Look at the final temptation.

"Final temptation?"

Rome and the power that it wields were offered to Jesus. Jesus rejected this one, too.

"Of course He rejected it. You can't force people to see the truth, or to love, or to believe in God."

Yes, you can. In fact, that's just what people want, force. You want to be forced to believe, or not to believe. You need to be coerced, manipulated, and forced. Sometimes the force can be softly applied, through miracles, mystery, and authority. Guidance is all people want. And that's just what Jesus fails to understand.

"Is that *all* people want? Or only according to you and the Inquisitor?"

No, there is one other want. It goes along with the power of Rome. What is really offered in the third temptation is universal unity.

"I don't quite follow you."

It is a difficult concept in our age, but the desire is still around. People want everyone to unite in one unanimous antheap. Human beings want certainty. That's the third anguish of humanity. Diverse beliefs make humans uncertain of their own beliefs.

"But why do you think we want that?"

Do you mean why do I think this is true? What evidence do I have? Or do you mean, why do people want to be part of the universal antheap?

"Both. Take the second question first. That's the one I meant."

You Can't Handle Intense Experiences

People want security, comfort, peace. You cannot handle intense experiences. Intense pleasures and pains frighten you.

"Wait a minute. I have intense experiences. I feel pleasure and pain just like everyone else!"

Not true. You and all your friends are too moral. You worry about the future, about consequences. You even worry about the effect you have on other people. You do not dwell in your passions and pleasures. You cannot live in the moment. No, my friend, your pleasures are mere shadows of what free people can feel.

"But there's no way to show that. You're just saying this, but there's no way to prove it."

I think your challenge is a legitimate one. And I do not think I can fully respond yet.

"Why, because the flock can't understand? Is that your excuse?"

Not at all, though you cannot yet understand. What I suggest is that I give you a brief reply now. I would have to tell a long story to make the point fully, and I do not think this is the place.

"Why can't people—the flock, as you call us—why can't we feel emotion the way free people can? Give me your answer. If I'm not satisfied, I'll ask for the more elaborate answer later."

You cannot let yourselves experience intensely. You are preoccupied with the past and the future. The present moment has barely any existence for you. The moment is the tick of a clock for you. Your memory, your sense of duty and obligation, your promises, all these distract you from experiencing what is going on now. Now! The best you can do is schedule your spontaneous moments.

"All you're saying is that we don't concentrate on every little detail in the present because we are concerned with what is coming. So what? We're not into contemplating our bellybuttons or watching dust settle."

Distractions.   There are a couple of other reasons why you cannot feel intensely. Do you know what happens when opposing forces pull at one object?

"Now this is a physics discussion? When two forces act on an object, the object is pulled (or pushed) in a direction that reflects the resulting direction and force of the pull (or push) from each force. Pull north plus pull east equals pull northeast. Opposing forces play a tug of war. What do opposing forces have to do with feelings and pleasure? Or is this just another of your distractions?"

Distractions? That's the word I was searching for. You sheeplike people have too many distractions. Each distraction pulls (or pushes) you, but because there are so many distractions, you do not go where (or feel what) you want.

"What do you mean? I'm not following you."

Let me try again. Distractions. All your rules and roles, duties and obligations, promises and responsibilities are distractions. You are distracted by consequences, by the past and the future. All these distractions create wants. You want to fulfill all the moral demands that the Inquisitor and I make on you, right?

"Right. It's important to fulfill one's promises and duties—"

Excuse me for interrupting. So you have all this moral baggage. Distracting wants! These alone can act as opposing forces. You may have inadvertently made two promises but find you cannot keep both. Or your role as a student may conflict with your role as a friend or as a worker. Already you're pulled (or pushed) in different directions. Opposing forces.

Then we add feelings and emotions. Some of your passions are not safe. That is why you demand that we establish morality in the first place, to keep your passions under control. Now we have several conflicting forces. Little wonder you cannot concentrate on the present. You have too many distractions. You have too many opposing and conflicting moral wants and natural passions. You are too weak to keep your obligations.

"Well, I'm not sure about this. Why can't someone be truly moral? That way there'd be no conflict."

Where's the Intensity?   I agree. But look at what it means to be truly moral. You have to be objective, concerned with responsibilities, etc. You aren't involved in the pleasure of the moment. Where's the intensity!

"I don't understand."

Let me see if I can explain this with an analogy. Moral people are like buckets.

"Buckets!"

Buckets with holes in them. What happens to a bucket of water that has a lot of holes in it?

"It loses its water. This is ridiculous."

I know it loses its water. But how does it lose the water? How strong are the streams of water running out of all the holes?

"The more holes, the weaker the streams of water. The streams at the lower levels will be slightly stronger because of the weight of the water."

Ha!

"Ah, yes! I get it."

You weak humans, with all your moral distractions, are like holey buckets.

"Not holy buckets; we'd like that."

You experience like the streams of water, weakly. Each stream of water dribbling out of the bucket is like your wants and obligations. Each represents an avenue of experience. You have so many that you experience everything, but too weakly. You don't have the energy for it. That's why I, as the Inquisitor, can allow you to sin. You cannot muster up the concentration and energy for a truly dangerous sin. So I forgive you. And—wouldn't you know it—you thank me for it. The closest you get to real intensity is your fear of genuine, free creation of your values.

"We do make decisions, free decisions. We do decide on our values."

Is that why you had so much trouble coming up with reasons for your values?

"Well—"

You still haven't found a way to guarantee them. And that is just what Religion, Inc. and I do for you. Our authority guarantees your values. We remove the "anxiety and terrible agony" that freedom brings. The reward is that you do not have to decide on values.

A Person in Sheep's Clothing

"But I want to make my own decisions on values. I don't want you and the Inquisitor and Religion, Inc. making my decisions for me. I want to control my own life."

I think you're serious. Maybe you're a person in sheep's clothing.

"Of course I'm a person. And I—that is, we—don't want you running our lives."

But you all flock to morality and religion. All I've been doing is reflecting the wants you expressed in our earlier talks. You said you want security, comfort, stability, safety. You're the ones who think religion and morality make a contribution to humanity.

"We resent the word 'flock.' We do not flock to religion and morality. We freely choose to follow the moral and religious tenets. Which moral and religious values, you're going to ask."

Very well, which moral values?

"I don't know. From what you say, we humans are too weak, vicious, and worthless to choose our own values. There doesn't seem to be any way out of this. Maybe we are too weak to choose. Maybe our natures are too frail. What a depressing idea!"

The Possibility of Freedom

That is why it is necessary to keep you ignorant. The truth of human frailty, coupled with your rebellious nature, leads to anguish.

"Yes, if what you say is true, then anguish does follow. If we are no more than socialized, moralized, religionized beings, then there is no chance of freedom. If we are as weak and worthless as you say, then we should be despairing."

There is no alternative. You must be cared for and protected from yourselves.

"But I wonder about all this. The fact that we know that we are socialized and all the rest gives us a chance to fight against your influence. Our ability to analyze our own situation gives us the power to change the effects that you and advertising, and schooling, and religion have on us."

Why not just accept your fate and be happy?

The Inquisitor Has Misled Us!

"I think you have misled us, Art. There is more to be said for humans' ability to be free than you have admitted. There is more to be said for conscience and roles than you have suggested. Maybe morality and religion are not the effect of our sheeplike need for security and safety."

Oh, I see. Maybe morality and religion are the cause of your submissive approach. Is that it?

"Right. Maybe people cannot handle living intensely because morality and religion have weakened us. You are forgetting that there are people who remain strong enough to be free in the knowledge of good and evil. If they are able to do it, human nature is not overly frail. Perhaps it is our leaders who are doing this to us."

The moral and religious leaders manipulate you?

"I think we're going about it the wrong way. It is not a conspiracy. The people who teach us our morality and religion are caught up in these ways of thinking and experiencing just as much as we are. You mean well; at least, most of you mean well. Where Religion, Inc. has gone wrong is in assuming that human nature calls for protection. You and the Grand Inquisitor are merely part of a story. The real truth is not so easily explained by a conspiracy of wicked people."

You are saying that human nature is not weak?

"Right. It is the blindly followed moral and religious points of view that weaken and sicken people. Once we've been convinced that morality and religion offer the truth, we're caught."

When were we convinced that morality and religion were correct?

"In our training institutions, of course. Schools, churches, and synagogues. Why?"

No, the right answer is, "Never!" We were never actually convinced. We just grew up believing. Morality and religion have always been a part of our lives.

"Are you saying that our society manipulated us? Are you agreeing with me?"

Yes, and when I think about the idea, I discover an interesting coincidence. Psychologists from different schools of psychology disagree about all sorts of things. They cannot agree about what is innate and what is learned. Some put (almost) complete emphasis on one alternative; others opt for the opposite. Even those who agree that there are innate drives rarely agree on what those drives are.

"Yes, so?"

They all pretty much agree that a person's fundamental character is formed between three and five years of age.

"Some say people continue to grow and develop throughout their lives."

We do continue to change. Even if we did not change, society would tell us that we continue to grow and to progress. Without society's compliments we would stop believing in it.

"Cynical, aren't you?"

I did not mean to be cynical. Sorry. The point still stands, though. Even if we continue to grow and prosper, our character and our outlook are fundamentally formed in early childhood. It takes a lot to change. It takes a lot of therapy or reconditioning.

Blind Obedience Hinders Growth

"What does that show?"

A person's character is basically formed by the time she is three to five years old. What else happens at this time? We learn right and wrong, good and bad. Before we are old enough to know right and wrong, good and bad, people don't hold us responsible. They figure we're too little to know the difference. And they're correct.

"What's the connection between learning moral responsibility and character formation? What's the problem?"

We stop growing when we hit three to five years old. We grow in physical size, but our character growth stops. Okay, maybe it doesn't stop entirely. It slows to a snail's pace. And snails pace pretty slowly. Once we learn good and bad, right and wrong, once we get a conscience, we're through. We obey morality blindly; we obey society blindly.

"But haven't you learned a lot since you were three! You could not read or write when you were three. You did not know math and science and history. Your hypothesis just doesn't hold up."

You're so manipulative! Yes, we change in insignificant ways, but—

"Insignificant! How can you say that all you have learned and done and experienced in the years since you were three has been insignificant!"

All I mean is that our values and our basic outlook on the world haven't changed much. We learned to respect authority, and we still do. Morally speaking, we haven't gone very far. Here's an example. A friend of mine told me several years ago that he realized that many people still believe in the God they believed in when they were two.

"Why should their God not be the same God?"

He was a firm believer. What he was saying, I think, was that the adult's God should not be the child's God. Jesus misunderstood. He overestimated humanity. Adults are children in their understanding.

"Why do you say that?"

The child has a conception of God as a man with a long flowing beard sitting on a cloud. Or, if the child is somewhat more enlightened, the God will be a unisex god sitting on a white cloud. Angels, perhaps a few cherubs. Children learn about their God and usually conceive of God visually, as a person in the sky.

"What's the harm in that? Adults don't continue with that belief, if that's what you're driving at. Adults have a more sophisticated vision of God."

More intellectual, yes; more sophisticated, no. The problem in our discussion of God's existence was caused by our intellect's outdistancing our childlike conception of God. People still believe in pretty much the same God. God protects them. God organizes their world. It explains the unexplainable.

"You needn't recite the whole conversation on God's nature. You're saying that the child's God is in the form of a protector, and so is the adult's God. That is what we teach them."

Yes. The protection required is different, but the protector is still there. God also serves as a "person" to make adults and children feel less alone. God answers their questions. And when the questions change, the answering God merely changes the answers.

"That is as much as the people can endure. Perhaps I shall have you burned as a heretic, as an atheist."

What I say doesn't mean there is no God. All it means is that people stop developing their views of the world. When do they do this? At about three to five years old. Baa! That's how society has manipulated and weakened us. Baa.

What's the Harm?

"That is all most people can accomplish. What's the harm in believing in a childlike way?"

Nothing. That would be great, except that the belief is not childlike; it's childish. You are correct. Religion and morality make people submissive. It subjects people to Inquisitors. It means people become content being clones of one another.

"Instead, people should be individuals and as creative as they can be."

Your optimism sounds like Jesus' own. There is no way you will ever be able to prove your point to the Inquisitor's followers, however. Their need for obedience makes them compliant. And look what you risk. What if you and Jesus are incorrect? What if you overestimate the strength of humanity? What horror will follow! You will cast them out of our control and set them into the vast ocean of despair. It is not worth the risk. And the evidence of humanity's desire for unity and security is all around you.

The Desire for Universal Unity

"You haven't given any evidence that we need universal unity. You say we need to be part of the antheap, but you haven't shown it. We are individuals. We want to be free. We want to choose our own course in life."

Individuals? I don't think so. Look at most housing developments. A huge sign hangs over the main road, "Homes for the Discriminating." There are magnificent houses at varying stages of completion. Turn down the street and take a look. Every block is perfectly shaped. Every house is identical to every other house. Where there are differences, they are insignificant. Some may have the front door toward the double garage on the left side and the maple tree on the right side. Others may have just the reverse. In fact, usually the pattern alternates, right door with left tree, left door with right tree. Discriminating!"

"What's that prove?"

Isn't it obvious? These are beautiful, expensive houses. But they are all fashionably the same.

"But the people who live in them are not necessarily the same."

Choice.   I don't think you would know creative intensity or individuality if it hit you in the face. What sheep-people lack is strength, self-direction, self-discipline, and a sense of drive (necessity) that is internally created. Look how you act in school or on the job. You don't act like individual people. You take the same tests in school. Every student is expected to answer the same questions, as though the questions are somehow really important. What you're really learning is to follow orders. Teachers work for us. They don't always know it, but why else would they work for so little pay? They're sheep, too. Baa. You learn what we tell you to learn, and then if you're a good student, you forget it.

"But we choose our own careers."

When did that start to happen?

"I decide which course of study to major in. No one decides it for me. Even if my parents and peers tell me to do one thing, I decide what I want to do with my life."

Maybe so. I do not feel like arguing about it.

"Maybe nothing. I decide my own fate. That's part of the freedom that

I want. You and the other Grand Inquisitors can deny it all you want. But I know what I decide and what I don't decide."

Then all the Madison Avenue advertising firms are going to go broke. Do you really think that advertising has no effect on you?

"It has some effect, yes. But what it really does is let me know what products are out there. I decide what to buy and what I want."

Then why would so much money be spent on advertising? Are you telling me that billions of dollars are being wasted? And that people buy the things they buy because they want those things? Incredible.

"I don't know about everyone else. I buy things because I want or need them. I'm free."

Careers.   Go back to your example of careers. Do you really think you choose your career?

"Absolutely."

Then explain this. Twenty-five years ago or so, people sitting in classrooms across the country looked pretty much like students do today. They were from the same socioeconomic groups, same races, same sexes. In different academic environments, they differed. But that's true today in pretty much the same proportions.

"Yeah, so?"

They majored in English and history and political science and sociology. They majored in the arts and sciences. Today, at least at most colleges and universities, the largest demand is away from the liberal arts and sciences. Careers are in; the arts are out.

"So? Are you going to become nostalgic on me? Are you going to tell me that people were freer twenty-five years ago?"

Hardly. The human condition is fixed. You are weak, vicious, worthless, and rebellious if not by nature, then as a result of socialization. No, the students then were just as unfree as they are now. They and you believe you are free to choose your majors. But the market conditions decide what your majors will be. The names change, but I decide which careers are acceptable, and to whom. What else would account for the nationwide swing in academic styles? It's the same with clothing styles and hair styles, and car styles, and movie styles, and music styles, and—

"What is the point?"

Only that your freedom is very restricted. You get to choose your career from a list of careers that we give you.

"But I'm still happy doing this."

Exactly. It is happiness that we give to humanity.

"But aren't I happy when I am choosing?"

Do you think we would manipulate you in an obvious way? That wouldn't do at all. I manipulate you so that you think the choices are yours. I protect you from some obvious alternatives. Some actions are just immoral. Off limits because they're too dangerous to you. Other actions are safe. Still others are acceptable. Those are the ones most of you choose.

"And what happens if we choose from the safe but unacceptable list?"

Nothing. You just don't get the same rewards from society. You look weird. Or you risk being excluded. If you want to be a poet, go ahead. We'll read your work after you're dead and buried. At the worst, the other Inquisitors and I will forgive you. Remember, we accept the responsibility. We take care of your conscience.

Do Whatever You Want

"You're saying that we don't get to do what we want?"

Not at all. In fact, that's the best part. The Inquisitor and I manipulate you so that you do get to do what you want.

"Then I'm free?"

Yes. You're free in everything, except determining your wants. That's up to me. By determining your wants, I determine every action and every value. And you're happy. You don't even know it's happening. You can do whatever you want. And you're safe doing it.

"But I thought doing whatever I want is freedom."

It is.

"But you just said—"

I just said that it's freedom. But an empty freedom. An empty freedom is a freedom. So you are free, in an empty sort of way. You are as free as humans are capable of being free.

"How exactly does this make me unfree?"

Not unfree, empty free.

"Okay, how does this make my freedom empty?"

There Are Wants and There Are Wants.   There are wants and there are wants.

"Another helpful distinction?"

All I mean is that there are wants and then there are desirable wants.

"Try again."

Your wants are given to you. However, that does not mean that your want is desirable to you. Once I forcefully implant the want, you are fanatically, compulsively dedicated to your want.

"This is weird."

It's not weird. It's common. There are a lot of compulsive shoppers. There are a lot of compulsive people. Alcoholics, workaholics, cigarette-aholics, religion-aholics, moral-aholics. Just because the addiction is common does not make it any less implanted. Just the opposite is probably true.

"You're saying we're all manipulated in our wants?"

No, I'm not saying that. All I'm saying is that there are wants and there are wants. Some wants are undesirable because they're compulsive. Some wants are desirable. In the case of compulsive handwashers, the want is unwanted. That's why these people seek therapy or help of some kind. They don't want their want.

"But the wants feel just like ours?"

Right. Some are strong, even overpowering. People try to remove those wants. Other wants are weaker or make us less "weird." We get along pretty well with those wants. And then there are wants that we genuinely want.

"So we don't always want what we want?"

Right. Some of the wants you may not want are compulsions. But that's pretty extreme. Most of your wants are determined by—

"You and the Grand Inquisitor?"

And Religion, Inc. We give you your wants. We use the institutions of education and religion. We use advertising and parents. We're everywhere. We give you your wants. But we're careful. We only give you wants that you can satisfy, or hope for. We give you safe wants. We give you values. And not a shred of anguish of indecision or of responsibility.

Morality Doesn't Make Us Free?   "Then morality doesn't make us free?"

You are free, all right. Just not in a very interesting way. To be free, you have to create your own wants. Ooh, pressure! That's why we give you your wants. You can have what you want. You just cannot want (or decide) what you want. We do that.

"Wait, you've distracted me from my objection. What you say is correct. People are sheeplike in their everyday living. We are sheeplike in our values. We just accept what we are given. And maybe we do that because we want certainty."

Then our conversation is concluded.

"Not quite. We are the way you say, but I don't think we have to be this way."

What alternative do you propose? And be wary. Even Jesus was bent by our will. He gave the Inquisitor a kiss on the lips of agreement before He left.

"I'm not so sure of that. That kiss He gave before He left the jail cell could be understood in different ways. But that's not the point I want to discuss. There are alternatives to mindless obedience where contentment and happiness are synonymous."

State them.

"I'm not sure I can. But I can point to a few. You say that people lack self-discipline and therefore lack freedom."

Epictetus writes to this point. I'm going to have a talk with him in just a bit. Anything else?

"Yes, though again I have only a guess. Not all philosophers believe that morality is blind obedience, do they?"

Mill and Kant and Sartre all reject this brand of mindless obedience. Each tries to define human freedom and happiness.

"How do they go about that?"

Well, I'm not exactly sure. I think Mill and Kant work on reason as the tool to free us from blind moral authority. Sartre's ideas are more extreme. He says that we are free.

"This reply of yours is hardly satisfactory."

I agree, as it stand now. I invite you to accompany me through the next few talks.

Summary of Discussion

The Grand Inquisitor and I know that people do not want to be free. Of course, you are taught that freedom is desirable, but that is only an illusory type of freedom. You believe that doing whatever you want makes you free. However, the Inquisitor and I know that we direct your values and your wants.

The story opens with the Inquisitor and Jesus discussing the three temptations that Jesus endured in the desert. The Inquisitor says that each temptation reveals an essential feature of human nature. We prefer security and material well-being to the knowledge of good and evil. We fear the burden of our own conscience, so we seek relief from its hold. Forgiveness given by the authority figure depends on the masses' ignorance of good and evil.

How does a person become an authority? People demand miracles and mystery, then they empower "inquisitors" with authority. Taken together, these three qualities remove the fundamental responsibility for the creation of moral values from individuals themselves. People strenuously demand universal unity. Almost no other cause brings the masses to such a frenzied pitch of passion. If everyone believes as we do, then our beliefs will go unchallenged. There's nothing more reassuring than having no challenges to one's belief.

Objections can be raised against the Inquisitor's perspective. By nature, people may not be uncritical and fearful. Institutional religion and morality have made people uncritical. By making questions sinful, the authority has diminished our ability to exercise our thinking.

The Inquisitor's claim that people do not want knowledge of good and evil, however, is still forceful. Our inability to do more than recite the moral restrictions in our society is telling. To demonstrate that people are strong enough to shoulder the responsibility entailed in the knowledge of right and wrong, you need to define good and evil carefully.

Discussion Highlights

I. People do not want to be free
　　1. Instead, they want bread (security).
　　2. They want relief from the anxiety of indecision.
　　3. They want relief of their consciences.
II. People are willing to sacrifice the knowledge of good and evil
　　1. They prefer miracles, mystery, and authority.
　　2. People fear their weakness and desire care.
　　3. People demand universal unity, so that
　　　　a. they can feel a sense of community.
　　　　b. criticism of values is eliminated.
III. Freedom is doing whatever one wants
　　1. There are wants and there are wants.
　　2. Morality doesn't make us free, only content.
IV. Baa!

Questions for Thought/Paper Topics

1. The Bible tells us that God expelled Adam and Eve from Paradise. One reason for the forced exit was that Adam and Eve ate from the Tree of Knowledge of Good and Evil. Does this story agree with the Inquisitor's insistence that people would rather live in ignorance of good and evil?

2. Is there any historical evidence that people prefer bread (security) to freedom in the knowledge of good and evil? Is there any historical evidence to the contrary?

3. Is there any way to protect ourselves from the mind-altering effects of early education? Can we protect ourselves from institutional authority? How?

4. You may believe that blind obedience hinders growth. The Inquisitor argues that obedience gives us just what we want: security, relief of conscience, miracle, mystery, and authority. Which option is most desirable?

5. Is the Inquisitor's authority the result of our "nature," or is our nature the result of institutional religion and morality? That is, are we really sheep, or are we just acting like sheep? (A simple answer, "Baa," will not be sufficient, no matter how revealing.)

6. Can everyone handle the knowledge of good and evil? If we can, why do we resist going beyond the rules to an understanding of what makes an action good or a character trait evil?

7. What one argument would you use in reply to the Inquisitor? As you construct your response, imagine that he is sitting across from you.

For Further Reading

Certainly you should read Dostoevski's "The Grand Inquisitor." It's in print by both Frederick Ungar and Bobbs-Merrill. Plato also has an interesting discussion of individual responsibility to authority in two compatible works, *Apology* and *Crito. Crito* follows immediately. *Apology* accompanies Chapter 10. More recent ideas on the authority of morality can be found in Erich Fromm and others, *Zen Buddhism and Psychoanalysis* (Harper & Row, 1970). John Stuart Mill has a compelling reply to the Inquisitor in *On Liberty* (Hackett, 1978), where he argues that society benefits by allowing its members the widest latitude in individual expression.

Crito

PLATO

Could anyone possibly take seriously the constraints placed on us by our society? Sure, we all live by the rules to some degree, but does anyone submit completely to society's demands? In the following reading, we meet Socrates, one of the founders of Western philosophy. Charged, found guilty, and sentenced to death for crimes against his society,* in this reading Socrates is urged to escape by his life-long friend, Crito. I have selected this true story to give you an example of a person who apparently accepts his society's judgment and unfair sentence yet is strong willed and intelligent. Socrates both accepts and transcends the "Grand Inquisitor's" authority.

Crito argues that Socrates is not guilty of any wrongdoing and further believes that Socrates owes it to his children and friends to stay alive. For these reasons and others, he says, Socrates should escape. Socrates considers Crito's reasons, and examines whether or not he must accept his sentence. He acknowledges that the court mistakenly found him guilty, but he believes he owes a debt to society, to the Laws. His imagined discussion with the Laws settles the question for him: he must accept the decisions made by its courts. Socrates believes he owes his life to the Laws and maintains this conviction even though the Athenian courts and bureaucrats have erred in their judgments.

See what you think of Socrates' reasoning. He strives to set the proper example for all of us. In this century it has been endorsed by Gandhi and by Martin Luther King, Jr. Both of these leaders argued that one should show allegiance to the Laws, to justice, and must accept the punishments meted out by the society in which one lives.

Ask yourself a few questions. Knowing that he is wrongly convicted, should Socrates accept punishment (in his case, death)? Would you accept any punishment your society imposed on you? Do you owe a debt to society? To the Laws? Must you obey all the rules? Is there anything you would be willing to die for? Has Socrates given us the right example? Are his reasons for doing so compelling?

PERSONS OF THE DIALOGUE: *Socrates, Crito*
SCENE: *The Prison of Socrates*

SOCRATES: Why have you come at this hour, Crito? It must be quite early?

CRITO: Yes, certainly.

SOCRATES: What is the exact time?

CRITO: The dawn is breaking.

SOCRATES: I wonder that the keeper of the prison would let you in.

*For a fuller story about the trial of Socrates, read the *Apology* following Chapter 10.
From Plato, *Crito,* in *The Dialogues of Plato,* trans. Benjamin Jowett, 3d ed. (New York: Oxford University Press, 1892).

CRITO: He knows me, because I often come, Socrates; moreover, I have done him a kindness.

SOCRATES: And are you only just arrived?

CRITO: No, I came some time ago.

SOCRATES: Then why did you sit and say nothing, instead of awakening me?

CRITO: I should not have liked myself, Socrates, to be in such great trouble and unrest as you are—indeed I should not; I have been watching with amazement your peaceful slumbers; and for that reason I did not awake you, because I wished to minimize the pain. I have always thought you to be of a happy disposition; but never did I see anything like the easy, tranquil manner in which you bear this calamity.

SOCRATES: Why, Crito, when a man has reached my age he ought not to be repining at the approach of death.

CRITO: And yet other old men find themselves in similar misfortunes, and age does not prevent them from repining.

SOCRATES: That is true. But you have not told me why you come at this early hour.

CRITO: I come to bring you a message which is sad and painful; not, as I believe, to yourself, but to all of us who are your friends, and saddest of all to me.

SOCRATES: What? Has the ship come from Delos, on the arrival of which I am to die?

CRITO: No, the ship has not actually arrived, but she will probably be here today, as persons who have come from Sunium tell me that they left her there; and therefore tomorrow, Socrates, will be the last day of your life.

SOCRATES: Very well, Crito; if such is the will of God, I am willing; but my belief is that there will be a delay of a day.

CRITO: Why do you think so?

SOCRATES: I will tell you. I am to die on the day after the arrival of the ship.

CRITO: Yes; that is what the authorities say.

SOCRATES: But I do not think that the ship will be here until tomorrow; this I infer from a vision which I had last night, or rather only just now, when you fortunately allowed me to sleep.

CRITO: And what was the nature of the vision?

SOCRATES: There appeared to me the likeness of a woman, fair and comely, clothed in bright raiment, who called to me and said: O Socrates, "The third day hence to fertile Phthia shalt thou go."

CRITO: What a singular dream, Socrates!

SOCRATES: There can be no doubt about the meaning, Crito, I think.

CRITO: Yes; the meaning is only too clear. But, oh! my beloved Socrates, let me entreat you once more to take my advice and escape. For if you die I shall not only lose a friend who can never be replaced, but there is another evil: people who do not know you and me will believe that I might have saved you if I had been willing to give money, but that I did not care. Now, can there be a worse disgrace than this—that I should be thought to value money more than the life of a friend? For the many will not be persuaded that I wanted you to escape, and that you refused.

SOCRATES: But why, my dear Crito, should we care about the opinion of the many? Good men, and they are the only persons who are worth considering, will think of these things truly as they occurred.

CRITO: But you see, Socrates, that the opinion of the many must be regarded, for what is now happening shows that they can do the greatest evil to any one who has lost their good opinion.

SOCRATES: I only wish it were so, Crito; and that the many could do the greatest evil; for then they would also be able to do the greatest good—and what a fine thing this would be! But in reality they can do neither; for they cannot make a man either wise or foolish; and whatever they do is the result of chance.

CRITO: Well, I will not dispute with you; but please to tell me, Socrates, whether you are not acting out of regard to me and your other friends: are you not afraid that if you escape from prison we may get into trouble with the informers for having stolen you away, and lose either the whole or a great part of our property; or that even a worse evil may happen to us? Now, if you fear on our account, be at ease; for in order to save you, we ought surely to run this, or even a greater risk; be persuaded, then, and do as I say.

SOCRATES: Yes, Crito, that is one fear which you mention, but by no means the only one.

CRITO: Fear not—there are persons who are willing to get you out of prison at no great cost; and as for the informers, they are far from being exorbitant in their demands—a little money will satisfy them. My means, which are certainly ample, are at your service, and if you have a scruple about spending all mine, here are strangers who will give you the use of theirs; and one of them, Simmias the Theban, has brought a large sum of money for this very purpose; and Cebes and many others are prepared to spend their money in helping you to escape. I say, therefore, do not hesitate on our account, and do not say, as you did in the court, that you will have a difficulty in knowing what to do with yourself anywhere else. For men will love you in other places to which you may go, and not in Athens only; there are friends of mine in Thessaly, if you like to go to them, who will value and protect you, and no Thessalian will give you any trouble. Nor can I think that you are at all justified, Socrates, in betraying your own life when you might be saved; in acting thus you are playing into the hands of your enemies, who are hurrying on your destruction. And further I should say that you are deserting your own children; for you might bring them up and educate them; instead of which you go away and leave them, and they will have to take their chance; and if they do not meet with the usual fate of orphans, there will be small thanks to you. No man should bring children into the world

who is unwilling to persevere to the end in their nurture and education. But you appear to be choosing the easier part, not the better and manlier, which would have been more becoming in one who professes to care for virtue in all his actions, like yourself. And, indeed, I am ashamed not only of you, but of us who are your friends, when I reflect that the whole business will be attributed entirely to our want of courage. The trial need never have come on, or might have been managed differently; and this last act, or crowning folly, will seem to have occurred through our negligence and cowardice, who might have saved you, if we had been good for anything; and you might have saved yourself, for there was no difficulty at all. See now, Socrates how sad and discreditable are the consequences, both to us and you. Make up your mind, then, or rather have your mind already made up, for the time of deliberation is over, and there is only one thing to be done, which must be done this very night, and if we delay at all will be no longer practicable or possible; I beseech you therefore, Socrates, be persuaded by me, and do as I say.

SOCRATES: Dear Crito, your zeal is invaluable, if a right one; but if wrong, the greater the zeal the greater the danger; and therefore we ought to consider whether I shall or shall not do as you say. For I am and always have been one of those natures who must be guided by reason, whatever the reason may be which upon reflection appears to me to be the best; and now that this chance has befallen me, I cannot repudiate my own words: the principles which I have hitherto honoured and revered I still honour, and unless we can at once find other and better principles, I am certain not to agree with you; no, not even if the power of the multitude could inflict many more imprisonments, confiscations, deaths, frightening us like children with hobgoblin terrors. What will be the fairest way of considering the question? Shall I return to your old argument about the opinions of men?—we were saying that some of them are to be regarded, and others not. Now, were we right in maintaining this before I was condemned? And has the argument which was once good now proved to be talk for the sake of talking—mere childish nonsense? That is what I want to consider with your help, Crito:—whether, under my present circumstances, the argument appears to be in any way different or not; and is to be allowed by me or disallowed. That argument, which, as I believe, is maintained by many persons of authority, was to the effect, as I was saying, that the opinions of some men are to be regarded, and of other men not to be regarded. Now you, Crito, are not going to die tomorrow—at least, there is no human probability of this—and therefore you are disinterested and not liable to be deceived by the circumstances in which you are placed. Tell me, then, whether I am right in saying that some opinions, and the opinions of some men only, are to be valued, and that other opinions, and the opinions of other men, are not to be valued. I ask you whether I was right in maintaining this?

CRITO: Certainly.

SOCRATES: The good are to be regarded, and not the bad?

CRITO: Yes.

SOCRATES: And the opinions of the wise are good, and the opinions of the unwise are evil?

CRITO: Certainly.

SOCRATES: And what was said about another matter? Is the pupil who devotes himself to the practice of gymnastic supposed to attend to the praise and blame and opinion of every man, or of one man only—his physician or trainer, whoever he may be?

CRITO: Of one man only.

SOCRATES: And he ought to fear the censure and welcome the praise of that one only, and not of the many?

CRITO: Clearly so.

SOCRATES: And he ought to act and train, and eat and drink in the way which seems good to his single master who has understanding, rather than according to the opinion of all other men put together?

CRITO: True.

SOCRATES: And if he disobeys and disregards the opinion and approval of the one, and regards the opinion of the many who have no understanding, will he not suffer evil?

CRITO: Certainly he will.

SOCRATES: And what will the evil be, whither tending and what affecting, in the disobedient person?

CRITO: Clearly, affecting the body; that is what is destroyed by the evil.

SOCRATES: Very good; and is not this true, Crito, of other things which we need not separately enumerate? In questions of just and unjust, fair and foul, good and evil, which are the subjects of our present consultation, ought we to follow the opinion of the many and to fear them; or the opinion of the one man who has understanding? ought we not to fear and reverence him more than all the rest of the world: and if we desert him shall we not destroy and injure that principle in us which may be assumed to be improved by justice and deteriorated by injustice;—there is such a principle?

CRITO: Certainly there is, Socrates.

SOCRATES: Take a parallel instance:—if, acting under the advice of those who have no understanding, we destroy that which is improved by health and is deteriorated by disease, would life be worth having? And that which has been destroyed is—the body?

CRITO: Yes.

SOCRATES: Could we live, having an evil and corrupted body?

CRITO: Certainly not.

SOCRATES: And will life be worth having, if that higher part of man be destroyed, which is improved by justice and depraved by injustice? Do we suppose that principle, whatever it may be in man, which has to do with justice and injustice, to be inferior to the body?

CRITO: Certainly not.

SOCRATES: More honourable than the body?

CRITO: Far more.

SOCRATES: Then, my friend, we must not regard what the many say of us: but what he, the one man who has understanding of just and unjust, will say, and what the truth will say. And therefore you begin in error when you advise that we should regard the opinion of the many about just and unjust, good and evil, honourable and dishonourable.—"Well," some one will say, "But the many can kill us."

CRITO: Yes, Socrates; that will clearly be the answer.

SOCRATES: And it is true: but still I find with surprise that the old argument is unshaken as ever. And I should like to know whether I may say the same of another proposition—that not life, but a good life, is to be chiefly valued?

CRITO: Yes, that also remains unshaken.

SOCRATES: And a good life is equivalent to a just and honourable one—that holds also?

CRITO: Yes, it does.

SOCRATES: From these premises I proceed to argue the question whether I ought or ought not to try to escape without the consent of the Athenians: and if I am clearly right in escaping, then I will make the attempt; but if not, I will abstain. The other considerations which you mention, of money and loss of character and the duty of educating one's children, are, I fear, only the doctrines of the multitude, who would be as ready to restore people to life, if they were able, as they are to put them to death—and with as little reason. But now, since the argument has thus far prevailed, the only question which remains to be considered is, whether we shall do rightly either in escaping or in suffering others to aid in our escape and paying them in money and thanks, or whether in reality we shall not do rightly; and if the latter, then death or any other calamity which may ensue on my remaining here must not be allowed to enter into the calculation.

CRITO: I think that you are right Socrates; how then shall we proceed?

SOCRATES: Let us consider the matter together, and do you either refute me if you can, and I will be convinced; or else cease, my dear friend, from repeating to me that I ought to escape against the wishes of the Athenians: for I highly value your attempts to persuade me to do so, but I may not be persuaded against my own better judgment. And now please to consider my first position, and try how you can best answer me.

CRITO: I will.

SOCRATES: Are we to say that we are never intentionally to do wrong, or that in one way we ought and in another way we ought not to do wrong, or is doing wrong always evil and dishonourable, as I was just now saying, and as has been already acknowledged by us? Are all our former admissions which were made within a few days to be thrown away? And have we, at our age, been earnestly discoursing with one another all our life long only to discover that we are no better than children? Or, in spite of the opinion of the many, and in spite of consequences whether better or worse, shall we insist on the truth of what was then said, that injustice is always an evil and dishonour to him who acts unjustly? Shall we say so or not?

CRITO: Yes.

SOCRATES: Then we must do no wrong?

CRITO: Certainly not.

SOCRATES: Nor when injured injure in return, as the many imagine; for we must injure no one at all?

CRITO: Clearly not.

SOCRATES: Again, Crito, may we do evil?

CRITO: Surely, not, Socrates.

SOCRATES: And what of doing evil in return for evil, which is the morality of the many—is that just or not?

CRITO: Not just.

SOCRATES: For doing evil to another is the same as injuring him?

CRITO: Very true.

SOCRATES: Then we ought not to retaliate or render evil for evil to any one, whatever evil we may have suffered from him. But I would have you consider, Crito, whether you really mean what you are saying. For this opinion has never been held, and never will be held, by any considerable number of persons; and those who are agreed and those who are not agreed upon this point have no common ground, and can only despise one another when they see how widely they differ. Tell me, then, whether you agree with and assent to my first principle, that neither injury nor retaliation nor warding off evil by evil is ever right. And shall that be the premise of our argument? Or do you decline and dissent from this? For so I have ever thought, and continue to think; but, if you are of another opinion, let me hear what you have to say. If, however, you remain of the same mind as formerly, I will proceed to the next step.

CRITO: You may proceed, for I have not changed my mind.

SOCRATES: Then I will go on to the next point, which may be put in the form of a question:—Ought a man to do what he admits to be right, or ought he to betray the right?

CRITO: He ought to do what he thinks is right.

SOCRATES: But if this is true, what is the application? In leaving the prison against the will of the Athenians, do I wrong any? or rather do I not wrong those whom I ought least to wrong? Do I not desert the principles which were acknowledged by us to be just— what do you say?

CRITO: I cannot tell, Socrates; for I do not know.

SOCRATES: Then consider the matter in this way:—Imagine that I am about to play truant (you may call the proceeding by any name which you like), and the laws and the government come and interrogate me: "Tell us, Socrates," they say; "what are you about? are you not going by an act of yours to overturn us— the laws, and the whole state, as far as in you lies? Do you imagine that a state can subsist and not be overthrown, in which the deci-

sions of law have no power, but are set aside and trampled upon by individuals?" What will be our answer, Crito, to these and the like words? Any one, and especially a rhetorician, will have a good deal to say on behalf of the law which requires a sentence to be carried out. He will argue that this law should not be set aside; and shall we reply, "Yes; but the state has injured us and given an unjust sentence." Suppose I say that?

CRITO: Very good, Socrates.

SOCRATES: "And was that our agreement with you?" the law would answer; "or were you to abide by the sentence of the state?" And if I were to express my astonishment at their words, the law would probably add: "Answer, Socrates, instead of opening your eyes—you are in the habit of asking and answering questions. Tell us,—What complaint have you to make against us which justifies you in attempting to destroy us and the state? In the first place did we not bring you into existence? Your father married your mother by our aid and begat you. Say whether you have any objection to urge against those of us who regulate marriage?" None, I should reply. "Or against those of us who after birth regulate the nurture and education of children, in which you also were trained? Were not the laws, which have the charge of education, right in commanding your father to train you in music and gymnastic?" Right, I should reply. "Well, then, since you were brought into the world and nurtured and educated by us, can you deny in the first place that you are our child and slave, as your fathers were before you? And if this is true, you are not on equal terms with us; nor can you think that you have a right to do to us what we are doing to you. Would you have any right to strike or revile or do any other evil to your father or your master, if you had one, because you have been struck or reviled by him, or received some other evil at his hands?—you would not say this? And because we think right to destroy you, do you think that you have any right to destroy us in return, and your country as far as in you lies? Will you, O professor of true virtue, pretend that you are justified in this? Has a philosopher like you failed to discover that our country is more to be valued and higher and holier far than mother or father or any ancestor, and more to be regarded in the eyes of the gods and of men of understanding? also to be soothed, and gently and reverently entreated when angry, even more than a father, and either to be persuaded, or if not persuaded, to be obeyed? And when we are punished by her, whether with imprisonment or stripes, the punishment is to be endured in silence; and if she lead us to wounds or death in battle, thither we follow as is right; neither may any one yield or retreat to leave his rank, but whether in battle or in a court of law, or in any other place, he must do what his city and his country order him; or he must change their view of what is just: and if he may do no violence to his father or mother, much less may he do violence to his country." What answer shall we make to this, Crito? Do the laws speak truly, or do they not?

CRITO: I think that they do.

SOCRATES: Then the laws will say: "Consider, Socrates, if we are speaking truly that in your present attempt you are going to do us an injury. For, having brought you into the world, and nurtured and educated you, and given you and every other citizen a share in every good which we had to give, we further proclaim to any Athenian by the liberty which we allow him, that if he does not like us when he has become of age and has seen the ways of the city, and made our acquaintance, he may go where he pleases and take his goods with him. None of us laws will forbid him or interfere with him. Any one who does not like us and the city, and who wants to emigrate to a colony or to any other city, may go where he likes, retaining his property. But he who has experience of the manner in which we order justice and administer the State, and still remains, has entered into an implied contract that he will do as we command him. And he who disobeys us is, as we maintain, thrice wrong; first, because in disobeying us he is disobeying his parents; secondly, because we are the authors of his education; thirdly, because he has made an agreement with us that he will duly obey our commands; and he neither obeys them nor convinces us that our commands are unjust; and we do not rudely impose them, but give him the alternative of obeying or convincing us;—that is what we offer, and he does neither.

"These are the sort of accusations to which, as we were saying, you, Socrates, will be exposed if you accomplish your intentions; you, above all other Athenians." Suppose now I ask, why I rather than anybody else? they will justly retort upon me that I above all other men have acknowledged the agreement. "There is clear proof," they will say, "Socrates, that we and the city were not displeasing to you. Of all Athenians you have been the most constant resident in the city, which, as you never leave, you may be supposed to love. For you never went out of the city either to see the games, except once when you went to the Isthmus, or to any other place unless when you were on military service; nor did you travel as other men do. Nor had you any curiosity to know other States or their laws: your affections did not go beyond us and our State; we were your special favourites, and you acquiesced in our government of you; and here in this city you begat your children, which is a proof of your satisfaction. Moreover, you might in the course of the trial, if you had liked, have fixed the penalty at banishment; the State which refuses to let you go now would have to let you go then. But you pretended that you preferred death to exile, and that you were not unwilling to die. And now you have forgotten these fine sentiments, and pay no respect to us, the laws, of whom you are the destroyer; and are doing what only a miserable slave would do, running away and turning your back upon the compacts and agreements which you made as a citizen. And, first of all, answer this very question: Are we right in saying that you agreed to be governed according to us in deed, and now in word only? Is that true or not?" How shall we answer, Crito? Must we not assent?

CRITO: We cannot help it, Socrates.

SOCRATES: Then will they not say: "You, Socrates, are breaking the covenants and agreements which you made with us at your leisure, not in any haste or under any compulsion or deception, but after you have had seventy years to think of them, during which time you were at liberty to leave the city, if we were not to your mind, or if our covenants appeared to you to be unfair. You had your choice, and might have gone either to Lacedaemon or Crete, both which States are often praised by you for their good government, or to some other Hellenic or foreign State. Whereas you, above all other Athenians, seemed to be so fond of the State, or, in other words, of us, her laws (and who would care about a State which has no laws?), that you never stirred out of her; the halt, the blind, the maimed were not more stationary in her than you were. And now you run away and forsake your agreements. Not so, Socrates, if you will take our advice; do not make yourself ridiculous by escaping out of the city.

"For just consider, if you transgress and err in this sort of way, what good will you do either to yourself or to your friends? That your friends will be driven into exile and deprived of citizenship, or will lose their property, is tolerably certain; and you yourself, if you fly to one of the neighboring cities, as, for example, Thebes or Megara, both of which are well governed, will come to them as an enemy, Socrates, and their government will be against you, and all patriotic citizens will cast an evil eye upon you as a subverter of the laws, and you will confirm in the minds of the judges the justice of their own condemnation of you. For he who is a corrupter of the laws is more than likely to be a corrupter of the young and foolish portion of mankind. Will you then flee from well-ordered cities and virtuous men? and is existence worth having on these terms? Or will you go to them without shame, and talk to them, Socrates? And what will you say to them? What you say here about virtue and justice and institutions and laws being the best things among men? Would that be decent of you? Surely not. But if you go away from well-governed States to Crito's friends in Thessaly, where there is great disorder and licence, they will be charmed to hear the tale of your escape from prison, set off with ludicrous particulars of the manner in which you were wrapped in a goatskin or some other disguise, and metamorphosed as the manner is of runaways; but will there be no one to remind you that in your old age you were not ashamed to violate the most sacred laws from a miserable desire of a little more life? Perhaps not, if you keep them in a good temper; but if they are out of temper you will hear many degrading things; you will live, but how?—as the flatterer of all men, and the servant of all men; and doing what?—eating and drinking in Thessaly, having gone abroad in order that you may get a dinner. And where will be your fine sentiments about justice and virtue? Say that you wish to live for the sake of your children—you want to bring them up and educate them—will you take them into Thessaly and deprive them of Athenian citizenship? Is this the benefit which you will confer upon them? Or are you under the impression that they will be better cared for and educated here if you are still alive, although absent from them; for your friends will take care of them? Do you fancy that if you are an inhabitant of Thessaly they will take care of them, and if you are an inhabitant of the other world that they will not take care of them? Nay; but if they who call themselves friends are good for anything, they will—to be sure they will.

"Listen, then, Socrates, to us who have brought you up. Think not of life and children first, and of justice afterwards, but of justice first, that you may be justified before the princes of the world below. For neither will you nor any that belong to you be happier or holier or juster in this life, or happier in another, if you do as Crito bids. Now you depart in innocence, a sufferer and not a doer of evil; a victim, not of the laws but of men. But if you go forth, returning evil for evil: and injury for injury, breaking the covenants and agreements which you have made with us, and wronging those whom you ought least of all to wrong, that is to say, yourself, your friends, your country, and us, we shall be angry with you while you live, and our brethren, the laws in the world below, will receive you as an enemy; for they will know that you have done your best to destroy us. Listen, then, to us and not to Crito."

This, dear Crito, is the voice which I seem to hear murmuring in my ears, like the sound of the flute in the ears of the mystic; that voice, I say, is humming in my ears, and prevents me from hearing any other. And I know that anything more which you may say will be vain. Yet speak, if you have anything to say.

CRITO: I have nothing to say, Socrates.

SOCRATES: Leave me, then, Crito, to fulfill the will of God, and to follow whither he leads.

7 Freedom and Self-Control: A Discussion with Epictetus

I HOPE YOU ENJOY discussing Epictetus' *Enchiridion*. The word *enchiridion* means manual. I think this is an interesting little book. So kick off your shoes and let's learn something about how Epictetus thinks, as recorded in notes by his students and friends.

Let me tell you a little about Epictetus while I turn on the resurrection machine. As the story goes, he was born a slave in ancient Rome. He was educated, probably to serve as a teacher for his owners' children. Excelling at his studies and his intellectual tasks, he became a free man and a teacher. Cast out of Rome with all other philosophers, he settled in Nicopolis. He opened his own school and developed a reputation for sincerity as well as intelligence. Such wise people are rare, and many people came to study with Epictetus. Others turned to him for advice.

What makes Epictetus truly extraordinary is that he lived the truths that he offered to others. Like Socrates before him and Spinoza after him, Epictetus devoted himself to finding a doctrine that he could live. He immersed himself less in theory and almost completely in the human difficulties of his contemporaries. He developed a set of techniques and attitudes to ward off despair and frustration. Epictetus' doctrine is applied morality. His belief is that freedom holds the answer to life's problems.

"I appreciate your praise and generous introduction. I am prepared to speak to you about my philosophy. Do you have any questions or comments?"

What is Your Theory of the Best Life?

Could you summarize your theory of the best life?

"Inner freedom and independence. The best life is comprised of inner freedom and independence. If we are able to exercise inner freedom, then we can live in conformity with nature. No event will overwhelm us; no circumstances will be unbearable."

Material in this chapter taken from Epictetus, *Enchiridion* (New York: Macmillan Publishing Co., 1955). Thomas W. Higginson translation.

How does freedom protect a person from one's surroundings? I mean, how can doing what I want put me in conformity with nature and protect me?

"You have a mistaken conception of freedom, Art. Freedom is not doing whatever you want. Freedom is attained by distinguishing that which is in our power and that which is beyond our power. Bearing this distinction in mind, self-control is possible."

Are you saying that freedom is self-control? Only when I control myself, I'm free? How could this be?

"To be free is to control one's emotional and sensitive life. A person must examine and control her passions, her love, her tenderness. One must always be ready for the inevitable moment of farewell, death."

I don't get it. Where does the fun come in?

"Art, most of life is a struggle to accept fate and position. My technique is concerned with a way of bearing the frustrations, sufferings, and losses in life. I want to minimize states of disappointment and frustration, of grief and fear. That is why I offer the advice of section VIII in my little manual."

Passive Acceptance

Yes, I'm glad you mention that. You say, "Demand not that events should happen as you wish; but wish them to happen as they do happen, and you will go on well." Is that correct?

"Yes. Do you have any questions about it?"

Well, yes, I do have some questions. I guess I don't see how your theory allows for much aggressive action. This piece of advice tells a person to be subservient to fate and to the powerful people of the world. It tells people to be passive to social injustice. Look at some of your examples. At a banquet we are supposed to wait until the platters are brought around to us.

"And then we are to take a moderate amount. Yes, that is correct."

You say the same rule applies to our children, spouse, position, and riches. Don't you see, this is too passive. Or for example, in section XVII you say that we should act the part given us. Your examples just don't fit twentieth-century America. If a person is born poor, we don't believe that person has to remain poor.

"I see. What do you propose instead?"

I propose that people can be whatever they set their minds to become. With enough hard work, and a little luck, people can accomplish almost anything.

"Indeed. I have no objection to working hard toward a goal. Just don't take the goal too seriously."

What? How can a person have a goal and not take it seriously? That's what goals are all about. But wait, I don't see from what you say that you allow for goals at all. Your whole theory sounds like a theory of passive acceptance. Just take whatever life offers; don't ask for more.

"That's correct."

You're contradicting yourself. First you say we should accept whatever comes along in life. That's total passivity. Then you say that we can strive for goals, only we can't take goals seriously. Explain yourself.

Striving and Goals

"Perhaps I could be clearer. Look at my example of the Olympic athlete in section XXIX. There I make it clear that you can attempt to achieve very lofty, very difficult goals. All I request is that you understand fully what you are getting involved in. The athlete must conform to rules, submit to a diet, refrain from dainties; exercise at a stated hour, in heat and cold; drink no cold water, and sometimes no wine—in a word, must give himself or herself up to the trainer as if to a physician."

Okay, prudence is sensible. People should find out what it takes to become successful. And we should be aware of the likelihood of success and failure. Knowing all this is important.

"Then we agree?"

No, we do not agree. You look only at the possible negative points. You exaggerate the training, and diet restrictions, and possible injuries and accidents. You think that everyone is going to suffer a dislocated shoulder or a turned ankle. Why just look at the down side? Where's your enthusiasm?

"Art, you are unrealistic. All I am calling attention to is the reality of the situation. If you seek a goal, know what you are getting involved in. When you have reckoned up all this, if your inclination still holds, set upon the task."

But if people take your attitude, no one will ever try to accomplish anything.

"I cannot speak to what people will or will not do. Other people's activities are beyond my control."

Within and Beyond Our Power

Maybe that's where I can make my criticism more forcefully. You say that freedom is just a matter of knowing what is within one's power and what is beyond one's power. Is that correct?

"Yes. Within our power are opinion, aim, desire, aversion."

Excuse me. I thought people's opinions were not under my control.

"Correct. Only my own affairs, my own mental states are within my control. It is my own opinions, my own aims, my own desires, and my own fears that are within my power."

Okay, sorry for the misunderstanding. Beyond our power are body, property, reputation, office, and similar things. Correct?

"You quote me adequately. Do you have a question about this distinction?"

Body.   A question? No, only a comment. It's wrong! Maybe your society was just different than ours. See, in our society we can affect our reputation and our bodies and our property. Capitalism allows us to work to gain wealth. And lots of people today are conscious of their bodies. They eat well and exercise. Medical care has really developed since your day.

"I think that misses the point. No matter how much effort you invest in your health and wellness, no matter how technologically advanced your medicine becomes, there are still events you cannot control. You may suffer injury from an accident. You may contract an ailment for which there is no cure. AIDS is one of your current problems, isn't it?"

Sure, but people can take precautions.

"Just my point. Precautions are desirable, but you cannot fully control your well-being. The frailty of the human body is a given in nature. We must learn to accept that."

I think I see your point. I remember a couple of years ago a neighbor of mine saw me returning from a bicycle workout. He told me that when I die I will be the healthiest corpse he ever met. I guess there are things I can't control about my body. But wealth and reputation are different. There you are mistaken.

Reputation. "A person cannot control what other people think or how other people evaluate events in the world. Therefore, a person cannot control his or her reputation."

But people think whatever they think about me because of what I do. My reputation results from my actions. If I am hard working and fair, then people will see me this way. If I am superficial, then people will see this in me. How can you deny this?

"Your perspective arises from a certain naivete."

What does that mean?

"Your point of view shows a certain simplicity. Do not take offense at that. I merely state a fact."

What is so simple about my point of view?

"You believe that people evaluate you solely on your actions."

Yes, that's right. And on the consequences of my actions, I suppose.

"Very well, on your actions and on the consequences of your actions. What you fail to factor in is the other person's desires, aspirations, and political, religious, moral, and cultural beliefs."

How do you mean? Why is that important? If I work hard, people will see that. What do their political beliefs have to do with that?

"Say that you are a hard worker for one person's cause. We can name him Demodicus."

How about naming him Smith?

"An odd name, but all right; you work hard in the cause of Smith's political party. From Smith's point of view—"

I am a noble person.

"At least your work is appreciated, and you are held in some esteem. However, another person may not evaluate you this way. Another person may oppose Smith's political agenda. She may despise what Smith, and you, are trying to accomplish. From her point of view your actions are not so praiseworthy."

Let's call her Brown. Okay, Brown doesn't agree with my politics, but she has to acknowledge my effort.

"True, but her acknowledgment will not be complimentary. To Brown you are despicable. Your reputation for hard work makes you all the more dangerous. Where Smith would call you a dedicated loyalist, Brown would call you a fanatical ideologue."

Oh, I see. Not everyone interprets my actions the same way. Still, I'm not convinced.

"All right, an analogy. Suppose there is music playing in the background. To a person who associates this piece of music with pleasant events in his life, the music is pleasing. To a melancholy—"

Melancholy?

"To a sad person, the same music may worsen his mood. Perhaps he associates the music with the loss of a friend. Finally, to a deaf person—"

I get it, to a deaf person the music is neutral, neither pleasing nor displeasing. So how does this analogy fit our discussion?

"One and the same music may cause different evaluations. The difference does not reside in the music but in the moods of the listeners. Similarly, your reputation is less a result of your actions, and their consequences, and more a result of the frame of mind of other people. Since you cannot control how and what other people think and feel, you cannot control your reputation. And that is the point I was making when we started this aside."

Wealth. Hmm. And wealth? Surely wealth is within my control. After all, in our society at least, if I work, earn money, and invest wisely, I will make more money. What could be a clearer case of control?

"What I have to say about wealth is similar to our discussion of body. You overlook many events that could and do occur. For example, natural disasters can wipe our your property."

I have insurance. See, you guys didn't have insurance back in Rome in C.E. 80.

"Very well, but there are still events that can remove a person's wealth. War and large-scale disaster are two such happenings. In your capitalist economy, there is always the possibility of depressions and faulty investments. Perhaps your recent history can give us examples. No matter how wisely a person invests her money, if other factors work on your market economy, the person may lose her money. Investing in a savings and loan company brought financial disaster to some people."

Sure, but that's because other people were dishonest.

"And those dishonest people were not in the investor's control. The same can be said of any other investment. So one's wealth is not in one's control. Physically existing structures can be devastated by natural disaster. Insurance companies can fail. Paper money and banks can be rendered worthless by war."

How? I thought investors did well in wartime.

"Winners may gain new markets and profit from a war economy. However, losers can have their entire economies ruined. Look at the Confederacy in your own country. Overnight, Confederate money became worthless."

Are you saying that we can't have any effect on our wealth?

"No, of course not. You can have an effect on body, on reputation, and on wealth. I am merely pointing out that you cannot control these things. They are external to you, and therefore weak, dependent, restricted, and alien."

So I can affect these things! Then what's the big deal? Why bother with this distinction?

"People who do not realize the distinction between things within our power and things beyond our power can sacrifice the former while pursuing the latter. What I mean is, people suffer great frustration in their concern for that which is beyond their power. Happiness cannot be found in pursuit of fame, wealth, or sensual pleasures."

What do you suggest?

"We must recognize the transiency of people, things, relations."

What are you recommending?

"That we do not wish for permanence and stability in outer events. The only stability and constancy one can achieve is in one's temperament. So be self-effacing, accept ridicule, be passive and even self-denigrating. Self-denial will aid one also. Let the things pass at the banquet of life. In this way you will train yourself so that loss will not overwhelm you."

Death.   That brings me to a real problem I have with your philosophy of living. Death. You say we should have death before our eyes every day. Why? It sounds morbid.

"The entire quotation is, 'Let death and exile, and all other things which appear terrible, be daily before your eyes, but death chiefly.'

Oh, that sounds upbeat and encouraging.

"And you will never entertain an abject thought, nor too eagerly covet anything."

Why do you say that? What do you mean?

"Knowing that you, and those you love, will die keeps you from abject thoughts."

Thinking about my death and the death of my family sounds pretty abject. Knowing I'm going to die makes all my plans and goals and accomplishments look pretty trivial.

"That's one way of seeing it. On the contrary, knowing you will die gives you a motivation to truly live. The events of the day become less important, to be sure. That is just the point. The insults, provocations, ridicule, and injuries become less important. People are disturbed not by things, but by the views which they take of things. That is in section V."

Death prevents me from concentrating on and desiring externals. Is that what you're saying? And if I don't concentrate on externals, I'll be able to avoid frustration, disappointment, and suffering?

"Yes."

I've got to think about this. What you say sounds right, but I have been raised to be goal-directed and ambitious. I have another question.

"Yes?"

The Loss of One's Favorite Cup.   How can you compare a loved one with your favorite cup? You are heartless and unfeeling.

"You must be referring to section III. Very well, let's discuss it. For some reason people often strongly react to this sentiment."

I wonder why. All you say is that your favorite cup is like your wife or child. Breaking your cup is the same as your wife or child dying. Gee, why would anyone think this is cold blooded!

"I do not think you are doing justice to my statement."

Look, Mr. Epictetus, people just can't view their parents or spouses or children the way they view their cups. When a person suffers a loss, the person has to grieve; it's only natural.

"Let me respond with an exaggerated example. Last evening I sat before my meal eating with healthy appetite. As I came to the final bites I began to cry. My crying became almost uncontrollable. My friends, who were dining with me, asked me what was the matter."

What did you say?

"I told them that I was suffering a loss."

A loss?

"Yes, my meal was almost entirely finished, and I would never have this meal again. I was grieving the loss of my evening meal."

That's ridiculous! No one grieves the loss of a dinner.

"Ah, so it is not all losses that bring on grief?"

Of course not. You took me too literally. What I meant was, people naturally grieve the loss of people and things close to them.

"Certainly my meal was close to me; it was inside me."

Grief Is Not Necessary.   Very funny, but you know what I mean. Grief is natural and healthy. Some people say that grief is necessary when we suffer the loss of a loved one. Do you disagree?

"Absolutely. Grief is only a response to events for which one has not prepared. People do not need to grieve. If only you would recognize the nature of human beings! We are mortal. Therefore, each time you say goodbye to a loved one, say it as though you will never see the person again. That way you will experience no event unprepared."

This is crazy. How am I supposed to envision that my family and friends are going to die each time I leave them? Am I supposed to wallow in sadness each time I leave my loved ones?

"That is unnecessary. All I mean is that you should leave nothing unsaid or undone. Taking your leave as I suggest will minimize petty disagreements. You see, many times people grieve because there were words or deeds left unspoken and undone. Often people will remark at funerals that they wish they had the chance to tell the loved one something. Or they may want to say goodbye. That is at least part of their grief."

But another part of grief is that you will never be able to share your life with the person. You must admit that people occupy an important part of our lives. They are there when we need them. They can give support, advice, or needed criticism. That's what we grieve, the loss of the other person's companionship.

"That is why I say in section III 'With regard to whatever objects either delight the mind or contribute to use or are tenderly beloved, remind yourself of what nature they are.' "

But people are not like cups. You can't just look at a person as though she were a favorite cup. What you're asking is inhuman.

"I do not assert that people and cups are equivalent. You distort my meaning. What I do say is that we should take this attitude 'beginning with the merest trifle: if you have a favorite cup, that it is but a cup of which you are fond.' You see, the cup is an example of a trifle. The important aspect is to recognize its nature."

Its nature?

"That it is but a cup, and as such it is breakable. For thus, if it is broken, you can bear it. That sounds easy enough with a cup, doesn't it?"

Well, yes, it does. But it's not the same with a person. A loved person is completely different than a cup. That's why we grieve. Cups are replaceable; people are not replaceable.

"The point is, however, that if you embrace your child or your wife, know that you embrace a mortal—and thus, if either of them dies, you can bear it. People are more important than cups, but our attitude toward either people or cups is ours alone. Remember—"

I know, people are disturbed not by things, but by the views they take of things. I just don't see it that way. I still say, it's natural to grieve a loss of a loved one. Everyone grieves.

Not Everyone Grieves.   "Not everyone grieves. The expression of grief is much more tied to cultural and religious beliefs than you might realize."

How so?

"Some cultures place a great deal of emphasis on a show of grief; other cultures do not show grief in actions."

Sure, but whether they show it or not, they are all feeling grief.

"Fair response. Not all societies grieve, however. But let's put that aside. Any example I select you will look on as an oddity or else you will search for extenuating conditions."

I will?

"It would be reasonable to do so. Therefore, let me give you an example that does not fit your statement. Even in your own twentieth-century American culture there are deaths that people do not mourn."

Yeah, sure, we don't mourn the deaths of evil people. And I guess we should, but we don't mourn the deaths of people we don't know.

"Agreed, though these are not in keeping with our principle. I say that we need not grieve when a loved one dies. Your examples are of people for whom we presumably have no strong feelings."

Then what is your example?

"Suppose you have an ailing relative; say, your elderly great-grandfather is dying. He has been ill for several years, all the while slowly diminishing in strength. Each member of the family and his circle of friends has said goodbye. Your great-grandfather's mind and body slowly wither away. His pain increases with the passing days. Finally, he loses all sense of who or what is around him. His pain increases even beyond the aid of narcotics and painkillers. The suffering continues, then he dies in his sleep."

Not a very happy scenario.

"Would you feel grief, or relief?"

Well, I guess I would feel some of each. I mean, I would feel relieved that my great-grandfather is out of pain. I would feel good that everyone got to say their goodbyes while he was well enough to know them. So my overwhelming emotion would be relief. But there would still be a sense of loss.

"What if he were 110 years old?"

Gee, that's old. That's so much older than most people expect to live. I guess it would depend on the quality of his life.

"I do not understand."

It would matter to me if he lived a happy life. If his life was happy, then I guess his death wouldn't be so terrible.

"Fine, we can adjust the example. Don't you see where this is going? You would feel okay if your great-grandfather's life were happy and if his death were anticipated."

But I would still feel some grief.

"Assuredly. I do not doubt that the cultural habit of grieving would happen. However, let us return to my original point. Knowing that your great-grandfather is mortal, you are able to bear his death."

Yes, I could bear it. That's true of everyone's death.

"Exactly."

Experts Say Grief Is Healthy. But experts say that grief is necessary and healthy. Elizabeth Kübler-Ross says that there are stages a person must go through in order to deal with the death of a loved one.

"Indeed, and I am impressed with her work. What she says is quite insightful."

You're contradicting yourself again, Mr. Epictetus. Maybe my resurrection machine is not translating your thoughts clearly enough.

"Your device is working well enough. You see, Art, I am not in disagreement with Kübler-Ross. Her position is that people need to get over the death of a loved one. I agree. Our only difference is that I think most of one's difficulties with loss can be eliminated in advance."

What do you mean, "in advance"?

The Detached Perspective

"If we hold a detached perspective of the event of death, we can deal with our loss more adequately."

A detached perspective? What do you mean?

"To be free requires that we take a detached perspective on all our desires. We use reason to effect the distance we need. When, therefore, anyone provokes you, be assured that it is your own opinion which provokes you. If we learn to view ourselves impersonally, then we will enter the first stage of freedom."

You want me to be able to look at my own affairs as though they were happening in someone else's life?

"Yes. We need to seek the causes of our passions and desires. That is, we must ask ourselves why this event provokes this response in me. For we already know that—"

It is not the event but the views we take toward the event that disturb us.

"Just so."

Will understanding the cause of my passions and desires cure me of their effects?

"No, that will not be sufficient. However, dispassionately understanding the responses that we have toward events does let us judge the desirability of the response. We must discipline ourselves to be able to view our own calamity as though it belonged to someone else."

In what way is this freedom?

"It is not yet freedom, Art, but it is a start."

Freedom Is Not Doing What One Wants

I just don't understand what you mean by freedom. Isn't freedom doing whatever I want?

"No, I do not think so. Many times doing what we want is not being free at all. Let me give you an example. You have already thought about the life of the Stranger. He does whatever he wants, but he is passive and unfeeling."

Sure, but he's still free. He does what he wants.

"Does he? His sensual desires rule him, as does his external environment. He is not free, because he is not the master of his own passions. He is in control neither of his internal mental states nor of his environment."

I don't get it.

"Imagine that as we sit in your kitchen discussing freedom, a man runs into the room. He screams loudly, dashes to the sink, and turns on the water. You jump to your feet and move to the sink. There, previously unknown to us, is an explosive device. The man's action has rendered it harmless, and so we are free to continue our discussion in one piece."

I'd say we owe the man a sincere thank you. After all, he ran in from outside and risked his own welfare. His actions saved our lives. So what's the point of the example?

"You are assuming a great deal. First, you are assuming that the man knew about the device."

Did he?

"For the sake of the example, let's say that he did."

Then where is the problem? He knew the device was there, and he risked his own welfare to save us. He's courageous.

"You are also assuming that he was not the one who placed the explosive there in the first place."

Did he?

"No."

Then my judgment stands. He's a good guy. What else is there?

"You are assuming he acted freely."

He knew the bomb was there. He didn't have someone pushing him in or threatening him, did he?

"No."

So where's the problem? He's free.

"What if I tell you that he is a compulsive handwasher? Imagine his compulsion is extreme."

What's a compulsion?

"A person who is compulsive is someone who feels great internal coercion to act in certain ways. His inner passions compel him to action."

So?

"Our hero is acting on a compulsion. The danger present to us and to him is minor compared to his compulsion. He would have burst through the door and run to the sink whether or not we were there."

Still, he defused the bomb.

"But that was only incidental. He would have acted in just the same way even if no bomb existed. His compulsion was to get to the water."

And you're saying that this compulsion makes him—

"Unfree."

Okay, but most people do not suffer from compulsions like this.

"Agreed. My point is merely that doing what one wants is not necessarily being free. The handwasher does what he wants. He washes his hands. However, he does not want to be compelled in his actions."

How do you know?

"Since it is only an exaggerated example, I could say that he does not want to be compelled, but that would not be helpful. It would be too tied to a single example."

And an imaginary one at that.

"Yes. So let me ask you, Art. What if you and I were talking for an extended time, and every ten minutes or so I got up from my seat, walked to the sink, and washed my hands? What would you think?"

I'd think there was a problem.

"And what if we were friends? What would you tell a friend who *had* to wash his hands so often? Wouldn't you tell him to seek help?"

Yes, I guess I would, especially if I saw his behavior changing his life in ways he didn't want.

Wanting What We Want

"Therefore, we can conclude that freedom is not merely doing what we want, but also wanting what we want."

Run that by me again.

"Being free involves not merely acting on our wants, but acting on the wants we find desirable. Another way of saying this is that we are just as unfree when the coercion we experience is internal as external."

Okay. Then the Stranger and Kierkegaard's A are not free. The Stranger is controlled by his passions and by his surroundings.

"Yes, and A is not free, either. He is more difficult to analyze. However, his despairing attitude and his cynicism entrap him. His wants are frustrating to him."

Even when he fulfills his wants?

"Especially when he satisfies his wants. That is part of what he tells us in the *Either/or* talk. No matter what he does, he experiences regret and frustration. This is not being free!"

Control Is Freedom

What's the answer?

"Self-control is freedom."

That's where we started, isn't it? Are you saying that the Grand Inquisitor's idea is correct?

"What is the Grand Inquisitor's idea?"

Sorry, I just assumed you had read an earlier chapter. I forgot that you have been, well, you know—

"Death is not such a great evil. Haven't you been listening to our conversation? Tell me, what is the Inquisitor's idea?"

He thinks that people are free only when they give up their freedom. He says people don't want to be truly free, so he takes their freedom from them.

"In what ways does this conform to my statements?"

You say that control brings freedom, right? That's what the Grand Inquisitor says. He controls people's lives. He tells people what to think and do. Are you saying that people are free living like this?

"Of course not, Art. Living under the rule of another person is hardly living freely. If this Inquisitor fellow coerces the people, then they are not free. And this applies even when the people desire his control."

How can you say that they are not free? You just told me that control is freedom.

"Self-control is freedom. What the Inquisitor offers is a flight from freedom. Let me be clearer. Whether a person is internally compelled or externally controlled, that person is not free. Only self-control makes one free. And by self-control, I do not mean that one's desires control one. As we have seen, that won't do."

Oh, yes, I remember. There are things within our power and things beyond our control. Within our power are our desires, passions, and all the rest.

"Yes, and that is the only realm where freedom can be found. Falling prey to one's passions and desires is no more freeing than suffering the threats and power of the Inquisitor. Did you know that passion means suffering?"

What Freedom Is

Now that you have told me what freedom is not, tell me what it is.

"Our conversation has led us far from my *Enchiridion*, I am afraid. We have been extrapolating from what I wrote. I hope you know that."

No problem. I mean, I know you probably never thought of compulsions and unconscious motives. But these ideas do fit your point of view. They seem to be consistent with what you said centuries ago. So, I think it's okay to speculate about what you would say today. That's the advantage of having the resurrection machine.

"Indeed, but before you become convinced that this device works, let us warn your readers."

Stop stalling. What is freedom?

"What is your own? The use of the phenomena of existence. So that when you are in harmony with nature in this respect, you will be elated with some reason: for you will be elated at some good of your own."

How do I achieve this harmony with the things in the world?

"Demand not that events should happen as you wish; but wish them to happen as they do happen, and you will go on well."

Explain that, please.

"With the exception of our inner life, the phenomena of existence are beyond our control. Therefore, in order to avoid frustration, grief, fear—in a word, in order to avoid being overwhelmed by the phenomena of existence—we must wish for events to happen as they do happen."

So, for example, I see it is raining outside. Therefore, I wish it to be raining? Are you asking me to conform my beliefs and desires to what is out there? Surely, being subservient to reality is not freedom.

"Indeed, acquiescence as you describe it is incomplete. What I suggest is that you sincerely wish for events to happen as they happen. However, either way is acceptable. The free person is the one whose beliefs, desires, and goals harmoniously coincide with the necessity of reality."

Huh?

"That remark may become your trademark."

Huh?

"What I mean is that we are free of frustration, fear, despair, and so on whenever our wants, beliefs, and all else properly within our control coincide with the necessary laws of reality. We are free whenever what we want to happen actually happens. And we want it, but not because it is going to happen."

How can this be freedom? And how can I ever want what is going to happen, but not because it is going to happen?

"The answer to your second question first. The final chapter of this book is an examination of Spinoza's and Lao Tsu's theories of virtue. I think they answer your question."

Freedom From Externals

How can what you describe be freedom?

"There are two types of unfreedom. We have examined each, though in a cursory way. The one type is when a person is compelled or coerced to do something. When one's conduct and desires are dictated by external contingencies—"

By what?

"By events that happen outside the person but which are not part of the necessary laws of nature."

So whenever my actions or thoughts are dictated by externals, then what?

"Then you are unfree. And remember what we established as externals. The quests for fame, wealth, and pleasures of the senses are all externals. Each is also contingent. Fame, wealth, and pleasures are all dependent on what lies outside the self. Therefore, they are all dependent, weak, restricted, and alien."

When I am free from these externals, am I free?

"Yes, that is certainly part of the story. However, the quest for freedom is not nearly as easy as our casual reflection implies. If you would improve, be content to be thought foolish and dull with regard to externals. Do not desire to be thought to know anything; and though you should appear to others to be somebody, distrust yourself."

Virtue, Not Morality

I have to give up my desires for social acceptance and security?

"Indeed. You must abandon the essential motivation for social acceptance. You must cultivate either your own reason or externals; apply yourself either to things within or external to you—that is, be either a philosopher or one of the mob."

But what moral rules am I supposed to follow? I don't see any rules in your manual.

"Mine is not a moral theory, Art, but a theory of human excellence. I am proposing a way to the virtuous life. Socrates is one of my models. There is a man who lives by his own reasoning."

I should be independent like Socrates?

"When you do anything from a clear judgment that it ought to be done, never shrink from being seen to do it, even though the world should misunderstand it; for if you are not acting rightly, shun the action itself; if you are, why fear those who wrongly censure you?"

Hemlock?

"You fear death, but that is your own perception."

Conflicting Desires

I'll think about your suggestions. Before we close our talk, though, you mentioned a second kind of unfreedom a moment ago. What were you thinking?

"Happiness and freedom are obtained by enjoying a harmonious coincidence of one's inner life and the phenomena of existence."

When what you want fits with what is happening?

"Yes. Now part of the formulation depends on external reality."

With what is happening around you.

"And part is dependent on the harmony we experience internally. Whenever our desires conflict, we are unfree. We are frustrated and confused."

Give me an example.

"Imagine you are enjoying an evening at home. You are studying for an exam that means a lot to your final grade and to your academic career."

This is just the reason I stay away from books. Too much pressure.

"To continue my example. Imagine also that a friend comes by and tells you about a great concert that is just about to begin. She has tickets. Of course, you want to go to the concert."

Of course.

"However, you also want to stay home and study. Your sense of the importance of the exam is tied to your sense of self-worth, or to your identification of yourself as a student, or to your career goals."

I want to study, and I want to go to the concert?

"Your conflicting desires render you confused and frustrated."

I'm not confused. I'll go to the concert and study later.

"For the sake of argument, assume that you cannot do both. In fact, try as you will, usually you cannot do both in reality. Which do you choose?"

The concert. I'll pick up my grades later.

Self-Identification. "That reply is acceptable, but it says that you identify yourself as a concertgoer first and as a student second."

What's wrong with that?

"What happens when you receive your exam grade?"

I'll regret not studying. I know that, because I have been through this choice before. So you think I should skip the concert and stay home to study. All work and no play makes Art seriously frustrated!

"It is not for me to tell you which action is desirable. That is up to you. I am only pointing out the conflict that arises between competing desires. Whichever way you decide, you will feel regret and distraction."

I know. When I go to a concert or a movie, I keep thinking about my exam. But if I stay home to study, I am equally distracted. I keep wondering how the concert is going. Is there any way out of this conflict? Or do I just go crazy, like Kierkegaard's A?

Freedom and the Harmonious Inner Life. "What I am about to say goes well beyond my formal statements in my manual. I believe we need to find a way of identifying ourselves. Once a person identifies who she is, she will be able to use the method I will now explain.

"Order the desires you have according to their desirability. You can do this by ordering desires according to the image you believe is most desirable for a person."

I order my desires based on how important they are to my self-image?

"That is a fine way of putting it. From there, the remainder is relatively easy. The highest desires you identify with yourself. These most accurately describe you. The desires in the middle of the ordered hierarchy are desires peripheral to the self. Finally, the desires at the lowest level of the hierarchy are alien or even painful to the self."

How does this resolve my inner conflicts?

"Each time you are about to act on your desires, seek the higher desire over the lower desire. You are free whenever your actions are self-motivated. With this method, the higher-order desires are most closely identified with your self. This method allows you to be in control of your desires. In fact, the detachment we discussed earlier allows you to select your desires in a rationally sound way."

Four Unfreedoms Resolved

How does that guarantee my freedom?

"There are four internal unfreedoms caused by conflicting desires and emotions. It is worthwhile to explore each unfreedom.

First. "The first unfreedom occurs when a person has no internally motivated desires."

What kind of person would that be, a corpse? Someone in a coma?

"Actually, there are rarely people who are naturally like this."

How is this sort of person unfree?

"A person with no desires is overly passive to his environment. Without any desires, he is totally inactive, totally passive. That is unfree. Because he is free only in the realm of his own mental life, a free person must assert his desires."

I agree. But haven't you been advocating that we dispense with our desires? You know, you say, "For the present, altogether restrain desire." Aren't you advocating a comatose unfreedom?

"Good objection, Art. However, my advice is only meant to strengthen the person who accepts my method. My manual is a training manual. As in all training, the student is asked to accept an exaggerated regimen. My aim is to toughen the person for the trials of the real world, where temptation is so often met."

Second.   Okay. What is the second unfreedom?

"The second unfreedom is the case where no particular thing is desired. This sort of person is also passive to her environment."

How does this person differ from the first one we just discussed?

"This second type has desires. However, her desires are caused by her surroundings. Virtually whatever she sees in her environment, she desires."

The Stranger?

"Yes, that would be a likely candidate. He passively accepted whatever his surroundings offered. He was just as pleased being with Marie as smoking a cigarette, eating eggs from the pan, or watching the street scene below his balcony. His unfreedom lies in his nearly total passivity to his surroundings."

Again, this is hardly an interesting category. How many people live so passively?

"All of us live like this to some extent. We may not live our entire lives passively encountering the moment, but we do live this way for brief intervals."

Third.   What's the next category?

"People experience desires that pull equally, but in opposing directions. The desires may be equally compelling, even though only one can be satisfied."

Like the example you used just a few moments ago? I had trouble deciding whether or not to go to the concert.

"Exactly. Our short-term and long-term goals often conflict. It may be an oversimplification to say that these desires exert equal force on us. When we are called upon to determine which is more pressing, however, we are usually at a loss."

Yes, I experience conflicts like this pretty often. What is the final form of unfreedom?

Fourth.   "There are times when a stronger desire competes with a weaker desire."

Where's the conflict? Simply ignore the weaker desire and follow the stronger.

"This is the problem of the compulsive. The stronger desire is not always the preferred desire. But consider a case weaker than the compulsive personality. Often we experience this type of conflict in our desires. What we value more, we feel less pressed to achieve. What we value as relatively less important, we feel tempted by."

For example?

"What tastes good is rarely good for us. Intense short-term pleasures are almost always weighed against weak but longer-term, more important goals. I think this sort of conflict is the most common of all."

Resolving the Unfreedoms.   How does your method deal with these unfreedoms?

"By establishing a hierarchy of desires with which we identify, we can counter each type of unfreedom. Having a set of desires counteracts the first unfreedom."

The comatose guy is out.

"Similarly, the Stranger's type of unfreedom is resolved. The hierarchy of desires with which the person identifies gives him direction. The third and fourth types of unfreedom are also resolved. Whenever a person is pulled by conflicting desires, she need only consult her self-defining hierarchy of desires. In each case, acting on the relatively higher desire yields freedom."

What about regrets? Won't we still regret not doing what the less important desire demands?

"Not if we take our notion of self-identification seriously. And not if we desire freedom and happiness. I am not saying that the method is easily achieved. Nor is it achieved without some sacrifice. Yet it is the only way for us to avoid being overwhelmed by the phenomena of existence."

I'm sure there is more you might want to add to this. I think we ought to stop here, however. I would like a chance to absorb this odd notion of freedom that you propose.

"Odd?"

Choices

Yes. Your freedom doesn't allow for choices. Once we have this perfect picture of ourselves, we never need to make a choice. We merely follow the higher-placed desire. That's an odd notion of freedom.

"Choice brings a person into internal and external conflict. Real happiness and freedom avoid the frustrations and anxiety that choice brings."

Like I said, perhaps we need to stop here. I certainly have a lot to consider. Your notions of freedom and self are interesting. I hope we get to pursue these again sometime.

"The resurrection device is yours, Art. But listen, as I have remarked, Spinoza and Lao Tsu reflect a similar line of reasoning. Perhaps they will be able to explain the method of freedom more fully. I know they address the matters of internalizing one's hierarchy of desires. And I believe they go some way in showing which desires, beliefs, and the like are acceptable."

Oh?

"But that takes us well beyond what I have to say here. A fuller discussion of the point of values is essential. And a good deal more needs to be said concerning human nature. Thank you for your attention."

I thank you, Mr. Epictetus. Maybe freedom is practicing self-control.

Summary of Discussion

Epictetus distinguishes those things that are within our control from those things that are beyond our control. In principle, our internal, mental life is within our control. We have control over our beliefs, our desires, our wishes, our fears, and our aims. Beyond our control are our bodies, our reputations, our wealth, and death. Because these things are beyond our control, we should never become too emotionally attached to their outcome. For example, grief is unnecessary when we realize the nature of humans. People die. Once we face this fact, we can accept the death of a loved one.

The emotionally detached perspective that Epictetus endorses gives us a special kind of freedom. Freedom is found in self-control. It is vital for our freedom that we maintain our independence from the external environment and from our internal passions. The best life, then, is the life that accomplishes these two tasks.

External environmental control can be alleviated. We need to understand that events occur as they are determined to occur. If we can learn to accept the "unfolding" of reality, then we will be immune to frustration and disappointment. After all, we are not disturbed by events but by the attitudes we take toward events.

The greatest defense of freedom from the internal anarchy of our passions is to identify ourselves according to our most important desires and beliefs. An harmonious inner life is made possible once we can replace our passions with emotions and beliefs that are more appropriate to our personal identity.

There are four distinct ways in which we can be unfree. We can have no internally motivating desires, or we can have no particular desire. This makes us unfree because we are passive to the environment. We can also have desires that exert equal psychological force but that pull in incompatible directions. Finally, we can have a stronger but less important desire compete with a weaker but more important desire. Freedom is disciplining ourselves to always act on those desires and beliefs that define who we are as individuals. For Epictetus, freedom is not a matter of choice but an acquisition of knowledge.

Discussion Highlights

I. Beyond our power are
   1. Body
   2. Reputation
   3. Wealth
   4. Death
   5. Therefore, no one ought to strive to control these elements of life.
II. Freedom consists in
   1. Maintaining a detached perspective with respect to externals.
   2. Controlling the internal, including one's
      a. beliefs
      b. aims
      c. aversions
      d. fears, and so on.
   3. Resolving conflicting desires
      a. through self-identification,
      b. by creating an harmonious internal life
III. Unfreedoms
   1. Having no internally motivating desires.
   2. Having no particular desire; being passive to the environment.
   3. Having desires that exert equal psychological force but pull in incompatible directions.
   4. Having a stronger but less important desire compete with a weaker but more important desire.
IV. Hierarchy of desires
   1. Resolves unfreedoms.
   2. Eliminates the necessity of choice.

Questions For Thought/Paper Topics

1. Epictetus believes we can be enslaved by both our passions and by events that occur outside us. Do you agree with Epictetus' contention that freedom is self-control? If he is correct, what are we free to do?
2. Does Epictetus endorse passivity? Should we accept our station in life? Or should we work for a better life?
3. Do people have control over their bodies, their wealth, and their reputations? How much effect can one person have on these "externals"?
4. What is Epictetus' attitude toward death and grief? Do you find his point of view realistic?
5. Epictetus argues for an emotionally detached attitude toward events beyond our control, even the death of a loved one. Do you agree that this is the best way to encounter events?
6. How does Epictetus distinguish the moral life from the virtuous life? Why does he place more importance on the virtuous life?
7. What is Epictetus' theory of human freedom? Is it more than a coping mechanism for dealing with the trials of reality?

For Further Reading

Of course, reading Epictetus' *Enchiridion* (Macmillan, 1987) is the best place to start learning about Stoic philosophy. Another book by Epictetus is the *Discourses* (Loeb Classic Library). *Letter from a Stoic* (Penguin, 1975) by Seneca is yet another good place to read about the Stoic ideal of the best life. A fine contemporary discussion of freedom can be found in Frithjof Bergmann's *On Being Free* (Notre Dame, 1977). Finally, an excellent discussion and application of Stoic philosophy is given in Paul Tillich's *The Courage to Be* (Yale, 1980).

The Eightfold Path

SIDDARTHA GAUTAMA BUDDHA

Identifying obstacles to well-being, Gautama strikes a note similar to that sounded by Epictetus. Gautama realizes that our *real* problem is ignorance. Our ignorance is shown in our resolve to cling to our desires and to a strong sense of self. Because of our desires to seek pleasure and avoid death, people "can find no escape from the hell of their own making." People go astray because they prefer illusion to truth, what is pleasant to what is true. What appears to be pleasing, however, brings "anxiety, tribulation, and misery."

So Gautama Buddha offers a lecture on the truth. Our problems, he says, arise primarily from ignorance and secondarily from desires. Remove ignorance and desires, and all will go well. In this brief reading Gautama offers the four noble truths: The first three noble truths describe the existence, cause, and cessation of sorrow. The fourth noble truth is the "eightfold path," a set of rules that identifies character traits to be attained. Rules are useful only insofar as they create specific character traits that free us from illusions. Self is the illusion that separates us from reality, creating envy and hatred. The conventions of morality are also inadequate. There is no wrong, nor vice, nor sin, except ignorance; there is only reality and our understanding of it.

The Sermon at Benares elaborates these ideas. In this story Gautama Buddha, the Enlightened One, offers the "middle path." Extremes of tastes and behaviors are not the way to understanding. Living the rough life of constant denial does not free a person from delusions, nor is a person served by self-inflicted pain. As long as the self remains, these measures are useless. Because self-denial does not remove ignorance or desire, a person should eat and drink to satisfy the needs of the body. The way to truth is through self-discipline, not extreme self-denial. To achieve understanding, we must realize that a person's ultimate control is over her state of mind. Only truth is sublime and everlasting, and that is where the "path" leads.

As you read this selection, notice how little Buddha is concerned with rules and laws, and how much he wants us to concentrate on our character. Could Epictetus be understood as offering a manual by which to bring us to Gautama Buddha's "middle path"?

Enlightenment

BODHISATTVA HAVING TO PUT TO FLIGHT MĀRA, gave himself up to meditation. All the miseries of the world, the evils produced by evil deeds and the sufferings arising therefrom passed before his mental eye, and he thought:

"Surely if living creatures saw the results of all their evil deeds, they would turn away from them in disgust. But selfhood blinds them, and they cling to their obnoxious desires.

"They crave for pleasure and they cause pain; when death destroys their individuality, they find no peace; their thirst for existence abides and their selfhood reappears in new births.

"Thus they continue to move in the coil and can find no escape from the hell of their own making. And how empty are their pleasures, how vain are their endeavors! Hollow like the plantain-tree and without contents like the bubble.

"The world is full of sin and sorrow, because it is full of error. Men go astray because they think that delusion is better than truth. Rather than truth they follow error, which is pleasant to look at in the beginning but causes anxiety, tribulation, and misery."

And Bodhisattva began to expound the dharma. The dharma is the truth. The dharma is the sacred law. The dharma is religion. The dharma alone can deliver us from error, sin, and sorrow.

Pondering on the origin of birth and death,

From *The Gospel of Buddha According to Old Records*, 5th ed., ed. Paul Carus (Chicago: The Open Court Publishing Co., 1897), pp. 30–43.

the Enlightened One recognised that ignorance was the root of all evil; and these are the links in the development of life, called the twelve nidānas:

"In the beginning there is existence blind and without knowledge; and in this sea of ignorance there are appetences [strong appetites] formative and organising. From appetences, formative and organising, rises awareness or feelings. Feelings beget organisms that live as individual beings. These organisms develop the six fields, that is, the five senses and the mind. The six fields come in contact with things. Contact begets sensation. Sensation creates the thirst of individualised being. The thirst of being creates a cleaving to things. The cleaving produces the growth and continuation of selfhood. Selfhood continues in renewed births. The renewed births of selfhood are the cause of suffering, old age, sickness, and death. They produce lamentation, anxiety, and despair.

"The cause of all sorrow lies at the very beginning; it is hidden in the ignorance from which life grows. Remove ignorance and you will destroy the wrong appetences that rise from ignorance; destroy these appetences and you will wipe out the wrong perception that rises from them. Destroy wrong perception and there is an end of errors in individualised beings. Destroy errors in individualised beings and the illusions of the six fields will disappear. Destroy illusions and the contact with things will cease to beget misconception. Destroy misconception and you do away with thirst. Destroy thirst and you will be free of all morbid cleaving. Remove the cleaving and you destroy the selfishness of selfhood. If the selfishness of selfhood is destroyed you will be above birth, old age, disease, and death, and you escape all suffering."

The Enlightened One saw the four noble truths which point out the path that leads to nirvana or the extinction of self:

"The first noble truth is the existence of sorrow. Birth is sorrowful, growth is sorrowful, illness is sorrowful, and death is sorrowful. Sad it is to be joined with that which we do not like. Sadder still is the separation from that which we love, and painful is the craving for that which cannot be obtained.

"The second noble truth is the cause of suffering. The cause of suffering is lust. The surrounding world affects sensation and begets a craving thirst, which clamors for immediate satisfaction. The illusion of self originates and manifests itself in a cleaving to things. The desire to live for the enjoyment of self entangles us in the net of sorrow. Pleasures are the bait and the result is pain.

"The third noble truth is the cessation of sorrow. He who conquers self will be free from lust. He no longer craves, and the flame of desire finds no material to feed upon. Thus it will be extinguished.

"The fourth noble truth is the eightfold path that leads to the cessation of sorrow. There is salvation for him whose self disappears before Truth, whose will is bent upon what he ought to do, whose sole desire is the performance of his duty. He who is wise will enter this path and make an end of sorrow.

"The eightfold path is (1) right comprehension; (2) right resolutions; (3) right speech; (4) right acts; (5) right way of earning a livelihood; (6) right efforts; (7) right thoughts, and (8) the right state of a peaceful mind."

This is the dharma. This is the truth. This is religion. And the Enlightened One uttered this stanza:

Long have I wandered! Long!
Bound by the chain of desire
Through many births,
Seeking thus long in vain,
Whence comes this restlessness in man?
Whence his egotism, his anguish?
And hard to bear is samsara
When pain and death encompass us.
Found! it is found!
Author of selfhood,
No longer shalt thou build a house for me.

Broken are the beams of sin;
The ridge-pole of care is shattered,
Into nirvana my mind has passed,
The end of cravings has been reached at last.

There is self and there is truth. Where self is, truth is not. Where truth is, self is not. Self is the fleeting error of samsara; it is individual separateness and that egotism which begets envy and hatred. Self is the yearning for pleasure and the lust after vanity. Truth is the correct comprehension of things; it is the permanent and everlasting, the real in all existence, the bliss of righteousness.

The existence of self is an illusion, and there is no wrong in this world, no vice, no sin, except what flows from the assertion of self.

The attainment of truth is possible only when self is recognised as an illusion. Righteousness can be practised only when we have freed our mind from the passions of egotism. Perfect peace can dwell only where all vanity has disappeared.

Blessed is he who has understood the dharma. Blessed is he who does no harm to his fellow-beings. Blessed is he who overcomes sin and is free from passion. To the highest bliss has he attained who has conquered all selfishness and vanity. He has become Buddha, the Perfect One, the Blessed One, the Holy One. . . .

Now the Blessed One thought: "To whom shall I preach the doctrine first? My old teachers are dead. They would have received the good news with joy. But my five disciples are still alive. I shall go to them, and to them shall I first proclaim the gospel of deliverance."

At that time the five bhiksus dwelt in the Deer Park at Benares, and the Blessed One not thinking of their unkindness in having left him at a time when he was most in need of their sympathy and help, but mindful only of the services which they had ministered unto him, and pitying them for the austerities which they practised in vain, rose and journeyed to their abode. . . .

The Sermon at Benares

The five bhiksus saw their old teacher approach and agreed among themselves not to salute him, nor to address him as a master, but by his name only. "For," so they said, "he has broken his vow and has abandoned holiness. He is no bhiksu but Gautama, and Gautama has become a man who lives in abundance and indulges in the pleasures of worldliness."

But when the Blessed One approached in a dignified manner, they involuntarily rose from their seats and greeted him in spite of their resolution. Still they called him by his name and addressed him as "friend."

When they had thus received the Blessed One, he said, "Do not call the Tathāgata by his name nor address him 'friend,' for he is Buddha, the Holy One. Buddha looks equally with a kind heart on all living beings and they therefore call him 'Father.' To disrespect a father is wrong; to despise him, is sin.

"The Tathāgata," Buddha continued, "does not seek salvation in austerities, but for that reason you must not think that he indulges in worldly pleasures, nor does he live in abundance. The Tathāgata has found the middle path.

"Neither abstinence from fish or flesh, nor going naked, nor shaving the head, nor wearing matted hair, nor dressing in a rough garment, nor covering oneself with dirt, nor sacrificing to Agni, will cleanse a man who is not free from delusions.

"Reading the Vedas, making offerings to priests, or sacrifices to the gods, self-mortification by heat or cold, and many such penances performed for the sake of immortality, these do not cleanse the man who is not free from delusions.

"Anger, drunkenness, obstinacy, bigotry, deception, envy, self-praise, disparaging others, superciliousness, and evil intentions constitute uncleanness; not verily the eating of flesh.

"Let me teach you, O bhiksus, the middle path, which keeps aloof from both extremes. By suffering, the emaciated devotee produces confusion and sickly thoughts in his mind. Mortification is not conducive even to worldly knowledge; how much less to a triumph over the senses!

"He who fills his lamp with water will not dispel the darkness, and he who tries to light a fire with rotten wood will fail.

"Mortifications are painful, vain, and profitless. And how can any one be free from self by leading a wretched life if he does not succeed in quenching the fires of lust.

"All mortification is vain so long as self remains, so long as self continues to lust after either worldly or heavenly pleasures. But he in whom self has become extinct is free from lust; he will desire neither worldly nor heavenly pleasures, and the satisfaction of his natural wants will not defile him. Let him eat and drink according to the needs of the body.

"Water surrounds the lotus-flower, but does not wet its petals.

"On the other hand, sensuality of all kind is enervating. The sensual man is a slave of his passions, and pleasure-seeking is degrading and vulgar.

"But to satisfy the necessities of life is not evil. To keep the body in good health is a duty, for otherwise we shall not be able to trim the lamp of wisdom, and keep our mind strong and clear.

"This is the middle path, O bhikṣus, that keeps aloof from both extremes."

And the Blessed One spoke kindly to his disciples, pitying them for their errors, and pointing out the uselessness of their endeavors, and the ice of ill-will that chilled their hearts melted away under the gentle warmth of the Master's persuasion.

Now the Blessed One set the wheel of the most excellent law a-rolling, and he began to preach to the five bhikṣus, opening to them the gate of immortality, and showing them the bliss of nirvana.

And when the Blessed One began his sermon, a rapture thrilled through all the universes.

The devas left their heavenly abodes to listen to the sweetness of the truth; the saints that had parted from life crowded around the great teacher to receive the glad tidings; even the animals of the earth felt the bliss that rested upon the words of the Tathāgata; and all the creatures of the host of sentient beings, gods, men, and beasts, hearing the message of deliverance, received and understood it in their own language.

Buddha said:

"The spokes of the wheel are the rules of pure conduct; justice is the uniformity of their length; wisdom is the tire; modesty and thoughtfulness are the hub in which the immovable axle of truth is fixed.

"He who recognises the existence of suffering, its cause, its remedy, and its cessation has fathomed the four noble truths. He will walk in the right path.

"Right views will be the torch to light his way. Right aims will be his guide. Right words will be his dwelling-place on the road. His gait will be straight, for it is right behavior. His refreshments will be the right way of earning his livelihood. Right efforts will be his steps: right thoughts his breath; and peace will follow in his footprints."

And the Blessed One explained the instability of the ego.

"Whatsoever is originated will be dissolved again. All worry about the self is vain; the ego is like a mirage, and all the tribulations that touch it will pass away. They will vanish like a nightmare when the sleeper awakes.

"He who has awakened is freed from fear; he has become Buddha; he knows the vanity of all his cares, his ambitions, and also of his pains.

"It easily happens that a man, when taking a bath, steps upon a wet rope and imagines that it is a snake. Horror will overcome him, and he will shake from fear, anticipating in his mind all the agonies caused by the serpent's venomous bite. What a relief does this man experience when he sees that the rope is no snake. The cause of his fright lies in his error, his ignorance, his illusion. If the true nature of the rope is recognised, his tranquillity of mind will come back to him; he will feel relieved; he will be joyful and happy.

"This is the state of mind of one who has recognised that there is no self, that the cause of all his troubles, cares, and vanities is a mirage, a shadow, a dream.

"Happy is he who has overcome all selfishness; happy is he who has attained peace; happy is he who has found the truth.

"The truth is noble and sweet; the truth can deliver from evil. There is no saviour in the world except the truth.

"Have confidence in the truth, although you may not be able to comprehend it, although you may suppose its sweetness to be bitter, although you may shrink from it at first. Trust in the truth.

"The truth is best as it is. No one can alter it; neither can any one improve it. Have faith in the truth and live it.

"Errors lead astray; illusions beget miseries. They intoxicate like strong drinks; but they fade away soon and leave you sick and disgusted.

"Self is a fever; self is a transient vision, a dream; but truth is wholesome, truth is sublime, truth is everlasting. There is no immortality except in truth. For truth alone abideth forever."

And when the doctrine was propounded, the venerable Kauṇḍinya, the oldest one among the five bhikṣus, discerned the truth with his mental eye, and he said: "Truly, O Buddha, our Lord, thou has found the truth."

And the devas and saints and all the good spirits of the departed generations that had listened to the sermon of the Tathāgata, joyfully received the doctrine and shouted: "Truly, the Blessed One has founded the kingdom of righteousness. The Blessed One has moved the earth; he has set the wheel of Truth rolling, which by no one in the universe, be he god or man, can ever be turned back. The kingdom of Truth will be preached upon earth; it will spread; and righteousness, good-will, and peace will reign among mankind."

8

The Greatest Good for the Greatest Number: The Philosophy of John Stuart Mill

A Lifeboat Example

Like all philosophers do, I am going to place you in a lifeboat out at sea. This happens a lot more often than you think. No, no, not that people are often in lifeboats at sea! Philosophers often place people on lifeboats, at least in their examples. Either philosophers are a notoriously nasty but water-loving bunch, or they use the lifeboat example to isolate possible answers and to bring our intuitions into clearer light—take your pick.

Okay, you're in a lifeboat in the middle of the Pacific Ocean, and your ship has just gone down. This hasn't been a very good day. As the smoke clears, you see three people swimming toward your boat. There's a problem. Your lifeboat is large enough for only two people. There is enough food, water, and space for only one other person. To simplify the example, assume that you cannot sacrifice yourself and also allow two of the people to board your boat. Which person do you allow on the boat? Which two do you let drown?

Perhaps you need more information. Okay, imagine that before your ship went down, you had a chance to get to know all three people. One is a sickly, seventy-year-old scientist who has just discovered the cure to AIDS. She has the formula and process stored away in her head. If she is saved, she will in turn save the lives of perhaps millions. The second person is a healthy, robust twelve-year-old boy. He is not remarkable, nor does he show much promise of living anything but an ordinary life. The third person is an eighty-year-old billionaire. He has been very successful in business and has recently given virtually all of his money to causes that you admire. If he is saved, he has just enough money to live on. (This fact puts out of the question any impulse to save him and get a reward.)

Material in this chapter taken from John Stuart Mill, *Utilitarianism*. Originally published in 1861. Reprinted by Hackett Publishing Company, Indianapolis, IN.

There are several ways to go with this decision. You could save the one who gets to your boat first. That has the appearance of fairness, but it probably discriminates against the older people. By the same token, you may decide to determine who survives by appealing to chance and having them draw straws. (This is a well-stocked lifeboat.) You may believe that it is right to save a life and that the decision must be determined by reasoned impartiality and fairness. If so, then your intuitions follow Immanuel Kant's ideas. (We'll get to Kant in the next discussion.) Kant argues that the outcomes to you or to society are irrelevant to moral decisions. Kant says that you must look at these people as moral equals. Each has to be treated as equally significant. That's another alternative.

A third way to decide is to appeal to the results of your action. And, of course, in our example there are three options. You may be sympathetic to the billionaire. As a moral rule of thumb, it's probably a good idea to reward people for their generosity. The effect of rewards will encourage others to be generous, and that would be socially beneficial. Not much good, however, will come directly from saving an eighty-year-old retiree.

The young boy gets some consideration, of course. Without promise of being socially valuable, however, he doesn't fare well, does he? He has a promise of a longer lifespan than his two companions. But he shows little promise of making a contribution to society. And he hasn't done anything to merit our indebtedness. He has not and probably will not ever give anything special to society.

The scientist has the cure to AIDS. Saving her will lead to millions of lives saved and to many more millions of people being spared the pain of the death of a loved one. She's the most likely candidate, isn't she?

John Stuart Mill tells us to calculate the overall outcome of our moral decisions. How much or how little will society benefit from saving each person? Calculate the probable results of your action, and that is your moral decision. Mill says that proper moral decisions increase the social benefit. If that's the way you decide, too, then your intuitions agree with Mill's analysis of morality.

Should We Always Tell the Truth?

My second example is far simpler. What if you had the chance to tell a lie? The lie will hurt no one and will help many people. Now you may believe that some moral actions have intrinsic worth. That means some actions are always right to perform, no matter what the consequences. Telling the truth may be one example of this type of action. Even if it hurts no one and benefits many people, you may argue that it is wrong to lie. Why? Perhaps people need to know that others will not lie to them. Without this assurance, human communication would be impossible.

Mill believes that actions have no moral worth apart from their consequences. All things being equal, if your lie hurts no one and leads to an increase in pleasure or happiness, then the act of lying is morally justified.

Utilitarianism

With that as an introduction, let's talk to Mill. Let's see if we can understand Mill's point of view in *Utilitarianism*. Mill himself has been kind enough to give us a little bit of his time.

Mr. Mill, welcome. It's generous of you to join us. We're hoping you can help us understand what utilitarianism is and how the theory can be justified.

"Thank you for giving me the opportunity to explain my theory, Art."

Can I start with a question? I don't mean to be disrespectful, but who are you to tell me how I ought to act and live?

The Purpose of the Theory

"Excellent. The way you understand the purpose of my project is important. The theory of utilitarianism is not trying to dictate how we ought to act."

It sure looks that way to me. If that isn't the point, what are you doing in your essay? I thought you were trying to give us a new way of defining right and wrong, and good and bad. Aren't you giving us a new foundation for morality?

"Hardly, Art. I can see why you have that impression, but proposing a new morality is far from my intentions. The institution of morality has been around for thousands of years. The question concerning the foundation of morality has occupied the most gifted intellects. And after more than two thousand years the same discussions continue. Philosophers still find basic disagreement, and neither thinkers nor mankind at large seem nearer to being unanimous on the subject."

But if you are not giving a new foundation of morality, what is the point of your essay?

"Utilitarianism is an attempt to define the foundation of morality. It is an old theory, at least as old as Socrates (470?–399 B.C.E.). Protagoras attributed the theory to Socrates in ancient Athens. So utilitarianism is not a new morality."

Okay, so it isn't new, but why bother worrying about defining the foundation of morality?

"The search for the foundation of morality is the search for a theory that will explain morality. I have made explicit the thread that ties moral judgments."

I'm lost. What do you mean by "explaining morality" and the "thread that ties moral judgments"?

"We need to account for the common underlying principles of our moral judgments. When we look at all our moral judgments, we desire to have a principle or set of principles by which to understand them."

Can you give me a nonmoral example?

"Take the example of gravity, Art. Many objects fall to the ground. Our experience finds nothing unusual in this. Our natural curiosity, however, asks whether or not these falling objects have any principle by which to understand their fall."

Gravity?

"Exactly. The principle or law of gravity describes the fall. A moral theory ought to do the same for moral judgments. It ought to show what common elements moral judgments share."

I think I'm with you.

Accounting for Moral Facts. "It's not so very complicated. We look at the moral judgments that people make. Basically we find two kinds of judgments. First, there are judgments that all or nearly all people agree on. For example, it is wrong to murder innocent people. Or again, offering aid to a person in need is desirable. Of course, there are exceptional circumstances where these principles do not hold."

Okay.

"Second, there are judgments about which we are not so certain. Whether or not abortion or mercy killing is morally permissible is hotly debated. Or again, in a politically free and democratic society, we also contend with striking a balance between free expression on one hand and pornography and erotica on the other. These questions provoke vigorous intellectual warfare among reasonable people of good will."

Huh?

"These issues are open to moral disagreement."

That's why I think morality is just personal bias. You know, morality is relative to each person. There's no theory that will get people to agree on these moral issues.

"It is certainly possible that morality is relative, but I think your conclusion is premature. You have misunderstood moral disagreement and the point of a moral theory."

Moral Disagreement. "Moral disagreement is like any other sort of disagreement. Within every branch of knowledge disagreement is found. That does not make the entire body of knowledge automatically suspect."

Where do you find similar disagreement?

"There are many examples. Examine the natural and the social sciences. In chemistry, well-trained chemists disagree about interpretations of evidence, theoretical points, and many other items. That does not do away with the foundation of chemistry, however. Chemistry does not become a relative and therefore transitory study just because people disagree. Economics is similarly constituted. Economists disagree about the nature and cause of recessions, depressions, and boom times. Their disagreement does not mean that the study of economy is worthless, nor that the results of such study are purely and viciously relative."

So I shouldn't be so concerned about moral differences?

The Point of a Moral Theory

"Right. Now the second misunderstanding. A theory defining the foundation of morality should not force people to conform to it. The theory should account for the facts."

Facts? What facts are there in morality?

"The moral judgments people make are the moral facts that a theory must describe. A theory accounts for these facts. An adequate theory gives us a way of describing the moral judgments people actually make. Where virtually all people agree in their moral judgments, the theory should show near certainty. Where people disagree in their moral judgments, the theory should reflect the disagreement or uncertainty of the moral worth of the action being debated. In so doing, it also sets out the ground rules for acceptable moral debate. Certain types of reasons count; other types of reasons are irrelevant."

So in the case of murdering innocent people, a theory should tell us that the action is wrong. And it's irrelevant that it's Tuesday?

"Exactly. An adequate theory will account for the moral fact that murdering innocent people is wrong. It will also set out circumstances where murder would be acceptable, if there are such cases."

When would murder be morally acceptable?

Offer Priority Rules.   "That's not the point, Art. An adequate moral theory will give priorities to our moral principles. It will accurately reflect what our priorities are and how we arrive at them."

I see. My complaint about the Ten Commandments was that there were no priorities listed in the commandments. So you think your theory can account for moral judgments—and for priority rules when moral principles come in conflict with each other? This I've got to see.

"An adequate theory also reflects the way that people arrive at their conclusions. It must show the real reasoning and moral calculation underlying our moral conclusions. Now that we have a clearer sense about what a moral theory intends to accomplish, let's address the utilitarian theory of morality."

The Foundation of Morality.   Are we going to answer my questions about why I should be moral and what guarantees that morality works?

"Art, you need to slow down. You are asking questions that are not equivalent by any means. I will answer each of your questions in due course. Let's begin with your question about guarantees. I am at a loss to understand what you mean."

My friends and I discussed moral relativism. You know, values seem to vary from person to person, culture to culture, historical period to historical period. Is there any way of discovering the correct principles? Can you show us that your principles are correct and unchanging?

"Are you asking if there are any universally valid moral claims? Yes, there are. People ought to perform actions that lead to good consequences. They ought to avoid actions that lead to bad consequences."

Good and Bad Consequences.   I'm afraid that's not very helpful, Mr. Mill. How do we determine which are the good consequences and which are the bad consequences?

"The highest good is the criterion of right and wrong. The highest good is the foundation of morality. Now, I grant you people have been concerned with these issues for a very long time. As with any pursuit, a clear and precise conception of what we are seeking would seem the first thing we need.

"Each of our actions is directed toward some goal, Art. We may not always be aware of the goal, but a little thought usually reveals it. Here's a modern analogy. If you see someone walk up to a vending machine, put the correct amount of money into the slot, and push a button, you are pretty safe in assuming that the person wants a cold drink. He is thirsty. Watch a little longer and you see the person pick up the can, pop the tab, and drink. This "complicated" set of actions is directed toward a goal, to quench his thirst. The 'foundation' of this action is his motivation or desire. He is thirsty."

How does this give us the criterion of right and wrong? What is the highest good?

"Imagine that our thirsty man goes through the actions we have just described, except that nothing comes out of the machine. He has nothing to drink. His actions did not produce the desired result. If he is like many of us, he will calmly consider his options. I think it's safe to say that he judges the result as bad. First, he will press the coin return."

Right, and when that fails he will strike and then kick the machine. He may even add some colorful language to his actions. Maybe he doesn't realize that vending machines don't listen to people.

"What we have, then, is a man with a goal. His goal is to satisfy his thirst." His desire motivates him to act. The results of his actions are important to him. He judges the consequences of his actions by whether or not they lead to the satisfaction of his desire. If the machine gives him a cold drink, then his actions are 'good' and the machine avoids abuse. If the machine does not provide a drink, then his actions are 'bad.' In this case the evaluation is based on his goal, to satisfy his thirst."

But no one judges his life this way. Your example is trivial.

"Of course, Art. But all action is for the sake of some end. Don't you agree?"

Yes, I agree. People don't act without some goal, even if the goal is not always apparent to them.

What Do All People Want?

"Excellent. The ultimate end of all human action is the standard of morality. Whatever all people want is the basis of morality. Rules of action, the moral rules, take their whole character and color from the end. Whatever we all strive for determines the basis of morality. Whatever satisfies our most basic desire is the foundation."

So what makes an action good?

"You see, Art, it is not the action itself that has value. It is the goals, the consequences of one's actions, that determine whether an action is good or bad. In our analysis, the thirsty man's actions were 'good' when he received the can and drank. His actions were 'bad' when he could not satisfy his thirst. And yet his actions were identical. It is the result of one's actions, therefore, that determines their worth.

Since situations vary, the same action may appear in different lights. It is always the desires and consequences that determine the worth of any action."

The Greatest Happiness Principle

I think I follow you, Mr. Mill. What goal do all people desire? What is the foundation of morality?

"Happiness!"

Wow, big surprise!

"I call this the principle of utility, or the greatest happiness principle. Actions are right in proportion as they tend to promote happiness, wrong as they tend to produce the reverse of happiness. To see how well this principle fits our moral judgments, let's look at some of the examples of moral rules you have already discussed."

Earlier we decided that it is wrong for me to steal.

"Exactly, Art. Stealing is wrong because it produces the reverse of happiness. If you steal from other people, they will be unhappy. So, generally speaking, stealing is wrong."

I know, that's what the readers told me at the beginning of the book.

"You should listen to them, Art."

Does this work with any other example?

"Certainly. It is wrong to murder because the total unhappiness produced outweighs the happiness produced."

Does the happiness of the murderer count?

"Yes, the total happiness produced includes everyone who is affected. Let me give another example."

Why bother?

"An adequate moral theory ought to be certain on moral decisions where we are certain."

Like murder and stealing are wrong?

"Yes. And it should show uncertainty where we are uncertain. Remember, a theory should represent not only our moral decisions. It should also show our ambivalence where that exists in our moral decisions. Where we have contrary decisions, the theory ought to reflect that. It should reflect how we arrive at our decisions."

Yes, I guess it should.

"Then consider the cases of mercy killing, or coming to the aid of a person committing suicide. People of good will differ in their moral judgments. Some say mercy killing is acceptable; others disagree."

What does utilitarianism say?

"The theory is indecisive. The greatest happiness principle reflects what conclusions moral people reach. It also reflects their way of thinking. On an issue like coming to the aid of a person committing suicide, moral people disagree because they cannot agree on how to calculate the total happiness and unhappiness produced."

Interesting point, Mr. Mill.

Happiness Is Pleasure.   I'd like to know what you mean by happiness. If the moral worth of actions is determined by how much happiness they produce, it's important to figure out what happiness is.

"It's just as I've written in my pamphlet, *Utilitarianism*. By happiness is intended pleasure, and the absence of pain; by unhappiness, pain, and the privation of pleasure."

You mean, how much pleasure is intended?

"No, no. By happiness I mean pleasure and the absence of pain."

That's all there is to it? Happiness is pleasure?

"Yes, happiness is pleasure. Pleasure is the only desirable end in itself. Every other activity is directed to produce pleasure."

No offense, Mr. Mill, but this sounds pretty crude.

"How do you mean, Art?"

Is Pleasure Seeking Degrading?   Well, first, you're saying that people strive for pleasure. You're saying that pleasure is the ultimate end. That sounds pretty degrading to—

"To suppose that life has no higher end than pleasure . . . is a doctrine worthy only of swine. Is that the substance of your objection?"

Yes.

"But surely, Art, you have misunderstood. I respond to this misunderstanding just as the Epicureans responded."

That may be, but I'd like you to reply.

"All right. It is not I, but you, who represent human nature in a degrading light. You are the one who supposes that people are capable of no pleasures except those of swine. You assume, when I say pleasure is an ultimate goal of all human action, that I belittle people. It is your assumption about pleasure, however, that diminishes us."

I don't understand.

"You are saying that pleasure alone is not sufficiently dignified for people to pursue as an ultimate goal. To pursue pleasure is vulgar and demeaning. Is that your objection?"

Yes, Mr. Mill, though I wouldn't be able to put it in such fancy language. Pursuing only pleasure is demeaning. At least that's what people tell me.

"An animal's pleasures do not satisfy a human being's conceptions of happiness. I grant you that point. It is precisely this misunderstanding, however, that often leads to a rejection of utilitarianism. Look how erroneous your assumption is. People have the ability to experience pleasures that are beyond animal appetites. We would not consider anything as happiness that does not include gratification of higher pleasures. Human pleasures and animal pleasures differ."

Differences in the Qualities of Pleasures.   How do you mean? What are examples of higher pleasures?

"Some kinds of pleasures are more desirable and more valuable than others. The pleasures of the intellect, of the feelings and imagination, and of moral sentiments are much preferred over mere sensations."

How do we decide which pleasure is higher and which is lower?

"If we present people with two pleasures, the higher pleasure is defined as the one that all or nearly all people will decidedly prefer. I qualify this definition by adding that moral obligation to prefer one pleasure over another cannot enter into the decision of the people."

So if we take a group of people and ask them to decide which of two pleasures they prefer—

"If one of the two is, by those who are competently acquainted with both, placed so far above the other that they prefer it . . . we are justified in ascribing to the preferred enjoyment a superiority in quality."

Hold on. I thought you were offering a kind of democratic way of determining which kinds of pleasures are superior. Why do the judges have to be people "competently acquainted with both" pleasures? It sounds elitist!

"Who could be a fair judge? Only people who have experienced both kinds of pleasures can fairly judge. Once we determine our group of competent judges, then a democratic voice is possible. And remember, Art, I also exclude contamination brought in by any moral obligation to prefer one pleasure to another pleasure."

I'm glad you reminded me. What do you mean by having a moral obligation to prefer one pleasure to another? I thought people's pleasures were pretty much independent of morality.

"Hardly independent. People's desires and pleasures are subject to moral appraisal. Just look at the response you received in the first part of this book! Your pleasures were suspect. They did not conform to the moral norm. My position is that even if we disallow moral obligation, still some pleasures will be judged superior to other pleasures."

Which Pleasures Are Superior?   Which pleasures will be judged superior, do you think?

"Surely the mental pleasures will be preferred to the bodily pleasures."

I'm not so sure. Some of my favorite pleasures involve my physical lusts!

"You may be as outrageous as you like, Art, but your extreme statements do not surprise me. You say you want bodily pleasures and that you prefer these to mental pleasures, do you?"

Absolutely. Your utilitarian theory is a pleasure seeker's dream! As long as I'm allowed to pursue my pleasures, I'm happy. I just don't see any reason for accepting your distinction that pleasures are qualitatively different. You'll need something more compelling than telling me that nearly everyone else prefers one pleasure to another. If I don't prefer the mental pleasures to the physical pleasures, your theory has nothing to say to me.

"Interesting defensive move. But look more closely, Art. Say I offer you a large quantity of lower pleasures. The only stipulation is that you must renounce the higher pleasures. Would you agree?"

Let me get this right. You will guarantee me the lower pleasures, the physical pleasures. All I have to do is give up the higher pleasures? What's the catch?

"There is no catch, as you call it. Would you sacrifice a lifetime of higher pleasures for a lifetime of nothing but the lower pleasures?"

Yes, I think I would.

"Ah, but think about it. In fact, you have the option at any time. All you need to do is have a frontal lobotomy performed on yourself. You would lose your intellectual functions. If I could guarantee that you will be cared for in a pleasant institution, would you forsake your mental capacities? I doubt it. Few people would consent to such a transition.

"Art, no intelligent being would consent to be a fool. . . . no person of feeling and conscience would be selfish and base. Only in extreme circumstances would a person even entertain such thoughts. A being of higher faculties—"

Huh?

"A cultivated person requires more to make him happy, is capable probably of more acute suffering . . . but he can never really wish to sink into what he feels to be a lower grade of existence."

Okay, okay, perhaps you're correct. I need to think about the difference in qualities of pleasures. We are still at the stage of clarifying your theory, anyway. Just let's not forget to return to this.

"Agreed."

Happiness and Contentment.   Even if I grant that I do not want to become an animal, aren't I sacrificing pleasure? And if I am sacrificing pleasure, then according to your theory, I'm sacrificing happiness. What do you say to that?

"To suppose that the superior person is not happier than the inferior person confounds the very different ideas of happiness and contentment."

I'm not sure I see the difference. When my desires are satisfied, that's happiness, isn't it? When I feel contented and peaceful, I'm happy.

"Your description is the happiness of a cow, a contented cow. People are more dignified, and more demanding, than that. I grant you that people do enjoy bodily pleasures. But, we must not confuse satisfaction or contentment on the one hand and happiness on the other hand.

"I have already said it in my little pamphlet. It is better to be a human being dissatisfied than a pig satisfied; better to be a Socrates dissatisfied than a fool satisfied."

Yes, you wrote this passage, but I'm not sure I can agree with it. The fool thinks he is happy. Isn't that good enough? If I think I am happy, then I am happy.

"Not quite. You forget, Art, that people often reflect back on their own past. They said that they were happy then, but now they realize that they were not happy. They thought they were happy, but now they see that they were mistaken."

Maybe that's because what makes them happy now isn't what made them happy then.

"Perhaps that is true in some cases. Many times, however, the person looks at her recent past and recognizes that she was only deceiving herself. Just the fact that that statement makes sense to us shows that we can be mistaken when we say we are happy. Sometimes we mistake happiness for contentment."

Yes, I know that is the distinction you are trying to make, but I still resist it.

A Hierarchy of Needs.   "Then let me try another tack. In your own century there is a psychologist named Abraham Maslow."

You've read Maslow's work? This is becoming a religiously spooky book. First I resurrect you, then I find out you've been reading all these years.

"Art, reading is a great pleasure for me, but don't get carried away. This whole dialogue is just a thought experiment on your part. Let's get back to my point.

Which is what?

"Maslow argues from his observations that there is a hierarchy of needs. Each person climbs the ladder of needs, each in pretty much the same order as every other person."

What is the point of the hierarchy?

"Maslow defines mental health in terms of ascending to the top. He calls the mentally healthy person self-actualizing. The hierarchy of needs begins with the physiological needs. These are the biological survival needs. Once these needs have been met, other, higher needs emerge. We have safety needs, the need to belong, to love and to be loved, to have self-esteem and esteem from others, the desires to know and to understand, and, finally, aesthetic needs."

Are you telling me that people need to read and to study?

"According to Maslow's theory of motivation, the desire to learn is basic to human nature."

I don't experience that desire in a very strong way.

"That may indicate that your other, lower needs have not been sufficiently addressed. Higher needs emerge only after lower needs have been satisfied."

So what you are calling contentment is satisfying the lower, bodily needs?

"Yes. Happiness is a more dignified, higher aspiration. What Maslow has hit upon substantiates my distinction. People are not happy until they experience the higher pleasures."

Monotony or Activity?   Can you give me an example?

"Which life would you rather live, a life of monotonous assembly-line work or a life like Leonardo Da Vinci's?"

Lots of people work on assembly lines and they're happy, aren't they?

"Imagine that you are locked into a life where you have to repeat the same simple action over and over."

Wait, I think I've lived that job. One summer I worked in a meat-packing plant. (I really did.) I was a wiener stringer. What I did every day was string hot dogs. Hot dogs would come out of a cooking machine in endless strings. The stringer stood on a metal grate platform about eighteen inches off the floor. As the hot dogs came out of the machine, I would have to reach up, take the string off a hook, count five hot dogs down the string, and place the wieners across a metal bar in front of me. Then I'd cut the string to leave ten wieners hanging on the bar, five on either side. Then I'd start the whole process again. When there were twenty strings of hot dogs on a bar, I would move the bar to a rack, replace it with another bar, and start the process again. Ten hot dogs to a string, twenty strings to a bar, twenty bars to a rack, start again. On a normal eight-hour shift, I'd string 160,000 hot dogs.

"Excellent example. Now imagine—"

I'm not through. The job was even worse because they placed me in an alcove where I could see only the rack I was working on, the metal wall of the machine behind me, and two blank brick walls close by on either side. The place was hot, damp, and boring.

"I understand, Art. This experience has left its mark on you. And that serves my point. Imagine just this job, but exaggerate it. Imagine that you have to perform this task for your entire waking life."

No way! I used to shudder when I had to work two hours overtime.

"Compare this life to a life like Da Vinci's. He was a man of incredibly diversified interests and talents. He was an artist, a scientist, an engineer, a mathematician, and a naturalist. He possessed many other talents. Imagine that your family and social life are rich and rewarding, that you enjoy health, and that your wealth is sufficient to allow you to enjoy leisure time. Would a life of such diverse and higher interests be more fulfilling than a life of monotony and boredom?"

Maybe, but your comparison isn't fair. You grant your Da Vinci character all the higher and the lower pleasures. But you begrudge the assembly-line worker even the lower pleasures. I know what you're going to say. You are willing to give the worker the lower pleasures, right?

"Yes, that would make the example appropriate."

Appropriate, but still unfair. All you have shown is that a life of lower and higher pleasures is preferable to a life of lower pleasures alone.

Is the Life of Higher Pleasure Preferred to a Life of Lower Pleasure?   "I think we have entered into the criticism part of our discussion. Very well, let's entertain objections. You are questioning whether a life of higher pleasures is to be preferred to a life of lower pleasures."

I am questioning your distinction and your way of arriving at it. You say that people who experience both kinds of pleasures nearly always choose one (the higher) over the other (the lower). But that just doesn't fit the facts. Lots of times when I am offered a lower pleasure and a higher pleasure, I choose the lower. Sometimes it just depends on my mood.

"For example?"

For example, when I have been reading or studying for a few hours, and a friend comes by and suggests we go out to get something to eat, I often put aside my reading and go. I forego my higher pleasure for a lower pleasure. I prefer a burger and fries to a good book. And before you reply, let me add that I usually prefer a burger and fries to a good book. The only reason I'm reading the book is because I am supposed to read it. But if we strip away any moral obligation to read and study, then I think I might always choose the lower pleasure. Now it's your turn.

Temptations.   "Under the influence of temptation, people occasionally postpone the higher pleasures to the lower. People often, from infirmity of character, make their election for the nearer good, though they know it to be the less valuable."

Hold on, Mr. Mill. First you tell me that the estimation of two competing pleasures is determined by people who have experienced both. You claim that nearly all people place one pleasure above the other. The determination of the clear majority determines the relative merit of a pleasure. Now you are telling me that people *often* make their choice for the lower pleasure and forsake the higher pleasure.

"It is caused by infirmity of character. A character unschooled in self-discipline will often gravitate to the lower pleasures."

You can't have it both ways. How can the majority decide which pleasure is more valuable yet continue to seek the less valuable pleasure?

"People pursue sensual indulgences to the injury of health, though perfectly aware that health is the greater good. In your time, people smoke cigarettes, drink alcohol to excess, and use other dangerous drugs. They know full well that they are pursuing the lower, closer pleasure. Even when they choose the lower pleasure, they are aware of the qualitative differences in pleasures. They are simply too weak of character to restrain themselves. So you see, the qualitative distinctions between pleasures still holds.

"Of course, Art, there is another category of people who seek the lesser pleasures. The capacity for the nobler feelings is in most natures a very tender plant, easily killed, not only by hostile influences, but by mere want of sustenance. For far too many people, perhaps the majority of young people, it speedily dies away."

So the majority of people are unable to enjoy the higher pleasures?

"I am afraid so. People do not have the time or the opportunity for developing and pursuing the higher pleasures. They addict themselves to inferior pleasures, not because they deliberately prefer them, but because they are either the only ones to which they have access or the only ones which they are any longer capable of enjoying."

Are you saying that the majority of people are idiots?

"Of course the majority of people are not idiots. But the majority does lack the opportunity to cultivate and entertain the higher pleasures. Most people are so caught up in making a living, or pursuing their careers and educational goals, that they are unable to develop their capacities for the higher pleasures. When you are tired from working or studying, you are less likely to engage in the superior activities."

I guess so.

"Further, we must be careful to note that this all-too-common transition to indolence and selfishness is not voluntary. Devoting oneself solely to one goal renders a person incapable of the other."

I don't understand.

"Pursuing school and career opportunities with the kind of focused drive required for success is too much. People who are driven to succeed in these occupations lose the ability to experience the nobler feelings. Single-minded drive for a career goal, or for wealth, is just that, single minded. Capacity for the higher pleasures is forfeited."

Morality Is Not the Pursuit of My (Higher) Pleasures!   So where does this leave us, Mr. Mill? Say I accept the qualitative distinction between higher and lower pleasures. And I accept the distinction between happiness and contentment. Now what? Is your theory saying that as long as I pursue the higher pleasures, then I am moral?

"Not quite. The utilitarian standard is not the agent's own greatest happiness, but the greatest amount of happiness altogether. As between his own happiness and that of others, utilitarianism requires him to be as strictly impartial as a disinterested and benevolent spectator."

Hold on. Your theory sounded pretty compelling when I thought it was *my* happiness I was pursuing. I was even willing to acknowledge that the intellectual pleasures are higher than the bodily pleasures. But now you tell me that it is not my pleasures, but everyone else's, that I have to produce?

"That's right. Your pleasures count, too, of course. However, utilitarianism requires you to count yourself as one among many equals. Everyone concerned receives equal weight. This is not peculiar to the utilitarian standard of right, it is what is demanded by morality. Why should this revelation shock you? I assumed all along that you were aware of it."

I feel deceived. Sorry, Mr. Mill, but your theory lacks incentive. Why should I bother concerning myself with everyone else's benefit?

"Because, Art, the nobler, more social pleasures are yours whenever you concern yourself with others. Since these are among the higher pleasures, you bring happiness to yourself whenever you bring benefit to others in your community. The sense of community itself is a reward."

Does this requirement mean that I am bound to do what is best for everyone? It sounds like it demands that I put my own happiness on hold and that I act in a special way for friends. Do I have to calculate the impact of my actions as they apply to the entire human race? And to animals? Is that what impartiality means?

"The great majority of good actions are intended not for the benefit of the world, but for that of individuals. Only public benefactors, like congressional representatives and judges, are held to account for their actions in terms of public utility. In every other case, the interest or happiness of some few persons is all one has to attend to."

Classes of Actions and the General Rule. So I can pretty much do what I want as long as I don't intend to bring pain to people close to me?

"Yes and no. You see there are certain actions you might perform that would have no ill effects in your particular case but from which you should abstain."

Why? I thought you just said that I could act any way I want as long as my actions are not intended to cause pain to those around me!

"It would be unworthy of an intelligent agent not to be consciously aware that the action is of a class which, if practiced generally, would be generally injurious, and that this is the ground of the obligation to abstain from it."

Huh?

"You cannot do whatever you want in particular cases, even when your actions bring pleasure to those around you."

Even if I create higher pleasures?

"Even then. Certain types of actions should be avoided as a general rule. What might be immediately useful may have adverse social effects."

For example?

Lying Is Wrong. "Deviation from truth weakens the trustworthiness of human assertion, which is . . . the principle support of all present social well-being. More than any one thing, untrustworthiness keeps back civilization . . . and everything upon which human happiness on the largest scale depends. Therefore, it is wrong to lie."

Are you telling me that I should not lie because my lie will bring civilization to its knees? My little lie!

"I do not want to exaggerate your importance, but lying weakens the social fabric. Therefore, utilitarians make it a general principle that lying is morally wrong."

Why? Because my particular lie is so important? Doubtful. Is it because I am such a pillar of society that everyone uses me as a role model. Wow, I can just see it now. People will say to their kids, "Look at Art, Johnny. He's such a fine example. Do whatever he does." Is that what you're saying?

"Of course not. Utilitarians suggest that as a general rule lying is not permitted. It is not because you are an exemplary specimen of virtue. If you do not mind my being blunt, in your particular case, Art, that is certainly not true. Even in your case, however, it is useful and socially important to cultivate a sense of the importance of truth telling."

Let me get this right. I have to be impartial like a benevolent spectator. Yet it's okay for me to restrict the calculation of the effects of my actions to a small group. But when I want to lie to someone in this small group, you tell me that I shouldn't lie because it will make the world a terrible mess. Do you wonder why I am confused by you moralists!

"Art, the waters of morality are difficult to fathom."

What does that mean?

"Morality is a complex business. You are expecting more precision than you are likely to get. For example, in the case of our present discussion, there are even exceptions."

You're kidding, right? I don't mean to be disrespectful, but this is beyond confusing.

"Even the rule against lying admits of exceptions by *all* moralists. If withholding some fact would save an individual from great and unmerited evil, then lying is acceptable. Of course, we want to prevent the exception from extending itself."

Of course. I know you have an example. You probably think it's acceptable to keep bad news from a person who is dangerously ill.

"Think for a moment. Say your Uncle Charlie is dreadfully ill. He is lying on his deathbed with no more than a few days of life left. He asks you to bend close to him. You do. He asks you if the mail has arrived. He is anxious to hear whether or not his manuscript has been accepted by a publisher. It is his life's ambition. In this circumstance, it may be morally permissible to withhold the fact that a letter of rejection came in the day's mail."

Morality is a messy business. I guess I just don't see how we are to distinguish an important lie from an acceptable lie.

"Agreed. The limits must be defined. I am confident that the principle of utility can outweigh the conflicting utilities."

Utilitarian Morality Is Vague

It just looks to me that morality is incredibly vague. What I perceived as a strength of your system is that it answers every moral question. Your system has only one principle, so there is no need for priorities, and it is relatively easy to apply. Just calculate the amount of happiness and act accordingly. But now the merits appear very different to me.

"How is that?"

Your utilitarian theory is the same as the Golden Rule.

"I acknowledge that. In the Golden Rule of Jesus of Nazareth we read the complete spirit of the ethics of utility. I consider that to be a strength, Art."

The same defect that applies to the Golden Rule applies to your system. Although it appears to be straightforward and simple, there is no way to know how to apply it. In actual cases, the values become vague and indefinite. The conclusion of my moral calculation depends more on how I interpret the situation than on morality.

Let's use your example. Do I lie to Uncle Charlie or don't I? On one level, I admit that lying to people leads to undesirable consequences. It is tempting to think, though, that in the case of poor Uncle Charlie, no harm, and a great deal of happiness, will be created by lying to him. This is confusing. Do I lie or do I crush his dreams? I think my objection can be put in different terms.

"Proceed."

Knowledge of the Future

I know it isn't exactly fair to criticize a dead guy, because you can't really reply. But here's the problem I have with your system. You suggest that consequences are what determine whether or not an action is morally acceptable. But this is unfair.

"In what ways?"

Well, you expect too much of people. How can anyone know what the future will bring? How can anyone know what will actually happen as a result of one's own action?

"Morality is not an exacting science, that's certain. Why would we expect more certainty than is available to our natures as human beings?"

That may be, but let me give you an example. Imagine that there was a guy named Fritz who lived in a small town. Now Fritz is a happy person, and he wants to share his happiness. He has two unmarried friends. Both are shy, but Fritz knows that they have a lot in common. So he arranges a blind date for them.

"This seems like an admirable action."

The couple dates, becomes engaged, and finally marries. We might even imagine that Fritz is the best man at the wedding. Several years later, the couple has a child, little Adolph. Adolph grows up to lead the world into the most violent and destructive war in human history.

"Causing mass destruction and pain is certainly morally blameworthy, to be sure. How is this a problem for utilitarianism?"

It's not Adolph's actions that I am pointing to, but Fritz's actions. Should we hold Fritz responsible for Hitler's actions? After all, if it wasn't for Fritz and the blind date, Hitler would not have been born. Surely we can't blame Fritz for World War II.

Contributing Causes

I know you don't actually take up this question in your writing, but could you speculate how a utilitarian might answer?

"Very well. There are two types of response. A utilitarian would reply that a person's actions may be a necessary but not sufficient cause for events in the world."

Huh?

"Take your example of Fritz. Of course, it is unlikely that Hitler would have been born had it not been for Fritz. This assumes that Hitler's parents would not have met under other circumstances, and so on. Let's say this is so unlikely as to be impossible. Still, even though introducing the two was necessary for Hitler to have been born, it was not significant enough to hold Fritz totally blameworthy for World War II."

Is one option to hold people accountable only to the degree that their actions have an effect on the consequences? That sounds pretty difficult to calculate. It also sounds like you are taking virtually all responsibility away from people.

"How does that follow?"

I can be held responsible only to the degree that my actions contribute to an event, right? Aren't my actions also events, with causes of their own? Therefore, a utilitarian who uses this strategy has to trace the causes of my actions and intentions. It wasn't my fault, my Uncle Charlie taught Fritz to be a caring, considerate romantic. So Uncle Charlie is also to blame? Perhaps this is true, but then human responsibility becomes meaningless. What is the other utilitarian reply?

Three Types of Consequences

"A utilitarian would distinguish three kinds of consequences by asking three questions. First, what actually happened as a result of this action? Second, what was intended to happen as a result of this action? Third, what consequences were reasonable to expect as a result of this action?

"The moral worth of the action itself must be determined by the actual results, by what actually happened. We can see that people's intuitions agree with this reasoning. Ultimately, we see what actually happens before we render final moral judgment. If events go in an unanticipated and unintended direction, we feel upset, though rarely guilty. Of course, it would be unnecessarily harsh to judge people on this first standard, by the actual consequences of their actions.

"The moral worth of the action can also be determined by the intended results. However, although this option is appealing, it is inadequate."

Why is that? Why shouldn't we judge a person's actions by intended consequences?

"One may intend to perform a good action but misunderstand the implication of the consequences. For example, a person may wish to save a village from being overtaken by the enemy. With that end in mind, he may decide to destroy the village in order to save it."

But that would bring more pain than pleasure, and it's likely to bring even more pain than the feared capture of the village.

"Agreed. The intended result may be praiseworthy, but the strategy is too extreme. Therefore, intended consequences are inappropriate ways of judging actions. Intentions, however, do indicate the moral quality of one's character.

"The moral worth of actions should be determined by what is reasonable to expect as the result of one's action. This provision takes care of your difficulty with Fritz. It is reasonable to believe that bringing two people together is desirable. It is not reasonable to believe that such an action will result in a world war or the deaths of tens of millions of people. Therefore, Fritz's action was praiseworthy because his reasonable expectation was for more pleasure than pain to be a result of his action."

I agree with you, but I am becoming increasingly suspicious of your system. Now you say that moral worth is not based on the actual consequences. Moral worth is determined by the consequences that could be reasonably expected.

"Yes. Actions are judged by what could be reasonably expected to be a result. The action itself is evaluated according to the actual consequences, by the amount of pleasure and pain created."

Two judgments? One for the actor, or agent as you call him, and one for the action? And you wonder why I'm confused!

Integrity

I have another question. How does integrity fit in?

"Integrity is traditionally construed as a positive character trait. Why would you expect utilitarianism to differ from this assessment?"

Say I am eligible to vote and I am registered. I calculate that it is reasonable to expect desirable consequences to come from voting. So I am morally obligated to vote in the upcoming election.

"Yes, that is sound."

Great. My problem is that I disapprove of both candidates. Neither has the personal characteristics or the experience to be qualified to hold an important office. I am forced, yet again, to vote for the "lesser of two evils." Where is the integrity in that? I have to endorse a candidate who is unqualified, or worse. According to your system, my action is praiseworthy because the reasonably expected results are better than the alternative. But sometimes the alternative is distasteful. What is so noble about choosing the poison that kills you?

Justice

I have another objection, Mr. Mill. Your system of morality overlooks justice. I think it is unjust to sacrifice innocent people, even if it is for the greater good.

"Do you have an example?"

Certainly. What if someone suggests that we harvest the organs of healthy people in order to save many more people? For example, we have a perfectly healthy twenty-five year old. Not only is this guy healthy, but he works at it. He exercises every day. He doesn't smoke cigarettes. He does not use any drug stronger than aspirin, and even those only reluctantly. He never drinks. (Now that I think of it, perhaps he should be killed to save him from a life of noble boredom.) Would it be right to harvest his organs in order to save twenty people's lives?

You don't have to answer. I can make the example even more compelling. We can imagine that the twenty people we can save are all valuable, contributing members of society. Poor Joe Healthy doesn't have much time for contributing to society. He's too busy being healthy. Your system of morality says we should promote the greatest good for the greatest number. But sacrificing poor, innocent Joe is unjust.

"My reply is that we all acknowledge that justice is an essential characteristic in any society. Because it is socially advantageous to have just institutions, your example, Joe, would be safe. We could argue that it does more harm to society to abridge justice and to place innocent people in jeopardy than it does to save the lives of contributing members of society. For everyone to live in a just society is a higher pleasure than saving the lives of any number of people. The superiority in quality so far outweighs quantity as to render it, in comparison, of small account."

Rule Utilitarianism

Again your position is vague and indefinite. Every time I come up with what seems to be a telling criticism, you incorporate it into your system. From a theoretical point of view, it's great. But in practice, it leaves me not knowing what to do.

"For the people who have neither the training nor the time to calculate consequences, there are rules received by society. We do not expect people to be inactive until they can determine the appropriate behavior. They have the combined learning of the human species. That is why we have general rules of conduct."

Vessels of Experience

Okay, let me ask a few other questions. I think these are objections. Doesn't the utilitarian theory make me calculate how much pleasure is likely to be produced by my actions?

"Don't forget to factor in quality of pleasures."

Fair enough. When faced with a moral decision, I simply calculate how much of the higher and lower pleasures are going to come from my actions. What bothers me is that this makes everyone just a vessel of experience. People lose their humanity when I calculate consequences in this way. Or have I misunderstood?

"Evidently, Art, you are not listening quite carefully enough. Your complaint, also raised by others, is that many utilitarians look on the morality of actions and do not lay sufficient emphasis on the other beauties of character which go toward making a human being lovable and admirable. I have already admitted this. Utilitarians who have cultivated their moral feelings, but not their sympathies, nor their artistic perceptions, do fall into this mistake; and so do all other moralists under the same conditions."

I'm sorry I haven't been more attentive. So far you have been extraordinary in your ability to anticipate my questions, but sometimes my questions do not follow the order of your presentation.

"A little more care should remedy that."

Perhaps, but my present question still remains. Telling me that other moral theories also fail to develop a fuller sense of other people does not satisfy me. You see, Mr. Mill, I have not accepted any moral description of morality. It isn't that your description of morality is inadequate. Quite the contrary! You're probably right. But knowing more about morality only shows me how undesirable it is to be moral.

But perhaps we should let our audience take a break. Thank you for visiting with us.

"It has been interesting speaking with you, Art. If nothing else, your resurrection machine is a work of genius."

You know it's just an imaginary device. There is no genius in it.

"Precisely."

Summary of Discussion

Utilitarianism states that the right action to perform is the one that creates the most good as a consequence. Mill says that happiness is defined by all people as the chief good. So the right action is the one that promotes the greatest amount of happiness (or minimizes the greatest amount of unhappiness). Any action can create some happiness and some unhappiness. Mill says that a person can calculate the net amount of happiness produced by any action and then can compare actions based on their results. Actions that result in a greater amount of happiness (or in less unhappiness) have more moral worth than actions that promise relatively less happiness.

What does Mill mean by happiness? By happiness he means pleasure, or the absence of pain. By unhappiness he means the reverse. So far, so good. Rather than degenerating into a crude pleasure-seeking way of thinking, Mill suggests two other conditions on moral actions. First, the pleasures and pains one considers must apply to all the people affected by the action. That way, one does not necessarily get to do whatever one wants. Morality demands that we consider other people as much as we consider ourselves.

Second, Mill distinguishes pleasures according to their quality. Superior pleasures are those that people select when they have a choice between two or more pleasures. Mill argues that superior pleasures are to be preferred to inferior pleasures. In saying this, he avoids defining morality as mere pleasure seeking by the majority. Superior pleasures might include intelligent conversation, appreciating works of art, and so on. What Mill suggests is that moral people are not crude pleasure seekers. However, Mill does not make the mistake of thinking that pleasures are not important in moral living.

There are both advantages and disadvantages to Mill's understanding of morality. One distinct advantage is that Mill accurately describes how we arrive at moral decisions. As moral people, we do calculate the amount and types of pleasures and pains that our actions produce. Because of this, morality demands that we calculate all people's happiness into our moral decisions. The ends may justify the means, but they must be the ends as they affect everyone involved.

Mill's analysis also permits priority rules to be set up. Whatever produces the greatest good takes priority over alternatives. In this way Mill can explain moral disagreements, and he can remedy them.

A possible weakness of Mill's understanding of morality is that he places too much emphasis on consequences. Consequences are not always easy to foresee. Mill also underestimates the importance of intentions. Imagine that I intend to cause a great deal of pain but that I am socially inept. My actions may not reflect my intentions. Mill's theory evaluates actions but fails to concern itself sufficiently with a person's character.

Accounting for justice is another apparent weakness in Mill's theory. The same may be said for other moral "absolutes." For example, lying may be permissible so long as the greatest happiness results. Finally, Mill's notion of other people is a problem. Other people appear to be valued only for their social worth. We relate to them morally as though they were vessels of experience.

Discussion Highlights

I. Mill endorses the greatest happiness principle
    1. All actions receive their worth from the consequences (or goals or ends) they create.

   2. Everyone ought to act in a way that produces the greatest good for the greatest number.

   3. Happiness is the ultimate good sought by all people.
   a. happiness is defined either as pleasure
   b. or as the absence of pain

   4. There are differences in the qualities of pleasures.
   a. higher and lower pleasures are determined by those people who have experienced both
   b. virtually no amount of a lower pleasure equals the worth of any amount of a higher pleasure

II. Strengths of utilitarianism
   1. Utilitarianism mirrors our method of moral reasoning.
   2. It offers priority rules.
   3. It solves every moral problem by weighing the pleasures and pains produced by one's possible actions.
   4. It explains moral disagreements.

III. Criticisms
   1. Application of utilitarian principles is difficult.
   2. Justice may be sacrificed by concern for the greatest happiness of the greatest number.
   3. Utilitarianism reduces people to their social worth.
   4. Utilitarianism reduces people to "vessels of experiences" of pleasure or pain.
   5. Utilitarianism demands an unrealistic knowledge of future consequences.

Questions For Thought/Paper Topics

As you criticize Mill, remember the V-8 principle and Mill's reply.

1. Should Congress make utilitarian decisions? Would it be fulfilling our wishes by creating the greatest happiness for the greatest number? Should the court system also make its decisions based on utilitarianism? What would happen to minority rights?

2. Does Mill's theory justify some lies? Are you justified in lying to a loved one if your lie will save that person some pain? Do you mind that your elected officials and the press routinely lie to you?

3. Apparently Mill defines other people according to their social worth, as bearers of rights, and as "vessels of experiences." How does Mill define the individual person who is making moral decisions? How are you as a moral decision maker different from other people?

4. Are any values absolute? Which values would you be willing to endorse even if they did not produce the greatest happiness for the greatest number?

5. Does Mill's explanation of morality let people relate to each other in an intimate way? Does morality promote people being in touch with each other?

6. Mill suggests that the happiness of the greatest number should be my motivation for acting. Why should I agree to this?

7. Remember that pen I stole? Is my action immoral if no one is adversely affected?
8. Is there any room for freedom in Mill's explanation of morality?

For Further Reading

There are three short works by Mill you might want to read. *Utilitarianism* (Hackett, 1979) is the one we have been talking to Mill about. Mill also wrote a short book, *On Liberty* (Hackett, 1978) about the limits of power that a society can rightly exercise over an individual. He argues for extensive individual freedom and that giving freedom will benefit society. A selection from *On Liberty* follows. Mill offers another insightful discussion in *The Subjection of Women* (Hackett, 1988). If you want to look at recent discussion of utilitarianism, look at Dan Brock's essay, "Recent Work in Utilitarianism," *American Philosophical Quarterly* 10, 1973. Finally, there is a compact discussion of Utilitarianism in Louis Pojman's book, *Ethics: Discovering Right and Wrong* (Wadsworth, 1990).

Introduction to *On Liberty*

JOHN STUART MILL

In the following selection from another of his works, Mill applies his theory to the social question of the limits that society can rightly place on the individual. Mill fears that democracy allows a "tyranny of the majority" against the minority or against the individual person, and he argues strenuously for allowing the greatest amount of individual differences as practicable. Mill urges us to allow complete freedom in thought and opinion, in spoken and written word; the sole restriction that should be placed on any person's actions is to prevent harm to others. The only part of a person's conduct that can rightly be subjected to social scrutiny is that which concerns others. How does this argument fit in with Mill's insistence that the greatest good for the greatest number should be our only criterion of right action? Mill appeals to "utility in the largest sense, grounded on the permanent interests of man as a progressive being."

As you read this selection, give Mill credit for formulating a unique and consistent idea. Try to figure out not only his reasons for promoting absolute liberty of conscience and tastes, but also what he has in mind by our "permanent interests." What could he mean by labeling people as "progressive beings"? He does say that his principles of liberty apply only to people who can be improved by free and equal discussion. Is there a connection?

What makes this essay provocative is that Mill appears to be arguing for the collective interest in our discussion of the principle of the greatest good for the greatest number. Here Mill champions the individual, advocating the greatest amount of freedom for experimentation in living. Yet he insists his argument is based on utility, on the greatest good.

THE SUBJECT OF THIS ESSAY is not the so-called "liberty of the will," so unfortunately opposed to the misnamed doctrine of philosophical necessity; but civil, or social liberty: the nature and limits of the power which can be legitimately exercised by society over the individual. A question seldom stated, and hardly ever discussed in general terms, but which profoundly influences the practical controversies of the age by its latent presence, and is likely soon to make itself recognized as the vital question of the future. It is so far from being new that, in a certain sense, it has divided mankind almost from the remotest ages; but in the stage of progress into which the more civilized portions of the species have now entered, it presents itself under new conditions and requires a different and more fundamental treatment.

The struggle between liberty and authority is the most conspicuous feature in the portions of history with which we are earliest familiar, particularly in that of Greece, Rome, and England. But in old times this context was between subjects, or some classes of subjects, and the government. By liberty was meant protection against the tyranny of the political rulers. The rulers were conceived (except in some of the popular governments of Greece) as in a necessarily antagonistic position to the people whom they ruled. They consisted of a governing One, or a governing tribe or caste, who derived their authority from inheritance or conquest, who, at all events, did not hold it at the pleasure of the governed, and whose supremacy men did not venture, perhaps did not desire, to contest, whatever precautions might be taken against its oppressive exercise. Their power was regarded as necessary, but also as highly dangerous; as a weapon which they would attempt to use against their subjects, no less than against external enemies. To prevent the weaker members of the community from being preyed upon by innumerable vultures, it was needful that there should be an animal of prey stronger than the rest, commissioned to keep them down. But as the king of the vultures would be no less bent upon preying on the flock than any of the minor harpies, it was indispensable to be in a perpetual attitude of defense against his beak and claws. The aim, therefore, of patriots was to set limits to the power which the ruler should be suffered to exercise over the community; and this limitation was what they meant by liberty. It was attempted in two ways. First, by obtaining a recognition of certain immunities, called political liberties or rights, which it was to be regarded as a breach of duty in the ruler to infringe, and which if he did infringe, specific resistance or general rebellion was held to be justifiable. A second, and generally a later, expedient was the establishment of constitutional checks by which the consent of the community, or of a body of some sort, supposed to represent its interests, was made a necessary condition to some of the more important acts of the governing power. To the first of these modes of limitation, the ruling power, in most European countries, was compelled, more or less, to submit. It was not so with the second; and, to attain this, or, when already in some degree possessed, to attain it more completely, became everywhere the principal object of the lovers of liberty. And so long

From John Stuart Mill, *Utilitarianism* (1861).

as mankind were content to combat one enemy by another, and to be ruled by a master on condition of being guaranteed more or less efficaciously against his tyranny, they did not carry their aspirations beyond this point.

A time, however, came, in the progress of human affairs, when men ceased to think it a necessity of nature that their governors should be an independent power opposed in interest to themselves. It appeared to them much better that the various magistrates of the state should be their tenants or delegates, revocable at their pleasure. In that way alone, it seemed, could they have complete security that the powers of government would never be abused to their disadvantage. By degrees this new demand for elective and temporary rulers became the prominent object of the exertions of the popular party wherever any such party existed, and superseded, to a considerable extent, the previous efforts to limit the power of rulers. As the struggle proceeded for making the ruling power emanate from the periodical choice of the ruled, some persons began to think that too much importance had been attached to the limitation of the power itself. *That* (it might seem) was a resource against rulers whose interests were habitually opposed to those of the people. What was now wanted was that the rulers should be identified with the people, that their interest and will should be the interest and will of the nation. The nation did not need to be protected against its own will. There was no fear of its tyrannizing over itself. Let the rulers be effectually responsible to it, promptly removable by it, and it could afford to trust them with power of which it could itself dictate the use to be made. Their power was but the nation's own power, concentrated and in a form convenient for exercise. This mode of thought, or rather perhaps of feeling, was common among the last generation of European liberalism, in the Continental section of which it still apparently predominates. Those who admit any limit to what a government may do, except in the case of such governments as they think ought not to exist, stand out as brilliant excep-

tions among the political thinkers of the Continent. A similar tone of sentiment might by this time have been prevalent in our country if the circumstances which for a time encouraged it had continued unaltered.

But, in political and philosophical theories as well as in persons, success discloses faults and infirmities which failure might have concealed from observation. The notion that the people have no need to limit their power over themselves might seem axiomatic, when popular government was a thing only dreamed about, or read of as having existed at some distant period of the past. Neither was that notion necessarily disturbed by such temporary aberrations as those of the French Revolution, the worst of which were the work of a usurping few, and which, in any case, belonged, not to the permanent working of popular institutions, but to a sudden and convulsive outbreak against monarchical and aristocratic despotism. In time, however, a democratic republic came to occupy a large portion of the earth's surface and made itself felt as one of the most powerful members of the community of nations, and elective and responsible government became subject to the observations and criticisms which wait upon a great existing fact. It was now perceived that such phrases as "self-government," and "the power of the people over themselves," do not express the true state of the case. The "people" who exercise the power are not always the same people with those over whom it is exercised; and the "self-government" spoken of is not the government of each by himself, but of each by all the rest. The will of the people, moreover, practically means the will of the most numerous or the most active *part* of the people—the majority, or those who succeed in making themselves accepted as the majority; the people, consequently, *may* desire to oppress a part of their number, and precautions are as much needed against this as against any other abuse of power. The limitation, therefore, of the power of government over individuals loses none of its importance when the holders of power are regularly accountable to the community, that is, to the strongest party therein. This view of things, recommending itself equally to the intelligence of thinkers and to the inclination of those important classes in European society to whose real or supposed interests democracy is adverse, has had no difficulty in establishing itself; and in political speculations "the tyranny of the majority" is now generally included among the evils against which society requires to be on its guard.

Like other tyrannies, the tyranny of the majority was at first, and is still vulgarly, held in dread, chiefly as operating through the acts of the public authorities. But reflecting persons perceived that when society is itself the tyrant—society collectively over the separate individuals who compose it—its means of tyrannizing are not restricted to the acts which it may do by the hands of its political functionaries. Society can and does execute its own mandates; and if it issues wrong mandates instead of right, or any mandates at all in things with which it ought not to meddle, it practices a social tyranny more formidable than many kinds of political oppression, since, though not usually upheld by such extreme penalties, it leaves fewer means of escape, penetrating much more deeply into the details of life, and enslaving the soul itself. Protection, therefore, against the tyranny of the magistrate is not enough; there needs protection also against the tyranny of the prevailing opinion and feeling, against the tendency of society to impose, by other means than civil penalties, its own ideas and practices as rules of conduct on those who dissent from them; to fetter the development and, if possible, prevent the formation of any individuality not in harmony with its ways, and compel all characters to fashion themselves upon the model of its own. There is a limit to the legitimate interference of collective opinion with individual independence; and to find that limit, and maintain it against encroachment, is as indispensable to a good condition of human affairs as protection against political despotism.

But though this proposition is not likely to be contested in general terms, the practical question where to place the limit—how to make the fitting adjustment between individual independence and social control—is a subject on which nearly everything remains to be done. All that makes existence valuable to anyone depends on the enforcement of restraints upon the actions of other people. Some rules of conduct, therefore, must be imposed—by law in the first place, and by opinion on many things which are not fit subjects for the operation of law. What these rules should be is the principal question in human affairs; but if we except a few of the most obvious cases, it is one of those which least progress has been made in resolving. No two ages, and scarcely any two countries, have decided it alike; and the decision of one age or country is a wonder to another. Yet the people of any given age and country no more suspect any difficulty in it than if it were a subject on which mankind had always been agreed. The rules which obtain among themselves appear to them self-evident and self-justifying. This all but universal illusion is one of the examples of the magical influence of custom, which is not only, as the proverb says, a second nature but is continually mistaken for the first. The effect of custom, in preventing any misgiving respecting the rules of conduct which mankind impose on one another, is all the more complete because the subject is one on which it is not generally considered necessary that reasons should be given, either by one person to others or by each to himself. People are accustomed to believe, and have been encouraged in the belief by some who aspire to the character of philosophers, that their feelings on subjects of this nature are better than reasons and render reasons unnecessary. The practical principle which guides them to their opinions on the regulation of human conduct is the feeling in each person's mind that everybody should be required to act as he, and those with whom he sympathizes, would like them to act. No one, indeed, acknowledges to himself that his standard of judgment is his own liking; but an opinion on a point of conduct, not supported by reasons, can only count as one person's preference; and if the reasons, when given, are a mere appeal to a similar preference felt by other people, it is still only many people's liking instead of one. To an ordinary man, however, his own preference, thus supported, is not only a perfectly satisfactory reason but the only one he generally has for any of his notions of morality, taste, or propriety, which are not expressly written in his religious creed, and his chief guide in the interpretation even of that. Men's opinions, accordingly, on what is laudable or blamable are affected by all the multifarious causes which influence their wishes in regard to the conduct of others, and which are as numerous as those which determine their wishes on any other subject. Sometimes their reason; at other times their prejudices or superstitions; often their social affections, not seldom their antisocial ones, their envy or jealousy, their arrogance or contemptuousness; but most commonly their desires or fear for themselves—their legitimate or illegitimate self-interest. Wherever there is an ascendant class, a large portion of the morality of the country emanates from its class interests and its feelings of class superiority. The morality between Spartans and Helots, between planters and Negroes, between princes and subjects, between nobles and roturiers, between men and women has been for the most part the creation of these class interests and feelings; and the sentiments thus generated react in turn upon the moral feelings of the members of the ascendant class, in their relations among themselves. Where, on the other hand, a class, formerly ascendant, has lost its ascendancy, or where its ascendancy is unpopular, the prevailing moral sentiments frequently bear the impress of an impatient dislike of superiority. Another grand determining principle of the rules of conduct, both in act and forbearance, which have been enforced by law or opinion, has been the servility of mankind toward the supposed preferences or aversions of their temporal masters or of their gods. This servility, though essentially selfish, is not hypocrisy; it gives rise to perfectly genuine sentiments of abhorrence; it made men burn magicians and heretics. Among so many baser influences, the general and obvious interests of society have, of course, had a share, and a large one, in the direction of the moral sentiments; less, however, as a matter of reason, and on their own account, than as a consequence of the sympathies and antipathies which grew out of them; and sympathies and antipathies which had little or nothing to do with the interests of society have made themselves felt in the establishment of moralities with quite as great force.

The likings and dislikings of society, or of some powerful portion of it, are thus the main thing which has practically determined the rules laid down for general observance, under the penalties of law or opinion. And in general, those who have been in advance of society in thought and feeling have left this condition of things unassailed in principle, however they may have come into conflict with it in some of its details. They have occupied themselves rather in inquiring what things society ought to like or dislike than in questioning whether its likings or dislikings should be a law to individuals. They preferred endeavoring to alter the feelings of mankind on the particular points on which they were themselves heretical rather than make common cause in defense of freedom with heretics generally. The only case in which the higher ground has been taken on principle and maintained with consistency, by any but an individual here and there, is that of religious belief: a case instructive in many ways, and not least so as forming a most striking instance of the fallibility of what is called the moral sense; for the *odium theologicum,* in a sincere bigot, is one of the most unequivocal cases of moral feeling. Those who first broke the yoke of what called itself the Universal Church were in general as little willing to permit difference of religious opinion as that church itself. But when the heat of the conflict was over, without giving a complete victory to any party, and each church or sect was reduced to limit its hopes to retaining possession of the ground it already occupied, minorities, seeing that they had no chance of becoming majorities, were under the necessity of pleading to those whom they could not convert for permission to differ. It is accordingly on this battlefield, almost solely, that the rights of the individual against society have been asserted on broad grounds of principle, and the claim of society to exercise authority over dissentients openly controverted. The great writers to whom the world owes what religious liberty it possesses have mostly asserted freedom of conscience as an indefeasible right, and denied absolutely that a human being is accountable to others for his religious belief. Yet so natural to mankind is intolerance in whatever they really care about that religious freedom has hardly anywhere been practically realized, except where religious indifference, which dislikes to have its peace disturbed by theological quarrels, has added its weight to the scale. In the minds of almost all religious persons, even in the most tolerant countries, the duty of toleration is admitted with tacit reserves. One person will bear with dissent in matters of church government, but not of dogma; another can tolerate everybody, short of a Papist or a Unitarian; another, everyone who believes in revealed religion; a few extend their charity a little further, but stop at the belief in a God and in a future state. Wherever the sentiment of the majority is still genuine and intense, it is found to have abated little of its claim to be obeyed.

In England, from the peculiar circumstances of our political history, though the yoke of opinion is perhaps heavier, that of law is lighter than in most other countries of Europe; and there is considerable jealousy of direct interference by the legislative or the executive power with private conduct, not so much from any just regard for the independence of the individual as from the still subsisting habit of looking on the government as representing an opposite interest to the public. The majority have not yet learned to feel the power of the government their power, or its opinions their opinions. When they do so, individual liberty will probably be as much exposed to invasion from the government as it already is from public opinion. But, as yet, there

is a considerable amount of feeling ready to be called forth against any attempt of the law to control individuals in things in which they have not hitherto been accustomed to be controlled by it; and this with very little discrimination as to whether the matter is, or is not, within the legitimate sphere of legal control; insomuch that the feeling, highly salutary on the whole, is perhaps quite as often misplaced as well grounded in the particular instances of its application. There is, in fact, no recognized principle by which the propriety or impropriety of government interference is customarily tested. People decide according to their personal preferences. Some, whenever they see any good to be done, or evil to be remedied, would willingly instigate the government to undertake the business, while others prefer to bear almost any amount of social evil rather than add one to the departments of human interests amenable to governmental control. And men range themselves on one or the other side in any particular case, according to this general direction of their sentiments, or according to the degree of interest which they feel in the particular thing which it is proposed that the government should do, or according to the belief they entertain that the government would, or would not, do it in the manner they prefer; but very rarely on account of any opinion to which they consistently adhere, as to what things are fit to be done by a government. And it seems to me that in consequence of this absence of rule or principle, one side is at present as often wrong as the other; the interference of government is, with about equal frequency, improperly invoked and improperly condemned.

The object of this essay is to assert one very simple principle, as entitled to govern absolutely the dealings of society with the individual in the way of compulsion and control, whether the means used be physical force in the form of legal penalties or the moral coercion of public opinion. That principle is that the sole end for which mankind are warranted, individually or collectively, in interfering with the liberty of action of any of their number is self-protection. That the only purpose for which power can be rightfully exercised over any member of a civilized community, against his will, is to prevent harm to others. His own good, either physical or moral, is not a sufficient warrant. He cannot rightfully be compelled to do or forbear because it will be better for him to do so, because it will make him happier, because, in the opinions of others, to do so would be wise or even right. These are good reasons for remonstrating with him, or reasoning with him, or persuading him, or entreating him, but not for compelling him or visiting him with any evil in case he do otherwise. To justify that, the conduct from which it is desired to deter him must be calculated to produce evil to someone else. The only part of the conduct of anyone for which he is amenable to society is that which concerns others. In the part which merely concerns himself, his independence is, of right, absolute. Over himself, over his own body and mind, the individual is sovereign.

It is, perhaps, hardly necessary to say that this doctrine is meant to apply only to human beings in the maturity of their faculties. We are not speaking of children or of young persons below the age which the law may fix as that of manhood or womanhood. Those who are still in a state to require being taken care of by others must be protected against their own actions as well as against external injury. For the same reason we may leave out of consideration those backward states of society in which the race itself may be considered as in its nonage. The early difficulties in the way of spontaneous progress are so great that there is seldom any choice of means for overcoming them; and a ruler full of the spirit of improvement is warranted in the use of any expedients that will attain an end perhaps otherwise unattainable. Despotism is a legitimate mode of government in dealing with barbarians, provided the end be their improvement and the means justified by actually effecting that end. Liberty, as a principle, has no application to any state of things anterior to the time when mankind have become capable of being im-

proved by free and equal discussion. Unlike then, there is nothing for them but implicit obedience to an Akbar or a Charlemagne if they are so fortunate as to find one. But as soon as mankind have attained the capacity of being guided to their own improvement by conviction or persuasion (a period long since reached in all nations with whom we need here concern ourselves), compulsion, either in the direct form or in that of pains and penalties for noncompliance, is no longer admissible as a means to their own good, and justifiable only for the security of others.

It is proper to state that I forego any advantage which could be derived to my argument from the idea of abstract right as a thing independent of utility. I regard utility as the ultimate appeal on all ethical questions; but it must be utility in the largest sense, grounded on the permanent interests of man as a progressive being. Those interests, I contend, authorize the subjection of individual spontaneity to external control only in respect to those actions of each which concern the interest of other people. If anyone does an act hurtful to others, there is a *prima facie* case for punishing him by law or, where legal penalties are not safely applicable, by general disapprobation. There are also many positive acts for the benefit of others which he may rightfully be compelled to perform, such as to give evidence in a court of justice, to bear his fair share in the common defense or in any other joint work necessary to the interest of the society of which he enjoys the protection, and to perform certain acts of individual beneficence, such as saving a fellow creature's life or interposing to protect the defenseless against ill usage—things which whenever it is obviously a man's duty to do he may rightfully be made responsible to society for not doing. A person may cause evil to others not only by his actions but by his inaction, and in either case he is justly accountable to them for the injury. The latter case, it is true, requires a much more cautious exercise of compulsion than the former. To make anyone answerable for doing evil to others is the rule; to make him answerable for not preventing evil is, comparatively speaking, the exception. Yet there are many cases clear enough and grave enough to justify that exception. In all things which regard the external relations of the individual, he is *de jure* amenable to those whose interests are concerned, and, if need be, to society as their protector. There are often good reasons for not holding him to the responsibility; but these reasons must arise from the special expediencies of the case: either because it is a kind of case in which he is on the whole likely to act better when left to his own discretion than when controlled in any way in which society have it in their power to control him; or because the attempt to exercise control would produce other evils, greater than those which it would prevent. When such reasons as these preclude the enforcement of responsibility, the conscience of the agent himself should step into the vacant judgment seat and protect those interests of others which have no external protection; judging himself all the more rigidly, because the case does not admit of his being made accountable to the judgment of his fellow creatures.

But there is a sphere of action in which society, as distinguished from the individual, has, if any, only an indirect interest: comprehending all that portion of a person's life and conduct which affects only himself or, if it also affects others, only with their free, voluntary, and undeceived consent and participation. When I say only himself, I mean directly and in the first instance; for whatever affects himself may affect others through himself: and the objection which may be grounded on this contingency will receive consideration in the sequel. This, then, is the appropriate region of human liberty. It comprises, first, the inward domain of consciousness, demanding liberty of conscience in the most comprehensive sense, liberty of thought and feeling, absolute freedom of opinion and sentiment on all subjects, practical or speculative, scientific, moral, or theological. The liberty of expressing and publishing opinions may seem to fall under a different principle, since it belongs to that part

of the conduct of an individual which concerns other people, but, being almost of as much importance as the liberty of thought itself and resting in great part on the same reasons, is practically inseparable from it. Secondly, the principle requires liberty of tastes and pursuits, of framing the plan of our life to suit our own character, of doing as we like, subject to such consequences as may follow, without impediment from our fellow creatures, so long as what we do does not harm them, even though they should think our conduct foolish, perverse, or wrong. Thirdly, from this liberty of each individual follows the liberty, within the same limits, of combination among individuals; freedom to unite for any purpose not involving harm to others: the persons combining being supposed to be of full age and not forced or deceived.

No society in which these liberties are not, on the whole, respected is free, whatever may be its form of government; and none is completely free in which they do not exist absolute and unqualified. The only freedom which deserves the name is that of pursuing our own good in our own way, so long as we do not attempt to deprive others of theirs or impede their efforts to obtain it. Each is the proper guardian of his own health, whether bodily *or* mental and spiritual. Mankind are greater gainers by suffering each other to live as seems good to themselves than by compelling each to live as seems good to the rest.

Though this doctrine is anything but new and, to some persons, may have the air of a truism, there is no doctrine which stands more directly opposed to the general tendency of existing opinion and practice. Society has expended fully as much effort in the attempt (according to its lights) to compel people to conform to its notions of personal as of social excellence. The ancient commonwealths thought themselves entitled to practice, and the ancient philosophers countenanced, the regulation of every part of private conduct by public authority, on the ground that the State had a deep interest in the whole bodily and mental discipline of every one of its citizens—a mode of thinking which may have been admissible in small republics surrounded by powerful enemies, in constant peril of being subverted by foreign attack or internal commotion, and to which even a short interval of relaxed energy and self-command might so easily be fatal that they could not afford to wait for the salutary permanent effects of freedom. In the modern world, the greater size of political communities and, above all, the separation between spiritual and temporal authority (which placed the direction of men's consciences in other hands than those which controlled their worldly affairs) prevented so great an interference by law in the details of private life; but the engines of moral repression have been wielded more strenuously against divergence from the reigning opinion in self-regarding than even in social matters; religion, the most powerful of the elements which have entered into the formation of moral feeling, having almost always been governed either by the ambition of a hierarchy seeking control over every department of human conduct, or by the spirit of Puritanism. And some of those modern reformers who have placed themselves in strongest opposition to the religions of the past have been noway behind either churches or sects in their assertion of the right spiritual domination: M. Comte, in particular, whose social system, as unfolded in his *Système de Politique Positive,* aims at establishing (though by moral more than by legal appliances) a despotism of society over the individual surpassing anything contemplated in the political ideal of the most rigid disciplinarian among the ancient philosophers.

Apart from the peculiar tenets of individual thinkers, there is also in the world at large an increasing inclination to stretch unduly the powers of society over the individual both by force of opinion and even by that of legislation; and as the tendency of all the changes taking place in the world is to strengthen society and diminish the power of the individual, this encroachment is not one of the evils which tend spontaneously to disappear, but, on the contrary, to grow more and more formidable. The disposition of mankind, whether as rulers or as fellow citizens, to impose their own opinions and inclinations as a rule of conduct on others is so energetically supported by some of the best and by some of the worst feelings incident to human nature that it is hardly ever kept under restraint by anything but want of power; and as the power is not declining, but growing, unless a strong barrier of moral conviction can be raised against the mischief, we must expect, in the present circumstances of the world, to see it increase.

It will be convenient for the argument if, instead of at once entering upon the general thesis, we confine ourselves in the first instance to a single branch of it on which the principle here stated is, if not fully, yet to a certain point, recognized by the current opinions. This one branch is the Liberty of Thought, from which it is impossible to separate the cognate liberty of speaking and of writing. Although these liberties, to some considerable amount, form part of the political morality of all countries which profess religious toleration and free institutions, the grounds, both philosophical and practical, on which they rest are perhaps not so familiar to the general mind, nor so thoroughly appreciated by many, even of the leaders of opinion, as might have been expected. Those grounds, when rightly understood, are of much wider application than to only one division of the subject, and a thorough consideration of this part of the question will be found the best introduction to the remainder. Those to whom nothing which I am about to say will be new may therefore, I hope, excuse me if on a subject which for now three centuries has been so often discussed I venture on one discussion more.

9

Absolute Moral Values and Reason: A Conversation with Immanuel Kant

What Should You Do?

What should you do? Your poor Uncle Charlie is lying on his deathbed. His life is ebbing away and you know he will most certainly die. Uncle Charlie motions to you to come closer. You bend close to hear his words. Marshalling his diminishing strength, he whispers to you. Has the mail brought any word about his book? Has the publisher accepted as worthy his life's work? Poor Uncle Charlie desperately wants to know the fate of his book.

You have checked the mail. The letter has come in the day's mail. Should you tell the dying man that the letter has not arrived? Or should you tell him the truth? The letter has arrived. It is a rejection of his masterpiece. What should you do?

Of course, telling the truth is the morally correct action in most cases. But the truth will make poor, dying Uncle Charlie's last moments very painful. He will know that his work is unacceptable. He will feel like a failure. You could try to explain that publishers and editors are not reliable judges of quality work. But Uncle Charlie has put all his confidence in them. He will not accept that as an answer.

If you lie, Uncle Charlie will die with a smile on his parched, thin lips. No other consequence will follow. The lie will die with him. If you tell the truth, Uncle Charlie will feel the emotional pain. The truth will be buried with him.

So is the obvious answer to lie? But what if Uncle Charlie thought you would lie? He would not have asked you. He may have asked you only because he trusts you. He may have asked you because he wants the truth. His dying wish may be to know the truth. What should you do?

Material in this chapter taken from Immanuel Kant, *Groundwork of the Metaphysics of Morals,* originally published in 1785, (London: Hutchinson Publishing Ltd.) H. J. Paton translation. Reprinted by permission of the publisher.

Another Example

I once heard of a case where a man was discovered to have inoperable cancer. His death was likely to come in three to six months. No, this is not one of those "miraculous" stories where the doctors are proved mistaken. The man did die four months after the diagnosis.

The dilemma comes in because the physician was asked by the family not to reveal to the man that he was dying. In recent months, he had already suffered several serious setbacks in his life. His business had failed. One of his grandchildren had died. His wife, children, and clergyman believed his own illness would depress him to the point that he would commit suicide. For religious reasons, and out of genuine concern for him, they counseled the physician to withhold information. He did.

As the man's health rapidly deteriorated, he approached his doctor. The doctor respected the family's wishes. He lied to the patient. Finally, in what turned out to be the final week of the man's life, he directly confronted the doctor. Yes, he was dying. He had not been told in order to protect his feelings.

Of course, the physician violated a promise he had with his patient. He had lied by omitting the true diagnosis. Isn't this what we were tempted to do with Uncle Charlie? The man was desperately unhappy. There had been one thing he had wanted to do in his life. He had wanted to see the Grand Canyon. He had never told anyone about his wish. An earlier diagnosis would have given him time to fulfill his childhood wish. By "saving" him grief, his own family and his doctor robbed him of his one and only wish. What should they have done?

Each of these examples plays on our sensitivity toward another human being. They are manipulative in that they confuse us over whether or not consequences matter. Can lying be excused by correct intentions or desirable consequences? Or must we never lie?

In his work, *Groundwork of the Metaphysics of Morals,* Immanuel Kant defines morality as an absolute standard. He is committed to an absolute morality where moral rules apply no matter what the consequences of one's action may be.

Kant provides a groundwork for morality. I know, you got that from the title. Kant shows that morality does not depend on human nature or on our definition of happiness. He guards morality against charges of historical or personal relativism. And he defines morality so that there is a reason to be moral. It's an impressive project.

How does Kant do all this? We'll get to the details in a moment. Basically, he argues that the nature of reason imposes conditions on our way of thinking about morality. He argues that reason leads to moral principles that cannot be violated. So our desires, our passions and our wants, must be placed aside in order for us to make moral decisions.

Kant's insight might fit our own thinking to a certain extent. Think about the examples of morality that we discussed earlier. The Ten Commandments was one example. If you look at the commandments, they are appealing in their simplicity and directness. Do not murder. Do not steal. On the tablets it does *not* say "Do not murder, except for the following cases." Right?

Nor do the rules exempt certain people. I've checked! The Ten Commandments does *not* say that it is wrong to steal, except for Art. Too bad, but it's true. It doesn't even let ethics-book writers steal. Nope, everyone is bound by the rule.

The rules are definite and unchanging. There are no references to consequences or to differing situations. I've checked that, too. The commandment against stealing does not say, "Do not steal, except when you really want that sports car." It doesn't even say, "Do not steal, except when you need to steal." There are no loopholes! The commandments are absolute, absolutely absolute.

Kant too builds in an absolute dimension to moral principles. Moral principles do not change with the circumstances, or with their projected or real results, or with the customs of the society. Kant's moral principles apply to every rational being.

Now let's talk to Kant about his theory. Through the miracle of Art's philosopher resurrection and time machine, I present for your education Immanuel Kant. Welcome, Professor Kant. (Kant is not the kind of guy who would ask us to call him Immanuel. Pretty formal, if you know what I mean.) We have some questions. Would you be kind enough to help us understand your theory?

"Certainly, Art. That is why I am here."

(Since Kant was a German university professor, it would be helpful if you would read this with a German accent. A slow, measured, and deliberate pace would help, too. Think of a sort of intellectual Terminator, or is that a contradiction? Now go back and read it again. "Certainly, Art. That is why I am here." Thanks.)

"Art, stop babbling to your readers. Before our conversation is completed, I should also like to comment on Mill's utilitarian doctrine. Unfortunately, Mill wrote after my death, so I did not have an opportunity to respond to his analysis of moral philosophy. I should like that opportunity. For example, moral goodness is definitely not based on consequences."

Anything you say, Professor Kant. And I'll try to be more serious.

The Aim of Kant's Theory

"Fine, Art. Now what questions do you have for me?"

Well, first, what are the aims of your book?

"The sole aim of the present *Groundwork* is to seek out and establish the supreme principle of morality."

What determines whether or not someone has done the right thing?

"If you mean what constitutes right action, the answer is doing one's duty."

Act From a Sense of Duty

Okay, and what gives me these duties?

"As a being who has reason, you are obliged to be an impartial, rational agent. The essence of morality is to act not from inclination—"

Time out. I don't mean to interrupt, but what do you mean by "inclination"?

"An inclination is a personal want, desire, or passion. It is anything that could bias the person. As I was saying, the essence of morality is to act not from inclination or passion, but from reason. One must act from a sense of duty that has been derived by reason. No other motivation is proper.

"You were on the correct path just a moment ago, Art. A law has to carry with it absolute necessity if it is to be valid morally. Consequently, the ground of moral obligation must be looked for, not in the nature of man nor in the circumstances of the world in which he is placed, but solely a priori in the concepts of pure reason."

I said that? I don't even know what a priori looks like.

"The words *a priori* mean logically necessary. What we are searching for is a completely rational basis for morality. Moral philosophy gives humanity laws a priori as rational beings. We don't need to look into the particular circumstances of people, either individually or collectively. The moral principles must apply to all rational beings, not only humans."

Who else is there? Vulcans?

"If any action is to be morally good, it is not enough that it should conform to the moral law—it must also be done for the sake of the moral law."

How does that answer my question?

Why Start with the Good Will?

"Don't you see, where this is not so, the conformity is only too contingent and precarious, since the nonmoral ground at work will now and then produce actions which accord with the law, but very often actions which transgress it."

Let me see if I have this right. Simply acting in a morally acceptable way is not good enough. My actions have to be done because they are moral?

"Yes. There is a problem with grounding morality on human nature."

What if it were possible to train a person to want to perform the morally praiseworthy action?

"People's wants and perceived needs are too subject to change. They are at best contingent."

Contingent?

"Possible. They are easily set aside for psychologically stronger desires. Therefore, morality must be based on reason alone. A metaphysic of morals has to investigate the idea and principles of a possible *pure* will, and not the activities and conditions of human willing as such."

So that's why you start out discussing the good will.

The Good Will Is Unconditionally Good.   "Then that is where we must begin. The good will is the only thing, real or imaginable, that is unconditionally good. It is good without qualification. All other qualities and goals are only conditionally good."

What do you mean? Aren't intelligence, wit, judgment, and courage also good? When could any of these traits be bad?

"These qualities of temperament are without doubt good and desirable in many respects, but they can also be extremely bad and hurtful."

How do you figure that? When would they be hurtful and undesirable?

"When the will is not good which has to make use of these gifts of nature. It is exactly the same with gifts of fortune. Power, wealth, honor, even health and that complete well-being and contentment with one's state that goes by the name of happiness, can have a dangerous influence on the mind. For example, they can cause over-boldness and lead one to serious injury."

The Good Will and Its Effects.   I thought your justification of moral principles was not going to use consequences as a justification. Aren't you making a utilitarian argument here?

"Good objection, and one I want to answer. In the present discussion I am appealing to ordinary rational knowledge."

Huh?

"You do have a way with language, Art. All I mean is that I am appealing to ordinary and reasonable insights into morality. My audience has a good grasp of morality and can be brought to a high degree of precision and accuracy. At this point I am merely applying clear examples of morality to shed light on its nature and on the nature of the good will."

Later you will draw your argument from pure reason?

"Exactly, for when moral value is in question we are concerned, not with the actions which we see, but with their inner principles, which we cannot see. For now, however, using examples is practical and will establish a common understanding between us."

I think I'm being told that I can't jump into the intellectually deep waters yet. Is that it?

"Don't be so insecure, Art. We are first going to work from ordinary rational knowledge of morality to the philosophical. You should know that from reading the title from chapter 1 of *my* book."

So where are we?

An Example of the Good Will.   "A good will is not good because of what it effects or accomplishes. It is good in itself. In fact, a good will seems to constitute the indispensable condition of our very worthiness to be happy."

I understand that later you intend to prove your theory without the use of examples, but could you give me an example to help me grasp your intuition?

"Certainly. Imagine that we have two shopkeepers. Their clothing shops are next door to each other. They carry the same brands of clothing. Let's name one shopkeeper Smith and the other Jones. When you do comparison shopping, you find that both charge the same price for the same item. Both have the same selection, and each store interior is qualitatively similar to the other. Our question is, in which store would you rather do business?"

You make everything equal. The location, the price, the merchandise, the selection; everything is equal. How can I choose? Is Smith nicer than Jones?

"Good question. Let me tell more of the story. Remember, we are seeking to discover if the effect of the good will has any impact on its worth. So to continue, imagine that Smith and Jones are both affable, polite, and helpful. Each treats you with courtesy and competence."

What's the difference? The way you describe them, there's no way of preferring one over the other.

"Excellent. Now imagine that we have proof that Smith is honest because he believes that honesty is the duty of every businessperson. Jones is equally honest, but only because he believes that dishonesty will be detected and he will lose business."

Let me get this right. Smith is honest because honesty is a duty. He believes in honesty. On the other hand, Jones is honest, but only for his self-interest. He's afraid people will detect his dishonesty and he will be run out of business. The choice is obvious. I would rather deal with Jones.

"What?"

I'm kidding. Of course, everyone would rather deal with Smith, the one who is honest because honesty is a moral duty.

"Just so, Art. If consequences were all that mattered, the choice would not be obvious. If consequences were all that mattered, you could not reasonably prefer one over the other. Why then do you prefer Smith?"

Well, Smith would be honest even if he knows he can't get caught. I'd feel better knowing that. He won't be tempted to cheat me.

"More accurately, even if he is able to cheat you, he will have a reverence for his moral duty. He will not cheat you even if he could."

Yes, that's right. Oh, now I get it. It's not the consequence. Even if Jones never cheats me, the fact is he would if he could. His character and values would let him.

"Therefore?"

Therefore, Smith, the one who is honest as a matter of duty, is my choice. Does he have dark blue, light-weight, V-neck sweaters?

"Art, you're getting off the point. Regain your concentration."

The Function of Reason.   Sorry. On to the next question. How does reason function in your system? The reason I ask is that reason seems to be worthwhile as a way of getting what we want.

"Are you backsliding again into that old 'do whatever you want' perspective?"

Actually, I guess that may be part of it. But Mill's theory also impresses me. Reason is useful in bringing happiness. I don't expect you to agree with this.

"Reason is not sufficiently serviceable for guiding the will safely as regards its objects and satisfaction of all our needs—a purpose for which an implanted natural instinct would have led us much more surely."

I don't understand.

"Let us take as a principle that in an organic being no organ is to be found for any end unless it is also the most appropriate to that end and best fitted for it."

All our mental and physical qualities and talents are there for some goal? Is that what you're saying? If I have serviceable legs, they are for walking? Arms are for reaching? Teeth are best suited for biting and chewing? Is this what you mean?

"Yes. Further, let us suppose for argument that the real purpose of reason is for humankind's preservation, welfare, or, in a word, our happiness. If we make these assumptions, then we can see that nature would have hit upon a very bad arrangement by choosing reason . . . to carry out this purpose of sustaining our preservation, welfare, or happiness."

Am I allowed to make an objection?

"Certainly."

Why would we assume any of this? It sounds to me that you're assuming that there is a God who creates our natures, each element having its own function or purpose.

"No, I would like to construct my argument without recourse to the divine. Your objection is well taken on this account. Still, there must be some end for which reason is specially suited."

I guess I'm having a problem thinking of the universe as purposive, as working toward some end. Why not assume that reason is like the appendix, unnecessary at best, a pain in the side at worst?

"We could do that, I suppose. You are, however, again losing track of the nature of our project. I am appealing to ordinary rational knowledge to lead us into a purer discussion of the foundations of morality. Let my assumptions be suggestive, if not fully compelling."

Okay, so where does this leave us?

"Reason's true function must be to produce a will which is good, not as a means to some further end, but in itself. The highest practical function of reason is to produce a good will."

What about happiness or contentment?

"A good will is capable of its own peculiar kind of contentment, a contentment determined by reason alone."

And what if reason and the good will interfere with more physical desires?

The Good Will Is Superior to Passions.   "A will must be the highest good and the condition of all the rest, even of all our demands for happiness. This happiness is desired even if its fulfillment should often involve interference with the purposes of inclination."

Then you're saying that reason and the good will are superior to physical desires? Have I gotten that right?

"Yes, I think so. I cannot justify that assumption here, but you will admit that that is exactly what morality claims, too. Remember, what we are after, Art, is to establish the supreme principle of morality."

Okay, but I just want it noted that you are making judgments about the relative worth of the mind over the body. I for one like my body very much. Let's go on to see what else you have to say.

The Motive of Duty

"First, I would like to point out a distinction, doing an action from duty or from some purpose of self-interest."

What's the difference? I mean, why do we need bother with the distinction? Are we going to be able to see the difference in real-life situations? Does it matter when the same actions will result from either motive?

"Good questions. You have a pretty optimistic view of people. Let's go through the distinction carefully. The distinction is certainly far more difficult to perceive when the action accords with duty and the person has an immediate inclination to perform the action."

For example?

"The example I give of the grocer is appropriate, I think. Because of competition, a sensible shopkeeper will not cheat inexperienced customers, including children."

Perfect. Everyone is treated fairly; no one is cheated.

"The people are served honestly, but we need to see and to know more. We are not justified in concluding that the shopkeeper acted from the principles of fair dealing."

Why not?

"Because his interests required him to do so. We can no more assume that he acted from a sense of duty than from a universal love of humanity."

Is this like the Eddie Haskell example that came up in Chapter 2?

"Yes, I think so. Even when Mr. Haskell is acting in accord with the dictates of morality, he is doing so for the wrong reasons.

Living in Conformity with Duty and from the Motive of Duty. "Examine another example. We all have a duty to preserve our own life. Everyone also has a desire to live. It's a natural inclination. We can see that people have the natural desire to live and to avoid pain. They take all kinds of precautions to this end. Although their precautions conform with duty, however, they have no moral worth."

Why not? Here you have people doing just what they are supposed to do, and you say their actions have no moral worth?

"Exactly right. Their actions are not done from the motive of duty. It's as though there is a fortunate overlap of inclination and duty. The people appear to be moral, but their motives are not the right sort."

What's wrong with that? Am I being too practical here? We have a moral duty to do something. We have people doing that action in just the right way. What's the problem?

Actions with Moral Worth

"Imagine that a person's life is suddenly filled with disappointment and hopeless misery. Imagine that such a person's misery takes away all of his taste for life, and he wants to commit suicide. He longs for death yet still preserves his life without loving it. That action has moral worth."

Why?

"Because his action (of preserving his life) was performed not from inclination or fear but from duty."

How do you figure?

"His strongest inclination is to kill himself, yet he resists and overcomes this desire."

Is that where the moral worth comes in, because he struggles with his stronger desires?

"No, while self-control and sober reflection are good in many respects, they are not good without qualification. Look at the self-controlled criminal who plans his crimes. Self-control and the ability to reflect make this person all the more dangerous and criminal. This is not a person of moral worth."

Then how is the suicidal person who resists suicide being moral?

"The morally decisive feature of the suicidal person is that he acts from a sense of duty. It is precisely in this that the worth of character begins to show—a moral worth and beyond all comparison the highest—namely, that he does good, not from inclination, but from duty."

Is Mr. Spock the Ideal Moral Person?

Are you saying that the ideal moral person is someone like Mr. Spock? I mean, Spock is supposed to be calm and self-controlled, and he always resists temptations.

"Mr. Spock may be a good candidate for the moral ideal, yes. It is not, however, because he exercises self-control or resists temptations. You are confusing qualities of the moral person with the essential feature of morality."

How's that again?

"Your example of Mr. Spock is interesting, but you have focused on the wrong personality traits. Let me put it this way. The kind of personal traits you suggest almost always attend the moral person, but they are not what makes the person morally worthy."

I still don't understand.

"Very good people and very bad people will exhibit the qualities of self-control, calm reflection, and the like. Because of this, it is not these qualities alone that describe the moral person's character. Romulans also exhibit self-control and calm reflection, and yet they are very bad. Does that help you?"

Yes, I think so. I guess I have always heard that moral people are self-controlled and all the rest. I just assumed that this is what makes them moral. Now you're telling me that acting from a sense of duty is what morality is about.

"Right. You see, it's one thing to want to help other people and another, very different thing to help people because it's your duty. Your example of Mr. Spock demonstrates this point. Spock is entirely logical."

That's not quite true. He has a human side that causes inner struggles.

"Granted. I'm sorry, but I never got very good reception of the show in my day. At any rate, Spock's human side can be put aside for our purposes. Morally speaking, the human side of Spock is irrelevant."

That's where I have a problem with your theory. I just don't see how you can exclude the feeling part of us!

"Art, I am not eliminating the feeling side of people. I am merely showing that the feeling side is not morally relevant. Morality is based on duty, not on feelings. Feelings are too changeable and capricious to stand as the foundation of morality."

Can't a person have an unchanging, stable emotion?

"I don't think so. Can you name one?"

Love Cannot Be a Moral Motivation

Can love be a moral motivation? I don't mean romantic love. I've seen people fall into and out of love. That's pretty unstable, I agree. But what about the love a person may feel toward her parents, or the love another person may feel toward his child?

"We do speak of some forms of love as unconditional. Even the types of love you forward for consideration are unacceptable, however."

Why, because you say so?

"It has nothing to do with what I say, Art. It is the nature and foundation of morality. There are several features of unconditional love that make it a problematic foundation for morality."

Like what?

"First, it distorts the relative worth of everything in the reality external to the loved person."

Huh?

"If you unconditionally love your child or parent, you place that person's welfare and interests above the welfare and interests of everyone else. That is biased. That distorts the importance of other people with whom you come into contact."

That isn't quite what I have in mind. Let me give you an example. Tell me what's wrong, morally wrong, with this picture. Say a parent has two small children. He loves each child unconditionally. By that I do not mean that he is blind to their weaknesses or undesirable traits. He sees them for who and what they really are. So far, he's not distorting reality. His unconditional love for each child makes his attitude toward them unwavering. I submit this as an argument that love can be a foundation for morality. What do you think so far?

"I am listening."

Okay. This parent has both kids come to him with a disagreement. They both want the same toy, or book. He resolves the dispute, not by being unfeeling. I guess I see Mr. Spock tearing the book exactly in half and giving one half to each child. No, the loving parent will give the book to the child who needs it more.

"Needs it more? How is this a moral decision? How is this impartial and objective?"

The child who needs it more gets the book. One child may need the parent's attention more at that moment, or she may need to be distracted from a hurt knee, or many other reasons. An hour later, the reverse decision may be desirable. The parent does what is best for both children by lovingly doing what is best in the present circumstances. Have I gotten you on this one?

"To use your vernacular, 'I should have had a V-8!' In truth, Art, I fail to see how this decision has moral worth."

Love Cannot Be Impartial.   But my example gives impartial treatment to the two children. Isn't that the essence of morality? Rather than inhibiting the impartial treatment of the two children, the parent's love for his children guarantees that each child will be treated just as the child needs to be treated.

"It is a decision that mirrors a moral decision, perhaps, but it is done entirely from inclination. But perhaps that misses the point, or merely restates my point. Doesn't the parent's attention to both children create a state of more attention given to them and less attention given to all other children?"

Are you saying that a moral parent is supposed to cater to the needs of other people's children as much as to his own children's needs? That's crazy! What you're suggesting is impractical.

"In Scripture we are commanded to love our neighbor and even our enemy. Love out of inclination cannot be commanded; but kindness from duty is practical. It is doubtless in this sense that we should understand the passages from Scripture. As a moral person, you have to act on duty."

I still do not see what is wrong with my example. Your objection to a morality based on emotion is that emotions are too transitory. Because you see the foundation of morality as stable, you reject emotion. But a parent's unconditional love is completely stable.

Love Is Not Objective.   "But love, even unconditional love, is not objective. Let me expand your example to show you that we are not disagreeing as you think. It is only your example that misleads you to a rash and inappropriate conclusion. Think about a judge in a court of law. The judge is the physical embodiment of the moral principle of justice. Now imagine that the judge listens to all the evidence, weighs it for its importance and truth value, and arrives at a decision."

Are we talking about a crooked judge who is running for reelection?

"Don't be so cynical. But let me use your sense of moral disapproval. Imagine that the judge renders her decision, against you, and then turns to the other party, smiles, and says, 'I'll see you at home tonight, son.' "

That's not fair. She can't judge a case involving her own son!

"Just the point."

Are you saying that a person cannot treat a loved one in a moral way?

"Of course not. The point is that objectivity is required for a decision to have moral worth. The example we constructed together portrayed a judge who we have reason to believe judged with bias. We suspected, prematurely and without hearing the evidence, that the judge could not stay objective. Her feelings toward her son may have hindered her making a moral decision. The same result would happen if she turned to you and said that she did not like the way you combed your hair."

Oh, I see what you mean. Look, I agree that emotional bias is a problem, morally speaking. You still haven't shown me how my original example of the parent is mistaken.

"For your parent-child example to work, you had to maintain a relationship of unconditional love toward both disputants."

You mean toward both children?

"Yes. If that was the entire world, then your example would be appropriate, but then the analysis you give would not be the correct one."

Explain, please.

"Certainly. Your example works as long as the children are loved from what I have been calling a sense of duty. This sense of duty becomes clearer when it is violated."

Like in your example of the judge?"

"Love must reside in the will and not in . . . feeling, in principles of action and not of melting compassion. It is this practical love alone which can be an object of command. And only actions that spring from the command of duty have moral worth. Duty, not inclination."

Principles, Maxims, and Laws

I think I'm getting the drift of your analysis of morality. I have a question about the categorical imperative. I want to make certain that I understand what you mean by this idea.

"Very well. We have established that an action done from duty has its moral worth, not in the purpose to be attained by it, but in the maxim in accordance with which it is decided upon."

What do you mean by a maxim?

"A maxim is a principle of the will. It's what we have been slowly defining in our discussion. A maxim is a principle that moves the will to act. It must not include desires or inclinations, of course."

What's the difference between a maxim and a law, or don't I want to know?

"A maxim is the subjective principle of a volition, of the will. An objective principle is what I have been calling a practical law."

Practical? Are you sneaking in consequences?

"No, by the word *practical,* I am referring to practical reason as opposed to theoretical reason. However, I think further discussion of this point will muddy the waters."

Subjective and Objective Principles.   Okay. But let me ask one more question. What is the difference between a subjective principle and an objective principle? This must be an important distinction for your theory.

"Yes, absolutely (no pun intended). A subjective principle is an action-guiding principle. An objective principle is one which also serves subjectively as a practical principle for all rational beings if reason had full control over the faculty of desire."

Say that again?

"A person may perform actions based on her rational principles formed by her reason. This is subjective because it resides in her. The principle becomes objective when all rational beings using reason would arrive at the same principle."

Are you saying that if I am rational and I decide on a course of action, my decision is subjective? And that's because there is only one of me? But if all rational people vote on the same guiding principle, then the principle is objective?

"It is something like that, yes. But look, Art. Mathematics and science operate on a similar distinction. A mathematician uses reason to construct mathematical proofs. One mathematician conjecturing about a proof makes it a subjective conclusion. After other rational mathematicians employ reason and arrive at the same results, then the proof is objective. All mathematicians will arrive at the same conclusion. Similarly, all rational beings will arrive at the same principles, as long as they all use reason to control their desires and inclinations."

The Categorical Imperative. So what is the categorical imperative? Or, to put it in your words, "What kind of law can this be the thought of which, even without regard to the results expected from it, has to determine the will?" What is the law that you believe defines morality?

"I ought never to act except in such a way that I can also will that my maxim should become a universal law."

Agreed. That's what you mean by objectivity, I guess. But what is the categorical imperative?

"You don't read very carefully, do you? I have just stated the categorical imperative. Bare conformity to universal law is what serves the will as its principle. Reason determines morality."

Could you put this into a form I can understand better? How can I test one of my principles to see whether or not it's a moral principle in line with your categorical imperative, with objectivity, and with reason? I guess I'm asking for something a little less theoretical. Is that okay?

"Assuredly. The quickest way and yet unerringly how to solve the problem . . . is to ask oneself, 'Should I really be content that my maxim should hold as a universal law?' That means, am I willing for this maxim to apply validly to myself and to others?"

What If Everyone Did That? So I ask myself: What if everyone did that? If I am content with that possibility, then my action is morally acceptable?

"A bit crudely stated, but you have the general idea."

I'm sorry, but this still sounds like you're looking to see what the results are. If I am some kind of fanatic and I invent a maxim that I am willing to apply universally to myself and to others, how does that make my action morally acceptable?

"Give me an example."

Well, earlier in the book we discussed variations of the Golden Rule. Oops, sorry! I forgot, you were still dead when we were discussing the Golden Rule.

"Art, control yourself. You are getting too much involved in your own role. Remember, this discussion is merely imaginary."

Gee, I was getting to like you. I guess this means you won't be coming over for dinner next week.

"Back to your point about the fanatic and the Golden Rule."

Oh, yes, the fanatic. Does your theory suggest that a fanatic's maxim is a moral principle if she is willing to make it a universal law?

"This is where you go astray. The rejection of a maxim is not because of a prospective loss to you or even to others, but because it cannot fit as a principle into a possible enactment as a universal law."

But if not because of the consequences of the action, why not?

"Because duty . . . is the condition of the will good in itself, whose value is above all else."

Come again. Could you translate that?

"Your fanatic is willing to apply her fanaticism to everyone. This fulfills one of the requirements of morality. Her fanaticism fails, however, because it is not acceptable to all rational beings who use reason to control their desires. The fanatic is consistent, but consistency is not enough. Do you understand?"

Let me try again with a more moderate case. What if I decide that I want to take a shower. I decide that I'm going to take a shower at noon on Saturday. Now I want to make sure that my action is morally acceptable. Right so far?

"Continue."

I state my maxim. Everyone ought to take a shower at noon on Saturday. It's universal. Now I ask, could I will that everyone take a shower at noon on Saturday?

"I think you have misunderstood."

Wait, let me finish. Could I will that everyone take a shower at noon on Saturday? No, I could not will that because the results would be disastrous. The water pressure would become nonexistent; the sewer line would burst from all that water going down the drains.

"Have you finished?"

Yes.

"I can see that my use of examples has misled you. We agreed that examples would be used only to bring your ordinary knowledge into harmony with moral philosophy. Examples serve us only as encouragement. We cannot do morality a worse service than by seeking to derive it from examples. Every example of it presented to me must first itself be judged by moral principles in order to decide if it is fit to serve as an original example."

Using examples is going about the process in the wrong direction? It's backward?

Two Imperatives.   "Yes. But let us return to your example of the fanatical shower taker. There are two distinct types of imperatives. One we call the hypothetical imperative; the other is the categorical imperative."

I don't see what your point is. Please pardon me for saying this, but you philosophers make a lot of distinctions for no good reason.

"We shall see. The 'unimportant' distinction between hypothetical and categorical imperatives answers your objection. Hypothetical imperatives declare a possible action to be practically necessary as a means to the attainment of something else that one wills. A categorical imperative would be one which represented an action as objectively necessary in itself apart from its relation to a further end."

So?

"I sense from your answer that you do not yet sufficiently understand. If the action would be good solely as a means to something else, the imperative is hypothetical; if the action is represented as good in itself and therefore as necessary, in virtue of its principle, for a will which of itself accords with reason, then the imperative is categorical."

Your entire theory comes down to reason and what reason implies. Morality is just acting like Mr. Spock.

"Slow down, Art. We'll get to that. First, let's resolve your problem. In your example of taking a shower, the shower taking is certainly not being done for its own sake. Enjoyable as showers are, they are a means to an end, whether that be cleanliness, or good grooming, or health. Therefore, the maxim is not a moral maxim at all. It need not be tested as a moral principle; it need not be universalized."

Oh, I see.

"Further, you are rightly tempted to consider the effects of that maxim just because it is a means to an end. What you are implicitly weighing—"

Hold on. What does "implicitly" mean?

"You are doing it without stating it, and in this case without realizing it. For example, if I tell you that all men are mortal, what does that tell you about Socrates?"

Socrates is mortal.

"Yes, and implicit in your reasoning is the idea that Socrates is a man. Many implicit ideas are so obvious that they go unstated. Many of our beliefs are taken for granted and never stated. Unfortunately, many of our obvious beliefs are mistaken. But I digress."

Sorry for the distraction.

"What you are implicitly weighing are the effects of everyone's taking a shower at the same time and everyone's being newly showered at the same time. Obviously, given the practical results, we would be willing to allow that people ought to bathe at different times. Don't you agree?"

You are one persuasive gent. Yes, I agree. Now what about the role of reason in your analysis of morality?

"Ask your questions."

Why Reasoned Objectivity?   Your whole analysis of morality comes down to reason. When we use reason properly, we are creating moral principles. In other words, moral action must be done for the sake of duty. And neither inclination nor consequences are acceptable motives; only duty is acceptable. What this all comes down to is that morality is objective and impartial. We are supposed to use reason to derive our moral laws. That brings moral worth. The fact that my actions are derived from reason, and not from consequences or from desires gives them moral worth?

"Right. The categorical imperative alone purports to be an unconditional command. It does not leave open to the will to do the opposite at its discretion. Therefore, the categorical imperative alone carries with it that necessity which we demand from a law."

The Formula of Universal Law: The Categorical Imperative.   And the formula for universal law is a single categorical imperative?

"Act only on that maxim through which you can at the same time will that it should become a universal law."

Now that you have stated it, I guess this seems pretty obvious from what we've discussed. You are looking for a universal law and logical consistency in creating applications of your principle, aren't you?

"Certainly one feature of the moral law is that it is self-consistent. That is why promises must be kept. If you read attentively, you will see that making an excuse for myself is inconsistent with promise making when the law is made universal. Making promises with the intention of not keeping them would make promising, and the very purpose of promising, itself impossible."

Cultivating One's Talents

While you refer to your illustrations, I have a question about one of them.

"The third one, no doubt. You seek to indulge yourself rather than to develop your talents."

Yup. What's wrong with that? I'm willing to make it a universal law. I don't see any contradiction or inconsistency in letting everyone live under this law.

"Every man should let his talents rust and should be bent on devoting his life solely to idleness, indulgence, procreation, and, in a word, enjoyment. Is that your candidate for a universal law?"

Absolutely!

"But one cannot possibly *will* that this should be a universal law. For as a rational being he necessarily wills that all his powers should be developed, since they serve him, and are given him, for all sorts of possible ends."

This is Mr. Spock! Everything has to be rational! Where is the inconsistency in my desire for everyone to seek enjoyment?

"You have not yet grasped the import of the notion of the will. It is not logically impossible—nor certainly impossible, in fact—for all people to devote their lives to idleness, indulgence, and procreation. In my own time, the South Sea Islanders appeared to live just this way."

I wonder if my time travel machine can take me there?

"Put your musings aside and stay with the subject. The consistency that morality demands goes beyond logical rigor. There is also a component that touches reality, so to speak. The rational being knows that in the future reality may deem him to use talents that he has not yet been called to use."

Star Fleet has made an investment in me and I am obliged to develop my talents, so I sit around playing chess with a computer instead of chasing members of the sex that attracts me?

"Mock morality if you will, but the rational being seeks to cultivate his talents because the future is not without surprises."

I get your point. I can't help resisting morality. It just demands so much.

Coming to the Aid of Others

"Ah, but morality offers quite a lot. In my fourth illustration, I point out that moral law requires that we aid others who are struggling with great hardships."

Yes, that's an interesting example. You say that humanity could get along perfectly well without people helping the less fortunate. I agree with that. Why should I help someone else just because she is struggling against great hardships?

"That is not what I said, Art. You have taken only one statement and removed it from its context. What I said was that one could make a universal law of nature that aid for the less fortunate be withheld. I also assert, however, that it is impossible to *will* that such a principle should hold everywhere as a law of nature."

I don't get it.

"A person who decides to make it universal that people merely tolerate each other——"

Tolerate? What do you mean?

"You, Art, may believe that each person should be as happy as circumstances allow, or as happy as she alone can make herself. Art, you may also believe that depriving others of anything is wrong, even that envying others is wrong."

Yes, this all sounds reasonable.

"But you cannot will this as a universal law."

Why not? I do not harm anyone, and do not wish harm to anyone else, and do not envy anyone else. And I'm willing to make this a universal law that applies to everyone else. What more could you ask?

"A will which decided in this way would be in conflict with itself."

You mean I would feel guilty or bothered if I felt this way?

"No, that is not what I mean. I am not referring to guilt or any other feelings. I am discussing the will, not inclinations."

Then what sort of conflict would the will be in?

"Think about it this way. Many situations might arise in which a person would need love and sympathy from others. By endorsing the law of nature that we need only refrain from interfering with others, the person would rob himself of all hope of the help he wants for himself."

Do unto others as you would have them do unto you? Is that what all this boils down to? Are you saying that because I can imagine someday needing love and sympathy, I am therefore required to give love and sympathy to others?

"Yes. Do you object to this?"

This just sounds like, "There but for the grace of God go I," so I ought to help the less fortunate. Yes, I object to this.

"Why?"

Because it isn't I who is in need, for one. And for two, most of the time it's the person's fault that his life is going the way it is going. Why should I have to help people like that? Tell me that.

"You are losing the focus of moral principles. Remember that you must be able to universalize your principles. There may be circumstances where you will need love and sympathy."

Fine, but I have friends and family who will help me. Why should I help strangers? Let everyone get love and sympathy from people they know.

"It's quite obvious that you come from a background where at least some of your close associates have stable, even prosperous lives. This is keeping you from making a leap of moral imagination. You are overly conservative with your principle because you cannot imagine fortune really turning on you."

How do you know? Maybe I've come up the hard way, and I wasn't offered any help, and I made it.

"Indeed, but made it in what way? Although you may prosper materially, you have not yet come to grips with morality and its requirements. You are losing track of the essential feature of morality."

Which is what?

The Veil of Ignorance

"The good will. At least in your imagination, you have to place yourself in an impartial, objective perspective. It is what Professor Rawls* calls the veil of ignorance. That example dramatizes the objectivity required in asserting the will."

You want me to ignore my own personal circumstances?

"Exactly. Theoretically, the veil places you in ignorance of your own situation. If you do not know your own personal situation, you are forced to create laws that can be universally applied. By adopting this 'blind' point of view, you are able to remove your own inclinations, talents, desires, and everything else that is personal."

But all that would remain is reason. Oh, I see, that's just what you're after, reason.

Objection: Isn't This an Appeal to Results?

I have an objection. Isn't this an appeal to results? What I mean is, aren't you arguing that I should help other people because I may need love and sympathy someday? This reason sounds like enlightened self-interest.

* John Rawls, *A Theory of Justice* (Harvard, 1971).

"Unfortunately, that is the problem with examples. Giving examples often over-personalizes the principle. Examples can make it appear that the ground for the moral decision is self-interest. That is not the case, however. Let me expand the example."

Go for it.

Primary Goods

"I will borrow another of Rawls's concepts, that of primary goods. Primary goods are 'things which it is supposed a rational man wants whatever else he wants. . . . Regardless of what an individual's rational plans are in detail, it is assumed that there are various things which he would prefer more of rather than less. With more of these goods men can generally be assured of greater success in carrying out their intentions and in advancing their ends, whatever these ends may be.'"

Okay, now what?

"Every rational person wills that she be granted as much and as many of the primary goods as is possible. Every rational being wills this, and not just for herself, but for everyone. You see, Art, it is the nature of the will that determines universal principles as laws of nature. The consequences do not matter. Each person as a rational being wills to enjoy the primary goods."

What sort of things count as primary goods?

"Rawls distinguishes two types of primary goods, social primary goods and natural goods. The first are things like 'rights and liberties, powers and opportunities, income and wealth.' Some of the natural primary goods are 'health and vigor, intelligence and imagination.' The idea is that these are desirable for just about any rational plan of life."

Are you saying that if you are denied all the social liberties, or that if you are not particularly healthy, you cannot pursue a rational plan of life? This doesn't make sense. For example, certainly a blind person is capable of achieving a lot in life.

"Of course, that's true. No rational person, though, would willingly give up sight without very compelling reason. Nor would a rational person willingly give up rights and liberties. Why? Because giving up these primary goods inhibits one's flexibility in pursuing the variety of goals that rational people set for themselves."

All right, this makes sense, but how does it apply to the illustration you are explaining?

"It's good you keep track of the argument. Sometimes people get distracted from the main point in justifying the lesser points. Love and sympathy are also primary goods. You may never need them, but it would not be rational to give them up without compelling reason. In times of struggle, if you do need them, they are important to have. Don't you agree?"

Yes, I guess so.

"Good, then the will demands that we help others when they need our sympathy and aid. This same reasoning applies to all primary goods. That is why I say that a will would be in conflict with itself if it denied people their primary goods."

Making Exceptions

"One other thing bothers me about what you said just a few moments ago, Art. By singling out yourself, you show a callous attitude toward others. Your attitude is: 'What does it matter to me that others are struggling with great hardships?' Of course, morally that is unacceptable."

I have come to realize that. How much more are you going to criticize me?

"What your attitude demonstrates is an ability to make an exception of yourself. Some maxims cannot be conceived as a universal law of nature. Others can be conceived, but they cannot be willed for the reasons we have just enunciated."

Because they would contradict the will?

"Yes. There is yet another test. We may experience a contradiction in our own will when we assert that a certain principle should be objectively necessary as a universal law and yet subjectively should not hold universally but should admit of exceptions."

Huh? Could you explain that?

"Huh, indeed. What I mean is that you may assert a certain principle and claim that it is universally necessary, yet you believe that it should not hold for everyone. I anticipate another 'huh?' "

Sorry.

"To explain, imagine that you advocate that everyone ought to keep promises. In this case, however, you find it difficult to obey your own principle. Imagine a case where you will be embarrassed if you keep your promise. Now you may be tempted to make an exception of your own case, but this will bring a contradiction to your own will."

Sometimes my will, my reason, conflicts with my desires?

"Exactly, and those times the will must be preferred to subjective inclination. That is what morality is about."

Reason and Autonomy

Why should I be moral? That's really what I want to know.

"Isn't it obvious why you should be moral? No, I guess it is not clear to you. Very well, like many others who have come before you, you see people as tied to laws by their duty. Isn't that correct?"

Yes, that's why I ask: Why should I be moral? Why should I give up self-interest and obey the laws that are imposed on me?

"What has not yet occurred to you is that you are subject only to laws which are made by you and yet are universal. You are bound only to act in uniformity with a will which is your own but has as nature's purpose for it the function of making universal law."

Are you saying that I am most free when I follow laws or principles that are my own creation?

"Absolutely, and the laws of your own making as a rational being are also laws that apply universally to all rational beings. Therefore, freedom, or what I call autonomy, is produced only by obedience to moral principle. Don't you see, Art, the constraint and coercion of moral principle is lifted. You follow your own laws, which are also moral laws."

And you are suggesting that I want autonomy.

"Yes, again. Autonomy is the ground of the dignity of human nature and of every rational nature. In fact, autonomy of the will is the supreme principle of morality."

The Formula of the End in Itself

According to your analysis, Professor Kant, reason and autonomy are valuable in themselves. Have I got that right?

"That is a good way of looking at the key points of morality. You ask, is there something whose existence has in itself an absolute value, something which as an end in itself could be a ground for determinate laws. If we could find such a valuable existing thing, then in it, and in it alone, would be the ground of a possible categorical imperative."

Is that what I'm asking?

"You are asking about something valuable in itself. You have surmised from our brief discussion that autonomy and reason qualify. Now I say that man, and in general every rational being, exists as an end in himself, not merely as a means for arbitrary use by this or that will. You see, Art, rational nature exists as an end in itself."

Doesn't nonrational nature exist in itself? I mean, trees and tables and chairs exist. Why give priority to rational nature?

"This is the way in which a man necessarily conceives his own existence. . . . But it is also the way in which every other rational being conceives his existence on the same rational ground which is valid also for me; hence it is . . . an objective principle."

How do you know that every rational—

"Excuse me, Art, please. Allow me to finish my thought, and then you may ask all the questions you like. The practical imperative is: Act in such a way that you always treat humanity, whether in your own person or in the person of any other, never simply as a means, but always at the same time as an end."

How Do We Conceive Our Existence?

I do have several comments. First, how do you know that all rational beings conceive their existence as an end in itself, as valuable in itself? Why can't we imagine rational creatures from another star system who value the whole and not the individual? You seem to be imposing on all rational beings our basic, and nearly universal, desire to survive. I don't see that as necessary.

"It is not rational to *will* your own annihilation. To will your own demise involves a contradiction. Let us suppose that from self-love I make it my principle to shorten my life. A system of nature by whose law the very same feeling whose function is to stimulate the furtherance of life should actually destroy life would contradict itself. Consequently, it could not subsist as a system of nature. Hence this maxim could not hold as a universal law of nature. It is therefore entirely opposed to the supreme principle of all duty."

Then your objection to suicide is not that if I kill myself, and everyone else follows, then there would be no one left to follow the same principle? Is that the inconsistency you mean?

"Of course not. The inconsistency is in the motivation of the principle."

Having Children.   To see if I understand, can I try an example from my time?

"Certainly, you may."

Imagine that I decide that a certain way of life or a certain attitude is wrong for people. I ask myself if I can universalize this, and I find that I can. I will that no one live this certain lifestyle.

"But by willing this prohibition, are you saying that there is an inconsistency in the way of life you condemn? Remember, mere consistency in a fanatic is not sufficient to warrant us saying you have a rational principle, a moral law."

Hmm. Okay, let me try this. Say that I value people as important.

"As intrinsically and unconditionally valuable?"

Yes, okay, just what you said. Say that I value them, and I find that people who do not wish to have children are living in offense of the natural order.

"How's that?"

Say they prevent pregnancy in their relationships. They do not want children, so they use contraceptives. Now people cannot will that no one have children. To say that would be to say that sex is for begetting children, yet they want sexual activity but no children. They live in contradiction to nature.

"No, you have misunderstood. People who do not desire children are not acting inconsistently with any principle. Your example is very different from my prohibition against suicide. In the case of suicide, the principle of self-love drives the person to the act of suicide. That is where the contradiction lies with suicide. Your example is an attempt to transform a natural, biological inclination into a moral principle. The analogy does not work."

So there is nothing inconsistent in principle about using contraceptives or being gay?

"Not that I can determine from your comments."

"We Destroyed the Village in Order to Save It."   Let me try one more example, Professor Kant. Imagine again that I decide that a certain way of life or a certain attitude is wrong for people. It is wrong for people to have to live under a dictatorship. I see my opportunity to prevent people from having to be oppressed. So I—

"Destroy the village in order to save it? That is what you were going to say?"

Yup. See, I value the people enough to try to come to their aid. By destroying their village, people and all, the dictator's army will have nothing to hold. Pretty good, huh?

"This is quite unacceptable. What you suggests involves killing innocent people, people about whom you profess to care. You kill some and destroy the homes of the others, all in the name of saving them. No, Art, this reasoning violates the formulation of people as ends in themselves."

How so? I'm doing it for them.

"So you say, but you are treating them as a means to your own desires and political bias. You cannot kill an innocent person and claim you are doing it to save him. This reasoning is analogous to the suicide example. One cannot kill oneself in order to save oneself. One cannot kill others in order to save them. Self-love or love of others cannot consistently be used as grounds for either suicide or murder. Do you have any other questions you wish to ask me? My time with you grows short."

One Final Criticism

At the end of chapter 2 of your *Groundwork,* you say, "We have merely shown by developing the concept of morality generally in vogue that autonomy of the will is unavoidably bound up with it or rather is its very basis." Is that all you have shown?

"What I claim is that the fitness of the maxim of every good will to make itself a universal law is itself the sole law which the will of every rational being spontaneously imposes on itself without basing it on any impulse or interest. . . . We have not here asserted the truth of this proposition, much less pretended to have a proof of it in our power."

Then all this only shows what morality is. You haven't shown why I should be moral.

"No, that's true, though I have more to say about that in future chapters and in other of my works."

Have you shown that the moral life as you define it is the best life?

"No, I have not done that here."

Summary of Discussion

Kant argues that there is only one purely good thing, the good will. The good will is unconditionally good. It uses reason to come to its principles for action. Superior to passions, the good will directs us to act according to our duties. It is important not merely to live in conformity with duty, but to have duty as one's motive. A moral action takes its worth from being motivated solely by duty and reason. Consequences play no role in moral reasoning.

It probably seems odd to many of us that love and other "gentler" emotions cannot be the motive for moral action. Kant rejects all emotional motivations because emotions are not impartial. Morality must be impartial and susceptible to universal application. Only reason can play this vital role.

Why does Kant require reasoned objectivity? Kant understands that morality is our vehicle for communicating and forming community. Communication is possible only if all people share in the ability to communicate. This ability is possible only if everyone shares the "language" of communication. That shared language is reason. By its very nature, reason is objective. Emotions, even emotions like love and sympathy, are subjective. Emotions allow for partiality. Therefore, emotions cannot be motivators for morality.

Kant also argues for the efficacy of reason because reason gives us autonomy, freedom. The only laws that are acceptable are those that apply to everyone. Reason defines us as human. By living in accordance with reason, we fulfill our natures. Isn't that one of the reasons you urged me to be moral? To be moral is to fulfill one's human nature.

Kant invents the categorical imperative to exemplify the formula of universal law. "Act only on that maxim through which you can at the same time will that it should become a universal law." Acting in accordance with this imperative guarantees that one's will accords with reason. Kant's application of the categorical imperative is instructive. He writes that you should "act in such a way that you always treat humanity, whether in your own person or in the person of any other, never simply as a means, but always at the same time as an end." Morality requires us to treat people as valuable just because they are reasoning agents.

What Kant derives from this is a set of duties to oneself and to others. One is duty-bound to cultivate one's talents. One is responsible to come to the aid of other people. One must treat other people with respect and objectivity. Morality, through reason, requires each of us to understand ourselves as one person among many equals. Only a good will informed by impartial, objective reason can be the source of morality.

Discussion Highlights

    I. The good will is
        1. Unconditionally good.
        2. A function of reason.
        3. Superior to the passions.
    II. The motive of duty
        1. Requires that we live in conformity with duty.
        2. And requires that we live from the motive of duty.
        3. Actions take their moral worth from the motive of duty.
        4. Love cannot be a moral motivation.
          a. love is not impartial
          b. love is not objective
    III. The categorical imperative
        1. Embodies reasoned objectivity.
        2. Requires that we come to the aid of other people.

3. Requires that we treat other people with respect and objectivity.
4. Requires each person as well to cultivate his or her talents.

IV. Autonomy or freedom
1. Comes only with acting on reason.
2. Allows people to communicate and to form communities.

Questions for Thought/Paper Topics

1. Kant argues that only reason is impartial. Do you agree? Can a parent's love for her children cause her to treat them differently but fairly?
2. Must morality always be equal treatment? What does it mean to treat equally people whose social position is unequal?
3. Kant argues that we have a duty to ourselves to cultivate our duties. How strong is that requirement? Do you agree with him?
4. If last week I promised you that I would meet you today at 10 A.M. and you later released me from the promise, I would not be obligated to meet you. We can be released from promises and other like duties. Does Kant's sense of duty to oneself allow for this? Can I release myself from the duty to myself to cultivate my talents?
5. Is Mr. Spock the ideal moral person? Does he fit Kant's criteria?
6. Describe how the "veil of ignorance" works. Does it capture our sense of morality?
7. Do you agree that reasoned objectivity is autonomy? Discuss Kant's vision of autonomy. Do you agree?

For Further Reading

The best way to learn Kant's thoughts is to read the *Groundwork of the Metaphysics of Morals* (Harper & Row, 1964). John Rawls's *A Theory of Justice* (Harvard, 1971) is sympathetic to Kant's approach to moral theory. I have included chapter 3, section 24, for this present discussion. Commentaries on Kant are numerous. C. D. Broad's *Five Types of Ethical Theory* (Routledge & Kegan Paul, 1930) is a good secondary source. Robert Paul Wolff's *The Autonomy of Reason: A Commentary on Kant's "Groundwork of the Metaphysics of Morals"* (Harper & Row, 1973) is more than just a catchy title.

The Veil of Ignorance

JOHN RAWLS

John Rawls is a contemporary philosopher who is sympathetic to the program of morality developed by Kant. The "veil of ignorance" is an interesting device designed to force us to exercise our reason in making moral judgments. Rawls suggests that we can become impartial if we situate ourselves behind a veil of ignorance. What he means is that if we are to make fair and impartial judgments, certain kinds of knowledge must be unknown to us; no one is to know one's own position in society, one's own fortune, talents, or social status.

I think what Rawls has in mind is similar to the procedure my brothers and I used to share cake when we were young. One of us would cut the cake. Then we would decide the order of choice of pieces, with the cutter normally going last. There was no incentive to cut any one piece too large because one of my other brothers would choose that piece. Following Rawls's idea, the cake cutter calculated how large each piece was to be before the cut was made. Most important, each brother automatically gained veto power over the decisions. Not knowing initially who would be first to choose a piece, I am sure we would all argue for equal-sized pieces of cake.

Does Rawls provide an adequate metaphor for making moral decisions? Is it important to remove emotional involvement and personal biases from moral decision making? Does the veil of ignorance accomplish its task? Is there any other, better way of deciding who gets a larger or a smaller piece of the cake? For example, would it be fair to give equal-sized pieces of cake to a hungry twelve-year-old and a well-fed two-year-old? Or should we consider need—in this case, body size and hunger—as more relevant?

THE IDEA OF THE ORIGINAL POSITION is to set up a fair procedure so that any principles agreed to will be just. The aim is to use the notion of pure procedural justice as a basis of theory. Somehow we must nullify the effects of specific contingencies which put men at odds and tempt them to exploit social and natural circumstances to their own advantage. Now in order to do this I assume that the parties are situated behind a veil of ignorance. They do not know how the various alternatives will affect their own particular case and they are obliged to evaluate principles solely on the basis of general considerations.[1]

---

[1] The veil of ignorance is so natural a condition that something like it must have occurred to many. The closest express statement of it known to me is found in J. C. Harsanyi, "Cardinal Utility in Welfare Economics and in the Theory of Risk-Taking," *Journal of Political Economy*, vol. 61 (1953). Harsanyi uses it to develop a utilitarian theory, discussed [elsewhere].

It is assumed, then, that the parties do not know certain kinds of particular facts. First of all, no one knows his place in society, his class position or social status; nor does he know his fortune in the distribution of natural assets and abilities, his intelligence and strength, and the like. Nor, again, does anyone know his conception of the good, the particulars of his rational plan of life, or even the special features of his psychology such as his aversion to risk or liability to optimism or pessimism. More than this, I assume that the parties do not know the particular circumstances of their own society. That is, they do not know its economic or political situation, or the level of civilization and culture it has been able to achieve. The persons in the original position have no information as to which generation they belong. These broader restrictions on knowledge are appropriate in part because questions of social justice arise between generations as well as within them, for example, the question of the appropriate rate of capital saving and of the conservation of natural resources and the environment of nature. There is also, theoretically anyway, the question of a reasonable genetic policy. In these cases too, in order to carry through the idea of the original position, the parties must not know the contingencies that set them in opposition. They must choose principles the consequences of which they are prepared to live with whatever generation they turn out to belong to.

As far as possible, then, the only particular facts which the parties know is that their society is subject to the circumstances of justice and whatever this implies. It is taken for granted, however, that they know the general facts about human society. They understand political affairs and the principles of economic theory; they know the basis of social organization and the laws of human psychology. Indeed, the parties are presumed to know whatever general facts affect the choice of the principles of justice. There are no limitations on general information, that is, on general laws and theories, since conceptions of justice must be adjusted to the characteristics of the systems of social cooperation which they are to regulate, and there is no reason to rule out these facts. It is, for example, a consideration against a conception of justice that in view of the laws of moral psychology, men would not acquire a desire to act upon it even when the institutions of their society satisfied it. For in this case there would be difficulty in securing the stability of social cooperation. It is an important feature of a conception of justice that it should generate its own support. That is, its principles should be such that when they are embodied in the basic structure of society men tend to acquire the corresponding sense of justice. Given the principles of moral learning, men develop a desire to act in accordance with its principles. In this case a conception of justice is stable. This kind of general information is admissible in the original position.

The notion of the veil of ignorance raises several difficulties. Some may object that the exclusion of nearly all particular information makes it difficult to grasp what is meant by the original position. Thus it may be helpful to observe that one or more persons can at any time enter this position, or perhaps, better, simulate the deliberations of this hypothetical situation, simply by reasoning in accordance with the appropriate restrictions. In arguing for a conception of justice we must be sure that it is among the permitted alternatives and satisfies the stipulated formal constraints. No considerations can be advanced in its favor unless they would be rational ones for us to urge were we to lack the kind of knowledge that is excluded. The evaluation of principles must proceed in terms of the general consequences of their public recognition and universal application, it being assumed that they will be complied with by everyone. To say that a certain conception of justice would be chosen in the original position is equivalent to saying that rational deliberation satisfying certain conditions and restrictions would reach a certain conclusion. If necessary, the argument to this result could be set out more formally. I shall, however, speak throughout in terms of the notion of the original position. It is more economical and suggestive, and brings out certain essential features that otherwise one might easily overlook.

These remarks show that the original position is not to be thought of as a general assembly which includes at one moment everyone who will live at some time; or, much less, as an assembly of everyone who could live at some time. It is not a gathering of all actual or possible persons. To conceive of the original position in either of these ways is to stretch fantasy too far; the conception would cease to be a natural guide to intuition. In any case, it is important that the original position be interpreted so that one can at any time adopt its perspective. It must make no difference when one takes up this viewpoint, or who does so: the restrictions must be such that the same principles are always chosen. The veil of ignorance is a key condition in meeting this requirement. It insures not only that the information available is relevant, but that it is at all times the same.

It may be protested that the condition of the veil of ignorance is irrational. Surely, some may object, principles should be chosen in the light of all the knowledge available. There are various replies to this contention. Here I shall sketch those which emphasize the simplifications that need to be made if one is to have any theory at all . . . To begin with, it is clear that since the differences among the parties are unknown to them, and everyone is equally rational and similarly situated, each is convinced by the same arguments. Therefore, we can view the choice in the original position from the standpoint of one person selected at random. If anyone after due reflection prefers a conception of justice to another, then they all do, and a unanimous agreement can be reached. We can, to make the circumstances more vivid, imagine that the parties are required to communicate with each other through a referee as intermediary, and that he is to announce which alternatives have been suggested and the reasons offered in their support. He forbids the attempt to form coalitions, and

he informs the parties when they have come to an understanding. But such a referee is actually superfluous, assuming that the deliberations of the parties must be similar.

Thus there follows the very important consequence that the parties have no basis for bargaining in the usual sense. No one knows his situation in society nor his natural assets, and therefore no one is in a position to tailor principles to his advantage. We might imagine that one of the contractees threatens to hold out unless the others agree to principles favorable to him. But how does he know which principles are especially in his interests? The same holds for the formation of coalitions: if a group were to decide to band together to the disadvantage of the others, they would not know how to favor themselves in the choice of principles. Even if they could get everyone to agree to their proposal, they would have no assurance that it was to their advantage, since they cannot identify themselves either by name or description. The one case where this conclusion fails is that of saving. Since the persons in the original position know that they are contemporaries (taking the present time of entry interpretation), they can favor their generation by refusing to make any sacrifices at all for their successors; they simply acknowledge the principle that no one has a duty to save for posterity. Previous generations have saved or they have not; there is nothing the parties can now do to affect that. So in this instance the veil of ignorance fails to secure the desired result. Therefore I resolve the question of justice between generations in a different way by altering the motivation assumption. But with this adjustment no one is able to formulate principles especially designed to advance his own cause. Whatever his temporal position, each is forced to choose for everyone.[2]

The restrictions on particular information in the original position are, then, of fundamental importance. Without them we would not be

---

[2] Rousseau, *The Social Contract*, bk. II, ch. IV, par. 5.

able to work out any definite theory of justice at all. We would have to be content with a vague formula stating that justice is what would be agreed to without being able to say much, if anything, about the substance of the agreement itself. The formal constraints of the concept of right, those applying to principles directly, are not sufficient for our purpose. The veil of ignorance makes possible a unanimous choice of a particular conception of justice. Without these limitations on knowledge the bargaining problem of the original position would be hopelessly complicated. Even if theoretically a solution were to exist, we would not, at present anyway, be able to determine it.

The notion of the veil of ignorance is implicit, I think, in Kant's ethics. Nevertheless the problem of defining the knowledge of the parties and of characterizing the alternatives open to them has often been passed over, even by contract theories. Sometimes the situation definitive of moral deliberation is presented in such an indeterminate way that one cannot ascertain how it will turn out. Thus Perry's doctrine is essentially contractarian: he holds that social and personal integration must proceed by entirely different principles, the latter by rational prudence the former by the concurrence of persons of good will. He would appear to reject utilitarianism on much the same grounds suggested earlier: namely, that it improperly extends the principle of choice for one person to choices facing society. The right course of action is characterized as that which best advances social aims as these would be formulated by reflective agreement given that the parties have full knowledge of the circumstances and are moved by a benevolent concern for one another's interests. No effort is made, however, to specify in any precise way the possible outcomes of this sort of agreement. Indeed, without a far more elaborate account, no conclusions can be drawn.[3] I do not wish here

to criticize others; rather, I want to explain the necessity for what may seem at times like so many irrelevant details.

Now the reasons for the veil of ignorance go beyond mere simplicity. We want to define the original position so that we get the desired solution. If a knowledge of particulars is allowed, then the outcome is biased by arbitrary contingencies. As already observed, to each according to his threat advantage is not a principle of justice. If the original position is to yield agreements that are just, the parties must be fairly situated and treated equally as moral persons. The arbitrariness of the world must be corrected for by adjusting the circumstances of the initial contractual situation. Moreover, if in choosing principles we required unanimity even when there is full information, only a few rather obvious cases could be decided. A conception of justice based on unanimity in these circumstances would indeed be weak and trivial. But once knowledge is excluded, the requirement of unanimity is not out of place and the fact that it can be satisfied is of great importance. It enables us to say of the preferred conception of justice that it represents a genuine reconciliation of interests.

A final comment. For the most part I shall suppose that the parties possess all general information. No general facts are closed to them. I do this mainly to avoid complications. Nevertheless a conception of justice is to be the public basis of the terms of social cooperation. Since common understanding necessitates certain bounds on the complexity of principles, there may likewise be limits on the use of theoretical knowledge in the original position. Now clearly it would be very difficult to classify and to grade for complexity the various sorts of general facts. I shall make no attempt to do this. We do however recognize an intricate theoretical construction when we meet one. Thus it seems reasonable to say that other things equal one conception of justice is to be preferred to another when it is founded upon markedly simpler general facts, and its choice does not depend

---

[3] See R. B. Perry, *The General Theory of Value* (New York, Longmans, Green and Company, 1926), pp. 674–682.

upon elaborate calculations in the light of a vast array of theoretically defined possibilities. It is desirable that the grounds for a public conception of justice should be evident to everyone when circumstances permit. This consideration favors, I believe, the two principles of justice over the criterion of utility.

10 Existentialist Ethics: Jean-Paul Sartre's Ideas on Being Free

Before we conjure up Jean-Paul Sartre, I would like to introduce existentialism. As I understand it, existentialism tells us that life is pointless; or, even worse, it tells us that life is filled with despair, forlornness, abandonment, and loneliness. If all this isn't bad enough, existentialism says that we can do whatever we want because moral values cannot be justified. Unfortunately, however, the theory isn't permissive in the way I wanted at the beginning of the book. We are allowed to do whatever we want, but we are responsible for our actions.

I think Sartre also says that values are vague. Someone told me once that Sartre believes that moral values are absurd. Given all this, why would anyone accept such a depressing picture of life?

"Art, I am disappointed with your analysis of my work."

Why? Haven't I adequately depressed my readers just the way you want?

"Don't be sarcastic. Your conclusions about existentialism are inadequate and misleading."

How? All you write about is depressing stuff. Life is filled with anguish, responsibility, forlornness, and loneliness. Do you deny it?

Two Insights

"I do not deny that existentialism carefully examines these attitudes, but you portray them in the most negative light. You also completely overlook the two most important insights of existentialism. Existentialism is the one doctrine that looks realistically, even optimistically, at people. We do not rule out generosity by saying that it is human nature to be greedy. We do not say that people are born and live in sin. We open the entire range of possibilities to humanity. People may choose to be generous or greedy, sinful or loving. What could be more refreshing and more encouraging? I believe existentialism is the doctrine that makes human life possible."

Material in this chapter taken from *Existentialism and Human Emotions* by Jean-Paul Sartre. Copyright © 1957, 1985 by Philosophical Library, Inc. Published by arrangement with Carol Publishing Group.

Two insights?

"Man's existence precedes his essence. And man is free."

Is that all there is to existentialism?

Existence Precedes Essence: There is No Human Nature

"I would also say that existentialism defines a set of questions and problems that have not been sufficiently addressed in recent philosophy. You are too casual, however, in dismissing the two defining features of the thought of existentialists. First, existentialists assert the importance of choice. We also believe that existence precedes essence."

What do you mean, existence precedes essence?

"Subjectivity must be the starting point."

To be honest, that doesn't ring any bells of understanding in my head. Could you explain it?

"In my essay I include the example of a paper cutter. A paper cutter is designed in a person's mind before the cutter exists. Its essence precedes its existence. With human beings, the opposite is true. We humans exist and then we define our essence."

Maybe, but I'm still in a fog.

"All right, let me put it this way. There is no human nature."

How can that be? Humans think; we are rational. Isn't that at least part of our nature?

"No, I don't think so. Human essence refers to human nature. What I mean when I say that existence precedes essence is that man exists, appears on the scene, and only afterwards defines himself."

How could that be? Surely you aren't denying the impact that instincts have on people's lives?

Man Is Nothing Else but What He Makes of Himself.   "I am denying exactly that. No matter what a person believes, she is free. That is what I am asserting most strenuously."

So that is where choice comes in?

"Very good, yes. Man is what he makes of himself; man is what he conceives himself to be and what he wills himself to be."

Are you saying that we exist, and then we define ourselves?

"Exactly. First comes a person's existence, then the person defines herself. There is no preordained purpose or function for humans. Human consciousness and choice must be called on to forge a self. That's freedom! Man is nothing else but what he makes of himself. That's the first principle of existentialism."

Consciousness?

"Humans are self-conscious and therefore free."

What do you mean, we're self-conscious?

"Not in the sense of being easily embarrassed. We humans are conscious of our own future. Man is a plan that is aware of itself. You, for example, know that you have a future, so you plan your life with some future in mind. That's what separates us from inanimate objects, plants and animals. Man will be what he plans to be."

Bad Faith.   What does that do to my idea of living in the moment?

"If by living in the moment you plan to pursue pleasure or intense experience, then your idea is unrealistic."

Unrealistic? Why do you say that?

"Because man knows he has a future. We are conscious of our lives. To play with the idea of merely living in one fixed moment of pleasure is an example of bad faith."

Bad faith? You're throwing too many new concepts at me.

"All I mean here by bad faith is that you are making efforts to establish that you are not what and where you are. You imagine a most pleasurable experience. Then you wish to block out the ever-changing present. To accomplish this, you lie to yourself. You go beyond the given facts of reality."

How Do We Create Our Own Obstacles?

But my plans don't always work out!

"Of course not, but existentialism does not suggest that your plans will always succeed. Instead, I mean that each person shapes his or her own future. There are facts of the world that must be accounted for, but even these facts are our choice to a great extent."

How are facts our choice? That doesn't make sense.

"We create our own obstacles."

Huh? Either something is in the way or it is not in the way.

"Take insults as an example. The Stoic Epictetus was correct in saying that it is up to me to determine my response to any action. It is also up to me to define what does and what does not count as an insult. Don't you agree?"

Maybe that works with insults, but some facts, some obstacles, are just there. A person can't choose not to see a mountain. Nor can a person choose to ignore his family relationships.

"Of course, both these alleged facts are up to me. If I choose to see the mountain as hindering my travels, then I acknowledge it. If I choose to see it as beautiful, or as ugly, it is my choice that gives it reality. As for family relationships, it is clearly I who determines them. If I am married, I must choose at each moment to be married to this woman and not to leave her. The point is I cannot use the fact of the mountain or the marriage to excuse myself from action."

Should I Do Whatever I Want?

Is existentialism advocating that I do whatever I want?

"No, that is oversimplifying the theory and distorting it. Man is at the start a plan which is aware of itself. Man consciously chooses his plan of life. Wants are merely symptoms of the fundamental choices we make."

I'm not sure I see the difference.

"First, there is the spontaneous choice of who you are. After that come your wants. The wants are connected to the earlier choice; the wants are a result of the choices we make. But choice comes first."

Are you saying that I choose my wants? I choose to be hungry or thirsty, a heterosexual or a homosexual?

"Yes, in an important way. You choose how, when, and why you will satisfy your hunger and thirst. For example, under certain circumstances you may choose to starve yourself, or to commit suicide by some other means. And yes, you choose your sexual preferences. You must recognize that your wants are yours. They define who you are."

And it's this spontaneous choice that you call the will?

"Right."

How Do I Choose?

I think we're getting somewhere. How do I choose? What I mean by that is, what are the standards by which I choose?

"Standards?"

Sure. With everyday garden-variety morality, choice is limited, or maybe it's better to say that choice is directed by moral values and goals. Now that I think of it, even the pleasure seeker's choices are directed toward achieving pleasure and avoiding pain. But you are saying that choice is more basic.

"If I choose to live a moral life, it is my choice. If I choose to be a hedonist, a pleasure seeker, that too is my choice."

But which choice is right?

"If you mean by right, morally right, then the moral life is obviously preferred."

No, that's not what I mean. Which life is more desirable? Which is the best life?

"The one that you choose, Art."

Huh?

"We always choose the good. To choose this or that is to affirm at the same time the value of what we choose. The fact that you choose it means you value it."

The ideas of choice and will are pretty powerful in your theory.

"Yes."

So What Gives Existentialism a Bad Name?

So what gives your existentialism a bad name? (Is there an echo in here?)

"In part it is the atheistic element, although there are many existentialists who are theists. Your book includes at least three—Dostoevski, Kierkegaard, and Buber—though you have not presented their religious writings."

Maybe my next book will include a philosophy of religion section. But why is existentialism attacked?

"Existentialism is a doctrine which declares that every truth and every action implies a human setting and a human subjectivity. Human choice is what makes human life possible."

Okay, Professor Sartre, but you must admit that the existentialism you present gives a pretty dark description of human living.

"Why do you say that?"

You say people live in a state of anguish, forlornness, and despair. I still think that's pretty depressing. Won't you admit that?

"I think with a little explanation you will find these words less frightening and depressing. It all starts with choice, of course."

How is choice objectionable to people?

Choice and Responsibility

"The objection is probably due to the extreme responsibility that existentialism places on each individual. The attacks come in different forms. From the Christian standpoint, we are charged with denying God's commandments and the eternal truths. Therefore, it is claimed, we deny the seriousness of human undertakings. From the politically conservative perspective, we are charged with resisting authority. This point of view says that we should not try to rise above our stations in life and that the reigning powers know what they are doing. Both these points of view, the Christian and the political, hold that there is a human nature. They believe, as do many people, that man's bent is always toward trouble."

Isn't it? The reason I ask is because that's been the attack made against me throughout this book.

"Art, the existentialist asserts that there is no human nature, remember? Therefore, everything is choice! There are no human inclinations except the ones we will."

Aren't some desires natural and others unnatural, or against our nature? I know many people say that we are evil by nature.

"Look at the evidence of reality, though. Not everyone responds in the same way to situations."

That's because we are all raised differently.

"What you say is true; we are all raised differently. But do you mean to say that all our actions are merely reflections of earlier training?"

That idea makes me uncomfortable, but yes, our family, friends, and society give us our values. Are you denying this?

"I do not deny that most people believe this. Indeed, the problem today, as always, is that people fear responsibility for their choices. What really scares people in the existentialist doctrine is that it leaves man a possibility of choice."

And they think we will misuse our ability to choose?

"I think that is the concern."

Say I accept that I am responsible for my choices and for my wants. What else is there?

"You are responsible for your choices and for all of mankind."

Wait a minute, I thought my choices were mine, and yours were yours, and that was the end of it. Why am I responsible for all humanity?

"Let's look at each part of responsibility separately."

Anguish.   Okay. According to you, I choose for myself. I am whatever I will myself to be. If I will that I am a moral person or a pleasure seeker, then I am. What's the big deal? I choose and I willingly accept the responsibility.

"The 'big deal' as you call it, is that you overlook the extreme responsibility of choice, the anguish. Even in your own case, apart from the rest of humanity, your choice is completely your own, completely. For example, say you choose to live a morally praiseworthy life. What that involves is a creative act."

Creative?

"Yes, you and you alone must create your own values. Remember, atheistic existentialism denies that there is any God with eternal truths and commandments. We also deny that there is any human nature. Therefore, you cannot resort to these sources for your values."

You've already ruled out my wants. You say that my wants come after my basic choice of a lifestyle. Where am I going to get my values?

"That question is the source of anguish."

And what's your answer?

"Choice! Oddly enough, most of the first part of your book has been devoted to the kind of thinking that I endorse."

You mean I am an existentialist without knowing it?

"Not quite. Your discussion, though, pits the moralist against a person who wants to live in the moment. In forcing that conversation, you set the right questions in motion."

How have I done that?

"You have consistently challenged your reader to justify morality generally and individual moral principles specifically. Your reluctance and theirs to grapple honestly with these challenges shows one element of existential anguish."

But I *have* been honest.

"If you believe that, then you are in bad faith. Your discomfort with morality causes you to run for cover. You find living in the moment to be an intellectually safe place to hide."

Safe?

"Defending morality is far more difficult than taking the relativist, or subjectivist, or hedonist, or egoist way out. Let me put it differently. You find morality perched on an unstable foundation. Your challenge to morality is commendable; however your recourse to hiding in some kind of vague self-centeredness is bad faith. You're avoiding the responsibility of choice. You prefer not to choose, because every choice frightens you. What you fail to realize is that not choosing is also a choice."

Choice frightens me? Why do you say that? I like the idea of doing whatever I want. What I don't like about morality is all the restrictions.

The Inability to Discover a Foundation of Morality.   "You cannot guarantee morality by reference to some other, better-grounded thought, so you flee from it."

Is that why Kant tries to ground morality in reason? And why Mill seeks to establish morality as impartial and based on happiness? Each is trying to discover an unshakeable foundation for morality?

"I think so, yes."

So what do you think is wrong with their theories?

"We'll get to that. First, however, we need to explain anguish. You cannot find any foundation for morality except some arbitrary beliefs that many people hold, right? You are asking for proof of morality, but you cannot figure out what proof would look like?"

Right. Nor can I see why I should be moral.

"So you are forced to choose your own values, just as you have been trying to force the reader to justify moral values. What is wrong with stealing? you ask. Failing to find an adequate answer, you and your reader either reject or accept the value of honesty. Here is where anguish comes in. By either accepting or rejecting the value of honesty, you are choosing either to be or not to be honest. Now take responsibility for your choice."

So at the beginning of the book, when I asked about honesty, all the reader had to answer was, "Because I will it," and that would be enough?

The Depth of Responsibility.   "After looking at a number of possibilities, one chooses. The value one chooses has value only because it is chosen."

Then it's easy! All I have to do is look at the alternatives and choose. Why do you call this anguish?

"You are overlooking the depth of responsibility involved. Think of yourself as a book writing itself. Each word, each sentence, is you. Each of your actions reveals who you are. You exist, then you create yourself. There are no excuses; you are your actions. That places all the responsibility onto you and no one else. You cannot make excuses for your values. You cannot turn to your cultural or religious values. You cannot blame the people who have raised and educated you. You cannot blame a commanding officer, or leader, or employer for your actions."

But sometimes a person has to do what she doesn't want to do. I mean, if I want to pass a course, I have to at least take the exams or write the papers. If I work for a company and they order me to do something, I have to do it. How can I get around that?

Do What You Will.   "You and you alone bear the responsibility. If you find that your orders are inappropriate, then disobey. For example, if your employer tells you to act in a way that you do not will, then don't follow the order."

Easy for you to say. If I do whatever I want, I'll get fired. There are lots of times I don't want to attend my classes or go to work at my job. But I have to go. If I don't, I'll get fired.

"Exactly. The choice is yours. I did not say that you should do what you want. You should do what you will. Remember, the will, the spontaneous choice, comes before your wants."

I think we're just getting caught up in a word game here. If I do whatever I "will," I'll flunk my courses or I'll get fired.

"The fact that you do not miss too many of your classes, the fact that you regularly go to work, shows what you will."

How? If I could do whatever I want, I'd—

"Your actions indicate your preferences. Your problem is that you want choice, but you fail to accept responsibility. I think, though, that your reaction to my questions shows that you do experience anguish."

How do my answers show that?

"In real life, you recognize that your choices have real-life impact. Your actions do have consequences. In choosing one action over another action, you calculate the impact. That's a recognition of anguish. The action is yours; the results are yours."

Go back a little. You said I could do whatever I want—I mean, whatever I will. But that's just not realistic. The teachers, the bosses, the commanding officers in the military all dictate the actions of their subordinates. A person can't just disobey.

"Ah, more anguish. You can disobey. However, you are evidently not prepared to accept the responsibility for your choice."

I'm not getting this. How can I disobey?

"Simply choose. Why are you blind to the possibilities? Anguish."

Blind to the possibilities?

"Imagine that your commanding officer orders you to do what you will not to do."

For example?

"Imagine that it is wartime and you are ordered to place deadly poison into the water supply for an entire city. Innocent people will die painful deaths, and you object to this tactic."

Wouldn't that be against my commanding officer's values?

"You do not have the luxury of putting the responsibility onto someone else's shoulders. Your actions are your own. Choose."

But if I disobey—no, I couldn't do that.

"Then you have chosen. You have chosen cowardice."

How?

"You have chosen to save your own life and to kill millions of other people. You have chosen to protect yourself and to forfeit your values."

Under other circumstances—

"One's actions are all there are. Choices are meaningless unless they are acted upon."

So the anguish is that I refuse to let myself be punished?

"The anguish is revealed in your initial inability to imagine the possibilities available to you. Then the anguish is compounded by your inability to take responsibility for your actions."

Up Against the Wall.   Are you saying that the results of my choices determine their value? Isn't that like utilitarianism?

"It is not the result of your choices that gives them value, it is the choices themselves. For example, say you are placed in a situation where you can be either cowardly or courageous. Your choice itself, and acting on your choice, makes you a coward or a courageous person. Consequences have nothing to do with it."

How could that be?

"I have depicted this sort of situation in a short story, 'The Wall.' Imagine again that it is wartime. You are captured by soldiers of the enemy. They threaten to execute you if you do not tell them the location of the leader of the resistance unit of which you are a member. If you tell them the location and save your life, you make one statement in the book that is you. If you mislead the enemy and buy more time for your leader and for the resistance, you make a different entry into your book. In sacrificing your life, you make a very different statement. Choose. The consequences are irrelevant."

How can the results of my choice be irrelevant? You say that the choice creates the person I am. If I save my leader and sacrifice myself for the resistance, then my action has worth because my leader is saved and the resistance is not weakened. The results do matter.

"Look at the example again. Imagine that you choose to lie to the enemy. You tell them that the leader of the resistance is hiding in the village cemetery just south of town. In fact, earlier in the day the resistance leader told you he would be hiding at his cousin's house to the north of town."

Yes, saving the leader would be the aim of my action. The result is what gives the action its worth.

"Suppose that the fellow had a fight with his cousin and decided to leave his hideout. Imagine that he came to hide in the cemetery, in the gravediggers' shack. He is captured and shot. Is your action any less heroic?"

But I chose to mislead the enemy! I lied to the soldiers!

"Exactly, and that is what makes your action courageous. The result is irrelevant. Look, there is never any guarantee that your action will succeed. There is never any guarantee that the resistance will succeed. That does not rob your action of its courage. Imagine an even more extreme possibility. Imagine that you die defending the resistance. It's heroic. However, you cannot foretell what will happen after your death. Your former comrades may decide that they have had enough fighting. They may even side with the enemy. They may see your death as the sign that resistance is futile."

You are cynical.

"Not at all. I am merely mapping out the possibilities, and each one is very real. No doubt each has happened many times. The point is that your action is courageous, and it has value because you chose and acted on it."

Oh, I see. You think that whatever I choose is good, from my perspective. Good is relative to each person. That's what you're advocating, isn't it?

"Yes and no. Your question is more subtle than you think."

In Choosing Myself, I Choose Man

What if I chose cowardice? In your example, what if I chose cowardice? I decide that my life is worth more than all the resistance. I decide that I am more important than my comrades. Even you admit that they may go over to the other side. What if I choose to live?

"Then you choose for all humankind that people should act in cowardly, self-serving ways."

I knew you were going to say that. And to be honest, I have been waiting for this. I think the idea of being responsible for all humanity is a weakness in your theory.

"Excellent. Not only do your choices elicit anguish because they reflect who you are, anguish also involves all humanity. Understanding this is important to the existentialist perspective."

How am I choosing all of humankind when I choose myself?

"Every one of us must choose himself. Each of us must create who he is. That is part of what we mean when we say that man must choose himself. But we also mean that in making this choice he also chooses all men."

This is the part I do not understand.

"In creating the man that we want to be . . . we are creating an image of man as we think he ought to be."

Are you telling me that I somehow get to dictate people's values to them? If that's true, how can they be free?

"Existentialism does not advocate dictating people's values to them. It vigorously affirms individual freedom. For an individual to choose to be this or that, however, is to affirm at the same time the value of what we choose, because we can never choose evil."

Of course we can choose evil. People commit all kinds of heinous crimes against each other. Entire countries go to war and kill innocent children. People can be incredibly cruel. You don't call that evil?

"I do call that evil."

Then how can you say that we can never choose evil?

We Always Choose the Good.   "We always choose the good, and nothing can be good for us without being good for all."

Hello? Hello? Somehow I don't think we are communicating very well. Maybe my philosopher resurrection machine is having electrical problems. The translator must be malfunctioning.

"I think I understand you. What's the problem?"

I know you are a great philosopher and all, but your statements are contradictory. You say that people can never choose evil, that they always choose good.

"Yes."

Then you agree with me that people have performed evil actions. Are you going to say that they weren't free when they acted so cruelly?

"That solution would get me out of the contradiction, but I reject it. People are free in all their actions, even in not choosing. If a person follows the orders of her government or of her commanding officer, she is free. I insist that her action is free, because she could have refused. There are always possibilities; there is always choice."

So people always freely choose their actions. And they always choose good and never evil. But we have people doing all kinds of evil things to each other, to animals, to the environment. How can you explain evil?

"When I say that man always chooses good and never evil, I mean that I am creating a certain image of man when I choose. Therefore, I am responsible for myself and for everyone else."

Oh, I see. You think that whatever you choose is good, from your perspective. You're a relativist! And you want to impose your values on everyone else.

Subjectivism and Simple Relativism.

"Not at all. I distinguish subjectivism and simple relativism. The simple relativist believes that each person has his own values, and that is the end of the story. Your values are yours; my values are mine; and the differences in values are like differences in tastes."

Isn't this your position?

"Not at all. I acknowledge that people do choose differently. Free choice is the essence of being human. However, simple relativism refuses to acknowledge responsibility. The existentialist affirms responsibility, not only for oneself, but for everyone. So I shall answer your questions more directly. Yes, values are relative to each person in that a person may choose a different plan of life. However, values are not merely relative, and no more can be told about them."

I'm still confused. Let me see if I can say why. I see that you want to avoid relativism. Okay, but how can my decisions be binding on others?

"Ah, so this is the difficulty. You believe that your actions are binding only on yourself. To make you take your choices seriously, you must see them in their proper light. An example may help. Suppose you are living by casually choosing your plan of life, your wants and fears, your values, and all the rest."

Involvement in Choice.

Casually choosing?

"Yes, for example, suppose that your sense of choice involves no one but you. Suppose further that you can change your plan of life at a moment's notice. That would be casually choosing. Casually choosing your plan of life does not sufficiently involve you in your choice."

What more do you want? I thought you wrote that our past choices do not have any effect on our present choices and actions. Isn't that correct?

"Yes, it would be bad faith, and a denial of freedom, to insist that the momentum from one's past forced one to similar choices in the future. The coward can change his life by choosing courage. The miser can become liberal and giving. Scrooge in Charles Dickens's "A Christmas Carol" is an example of such a transition. His choice was not a casual one; he chose for all humanity."

But Scrooge changed because he was visited by the three ghosts of Christmas.

"Ah, and this is another element of anguish. Who can deny that choice was involved here? As the story goes, Scrooge goes to bed and is awakened three times, each time by a different apparition. Look at the possible interpretations. Obviously, he could have been dreaming."

Or three angels of Christmas came to visit him.

"Let's take that interpretation. Even if three apparitions visited him, how did he determine that they were angels, that they were revealing the truth, that he should obey their directives? Choice goes so deep that one even chooses one's own interpretation of reality."

Okay, I get the point. But I still don't see how my choices apply to all humanity.

"Imagine that space creatures come to earth. Like all good biologists, they want to examine specimens to understand the life forms on earth. So they watch you. Each of your decisions and actions is recorded. You are acting not only for yourself, but as an example for all humanity."

Come on, Sartre, space creatures aren't going to come to earth to watch my actions.

"It's an example, Art. The point is, you always choose what you believe is the best way. You always choose according to your sense of the good. You always choose to act in ways consonant with your image of the best life. Therefore, your choices apply to all people."

Forlornness

Perhaps. I need to think more about this. Let me ask about forlornness. When you say this, you mean "that God does not exist and that we have to face all the consequences of this." What consequences?

"Beginning late in the last century and running into this century, there has been an intellectual movement denying the existence of God. However, what this movement did was to keep all the values of the 'God-inspired' society—"

I don't understand. Could you put this into more personal terms?

"Good idea. I know people who are atheists."

Well, you say that you're an atheist, too.

"Yes, but there are differences in atheists' perspectives."

I thought all atheists believe that there is no God.

"Many atheists merely deny that a God exists. However, they struggle mightily with this both intellectually and emotionally. After all, for most people denying

God's existence is emotionally difficult. Such a denial challenges all one's emotional attachments to family and friends who continue to believe."

I know people who would like intellectually to give up the idea of a God but who can't because their dead parents or grandparents were believers. Is that what you have in mind?

"Yes. Dead or living, parents and friends affect us, if we choose."

I'm sorry for interrupting again, but what does this have to do with existentialism?

"For many people who merely give up the belief in God, the values and view-point of religious morality are still binding. These people believe that nothing will be changed if God does not exist. They believe that God is an outdated hypothesis that will peacefully die off by itself. Yet they continue to live by the moral rules of their youth. Then there is a second group of atheists who go beyond denying God's existence."

I know a lot of people whose religious beliefs are intense. I don't think news of God's death is going to be taken so passively.

"Just the point. I think it is very distressing that God does not exist."

You do? Why?

"Because all possibility of finding values in a heaven of ideas disappears along with Him. We are left on a plane where there are only people. As Dostoevski said, 'If God didn't exist, everything would be possible.'"

Doesn't this allow us to be completely free? I mean, with no God, there are no restrictions.

"Nor can we find anything to cling to. We can't start making excuses for ourselves. That is what I mean when I say man is forlorn."

I don't quite get it. I think being completely unrestricted is good. I can do whatever I want!

"Before you leap into an ecstatic state of abandon, think what this means. If existence precedes essence, there is no explaining things away by reference to a fixed and given human nature. There is no determinism, man is free, man is freedom. What this means is that you must invent your own values and the image of humanity. You must invent these values completely by your own devices."

Okay. You warned me about this before.

"There's more to it. If God does not exist, we find no values or commands to turn to which legitimize our conduct. We are alone, with no excuses. The values that are you are completely up to you. For example, look how much you and your reader struggled to justify your particular values, and then morality generally. We are forlorn when we recognize that in creating our own life we are on our own, forlorn and lonely."

Condemned To Be Free

So that is why you say we are condemned to be free.

"Yes. Once you exist, you are responsible for everything you do. You are completely and unavoidably responsible. You are responsible for every passion that sweeps you into action. You are responsible for every omen, because it is you who interprets the omen."

You don't make freedom sound as appealing as I once thought it was.

Morality is Clouded

"To clarify the idea of forlornness, I've cited the example of one of my students. The boy was faced with the choice of leaving for England and joining the Free French Forces or remaining with his mother and helping her carry on."

I recall the example. What is your point?

"Who could help him choose? Christian doctrine speaks in generalities that support each action. No ethics book can tell him. Kantian ethics tells him to treat every person as an end, never merely as a means. But each alternative before him involves treating some people as means and others as ends."

How about utilitarianism? Can't he do what will bring the greatest good to the greatest number?

"How is he to know what will bring the most and the highest good? The future is always clouded. For example, how can he guarantee that joining the Free French Forces will have important results? He might make his way to England and arrive just as the war ends. Or he might make it to England, join the Free French, and be placed on some insignificant detail. Should he leave his mother so that he can be placed on garbage duty by the Free French Forces? Staying with his mother is just as uncertain. No, the effects of his actions are clouded. They give no indication of which alternative to choose."

I guess you would also say that the value of the results of his actions are also his choosing.

"Very good, you're showing promise. Mill argues for utility, but it is up to you to decide what utility consists in."

Feelings Are No Help in Choosing.   Your student friend finally just trusted his instincts, his feelings. Isn't that the only way to go? I mean, I don't see any other options.

"But how is the value of a feeling determined? What gives your feeling value?"

I don't understand. I feel my feelings; that's what gives them value.

"The only way to determine the value of an affection is precisely to perform an act which confirms or denies it. Since you require a feeling to justify your act, you are in a vicious circle."

I don't agree. My feelings do motivate me to action.

"But it does not make sense to say that, for example, 'I love my mother enough to remain with her' unless I have remained with her. Art, look at all the people who idly speculate on their actions. Look how many heroes there would be if only they could be in the trenches with the troops. Look how many naive, self-deceptive boasts we feel. The only way to be able to say that you are moved by courage is to act courageously. The feeling itself is formed by the acts one performs."

What does this leave us with?

"I can neither seek within myself the true condition which will impell me to act, nor apply a system of ethics for concepts which will permit me to act."

I think I am feeling forlorn. The puzzle you present is irresolvable.

Choosing the Advisor Is Choosing the Advice.   "Well, there are other attempts to resolve the dilemma. For example, someone may say of my student friend, 'At least, he did go to a teacher for advice.'"

Yes, that's true. If there is no other way to go, I suppose one can always seek advice.

"But choosing your advisor is involving yourself."

I don't get it.

"If someone seeking advice comes to me, Sartre, that person is pretty much aware of how I will answer. That person has chosen to seek advice from me, an atheistic existentialist, and not from a priest. So—"

I see, choosing your advisor *is* choosing the advice you'll get.

"The same reasoning applies to interpreting successes and failures in life. Each of us is responsible for his own interpretation. Forlornness implies that we ourselves choose our being. Forlornness and anguish go together."

And each happens because we are responsible, because of our complete freedom to choose. In that light, anguish and forlornness do not sound quite as hopeless as I first thought.

"Why? Did you think they implied hopelessness?"

They seemed to make us passive victims unable to live dignified lives. I think my interpretation was mistaken.

"Good."

Despair

What about despair? What do you mean by this and why must I despair?

"As for despair, the term has a very simple meaning. It means that we shall confine ourselves to reckoning only with what depends upon our will, or on the ensemble of probabilities which make our action possible."

Simple? I don't understand at all. What do you mean?

"When we want something, we always have to reckon with probabilities. You cannot hope for something to happen. Hoping is an act which leaves the realm of possibilities that are beyond me. Possibilities are to be reckoned with only to the point where my action comports with the ensemble of these possibilities, and no further."

So you're saying that you should never bet on anything but yourself and what you are involved in?

"Right, I will always rely on . . . the unity of the party or a group in which I can more or less make my weight felt. But, given that man is free and that there is no human nature for me to depend on, I can not count on men whom I do not know by relying on human goodness or man's concern for the good of society."

And this attitude doesn't make you just give up?

"No. I should involve myself. . . . but I shall have no illusions and shall do what I can. Quietism is the attitude of people who say, 'Let others do what I can't do.' "

You are telling us to be much more active than that, right?

There is No Reality Except in Action

"You have to ask yourself about each issue and each decision, 'Where else can I be; what else can I be doing?' There is no reality except in action. Man is nothing else than his plan; he exists only to the extent that he fulfills himself; he is therefore nothing else than the ensemble of his acts, nothing else than his life."

I can see the importance of setting up a hierarchy of personal values. But I don't agree that people are nothing except their actions. How do you justify this? Or have I misunderstood?

"People resist this idea because it, too, places responsibility squarely on them. It removes the excuse that 'circumstances are against me.' There is no reality except in action. There really is no love other than one which manifests itself in a person's being in love. There is no genius other than one which is expressed in works of art."

This leaves most people with worthless lives!

"It prompts people to understand that reality alone is what counts."

Aren't you reducing a person to what he or she accomplishes? I think this is too narrow. I mean, a great artist may be a terrible person in other respects. And an average person may be wonderful as a family member, as a friend, and so on.

"Of course. A thousand other things will contribute toward summing him up. A man is nothing else than a series of undertakings. He is the sum, the organization, the ensemble of the relationships which make up these undertakings."

Are you denying the inner life?

"Inner life?"

Yes, the inner life. Are you suggesting that we are merely our behavior?

"I have already said that feelings are formed by the actions we perform. This does not address the point, however. The value of our feelings is determined by our actions. That's one point. If I claim to have a burning love deep within me, but I never act on it, then what is the sense, what is the value of that feeling?"

I see your point. And what is your second point?

"We are not merely the product of heredity, the workings of the environment, and society. I deny biological and psychological determinism."

That's great; what does it mean?

"A person is not the way he is because of physiological makeup. A coward is not cowardly because of a cowardly constitution. What makes cowardice is the act of renouncing or yielding."

Total Involvement

People aren't born cowards or heroes? Then what makes them that way? You say it cannot be their training or their environment. What's left?

"Actions. The person chooses to act in a cowardly or heroic way. You see, Art, what counts is total involvement. Some one particular action or set of circumstances is not total involvement."

Then no one can ever be described as a coward or a hero. At some later time the coward may act heroically, and vice versa.

"Exactly, and that is what we mean by freedom. That is the full force of freedom. Your destiny lies within you. We are dealing here with an ethics of action and involvement."

Loneliness

Doesn't your insistence on complete human freedom make life pretty lonely? You even base your theory on Descartes's *cogito*: "I think; therefore, I exist." Doesn't that cut you off from other people?

"That's correct; my perspective does spring from Descartes's *cogito*. There we have the absolute truth of consciousness becoming aware of itself."

Huh?

"The one thing we know with certainty is the experience of being conscious, of existing as a conscious being. You ask if this commits the existentialist to a lonely existence. One discovers in the *cogito* not only himself but others as well."

How do you get this? If "I think; therefore, I exist" is true, it shows only that I exist. It does not show that others exist, too. The best we can say for others is that each person knows that he or she exists. Or have I missed something?

"Through the 'I think' we reach our own self in the presence of others, and the others are just as real to us as our own self."

Saying this is nice enough, but I just don't see how it follows.

"In order to get any truth about myself, I must have contact with another person."

Why?

"Well, what sense does it make to say that I am nasty or selfish or clever except that it is recognized by other people? For example, say you think you are adept at comedy. You tell your jokes to people and no one laughs. No one shows any sign of the least amusement. Undeterred, you continue to tell your jokes. You perform for a large number of people. No one finds any humor in your stories. In what sense could you be said to be adept at comedy?"

Maybe I'm just ahead of my time.

"Even if this were true, we wouldn't know that except for people's responses to you. People in the future would see the humor in your material. You only get truth about yourself in your contact with others."

How Do You Know Other People Exist?

Aren't you making a mistake here? Aren't you confusing an argument for other people's existence with how we know that other people exist?

"The two are identical. The man who becomes aware of himself . . . also perceives all others, and he perceives them as the condition of his own existence. The other is indispensable to my own existence as well as to my knowledge about myself."

I'm not following this very well. Maybe I can state my objection in a different way. At the heart of my objection is a worry that your subjectivism leads to relativism. So let me ask directly, are you a relativist?

"How do you mean? I assert a position that we call intersubjectivity; this is the world in which man decides what he is and what others are."

The Limits of the Human Condition

Yes, I understand that from our talk about responsibility. But you deny that there is a human nature. If there is no human nature, how can we ever understand other people?

"Good question. I'm glad you asked this. There does exist a human condition. What I mean by that is that there are limits which outline man's fundamental situation in the universe."

Finally, there is going to be a stable piece of ground to stand on!

"What does not change is the necessity of man to exist in the world, to be at work there, to be there in the midst of other people, and to be mortal there."

I knew that.

"We freely choose our existence with reference to the human condition. Every configuration—"

Huh?

"Oh, all I mean by that is how a person confronts, or denies, or wishes to pass beyond the limits."

I don't get it.

"Each person has his or her own strategy for living. Each of us approaches the limits of the human condition with different choices. That's freedom. That's what I mean by configuration, the way a person approaches the limits of the human condition. Every configuration, however individual it may be, has a universal value."

Here we go again. I understand you up to this point. We are all different. Each of us chooses to live differently. That's the kind of talk that leads me to think that you're a relativist. How does this talk of universal value fit in?

"Every attempt at living, every configuration has universality in the sense that it can be understood by every man."

Are you saying that I can understand the life of someone who lives in a completely different culture, and maybe in a different historical period? Are you saying that I can understand the point of view of the psychotic, of the serial killer?

"Yes, there is always a way to understand the idiot, the child, the savage, the foreigner, provided one has the necessary information."

Why do you say that?

"At heart, what existentialism shows is the connection between the absolute character of free involvement, by virtue of which every man realizes himself in realizing a type of mankind—"

Hold on. How does absolute involvement translate into an understanding of anyone else? If the other person is not involved in what I am involved in, how can I understand the other person?

"Involvement is always comprehensible in any age whatsoever and by any person whosoever, and the relativeness of the cultural ensemble which may result from such a choice."

Can you give me examples?

"Each of us performs an absolute act in breathing, eating, sleeping, or behaving in any way whatever. There is no difference between being free . . . and being absolute."

I'm at a loss. All you are saying is that people share common physical needs. Is that all it means to understand the other person?

"It means that we need not be thoroughly isolated from others. It means we can cross historical and cultural boundaries and understand people from beyond those boundaries."

This "connection" is not very intimate, or so it seems. But let's move on to objections.

Existentialism Does Not Advocate Caprice

I understand that existentialism does not advocate caprice. All my actions emerge from choice. So although my actions may look capricious, they are reflections of me.

"If I in any way assume responsibility for a choice . . . this has nothing to do with caprice. Ethics, like art, involves invention and creativity, but it is unfair to say this is capricious."

Okay, and I agree that your emphases on total involvement and responsibility make it absurd to charge your theory with arbitrariness of choice. But—

Are We Able to Pass Judgments on Others?

"But we are unable to pass judgment on others. That's your objection, isn't it?"

Yes.

"One can still pass judgment, for, as I have said, one makes a choice in relationship to others."

But that just means that I choose from the plan of life I have adopted. There isn't any way of deciding which plan is better?

"First, one can judge (and this is perhaps not a judgment of value, but a logical judgment) that certain choices are based on error and others on truth."

Consistency is desirable, but I was looking for something more substantial. What is the best life? Can you tell me what it is?

"If we have defined man's situation as a free choice, with no excuses and no recourse, every man who takes refuge behind the excuse of his passions, every man who sets up a determinism, is a dishonest man."

Okay, put to the side all logical and factual errors. And we admit complete honesty in our choice. So our attitude is strictly coherent. What constitutes the best life?

Freedom is the Basis of All Values

"Freedom is the basis of all values."

What do you mean?

"The ultimate meaning of the acts of honest men is the quest for freedom as such. We want freedom for freedom's sake and in every particular circumstance."

Ah, Sartre, you have been hiding a value all along. Your theory's ultimate value is freedom.

"In wanting freedom, we discover that it depends entirely on the freedom of others and that the freedom of others depends on ours."

Are you defining humanity as dependent on one another?

"No, but as soon as there is involvement, I am obliged to want others to have freedom at the same time that I want my own freedom."

You're assuming that people are alike, at least with respect to freedom. I know you are struggling to avoid loneliness and complete isolation between people. But you are defining humans as essentially free. You are saying that humans have a nature, which is to be free.

"I've recognized that man is a being in whom existence precedes essence, that he is a free being who . . . can want only his freedom."

And that allows you to judge other people?

"I may pass judgment on those who seek to hide from themselves the complete arbitrariness and the complete freedom of their existence. Therefore, though the content of ethics is variable, a certain form of it is universal."

And what is that, as if I don't know?

"The one thing that counts is knowing whether the inventing that has been done has been done in the name of freedom."

But Which Way Does Freedom Tell Me to Act?

But which way does freedom tell me to act? Take your example of the guy who couldn't decide whether he should stay with his mother or go off to fight for the

Free French. If morality and religion are at fault for being vague in concrete circumstances, how is your value of freedom any less vague? Telling me to choose freely doesn't give me any direction.

"Admittedly, but at least the choice will be honest, consistent, and free. At least you will be creating your own life in inventing your own values."

But what if someone freely chooses to be cruel?

"That is possible. All we can judge is whether or not he chose in the name of his freedom and the freedom of other people."

Ah, now I see why you're emphasizing our relation to others. If I have to take others into account, as a reflection of my own reality, then my freedom restricts me in certain ways.

"Yes."

Then I think a lot more needs to be said to ensure that the connection you claim does exist.

"Your Chapter 12 will give you a chance to understand the connections more fully."

I will look at the discussion. But before you leave, could you tell me one more thing? Do you think life is meaningful or absurd?

"Before you come alive, life is nothing; it's up to you to give it a meaning, and value is nothing else but the meaning that you choose."

So the best life is—?

"The life plan freely chosen."

I guess you're right; choosing the advisor is choosing the advice. Thanks, Mr. Sartre. You have given me quite a lot to consider.

Summary of Discussion

Sartre presents us with two unique insights on the human condition. There is no human nature. We are totally and irreversibly free. Although we often deny our freedom, Sartre contends that each person is nothing but what she makes of herself. Each action, each value, each belief is freely chosen. What this means is that each person is the author of his or her own life. Clearly, we do not choose the century, the country, or the class we are born in. Nor do we choose our parents. We do, however, choose our attitudes toward these "givens."

Recognizing our total freedom is a terrifying burden. It is probably terrifying because morality has convinced us that values are independent of us. Now, however, Sartre shows us that each person is responsible and independent. If you live by a certain set of values, then you are responsible for them. After all, in choosing your advisor, you choose your advice.

One of Sartre's best insights is embodied in his example of the young man who cannot decide whether he should stay with his mother, or go off to join the Resistance. Sartre claims that our freedom forces us to choose between conflicting values and desires. No moral or religious principle is going to help us resolve such dilemmas. Neither Mill's utilitarianism nor Kant's categorical imperative helps. Religion is too general when it comes to real-life cases. Sartre says we must simply choose. It is our choice and action that creates the value. Freedom is the basis of all values and the prerequisite of human existence.

Sartre is probably correct when he forces us to confront our own responsibility and freedom. His idea that religion and morality are vague, and therefore unhelpful, is to the point. Sartre's own instruction—simply to choose—is not adequate, however. On what basis does one choose? What is lacking is a determination of the point of choosing. If my actions are directed toward pleasure, then I know what counts as a good choice. If loneliness is the defining problem, then a very different set of choices is appropriate.

By telling us to be free, Sartre is not advocating caprice. Freedom defines the human being. Freedom carries all the responsibility and importance of our human existence. If I choose to act in a cowardly way, then I am a coward. However, human freedom is radical. No previous action determines any subsequent action. Yesterday's coward can be today's courageous person. Choice and action are everything.

Finally, Sartre urges us to be totally involved. This is a remarkable insight that other moral theories overlook. In fact, Sartre is at his most insightful with ideas and concerns about our emotions and inner conflicts.

Discussion Highlights

I. Existence precedes essence
   1. There is no human nature.
   2. Man is nothing else than what he makes of himself.
II. Choice and responsibility
   1. Choice brings anguish.
      a. we are condemned to be free
      b. each person is responsible for his or her own actions
      c. there are no excuses
   2. In choosing myself, I choose all mankind.
      a. each person always chooses what he or she believes is good
      b. each person is a representative of the entire human race
III. We are condemned to be free
   1. Abandonment: there is no God to direct our lives.
   2. Despair: we are alone in our lives, in our actions, in our existence.
   3. Anguish: we experience a profound responsibility for ourselves and for others.
   4. Alienation: we are separated from others.
   5. Total involvement: we can immerse ourselves in creating our own lives.

Questions for Thought/Paper Topics

1. Sartre says we experience anguish because we are responsible for all humankind. Explain his position and discuss how he defends it. Do you agree with him?

2. What does Sartre mean when he says we are condemned to be free?
3. If choice is the basis of all values, is every action permissible?
4. Can anyone make a choice without knowing what counts as a good choice? Does Sartre's emphasis on "total commitment" give any guidelines by which to live?
5. Sartre claims that moral and religious values are vague. They are unhelpful in real-life situations. What are his examples? Is Sartre's system any less vague and unhelpful?
6. According to Sartre, there is no human nature. What does he mean by this? Do you think there are human instincts and natural responses to events? Do you think emotions are natural or culturally determined? Do people choose their emotions?
7. Do you agree that there is no human reality except in human action? In what sense are we free except in our actions?

For Further Reading

The essay "Existentialism Is a Humanism" (Citadel, 1971) is the source of our discussion with Sartre. Sartre also wrote *Being and Nothingness* (Simon & Schuster, 1966). While this is an imposing book, you might want to look at his chapters on "Bad Faith," "Being and Doing: Freedom." I find his discussion of "existential psychoanalysis" very interesting. Another way to get into Sartre's point of view is to read one of his novels, short stories or plays, such as *Nausea* (New Directions, 1959), *The Wall* (New Directions, 1969), and *No Exit* (Random House, 1955).

Apology

PLATO

Though Socrates was not an existentialist, he stands as an example of a person who chooses his own values and takes responsibility for his own actions. Far from offering an apology, Socrates is portrayed in this work as a person determined to live as he believes he should live.

How does he exemplify Sartre's theory? Socrates says that his life is a constant pursuit of wisdom. Knowing his own ignorance, he has questioned experts and authorities for years. His thirst for wisdom has brought him poverty, ridicule, and now a public trial for treason. His questioning has also brought him a unique kind of wisdom; he knows the limit of his knowledge. So Socrates maintains his values, and he believes that society and every one of its members would be well served by following his example.

As you read this selection, notice how independent Socrates is. He refuses to act in any way that he believes is wrong. When asked by the democratic authorities to sit in judgment of the naval generals, Socrates refuses because trying the generals together violates the constitution of Athens. Is Socrates antidemocratic? Perhaps, but when the powerful tyrants demand that he arrest Leon of Salamis, Socrates refuses. He knows Leon is innocent of any wrongdoing. In each case Socrates refuses to contribute knowingly to any injustice. Just as Sartre urges us to do, Socrates risks punishment, even death, to maintain his values. Socrates knows that a person is no more than the actions he performs.

What do you think of the moral worth of Socrates? Do you believe he stands as a viable example of Sartre's theory? Does he impress you as a person of integrity? How would you vote if you were on the jury? Are you moved by his defense of his actions? If he is guilty of atheism and corrupting youth, does Socrates deserve death or exile?

Hᴏᴡ ʏᴏᴜ, O Aᴛʜᴇɴɪᴀɴs, have been affected by my accusers, I cannot tell; but I know that they almost made me forget who I was—so persuasively did they speak; and yet they have hardly uttered a word of truth. But of the many falsehoods told by them, there was one which quite amazed me;—I mean when they said that you should be upon your guard and not allow yourselves to be deceived by the force of my eloquence. To say this, when they were certain to be detected as soon as I opened my lips and proved myself to be anything but a great speaker, did indeed appear to me most shameless—unless by the force of eloquence they mean the force of truth; for if such is their meaning, I admit that I am eloquent. But in how different a way from theirs! Well, as I was saying, they have scarcely spoken the truth at all; but from me you shall hear the whole truth: not, however, delivered, after their manner in a set oration duly ornamented with words or phrases. No, by heaven! but I shall use the words and arguments which occur to me at the moment; for I am confident in the justice of my cause: at my time of life I ought not to be appearing before you, O men of Athens, in the character of a juvenile or-

ator—let no one expect it of me. And I must beg of you to grant me a favour:—If I defend myself in my accustomed manner, and you hear me using the words which I have been in the habit of using the agora, at the tables of the money-changers, or anywhere else, I would ask you not to be surprised, and not to interrupt me on this account. For I am more than seventy years of age, and appearing now for the first time in a court of law, I am quite a stranger to the language of the place; and therefore I would have you regard me as if I were really a stranger, whom you would excuse if he spoke in his native tongue, and after the fashion of his country:— Am I making an unfair request of you? Never mind the manner, which may or may not be good; but think only of the truth of my words, and give heed to that: let the speaker speak truly and the judge decide justly.

And first, I have to reply to the older charges and to my first accusers, and then I will go on to the later ones. For of old I have had many accusers, who have accused me falsely to you during many years; and I am more afraid of them than of Anytus and his associates, who are dangerous, too, in their own way. But far more dangerous

From Plato, *Apology*, in *Dialogues of Plato*, trans. Benjamin Jowett, 3d ed. (New York: Oxford University Press, 1892).

are the others, who began when you were children, and took possession of your minds with their falsehoods, telling of one Socrates, a wise man, who speculated about the heaven above, and searched into the earth beneath, and made the worse appear the better cause. The disseminators of this tale are the accusers whom I dread; for their hearers are apt to fancy that such enquirers do not believe in the existence of the gods. And they are many, and their charges against me are of ancient date, and they were made by them in the days when you were more impressible than you are now—in childhood, or it may have been in youth—and the cause when heard went by default, for there was none to answer. And hardest of all, I do not know and cannot tell the names of my accusers; unless in the chance case of a Comic poet. All who from envy and malice have persuaded you—some of them having first convinced themselves—all this class of men are most difficult to deal with; for I cannot have them up here, and cross-examine them, and therefore I must simply fight with shadows in my own defence, and argue when there is no one who answers. I will ask you then to assume with me, as I was saying, that my opponents are of two kinds; one recent, the other ancient: and I hope that you will see the propriety of my answering the latter first, for these accusations you heard long before the others, and much oftener.

Well, then, I must make my defence, and endeavor to clear away in a short time, a slander which has lasted a long time. May I succeed, if to succeed be for my good and yours, or likely to avail me in my cause! The task is not an easy one; I quite understand the nature of it. And so leaving the event with God, in obedience to the law I will now make my defence.

I will begin at the beginning, and ask what is the accusation which has given rise to the slander of me, and in fact has encouraged Meletus to prefer this charge against me. Well, what do the slanderers say? They shall be my prosecutors, and I will sum up their words in an affidavit: "Socrates is an evil-doer, and a curious person, who searches into things under the earth and in heaven, and he makes the worse appear the better cause; and he teaches the aforesaid doctrines to others." Such is the nature of the accusation: it is just what you have yourselves seen in the comedy of Aristophanes, who has introduced a man whom he calls Socrates, going about and saying that he walks in air, and talking a deal of nonsense concerning matters of which I do not pretend to know either much or little—not that I mean to speak disparagingly of any one who is a student of natural philosophy. I should be very sorry if Meletus could bring so grave a charge against me. But the simple truth is, O Athenians, that I have nothing to do with physical speculations. Very many of those here present are witnesses to the truth of this, and to them I appeal. Speak then, you who have heard me, and tell your neighbours whether any of you have ever known me hold forth in few words or in many upon such matters. . . . You hear their answer. And from what they say of this part of the charge you will be able to judge of the truth of the rest.

As little foundation is there for the report that I am a teacher, and take money; this accusation has no more truth in it than the other. Although, if a man were really able to instruct mankind, to receive money for giving instruction would, in my opinion, be an honour to him. There is Gorgias of Leontium, and Prodicus of Ceos, and Hippias of Elis, who go the round of the cities, and are able to persuade the young men to leave their own citizens by whom they might be taught for nothing, and come to them whom they not only pay, but are thankful if they may be allowed to pay them. There is at this time a Parian philosopher residing in Athens, of whom I have heard; and I came to hear of him in this way:—I came across a man who has spent a world of money on the Sophists, Callias, the son of Hipponicus, and knowing that he had sons, I asked him: "Callias," I said, "if your two sons were foals or calves, there would be no difficulty in finding some one to put over them; we should hire a trainer of horses, or a farmer probably, who would improve and perfect them in their own proper virtue and excellence; but as they are human beings, whom are you thinking of placing over them? Is there any one who understands human and political virtue? You must have thought about the matter, for you have sons; is there any one?" "There is," he said. "Who is he?" said I; "and of what country? and what does he charge?" "Evenus the Parian," he replied; "he is the man, and his charge is five minae." Happy is Evenus, I said to myself, if he really has this wisdom, and teaches at such a moderate charge. Had I the same, I should have been very proud and conceited; but the truth is that I have no knowledge of the kind.

I dare say, Athenians, that some one among you will reply, "Yes, Socrates, but what is the origin of these accusations which are brought against you; there must have been something strange which you have been doing? All these rumours and this talk about you would never have arisen if you had been like other men: tell us, then, what is the cause of them, for we should be sorry to judge hastily of you." Now I regard this as a fair challenge, and I will endeavour to explain to you the reason why I am called wise and have such an evil fame. Please to attend then. And although some of you may think that I am joking, I declare that I will tell you the entire truth. Men of Athens, this reputation of mine has come of a certain sort of wisdom which I possess. If you ask me what kind of wisdom, I reply, wisdom such as may perhaps be attained by man, for to that extent I am inclined to believe that I am wise; whereas the persons of whom I was speaking have a superhuman wisdom, which I may fail to describe, because I have it not myself; and he who says that I have, speaks falsely, and is taking away my character. And here, O men of Athens, I must beg you not to interrupt me, even if I seem to say something extravagant. For the word which I will speak is not mine. I will refer you to a witness who is worthy of credit; that witness shall be the God of Delphi—he will tell you about my wisdom, if I have any, and of what sort it is. You must have known Chaerephon; he was

early a friend of mine, and also a friend of yours, for he shared in the recent exile of the people, and returned with you. Well, Chaerephon, as you know, was very impetuous in all his doings, and he went to Delphi and boldly asked the oracle to tell him whether—as I was saying, I must beg you not to interrupt—he asked the oracle to tell him whether any one was wiser than I was, and the Pythian prophetess answered, that there was no man wiser. Chaerephon is dead himself; but his brother, who is in court, will confirm the truth of what I am saying.

Why do I mention this? Because I am going to explain to you why I have such an evil name. When I heard the answer, I said to myself, What can the god mean? and what is the interpretation of his riddle? for I know that I have no wisdom, small or great. What then can he mean when he says that I am the wisest of men? And yet he is a god, and cannot lie; that would be against his nature. After long consideration, I thought of a method of trying the question. I reflected that if I could only find a man wiser than myself, then I might go to the god with a refutation in my hand. I should say to him, "Here is a man who is wiser than I am; but you said that I was the wisest." Accordingly I went to one who had the reputation of wisdom, and observed him—his name I need not mention; he was a politician whom I selected for examination—and the result was as follows: When I began to talk to him, I could not help thinking that he was not really wise, although he was thought wise by many, and still wiser by himself; and thereupon I tried to explain to him that he thought himself wise, but was not really wise; and the consequence was that he hated me, and his enmity was shared by several who were present and heard me. So I left him, saying to myself, as I went away: Well, although I do not suppose that either of us knows anything really beautiful and good, I am better off than he is,—for he knows nothing, and thinks that he knows; I neither know nor think that I know. In this latter particular, then, I seem to have slightly the advantage of him.

Then I went to another who had still higher pretensions to wisdom, and my conclusion was exactly the same. Whereupon I made another enemy of him, and of many others besides him.

Then I went to one man after another, being not unconscious of the enmity which I provoked, and I lamented and feared this: But necessity was laid upon me,—the word of God, I thought, ought to be considered first. And I said to myself, Go I must to all who appear to know, and find out the meaning of the oracle. And I swear to you, Athenians, by the dog I swear!— for I must tell you the truth—the result of my mission was just this: I found that the men most in repute were all but the most foolish; and that others less esteemed were really wiser and better. I will tell you the tale of my wanderings and of the "Herculean" labours, as I may call them, which I endured only to find at last the oracle irrefutable. After the politicians, I went to the poets; tragic, dithyrambic, and all sorts. And there, I said to myself, you will be instantly detected; now you will find out that you are more ignorant than they are. Accordingly, I took them some of the most elaborate passages in their own writings, and asked what was the meaning of them—thinking that they would teach me something. Will you believe me? I am almost ashamed to confess the truth, but I must say that there is hardly a person present who would not have talked better about their poetry than they did themselves. Then I knew that not by wisdom do poets write poetry, but by a sort of genius and inspiration; they are like diviners or soothsayers who also say many fine things, but do not understand the meaning of them. The poets appeared to me to be much in the same case; and I further observed that upon the strength of their poetry they believed themselves to be the wisest of men in other things in which they were not wise. So I departed, conceiving myself to be superior to them for the same reason that I was superior to the politicians.

At last I went to the artisans, for I was conscious that I knew nothing at all, as I may say, and I was sure that they knew many fine things; and here I was not mistaken, for they did know many things of which I was ignorant, and in this they certainly were wiser than I was. But I observed that even the good artisans fell into the same error as the poets;—because they were good workmen they thought that they also knew all sorts of high matters, and this defect in them overshadowed their wisdom; and therefore I asked myself on behalf of the oracle, whether I would like to be as I was, neither having their knowledge nor their ignorance, or like them in both; and I made answer to myself and to the oracle that I was better off as I was.

This inquisition has led to my having many enemies of the worst and most dangerous kind, and has given occasion also to many calumnies. And I am called wise, for my hearers always imagine that I myself possess the wisdom which I find wanting in others: but the truth is, O men of Athens, that God only is wise; and by his answer he intends to show that the wisdom of men is worth little or nothing; he is not speaking of Socrates, he is only using my name by way of illustration, as if he said, He, O men, is the wisest, who, like Socrates, knows that his wisdom is in truth worth nothing. And so I go about the world, obedient to the god, and search and make enquiry into the wisdom of any one, whether citizen or stranger, who appears to be wise; and if he is not wise, then in vindication of the oracle I show him that he is not wise; and my occupation quite absorbs me, and I have no time to give either to any public matter of interest or to any concern of my own, but I am in utter poverty by reason of my devotion to the god.

There is another thing:—young men of the richer classes, who have not much to do, come about me of their own accord; they like to hear the pretenders examined, and they often imitate me, and proceed to examine others; there are plenty of persons, as they quickly discover, who think that they know something, but really know little or nothing; and then those who are examined by them instead of being angry with themselves are angry with me: This confounded Socrates, they say; this villainous misleader of youth!—and then if somebody asks them, Why, what evil does he practise or teach? they do not know, and cannot tell; but in order that they may not appear to be at a loss, they repeat the ready-made charges which are used against all philosophers about teaching things up in the clouds and under the earth, and having no gods, and making the worse appear the better cause; for they do not like to confess that their pretence of knowledge has been detected—which is the truth; and as they are numerous and ambitious and energetic, and are drawn up in battle array and have persuasive tongues, they have filled your ears with their loud and inveterate calumnies. And this is the reason why my three accusers, Meletus and Anytus and Lycon, have set upon me; Meletus, who has a quarrel with me on behalf of the poets; Anytus, on behalf of the craftsmen and politicians; Lycon, on behalf of the rhetoricians; and as I said at the beginning, I cannot expect to get rid of such a mass of calumny all in a moment. And this, O men of Athens, is the truth and the whole truth; I have concealed nothing, I have dissembled nothing. And yet, I know that my plainness of speech makes them hate me, and what is their hatred but a proof that I am speaking the truth?—Hence has arisen the prejudice against me; and this is the reason of it, as you will find out either in this or in any future enquiry.

I have said enough in my defence against the first class of my accusers; I turn to the second class. They are headed by Meletus, that good man and true lover of his country, as he calls himself. Against these, too, I must try to make a defence:—Let their affidavit be read: it contains something of this kind: It says that Socrates is a doer of evil, who corrupts the youth; and who does not believe in the gods of the state, but has other new divinities of his own. Such is the charge; and now let us examine the particular counts. He says that I am a doer of evil, and corrupt the youth; but I say, O men of Athens, that Meletus is a doer of evil, in that he pretends to be in earnest when he is only in jest, and is so eager to bring men to trial from a pretended zeal

and interest about matters in which he really never had the smallest interest. And the truth of this I will endeavour to prove to you.

Come hither, Meletus, and let me ask a question of you. You think a great deal about the improvement of youth?

Yes, I do.

Tell the judges, then, who is their improver; for you must know, as you have taken the pains to discover their corrupter, and are citing and accusing me before them. Speak, then, and tell the judges who their improver is.—Observe, Meletus, that you are silent, and have nothing to say. But is not this rather disgraceful, and a very considerable proof of what I was saying, that you have no interest in the matter? Speak up, friend, and tell us who their improver is.

The laws.

But that, my good sir, is not my meaning. I want to know who the person is, who, in the first place, knows the laws.

The judges, Socrates, who are present in court.

What, do you mean to say, Meletus, that they are able to instruct and improve youth?

Certainly they are.

What, all of them, or some only and not others?

All of them.

By the goddess Hera, that is good news! There are plenty of improvers, then. And what do you say of the audience,—do they improve them?

Yes, they do.

And the senators?

Yes, the senators improve them.

But perhaps the members of the assembly corrupt them?—or do they too improve them?

They improve them.

Then every Athenian improves and elevates them; all with the exception of myself; and I alone am their corrupter? Is that what you affirm?

That is what I stoutly affirm.

I am very unfortunate if you are right. But suppose I ask you a question: How about horses? Does one man do them harm and all the world good? Is not the exact opposite the truth? One man is able to do them good, or at least not many;—the trainer of horses, that is to say, does them good, and others who have to do with them rather injure them? Is not that true, Meletus, of horses, or of any other animals? Most assuredly it is; whether you and Anytus say yes or no. Happy indeed would be the condition of youth if they had one corrupter only, and all the rest of the world were their improvers. But you, Meletus, have sufficiently shown that you never had a thought about the young: your carelessness is seen in your not caring about the very things which you bring against me.

And now, Meletus, I will ask you another question—by Zeus I will: Which is better, to live among bad citizens, or among good ones? Answer, friend, I say; the question is one which may be easily answered. Do not the good do their neighbours good, and the bad do them evil?

Certainly.

And is there any one who would rather be injured than benefited by those who life with him? Answer, my good friend, the law requires you to answer—does any one like to be injured?

Certainly not.

And when you accuse me of corrupting and deteriorating the youth, do you allege that I corrupt them intentionally or unintentionally?

Intentionally, I say.

But you have just admitted that the good do their neighbours good, and evil do them evil. Now, is that a truth which your superior wisdom has recognized thus early in life, and am I, at my age, in such darkness and ignorance as not to know that if a man with whom I have to live is corrupted by me, I am very likely to be harmed by him; and yet I corrupt him, and intentionally, too—so you say, although neither I nor any other human being is ever likely to be convinced by you. But either I do not corrupt them, or I corrupt them unintentionally; and on either view of the case you lie. If my offence is unintentional, the law has no cognizance of un-

intentional offences: you ought to have taken me privately, and warned and admonished me; for if I had been better advised, I should have left off doing what I only did unintentionally—no doubt I should; but you would have nothing to say to me and refused to teach me. And now you bring me up in this court, which is a place not of instruction, but of punishment.

It will be very clear to you, Athenians, as I was saying, that Meletus has no care at all, great or small, about the matter. But still I should like to know, Meletus, in what I am affirmed to corrupt the young. I suppose you mean, as I infer from your indictment, that I teach them not to acknowledge the gods which the state acknowledges, but some other new divinities or spiritual agencies in their stead. These are the lessons by which I corrupt the youth, as you say.

Yes, that I say emphatically.

Then, by the gods, Meletus, of whom we are speaking, tell me and the court, in somewhat plainer terms, what you mean! for I do not as yet understand whether you affirm that I teach other men to acknowledge some gods, and therefore that I do believe in gods, and am not an entire atheist—this you do not lay to my charge,—but only you say that they are not the same gods which the city recognizes—the charge is that they are different gods. Or, do you mean that I am an atheist simply, and a teacher of atheism?

I mean the latter—that you are a complete atheist.

What an extraordinary statement! Why do you think so, Meletus? Do you mean that I do not believe in the godhead of the sun or moon, like other men?

I assure you, judges, that he does not; for he says that the sun is stone, and the moon earth.

Friend Meletus, you think that you are accusing Anaxagoras: and you have but a bad opinion of the judges, if you fancy them illiterate to such a degree as not to know that these doctrines are found in the books of Anaxagoras the Clazomenian, which are full of them. And so, forsooth, the youth are said to be taught them by

Socrates, when there are not unfrequently exhi-
bitions of them at the theatre (price of admission
one drachma at the most); and they might pay
their money, and laugh at Socrates if he pretends
to father these extraordinary views. And so, Meletus, you really think that I do not believe in any
god?

I swear by Zeus that you believe absolutely in
none at all.

Nobody will believe you, Meletus, and I am
pretty sure that you do not believe yourself. I
cannot help thinking, men of Athens, that Meletus is reckless and impudent, and that he has
written this indictment in a spirit of mere wan-
tonness and youthful bravado. Has he not compounded a riddle, thinking to try me? He said to
himself:—I shall see whether the wise Socrates
will discover my facetious contradiction, or
whether I shall be able to deceive him and the
rest of them. For he certainly does appear to me
to contradict himself in the indictment as much
as if he said that Socrates is guilty of not believing in the gods, and yet of believing in them—
but this is not like a person who is in earnest.

I should like you, O men of Athens, to join
me in examining what I conceive to be his inconsistency; and do you, Meletus, answer. And
I must remind the audience of my request that
they would not make a disturbance if I speak in
my accustomed manner:

Did ever man, Meletus, believe in the existence of human things, and not of human
beings? . . . I wish, men of Athens, that he
would answer, and not be always trying to get
up an interruption. Did ever any man believe in
horsemanship, and not in horses? or in flute-
playing, and not in flute-players? No, my friend;
I will answer to you and to the court, as you
refuse to answer for yourself. There is no man
who ever did. But now please to answer the next
question: Can a man believe in spiritual and divine agencies, and not in spirits or demigods?

He cannot.

How lucky I am to have extracted that answer, by the assistance of the court! But then you
swear in the indictment that I teach and believe

in divine or spiritual agencies (new or old, no
matter for that); at any rate, I believe in spiritual
agencies,—so you say and swear in the affidavit;
and yet if I believe in divine beings, how can I
help believing in spirits or demigods;—must I
not? To be sure I must; and therefore I may assume that your silence gives consent. Now what
are spirits or demigods? are they not either gods
or the sons of gods?

Certainly they are.

But this is what I call the facetious riddle invented by you: the demigods or spirits are gods,
and you say first that I do not believe in gods,
and then again that I do believe in gods; that is,
if I believe in demigods. For if the demigods are
the illegitimate sons of gods, whether by the
nymphs or by any other mothers, of whom they
are said to be the sons—what human being will
ever believe that there are no gods if they are the
sons of gods? You might as well affirm the existence of mules, and deny that of horses and
asses. Such nonsense, Meletus, could only have
been intended by you to make trial of me. You
have put this into the indictment because you
had nothing real of which to accuse me. But no
one who has a particle of understanding will
ever be convinced by you that the same men can
believe in divine and superhuman things, and
yet not believe that there are gods and demigods
and heroes.

I have said enough in answer to the charge of
Meletus: any elaborate defence is unnecessary;
but I know only too well how many are the en-
mities which I have incurred, and this is what
will be my destruction if I am destroyed;—not
Meletus, nor yet Anytus, but the envy and de-
traction of the world, which has been the death
of many good men, and will probably be the
death of many more; there is no danger of my
being the last of them.

Some one will say: And are you not ashamed,
Socrates, of a course of life which is likely to
bring you to an untimely end? To him I may
fairly answer: There you are mistaken: a man
who is good for anything ought not to calculate
the chance of living or dying; he ought only to

consider whether in doing anything he is doing right or wrong—acting the part of a good man or of a bad. Whereas, upon your view, the heroes who fell at Troy were not good for much, and the son of Thetis above all, who altogether despised danger in comparison with disgrace; and when he was so eager to slay Hector, his goddess mother said to him, that if he avenged his companion Patroclus, and slew Hector, he would die himself—"Fate," she said, in these or the like words, "waits for you next after Hector"; he, receiving this warning, utterly despised danger and death, and instead of fearing them, feared rather to live in dishonour, and not to avenge his friend. "Let me die forthwith," he replies, "and be avenged of my enemy, rather than abide here by the beaked ships, a laughing-stock and a burden of the earth." Had Achilles any thought of death and danger? For wherever a man's place is, whether the place which he has chosen or that in which he has been placed by a commander, there he ought to remain in the hour of danger; he should not think of death or of anything but of disgrace. And this, O men of Athens, is a true saying.

Strange, indeed, would be my conduct, O men of Athens, if I who, when I was ordered by the generals whom you chose to command me at Potidaea and Amphipolis and Delium, remained where they placed me, like any other man, facing death—if now, when, as I conceive and imagine, God orders me to fulfill the philosopher's mission of searching into myself and other men, I were to desert my post through fear of death, or any other fear; that would indeed be strange, and I might justly be arraigned in court for denying the existence of the gods, if I disobeyed the oracle because I was afraid of death, fancying that I was wise when I was not wise. For the fear of death is indeed the pretence of wisdom, and not real wisdom, being a pretence of knowing the unknown; and no one knows whether death, which men in their fear apprehend to be the greatest evil, may not be the greatest good. Is not this ignorance of a disgraceful sort, the ignorance which is the conceit that man knows what he does not know? And in this respect only I believe myself to differ from men in general, and may perhaps claim to be wiser than they are:—that whereas I know but little of the world below, I do not suppose that I know: but I do know that injustice and disobedience to a better, whether God or man, is evil and dishonourable, and I will never fear or avoid a possible good rather than a certain evil. And therefore if you let me go now, and are not convinced by Anytus, who said that since I had been prosecuted I must be put to death (or if not that I ought never to have been prosecuted at all); and that if I escape now, your sons will all be utterly ruined by listening to my words—if you say to me, Socrates, this time we will not mind Anytus, and you shall be let off, but upon one condition, that you are not to enquire and speculate in this way any more, and that if you are caught doing so again you shall die;—if this was the condition on which you let me go, I should reply: Men of Athens, I honour and love you; but I shall obey God rather than you, and while I have life and strength I shall never cease from the practice and teaching of philosophy, exhorting any one whom I meet and saying to him after my manner: You, my friend,—a citizen of the great and mighty and wise city of Athens,—are you not ashamed of heaping up the greatest amount of money and honour and reputation, and caring so little about wisdom and truth and the greatest improvement of the soul, which you never regard or heed at all? And if the person with whom I am arguing, says: Yes, but I do care; then I do not leave him or let him go at once; but I proceed to interrogate and examine and cross-examine him, and if I think that he has no virtue in him, but only says that he has, I reproach him with undervaluing the greater, and overvaluing the less. And I shall repeat the same words to every one whom I meet, young and old, citizen and alien, but especially to the citizens, inasmuch as they are my brethren. For know that this is the command of God; and I believe that no greater good has ever happened in the state than my service to the God. For I do nothing but go about persuading you all, old and young alike, not to take thought for your persons or your properties, but first and chiefly to care about the greatest improvement of the soul. I tell you that virtue is not given by money, but that from virtue comes money and every other good of man, public as well as private. This is my teaching, and if this is the doctrine which corrupts the youth, I am a mischievous person. But if any one says that this is not my teaching, he is speaking an untruth. Wherefore, O men of Athens, I say to you, do as Anytus bids or not as Anytus bids, and either acquit me or not; but whichever you do, understand that I shall never alter my ways, not even if I have to die many times.

Men of Athens, do not interrupt, but hear me; there was an understanding between us that you should hear me to the end: I have something more to say, at which you may be inclined to cry out; but I believe that to hear me will be good for you, and therefore I beg that you will not cry out. I would have you know, that if you kill such an one as I am, you will injure yourselves more than you will injure me. Nothing will injure me, not Meletus nor yet Anytus—they cannot, for a bad man is not permitted to injure a better than himself. I do not deny that Anytus may, perhaps, kill him, or drive him into exile, or deprive him of civil rights; and he may imagine, and others may imagine, that he is inflicting a great injury upon him: but there I do not agree. For the evil of doing as he is doing—the evil of unjustly taking away the life of another—is greater far.

And now, Athenians, I am not going to argue for my own sake, as you may think, but for yours, that you may not sin against the God by condemning me, who am his gift to you. For if you kill me you will not easily find a successor to me, who, if I may use such a ludicrous figure of speech, am a sort of gadfly, given to the state by God; and the state is a great and noble steed who is tardy in his motions owing to his very size, and requires to be stirred into life. I am that gadfly which God has attached to the state, and

all day long and in all places am always fastening upon you, arousing and persuading and reproaching you. You will not easily find another like me, and therefore I would advise you to spare me. I dare say that you may feel out of temper (like a person who is suddenly awakened from sleep), and you think that you might easily strike me dead as Anytus advises, and then you would sleep on for the remainder of your lives, unless God in his care of you sent you another gadfly. When I say that I am given to you by God, the proof of my mission is this:—if I had been like other men, I should not have neglected all my own concerns or patiently seen the neglect of them during all these years, and have been doing yours, coming to you individually like a father or elder brother, exhorting you to regard virtue; such conduct, I say, would be unlike human nature. If I had gained anything, or if my exhortations had been paid, there would have been some sense in my doing so; but now, as you will perceive, not even the impudence of my accusers dares to say that I have ever exacted or sought pay of any one; of that they have no witness. And I have a sufficient witness to the truth of what I say—my poverty.

Some one may wonder why I go about in private giving advice and busying myself with the concerns of others, but do not venture to come forward in public and advise the state. I will tell you why. You have heard me speak at sundry times and in divers places of an oracle or sign which comes to me, and is the divinity which Meletus ridicules in the indictment. This sign, which is a kind of voice, first began to come to me when I was a child; it always forbids but never commands me to do anything which I am going to do. This is what deters me from being a politician. And rightly, as I think. For I am certain, O men of Athens, that if I had engaged in politics, I should have perished long ago, and done no good either to you or to myself. And do not be offended at my telling you the truth: for the truth is, that no man who goes to war with you or any other multitude, honestly striving against the many lawless and unrighteous deeds which are done in a state, will save his life; he who will fight for the right, if he would live even for a brief space, must have a private station and not a public one.

I can give you convincing evidence of what I say, not words only, but what you value far more—actions. Let me relate to you a passage of my own life which will prove to you that I should never have yielded to injustice from any fear of death, and that "as I should have refused to yield" I must have died at once. I will tell you a tale of the courts, not very interesting perhaps, but nevertheless true. The only office of state which I ever held, O men of Athens, was that of senator: the tribe Antiochis, which is my tribe, had the presidency at the trial of the generals who had not taken up the bodies of the slain after the battle of Arginusae; and you proposed to try them in a body, contrary to law, as you all thought afterwards; but at the time I was the only one of the Prytanes who was opposed to the illegality, and I gave my vote against you; and when the orators threatened to impeach and arrest me, and you called and shouted, I made up my mind that I would run the risk, having law and justice with me, rather than take part in your injustice because I feared imprisonment and death. This happened in the days of democracy. But when the oligarchy of the Thirty was in power, they sent for me and four others into the rotunda, and bade us bring Leon the Salaminian from Salamis, as they wanted to put him to death. This was a specimen of the sort of commands which they were always giving with the view of implicating as many as possible in their crimes; and then I showed, not in word only but in deed, that, if I may be allowed to use such an expression, I cared not a straw for death, and that my great and only care was lest I should do an unrighteous or unholy thing. For the strong arm of that oppressive power did not frighten me into doing wrong; and when we came out of the rotunda the other four went to Salamis and fetched Leon, but I went quietly home. For which I might have lost my life, had not the power of the Thirty shortly afterwards come to an end. And many will witness to my words.

Now do you really imagine that I could have survived all these years, if I had led a public life, supposing that like a good man I had always maintained the right and had made justice, as I ought, the first thing? No indeed, men of Athens, neither I nor any other man. But I have been always the same in all my actions, public as well as private, and never have I yielded any base compliance to those who are slanderously termed my disciples, or to any other. Not that I have any regular disciples. But if any one likes to come and hear me while I am pursuing my mission, whether he be young or old, he is not excluded. Nor do I converse only with those who pay; but any one, whether he be rich or poor, may ask and answer me and listen to my words; and whether he turns out to be a bad man or a good one, neither result can be justly imputed to me; for I never taught or professed to teach him anything. And if any one says that he has ever learned or heard anything from me in private which all the world has not heard, let me tell you that he is lying.

But I shall be asked, Why do people delight in continually conversing with you? I have told you already, Athenians, the whole truth about this matter: they like to hear the cross-examination of the pretenders to wisdom; there is amusement in it. Now this duty of cross-examining other men have been imposed upon me by God; and has been signified to me by oracles, visions, and in every way in which the will of divine power was ever intimated to any-one. This is true, O Athenians; or, if not true, would be soon refuted. If I am or have been corrupting the youth, those of them who are now grown up and become sensible that I gave them bad advice in the days of their youth should come forward as accusers, and take their revenge; or if they do not like to come themselves, some of their relatives, fathers, brothers, or other kinsmen, should say what evil their families have suffered at my hands. Now is their time. Many of them I see in the court. There is

Crito, who is of the same age and of the same deme with myself, and there is Critobulus his son, whom I also see. Then again there is Lysanias of Sphettus, who is the father of Aeschines—he is present; and also there is Antiphon of Cephisus, who is the father of Epigenes; and there are the brothers of several who have associated with me. There is Nicostratus the son of Theosdotides, and the brother of Theodotus (now Theodotus himself is dead, and therefore he, at any rate, will not seek to stop him); and there is Paralus the son of Demodocus, who had a brother Theages; and Adeimantus the son of Ariston, whose brother Plato is present; and Aeantodorus, who is the brother of Apollodorus, whom I also see. I might mention a great many others, some of whom Meletus should have produced as witnesses in the course of his speech; and let him still produce them, if he has forgotten—I will make way for him. And let him say, if he has any testimony of the sort which he can produce. Nay, Athenians, the very opposite is the truth. For all these are ready to witness on behalf of the corrupter, of the injurer of their kindred, as Meletus and Anytus call me; not the corrupted youth only—there might have been a motive for that—but their uncorrupted elder relatives. Why should they too support me with their testimony? Why, indeed, except for the sake of truth and justice, and because they know that I am speaking the truth, and that Meletus is a liar.

Well, Athenians, this and the like of this is all the defence which I have to offer. Yet a word more. Perhaps there may be some one who is offended at me, when he calls to mind how he himself on a similar, or even a less serious occasion, prayed and entreated the judges with many tears, and how he produced his children in court, which was a moving spectacle, together with a host of relations and friends; whereas I, who am probably in danger of my life, will do none of these things. The contrast may occur to his mind, and he may be set against me, and vote in anger because he is displeased at me on this account. Now if there be such a person among

you,—mind, I do not say that there is,—to him I may fairly reply: My friend, I am a man, and like other men, a creature of flesh and blood, and not "of wood or stone," as Homer says; and I have a family, yes, and sons, O Athenians, three in number, one almost a man, and two others who are still young; and yet I will not bring any of them hither in order to petition you for an acquittal. And why not? Not from any self-assertion or want of respect for you. Whether I am or am not afraid of death is another question, of which I will not now speak. But, having regard to public opinion, I feel that such conduct would be discreditable to myself, and to you, and to the whole state. One who has reached my years, and who has a name for wisdom, ought not to demean himself. Whether this opinion of me be deserved or not, at any rate the world has decided that Socrates is in some way superior to other men. And if those among you who are said to be superior in wisdom and courage, and any other virtue, demean themselves in this way, how shameful is their conduct! I have seen men of reputation, when they have been condemned, behaving in the strangest manner: they seemed to fancy that they were going to suffer something dreadful if they died, and that they could be immortal if you only allowed them to live; and I think that such are a dishonour to the state, and that any stranger coming in would have said of them that the most eminent men of Athens, to whom the Athenians themselves give honour and command, are no better than women. And I say that these things ought not to be done by those of us who have a reputation; and if they are done, you ought not to permit them; you ought rather to show that you are far more disposed to condemn the man who gets up a doleful scene and makes the city ridiculous, than him who holds his peace.

But, setting aside the question of public opinion, there seems to be something wrong in asking a favour of a judge, and thus procuring an acquittal, instead of informing and convincing him. For his duty is, not to make a present of justice, but to give judgment; and he has sworn that he will judge according to the laws, and not according to his own good pleasure; and we ought not to encourage you, nor should you allow yourself to be encouraged, in this habit of perjury—there can be no piety in that. Do not then require me to do what I consider dishonourable and impious and wrong, especially now, when I am being tried for impiety on the indictment of Meletus. For if, O men of Athens, by force of persuasion and entreaty I could overpower your oaths, then I should be teaching you to believe that there are no gods, and in defending should simply convict myself of the charge of not believing in them. But that is not so—far otherwise. For I do believe that there are gods, and in a sense higher than that in which any of my accusers believe in them. And to you and to God I commit my cause, to be determined by you as is best for you and me.

There are many reasons why I am not grieved, O men of Athens, at the vote of condemnation. I expected it, and am only surprised that the votes are so nearly equal; for I had thought that the majority against me would have been far larger; but now, had thirty votes gone over to the other side, I should have been acquitted. And I may say, I think, that I have escaped Meletus. I may say more; for without the assistance of Anytus and Lycon, any one may see that he would not have had a fifth part of the votes, as the law requires, in which case he would have incurred a fine of a thousand drachmae.

And so he proposes death as the penalty. And what shall I propose on my part, O men of Athens? Clearly that which is my due. And what is my due? What return shall be made to the man who has never had the wit to be idle during his whole life; but has been careless of what the many care for—wealth, and family interests, and military offices, and speaking in the assembly, and magistracies, and plots, and parties. Reflecting that I was really too honest a man to be a politician and live, I did not go where I could do no good to you or to myself; but where I could do the greatest good privately to every one of you, thither I went, and sought to persuade every man among you that he must look to himself, and seek virtue and wisdom before he looks to his private interests, and look to the state before he looks to the interests of the state; and that this should be the order which he observes in all his actions. What shall be done to such an one? Doubtless some good thing, O men of Athens, if he has his reward; and the good should be of a kind suitable to him. What would be a reward suitable to a poor man who is your benefactor, and who desires leisure that he may instruct you? There can be no reward so fitting as maintenance in the Prytaneum, O men of Athens, a reward which he deserves far more than the citizen who has won the prize at Olympia in the horse or chariot race, whether the chariots were drawn by two horses or by many. For I am in want, and he has enough; and he only gives you the appearance of happiness, and I give you the reality. And if I am to estimate the penalty fairly, I should say that maintenance in the Prytaneum is the just return.

Perhaps you think that I am braving you in what I am saying now, as in what I said before about the tears and prayers. But this is not so. I speak rather because I am convinced that I never intentionally wronged any one, although I cannot convince you—the time has been too short; if there were a law at Athens, as there is in other cities, that a capital cause should not be decided in one day, then I believe that I should have convinced you. But I cannot in a moment refute great slanders; and, as I am convinced that I never wronged another, I will assuredly not wrong myself. I will not say of myself that I deserve any evil, or propose any penalty. Why should I? Because I am afraid of the penalty of death which Meletus proposes? When I do not know whether death is a good or an evil, why should I propose a penalty which would certainly be an evil? Shall I say imprisonment? And why should I live in prison, and be the slave of the magistrates of the year—of the Eleven? Or shall the penalty be a fine, and imprisonment until the fine is paid? There is the same objection. I should have to lie in prison, for money I have none, and cannot pay. And if I say exile (and this may possibly be the penalty which you will affix), I must indeed be blinded by the love of life, if I am so irrational as to expect that when you, who are my own citizens, cannot endure my discourses and words, and have found them so grievous and odious that you will have no more of them, others are likely to endure me. No indeed, men of Athens, that is not very likely. And what a life should I lead, at my age, wandering from city to city, ever changing my place of exile, and always being driven out! For I am quite sure that wherever I go, there, as here, the young men will flock to me; and if I drive them away, their elders will drive me out at their request; and if I let them come, their fathers and friends will drive me out for their sakes.

Some one will say: Yes, Socrates, but cannot you hold your tongue, and then you may go into a foreign city, and no one will interfere with you? Now I have great difficulty in making you understand my answer to this. For if I tell you that to do as you say would be a disobedience to the God, and therefore that I cannot hold my tongue, you will not believe that I am serious; and if I say again that daily to discourse about virtue, and of those other things about which you hear me examining myself and others, is the greatest good of man, and that the unexamined life is not worth living, you are still less likely to believe me. Yet I say what is true, although a thing of which it is hard for me to persuade you. Also, I have never been accustomed to think that I deserve to suffer any harm. Had I money I might have estimated the offence at what I was able to pay, and not have been much the worse. But I have none, and therefore I must ask you to proportion the fine to my means. Well, perhaps I could afford a mina, and therefore I propose that penalty: Plato, Crito, Critobulus, and Apollodorus, my friends here, bid me say thirty minae, and they will be the sureties. Let thirty minae be the penalty; for which sum they will be ample security to you.

* * *

Not much time will be gained, O Athenians, in return for the evil name which you will get from the detractors of the city, who will say that you killed Socrates, a wise man; for they will call me wise, even although I am not wise, when they want to reproach you. If you had waited a little while, your desire would have been fulfilled in the course of nature. For I am far advanced in years, as you may perceive, and not far from death. I am speaking now not to all of you, but only to those who have condemned me to death. And I have another thing to say to them: You think that I was convicted because I had no words of the sort which would have procured my acquittal—I mean, if I had thought fit to leave nothing undone or unsaid. Not so; the deficiency which led to my conviction was not of words—certainly not. But I had not the boldness or impudence or inclination to address you as you would have liked me to do, weeping and wailing and lamenting, and saying and doing many things which you have been accustomed to hear from others, and which, as I maintain, are unworthy of me. I thought at the time that I ought not to do anything common or mean when in danger: nor do I now repent of the style of my defence; I would rather die having spoken after my manner, than speak in your manner and live. For neither in war nor yet at law ought I or any man to use every way of escaping death. Often in battle there can be no doubt that if a man will throw away his arms, and fall on his knees before his pursuers, he may escape death; and in other dangers there are other ways of escaping death, if a man is willing to say and do anything. The difficulty, my friends, is not to avoid death, but to avoid unrighteousness; for that runs faster than death. I am old and move slowly, and the slower runner has overtaken me, and my accusers are keen and quick, and the faster runner, who is unrighteousness, has overtaken them. And now I depart hence condemned by you to suffer the penalty of death,—they too go their ways condemned by the truth to suffer the penalty of villainy and wrong; and I must abide by my award—let them abide by theirs. I suppose that these things may be regarded as fated,—and I think that they are well.

And now, O men who have condemned me, I would fain prophesy to you; for I am about to die, and in the hour of death men are gifted with prophetic power. And I prophesy to you who are my murderers, that immediately after my departure punishment far heavier than you have inflicted on me will surely await you. Me you have killed because you wanted to escape the accuser, and not to give an account of your lives. But that will not be as you suppose: far otherwise. For I say that there will be more accusers of you than there are now; accusers whom hitherto I have restrained: and as they are younger they will be more inconsiderate with you, and you will be more offended at them. If you think that by killing men you can prevent some one from censuring your evil lives, you are mistaken; that is not a way of escape which is either possible or honourable; the easiest and the noblest way is not to be disabling others, but to be improving yourselves. This is the prophecy which I utter before my departure to the judges who have condemned me.

Friends, who would have acquitted me, I would like also to talk with you about the thing which has come to pass, while the magistrates are busy, and before I go to the place at which I must die. Stay then a little, for we may as well talk with one another while there is time. You are my friends, and I should like to show you the meaning of this event which has happened to me. O my judges—for you I may truly call judges—I should like to tell you of a wonderful circumstance. Hitherto the divine faculty of which the internal oracle is the source has constantly been in the habit of opposing me even about trifles, if I was going to make a slip or error in any matter; and now as you see there has come upon me that which may be thought, and is generally believed to be, the last and worst evil. But the oracle made no sign of opposition, either when I was leaving my house in the morning, or when I was on my way to the court, or while I was speaking, at anything which I was going to say; and yet I have often been stopped in the middle of a speech, but now in nothing I either said or did touching the matter in hand has the oracle opposed me. What do I take to be the explanation of this silence? I will tell you. It is an intimation that what has happened to me is a good, and that those of us who think that death is an evil are in error. For the customary sign would surely have opposed me had I been going to evil and not to good.

Let us reflect in another way, and we shall see that there is great reason to hope that death is a good; for one of two things—either death is a state of nothingness and utter unconsciousness, or, as men say, there is a change and migration of the soul from this world to another. Now if you suppose that there is no consciousness, but a sleep like the sleep of him who is undisturbed even by dreams, death will be an unspeakable gain. For if a person were to select the night in which his sleep was undisturbed even by dreams, and were to compare with this the other days and nights of his life, and then were to tell us how many days and nights he had passed in the course of his life better and more pleasantly than this one, I think that any man, I will not say a private man, but even the great king will not find many such days or nights, when compared with the others. Now if death be of such a nature, I say that to die is gain; for eternity is then only a single night. But if death is the journey to another place, and there, as men say, all the dead abide, what good, O my friends and judges, can be greater than this? If indeed when the pilgrim arrives in the world below, he is delivered from the professors of justice in this world, and finds the true judges who are said to give judgment there, Minos and Rhadamanthus and Aeacus and Triptolemus, and other sons of God who were righteous in their own life, that pilgrimage will be worth making. What would not a man give if he might converse with Orpheus and Musaeus and Hesiod and Homer? Nay, if this be true, let me die again and again. I myself, too, shall have a wonderful interest in there meeting and conversing with Palamedes, and Ajax the son of Telamon, and any other ancient hero who has suffered death through an unjust judgment; and there will be no small pleasure, as I think, in comparing my own sufferings with theirs. Above all, I shall then be able to continue my search into true and false knowledge; as in this world, so also in the next; and I shall find out who is wise; and who pretends to be wise, and is not. What would not a man give, O judges, to be able to examine the leader of the great Trojan expedition; or Odysseus or Sisyphus, or numberless others, men and women too! What infinite delight would there be in conversing with them and asking them questions! In another world they do not put a man to death for asking questions: assuredly not. For besides being happier than we are, they will be immortal, if what is said is true.

Wherefore, O judges, be of good cheer about death, and know of a certainty, that no evil can happen to a good man, either in life or after death. He and his are not neglected by the gods;

nor has my own approaching end happened by mere chance. But I see clearly that the time had arrived when it was better for me to die and be released from trouble; wherefore the oracle gave no sign. For which reason, also, I am not angry with my condemners, or with my accusers; they have done me no harm, although they did not mean to do me any good; and for this I may gently blame them.

Still I have a favour to ask of them. When my sons are grown up, I would ask you, O my friends, to punish them; and I would have you trouble them, as I have troubled you, if they seem to care about riches, or anything, more than about virtue; or if they pretend to be something when they are really nothing,—then reprove them, as I have reproved you, for not caring about that for which they ought to care, and thinking that they are something when they are really nothing. And if you do this, both I and my sons will have received justice at your hands.

The hour of departure has arrived, and we go our ways—I to die, and you to live. Which is better God only knows.

Part Three

Does Morality Answer the Questions?

Introduction

Where Are We Going?

What is the best life? Is it living for pleasure? Is it living one of the versions of morality we have encountered? Is it best explained by Kant, by Mill, by Sartre, or by religions? Perhaps the conformity required by the Grand Inquisitor is really best. Maybe people don't want to be free and responsible. If you are like me, you are probably confused. We have looked at so many options of the best life that it's difficult to know how to decide which theory is most adequate. I think it is time to address our confusion.

Moral Objectivity and Impartiality

Morality requires that we internalize an impartial, objective "system" of belief. The moral point of view is essentially one in which we look at ourselves as one person among many moral equals. That doesn't mean that all people are equal in all ways, of course. But morality does require that each of us be thought of and treated with moral impartiality. So objectivity and impartiality are essential to morality.

Now you may ask what objection I could make against that? After all, it's only fair to ask that everyone abide by the same rules. That's a strength of morality. It's the feature that staves off chaos in society. If everyone follows the moral rules, then we will all be better off. At least that's what you thought when we started this book. Social stability, however, doesn't guarantee us the best life. It only promises to keep us away from the much worse life of chaos and fear.

Can We Have the Best of Each Life?

Is there a way to live that lets us fully experience the moment and at the same time keeps us living a life, and not just a series of chaotic, disjointed moments? Can we live *in* the here and now and still avoid a fragmented life? Can we be a part of our community without giving up our individuality? I think the answer to each of these questions is yes.

To see how we can find such a life, we need to look in two directions. We have already explored a number of traditional formulations of the moral point of view. First, we need to find and hold to the truths of each thinker we've read. Second, we need to ask: What is the value of moral values?

Hold to the Truths

What are the truths incorporated in each moralist's theory? Kierkegaard's A, Camus's Stranger, and even Mill assert that pleasure and intense experience are key elements in living the best life. At the same time, the Grand Inquisitor's insight rightly emphasizes our desire for security and certainty in our moral values. We want to be free of the dual anxieties of indecision and responsibility. When it comes to moral values, though, it would be better if we knew what made our rules correct.

Epictetus goes further. He tells us that our own pleasure is desirable, but self-control is better. Self-control is an important feature of the best life. Of course, the freedom Epictetus offers is not doing whatever we want. His freedom is a defense against being overwhelmed by one's external environment, or one's passions. Sartre's emphasis on freedom and self-determination endorses Epictetus' contribution.

Even after we wrestle with the questions of freedom, conformity, and good and bad, we are left wondering: What is the point of morality? Camus, Kierkegaard, Epictetus, Mill, Kant, Dostoevski, and Sartre all give impressive insights into what direction we want to go in our lives. We want to avoid boredom, and the dual anxieties of indecision and responsibility, and we want to experience our reality in an undistorted way.

What's the Value of Moral Values?

Now we need to ask: What is the value of moral values? Perhaps morality is not the best way to live. From what we've seen, morality does not successfully eliminate boredom, anxiety, and guilt. Nor does morality adequately give meaning to our lives, or allow us to relate to others and to reality in an intimate and intense way. The aim of the final three discussions is to create a better version of the best life.

Is Life Meaningful or Absurd?

Chapter 11 asks whether life is meaningful or absurd. This is an important question in its own right. As well, asking this question is a symptom of our dissatisfaction with the answers that moral philosophers produce in defining the best life. Here you will meet two of the ancient world's wisest people, Sisyphus and Solomon.

How Can We Relate With Other People?

Chapter 12 asks for alternate ways of relating with people. Here we resurrect Martin Buber. Although you probably have not heard of him, I think you will learn from his insights into the ways we experience and relate to others.

What is the Best Life?

Our final chapter is more of a "pointing" than a definitive answer to the question: What is the best life? Spinoza and Lao Tsu are two philosophers worth reading in full. Our more limited use of them, however, will be to draw out their conclusions on the best life. The "answers" given by Spinoza and Lao Tsu are interestingly similar. And yet Spinoza lived in seventeenth-century Holland and Lao Tsu lived in sixth-century B.C.E. China. Perhaps the question: What is the best life? transcends time and place. It is a uniquely human question. And if Spinoza and Lao Tsu are on the right track, then the answer to our question also transcends all the human differences that separate us.

Is Life Meaningful or Absurd? The Wisdom of Solomon and Sisyphus

Is LIFE MEANINGFUL? What does it mean to say that life is absurd? The two authors before us represent different approaches to our questions. In Ecclesiastes, Solomon laments the human condition as vain, meaningless, and futile. His answer to our meaningless existence is straightforward. "Fear God and keep his commandments. This is the whole duty of mankind." In *The Myth of Sisyphus*, Camus states that "the meaning of life is the most urgent of questions." He says that "there is but one truly serious philosophical problem, and that is suicide." Whether or not one commits suicide is one's response to the question of life's meaning.

How the Questions Arise

Before we talk to our time-traveling visitors, we ought to prepare ourselves. What circumstances raise the question of the meaning or absurdity of life? We ask about the meaning of life when our basic values and beliefs appear vague, or uncertain, or relative. We question life's meaning when we feel insignificant, or when our situation appears hopeless, or when our work is fruitless and unappreciated.

Two General Strategies

Our authors represent two general strategies to the question of the meaningful life. Not surprisingly, as part of the Bible, Ecclesiastes represents one religious reply to the question of meaning. Camus's *Myth of Sisyphus* is a nonreligious response. We need to be careful, of course, not to take too seriously the categories of the religious and the nonreligious. While Solomon clearly believes in his God, Camus's Sisyphus

Material in this chapter taken from *The Myth of Sisyphus and Other Essays* by Albert Camus, trans., J. O'Brien. Copyright © 1955 by Alfred A. Knopf, Inc. Reprinted by permission of the publisher.

is an atheistic response in that Sisyphus' attitude places him above the gods. We'll look into this shortly. For now, let's turn to the religious alternatives.

Solomon's Lament

Solomon's lament in Ecclesiastes affirms God's existence. Solomon is not convinced that there is an afterlife, however. Nor is he concerned with God's great and mysterious plan for the universe. Solomon's thoughts are more inwardly directed. He wants to know what this life offers. As the wisest man of ancient Israel, Solomon desires to know the purpose of his own life, not as a piece of the great unknown, but as a human being. Solomon does not believe that a longer life is necessarily a more meaningful, or fuller, or happier life. So an eternal life following this temporary stay on earth is not particularly appealing to him. Let's resurrect him now.

All is Vanity.   It is an honor to speak to the wisest of the ancient Hebrews.
   "Why?"
   Well, Mr. Solomon, because you must have a pretty good idea of what makes a life meaningful. Is the meaningful life a life of sensual pleasures, or fame, or wealth? Surely if anyone knows, you must.
   "Art, vanity of vanities! All is vanity."
   What does that mean?
   "Life is meaningless!"
   Why do you, the wisest of all ancient people, think that all is vain and hopeless?
   "Why do you insist on exaggerating the worth of my wisdom?"
   Isn't wisdom preferable to foolishness?
   "I gave my heart to know wisdom, and to know madness and folly; I perceived that this also is but a striving after the wind. For in much wisdom *is* much grief; and he that increases knowledge increases sorrow."
   But isn't one life better than the other? Isn't it better to know and understand the world than to live in it ignorantly?
   "The wise man's eyes are in his head; but the fool walks in darkness."
   So there is a difference.
   "And yet . . . one event happens to them all. When I perceived this I said to myself, 'As it happens to the fool, so it happens even to me: and why was I then more wise?'"
   But this can't be correct. Surely a wise person lives better than a fool!
   "This also is vanity. For there is no remembrance of the wise more than of the fool forever; seeing that which now is in the days to come shall be forgotten."
   What is the enduring fate that you speak of?
   "How the wise man dies just like the fool, of course!"
   So you believe that death robs life of its meaning?
   "Yes. And when I realized this truth, I hated life, for the work that is wrought under the sun *is* grievous to me; for all is vanity and a striving after the wind."

The Pleasurable Life.   Are you suggesting that we live for the pleasure of the moment? This will come as a great shock to people.

"Once I said in my heart, 'Go now, I will prove thee with pleasure: therefore enjoy pleasure.'"

And did you? I mean as king you could do whatever you want.

"This also is vanity. I said of laughter, 'It is mad,' and of pleasure, 'What use is it?'"

That's it? You gave up after just thinking about pleasure?

"I sought in my heart to give myself over to wine—my heart still acquainted with wisdom—and to lay hold on folly, till I might see what was good for the sons of men, which they should do under heaven all the days of their life."

Wow! You became a "professional" pleasure seeker? As an experiment?

"I made great works, houses, vineyards, gardens, and orchards. I got servants and maidens, and had possession of great and small cattle. I gathered gold and silver; I got singers, and women singers, man's delight. I became great and increased more than all who were before me in Jerusalem: also my wisdom remained with me. I held not my heart from any joy for my heart rejoiced in all my labor."

How did this work out? I mean, is this the best life?

"All was vanity and a striving after the wind."

Isn't Work Meaningful?   Can you find any meaning in your work?

"What has man from all his labor, wherein he has labored under the sun?"

Are you saying that work doesn't accomplish anything? That we should not have goals?

"What has a man from all the labor and vexation with which he labors beneath the sun? For all his days are sorrow and his work is grief."

Think of all that you contribute to the people who come after you.

"Who knows whether the man who will come after me shall be a wise man or a fool? Yet he will have rule over all my labor and where I showed myself wise. This is vanity."

I see what you mean. Nothing and nobody lasts. Life is transitory, unsatisfying, and boring. In life there is nothing novel. Even our work comes to nothing. Accomplishments perish and are forgotten. Or used by strangers who may misuse our works. So there is no point in working?

"On the contrary, there is nothing better for a man than that he should eat and drink, and enjoy good in his labor."

Isn't this just what you denied? How can a person find joy in pleasures and work? You've just said it is all pointless!

"It is from the hand of God. For God gives to a man that is good in his sight, wisdom and knowledge and joy: but to the sinner he gives the work of gathering and heaping, that he may give to him that is good before God."

How do you know what pleases God?

"To every thing there is a season and a time to every purpose under heaven."

I know, a time to plant and a time to reap, a time to be born and a time to die. This sounds pretty cynical.

"What profit has the worker from his work? All of this is vanity and a striving after the wind."

Justice.   Is there no justice, Solomon? Aren't hard-working people compensated for their labors?

"I said in my heart that God might show men that they are but beasts. For that which befalls the sons of men befalls beasts. As one dies, so dies the other. They all have one breath, and man has no preeminence above a beast: all is vanity."

What about heaven? Don't you believe that good people go to heaven?

"All go to one place; all are of the dust, and all turn to dust again. Who knows whether the spirit of man goes upward and the spirit of the beast goes downward to the earth?"

What's left?

"There is nothing better than that a man should rejoice in his own works; for that is his portion."

This sounds so passive. Must people just live as they live? Isn't there any justice in the world? Aren't the oppressed rewarded and the evil punished?

"I considered all the oppressions that are done under the sun . . . the tears of the oppressed, and they had no comforter! On the side of their oppressors there was power."

What comfort can be brought to the oppressed?

Oppression and the Happiest Person.   "There was no one to comfort them. And I praised the dead who are already dead more than the living who are still alive, but better than both is he who has not yet been born, who has not seen the evil work that is done under the sun."

I don't understand. Are you saying that a person who is dead is better off than a person who is alive? Solomon, do you praise the dead and feel grief for the living who must witness the evil-doing of oppressing peoples? And you think that those who have not been born, and so have not witnessed oppression, are happier yet?

"That is just what I say. The living person must witness the evil and oppression that men commit. The dead who are already dead are spared that torture of the spirit."

And the happiest person is the one who has not been born?

"The person who has not yet been born does not experience the torture of which I speak. Neither does this person see the oppression now. Therefore, he is the most fortunate."

It sounds like the best life is the one where the person is never born! Is that what you are saying?

"Yes, all else is vanity and a striving after the wind."

What does that mean?

"All else is futile and pointless, a striving after that which cannot be caught."

Envy.   "I considered all the right work, that for this a man is envied by his neighbor."

I know; it is vanity and a striving after the wind.

"The fool, the envious person, consumes himself in his attitude toward others. He removes himself from his companions, and suffers mightily."

What do you mean? What sort of person do you have in mind?

"A person who has no one, yet there is no end to all his labor: neither is his eye satisfied with riches. This also is vanity and a sore travail. Two are better than one. A threefold cord is not quickly broken."

Companionship, friendship, and loving relations are better than envy and the striving for wealth? Is that it?

"There is more. When you vow a vow to God, do not defer paying it; for he has no pleasure in fools. Pay what you have vowed."

How does this counter the injustice that we see?

Wealth.   "If you see the oppression of the poor, and violent perverting of judgment and justice in a province, do not be amazed at the matter, for a high official is watched by a higher."

I wonder about this. The rich seem to prosper and the poor lead difficult lives.

"He who loves silver will not be satisfied with silver; nor he who loves abundance with increase. The sleep of the laborer is sweet, whether he eats little or much; but the abundance of the rich will not let him sleep."

It's better to be a poor worker than a rich person? You're saying that the rich person's excessive wealth troubles him? This is difficult to believe. It sounds like a rationalization. No, it sounds like a way of keeping oppressed people from doing anything about their lives.

"Why do you say this, Art?"

What you say makes it sound like the rich live a more troubled life than the poor. What better way to keep the poor in their place than by convincing them that it is the rich who suffer? It doesn't look like suffering from where I stand.

"Yet there is a grievous evil which I have seen under the sun: riches kept for the owners to their hurt. But those riches perish by evil travail."

Yeah, so?

"As he came forth of his mother's womb, naked shall he return to go as he came, and shall take nothing of his labor, which he may carry away in his hand."

But a rich person's time on earth is more comfortable! Surely you don't deny that!

"What profit has he that he labors for the wind, and all his days he eats in darkness, in much sorrow and wrath with his sickness?"

You aren't talking about material comforts, are you? You think rich people suffer, and are sick and filled with resentment. Is that it? Are you saying that the joys of this world are worthless?

Eat, Drink, and Be Merry.   "What I have seen to be good and to be fitting is to eat and to drink and to enjoy the good of all the labor that he takes under the sun all the days of his life."

So it isn't the wealth or poverty, it's our attitude toward our work—or our labor, as you call it.

"Every man also to whom God has given riches and wealth and power to enjoy them, and to take his portion and to rejoice in his labor—this is the gift of God."

Then the key is to work and to live—

"With joy in his heart. What else is there to life than joy in living it? For who can tell a man what will be after him under the sun?"

Quiet Despair.   It sounds to me like you are inviting people to remain in a state of quiet despair. You concentrate so much on death that you leave little room for the joys of life. How do you answer that?

"The day of death is better than the day of birth. It is better to go to the house of mourning than to go to the house of feasting. Sorrow is better than laughter, for by sadness of the countenance the heart is made better."

You don't think this is depressing? This is more stoic than Epictetus!

"Perhaps, yes, a man must deal with the inevitable. In the day of prosperity be joyful, and in the day of adversity consider; God also has set the one over against the other, to the end that man should find nothing after him."

What are you directing us to do? How are we to live?

"He who fears God shall come forth of them all."

This doesn't help much. What does it mean? Is the perfect life living always according to your God's laws?

"There is not a just man on earth who does good and never sins."

Then what is the best life, Solomon?

"Be not righteous over much, and do not make yourself overwise; why should you destroy yourself? Be not wicked over much, neither be foolish; why should you die before your time?"

Nothing in excess; that's your formula for the best life?

Enjoy Life, for Death Comes to Us All.   "Go, eat your bread with joy and drink your wine with a merry heart. Let your garments be always white. Enjoy life with the wife whom you love, all the days of your vain life."

How can I enjoy my vain life knowing that everything is for nothing? You force me to think about the futility of living and working, then you tell me to enjoy it? How can I?

"Whatever your hand finds to do, do it with your might."

Is There No Value We Can Endorse?   Solomon, doesn't hard work pay off?

"The race is not to the swift, nor the battle to the strong, nor bread to the wise, nor riches to the intelligent, nor favor to the men of skill; but time and chance happen to them all."

Then is there no value we can endorse?

"Wisdom *is* better than strength. The words of wise men are heard in quiet more than the cry of a ruler among fools."

So wisdom is a virtue, an excellence that you believe in? Is the wise person better than the foolish?

"When the fool walks by the way, his wisdom fails him, and he says to every one that he is a fool."

Huh?

"A fool also is full of words; a man cannot tell what is to be. The labor of a fool wearies everyone. The foolish person's life lacks enjoyment because it lacks concentration."

Aren't we back to a quietism, an acceptance of what is? You say that we should accept whatever happens, but that is a depressing way to live.

"Light is sweet, and it is pleasant for the eyes to behold the sun. But if a man lives many years, and rejoice in them all, yet let him remember the days of darkness; for they will be many. All that comes is vanity."

So live life, for someday we will die? Is that your message? Live for the brief time we have, for death lasts forever?

"Yes. The conclusion of the matter is this. Fear God, and keep his commandments; for this is the whole duty of man."

Death Robs Life of Its Meaning? So you think that death robs life of its meaning?

"Assuredly, Art. I would gladly trade places with you and live your life! Not because you are particularly worthy, but because you are alive. And except for the brief moments that your resurrection machine sustains me, I am dead, and will always remain so."

What if your religious descendants are correct? What if you do live forever? Would you be happier? Would eternal life make it meaningful?

"As I have already said, a man cannot know whether life is eternal, whether men rise and animals descend. What we have to go on is what we see in this life. Men return to the dust from which they spring. That is the only truth we see."

Solomon, you sound remarkably like the existentialist who gets criticized in our discussion with Sartre. Would you mind if I distill our talk to a few brief statements?

"Proceed."

You say that life is meaningless because each of us will die.

"Yes, all is a torture of the spirit. The more one lives and enjoys life's experiences, the more one realizes the pain of impending death."

Okay, and you also say that God acts in ways that we cannot always understand.

"Nor do we always approve of God's actions. That is why we despair over the injustice practiced against the oppressed."

What you're saying is that reality goes on as it does. There is little we can do to understand, or at least to change reality, so we might as well—

"Deal with the inevitable. In the day of prosperity be joyful, and in the day of adversity consider; God also has set the one over against the other, to the end that man should find nothing after him."

Then death and the unchangeable laws of science are what drive you to believing that life is vain?

"Yes. And now I must leave, Art. I have remained here too long."

Thank you, and goodbye, King Solomon. You have given me a great deal to think about living and about dying.

Sisyphus' Immortality

Camus's *Myth of Sisyphus* gives an example of the meaningless life. According to Greek legend, Sisyphus is condemned to roll a rock ceaselessly to the top of a mountain. When his chore is accomplished, the rock rolls back to the valley below, where Sisyphus must return to begin the process again.

"They had thought with some reason, Art, that there is no more dreadful punishment than futile and hopeless labor."

Why is this such a horrible punishment? Because it lasts forever? You live forever. Your burden, your punishment, depends on your eternal life and your unending, eternal task. Isn't that it?

"Certainly not. Immortality is one of humanity's greatest hopes."

Then, Sisyphus, it must be the immensity of the stone and the struggle required. Is that it? You have to exert all your strength against the huge rock?

"It does require the whole effort of my body striving to raise the huge stone, to roll it and push it up a slope a hundred times over; my face screwed up, my cheek tight against the stone, my shoulder bracing the clay-covered mass, my foot wedging it, each fresh start with my arms outstretched. But that is not the torment."

Then what is the punishment, if not the endless struggle?

Nothing Comes of It.   "Nothing comes of it."

I don't understand.

"The punishment given me by the gods is pointless activity. I am not even saved by death. The task they have given me is endless repetition serving absolutely no purpose, except punishment."

Isn't this the same "punishment" that Solomon describes? People toil under the sun, but for no purpose? It's just that yours is endless toil.

"Nothing comes of my toil. I do not even receive credit toward my punishment. There is no success; not even small goals are reached. At first I would mentally place markers along the climb. I would cheer myself by reaching each marker."

Did your little goals keep you going? Did you feel better for reaching them?

"At first, yes."

What went wrong?

"The prospect of endlessly achieving pointless short-term goals fails after a brief time. I was merely deceiving myself. There is no point to goals, long-term or short-term."

Crime.   Perhaps I can get a handle on your punishment if I can understand the crime. What did you do?

"I was accused of a certain levity in regard to the gods."

How so?

"I stole their secrets. I tricked Aesopus into giving water to the citadel of Corinth."

You chose water and risked the gods' wrath!

"Homer tells of another crime. I had Death put in chains. Pluto could not endure the sight of his deserted, silent empire. So he dispatched the god of war, who liberated Death."

And you were punished for your hatred of Death?

"Yes. There is a third charge against me. When I was about to die, I wanted to test my wife's love. It was rash, but that is part of my nature."

How is it a crime to test your wife's love?

"I ordered her to cast my unburied body into the middle of the public square."

Gross.

"Even more detestable in my culture, where burial is a sacred right of a good man. When I awoke in the underworld, I was annoyed by an obedience so contrary to human love. Imagine!"

What did you do?

"I obtained permission from Pluto to return to earth to chastise my wife. The gods understand love and the indignity done to me."

I'm getting a sense of why you were considered the wisest and most prudent of mortals. Convincing Pluto to release you from death is certainly clever. But if you had permission to go, where's the problem?

"When I had seen the face of this world, enjoyed water and sun, warm stones and the sea, I no longer wanted to go back to the infernal darkness."

I'm sure there were recalls, anger and warnings from the gods, especially from Pluto.

"Oh, yes, but many years more I lived facing the curve of the gulf, the sparkling seas, and the smiles of the earth. Life is so full. Every experience is vital and intense. I could not willingly return to the darkness."

The gods must have been very angry!

"A decree of the gods was necessary. Mercury came and seized me by the collar, snatching me from my joys."

And Punishment.   Then your crime was—

"A passionate desire to live, to feel, to experience every morsel of reality. I hate Death. I love living, experiencing, breathing, tasting, seeing, hearing, thinking, feeling—all the senses. That is my crime!"

You were sentenced to futile and hopeless labor for being passionate? For really living?

"My scorn of the gods, my hatred of death, and my passion for life won me the unspeakable penalty in which the whole being is exerted toward accomplishing nothing. This is the price that must be paid for the passions of this earth."

What punishment could be more dreadful? I guess Solomon was mistaken. Death is not the worst outcome of a person's life. Eternal, pointless repetition is worse. How do you deal with this torture?

Consciousness.   "Consciousness. At each conscious moment when I leave the heights and gradually sink toward the lair of the gods, I am superior to my fate. I am stronger than my rock."

But if you were not conscious, there would be no torture. The tragedy is in the fact of your awareness of your punishment.

"No, Art. The lucidity that constitutes my torture at the same time crowns my victory. There is no fate that cannot be surmounted by scorn."

But your punishment is so unusual, so extreme. How does awareness make it more bearable?

"The workman of today works every day in his life at the same tasks, and this fate is no less absurd. It is tragic only at the rare moments when one becomes conscious."

You make us sound pathetic. Can't we change anything?

"I, too, am powerless, but I am a proletarian of the gods. I am their better because I am rebellious. I know the whole extent of my wretched condition."

A powerless worker can be better than her masters, just by being rebellious? Just by knowing how things are?

Sorrow and Joy.   What about on your descent? What do you think about?

"Sometimes my descent is performed in sorrow. When the images of earth cling too tightly to my memory, when the call of happiness is too insistent, it happens that melancholy rises in a man's heart; this is the rock's victory, this is the rock itself. The boundless grief is too heavy to bear."

Are you saying that there's no way to overcome the despair of a meaningless existence? Isn't there any way to combat the sorrow?

"Yes, the descent can also be performed in joy."

How?

"Crushing truths perish from being acknowledged, Art. Do you know the story of Oedipus?"

No, not really.

"Oedipus was destined to murder his father and marry his mother. The seers told his parents of his fate. To protect themselves and Oedipus from this terrible fate, they had the infant secretly taken to another couple in another province. The other couple raised Oedipus as their own son. He grew to adulthood believing that his 'adoptive' parents were his only family. Then Oedipus discovered that his fate 'required' the deeds predicted at his birth."

What did he do?

"Oedipus fled his homeland. He believed that if he left his parents and journeyed far away, he would avoid the horrible acts that were his fate."

Did it work?

"Well, Oedipus did not kill his adoptive father or marry his adoptive mother. But, journeying far from home, he did come upon a man. They argued and Oedipus killed the man."

His real father?

"Yes, though Oedipus did not know it. On he traveled. He came to a city. After solving a riddle presented by a Sphinx that was plaguing the city, Oedipus married the widowed queen of the city."

No way—his mother?

"His mother. They lived happily and prosperously. Then the truth was revealed to Oedipus."

What did he do?

"Horrified, he gouged out his eyes."

Where do you find joy in this story?

"Oedipus at the beginning obeys fate without knowing it. But from the moment he knows, his tragedy begins."

I thought you said that "crushing truths perish from being acknowledged." This one sure didn't perish. In fact, the tragedy begins only when he discovers the truth.

"Yet at the same moment, blind and desperate, he realizes that the only bond linking him to the world is the cool hand of a girl, his daughter."

Of course, she loves him. And I understand that she will care for him and be his eyes. But how is this joyful?

"A tremendous remark rings out from Oedipus: 'Despite so many ordeals, my advanced age and the nobility of my soul make me conclude that all is well.' "

All is well! Has he gone mad? Here's a guy who has lived his entire life hoping to avoid a terrible fate. And yet, although each of his actions is well intended, even heroic, each action leads him directly to his fate. What a terrible, joyless life. Nothing he desired happened. Everything he intended to avoid, he found. How can he conclude that all is well?

Absurd Victory.   "Oedipus gives the recipe for the absurd victory. Happiness and the absurd are two sons of the same earth. They are inseparable."

What do you mean by the absurd?

"In a world suddenly divested of illusions and lights, man feels an alien, a stranger."

And you're saying that the illusion is what?

"In Oedipus' case the illusion is that he has mastered, or at least escaped, his fate. His illusion is that his life is happy and meaningful. His exile is without remedy since he is deprived of the memory of a lost home or the hope of a promised land."

Okay, Oedipus cannot go back home. That's his problem; he is home. And he cannot hope for a better future. His past has dictated the rest of his life. But what is the absurdity? What is the illusion that the rest of us live with?

"This divorce between man and his life, the actor and his setting, is properly the feeling of absurdity."

Then the problem isn't that our lives are meaningless?

"It often happens that those who commit suicide were assured of the meaning of life."

What causes a person to go on living? From my conversation with Solomon and you, I can't see why people even bother to live. Take Oedipus as an example. What kept him going? What makes him say that all is well? How did he overcome the divorce between himself and his entire life? How did he bridge his separation from reality?

"In a man's attachment to life there is something stronger than all the ills in the world. The body's judgment is as good as the mind's, and the body shrinks from annihilation. Of course, intelligence, too, tells me that the world is absurd."

The Absurd Battle.   Look, Mr. Sisyphus, that doesn't tell me enough. What do I need to battle against the absurd? What do I have to do in order to fight against the absurd?

"Struggle implies a total absence of hope (which has nothing to do with despair), a continual rejection (which must not be confused with renunciation), and a conscious dissatisfaction (which must not be compared to immature unrest). Everything that destroys, conjures away, or exorcises these requirements (and, to begin with, consent which overthrows divorce) ruins the absurd and devaluates the attitude that may then be proposed."

What do you mean?

"The absurd has meaning only insofar as it is not agreed to. 'I conclude that all is well,' says Oedipus, and that remark is sacred."

How so?

"It teaches that all is not, has not been, exhausted. It drives out of this world a god who had come into it with dissatisfaction and a preference for futile sufferings. It makes of fate a human matter, which must be settled among men."

This is where you find your joy—in your suffering?

"My joy is contained therein. My fate belongs to me."

Divorced From Life

I know you said it already, but what do you mean by *absurd*?

"This divorce between man and his life, the actor and his setting, is properly the feeling of absurdity."

What divorce?

"Men, too, secrete the inhuman. At certain moments of lucidity, the mechanical aspects of their gestures, their meaningless pantomime makes silly everything that surrounds them. A man is talking on the telephone behind a glass partition; you cannot hear him, but you see his incomprehensible dumb show: you wonder why he is alive."

Can you explain this differently?

"This world in itself is not reasonable, that is all that can be said. But what is absurd is the confrontation of this irrational and the wild longing for clarity whose call echoes in the human heart. The absurd depends as much on man as on the world. For the moment it is all that links them together. It binds them one to the other as only hatred can weld two creatures together. This is all I can discern clearly in this measureless universe where my adventure takes place."

What brings you to this awareness?

"The 'why' arises and everything begins in that weariness tinged with amazement. Weariness comes at the end of the acts of a mechanical life, but at the same time it inaugurates the impulse to consciousness."

It's your very punishment that has made you aware?

"Yes. The mechanical life of pressing against the rock brings lucidity as I pause and turn to walk down the mountain. Likewise, the absurd man, when he contemplates his torment, silences all the idols."

Idols?

"All of the illusions that bring him false hopes; all of the false senses of meaning that bear him through the mundane monotony; all of the values that shield him from awareness of the separation between himself and the world."

You want us to get rid of the distortions and distractions in moral thinking, don't you?

"In the universe suddenly restored to its silence, the myriad wondering little voices of the earth rise up. There is no sun without shadow, and it is essential to know the night."

I have to see reality for what it is? Even the frightening parts of it?

"The absurd man says yes and his effort will henceforth be unceasing. If there is a personal fate, there is no higher destiny, or at least there is but one which he concludes is inevitable and despicable."

What good comes from this knowledge? Why should I want to be aware of my separation from reality? It all sounds terrifying.

"The absurd man knows himself to be the master of his days. At that subtle moment when man glances back over his life, my return to my rock, in that slight pivoting he contemplates that series of unrelated actions which becomes his fate, created by him, combined under his memory's eye and soon sealed by his death."

How can you say that fate is a series of unrelated actions?

"They are related only in that I have acted them."

Look at any biography. Surely there is a line of action that follows from child-hood right through the person's life until the person reaches her goal. A great dancer shows signs of musical interest from childhood. She enters dance class, drives herself, and succeeds. Or a businesswoman thinks creatively as a child. She later enters college, takes design and engineering classes, and goes on to become chief design engineer for a major manufacturer. And yet you call these actions unrelated?

"Another illusion to dispel the absurd. The biography is written after the per-son's fate has been sealed with his death. Only after the fact can we use our memo-ries or imagination to draw a thread connecting the person's actions. But I assure you, at the time of the actions, they were totally unrelated to the person. More to the point, however, is the wholly human origin of all that is human."

Everything is absurd, connected only by our wishes and illusions, by our basic beliefs and attitudes.

"Yes, great feelings take with them their own universe, splendid or abject. They light up with their own passion an exclusive world in which they recognize their climate. The universe is a universe of jealousy, of ambition, of selfishness, or of generosity."

It is my universe to make as I desire?

"I am back at the foot of my mountain, and so I must leave you now. One always finds one's burdens again. But you, too, can find a higher fidelity that negates the gods and raises rocks. All *is* well."

Haven't you reduced this life to meaningless drudgery?

"The universe henceforth without a master seems to me neither sterile nor futile. Each atom of my stone, each mineral flake of this night-filled mountain, in itself forms a world. The struggle itself toward the heights is enough to fill a man's heart."

Then one must imagine Sisyphus happy.

Summary of Discussion

Is life meaningful or absurd? In this chapter we speak to two "wise" men from ancient history, King Solomon and Sisyphus. Each believes that living can be meaningless, but for different reasons.

Solomon laments that death robs our life of meaning. He says that all that we do and accomplish is vain and futile. Both the pleasure-seeking life and the productive life are pointless. We will join the animals in the ground, and nothing follows death. He sees that the world is not just. People are oppressed and their oppressors thrive. Wise people are not revered for their wisdom, nor does hard work receive ample payment. The happiest person is the one who has never lived.

Even wealth is a torment, and the rich do not sleep well at night. So eat, drink, and find enjoyment in the everyday things. Since nothing brings meaning, just live in the momentary pleasures that life offers. There are no enduring values. Only if death were not total annihilation of the person would life be worth living. So, Solomon concludes somewhat puzzlingly, obey God's laws.

The example of Sisyphus is a reply to Solomon. Sisyphus does get to live beyond his death. His punishment depends on his immortality. His crime is that he lived too intensely. He enjoyed life fully. His punishment is that he must perform a task that cannot be accomplished. Nothing comes of it.

Sisyphus' only salvation from a meaningless existence comes in his moments of full consciousness. He becomes free, and surmounts his fate, when he knowingly chooses to perform his task. He is free when he willingly returns to his task. It is the doing and not the accomplishment of his task that brings him victory. When he is no longer divorced from his project, then he lives. So Sisyphus' "crime" is also his formula for victory. Living and acting passionately and with total involvement crown his life. "The struggle itself toward the heights is enough to fill a man's heart." One must imagine Sisyphus happy. He has learned to relate to himself, to others, and to reality.

Discussion Highlights

   I. Is life meaningful or absurd? How the question arises.
     1. Values are uncertain.
     2. We experience our insignificance.
     3. Our work is unappreciated and fruitless.
  II. Solomon's lament
     1. All is vanity.
     2. Pleasure and work are both meaningless.
     3. The world has no justice.
     4. Wealth is transitory and a problem unto itself.
     5. It is better to eat, drink, and find momentary enjoyment.
     6. Death comes to us all and robs life of meaning.
     7. So obey God's laws.
 III. Sisyphus' immortality
     1. Death does not rob life of meaning.

2. Meaninglessness occurs when nothing comes of one's actions.
3. Living passionately and fully is our crime.
4. Meaningless, passionless, alienated work is the punishment.
5. Consciousness of our life offers promise.
6. The absurd victory is found in lucidity and involvement.
7. We need to learn to relate better to ourselves, to others, and to reality.

Questions for Thought/Paper Topics

1. Solomon declares that all is vanity. Can one's work be meaningful? How about one's relationship with family and friends?
2. Remember Joe the Mesopotamian from Chapter 5? Was his life meaningful? In what ways was it worthwhile?
3. Solomon says that the happiest person is the one who was never born. Why does he say this? Do you agree? (By the way, oops! it's too late; you were already born. Sorry.)
4. Why does Solomon say that life is meaningless? Is it because we are going to die and become "dust" in the wind? How would Sisyphus reply?
5. Sisyphus gets to live forever, yet his punishment is meaningless activity. Is a life meaningless if it involves pointless repetition?
6. Sisyphus claims what he calls an "absurd victory" over the gods and over his burden. What does he mean by this?
7. Sisyphus says that "the divorce between man and his life . . . is properly the feeling of absurdity." How does he recommend that we dispel the absurd and live genuinely human lives?

For Further Reading

Obviously, you ought to read Camus's *The Myth of Sisyphus and Other Essays* (Vintage, 1955). Camus is one of the most insightful philosophers and best writers of our century. Read Ecclesiastes, too. You can find it in any Bible. There are other interesting discussions of life's meaning. *The Meaning of Life* (Prentice-Hall, 1980), by Steven Sandars and David Cheney, has a strong list of readings. Two other good works are by psychologists. Take a look at Viktor Frankl's *Man's Search for Meaning* (Beacon, 1963). A truly wonderful book about a true champion in living is *Zorba the Greek,* by Nikos Kazantzakis. You'll love Zorba once you understand him.

What Makes a Life Significant?

WILLIAM JAMES

Tens of centuries after Solomon offered his conclusions on human fate in Ecclesiastes, William James makes a modern response to the question of life's meaning. He claims that life is "soaked with values and meaning" if only we are sensitive to see them. Understanding that people are differently attuned to each other and to life's experiences allows us to be tolerant, even lovingly understanding. These are the attitudes that James wants us to embrace. Only a tolerant, open person can see another person's "inner secrets," the genuine self disguised under outward behavior.

After visiting a "utopian" community where the highest cultural ideals are realized, James comes to a startling conclusion. He accepts the importance of the cultivated person's experience, but he reacts against the cultural ideal in isolation. The real world of human experience gets its "moral style" from "strength and strenuousness, intensity and danger." James realizes that "what our human emotions seem to require is the sight of the struggle going on." The dullness of human life is caused by the absence of living the extremes. "An irremediable flatness is coming over the world." Living with the heights and the depths of human experience is part of the excitement of living a human life.

Ultimately, James rejects the cultural cultivation of the "utopian" society, the absolute virtue of common work, and ideals. He is not satisfied that any of these approaches in itself is adequate to give life significance. Ultimately, he believes, "there must be some sort of fusion" of these elements. How well do Solomon's advice that we take joy in our knowledge, in our work and in our loves, and Sisyphus' knowing and free struggle to reach the heights reconfirm James's thinking? Tolerance, humility, reverence, and love for others give us a "certain inner joyfulness" and "spiritual health," says James. Does this conclusion correspond to your experience?

IN MY PREVIOUS TALK, "On a Certain Blindness," I tried to make you feel how soaked and shot-through life is with values and meanings which we fail to realize because of our external and insensible point of view. The meanings are there for the others, but they are not there for us. There lies more than a mere interest of curious speculation in understanding this. It has the most tremendous practical importance. I wish that I could convince you of it as I feel it myself. It is the basis of all our tolerance, social, religious, and political. The forgetting of it lies at the root of every stupid and sanguinary mistake that rulers over subject-peoples make. The first thing to learn in intercourse with others is non-interference with their own peculiar ways of

From *The Will to Believe, and Other Essays in Popular Philosophy,* New York, Longmans, Green & Co., 1897.

being happy, provided those ways do not assume to interfere by violence with ours. No one has insight into all the ideals. No one should presume to judge them off-hand. The pretension to dogmatize about them in each other is the root of most human injustices and cruelties, and the trait in human character most likely to make the angels weep.

Every Jack sees in his own particular Jill charms and perfections to the enchantment of which we stolid onlookers are stone-cold. And which has the superior view of the absolute truth, he or we? Which has the more vital insight into the nature of Jill's existence, as a fact? Is he in excess, being in this matter a maniac? or are we in defect, being victims of a pathological anæsthesia as regards Jill's magical importance? Surely the latter; surely to Jack are the profounder truths revealed; surely poor Jill's palpitating little life-throbs *are* among the wonders of creation, *are* worthy of this sympathetic interest; and it is to our shame that the rest of us cannot feel like Jack. For Jack realizes Jill concretely, and we do not. He struggles toward a union with her inner life, divining her feelings, anticipating her desires, understanding her limits as manfully as he can, and yet inadequately, too; for he is also afflicted with some blindness, even here. Whilst we, dead clods that we are, do not even seek after these things, but are contented that that portion of eternal fact named Jill should be for us as if it were not. Jill, who knows her inner life, knows that Jack's way of taking it—so importantly—is the true and serious way; and she responds to the truth in him by taking him truly and seriously, too. May the ancient blindness never wrap its clouds about either of them again! Where would any of *us* be, were there no one willing to know us as we really are or ready to repay us for *our* insight by making recognizant return: We ought, all of us, to realize each other in this intense, pathetic, and important way.

If you say that this is absurd, and that we cannot be in love with everyone at once, I merely point out to you that, as a matter of fact, certain persons do exist with an enormous capacity for friendship and for taking delight in other people's lives; and that such persons know more of truth than if their hearts were not so big. The vice of ordinary Jack and Jill affection is not its intensity, but its exclusions and its jealousies. Leave those out, and you see that the ideal I am holding up before you, however impracticable today, yet contains nothing intrinsically absurd.

We have unquestionably a great cloud-bank of ancestral blindness weighing down upon us, only transiently riven here and there by fitful revelations of the truth. It is vain to hope for this state of things to alter much. Our inner secrets must remain for the most part inpenetrable by others, for beings as essentially practical as we are are necessarily short of sight. But, if we cannot gain much positive insight into one another, cannot we at least use our sense of our own blindness to make us more cautious in going over the dark places? Cannot we escape some of those hideous ancestral intolerances and cruelties, and positive reversals of the truth?

For the remainder of this hour I invite you to seek with me some principle to make our tolerance less chaotic. And, as I began my previous lecture by a personal reminiscence, I am going to ask your indulgence for a similar bit of egotism now.

A few summers ago I spent a happy week at the famous Assembly Grounds on the borders of Chautauqua Lake. The moment one treads that sacred enclosure, one feels one's self in an atmosphere of success. Sobriety and industry, intelligence and goodness, orderliness and ideality, prosperity and cheerfulness, pervade the air. It is a serious and studious picnic on a gigantic scale. Here you have a town of many thousands of inhabitants, beautifully laid out in the forest and drained, and equipped with means for satisfying all the necessary lower and most of the superfluous higher wants of man. You have a first-class college in full blast. You have magnificent music—a chorus of seven hundred voices, with possibly the most perfect open-air auditorium in the world. You have every sort of athletic exercise from sailing, rowing, swimming, bicycling, to the ball-field and the more artificial doings which the gymnasium affords. You have kindergartens and model secondary schools. You have general religious services and special clubhouses for the several sects. You have perpetually running soda-water fountains, and daily popular lectures by distinguished men. You have the best of company, and yet no effort. You have no zymotic diseases, no poverty, no drunkenness, no crime, no police. You have culture, you have kindness, you have cheapness, you have equality, you have the best fruits of what mankind has fought and bled and striven for under the name of civilization for centuries. You have, in short, a foretaste of what human society might be, were it all in the light, with no suffering and no dark corners.

I went in curiosity for a day. I stayed for a week, held spell-bound by the charm and ease of everything, by the middle-class paradise, without a sin, without a victim, without a blot, without a tear.

And yet what was my own astonishment, on emerging into the dark and wicked world again, to catch myself quite unexpectedly and involuntarily saying: "Ouf! what a relief! Now for something primordial and savage, even though it were as bad as an Armenian massacre, to set the balance straight again. This order is too tame, this culture too second-rate, this goodness too uninspiring. This human drama without a villain or a pang; this community so refined that ice-cream and soda-water is the utmost offering it can make to the brute animal in man; this city simmering in the tepid lakeside sun; this atrocious harmlessness of all things—I cannot abide with them. Let me take my chances again in the big outside worldly wilderness with all its sins and sufferings. There are the heights and depths, the precipices and the steep ideals, the gleams of the awful and the infinite; and there is more hope and help a thousand times than in this dead level and quintessence of every mediocrity."

Such was the sudden right-about face performed for me by my lawless fancy! There had

been spread before me the realization—on a small, sample scale of course—of all the ideals for which our civilization has been striving: security, intelligence, humanity, and order; and here was the instinctive hostile reaction, not of the natural man, but of a so-called cultivated man upon such a Utopia. There seemed thus to be a self-contradiction and paradox somewhere, which I, as a professor drawing a full salary, was in duty bound to unravel and explain, if I could.

So I meditated. And, first of all, I asked myself what the thing was that was so lacking in this Sabbatical city, and the lack of which kept one forever falling short of the higher sort of contentment. And I soon recognized that it was the element that gives to the wicked outer world all its moral style, expressiveness and picturesqueness—the element of precipitousness, so to call it, of strength and strenuousness, intensity and danger. What excites and interests the looker-on at life, what the romances and the statues celebrate and the grim civic monuments remind us of, is the everlasting battle of the powers of light with those of darkness; with heroism, reduced to its bare chance, yet ever and anon snatching victory from the jaws of death. But in this unspeakable Chautauqua there was no potentiality of death in sight anywhere, and no point of the compass visible from which danger might possibly appear. The ideal was so completely victorious already that no sign of any previous battle remained, the place just resting on its oars. But what our human emotions seem to require is the sight of the struggle going on. The moment the fruits are being merely eaten, things become ignoble. Sweat and effort, human nature strained to its uttermost and on the rack, yet getting through alive, and then turning its back on its success to pursue another more rare and arduous still—this is the sort of thing the presence of which inspires us, and the reality of which it seems to be the function of all the higher forms of literature and fine art to bring home to us and suggest. At Chautauqua there were no racks, even in the place's historical museum; and no sweat, except possibly the gentle moisture on the brow of some lecturer, or on the sides of some player in the ball-field.

Such absence of human nature *in extremis* anywhere seemed, then, a sufficient explanation for Chautauqua's flatness and lack of zest.

But was not this a paradox well calculated to fill one with dismay? It looks indeed, thought I, as if the romantic idealists with their pessimism about our civilization were, after all, quite right. An irremediable flatness is coming over the world. Bourgeoisie and mediocrity, church sociables and teachers' conventions, are taking the place of the old heights and depths and romantic chiaroscuro. And, to get human life in its wild intensity, we must in future turn more and more away from the actual, and forget it, if we can, in the romancer's or the poet's pages. The whole world, delightful and sinful as it may still appear for a moment to one just escaped from the Chautauquan enclosure, is nevertheless obeying more and more just those ideals that are sure to make of it in the end a mere Chautauqua Assembly on an enormous scale. *Was im Gesang soll leben muss im Leben untergehn.* Even now, in our own country, correctness, fairness, and compromise for every small advantage are crowding out all other qualities. The higher heroisms and the old rare flavors are passing out of life.[1]

With these thoughts in my mind, I was speeding with the train toward Buffalo, when, near that city, the sight of a workman doing something on the dizzy edge of a sky-scaling iron construction brought me to my senses very suddenly. And now I perceived, by a flash of insight, that I had been steeping myself in pure ancestral blindness, and looking at life with the eyes of a remote spectator. Wishing for heroism and the spectacle of human nature on the rack, I had never noticed the great fields of heroism lying around about me, I had failed to see it present and alive. I could only think of it as dead and embalmed, labelled and costumed, as it is in the pages of romance. And yet there it was before me in the daily lives of the laboring classes. Not in clanging fights and desperate marches only is heroism to be looked for, but on every railway bridge and fire-proof building that is going up today. On freight-trains, on the decks of vessels, in cattle-yards and mines, on lumber-rafts, among the firemen and the policemen, the demand for courage is incessant; and the supply never fails. There, every day of the year somewhere, is human nature *in extremis for you.* And wherever a scythe, an axe, a pick, or a shovel is wielded, you have it sweating and aching and with its powers of patient endurance racked to the utmost under the length of hours of the strain.

As I awoke to all this unidealized heroic life around me, the scales seemed to fall from my eyes; and a wave of sympathy greater than anything I had ever before felt with the common life of common men began to fill my soul. It began to seem as if virtue with horny hands and dirty skin were the only virtue genuine and vital enough to take account of. Every other virtue poses; none is absolutely unconscious and simple, and unexpectant of decoration or recognition, like this. These are our soldiers, thought I, these our sustainers, these the very parents of our life.

Many years ago, when in Vienna, I had had a similar feeling of awe and reverence in looking at the peasant-women, in from the country on their business at the market for the day. Old hags many of them were, dried and brown and wrinkled, kerchiefed and short-petticoated, with thick wool stockings on their bony shanks, stumping through the glittering thoroughfares, looking neither to the right nor the left, bent on duty, envying nothing, humble-hearted, remote; and yet at bottom, when you came to think of it, bearing the whole fabric of the splendors and corruptions of that city on their laborious backs. For where would any of it have been without their unremitting, unrewarded labor in the fields? And so with us: not to our generals and poets, I thought, but to the Italian and Hungarian laborers in the Subway, rather, ought the monuments of gratitude and reverence of a city like Boston to be reared.

If any of you have been readers of Tolstoï,

you will see that I passed into a vein of feeling similar to him, with its abhorrence of all that conventionally passes for distinguished, and its exclusive deification of the bravery, patience, kindliness, and dumbness of the unconscious natural man.

Where now is *our* Tolstoï, I said, to bring the truth of all this home to our American bosoms, fill us with a better insight, and wean us away from that spurious literary romanticism on which our wretched culture—as it calls itself—is fed? Divinity lies all about us, and culture is too hide-bound to even suspect the fact. Could a Howells or a Kipling be enlisted in this mission? or are they still too deep in the ancestral blindness, and not humane enough for the inner joy and meaning of the laborer's existence to be really revealed? Must we wait for some one born and bred and living as a laborer himself, but who, by grace of Heaven, shall also find a literary voice?

And there I rested on that day, with a sense of widening of vision, and with what it is surely fair to call an increase of religious insight into life. In God's eyes the differences of social position, of intellect, of culture, of cleanliness, of dress, which different men exhibit, and all the other rarities and exceptions on which they so fantastically pin their pride, must be so small as practically quite to vanish; and all that should remain is the common fact that here we are, a countless multitude of vessels of life, each of us pent in to peculiar difficulties, with which we must severally struggle by using whatever of fortitude and goodness we can summon up. The exercise of the courage, patience, and kindness, must be the significant portion of the whole business; and the distinctions of position can only be a manner of diversifying the phenomenal surface upon which these underground virtues may manifest their effects. At this rate, the deepest human life is everywhere, is eternal. And, if any human attributes exist only in particular individuals, they must belong to the mere trapping and decoration of the surface-show.

Thus are men's lives levelled up as well as lev-

elled down—levelled up in their common inner meaning, levelled down in their outer gloriousness and show. Yet always, we must confess, this levelling insight tends to be obscured again; and always the ancestral blindness returns and wraps us up, so that we end once more by thinking that creation can be for no other purpose than to develop remarkable situations and conventional distinctions and merits. And then always some new leveller in the shape of a religious prophet has to arise—the Buddha, the Christ, or some Saint Francis, some Rousseau or Tolstoï—to re-dispel our blindness. Yet, little by little, there comes some stable gain; for the world does get more humane, and the religion of democracy tends toward permanent increase.

This, as I said, became for a time my conviction, and gave me great content. I have put the matter into the form of a personal reminiscence, so that I might lead you into it more directly and completely, and so save time. But now I am going to discuss the rest of it with you in a more impersonal way.

Tolstoï's levelling philosophy began long before he had the crisis of melancholy commemorated in that wonderful document of his entitled 'My Confession,' which led the way to his more specifically religious works. In his masterpiece *War and Peace*—assuredly the greatest of human novels—the rôle of the spiritual hero is given to a poor little soldier named Karataïeff, so helpful, so cheerful, and so devout that, in spite of his ignorance and filthiness, the sight of him opens the heavens, which have been closed, to the mind of the principal character of the book; and his example evidently is meant by Tolstoï to let God into the world again for the reader. Poor little Karataïeff is taken prisoner by the French; and, when too exhausted by hardship and fever to march, is shot as other prisoners were in the famous retreat from Moscow. The last view one gets of him is his little figure leaning against a white birch-tree, and uncomplainingly awaiting the end.

"The more," writes Tolstoï in the work 'My Confession,' "the more I examined the life of these laboring folks, the more persuaded I became that they veritably have faith, and get from it alone the sense and the possibility of life. . . . Contrariwise to those of our own class, who protest against destiny and grow indignant at its rigor, these people receive maladies and misfortunes without revolt, without opposition, and with a firm and tranquil confidence that all had to be like that, could not be otherwise, and that it is all right so. . . . The more we live by our intellect, the less we understand the meaning of life. We see only a cruel jest in suffering and death, whereas these people live, suffer, and draw near to death with tranquility, and oftener than not with joy. . . . There are enormous multitudes of them happy with the most perfect happiness, although deprived of what for us is the sole good of life. Those who understand life's meaning, and know how to live and die thus, are to be counted not by twos, threes, tens, but by hundreds, thousands, millions. They labor quietly, endure privations and pains, live and die, and throughout everything see the good without seeing the vanity. I had to love these people. The more I entered into their life, the more I loved them; and the more it became possible for me to live, too. It came about not only that the life of our society, of the learned and of the rich, disgusted me—more than that, it lost all semblance of meaning in my eyes. All our actions, our deliberations, our sciences, our arts, all appeared to me with a new significance. I understood that these things might be charming pastimes, but that one need seek in them no depth, whereas the life of the hardworking populace, of that multitude of human beings who really contribute to existence, appeared to me in its true light. I understood that there veritably is life, that the meaning which life there receives is the truth; and I accepted it." [2]

In a similar way does Stevenson appeal to our piety toward the elemental virtue of mankind.

"What a wonderful thing," he writes, [3] "is this Man! How surprising are his attributes! Poor soul, here for so little, cast among so many hardships, savagely surrounded, savagely descended,

irremediably condemned to prey upon his fellow-lives—who should have blamed him, had he been of a piece with his destiny and a being merely barbarous? . . . [Yet] it matters not where we look, under what climate we observe him, in what stage of society, in what depth of ignorance, burdened with what erroneous morality; in ships at sea, a man inured to hardship and vile pleasures, his brightest hope a fiddle in a tavern, and a bedizened trull who sells herself to rob him, and he, for all that, simple, innocent, cheerful, kindly like a child, constant to toil, brave to drown, for others; . . . in the slums of cities, moving among indifferent millions to mechanical employments, without hope of change in the future, with scarce a pleasure in the present, and yet true to his virtues, honest up to his lights, kind to his neighbors, tempted perhaps in vain by the bright gin-palace, . . . often repaying the world's scorn with service, often standing firm upon a scruple; . . . everywhere some virtue cherished or affected, everywhere some decency of thought and courage, everywhere the ensign of man's ineffectual goodness—ah! if I could show you this! If I could show you these men and women all the world over, in every stage of history, under every abuse of error, under every circumstance of failure, without hope, without help, without thanks, still obscurely fighting the lost fight of virtue, still clinging to some rag of honor, the poor jewel of their souls."

All this is as true as it is splendid, and terribly do we need our Tolstoïs and Stevensons to keep our sense for it alive. Yet you remember the Irishman who, when asked, "Is not one man as good as another?" replied, "Yes; and a great deal better, too!" Similarly (it seems to me) does Tolstoï over-correct our social prejudices, when he makes his love of the peasant so exclusive, and hardens his heart toward the educated man as absolutely as he does. Grant that at Chautauqua there was little moral effort, little sweat or muscular strain in view. Still, deep down in the souls of the participants we may be sure that something of the sort was hid, some inner stress, some vital virtue not found wanting when required. And, after all, the question recurs, and forces itself upon us. Is it so certain that the surroundings and circumstances of the virtue do make so little difference in the importance of the result? Is the functional utility, the worth to the universe of a certain definite amount of courage, kindliness, and patience, no greater if the possessor of these virtues is in an educated situation, working out far-reaching tasks, than if he be an illiterate nobody, hewing wood and drawing water, just to keep himself alive? Tolstoï's philosophy, deeply enlightening though it certainly is, remains a false abstraction. It savors too much of that Oriental pessimism and nihilism of his, which declares the whole phenomenal world and its facts and their distinctions to be a cunning fraud.

A mere bare fraud is just what our Western common sense will never believe the phenomenal world to be. It admits fully that the inner joys and virtues are the *essential* part of life's business, but it is sure that *some* positive part is also played by the adjuncts of the show. If it is idiotic in romanticism to recognize the heroic only when it sees it labelled and dressed-up in books, it is really just as idiotic to see it only in the dirty boots and sweaty shirt of some one in the fields. It is with us really under every disguise: at Chautauqua; here in your college; in the stockyards and on the freight-trains; and in the czar of Russia's court. But, instinctively, we make a combination of two things in judging the total significance of a human being. We feel it to be some sort of a product (if such a product only could be calculated) of his inner virtue *and* his outer place, neither singly taken, but both conjoined. If the outer differences had no meaning for life, why indeed should all this immense variety of them exist? They *must* be significant elements of the world as well.

Just test Tolstoï's deification of the mere manual laborer by the facts. This is what Mr. Walter Wyckoff, after working as an unskilled laborer in the demolition of some buildings at West Point,

writes of the spiritual condition of the class of men to which he temporarily chose to belong:

"The salient features of our condition are plain enough. We are grown men, and are without a trade. In the labor-market we stand ready to sell to the highest bidder our mere muscular strength for so many hours each day. We are thus in the lowest grade of labor. And, selling our muscular strength in the open market for what it will bring, we sell it under peculiar conditions. It is all the capital that we have. We have no reserve means of subsistence, and cannot, therefore, stand off for a 'reserve price.' We sell under the necessity of satisfying imminent hunger. Broadly speaking, we must sell our labor or starve; and, as hunger is a matter of a few hours, and we have no other way of meeting this need, we must sell at once for what the market offers for our labor.

"Our employer is buying labor in a dear market, and he will certainly get from us as much work as he can at the price. The gang-boss is secured for this purpose, and thoroughly does he know his business. He has sole command of us. He never saw us before, and he will discharge us all when the dèbris is cleared away. In the meantime he must get from us, if he can, the utmost physical labor which we, individually and collectively, are capable of. If he should drive some of us to exhaustion, and we should not be able to continue at work, he would not be the loser; for the market would soon supply him with others to take our places.

"We are ignorant men, but so much we clearly see that we have sold our labor where we could sell it dearest, and our employer has bought it where he could buy it cheapest. He has paid high, and he must get all the labor that he can; and, by a strong instinct which possesses us, we shall part with as little as we can. From work like ours there seems to us to have been eliminated every element which constitutes the nobility of labor. We feel no personal pride in its progress, and no community of interest with our employer. There is none of the joy of responsibility, none of the sense of achievement, only the dull monotony of grinding toil, with the longing for the signal to quit work, and for our wages at the end.

"And being what we are, the dregs of the labor-market, and having no certainty of permanent employment, and no organization among ourselves, we must expect to work under the watchful eye of a gang-boss, and be driven, like the wage-slaves that we are, through our tasks.

"All this is to tell us, in effect, that our lives are hard, barren, hopeless lives."

And such hard, barren, hopeless lives, surely, are not lives in which one ought to be willing permanently to remain. And why is this so? Is it because they are so dirty? Well, Nansen grew a great deal dirtier on his polar expedition; and we think none the worse of his life for that. Is it the insensibility? Our soldiers have to grow vastly more insensible, and we extol them to the skies. Is it the poverty? Poverty has been reckoned the crowning beauty of many a heroic career. Is it the slavery to a task, the loss of finer pleasures? Such slavery and loss are of the very essence of the higher fortitude, and are always counted to its credit—read the records of missionary devotion all over the world. It is not any one of these things, then, taken by itself—no, nor all of them together—that make such a life undesirable. A man might in truth live like an unskilled laborer, and do the work of one, and yet count as one of the noblest of God's creatures. Quite possibly there were some such persons in the gang that our author describes; but the current of their souls ran underground; and he was too steeped in the ancestral blindness to discern it.

If there *were* any such morally exceptional individuals, however, what made them different from the rest? It can only have been this—that their souls worked and endured in obedience to some inner *ideal,* while their comrades were not actuated by anything worthy of that name. These ideals of other lives are among those secrets that we can almost never penetrate, although something about the man may often tell us when they are there. In Mr. Wyckoff's own case we know exactly what the self-imposed ideal was. Partly he had stumped himself, as the boys say, to carry through a strenuous achievement; but mainly he wished to enlarge his sympathetic insight into fellow-lives. For this his sweat and toil acquire a certain heroic significance, and make us accord to him exceptional esteem. But it is easy to imagine his fellows with various other ideals. To say nothing of wives and babies, one may have been a convert of the Salvation Army, and had a nightingale singing of expiation and forgiveness in his heart all the while he labored. Or there might have been an apostle like Tolstoï himself, or his compatriot Bondareff, in the gang, voluntarily embracing labor as their religious mission. Class-loyalty was undoubtedly an ideal with many. And who knows how much of that higher manliness of poverty, of which Phillips Brooks has spoken so penetratingly, was or was not present in that gang?

"A rugged, barren land," says Phillips Brooks, "is poverty to live in—a land where I am thankful very often if I can get a berry or a root to eat. But living in it really, letting it bear witness to me of itself, not dishonoring it all the time by judging it after the standard of the other lands, gradually there come out its qualities. Behold! no land like this barren and naked land of poverty could show the moral geology of the world. See how the hard ribs . . . stand out strong and solid. No life like poverty could so get one to the heart of things and make men know their meaning, could so let us feel life and the world with all the soft cushions stripped off and thrown away. . . . Poverty makes men come very near each other, and recognize each other's human hearts; and poverty, highest and best of all, demands and cries out for faith in God. . . . I know how superficial and unfeeling, how like mere mockery, words in praise of poverty may seem. . . . But I am sure that the poor man's dignity and freedom, his self-respect and energy, depend upon his cordial knowledge that his poverty is a true region and kind of life, with its own chances of character, its own springs of happiness and revelations of God. Let him resist the characterlessness which often goes with being poor. Let him insist on respecting the condition where he lives. Let him learn to love it, so that by and by, (if) he grows rich, he shall go out of the low door of the old familiar poverty with a true pang of regret, and with a true honor for the narrow home in which he has lived so long."[4]

The barrenness and ignobleness of the more usual laborer's life consist in the fact that it is moved by no such ideal inner springs. The backache, the long hours, the danger, are patiently endured—for what? To gain a quid of tobacco, a glass of beer, a cup of coffee, a meal, and a bed, and to begin again the next day and shirk as much as one can. This really is why we raise no monument to the laborers in the Subway, even though they be our conscripts, and even though after a fashion our city is indeed based upon their patient hearts and enduring backs and shoulders. And this is why we do raise monuments to our soldiers, whose outward conditions were even brutaller still. The soldiers are supposed to have followed an ideal, and the laborers are supposed to have followed none.

You see, my friends, how the plot now thickens; and how strangely the complexities of this wonderful human nature of ours begin to develop under our hands. We have seen the blindness and deadness to each other which are our natural inheritance; and, in spite of them, we have been led to acknowledge an inner meaning which passeth show, and which may be present in the lives of others where we least descry it. And now we are led to say that such inner meaning can be *complete* and *valid for us also,* only when the inner joy, courage, and endurance are joined with an ideal.

But what, exactly, do we mean by an ideal? Can we give no definite account of such a word?

To a certain extent we can. An ideal, for instance, must be something intellectually conceived, something of which we are not unconscious, if we have it; and it must carry with it that sort of outlook, uplift, and brightness that go with all intellectual facts. Secondly, there must be *novelty* in an ideal—novelty at least for him whom the ideal grasps. Sodden routine is incompatible with ideality, although what is sodden routine for one person may be ideal novelty for another. This shows that there is nothing absolutely ideal: ideals are relative to the lives that entertain them. To keep out of the gutter is for us here no part of consciousness at all, yet for many of our brethren it is the most legitimately engrossing of ideals.

Now, taken nakedly, abstractly, and immediately, you see that mere ideals are the cheapest things in life. Everybody has them in some shape or other, personal or general, sound or mistaken, low or high; and the most worthless sentimentalists and dreamers, drunkards, shirks and verse-makers, who never show a grain of effort, courage, or endurance, possibly have them on the most copious scale. Education, enlarging as it does our horizon and perspective, is a means of multiplying our ideals, of bringing new ones into view. And your college professor, with a starched shirt and spectacles, would, if a stock of ideals were all alone by itself enough to render a life significant, be the most absolutely and deeply significant of men. Tolstoï would be completely blind in despising him for a prig, a pedant and a parody; and all our new insight into the divinity of muscular labor would be altogether off the track of truth.

But such consequences as this, you instinctively feel, are erroneous. The more ideals a man has, the more contemptible, on the whole, do you continue to deem him, if the matter ends there for him, and if none of the laboring man's virtues are called into action on his part—no courage shown, no privations undergone, no dirt or scars contracted in the attempt to get them realized. It is quite obvious that something more than the mere possession of ideals is required to make a life significant in any sense that claims the spectator's admiration. Inner joy, to be sure, it may *have,* with its ideals; but that is its own private sentimental matter. To extort from us, outsiders as we are, with our own ideals to look after, the tribute of our grudging recognition, it must back its ideal visions with what the laborers have, the sterner stuff of manly virtue; it must multiply their sentimental surface by the dimension of the active will, if we are to have *depth,* if we are to have anything cubical and solid in the way of character.

The significance of a human life for communicable and publicly recognizable purposes is thus the offspring of a marriage of two different parents, either of whom alone is barren. The ideals taken by themselves give no reality, the virtues by themselves no novelty. And let the orientalists and pessimists say what they will, the thing of deepest—or, at any rate, of comparatively deepest—significance in life does seem to be its character of *progress,* or that strange union of reality with ideal novelty which it continues from one moment to another to present. To recognize ideal novelty is the task of what we call intelligence. Not every one's intelligence can tell which novelties are ideal. For many the ideal thing will always seem to cling still to the older more familiar good. In this case character, though not significant totally, may be still significant pathetically. So, if we are to choose which is the more essential factor of human character, the fighting virtue or the intellectual breadth, we must side with Tolstoï and choose that simple faithfulness to his light or darkness which any common unintellectual man can show.

But, with all this beating and tacking on my part, I fear you take me to be reaching a confused result. I seem to be just taking things up and dropping them again. First I took up Chautauqua, and dropped that; then Tolstoï and the heroism of common toil, and dropped them; finally, I took up ideals, and seem now almost dropping those. But please observe in what sense it is that I drop them. It is when they pretend *singly* to redeem life from insignificance. Culture and refinement all alone are not enough

to do so. Ideal aspirations are not enough, when uncombined with pluck and will. But neither are pluck and will, dogged endurance and insensibility to danger enough, when taken all alone. There must be some sort of fusion, some chemical combination among these principles, for a life objectively and thoroughly significant to result.

Of course, this is a somewhat vague conclusion. But in a question of significance, of worth, like this, conclusions can never be precise. The answer of appreciation, of sentiment, is always a more or a less, a balance struck by sympathy, insight, and good will. But it is an answer, all the same, a real conclusion. And, in the course of getting it, it seems to me that our eyes have been opened to many important things. Some of you are, perhaps, more livingly aware than you were an hour ago of the depths of worth that lie around you, hid in alien lives. And, when you ask how much sympathy you ought to bestow, although the amount is, truly enough, a matter of ideal on your own part, yet in this notion of the combination of ideals with active virtues you have a rough standard for shaping your decision. In any case, your imagination is extended. You divine in the world about you matter for a little more humility on your own part, and tolerance, reverence, and love for others; and you gain a certain inner joyfulness at the increased importance of our common life. Such joyfulness is a religious inspiration and an element of spiritual health, and worth more than large amounts of that sort of technical and accurate information which we professors are supposed to be able to impart.

To show the sort of thing I mean by these words, I will just make one brief practical illustration, and then close.

We are suffering today in America from what is called the labor-question; and, when you go out into the world, you will each and all of you be caught up in its perplexities. I use the brief term labor-question to cover all sorts of anarchistic discontents and socialistic projects, and the conservative resistances which they provoke. So far as this conflict is unhealthy and regrettable—and I think it is so only to a limited extent—the unhealthiness consists solely in the fact that one-half of our fellow-countrymen remain entirely blind to the internal significance of the lives of the other half. They miss the joys and sorrows, they fail to feel the moral virtue, and they do not guess the presence of the intellectual ideals. They are at cross-purposes all along the line, regarding each other as they might regard a set of dangerously gesticulating automata, or, if they seek to get at the inner motivation, making the most horrible mistakes. Often all that the poor man can think of in the rich man is a cowardly greediness for safety, luxury, and effeminacy, and a boundless affectation. What he is, is not a human being, but a pocket-book, a bank-account. And a similar greediness, turned by disappointment into envy, is all that many rich men can see in the state of mind of the dissatisfied poor. And, if the rich man begins to do the sentimental act over the poor man, what senseless blunders does he make, pitying him for just those very duties and those very immunities which, rightly taken, are the condition of his most abiding and characteristic joys! Each, in short, ignores the fact that happiness and unhappiness and significance are a vital mystery; each pins them absolutely on some ridiculous feature of the external situation; and everybody remains outside of everybody else's sight.

Society has, with all this, undoubtedly got to pass toward some newer and better equilibrium, and the distribution of wealth has doubtless slowly got to change: such changes have always happened, and will happen to the end of time. But if, after all that I have said, any of you expect that they will make any *genuine vital difference* on a large scale, to the lives of our descendants, you will have missed the significance of my entire lecture. The solid meaning of life is always the same eternal thing—the marriage, namely, of some unhabitual ideal, however special, with some fidelity, courage, and endurance; with some man's or woman's pains. And, whatever or

wherever life may be, there will always be the chance for that marriage to take place.

Fitz-James Stephen wrote many years ago words to this effect more eloquent than any I can speak: "The 'Great Eastern,' or some of her successors," he said, "will perhaps defy the roll of the Atlantic, and cross the seas without allowing their passengers to feel that they have left the firm land. The voyage from the cradle to the grave may come to be performed with similar facility. Progress and science may perhaps enable untold millions to live and die without a care, without a pang, without an anxiety. They will have a pleasant passage and plenty of brilliant conversation. They will wonder that men ever believed at all in clanging fights and blazing towns and sinking ships and praying hands; and, when they come to the end of their course, they will go their way, and the place thereof will know them no more. But it seems unlikely that they will have such a knowledge of the great ocean on which they sail, with its storms and wrecks, its currents and icebergs, its huge waves and mighty winds, as those who battled with it for years together in the little craft, which, if they had few other merits, brought those who navigated them full into the presence of time and eternity, their maker and themselves, and forced them to have some definite view of their relations to them and to each other."[5]

In this solid and tridimensional sense, so to call it, those philosophers are right who contend that the world is a standing thing, with no progress, no real history. The changing conditions of history touch only the surface of the show. The altered equilibriums and redistributions only diversify our opportunities and open chances to us for new ideals. But, with each new ideal that comes into life, the chance for a life based on some old ideal will vanish; and he would needs be a presumptuous calculator who should with confidence say that the total sum of significances is positively and absolutely greater at any one epoch than at any other of the world.

I am speaking broadly, I know, and omitting to consider certain qualifications in which I myself believe. But one can only make one point in one lecture, and I shall be well content if I have brought my point home to you this evening in even a slight degree. *There are compensations:* and no outward changes of condition in life can keep the nightingale of its eternal meaning from singing in all sorts of different men's hearts. That is the main fact to remember. If we could not only admit it with our lips, but really and truly believe it, how our convulsive insistencies, how our antipathies and dreads of each other, would soften down! If the poor and the rich could look at each other in this way, *sub specie æternatis,* how gentle would grow their disputes! what toler-

ance and good humor, what willingness to live and let live, would come into the world!

NOTES

1. This address was composed before the Cuban and Philippine wars. Such outbursts of the passion of mastery are, however, only episodes in social process which in the long run seems everywhere tending toward the Chautauquan ideals.

2. *My Confession,* X. (condensed).

3. *Across the Plains:* "Pulvis et Umbra" (abridged).

4. *Sermons, 5th Series,* New York, 1893, pp. 166, 167.

5. *Essays by a Barrister,* London, 1862, p. 318.

12

How Can We Relate With Other People? A Talk With Martin Buber

IN OUR CONVERSATIONS with Solomon and Sisyphus we were told that life is absurd. They say that we are divorced from our life. We are out of touch with ourselves, separated from other people and from reality. In this chapter we are going to examine the separation. In *I and Thou* Martin Buber's analysis takes us beyond the despair and resignation of Solomon. In what follows, Buber will suggest not only the nature and cause of our separation, but also a way to avoid absurdity in living. If our talk with Solomon and Sisyphus was a bit disheartening, our conversation with Buber should bring us optimism.

I-Thou, I-It

Welcome, Mr. Buber. Could you help me? For example, what is the difference between I-It and I-Thou?

"To man the world is twofold, in accordance with his twofold attitude."

I can have two attitudes toward the world? Kind of like there are two sets of things in the world, the ones I care about and the ones I am indifferent toward. Is that it?

"Primary words do not signify things, but they intimate relations."

Relations? Well, I guess I relate to the different types of things in different ways. Am I getting warm?

"Not quite, Art. The primary words are not isolated words, but combined words. The one primary word is the combination I-Thou. The other primary word is the word combination I-It."

Yeah, so?

"The I of the primary word I-Thou is a different I from that of the primary word

Material in this chapter reprinted with the permission of Charles Scribner's Sons, an imprint of Macmillan Publishing Company from *I and Thou* by Martin Buber, translated by Ronald Gregor Smith. Translation copyright © 1958 Charles Scribner's Sons.

I-It. If Thou is said, the I of the combination I-Thou is said along with it. If It is said, the I of the combination I-It is said along with it."

But there is only one me! How could I be different just because of what I relate to?

"There is no I taken in itself, but only the I of the primary word I-Thou and the I of the primary word I-It."

The Attitude of Man is Twofold. Oh, wait a minute. It's the same I! You mean that "the *attitude* of man is twofold."

"Just as I have already said, yes."

And if I relate to things with one attitude and not the other, then my sense of them will be different. But different in what way?

"The primary word I-Thou can only be spoken with the whole being. The primary word I-It can never be spoken with the whole being."

So, depending on my attitude, I experience things differently. Sometimes I experience things as inner experiences and sometimes as outer experiences. Is that what you mean? Some things I experience more deeply than other things?

"If we add 'inner' to 'outer' experiences, nothing in the situation is changed. Inner things or outer things, what are they but things and things!"

I really don't get it, Mr. Buber. What am I supposed to experience when I experience something?

"The life of human beings . . . does not exist in virtue of activities alone which have some *thing* for their object."

Okay?

"Art, like you, I perceive something. I am sensible of something. I imagine something. I will something. I feel something. I think something. The life of human beings does not consist of all this and the like alone. This and the like together establish the realm of It."

What else is there?

"The realm of Thou has a different basis. When Thou is spoken, the speaker has no thing for his object. When Thou is spoken, the speaker has no thing; he has indeed nothing. But he takes his stand in relation."

Are you saying that there is more than just experiencing the world?

"Man experiences his world. What does that mean? Man travels over the surface of things and experiences them. He extracts knowledge about their constitution from them. He experiences what belongs to the things. But the world is not presented to man by experiences alone. These present him only with a world composed of It and He and She and It again."

The In-Between. What's wrong with experiencing that way?

"The man who experiences has no part in the world. For it is 'in him' and not between him and the world that the experience arises."

Oh, I think I'm starting to understand. You're saying that I can distort reality by what's in me. If I am angry, then my perception of the world will be different than if I am happy. In that way, experiences arise in me. So I have no part in the world because my interpretation of the world is in me, in my moods.

"Yes, well done."

And now you're saying that the hyphen is important in your I-Thou, I-It words. It's what's in between me and the world that matters. Can I try a simple-minded example?

"Certainly."

If you and I are talking, and I look at you as a teacher, as my teacher, then I will be looking at myself as your student. As your student, I will treat you in a way that I would not treat you in another relationship. And I will treat myself as though I am merely a student.

"An apt example."

So I am only going to learn what you, the teacher, teach me. And I am going to put up with a lot that I would never want to put up with. Because you have the power to grade me.

"There are better ways to learn than to have a teacher hold a weapon over the students' heads. But let's put that aside. Your example is appropriate. As long as you regard me as your teacher, I am filling a role; I am an It."

And I am an It, too! As a "student" I become a passive information gatherer. And the intimacy that we want is lost. That's what Camus was saying.

"Yes."

Experiences and Relating

And if I look at things from the I-It point of view, I limit myself?

"Yes. Where there is a thing there is another thing. Every It is bounded by others. . . . But when Thou is spoken, there is no thing. Thou has no bounds."

Okay. Could you say this in a different way so that I can see if I have it?

"As experience, the world belongs to the primary word I-It. The primary word I-Thou establishes the world of relation."

Ah, so that's where the in-between happens. The I-It way makes me separate myself from the object of my experience. With I-Thou, I relate to the other thing. It's the importance of the relationship that you're pointing to, and not me or It.

"Yes. You take your stand in relation. . . . and we answer—forming, thinking, acting. We speak the primary word with our being, though we cannot utter Thou with our lips."

And you don't think this is a little unusual?

"In each sphere we are aware of a breath from the eternal Thou; in each Thou we address the eternal Thou."

Are you saying that each thing is a piece of the eternal reality, or Thou, as you name it? Once I heard a story about a Zen guy who said that the universe is like a shattered mirror. Each thing reflects the entire mirror, the entire reality. So in some sense, all of reality is in each piece of it. Each thing has a value simply because it exists. You might say the same idea by saying that the I-Thou attitude sees everything as sacred. Is that what you mean?

"I like that metaphor. It is in keeping with my distinction."

Okay, but for my sake, let's keep this in the sphere of this world for a little while. How can I relate to an object in nature in the I-Thou way?

The Power of Exclusiveness

"I consider a tree. I look on it as a picture. I can perceive it as movement. I can classify it in a species. I can subdue its actual presence and form so sternly that I recognize it only as the expression of law. I can dissipate it and perpetuate it in number, in pure numerical relation."

Good example. Is the I-Thou relationship the ability to see the tree the way the artist, poet, botanist, physicist, and mathematician see it?

"No, in all this the tree remains my object, occupies space and time, and has its nature and constitution. It can, however, also come about, if I have both will and grace, that in considering the tree I become bound up in relation to it. The tree is no longer It. I have been seized by the power of exclusiveness."

You want to see the tree as unique, as a one-of-a-kind. Does that mean you have to give up the other ways of seeing the tree?

"To effect this it is not necessary for me to give up any of the ways in which I consider the tree. Rather is everything, picture and movement, species and type, law and number, invisibly united in this event."

Yet you say that the totality of the It perspective does not make up the Thou. How are these points of view different?

"Everything belonging to the tree is in this . . . all present in a single whole."

Aren't you just describing a mood that a person gets into sometimes? The tree appears to you as a unique, single whole because you're feeling relaxed and "spiritual."

"Art, the tree is no impression, no play of my imagination, no value depending on my mood. Relation is mutual."

You feel the tree as it relates to you? It communicates to you as though it's another person? The tree is conscious?

"Of that I have no experience, Art. I encounter no soul, or dryad of the tree, but the tree itself."

How the Primary Words Evolve

Let's say for a moment that I like the sound of your description of the I-Thou attitude. How can I move from the I-It experience to the I-Thou way of relating? You say it's a matter of will and grace. I will it by preparing myself, and then if I'm lucky, it happens? If that's it, how do I prepare myself?

"Let us look at how the primary words evolve. The first primary word can be resolved, certainly, into I and Thou, but it did not arise from their being set together; by its nature the I-Thou attitude precedes I."

I-Thou comes before the distinction between them? You're suggesting that we have the I-Thou attitude before we even discover an I and a Thou? Does this apply to I-It as well?

"No, the second word arose from the setting together of I and It; by nature the I-It attitude comes after I."

Can you give me an example? And please don't start talking to trees again. Did premodern cultures relate this way to their moon gods? Is that the idea?

"Only brief glimpses into the context in time of the two primary words are given us by primitive man. We receive fuller knowledge from the child."

Thank you, that's much more manageable for me.

Natural Combination and Natural Separation.   "Here it becomes crystal clear to us that the spiritual reality of the primary words arises out of a natural reality, that of the primary word I-Thou out of natural combination, and that of the primary word I-It out of natural separation."

For example?

"This connection has such a cosmic quality that the mythical saying of the Jews, 'In the mother's body man knows the universe, in birth he forgets it,' reads like an imperfect decipherment of an inscription from earliest times."

No offense, Mr. Buber, but old sayings don't prove anything.

"Of course not, but it remains indeed in man as a secret image of desire. The yearning is for the cosmic connection, with its true Thou."

I'm still looking for a plausible example.

Establishing a Relation.   "The primal nature of the effort to establish relation is already to be seen in the earliest and most confined stage. Before anything isolated can be perceived, timid glances move out into indistinct space, towards something indefinite; and in times where there seems to be no desire for nourishment, hands sketch delicately and dimly in the empty air, apparently aimlessly seeking and reaching out to meet something indefinite."

Babies move their arms, so what?

"These very glances will after protracted attempts settle on the red carpet pattern and not be moved till the soul of the red has opened itself to them; and this very movement of the hands will win from the woolly teddybear its precise form, apparent to the senses, and become lovingly and unforgettably aware of a complete body."

Isn't that just the opposite of what you were saying? In your example, the infant knows itself as an I, and only after groping around discovers objects out there in the world. It sees the red carpet and feels the teddybear.

"Neither of these acts is experience of an object, but is the correspondence of the child."

I'm uncomfortable with your interpretation. The infant is merely exercising her imagination.

"To be sure it is only 'fanciful'—with what is alive and effective over against itself. . . . It is the instinct to make everything into Thou, to give relation to the universe."

An interesting idea, but why should we accept this interpretation? Babies look around; they move their little arms; they make sounds. How does any of this prove that they are relating to anything?

"Little, disjointed, meaningless sounds still go out persistently into the void. But one day, unforeseen, they will have become conversation—does it matter that it is perhaps with a simmering kettle? It is conversation."

Well, maybe.

"Art, it is simply not the case that the child first perceives an object, then, as it were, puts itself into relation with it. The effort to establish relation comes first —the hand of the child arched out so that what is over against him may nestle under it."

I see what you're saying. The child reaches or looks so that it can relate in its world.

Relating.   "Second is the actual relation, a saying of Thou without words, in the state preceding the word form."

You're saying that the conversation with the tea kettle or the teddybear comes as an unspoken relation?

"Yes, and the thing, like the I, is produced late, arising after the original experiences have been split asunder and the connected partners separated."

Then the teddy relationship is essential for the infant even to discover that she is a unique thing? You're saying that the relation between the teddy and the infant comes first, even before the infant is aware that she has a limited body?

"In the beginning is relation—as a category of being, readiness, grasping form . . . it is . . . *inborn Thou.*"

Say this again.

"The inborn Thou is realized in the lived relations with that which meets it. The fact that this Thou can be known as what is over against the child, can be taken up in exclusiveness, and finally can be addressed with the primary word, is based on the a priori (the essential nature) of relation."

Loving and Hating.   So our sense of loving and caring arises from this way of relating?

"In the instinct to make contact the inborn Thou is very soon brought to its full powers, so that the instinct ever more clearly turns out to mean mutual relation, 'tenderness.'"

Then you're saying that the I-Thou attitude is really loving and caring for everyone. Loving and caring are the only feelings we should have toward anyone. We should love our neighbors, and our enemies, and everyone else, no matter what type of people they are.

"You speak of love as though it were the only relation between men. But properly speaking, can you take it even as only an example, since there is such a thing as hate?"

I hadn't thought of hate as an intimate way of relating. I was just thinking that absolutely devoted love is what you were asking from me.

"So long as love is 'blind,' that is, so long as it does not see a *whole* being, it is not truly under the sway of the primary word of relation."

A whole being?

"Art, hate is by nature blind. Only a part of a being can be hated. He who sees a whole being and is compelled to reject it is no longer in the kingdom of hate, but is in that of human restriction of the power to say Thou."

Why do you say that?

"He finds himself unable to say the primary word to the other human being confronting him. This word consistently involves an affirmation of the being addressed."

Why can't a person who hates say Thou to the person he hates? Why can't I hate someone and affirm him at the same time?

"You are compelled to reject either the other or yourself."

So you're saying that if I hate someone, and I see their whole being, then I cannot see myself as fully affirmed as a human being? I am merely judging the other person by my own values. Then hate is always wrong?

"Yet the man who straightforwardly hates is nearer to relation than the man without hate and love."

Now I am confused. Why do you say this?

"Relation is mutual. My Thou affects me, as I affect it. . . . We live our lives inscrutably included within the streaming mutual life of the universe."

I understand that in some unintelligible way I am attached to everything. But how can you not have negative feelings toward the bad person?

Love Goes Beyond Feelings.   "Feelings accompany the metaphysical and metapsychical fact of love, but they do not constitute it."

Now it's my turn to have a V-8! Since you put it that way, it's so obvious!

"Why the sarcasm?"

What is the metaphysical and metapsychical fact of love? I don't have any idea what that means.

"The feeling of Jesus for the demoniac differs from his feeling for the beloved disciple; but the love is one love."

How could that be? Love is love.

"Feelings are 'entertained': love comes to pass. Feelings dwell in a man; but man dwells in his love."

That's a nice metaphor for saying that love is deeper than feelings.

"That is no metaphor, but the actual truth. Love does not cling to the I in such a way as to have the Thou only for its 'content,' its object; but love is *between* I and Thou."

Then the feelings involved in loving are only by-products of the fact, of the attitude of love?

"The man who does not know this, with his very being know this, does not know love."

Even though he has strong feelings of affection or caring for other people?

"Even though he ascribes to it feelings he lives through, experiences, enjoys, and expresses."

How is the person different who loves beyond the feelings?

"In the eyes of him who takes his stand in love, and gazes out of it, men are cut free from their entanglement in bustling activity. Good people and evil, wise and foolish, beautiful and ugly, become successively *real* to him."

You want people to become more and more real to me? What do you mean?

"Set free, they step forth in their singleness and confront you as Thou."

The Thou Relationship

What do I experience when I am in an I-Thou relation?

"In the act of experience Thou is far away. I do not experience the man to whom I say Thou."

I don't understand.

"I take my stand in relation to him—"

I'm sorry; I used the wrong words to ask my question. What does the world look like to a person who has the I-Thou attitude?

"If I face a human being as my Thou, and say the primary word I-Thou to him, he is not a thing among things, and does not consist of things. Thus a human being is not He or She, bounded from every other He or She, a specific point in space and time within the net of the world; nor is he a nature able to be experienced or described, a loose bundle of named qualities."

Well, that's what the Thou is not, but what is the Thou?

"Whole in himself . . . all else lives in his light."

All else lives in his light? What do we experience of Thou?

"Just nothing. For we do not experience it."

What, then, do we know of Thou?

"Just everything. For we know nothing isolated about it anymore."

Oh, I see. We understand all of reality as a setting for the Thou.

A Sacrifice and a Risk.   This all sounds pretty risky to me.

"Yes, Art, the act includes a sacrifice and a risk."

What's the sacrifice?

"The endless possibility that is offered up on the altar of form."

By that you mean that I can't act like I have been acting all this time? I have to take off my mask? I have to actually be who I am? Most people are so accustomed to acting according to social roles and people's expectations! We expect everybody else to act that way, too. Yes, that is a sacrifice. And the risk?

"The primary word can only be spoken with the whole being. He who gives himself to it may withhold nothing of himself."

You mean I have to tell the other person everything about myself, including my thoughts and desires?

"Things among things. This is the It world. Art, all real living is meeting."

But, Professor Buber, if I drop my mask, and if I withhold nothing of my self, what guarantee do I have that the other person will be aware of me?

"Even if the man to whom I say Thou is not aware of it in the midst of his experience, yet relation may exist. For Thou is more than It realizes."

Isn't the other person going to take advantage of me? Can't she deceive me?

"No deception penetrates here; here is the cradle of the Real Life."

To Man the World is Twofold.   I know that we can experience the world in an I-It way. When I do that, I can accomplish a lot. It's the practical life. What do I get by having the I-Thou attitude? You say my sense of myself is determined by how I relate to the other person or thing. What else do I understand in this Thou meeting?

"Man becomes always what is over against him, always simply a *single* being and each thing simply as being."

What do you mean?

"Nothing is present for you except this one being, but it implicates the whole world."

That's what you mean when you say that I see the whole world in his light?

"Yes. Measure and comparison have disappeared; it lies with yourself how much of the immeasurable becomes reality for you. These meetings are not organized to make the world, but each is a sign of the world order."

It sounds chaotic. What benefit do I get from this attitude?

"Each meeting assures you of your solidarity with the world."

The Relation to the Thou is Direct.   Solidarity with the world? That brings to my mind a question I have been wanting to ask.

"Yes?"

You say that the relation to the Thou is direct. What do you mean?

"No system of ideas, no foreknowledge, and no fancy intervene between I and Thou."

So I encounter the Thou as it really exists?

"Yes, no aim, no lust, and no anticipation intervene between I and Thou. Desire itself is transformed as it plunges out of its dream into the appearance."

Why is it so important that aims and desires and anticipations be left behind?

"Every means is an obstacle. Only when every means has collapsed does the meeting come about."

Oh, okay. I have to get myself out of the I-It frame of mind. But I still don't understand the nature of the I-Thou way of relating. For example, you say in your tree example that the tree isn't an impression or part of my imagination.

It Is Bodied Over Against Me.   "Correct. Nor is the tree a value depending on my mood; but it is bodied over against me and has to do with me, as I with it."

Now we are getting at what I don't understand. What does it mean for something to be "bodied over against me"?

"Art, I can neither experience nor describe the form which meets me, but only body it forth."

Wait, are you saying that the intellect doesn't have a part in the I-Thou relationship? That's it, isn't it? If I think in categories and make judgments, then I am only experiencing the thing. But if I suspend my intellectual way of understanding, then the thing is presented to me directly. That's what you mean when you say the relation is direct. I know the Thou with my whole being, not with my senses, my intellectual categories, and my judgments. The thing becomes real, a single, existing thing important just because it is here, because it is present. And I am present along with it.

The Present Is Filled. "That is why the real, filled present exists only insofar as actual presentness, meeting, and relation exist. The present arises only in virtue of the fact that the Thou becomes present."

This sounds like the pleasure seeker's experiences. Is the difference between the Thou way of relating and the pleasure seeker's way of experiencing that the pleasure seeker is goal directed?

"Insofar as man rests satisfied with the things that he experiences and uses, he lives in the past, and his moment has no present content."

Huh?

"True beings are lived in the present, the life of objects is in the past."

Every Thou Must Become an It

If the reality of our own selves depends on the I-Thou, why don't we all live with the I-Thou attitude all the time?

"Every Thou in our world must become an It."

Isn't there any way to prevent it?

"It does not matter how exclusively present the Thou was in direct relation. As soon as the relation has been worked out or has been permeated with a means, the Thou becomes an object among objects—perhaps the chief, but still one of them."

Then overcoming our separation from the real world is impossible?

"Every Thou in the world is by its nature fated to become a thing, or continually to reenter into the condition of things. Consider the speech of 'primitive' peoples, that is, of those that have a meager stock of objects, and whose life is built up within a narrow circle of acts highly charged with presentness."

Separation and Connection with Reality

What about them? Does their language show that separation is impossible to avoid?

"The nuclei of this speech . . . most indicate the wholeness of relation. We say 'far away'; the Zulu has for that a word which means, in our sentence form, 'There where someone cries out: O mother, I am lost.' "

Their language has a more emotional feel to it.

"The Fuegian soars above our analytic wisdom with a seven-syllabled word whose precise meaning is, 'They stare at one another, each waiting for the other to volunteer to do what both wish, but are not able to do.' "

What's your point?

"The chief concern is not with these products of analysis and reflection but with the true original unity, the lived relation."

Their language does express the sense of separation and the need for connection with reality. There is an immediacy about the "primitive" understanding that goes beyond our normal intellectual, moral way of relating.

"To accept what has no sensuous qualities at all as actually existing must strike him as absurd. The appearances to which he ascribes the 'mystical power' are all elementary incidents that are relational in character, that is, all incidents that disturb him by disturbing his body and leaving behind in him a stirring image."

Should the theme from *Twilight Zone* be racing through my mind?

"Not at all. I am merely presenting an example of knowledge that is bodied over against a person."

You Believe in Paradise?

Then you think that ancient people lived in a kind of paradise?

"Even if it was a hell—and certainly that time to which I can go back in historical thought was full of fury and anguish and torment and cruelty—at any rate it was not unreal."

Your whole emphasis is for us to encounter reality as it is. You think that our objective way of experiencing shields us from "feeling" what is out there. Your critique is really aimed at us. We have not shed the insulation of the moral way of thinking and relating. Isn't that it? You're saying that our modern way of experiencing doesn't let things be real. Is the "primitive" way better?

"Rather force exercised on being that is really lived, than shadowy solicitude for faceless numbers!"

Why Enter the Thou Attitude?

Professor Buber, I have several reservations about the Thou way of living. Before we part, may I state them?

"Yes, by all means, do."

What does the Thou attitude offer me? How does it compare with living in the It world? What I mean is, the Thou attitude sounds appealing, but also lonely, dangerous, and impractical. I hope you don't mind me saying this.

"Art, through the Thou a man becomes I. That which confronts him comes and disappears, relational events condense, then are scattered, and in the change consciousness of the unchanging partner, of the I, grows clear, and each time stronger."

I appreciate that part of your analysis. I'm even willing to concede that the child's sense of I arises from the I-Thou primary attitude. What comes of that?

"Only now can the other primary word be assembled. Hitherto the Thou of relation was continually fading away, but it did not thereby become an It for some I, an object of perception and experience, without real connection—as it will henceforth become."

I guess I'm asking a more practical, adult question.

"The man who becomes conscious of I, that is, the man who says I-It, stands before things, but not over against them in the flow of mutual action. Now with the magnifying glass of peering observation he bends over particulars and objectifies them, or with the fieldglass of remote inspection he objectifies them and arranges them as scenery, he isolates them in observation without any feeling of their exclusiveness, or he knits them into a scheme of observation without any feeling of universality."

That speaks in favor of the practical nature of the I-It experience. All science depends on objective observation.

"Art, the feeling of exclusiveness he would be able to find only in relation, the feeling of universality only through it."

Exclusiveness? So to be a unique individual, and not merely part of humanity, I should adopt the I-Thou attitude? But so much speaks in favor of the I-It!

"These are the two basic privileges of the world of It. They move man to look on the world of It as the world in which he has to live, and in which it is comfortable to live, as the world, indeed, which offers him all manner of incitements and excitements, activity and knowledge. In this chronicle of solid benefits the moments of the Thou appear as strange lyric and dramatic episodes, seductive and magical, but tearing us away to dangerous extremes, loosening the well-tried context, leaving more questions than satisfaction behind them, shattering security—in short, uncanny moments we can well dispense with."

That's exactly what I think. Maybe I'm being too moral in looking for the security of the familiar, but why should I venture out into Thou relations? Since we cannot hold for long anything in our consciousness as a Thou—

"Why not call to order what is over against us and send it packing into the realm of objects?"

Yes. Why not?

"It is not possible to live in the bare present. Life would be quite consumed if precautions were not taken to subdue the present speedily and thoroughly."

Exactly. You have forcefully stated my concerns.

"But it is possible to live in the bare past; indeed, only in it may a life be organized. We only need to fill each moment with experiencing and using, and it ceases to burn."

So why not live the safe, secure, predictable life?

"In all seriousness of truth, hear this: without It man cannot live."

Just as I thought.

"But he who lives with It alone is not man, is not human."

Summary of Discussion

Martin Buber suggests that each of us has two attitudes toward the world. The first and more easily identified attitude is what he calls the I-It attitude. This perspective understands objects and people as instrumental for achieving goals and the like. The second attitude is the I-Thou attitude. I-Thou is a most intimate way of knowing the other. I-Thou goes beyond the surface of the other person or thing. The I-Thou attitude sees the other for what is really there. Another way of putting this distinction is that the I-It attitude allows one to experience the other person or thing. The I-Thou attitude necessitates one person's relating to the other. In each case the nature of the I is determined by the attitude with which the I understands the other.

I-Thou is the only way for a person to alleviate his loneliness. It involves relating with one's whole being. I-Thou requires that one person openly view the other. There is a risk involved. One must drop one's pretense, one's "masks." Buber suggests that the I-Thou way of relating is the most natural way. He says that it predates the I-It experience. The infant relates to its first objects as Thou, defining itself and the other in this process of relating.

Unfortunately, this direct, intimate, and filled relation cannot be sustained. Every Thou must become an It. Every meeting must break apart into a separation. But the meeting can occur again. One can become connected with reality again.

For all its risks and sacrifices, the Thou way of relating is essential to us. We can live immersed in the I-It way of experiencing, but this does not make us human. The I-It way of experiencing is a safe, secure, and predictable life. Why not live exclusively with the I-It attitude? Buber answers, "Without It man cannot live. But he who lives with It alone is not man, is not human."

Discussion Highlights

I. The attitude of man is twofold.
  1. There is the I-It attitude and way of relating.
    a. One experiences reality and the surface of things.
    b. One lives in the purely "practical" world.
  2. There is the I-Thou attitude and way of relating.
    a. One relates to the other and experiences the world in light of the other.
    b. The power of exclusiveness occurs in the I-Thou relation.
II. The Thou relationship has several distinguishing features.
  1. It occurs with a sacrifice and a risk.
  2. The Thou is bodied over against me.
  3. The present is filled.
  4. Every Thou must become an It.
  5. The separation created by language can be overcome.
  6. Both attitudes, I-Thou and I-It, are necessary for us to live as humans.

Questions for Thought/Paper Topics

1. What characteristics distinguish the I-It and the I-Thou attitudes?
2. Buber defines three spheres of relating. First is nature, then come our fel-

low humans, and finally spiritual beings. What do you make of this distinction?

3. What is the significance of Buber's notion of the "in-between"? He claims it is the key to understanding the self and the other.

4. Discuss how Buber's discussion of the tree exemplifies the "power of exclusiveness."

5. What could Buber mean when he says that real meeting goes beyond loving and hating?

6. Does Buber succeed in integrating the individual person and all reality? Discuss how he accomplishes this.

7. Does Buber's notion of the "filled moment" sound similar to the Stranger's concentration on momentary pleasure? How do they differ?

For Further Reading

Read Buber's *I and Thou* (Scribner's Sons, 1958). That is where Buber first lays out his I-Thou, I-It distinction. You might also look at his *Between Man and Man* (Macmillan, 1965) for Buber's own explanation and application of his theory. There are very good works on human relating. In *An Inquiry Concerning the Principles of Morals* (Bobbs-Merrill, 1957), David Hume offers a remarkable analysis of morality and its requirement of relating through "gentler" emotions. An excerpt from Hume's *Inquiry* follows to give you an idea of this analysis. Another impressive book is Simone de Beauvoir's *The Second Sex* (Random House, 1974). Chapter 23, "The Woman in Love," is particularly appropriate to our discussion.

From *The Principle of Humanity, or Social Sympathy*

DAVID HUME

David Hume proposes that self-interest cannot be used to explain moral sentiment. Breaking with many other philosophers, Hume argues that morality is not based on self-love or on enlightened selfishness. He suggests that a sense of "humanity or a fellow-feeling with others" is the origin of morality and agrees with Buber that there is a capacity for intimacy between people that defines and determines many of our pleasures.

Seeing other people happy, joyful, and prosperous gives us pleasure. Think about your own reactions. When you enter a room and people are smiling and laughing, you feel pleasure. When people around you are sad or depressed, your mood reflects theirs also. Another way to think about this is in the context of watching a movie or play. Once you get into the story, you "forget" that the characters are really actors. When the heroine is successful in her quest, you feel pleasure. When she is injured, you feel sympathy. Even more remarkable, when she is cut on the arm, you wince and feel a "shadow" of the cut on your arm. Many people feel this kind of empathy for others.

Of course, we are most likely to sympathize with those whose lives resemble our everyday experience. Every person does not experience the same ups and downs in life. But, says Hume, "no passion, when well represented, can be entirely indifferent to us." Sympathy is natural to us. It is an underutilized emotion that can be desirable. Hume argues that this capacity for fellow-feeling is the true foundation and motivation for morality. Without fellow-feeling, we can enjoy only the sensual and intellectual pleasures. To be human, we need to appreciate and take pleasure in other people's feelings and experiences.

Think how Hume's notion of "humanity or fellow-feeling" can be used to combat racism, sexism, and other prejudices stemming from national, religious, and even educational biases. As you read this selection from Hume, question him. Does he accurately describe humans? Is his principle a step in creating the best life? How do the positions of Hume and Buber match your own considered judgments?

SELF-LOVE IS A PRINCIPLE in human nature of such extensive energy, and the interest of each individual is, in general, so closely connected with that of the community, that those philosophers were excusable, who fancied that all our concern for the public might be resolved into a concern for our own happiness and preservation. They saw every moment, instances of approbation or blame, satisfaction or displeasure towards characters and actions; they denominated the objects of these sentiments, *virtues,* or *vices*; they observed, that the former had a tendency to increase the happiness, and the latter the misery of mankind; they asked, whether it were possible that we could have any general concern for society, or any disinterested resentment of the welfare or injury of others; they found it simpler to consider all these sentiments as modifications of self-love; and they discovered a pretence, at least, for this unity of principle, in that close union of interest, which is so observable between the public and each individual.

But notwithstanding this frequent confusion of interests, it is easy to attain what natural philosophers, after Lord Bacon, have affected to call the *experimentum crucis,* or that experiment which points out the right way in any doubt or ambiguity. We have found instances, in which private interest was separate from public; in which it was even contrary: And yet we observed the moral sentiment to continue, notwithstanding this disjunction of interests. And wherever these distinct interests sensibly concurred, we always found a sensible increase of the sentiment, and a more warm affection to virtue, and detestation of vice, or what we properly call, *gratitude* and *revenge.* Compelled by these instances, we must renounce the theory, which accounts for every moral sentiment by the principle of self-love. We must adopt a more public affection, and allow, that the interest of society are not, even on their own account, entirely indifferent to us. Usefulness is only a tendency to a certain end; and it is a contradiction in terms, that anything pleases as means to an end, where the end

From *An Inquiry Concerning the Principles of Morals,* first published in 1777.

itself no wise affects us. If usefulness, therefore, be a source of moral sentiment, and if this usefulness be not always considered with a reference to self, it follows, that everything, which contributes to the happiness of society, recommends itself directly to our approbation and good-will. Here is a principle, which accounts, in great part, for the origin of morality: And what need we seek for abstruse and remote systems, when there occurs one so obvious and natural?[1]

Have we any difficulty to comprehend the force of humanity and benevolence? Or to conceive, that the very aspect of happiness, joy, prosperity, gives pleasure; that of pain, suffering, sorrow, communicates uneasiness? The human countenance, says Horace, borrows smiles or tears from the human countenance. Reduce a person to solitude, and he loses all enjoyment, except either of the sensual or speculative kind; and that because the movements of his heart are not forwarded by correspondent movements in his fellow-creatures. The signs of sorrow and mourning, though arbitrary, affect us with melancholy; but the natural symptoms, tears and cries and groans, never fail to infuse compassion and uneasiness. And if the effects of misery touch us in so lively a manner; can we be supposed altogether insensible or indifferent towards its causes; when a malicious or treacherous character and behaviour are presented to us?

---

[1] It is needless to push our researches so far as to ask, why we have humanity or a fellow-feeling with others. It is sufficient, that this is experienced to be a principle in human nature. We must stop somewhere in our examination of causes; and there are, in every science, some general principles, beyond which we cannot hope to find any principle more general. No man is absolutely indifferent to the happiness and misery of others. The first has a natural tendency to give pleasure; the second, pain. This every one may find in himself. It is not probable, that these principles can be resolved into principles more simple and universal, whatever attempts may have been made to that purpose. But if it were possible, it belongs not to the present subject; and we may here safely consider these principles as original: happy, if we can render all the consequences sufficiently plain and perspicuous!

We enter, I shall suppose, into a convenient, warm, well-contrived apartment: We necessarily receive a pleasure from its very survey; because it presents us with the pleasing ideas of ease, satisfaction, and enjoyment. The hospitable, good-humoured, humane landlord appears. This circumstance surely must embellish the whole; nor can we easily forbear reflecting, with pleasure, on the satisfaction which results to every one from his intercourse and good-offices.

His whole family, by the freedom, ease, confidence, and calm enjoyment, diffused over their countenances, sufficiently express their happiness. I have a pleasing sympathy in the prospect of so much joy, and can never consider the source of it, without the most agreeable emotions.

He tells me, that an oppressive and powerful neighbour had attempted to dispossess him of his inheritance, and had long disturbed all his innocent and social pleasures. I feel an immediate indignation arise in me against such violence and injury.

But it is no wonder, he adds, that a private wrong should proceed from a man, who had enslaved provinces, depopulated cities, and made the field and scaffold stream with human blood. I am struck with horror at the prospect of so much misery, and am actuated by the strongest antipathy against its author.

In general, it is certain, that, wherever we go, whatever we reflect on or converse about, everything still presents us with the view of human happiness or misery, and excites in our breast a sympathetic movement of pleasure or uneasiness. In our serious occupations, in our careless amusements, this principle still exerts its active energy.

A man who enters the theatre, is immediately struck with the view of so great a multitude participating of one common amusement; and experiences, from their very aspect, a superior sensibility or disposition of being affected with every sentiment, which he shares with his fellow-creatures.

He observes the actors to be animated by the appearance of a full audience, and raised to a degree of enthusiasm, which they cannot command in any solitary or calm moment.

Every movement of the theatre, by a skillful poet, is communicated, as it were by magic, to the spectators; who weep, tremble, resent, rejoice, and are inflamed with all the variety of passions, which actuate the several personages of the drama.

Where any event crosses our wishes, and interrupts the happiness of the favourite characters, we feel a sensible anxiety and concern. But where their sufferings proceed from the treachery, cruelty, or tyranny of an enemy, our breasts are affected with the liveliest resentment against the author of these calamities.

It is here esteemed contrary to the rules of art to represent anything cool and indifferent. A distant friend, or a confident, who has no immediate interest in the catastrophe, ought, if possible, to be avoided by the poet; as communicating a like indifference to the audience, and checking the progress of the passions.

Few species of poetry are more entertaining than *pastoral*; and every one is sensible, that the chief source of its pleasure arises from those images of a gentle and tender tranquility, which it represents in its personages, and of which it communicates a like sentiment to the reader. Sannazarius, who transferred the scene to the sea-shore, though he presented the most magnificent object in nature, is confessed to have erred in his choice. The idea of toil, labour, and danger, suffered by the fishermen, is painful; by an unavoidable sympathy, which attends every conception of human happiness or misery.

When I was twenty, says a French poet, Ovid was my favourite: Now I am forty, I declare for Horace. We enter, to be sure, more readily into sentiments, which resemble those we feel every day: But no passion, when well represented, can be entirely indifferent to us; because there is none, of which every man has not, within him, at least the seeds and first principles. It is the business of poetry to bring every affection near

to us by lively imagery and representation, and make it look like truth and reality: A certain proof, that, wherever that reality is found, our minds are disposed to be strongly affected by it.

Any recent event or piece of news, by which the fate of states, provinces, or many individuals is affected, is extremely interesting even to those whose welfare is not immediately engaged. Such intelligence is propagated with celerity, heard with avidity, and enquired into with attention and concern. The interest of society appears, on this occasion, to be in some degree the interest of each individual. The imagination is sure to be affected; though the passions excited may not always be so strong and steady as to have great influence on the conduct and behaviour.

The perusal of a history seems a calm entertainment; but would be no entertainment at all, did not our hearts beat with correspondent movements to those which are described by the historian.

Thucydides and Guicciardin support with difficulty our attention; while the former describes the trivial rencounters of the small cities of Greece, and the latter the harmless wars of Pisa. The few persons interested and the small interest fill not the imagination, and engage not the affections. The deep distress of the numerous Athenian army before Syracuse; the danger which so nearly threatens Venice; these excite compassion; these move terror and anxiety.

The indifferent, uninteresting style of Suetonius, equally with the masterly pencil of Tacitus, may convince us of the cruel depravity of Nero or Tiberius: But what a difference of sentiment! While the former coldly relates the facts; and the latter sets before our eyes the venerable figures of a Soranus and a Thrasea, intrepid in their fate, and only moved by the melting sorrows of their friends and kindred. What sympathy then touches every human heart! What indignation against the tyrant, whose causeless fear or unprovoked malice gave rise to such detestable barbarity!

If we bring these subjects nearer: If we remove all suspicion of fiction and deceit: What powerful concern is excited, and how much superior, in many instances, to the narrow attachments of self-love and private interest! Popular sedition, party zeal, a devoted obedience to factious leaders; these are some of the most visible, though less laudable effects of this social sympathy in human nature.

The frivolousness of the subject too, we may observe, is not able to detach us entirely from what carries an image of human sentiment and affection.

When a person stutters, and pronounces with difficulty, we even sympathize with this trivial uneasiness, and suffer for him. And it is a rule in criticism, that every combination of syllables or letters, which gives pain to the organs of speech in the recital, appears also from a species of sympathy harsh and disagreeable to the ear. Nay, when we run over a book with our eye, we are sensible of such unharmonious composition; because we still imagine, that a person recites it to us, and suffers from the pronunciation of these jarring sounds. So delicate is our sympathy!

Easy and unconstrained postures and motions are always beautiful: An air of health and vigour is agreeable: Clothes which warm, without burthening the body; which cover, without imprisoning the limbs, are well-fashioned. In every judgement of beauty, the feelings of the person affected enter into consideration, and communicate to the spectator similar touches of pain or pleasure. What wonder, then, if we can pronounce no judgement concerning the character and conduct of men, without considering the tendencies of their actions, and the happiness or misery which thence arises to society? What association of ideas would ever operate, were that principle here totally unactive.[2]

If any man from a cold insensibility, or narrow selfishness of temper, is unaffected with the images of human happiness or misery, he must be equally indifferent to the images of vice and virtue: As, on the other hand, it is always found, that a warm concern for the interests of our species is attended with a delicate feeling of all moral distinctions; a strong resentment of injury done to men; a lively approbation of their welfare. In this particular, though great superiority is observable of one man above another; yet none are so entirely indifferent to the interest of their fellow-creatures, as to perceive no distinctions of moral good and evil, in consequence of the different tendencies of actions and principles. How, indeed, can we suppose it possible in any one, who wears a human heart, that if there be subjected to his censure, one character or system of conduct, which is beneficial, and another which is pernicious, to his species or community, he will not as much as give a cool preference to the former, or ascribe to it the smallest merit or regard? Let us suppose such a person ever so selfish; let private interest have ingrossed ever so much his attention; yet in instances, where that is not concerned, he must unavoidably feel *some* propensity to the good of mankind, and make it an object of choice, if everything else be equal. Would any man, who is walking along, tread as willingly on another's gouty toes, whom he has no quarrel with, as on the hard flint and pavement? There is here surely a difference in the case. We surely take into consideration the happiness and misery of others, in

[2] In proportion to the station which a man possesses, according to the relations in which he is placed; we always expect from him a greater or less degree of good, and when disappointed, blame his inutility; and much more do we blame him, if any ill or prejudice arise from his conduct and behaviour. When the interests of one country interfere with those of another, we estimate the merits of a statesman by the good or ill, which results to his own country from his measures and councils, without regard to the prejudice which he brings on its enemies and rivals. His fellow-citizens are the objects, which lie nearest the eye, while we determine his character. And as nature has implanted in every one a superior affection to his own country, we never expect any regard to distant nations, where a competition arises. Not to mention, that, while every man consults the good of his own community, we are sensible, that the general interest of mankind is better promoted, than by any loose indeterminate views to the good of a species, whence no beneficial action could ever result, for want of a duly limited object, on which they could exert themselves.

weighing the several motives of action, and incline to the former, where no private regards draw us to seek our own promotion or advantage by the injury of our fellow-creatures. And if the principles of humanity are capable, in many instances, of influencing our actions, they must, at all times, have *some* authority over our sentiments, and give us a general approbation of what is useful to society, and blame of what is dangerous or pernicious. The degrees of these sentiments may be the subject of controversy; but the reality of their existence, one should think, must be admitted in every theory or system.

A creature, absolutely malicious and spiteful, were there any such in nature, must be worse than indifferent to the images of vice and virtue. All his sentiments must be inverted, and directly opposite to those, which prevail in the human species. Whatever contributes to the good of mankind, as it crosses the constant bent of his wishes and desires, must produce uneasiness and disapprobation; and on the contrary, whatever is the source of disorder and misery in society, must, for the same reason, be regarded with pleasure and complacency. Timon, who probably from his affected spleen more than any inveterate malice, was denominated the manhater, embraced Alcibiades with great fondness. *Go on my boy!* cried he, *acquire the confidence of the people: You will one day, I foresee, be the cause of great calamities to them.* Could we admit the two principles of the Manicheans, it is an infallible consequence, that their sentiments of human actions, as well as of everything else, must be totally opposite, and that every instance of justice and humanity, from its necessary tendency, must please the one deity and displease the other. All mankind so far resemble the good principle, that, where interest or revenge or envy perverts not our disposition, we are always inclined, from our natural philanthropy, to give the preference to the happiness of society, and consequently to virtue above its opposite. Absolute, unprovoked, disinterested malice has never perhaps place in any human breast; or if it had, must

there pervert all the sentiments of morals, as well as the feelings of humanity. If the cruelty of Nero be allowed entirely voluntary, and not rather the effect of constant fear and resentment; it is evident that Tigellinus, preferably to Seneca or Burrhus, must have possessed his steady and uniform approbation.

A statesman or patriot, who serves our own country in our own time, has always a more passionate regard paid to him, than one whose beneficial influence operated on distant ages or remote nations; where the good, resulting from his generous humanity, being less connected with us, seems more obscure, and affects us with a less lively sympathy. We may own the merit to be equally great, though our sentiments are not raised to an equal height, in both cases. The judgement here corrects the inequalities of our internal emotions and perceptions; in like manner, as it preserves us from error, in the several variations of images, presented to our external senses. The same object, at a double distance, really throws on the eye a picture of but half the bulk; yet we imagine that it appears of the same size in both situations; because we know that on our approach to it, its image would expand on the eye, and that the difference consists not in the object itself, but in our position with regard to it. And, indeed, without such a correction of appearances, both in internal and external sentiment, men could never think or talk steadily on any subject; while their fluctuating situations produce a continual variation on objects, and throw them into such different and contrary lights and positions.[3]

---

[3] For a like reason, the tendencies of actions and characters, not their real accidental consequences, are alone regarded in our moral determinations or general judgements; though in our real feeling or sentiment, we cannot help paying greater regard to one whose station, joined to virtue, renders him really useful to society, than to one, who exerts the social virtues only in good intentions and benevolent affections. Separating the character from the fortune, by an easy and necessary effort of thought, we pronounce these persons alike, and give them the same general praise. The judgement corrects or endeavours to correct the appearance:

The more we converse with mankind, and the greater social intercourse we maintain, the more shall we be familiarized to these general preferences and distinctions, without which our conversation and discourse could scarcely be rendered intelligible to each other. Every man's interest is peculiar to himself, and the aversions and desires, which result from it, cannot be supposed to affect others in a like degree. General language, therefore, being formed for general use, must be moulded on some more general views, and must affix the epithets of praise or blame, in conformity to sentiments, which arise from the general interests of the community. And if these sentiments, in most men, be not so strong as those, which have a reference to private good; yet still they must make some distinction, even in persons the most depraved and selfish; and must attach the notion of good to a beneficent conduct, and of evil to the contrary. Sympathy, we shall allow, is much fainter than our concern for ourselves, and sympathy with persons remote from us much fainter than that with persons near and contiguous; but for this very reason it is necessary for us, in our calm judgements and discourse concerning the characters of men, to neglect all these differences, and render our sentiments more public and social. Besides, that we ourselves often change our situation in this particular, we every day meet with persons who are in a situation different from us, and who could never converse with us were we to remain constantly in that position and point of view, which is peculiar to ourselves. The intercourse of sentiments, therefore, in society and conversation, makes us form some general unalterable standard, by which we may approve or disapprove of characters and man-

ners. And though the heart takes not part entirely with those general notions, nor regulates all its love and hatred, by the universal abstract differences of vice and virtue, without regard to self, or the persons with whom we are more intimately connected; yet have these moral differences a considerable influence, and being sufficient, at least, for discourse, serve all our purposes in company, in the pulpit, on the theatre, and in the schools.[4]

Thus, in whatever light we take this subject, the merit, ascribed to the social virtues, appears still uniform, and arises chiefly from that regard, which the natural sentiment of benevolence engages us to pay to the interests of mankind and society. If we consider the principles of the human make, such as they appear to daily experience and observation, we must, *a priori,* conclude it impossible for such a creature as man to be totally indifferent to the well or ill-being of his fellow-creatures, and not readily, of himself, to pronounce, where nothing gives him any particular bias, that what promotes their happiness is good, what tends to their misery is evil, without any farther regard or consideration. Here then are the faint rudiments, at least, or outlines, of a *general* distinction between actions; and in proportion as the humanity of the person is supposed to encrease, his connexion with those who are injured or benefited, and his lively conception of their misery or happiness; his consequent censure or approbation acquires proportionable vigour. There is no necessity, that a generous action, barely mentioned in an old history or remote gazette, should communicate any strong feelings of applause and admiration. Virtue,

---

But is not able entirely to prevail over sentiment.

Why is this peach-tree said to be better than that other; but because it produces more or better fruit? And would not the same praise be given it, though snails or vermin had destroyed the peaches, before they came to full maturity? In morals too, is not *the tree known by the fruit?* And cannot we easily distinguish between nature and accident, in the one case as well as in the other?

[4] It is wisely ordained by nature, that private connexions should commonly prevail over universal views and considerations; otherwise our affections and actions would be dissipated and lost, for want of a proper limited object. Thus a small benefit done to ourselves, or our near friends, excites more lively sentiments of love and approbation than a great benefit done to a distant commonwealth: But still we know here, as in all the senses, to correct these inequalities by reflection, and retain a general standard of vice and virtue, founded chiefly on general usefulness.

placed at such a distance, is like a fixed star, which, though to the eye of reason it may appear as luminous as the sun in his meridian, is so infinitely removed as to affect the senses, neither with light nor heat. Bring this virtue nearer, by our acquaintance or connexion with the persons, or even by an eloquent recital of the case; our hearts are immediately caught, our sympathy enlivened, and our cool approbation converted into the warmest sentiments of friendship and regard. These seem necessary and infallible consequences of the general principles of human nature, as discovered in common life and practice.

Again; reverse these views and reasoning: Consider the matter *a posteriori*; and weighing the consequences, enquire if the merit of social virtue be not, in a great measure, derived from the feelings of humanity, with which it affects the spectators. It appears to be a matter of fact, that the circumstance of *utility*, in all subjects, is a source of praise and approbation: That it is constantly appealed to in all moral decisions concerning the merit and demerit of actions: That it is the *sole* source of that high regard paid to justice, fidelity, honour, allegiance, and chastity: That it is inseparable from all the other social virtues, humanity, generosity, charity, affability, lenity, mercy, and moderation: And, in a word, that it is a foundation of the chief part of morals, which has a reference to mankind and our fellow-creatures.

It appears also, that, in our general approbation of characters and manners, the useful tendency of the social virtues moves us not by any regards to self-interest, but has an influence much more universal and extensive. It appears that a tendency to public good, and to the promoting of peace, harmony, and order in society,

does always, by affecting the benevolent principles of our frame, engage us on the side of the social virtues. And it appears, as an additional confirmation, that these principles of humanity and sympathy enter so deeply into all our sentiments, and have so powerful an influence, as may enable them to excite the strongest censure and applause. The present theory is the simple result of all these inferences, each of which seems founded on uniform experience and observation.

Were it doubtful, whether there were any such principle in our nature as humanity or a concern for others, yet when we see, in numberless instances, that whatever has a tendency to promote the interest of society, is so highly approved of, we ought thence to learn the force of the benevolent principle; since it is impossible for anything to please as means to an end, where the end is totally indifferent. On the other hand, were it doubtful, whether there were, implanted in our nature, any general principle of moral blame and approbation, yet when we see, in numberless instances, the influence of humanity, we ought thence to conclude, that it is impossible, but that everything which promotes the interest of society must communicate pleasure, and what is pernicious give uneasiness. But when these different reflections and observations concur in establishing the same conclusion, must they not bestow an undisputed evidence upon it?

It is however hoped, that the progress of this argument will bring a farther confirmation of the present theory, by showing the rise of other sentiments of esteem and regard from the same or like principles.

13

What Is the Best Life? The Virtuous Sage of Spinoza and Lao Tsu

W HAT IS THE BEST LIFE? How can I live it? These two questions have received very different answers in our discussions. We cannot help but notice the diversity of wants, values, and goals that people endorse. Responses to our question, "What is the best life?" have been categorized by their goals. The moralist seeks security and acceptance. The pleasure seeker's goal is pleasures of the senses. Either one lives for the pleasure of the moment like Camus's Stranger, Kierkegaard's A, and Art. Or one lives a moral life in one of the ways we have seen described by the Grand Inquisitor, Epictetus, Mill, Kant, or Sartre. In this, our final discussion, I'd like to bring together some "conclusions" from our talks.

Translating the Basic Questions in Living

Although we have categorized each vision of living according to its goals, goals alone do not help us figure out which is the most desirable strategy of living. Telling a pleasure seeker that she is living an immoral, meaningless life is a lot like arguing etiquette with a hungry lion as she is about to eat you. As long as there are different goals, there is apparently no way of resolving the debate. I think, however, that there is a more helpful way to proceed.

Instead of examining the answers to the question, "What is the best life?" I suggest we look at the question itself and how each vision of living interprets the question. For the moment, imagine that each vision of living asks the same basic question. Why, then, are the answers so apparently different, you ask? Perhaps the answers are not so different. Our confusion may be a result of how each vision distorts the questions and the answers. Does each vision interpret the question differently? Certainly we have seen that each vision has different beliefs about human nature, about other people, about the nature of reality. Since each way of living

Material in this chapter taken from Benedict de Spinoza, *The Ethics* (New York: Dover Publications, Inc.), R.H.M. Elwes translation; and from Lao Tsu, *Tao Te Ching* (New York: Random House, Inc., 1972), Gia-fu Feng and Jane English translation.

differently defines the question of the best life, each seeks apparently different goals. It's as though each vision of living speaks a different language. Each vision sees the same question, but each has a different translation. If my idea is correct, all we have to do is translate the question in a better way. Let me show you what I mean.

Living to Avoid Boredom.

We can best understand Camus's Stranger as a person wishing to avoid boredom. I know what you're thinking. The Stranger leads an incredibly boring life. But does he? Or does his life only appear boring to moral people?

The Stranger is engaged in the here and now. He says, "All that counts is the present and the concrete." He sees a reality of facts without meaning. Reality is a series of unconnected impressions. Each moment sweeps away the one before it and is swept away by the one that follows it. For the Stranger, one experience is as good as another. No thought, no responsibility, nothing interrupts his experience of the here and now.

So sensual experience is his answer to the question of the best life. Sensual experience negates boredom. He is not engaged by society; he is engaged only by his senses. The Stranger is never bored. His way of living in the here and now keeps away boredom. More important, it also reaffirms his experience of existing. To him, he is real only as long as he is intensely experiencing his surroundings.

Of course, defining oneself by experiencing in the here and now does not work too well. All of the Stranger's experiences occur on the surface. In Buber's language, they are confined to the I-It way of relating. This weakness is enough to discourage us from living for the moment alone. However, the Stranger has discovered two keys to living well. He has discovered that intensity of interaction with reality is vital. And he understands that increasing the concentration on experiencing makes him feel more real. Ultimately, the Stranger's question is not so much one of avoiding boredom. Ultimately, it is a question of how real he is, and how he is real. He is certain of his own reality in his moments of sensual experience. Think about it. When you are suffering intense pain, there is no question that you are real.

Living to Avoid Decisions.

Kierkegaard's A is a more sophisticated version of living for the moment. A is nearer to the moral way that we live. A avoids decisions. A wants to experience intensely, but he also wants to control his world. He realizes that some experiences are more intense than others; some are more rewarding, that is, more pleasurable, than others. Which experience he chooses is important to him. Choose correctly and he knows that he is alive. His pleasures, his pains, and his sensual feelings all tell him so with absolute certainty. Choose mistakenly and he suffers. He is forced to live morally, with only a bored, distracted, vague sense of his own reality. That's why choice makes him anxious. Anxiety of indecision springs from the possibility of choice and control over surroundings.

When we ask A what is the best life, he replies that it is a life where one does not suffer the anxiety of indecision. Remember, he regrets every choice. It's possible that that is all there is to it. However, A is depressed and cynical. Something more is going on. A attempts to experience himself in experiencing other people and reality. But his way of experiencing is too limited to the "surface" of things.

For both the Stranger and A, there is a confusion. In each case the basic question, "What is the best life?" is apparently answered differently. The real and more fundamental quest, however, is to be fully real by intimately and intensely experiencing and relating to reality. That's just what Buber suggested in Chapter 12!

Living to Avoid Decisions and Responsibility.   Does this same analysis work with the moral life? In answering the question, "What is the best life?" the moral person accepts the safety of low-intensity experiencing. As we have seen, morality replaces intensity with meaningfulness. However, in our discussion of life's meaning or absurdity, we saw that the question of life's meaning is really only a hidden plea for knowing and affirming one's own reality by experiencing and relating to others and to reality.

Is this really the moralist's point of view? The anxieties of indecision and of responsibility are resolved by reference to a fixed standard, by the moral rules. Not only formalized rules and roles but social expectations resolve the need to make decisions on ultimate values. They remain fixed. They continue from the venerable past through the present and into the enduring future.

We can understand the moralist as a person wishing to avoid the anxieties of indecision and of responsibility, and meaninglessness. Minimizing the anxieties and meaninglessness defines and *gives reality* to the moral self. The moralist has merely moved the Stranger's question of intensity to duration, from momentary experience to feeling secure. The moralist seeks social acceptance and security.

Why Morality Doesn't Work

Why doesn't the moral reply adequately answer the question of the best life? Look at our conclusions about morality. Kant, Mill, and Sartre do not agree on their interpretation of morality. They do agree, however, that morality is the perspective of objective, universal impartiality. We have already seen that the moral point of view requires objectivity and impartiality. And it is universal in that it applies to everyone.

Within the objective moral vision of living, the other person is well defined but emotionally distant. For example, as a representative of the moral point of view, we can pick a judge. As a judge, the person is supposed to be morally impartial. No matter what the judge is feeling emotionally and no matter what the judge's relationship with the accused person, the judgment is supposed to be impartial. Imagine what it would be like to take someone to court, offer your evidence, and then have the judge say to your opponent, "In spite of the overwhelming evidence to the contrary, I find in your favor. I'll see you at home for dinner, son." Not very impartial! Not morally acceptable. So morality is essentially impartial and objective.

The Self and Others

The moral self is an isolated and unchanging object living through the experiences of the present. Morality confines my experiencing to my own person. I can feel neither the pains nor the joys of another person. I can experience sympathy or pity, but not empathy. I can feel only my own pains and joys. I am secure, but isolated and alone.

My only effective tool for communication is provided by the universal perspective of morality. I remain objective, even caring in the moral fashion, but always experientially isolated. Others are defined by the rights, duties, and obligations assigned them. I relate to others by joining them in the commonality of the "social continuities." We communicate; we have commerce. We understand our historical connection with each other. We cooperate in creative (productive) efforts, and in a sense of community.

Because morality makes us out of touch with other people, they seem to be like me, but they are not as real as me. After all, I cannot directly experience their feelings. They are "surface" experiences. They are "inferences." Each moralist is tied to morality for his or her own reality. Each moralist's own experience of his or her reality depends on the objective, universal perspective.

Meaningfulness

For the moral person, a meaningful life is important. But why? Though it might be true in some instances, what the moralist calls the meaningful life is not necessarily more pleasurable. Nor is the meaningful life necessarily more secure materially. Why, then, do moralists worry about the prospect of a meaningless life? The fear cannot be that the meaningless life brings anonymity. Anonymity in the form of objective impartiality is precisely what the moral life advocates. Within morality we are all moral equals. Selfishness is condemned as dangerous; being morally anonymous is praised.

The question of life's meaningfulness reveals a disguised fear of being out of touch with reality. Without experiencing what is out there, a person's life is confirmed only insofar as she aids and affects others, insofar as she achieves social connectedness (acceptance). If a moralist loses contact with the "continuity" of humanity, she loses her experience of her own reality.

Relating to Reality

How one relates to other people and to the things within reality, and therefore how one experiences one's self becomes confused with one's very existence itself. Without the impartial, objective relating of the universal perspective, the moralist believes that the self does not exist. Without moral relating, the moralist is "no better than an animal." One's moral existence, one's membership in the moral community, is granted only when one's motives and one's conception of others spring from impartial reason.

As moralists, we relate to other people and to reality in an emotionally and sensually uncommitted way. We become bored with others and with reality. We cannot become actively and intimately engaged with any specific part of it. We become drained by our lack of engagement. We are not bored and lifeless because we lack energy; we lack energy because we are bored. We are separated from reality. We are out of touch. We cannot become engaged and creative, and therefore we fail to gain vitality from our interaction with the environment. Even brief moments of non-moral, genuine interaction with reality revitalize us. Creative work and play, for example, do not tire us.

Morality does not provide more attuned tools for relating. It is not the aim of moral relating to savor the intensity of experiencing. Nor is morality designed to let us feel the sensuous texture of reality. Moral understanding captures and solidifies what can be reproduced, organized and judged. It performs this task well, but it cannot do more. Morality creates objects from subjects, estranged people from creative, sensuous humans. From the moral point of view, everything is an object, people are just objects valued among other things. Our isolation is a by-product of the moral point of view.

The Real Question

Therefore, we can conclude that it is neither boredom, nor anxiety, nor meaninglessness, nor loneliness, nor deteriorating social relationships that plague us. These are symptoms. More fundamental than these problems is the way we relate to the self, to others, and to reality.

We can see that the fundamental quest is to be fully real. Each vision of living asks the "right" questions. Each vision goes astray not in motive, but in its interpretation of reality. The only genuine difference among visions of living is how they allow us to relate to reality.

The Virtuous Sage: The Life of Excellence

What's left? Isn't there a best way to live? That's what you're asking, isn't it? I have an answer. I think that the life of the virtuous sage is the best life. Let's end our book-long discussion with a short talk about Spinoza and Lao Tsu. I'll leave it to you to work out the details of the virtuous life, and to evaluate it.

Virtue and Morality.   Before I summarize the ideas of these two notable people, I should distinguish virtue and moral goodness for you. Virtue is often misunderstood as moral goodness. A virtuous person is sometimes thought to be someone who follows the moral rules with a special strictness and seriousness. That is not what Spinoza and Lao Tsu mean by virtue. Virtue means excellence. When a thing excels at its given task, it is virtuous. For example, if the pen I am holding is supposed to chop wood, then it isn't excellent. The pen is a pretty poor axe. However, if my intention is to write, then this pen is virtuous.

Excellence in a desired activity determines an object's virtue. Of course, it isn't clear what function or purpose or activity humans are supposed to fulfill. Can't you hear Sartre screaming through the pages from Chapter 10? "No, no, humans choose their essence!" Okay, Jean-Paul, there is no human nature. However, the common concern of each vision of living has been to bring each of us into closer, more intimate contact with our own selves, with other people, and with the rest of reality. The vision that makes possible intimate and intense relating is the one worthy of being called excellent. That's the project for Spinoza and Lao Tsu.

Spinoza and Lao Tsu.   Rather than carrying on a discussion with these two thinkers, I am going to summarize their thinking. I'm doing this for three reasons. First, it lets me show you that they are in agreement about the best life. This is amazing when we consider that they lived at least twenty-two centuries apart, and in culturally different areas of the world. Lao Tsu was a Chinese who lived perhaps twenty-six centuries ago. Spinoza was a Dutch Jew of either Spanish of Portuguese ancestry who lived during the seventeenth century. Lao Tsu's times were marked by feudal war and superstition. Spinoza lived in an era when science was taking hold and blind faith was being replaced with curiosity and knowledge.

Second, summarizing the ideas of these two thinkers places more responsibility on you. Even though I have an interpretation of their ideas, I want to lay the responsibility on you. Read their writings. We are nearly at the end of the book. I am hoping that my summary will tease you into reading on your own and to surpass your "teacher." What follows is only a summary of the virtuous life.

Third, I am asking you to look at this point of view because I think this is the reasonable conclusion of our long discussion. Another way of saying the same thing is that I agree with Spinoza and Lao Tsu, and I'd like you to see what they think.

What Is the Best Life?   Spinoza says that the virtuous person defines the "best" life as the "knowledge of the union existing between the mind and the whole of nature." Lao Tsu's sage's interpretation of the question of the best life is answered by the interaction of the self and reality. The virtuous sage faces the "mysterious abyss" of reality separating the self, others, and reality. However, the virtuous sage seeks neither moral security, nor acceptance, nor sensual pleasures. These are distractions. Instead the virtuous person develops his latent skill of awareness. He develops his reasoning so that he sees reality in an intimate way. As we've just seen, that is what each vision of living is really asking.

The virtuous sage is sensitive to the initial insecurity of his own reality and to the uncertainty of the reality of others. These states are initiated by noting a self-other distinction. He realizes that his loneliness is a symptom of a split between the self, others, and reality. Bridging the separation between the self, others, and reality prevents his sense of being out of touch. Intimately interrelating the self, others, and reality answers the question of the best life.

The Virtues.   What are the recommendations of Spinoza and Lao Tsu? The virtuous vision of living "creates" a self through fully experiencing the self, others, and reality. To be less alone, but uniquely human; to relate to others and to other things in the world in the most intimate human way, with neither expectation nor blind acceptance; to confirm the reality of others and of one's self without distortion; to produce a way of living and of conceiving of reality that guarantees our continued sensitivity to living—these are the elements that we must discover in creating the virtuous vision of living. For the virtuous sage, preparation involves affective and "intuitive" union of self, others, and reality. The sage relates through the virtue(s) of empathic understanding, of active listening, of active noninterference (*wu wei*), and of open and courageous questioning.

The Sage's Picture of Reality.   What is the sage's* picture of reality that produces these effects? On the most fundamental level, the sage rejects thinking in opposites as the moralist thinks. She minimizes any experiential distance in these distinctions. The sage conceives a single, unconditioned reality, a reality that is timelessly eternal, infinite, and indivisible, a reality involving no negation of reality, a reality whose "essence is existence." This undifferentiated reality is the "mother of all things"; it is "the indwelling and not the transient cause of all things." This is Spinoza's active Nature or God (*natura naturans*) and Lao Tse's Tao. (Neither thinker believes the name does justice to "the mystery.")

Beyond the fundamental Nature or God, or Tao, the sage's interpretation of reality becomes more complicated. The sage distinguishes between what Lao Tsu calls "heaven and earth," and what Spinoza calls the attributes of thought and of extension. The sage tentatively categorizes each item of the world as a thinking thing, as a mental item, or as an extended object. In fact, each thing is a subtle "combination" of the two categories. Beyond this primary discrimination, the sage sees individually differentiated objects. Finite pieces of reality are perceived as either part of thought or of extended matter. Either a "thing" is an idea or a material object. This is the conceptual distance she creates as her self-awareness emerges. In conceiving of reality as a set of finite things, as a set of the "ten thousand things," desires emerge. To desire is to see reality by distinguishing subject and object. This creates an experiential distance that must be crossed.

So the sage "suffers" the same initial problem that each other vision suffers. The sage is aware of her self and therefore is experientially distant from others and from reality. She experiences them as Its. Her discriminations make it possible for her to live in the world. Without differentiation, the world would be unacceptably defined as "nothingness." As Buber tells us, however, the conceptual distance requires experiential return.

Intimate Relating.   The virtuous sage's assumptions minimize conceptual distance and effect intimate return. He conceives of each "thing" not only as a part of the whole, but also as a contact point with reality. Each "thing" itself becomes the way to the whole of reality. To the virtuous sage, each "thing" has a being-value— that is, each "thing" mirrors the sage's own reality as he intimately relates with it.

The virtuous sage has no expectations. Grasping the "feel" of natural reality, the

---

*Since the Sage can be male or female, both pronouns will be used interchangeably.

pieces of reality "fall into place" in his understanding. Understanding the process of reality itself, the details of actual movements within reality become understandable. Nothing goes amiss because each event occurs within the necessity of the laws of nature. So the sage is neither overwhelmed by his passions, nor is he subject to the whims of his environment. He successfully creates his own life in such a way that he abides by the flow of Nature. Through intuitive knowledge he comes actively to accept the natural progression of reality. His is a special knowledge of union. Does he agree with the movement of reality? He understands it and knows not to waste his energy in the vain effort of interfering with reality.

"But," you are thinking, "what about social and political activities?" Are we supposed to be passive and just accept whatever the authorities offer? Spinoza and Lao Tsu distinguish reality and the artificial existence of the social and political. They do not ask that you be socially and politically passive. Those institutions can be changed by beliefs and actions. It is only the laws of reality that are unchanging. It is reality, not society, from which we are separated.

Paradoxical Relating. The sage's attitude toward others and toward the world is paradoxical. She is aloof and intimate. She finds that whatever "causes men to live together in harmony is useful," and yet she endorses neither the moral "continuities" nor the search for a meaningful life. Far from the indolence or melancholy of A's failed life of pleasure, Spinoza believes that "mirth cannot be excessive." The intensity of the sage's own existence gives her great pleasure.

Unlike the moralist, she is not future oriented and is therefore neither hopeful nor fearful. She neither overesteems nor disparages. She finds pity useless, even dangerous. Far from being emotionally reserved, however, the sage is compassionate. She can be "ruthless," and "detached" and free of desires while still maintaining an empathy toward others. Though she is not assertive, the sage is neither self-effacing nor repentant, nor does she suffer the "spiritual infirmities" of extreme pride or dejection.

Though she knows that others can be "mirrors" for her it is her and their reality that is most important to her. Her experiencing is intimate and spontaneous.

Spinoza says that the virtuous sage "performs those actions which follow from the necessity of [her] nature considered in itself alone." She is not susceptible to the moral persuasions of humility or guilt, but determines the course of her own actions.

The virtuous sage is not led by fear, nor by sensual pleasure. The sage is not motivated by conceptions of good and evil or of guilt. She forms no conceptions of good or of evil. Even death does not play a role in her living. The sage "thinks of death least of all things; his wisdom is a meditation not of death but of life." What motivates the virtuous sage is her experiential connectedness with her own reality and the reality of others and of the "mysterious abyss."

The sage does not wallow in her momentary passions and lusts. Ever desireless, the sage's "desireless" desires spring not from the "pleasures of a single part(s) of the body." Her wants spring from the commitment that each thing is connected with her in a web of reality. However, she does not deny her intimate feelings and her momentarily present experiences.

Though she experiences with an intensity as extreme as the most extreme plea-sure seeker, the virtuous sage is undisturbed in spirit. She avoids the pitfalls of the pleasure-seeking life. Self-mastery prevents her from becoming the passive playing field of her experiencing and her passions. Her repertoire of emotions shrinks be-cause it is determined by the prospect of relating to reality. This narrowed set of emotions allows her to devote the whole of her concentration to experiencing. Be-cause her emotions are fully informed by and conform to the necessity of her na-ture, and are also informed by her "union" with "the whole of Nature," they never require her to act unfreely. Her actions flow as effortlessly and as thoughtlessly as long grass swaying in the breeze.

Virtues and Freedom

Understanding the limits of concepts, Lao Tsu says, "the [virtuous] sage is guided by what he feels and not by what he sees." Above all, the sage is courageous, actively patient, and yielding (*wu wei*). He is open and quietly attentive. Though he is not an uncritical listener, he does not judge. His freedom consists in actively living according to the necessity of his nature. He does what he must do. However, ne-cessity does not impose the limits on him that the moralist and the pleasure seeker experience from necessity. The virtuous sage's freedom springs from his "intuitive" grasp of his connection with reality. The sage mirrors reality. He lives "in harmony with the order of nature as a whole," Spinoza tells us.

Each Thing Has Existence-Value.   The virtuous person's values are created by his relationship to reality. He values objects and other people not as means, but as things in reality with full and unconditional worth. This intuition is expressed in any number of different ways. Zen poets are fond of speaking of the "lowliest" objects as being part of Zen. "The Zen mind is the everyday mind," they tell us. One does not need to accomplish any great and mysterious task, nor achieve any goal, to experience reality. Intuitive understanding is not a state of mind but an activity. It is an activity of concrete and particular re-union. What is real, not what is good nor what is true, is the pressing concern of the virtuous person.

Freedom.   The virtuous sage does not have conflicting desires. He desires what will happen, but not because it will happen. His freedom is the harmonious coin-cidence of his own desirings, beliefs, and attitudes with what must happen in real-ity. Because he knows the workings of reality, he does not diffuse his desires to what will not be. The sage maintains an extraordinary spontaneity and intensity in expe-riencing. His emotions and beliefs are determined and supported by his project. Because he does not make decisions on the most fundamental level of values, he does not suffer from the anxieties of indecision and of responsibility. And because he does not experience himself as essentially divorced from reality, he does not ex-perience the separation and loneliness at the root of the moralist's drive for a meaningful life. The virtuous sage is intimately and intensely united with "the whole of nature" by his way of conceiving of and relating to nature.

Bridging the Abyss Between the Self and Others.   The virtuous sage recognizes that she is intimately connected with the reality she experiences and in the way she experiences it. Existence itself is a value. The virtuous sage conceives of and experiences reality with intensity and intimacy, and with full subjectivity. Yet the radical subjectivity of the virtuous sage does not separate the self and the other. Her subjectivity and intensity in experiencing are grounded in her own "pleasure" *and* in the intrinsic value of the other.

The self is recreated continually in just the form that it relates to the other. She does not separate the I and the Thou. The virtuous sage is at once selfish and selfless. The self dissolves (without loss of self) because the self-other distinction is blurred and finally "lost" altogether. Love for the sage is the extension of the boundaries of the self to include the other person or thing as fully real.

Therefore, the virtuous sage experiences the reality of herself in experiencing the reality of the other. With the self-other dichotomy dissolved, the tear between self and other is finally mended. The sage maintains a self-other differentiation; consciousness requires that. Yet the self-other opposition and confrontation are eliminated. The other is not there for the self. The notion of domination is a purely moral one, not a virtuous one. For the virtuous sage, the self and other become intimately intertwined through openness. The virtuous sage relates so that "subject" and "object" become more real together.

Freedom and Virtue

To finish our closing summary of the best life, let me say something about freedom. We can describe the freedom of the pleasure seeker as a freedom of doing what one wants to do—or, more accurately, of doing what one "most" wants to do. Moral freedom is a freedom of doing what is most "important" to one to do, what one ought to do.

The freedom of the virtuous sage is a freedom of necessity. What's that? To be free is to be self-creating and recreating at each moment. The freedom of the virtuous sage does not consist of doing what he wants to do, nor of doing what he wants to want to do, nor of doing what he is supposed to want to do. The freedom of the virtuous sage is an harmonious coincidence of beliefs and desires with the necessity of reality. The freedom of the virtuous sage involves what Spinoza describes as the knowledge that "nothing in the universe is contingent, but all things are conditioned to exist and operate in a particular manner by the necessity of [divine] nature." The virtuous sage understands that being free is acting according to the laws of nature. Following Epictetus, the sage "demands not that events happen as [he] wishes; but [he] wishes them to happen as they do happen."

The virtuous sage's beliefs and desires coincide with the necessary laws of reality in an important way. The coincidence of beliefs and desires with the necessary laws of nature is neither causal nor contrived. If the coincidence were caused by reality, this would be resignation or submission. Yet the sage believes and desires, but not *because* of the necessity of reality. He believes and he desires, and these beliefs and desires "coincidently" reflect the necessity of reality. How does he manage that? By knowing reality, he intuitively joins reality.

Ultimately, a "new" way of experiencing emerges. The whole of the virtuous sage's consciousness is submerged into his experiencing. His grasp of the necessity of reality narrows the range of emotions necessary for relating to reality. Because the sage has limited the repertoire of desires, emotions, and beliefs, the intensity of each emotion is increased; the sage's limited emotional energy becomes concentrated.

The virtuous sage's grasp of the self, of others, and of reality creates a reemphasis on many of our underdeveloped talents. The virtuous sage identifies and masters himself. To be his own author, to be self-created and recreated, the virtuous sage must be aware of his own nature.

The Virtues

Being "self-knowing" is essential for being free, but it is not enough. The sage must answer the questions placed before each vision of living. The sage must also connect with others and with reality. He must be an active listener and questioner of himself and of others. He must cultivate the underdeveloped abilities of listening beyond the words that are spoken. That's why, according to Buber, for the virtuous sage there are no lies, only hidden and unrevealed truths. The virtuous sage skillfully understands others.

He is intuitively aware of the whole of nature. For the virtuous sage, being free and being virtuous are one and the same. Spinoza says, "blessedness [freedom] is not the reward of virtue, but virtue itself." In the clarity and lucidity of an open mind, the virtuous sage possesses "true acquiescence of spirit." The "way" to being free is by being open, courageous, self-knowing, actively noninterfering (*wu wei*), "quietly" creating, actively listening, intuitively and affectively questioning.

The virtuous sage's way of living is not beyond our grasp; it is available to each of us. It involves an improved asking of the question of the best life. According to Spinoza and Lao Tsu, the virtuous sage lives the best life by "simply" being in the world.

Summary of Discussion

This discussion is the culmination of our entire search. Like you, the virtuous sage has examined the life of living for the moment, and the moral life. The virtuous sage realizes that the goals of these two approaches to living are misdirected. Each way of stating these goals, however, reveals the genuine question underlying them. When we want to avoid boredom, and the anxieties of indecision and responsibility, we are really asking to find a way to relate intimately to reality. Put another way, the searches for intense pleasure and for moral security and control are merely attempts to experience oneself as real. The virtuous sage builds on this better understanding of the basic question, "What is the best life?"

The best life must be more than a set of goals or values. It must involve an entire undistorted understanding of reality. The sage discovers herself in relating to reality. The virtuous sage knows that defining things according to categories distances her from the things in reality. Therefore, she uses distinctions only when necessary, always recognizing the distorting feature of this way of thinking. Ultimately, the sage recognizes that each thing in reality, not only each person, has an existence-value. It is valuable simply because it exists.

Virtuous freedom finally resolves inner conflicts and outer domination. The sage desires what happens, but not because it happens. Virtuous freedom is the harmonious coincidence of desires, beliefs, and attitudes with what must happen in reality. We found that with Epictetus freedom is not choice, but knowledge. The virtuous sage improves on this by replacing knowledge with understanding. The sage understands and agrees with the way reality unfolds. The virtuous sage experiences the reality of himself or herself in experiencing the reality of the other.

The result of this virtuous, free way of relating is that the abyss between the self and the other person or thing is bridged. The self-other opposition and confrontation is dissolved. "Subject" and "object" become more real together.

The virtuous "way" is to be open, courageous, self-knowing, actively noninterfering, quietly creating, actively listening, intuitively and affectively questioning.

Discussion Highlights

  I. The basic questions in living are living to avoid
     1. boredom.
     2. decisions.
     3. responsibility.
  II. Morality fails to work because it misunderstands the basic question of living.
  III. The real question is: How do I know and relate to
     1. the self.
     2. others.
     3. reality.
  IV. The virtuous sage's way of living
     1. demonstrates the necessity of the virtues.
     2. pictures reality in varying degree of accuracy.
     3. produces intimate relating.
     4. integrates the virtues and freedom.

Questions for Thought/Paper Topics

  1. What are the basic questions in living? Do these translate into the question, "What is the best life?"

2. What is the argument that morality doesn't work? Do you agree?
3. The virtuous life presented by Lao Tsu and Spinoza directly confronts the problem of intimately relating to the self, others, and reality? Is this the "real question"?
4. Describe how the virtues are derived. Think back over the strengths of the other theories we have examined. Does the virtuous life incorporate these strengths?
5. How does the sage's "picture" of reality fit in with a theory of correct living? Does Buber's analysis of the I-Thou attitude apply?
6. What is the connection between the virtues and freedom? Do Spinoza and Lao Tsu offer an acceptable notion of freedom?
7. This question is easy! What is the best life?

For Further Reading

Since our two subjects are Spinoza and Lao Tsu, it is only courtesy to read their chief works. Spinoza's *Ethics* is part of a volume entitled *On the Improvement of the Understanding: The Ethics* (Dover, 1955). Lao Tsu's *Tao Te Ching* (Random House, 1972) has been translated by a number of capable people. Because ancient Chinese is vague, it's instructive to get several translations to see what you can make of his ideas. A helpful little book that merits your attention is Stuart Hampshire's *Spinoza* (Penguin, 1951). Hampshire does a good job clarifying and organizing Spinoza's thoughts into digestible bites. For a secondary source on taoism, Lao Tsu's philosophical school, I suggest two books. Raymond Smullyan's *The Tao Is Silent* (Harper & Row, 1977) is a truly wonderful introduction to taoism. A more sophisticated work is Chang Chung-yuan's *Creativity and Taoism* (Harper & Row, 1963).

Nicomachean Ethics

ARISTOTLE

In this selection Aristotle discusses happiness as well as the virtues of the body and of the intellect. He calls the virtues of the body moral virtues and says that these virtues can be described as a mean between two more dramatic extremes. A moral virtue lies between two driving passions. We can understand battlefield courage, for example, as a mean between the extreme passions of cowardice and foolhardiness. One impulse is to run from the enemy, another is to foolishly charge the enemy; neither response is appropriate. More appropriately, a soldier should engage the enemy at the right time, in the right way, and with the right motives. Neither fear nor desire for fame should be the motivating factor. What lies between these two extremes? Courage.

Aristotle analyzes a number of moral virtues, and in almost every case the virtue can be understood as a mean between two extremes. Be careful, though. Aristotle does not argue that this is a hard and fast rule. It does no good, for example, to argue that one's desire to murder ten people and one's contrary desire not to murder at all indicate that murdering five people is virtuous. In the case of murder, the mean is not appropriate; some actions are simply wrong. Aristotle's moral virtues have more to do with character traits than with arithmetic average.

When it comes to intellectual virtues, however, Aristotle believes the extreme *is* desirable. There are different types of knowledge, and Aristotle urges us to develop our understanding of our own self, of other people, and of reality using the appropriate type of knowledge. Carefully examine each type of knowledge. Do you see a connection between Aristotle's approach to the best life and that of Spinoza and Lao Tsu?

Book I

EVERY ART AND EVERY INQUIRY, and similarly every action and pursuit, is thought to aim at some good; and for this reason the good has rightly been declared to be that at which all things aim. But a certain difference is found among ends; some are activities, others are products apart from the activities that produce them. Where there are ends apart from the actions, it is the nature of the products to be better than the activities. Now, as there are many actions, arts, and sciences, their ends also are many; the end of the medical art is health, that of ship-building a vessel, that of strategy victory, that of economics wealth. But where such arts fall under a single capacity—as bridlemaking and the other arts concerned with the equipment of horses fall under the art of riding, and this and every military action under strategy, in the same way other arts fall under yet others—in all of these the ends of the master arts are to be preferred to all the subordinate ends; for it is for the

sake of the former that the latter are pursued. It makes no difference whether the activities themselves are the ends of the actions, or something else apart from the activities, as in the case of the sciences just mentioned.

If, then, there is some end of the things we do, which we desire for its own sake (everything else being desired for the sake of this), and if we do not choose everything for the sake of something else (for at that rate the process would go on to infinity, so that our desire would be empty and vain), clearly this must be the good and the chief good. Will not the knowledge of it, then, have a great influence on life? Shall we not, like archers who have a mark to aim at, be more likely to hit upon what is right? If so, we must try, in outline at least, to determine what it is, and of which of the sciences or capacities it is the object. It would seem to belong to the most authoritative art and that which is most truly the

Reprinted from Aristotle's *Nicomachean Ethics* translated by W. D. Ross (1925) by permission of Oxford University Press.

master art. And politics appears to be of this nature; for it is this that ordains which of the sciences should be studied in a state, and which each class of citizens should learn and up to what point they should learn them; and we see even the most highly esteemed of capacities to fall under this, e.g. strategy, economics, rhetoric; now, since politics uses the rest of the sciences, and since, again, it legislates as to what we are to do and what we are to abstain from, the end of this science must include those of the others, so that this end must be the good for man. For even if the end is the same for a single man and for a state, that of the state seems at all events something greater and more complete whether to attain or to preserve; though it is worthwhile to attain the end merely for one man, it is finer and more godlike to attain it for a nation or for city-states. These, then, are the ends at which our inquiry aims, since it is political science, in one sense of that term.

Our discussion will be adequate if it has as much clearness as the subject-matter admits of, for precision is not to be sought for alike in all discussions, any more than in all the products of the crafts. Now fine and just actions, which political science investigates, admit of much variety and fluctuation of opinion, so that they may be thought to exist only by convention, and not by nature. And goods also give rise to a similar fluctuation because they bring harm to many people; for before now men have been undone by reason of their wealth, and others by reason of their courage. We must be content, then, in speaking of such subjects and with such premisses to indicate the truth roughly and in outline, and in speaking about things which are only for the most part true and with premisses of the same kind to reach conclusions that are no better. In the same spirit, therefore, should each type of statement be *received;* for it is the mark of an educated man to look for precision in each class of things just so far as the nature of the subject admits; it is evidently equally foolish to accept probable reasoning from a mathematician and to demand from a rhetorician scientific proofs.

Now each man judges well the things he knows, and of these he is a good judge. And so the man who has been educated in a subject is a good judge of that subject, and the man who has received an all-round education is a good judge in general. Hence a young man is not a proper hearer of lectures on political science; for he is inexperienced in the actions that occur in life, but its discussions start from these and are about these; and, further, since he tends to follow his passions, his study will be vain and unprofitable, because the end aimed at is not knowledge but action. And it makes no difference whether he is young in years or youthful in character; the defect does not depend on time, but on his living, and pursuing each successive object, as passion directs. For to such persons, as to the incontinent, knowledge brings no profit; but to those who desire and act in accordance with a rational principle knowledge about such matters will be of great benefit.

These remarks about the student, the sort of treatment to be expected, and the purpose of the inquiry, may be taken as our preface.

Let us resume our inquiry and state, in view of the fact that all knowledge and every pursuit aims at some good, what it is that we say political science aims at and what is the highest of all goods achievable by action. Verbally there is very general agreement; for both the general run of men and people of superior refinement say that it is happiness, and identify living well and doing well with being happy; but with regard to what happiness is they differ, and the many do not give the same account as the wise. For the former think it is some plain and obvious thing, like pleasure, wealth, or honour; they differ, however, from one another—and often even the same man identifies it with different things, with health when he is ill, with wealth when he is poor; but, conscious of their ignorance, they admire those who proclaim some great ideal that is above their comprehension. Now some thought that apart from these many goods there is another which is self-subsistent and causes the goodness of all these as well. To examine all the opinions that have been held were perhaps somewhat fruitless; enough to examine those that are most prevalent or that seem to be arguable. . . .

Let us, however, resume our discussion from the point at which we digressed. To judge from the lives that men lead, most men, and men of the most vulgar type, seem (not without some ground) to identify the good, or happiness, with pleasure; which is the reason why they love the life of enjoyment. For there are, we may say, three prominent types of life—that just mentioned, the political, and thirdly the contemplative life. Now the mass of mankind are evidently quite slavish in their tastes, preferring a life suitable to beasts, but they get some ground for their view from the fact that many of those in high places share the tastes of Sardanapallus. A consideration of the prominent types of life shows that people of superior refinement and of active disposition identify happiness with honour; for this is, roughly speaking, the end of the political life. But it seems too superficial to be what we are looking for, since it is thought to depend on those who bestow honour rather than on him who receives it, but the good we divine to be something proper to a man and not easily taken from him. Further, men seem to pursue honour in order that they may be assured of their goodness; at least it is by men of practical wisdom that they seek to be honoured, and among those who know them, and on the ground of their virtue; clearly, then, according to them, at any rate, virtue is better. And perhaps one might even suppose this to be, rather than honour, the end of the political life. But even this appears somewhat incomplete; for possession of virtue seems actually compatible with being asleep, or with life-long inactivity, and, further, with the greatest sufferings and misfortunes; but a man who was living so no one would call happy, unless he were maintaining a thesis at all costs. But enough of this; for the subject has been sufficiently treated even in the current discussions. Third comes the contemplative life, which we shall consider later.

The life of money-making is one undertaken under compulsion, and wealth is evidently not the good we are seeking; for it is merely useful and for the sake of something else. And so one might rather take the aforenamed objects to be ends; for they are loved for themselves. But it is evident that not even these are ends; yet many arguments have been thrown away in support of them. Let us leave this subject, then. . . .

Let us again return to the good we are seeking, and ask what it can be. It seems different in different actions and arts; it is different in medicine, in strategy, and in the other arts likewise. What then is the good of each? Surely that for whose sake everything else is done. In medicine this is health, in strategy victory, in architecture a house, in any other sphere something else, and in every action and pursuit the end; for it is for the sake of this that all men do whatever else they do. Therefore, if there is an end for all that we do, this will be the good achievable by action, and if there are more than one, these will be the goods achievable by action.

So the argument has by a different course reached the same point; but we must try to state this even more clearly. Since there are evidently more than one end, and we choose some of these (e.g. wealth, flutes, and in general instruments) for the sake of something else, clearly not all ends are final ends; but the chief good is evidently something final. Therefore, if there is only one final end, this will be what we are seeking, and if there are more than one, the most final of these will be what we are seeking. Now we call that which is in itself worthy of pursuit more final than that which is worthy of pursuit for the sake of something else, and that which is never desirable for the sake of something else more final than the things that are desirable both in themselves and for the sake of that other thing, and therefore we call final without qualification that which is always desirable in itself and never for the sake of something else.

Now such a thing happiness, above all else, is held to be; for this we choose always for itself and never for the sake of something else, but honour, pleasure, reason, and every virtue we choose indeed for themselves (for if nothing resulted from them we should still choose each of them), but we choose them also for the sake of happiness, judging that by means of them we shall be happy. Happiness, on the other hand, no one chooses for the sake of these, nor, in general, for anything other than itself.

From the point of view of self-sufficiency the same result seems to follow; for the final good is thought to be self-sufficient. Now by self-sufficient we do not mean that which is sufficient for a man by himself, for one who lives a solitary life, but also for parents, children, wife, and in general for his friends and fellow citizens, since man is born for citizenship. But some limit must be set to this; for if we extend our requirement to ancestors and descendants and friends' friends we are in for an infinite series. Let us examine this question, however, on another occasion; the self-sufficient we now define as that which when isolated makes life desirable and lacking in nothing; and such we think happiness to be; and further we think it most desirable of all things, without being counted as one good thing among others—if it were so counted it would clearly be made more desirable by the addition of even the least of goods; for that which is added becomes an excess of goods, and of goods the greater is always more desirable. Happiness, then, is something final and self-sufficent, and is the end of action.

Presumably, however, to say that happiness is the chief good seems a platitude, and a clearer account of what it is is still desired. This might perhaps be given, if we could first ascertain the function of man. For just as for a flute-player, a sculptor, or any artist, and, in general, for all things that have a function or activity, the good and the "well" is thought to reside in the function, so would it seem to be for man, if he has a function. Have the carpenter, then, and the tanner certain functions or activities, and has man none? Is he born without a function? Or as eye, hand, foot, and in general each of the parts evidently has a function, may one lay it down that man similarly has a function apart from all these? What then can this be? Life seems to be common even to plants, but we are seeking what is peculiar to man. Let us exclude, therefore, the life of nutrition and growth. Next there would be a life of perception, but it also seems to be common even to the horse, the ox, and every animal. There remains, then, an active life of the element that has a rational principle; of this, one part has such a principle in the sense of being obedient to one, the other in the sense of possessing one and exercising thought. And, as "life of the rational element" also has two meanings, we must state that life in the sense of activity is what we mean; for this seems to be the more proper sense of the term. Now if the function of man is an activity of soul which follows or implies a rational principle, and if we say "a so-and-so" and "a good so-and-so" have a function which is the same in kind, e.g. a lyre-player and a good lyre-player, and so without qualification in all cases, eminence in respect of goodness being added to the name of the function (for the function of a lyre-player is to play the lyre, and that of a good lyre-player is to do so well): if this is the case, [and we state the function of man to be a certain kind of life, and this to be an activity or actions of the soul implying a rational principle, and the function of a good man to be the good and noble performance of these, and if any action is well performed when it is performed in accordance with the appropriate excellence: if this is the case,] human good turns out to be activity of soul in accordance with virtue, and if there are more than one virtue, in accordance with the best and most complete.

But we must add "in a complete life." For one swallow does not make a summer, nor does one day; and so too one day, or a short time, does not make a man blessed and happy.

Let this serve as an outline of the good; for

we must presumably first sketch it roughly, and then later fill in the details. But it would seem that any one is capable of carrying on and articulating what has once been well outlined, and that time is a good discoverer or partner in such a work; to which facts the advances of the arts are due; for any one can add what is lacking. And we must also remember what has been said before, and not look for precision in all things alike, but in each class of things such precision as accords with the subject-matter, and so much as is appropriate to the inquiry. For a carpenter and a geometer investigate the right angle in different ways; the former does so in so far as the right angle is useful for his work, while the latter inquires what it is or what sort of thing it is; for he is a spectator of the truth. We must act in the same way, then, in all other matters as well, that our main task may not be subordinated to minor questions. Nor must we demand the cause in all matters alike; it is enough in some cases that the *fact* be well established, as in the case of the first principles; the fact is the primary thing or first principle. Now of first principles we see some by induction, some by perception, some by a certain habituation, and others too in other ways. But each set of principles we must try to investigate in the natural way, and we must take pains to state them definitely, since they have a great influence on what follows. For the beginning is thought to be more than half of the whole, and many of the questions we ask are cleared up by it.

Since happiness is an activity of soul in accordance with perfect virtue, we must consider the nature of virtue; for perhaps we shall thus see better the nature of happiness. . . .

Some things are said about it, adequately enough, even in the discussions outside our school, and we must use these; e.g. that one element in the soul is irrational and one has a rational principle. Whether these are separated as the parts of the body or of anything divisible are, or are distinct by definition but by nature inseparable, like convex and concave in the circumference of a circle, does not affect the present question.

Of the irrational element one division seems to be widely distributed, and vegetative in its nature, I mean that which causes nutrition and growth; for it is this kind of power of the soul that one must assign to all nurslings and to embryos, and this same power to full-grown creatures; this is more reasonable than to assign some different power to them. Now the excellence of this seems to be common to all species and not specifically human; for this part or faculty seems to function most in sleep, while goodness and badness are least manifest in sleep (whence comes the saying that the happy are no better off than the wretched for half their lives; and this happens naturally enough, since sleep is an inactivity of the soul in that respect in which it is called good or bad), unless perhaps to a small extent some of the movements actually penetrate to the soul, and in this respect the dreams of good men are better than those of ordinary people. Enough of this subject, however; let us leave the nutritive faculty alone, since it has by its nature no share in human excellence.

There seems to be also another irrational element in the soul—one which in a sense, however, shares in a rational principle. For we praise the rational principle of the continent man and of the incontinent, and the part of their soul that has such a principle, since it urges them aright and towards the best objects; but there is found in them also another element naturally opposed to the rational principle, which fights against and resists that principle. For exactly as paralysed limbs when we intend to move them to the right turn on the contrary to the left, so is it with the soul; the impulses of incontinent people move in contrary directions. But while in the body we see that which moves astray, in the soul we do not. No doubt, however, we must none the less suppose that in the soul too there is something contrary to the rational principle, resisting and opposing it. In what sense it is distinct from the other elements does not concern us. Now even this seems to have a share in a rational principle, as we said; at any rate in the continent man it obeys the rational principle—and presumably in the temperate and brave man it is still more obedient; for in him it speaks, on all matters, with the same voice as the rational principle.

Therefore the irrational element also appears to be twofold. For the vegetative element in no way shares in a rational principle, but the appetitive and in general the desiring element in a sense shares in it, in so far as it listens to and obeys it; this is the sense in which we speak of "taking account" of one's father or one's friends, not that in which we speak of "accounting" for a mathematical property. That the irrational element is in some sense persuaded by a rational principle is indicated also by the giving of advice and by all reproof and exhortation. And if this element also must be said to have a rational principle, that which has a rational principle (as well as that which has not) will be twofold, one subdivision having it in the strict sense and in itself, and the other having a tendency to obey as one does one's father.

Virtue too is distinguished into kinds in accordance with this difference; for we say that some of the virtues are intellectual and others moral, philosophic wisdom and understanding and practical wisdom being intellectual, liberality and temperance moral. For in speaking about a man's character we do not say that he is wise or has understanding but that he is good-tempered or temperate; yet we praise the wise man also with respect to his state of mind; and of states of mind we call those which merit praise virtues.

Book II

Virtue, then, being of two kinds, intellectual and moral, intellectual virtue in the main owes both its birth and its growth to teaching (for which reason it requires experience and time), while moral virtue comes about as a result of habit,

whence also its name is one that is formed by a slight variation from the word *habit*. From this it is also plain that none of the moral virtues arises in us by nature; for nothing that exists by nature can form a habit contrary to its nature. For instance the stone which by nature moves downwards cannot be habituated to move upwards, not even if one tries to train it by throwing it up ten thousand times; nor can fire be habituated to move downwards, nor can anything else that by nature behaves in one way be trained to behave in another. Neither by nature, then, nor contrary to nature do the virtues arise in us; rather we are adapted by nature to receive them, and are made perfect by habit.

Again, of all the things that come to us by nature we first acquire the potentiality and later exhibit the activity (this is plain in the case of the senses; for it was not by often seeing or often hearing that we got these senses, but on the contrary we had them before we used them, and did not come to have them by using them); but the virtues we get by first exercising them, as also happens in the case of the arts as well. For the things we have to learn before we can do them, we learn by doing them, e.g. men become builders by building and lyre-players by playing the lyre; so too we become just by doing just acts, temperate by doing temperate acts, brave by doing brave acts. . . .

First, then, let us consider this, that it is the nature of such things to be destroyed by defect and excess, as we see in the case of strength and of health (for to gain light on things imperceptible we must use the evidence of sensible things); both excessive and defective exercise destroys the strength, and similarly drink or food which is above or below a certain amount destroys the health, while that which is proportionate both produces and increases and preserves it. So too is it, then, in the case of temperance and courage and the other virtues. For the man who flies from and fears everything and does not stand his ground against anything becomes a coward, and the man who fears nothing at all but goes to meet every danger becomes rash; and similarly the man who indulges in every pleasure and abstains from none becomes self-indulgent, while the man who shuns every pleasure, as boors do, becomes in a way insensible; temperance and courage, then, are destroyed by excess and defect, and preserved by the mean. . . .

We must, however, not only describe virtue as a state of character, but also say what sort of state it is. We may remark, then, that every virtue or excellence both brings into good condition the thing of which it is the excellence and makes the work of that thing be done well; e.g. the excellence of the eye makes both the eye and its work good; for it is by the excellence of the eye that we see well. Similarly the excellence of the horse makes a horse both good in itself and good at running and at carrying its rider and at awaiting the attack of the enemy. Therefore, if this is true in every case, the virtue of man also will be the state of character which makes a man good and which makes him do his own work well.

How this is to happen we have stated already, but it will be made plain also by the following consideration of the specific nature of virtue. In everything that is continuous and divisible it is possible to take more, less, or an equal amount, and that either in terms of the thing itself or relatively to us; and the equal is an intermediate between excess and defect. By the intermediate in the object I mean that which is equidistant from each of the extremes, which is one and the same for all men; by the intermediate relatively to us that which is neither too much nor too little—and this is not one, nor the same for all. For instance, if ten is many and two is few, six is the intermediate, taken in terms of the object; for it exceeds and is exceeded by an equal amount; this is intermediate according to arithmetical proportion. But the intermediate relatively to us is not to be taken so; if ten pounds are too much for a particular person to eat and two too little, it does not follow that the trainer

will order six pounds; for this also is perhaps too much for the person who is to take it, or too little—too little for Milo, too much for the beginner in athletic exercises. The same is true of running and wrestling. Thus a master of any art avoids excess and defect, but seeks the intermediate and chooses this—the intermediate not in the object but relatively to us.

If it is thus, then, that every art does its work well—by looking to the intermediate and judging its works by this standard (so that we often say of good works of art that it is not possible either to take away or to add anything, implying that excess and defect destroy the goodness of works of art, while the mean preserves it; and good artists, as we say, look to this in their work), and if, further, virtue is more exact and better than any art, as nature also is, then virtue must have the quality of aiming at the intermediate. I mean moral virtue; for it is this that is concerned with passions and actions, and in these there is excess, defect, and the intermediate. For instance, both fear and confidence and appetite and anger and pity and in general pleasure and pain may be felt both too much and too little, and in both cases not well; but to feel them at the right times, with reference to the right objects, towards the right people, with the right motive, and in the right way, is what is both intermediate and best, and this is characteristic of virtue. Similarly with regard to actions also there is excess, defect, and the intermediate. Now virtue is concerned with passions and actions, in which excess is a form of failure, and so is defect, while the intermediate is praised and is a form of success; and being praised and being successful are both characteristics of virtue. Therefore virtue is a kind of mean, since, as we have seen, it aims at what is intermediate.

Again, it is possible to fail in many ways (for evil belongs to the class of the unlimited, as the Pythagoreans conjectured, and good to that of the limited), while to succeed is possible only in one way (for which reason also one is easy and the other difficult—to miss the mark easy, to hit it difficult); for these reasons also, then, excess and defect are characteristic of vice, and the mean of virtue;

> For men are good in but one way, but bad in many.

Virtue, then, is a state of character concerned with choice, lying in a mean, i.e. the mean relative to use, this being determined by a rational principle, and by that principle by which the man of practical wisdom would determine it. Now it is a mean between two vices, that which depends on excess and that which depends on defect; and again it is a mean because the vices respectively fall short of or exceed what is right in both passions and actions, while virtue both finds and chooses that which is intermediate. Hence in respect of its substance and the definition which states its essence virtue is a mean, with regard to what is best and right an extreme.

But not every action nor every passion admits of a mean; for some have names that already imply badness, e.g. spite, shamelessness, envy, and in the case of actions adultery, theft, murder; for all of these and suchlike things imply by their names that they are themselves bad, and not the excesses or deficiencies of them. It is not possible, then, ever to be right with regard to them; one must always be wrong. Nor does goodness or badness with regard to such things depend on committing adultery with the right woman, at the right time, and in the right way, but simply to do any of them is to go wrong. It would be equally absurd, then, to expect that in unjust, cowardly, and voluptuous action there should be a mean, an excess, and a deficiency; for at that rate there would be a mean of excess and of deficiency, an excess of excess, and a deficiency of deficiency. But as there is no excess and deficiency of temperance and courage because what is intermediate is in a sense an extreme, so too of the actions we have mentioned there is no mean nor any excess and deficiency, but however they are done they are wrong; for in general there is neither a mean of excess and deficiency, nor excess and deficiency of a mean.

* * *

We must, however, not only make this general statement, but also apply it to the individual facts. For among statements about conduct those which are general apply more widely, but those which are particular are more genuine, since conduct has to do with individual cases, and our statements must harmonize with the facts in these cases. We may take these cases from our table. With regard to feelings of fear and confidence courage is the mean; of the people who exceed, he who exceeds in fearlessness has no name (many of the states have no name), while the man who exceeds in confidence is rash, and he who exceeds in fear and falls short in confidence is a coward. With regard to pleasures and pains—not all of them, and not so much with regard to the pains—the mean is temperance, the excess self-indulgence. Persons deficient with regard to the pleasures are not often found; hence such persons also have received no name. But let us call them "insensible."

With regard to giving and taking of money the mean is liberality, the excess and the defect prodigality and meanness. In these actions people exceed and fall short in contrary ways; the prodigal exceeds in spending and falls short in taking, while the mean man exceeds in taking and falls short in spending. (At present we are giving a mere outline or summary, and are satisfied with this; later these states will be more exactly determined.) With regard to money there are also other dispositions—a mean, magnificence (for the magnificent man differs from the liberal man; the former deals with large sums, the latter with small ones), and excess, tastelessness and vulgarity, and a deficiency, niggardliness; these differ from the states opposed to liberality, and the mode of their difference will be stated later.

With regard to honour and dishonour the mean is proper pride, the excess is known as a sort of "empty vanity," and the deficiency is undue humility; and as we said liberality was related to magnificence, differing from it by dealing with small sums, so there is a state similarly related to proper pride, being concerned with small honours while that is concerned with great. For it is possible to desire honour as one ought, and more than one ought, and less, and the man who exceeds in his desires is called ambitious, the man who falls short unambitious, while the intermediate person has no name. The dispositions also are nameless, except that that of the ambitious man is called ambition. Hence the people who are at the extremes lay claim to the middle place; and we ourselves sometimes call the intermediate person ambitious and sometimes unambitious, and sometimes praise the ambitious man and sometimes the unambitious. The reason of our doing this will be stated in what follows; but now let us speak of the remaining states according to the method which has been indicated.

With regard to anger also there is an excess, a deficiency, and a mean. Although they can scarcely be said to have names, yet since we call the intermediate person good-tempered let us call the mean good temper; of the persons at the extremes let the one who exceeds be called irascible, and his vice irascibility, and the man who falls short an inirascible sort of person, and the deficiency inirascibility. . . .

Book VI

. . . Let it be assumed that the states by virtue of which the soul possesses truth by way of affirmation or denial are five in number, i.e. art, scientific knowledge, practical wisdom, philosophic wisdom, intuitive reason; we do not include judgement and opinion because in these we may be mistaken.

Now what *scientific knowledge* is, if we are to speak exactly and not follow mere similarities, is plain from what follows. We all suppose that what we know is not even capable of being otherwise; of things capable of being otherwise we do not know, when they have passed outside our observation, whether they exist or not. Therefore the object of scientific knowledge is of ne-

cessity. Therefore it is eternal; for things that are of necessity in the unqualified sense are all eternal; and things that are eternal are ungenerated and imperishable. Again, every science is thought to be capable of being taught, and its object of being learned. And all teaching starts from what is already known, as we maintain in the *Analytics* also; for it proceeds sometimes through induction and sometimes by syllogism. Now induction is the starting-point which knowledge even of the universal presupposes, while syllogism proceeds *from* universals. There are therefore starting-points from which syllogism proceeds, which are not reached by syllogism; it is therefore by induction that they are acquired. Scientific knowledge is, then, a state of capacity to demonstrate, and has the other limiting characteristics which we specify in the *Analytics;* for it is when a man believes in a certain way and the starting-points are known to him that he has scientific knowledge, since if they are not better known to him than the conclusion, he will have his knowledge only incidentally.

Let this, then, be taken as our account of scientific knowledge.

In the variable are included both things made and things done; making and acting are different (for their nature we treat even the discussions outside our school as reliable); so that the reasoned state of capacity to act is different from the reasoned state of capacity to make. Hence too they are not included one in the other; for neither is acting making nor is making acting. Now since architecture is an art and is essentially a reasoned state of capacity to make, and there is neither any art that is not such a state nor any such state that is not an art, *art* is identical with a state of capacity to make, involving a true course of reasoning. All art is concerned with coming into being, i.e. with contriving and considering how something may come into being which is capable of either being or not being, and whose origin is in the maker and not in the thing made; for art is concerned neither with things that are, or come into being, by necessity, nor with things that do so in accordance with nature (since these have their origin in themselves). Making and acting being different, art must be a matter of making, not of acting. And in a sense chance and art are concerned with the same objects; as Agathon says, "art loves chance and chance loves art." Art, then, as has been said, is a state concerned with making, involving a true course of reasoning, and lack of art on the contrary is a state concerned with making, involving a false course of reasoning; both are concerned with the variable.

Regarding *practical wisdom* we shall get at the truth by considering who are the persons we credit with it. Now it is thought to be the mark of a man of practical wisdom to be able to deliberate well about what is good and expedient for himself, not in some particular respect, e.g. about what sorts of thing conduce to health or to strength, but about what sorts of thing conduce to the good life in general. This is shown by the fact that we credit men with practical wisdom in some particular respect when they have calculated well with a view to some good end which is one of those that are not the object of any art. It follows that in the general sense also the man who is capable of deliberating has practical wisdom. Now no one deliberates about things that are invariable, nor about things that it is impossible for him to do. Therefore, since scientific knowledge involves demonstration, but there is no demonstration for things whose first principles are variable (for all such things might actually be otherwise), and since it is impossible to deliberate about things that are of necessity, practical wisdom cannot be scientific knowledge nor art; not science because that which can be done is capable of being otherwise, not art because action and making are different kinds of thing. The remaining alternative, then, is that it is a true and reasoned state of capacity to act with regard to the things that are good or bad for man. For while making has an end other than itself, action cannot; for good action itself is its end. It is for this reason that we think Pericles and men like him have practical wisdom, viz. because they can see what is good for themselves and what is good for men in general; we consider that those can do this who are good at managing households or states. (This is why we call temperance by this name; we imply that it preserves one's practical wisdom. Now what it preserves is a judgement of the kind we have described. For it is not any and every judgement that pleasant and painful objects destroy and pervert, e.g. the judgement that the triangle has or has not its angles equal to two right angles, but only judgements about what is to be done. For the originating causes of the things that are done consist in the end at which they are aimed; but the man who has been ruined by pleasure or pain forthwith fails to see any such originating cause—to see that for the sake of this or because of this he ought to choose and do whatever he chooses and does; for vice is destructive of the originating cause of action.)

Practical wisdom, then, must be a reasoned and true state of capacity to act with regard to human goods. But further, while there is such a thing as excellence in art, there is no such thing as excellence in practical wisdom; and in art he who errs willingly is preferable, but in practical wisdom, as in the virtues, he is the reverse. Plainly, then, practical wisdom is a virtue and not an art. There being two parts of the soul that can follow a course of reasoning, it must be the virtue of one of the two, i.e. of that part which forms opinions; for opinion is about the variable and so is practical wisdom. But yet it is not only a reasoned state; this is shown by the fact that a state of that sort may be forgotten but practical wisdom cannot.

Scientific knowledge is judgement about things that are universal and necessary, and the conclusions of demonstration, and all scientific knowledge, follow from first principles (for scientific knowledge involves apprehension of a rational ground). This being so, the first principle from which what is scientifically known follows cannot be an object of scientific knowledge, of art, or of practical wisdom; for that which can be scientifically known can be demonstrated, and art and practical wisdom deal with things that are variable. Nor are these first principles the objects of philosophic wisdom, for it is a mark of the philosopher to have *demonstration* about some things. If, then, the states of mind by which we have truth and are never deceived about things invariable or even variable are scientific knowledge, practical wisdom, philosophic wisdom, and intuitive reason, and it cannot be any of the three (i.e. practical wisdom, scientific knowledge, or philosophic wisdom), the remaining alternative is that it is *intuitive reason* that grasps the first principles.

Wisdom (1) in the arts we ascribe to their most finished exponents, e.g. to Phidias as a sculptor and to Polyclitus as a maker of portrait-statues, and here we mean nothing by wisdom except excellence in art; but (2) we think that some people are wise in general, not in some particular field or in any other limited respect, as Homer says in the *Margites*,

> Him did the gods make neither a digger nor
>   yet a ploughman
> Nor wise in anything else.

Therefore wisdom must plainly be the most finished of the forms of knowledge. It follows that the wise man must not only know what follows from the first principles, but must also possess truth about the first principles. Therefore wisdom must be intuitive reason combined with scientific knowledge—scientific knowledge of the highest objects which has received as it were its proper completion.

Of the highest objects, we say; for it would be strange to think that the art of politics, or practical wisdom, is the best knowledge, since man is not the best thing in the world. Now if what is healthy or good is different for men and for fishes, but what is white or straight is always the same, any one would say that what is wise is the same but what is practically wise is different; for it is to that which observes well the various matters concerning itself that one ascribes practical wisdom, and it is to this that one will entrust such matters. This is why we say that some even of the lower animals have practical wisdom, viz. those which are found to have a power of foresight with regard to their own life. It is evident also that philosophic wisdom and the art of politics cannot be the same; for if the state of mind concerned with a man's own interests is to be called philosophic wisdom, there will be many philosophic wisdoms; there will not be one concerned with the good of all animals (any more than there is one art of medicine for all existing things), but a different philosophic wisdom about the good of each species.

But if the argument be that man is the best of the animals, this makes no difference; for there are other things much more divine in their nature even than man, e.g., most conspicuously, the bodies of which the heavens are framed. From what has been said it is plain, then, that philosophic wisdom is scientific knowledge, combined with intuitive reason, of the things that are highest by nature. This is why we say Anaxagoras, Thales, and men like them have philosophic but not practical wisdom, when we see them ignorant of what is to their own advantage, and why we say that they know things that are remarkable, admirable, difficult, and divine, but useless; viz. because it is not human goods that they seek.

Practical wisdom on the other hand is concerned with things human and things about which it is possible to deliberate; for we say this is above all the work of the man of practical wisdom, to deliberate well, but no one deliberates about things invariable, nor about things which have not an end, and that a good that can be brought about by action. The man who is without qualification good at deliberating is the man who is capable of aiming in accordance with calculation at the best for man of things attainable by action. Nor is practical wisdom concerned with universals only—it must also recognize the particulars; for it is practical, and practice is concerned with particulars. This is why some who do not know, and especially those who have experience, are more practical than others who know; for if a man knew that light meats are digestible and wholesome, but did not know which sorts of meat are light, he would not produce health, but the man who knows that chicken is wholesome is more likely to produce health.

Now practical wisdom is concerned with action; therefore one should have both forms of it, or the latter in preference to the former. But of practical as of philosophic wisdom there must be a controlling kind.

Book X

If happiness is activity in accordance with virtue, it is reasonable that it should be in accordance with the highest virtue; and this will be that of the best thing in us. Whether it be reason or something else that is this element which is thought to be our natural ruler and guide and to take thought of things noble and divine, whether it be itself also divine or only the most divine element in us, the activity of this in accordance with its proper virtue will be perfect happiness. That this activity is contemplative we have already said.

Now this would seem to be in agreement both with what we said before and with the truth. For, firstly, this activity is the best (since not only is reason the best thing in us, but the objects of reason are the best of knowable objects); and, secondly, it is the most continuous, since we can contemplate truth more continuously than we can *do* anything. And we think happiness has pleasure mingled with it, but the activity of philosophic wisdom is admittedly the pleasantest of virtuous activities; at all events the pursuit of it is thought to offer pleasures marvellous for their purity and their enduringness, and it is to be expected that those who know will pass their time more pleasantly than those who inquire. And the self-sufficiency that is spoken of must belong most to the contemplative activity. For while a philosopher, as well as a just man or one possessing any other virtue, needs the necessaries of life, when they are sufficiently equipped with things of that sort the just man needs people towards whom and with

whom he shall act justly, and the temperate man, the brave man, and each of the others is in the same case, but the philosopher, even when by himself, can contemplate truth, and the better the wiser he is; he can perhaps do so better if he has fellow-workers, but still he is the most self-sufficient. And this activity alone would seem to be loved for its own sake; for nothing arises from it apart from the contemplating, while from practical activities we gain more or less apart from the action. And happiness is thought to depend on leisure; for we are busy that we may have leisure, and make war that we may live in peace. Now the activity of the practical virtues is exhibited in political or military affairs, but the actions concerned with these seem to be unleisurely. Warlike actions are completely so (for no one chooses to be at war, or provokes war, for the sake of being at war; any one would seem absolutely murderous if he were to make enemies of his friends in order to bring about battle and slaughter); but the action of the statesman is also unleisurely, and—apart from the political action itself—aims at despotic power and honours, or at all events happiness, for him and his fellow citizens—a happiness different from political action, and evidently sought as being different. So if among virtuous actions political and military actions are distinguished by nobility and greatness, and these are unleisurely and aim at an end and are not desirable for their own sake, but the activity of reason, which is contemplative, seems both to be superior in serious worth and to aim at no end beyond itself, and to have its pleasure proper to itself (and this augments the activity), and the self-sufficiency, leisureliness, unweariedness (so far as this is possible for man), and all the other attributes ascribed to the supremely happy man are evidently those connected with this activity, it follows that this will be the complete happiness of man, if it be allowed a complete term of life (for none of the attributes of happiness is *in*complete).

But such a life would be too high for man; for it is not in so far as he is man that he will live so, but in so far as something divine is present in him; and by so much as this is superior to our composite nature is its activity superior to that which is the exercise of the other kind of virtue. If reason is divine, then, in comparison with man, the life according to it is divine in comparison with human life. But we must not follow those who advise us, being men, to think of human things, and, being mortal, of mortal things, but must, so far as we can, make ourselves immortal, and strain every nerve to live in accordance with the best thing in us; for even if it be small in bulk, much more does it in power and worth surpass everything. This would seem, too, to be each man himself, since it is the authoritative and better part of him. It would be strange, then, if he were to choose not the life of his self but that of something else. And what we said before will apply now; that which is proper to each thing is by nature best and most pleasant for each thing; for man, therefore, the life according to reason is best and pleasantest, since reason more than anything else *is* man. This life therefore is also the happiest.

Part Four

Moral Questions

Introduction

Pᴀʀᴛs ᴛᴡᴏ ᴀɴᴅ ᴛʜʀᴇᴇ offer us a chance to compare our ideas and the thoughts of some certified "important" philosophers. Part Four gives us the opportunity to tackle current applied moral questions. Debate rages in our society over questions of sexual morality, abortion, discrimination and preferential treatment, capital punishment, and treatment of animals and our environment. The readings in this part let us enter into these current debates. I'm sure you have opinions about each of these issues, too. As you read the differing judgments on each issue, keep an open mind to any features of the debate you may not have thought about before your reading.

Sexual Morality

There is little question that sexual morality is a recurring social issue. Our society is once again struggling with questions surrounding the treatment of gays and lesbians. In this context questions of human nature often arise. Is homosexuality unnatural? Are all unnatural preferences and actions immoral just because they are unnatural? Do certain kinds of sexual practices raise the moral questions, or should regard people have for one another and the way they treat each other be our moral concern?

The articles you will find in Chapter 14 start with two competing Supreme Court decisions. Two noted justices, Byron White and Harry A. Blackmun, disagree about the right of people to do what they want to do in private. This discussion is followed by the Vatican's position on human sexuality. Based on its specific views of human nature, the Catholic Church argues that important components are missing in premarital, extramarital, and homosexual relationships. A reply to the Vatican argument about the "unnaturalness" of certain sexual orientations is offered by Burton Leiser, who analyzes the central concept of naturalness. Finally, Sara Ruddick offers ideas to achieve "better sex." Her discussion defines "complete" sex acts and emphasizes that having respect for one's partner(s) and preserving their dignity must be considered in any discussion of sexual morality.

Abortion

The discussion of abortion also begins with a Supreme Court decision. *Roe v. Wade* is the court decision that set the debate in contemporary U.S. society. Representing the majority, Justice Blackmun raises questions of privacy, the mother's health, when life begins, the viability of a fetus, and the potential that the human fetus represents. Representing a minority of the Court, Justice White raises a serious question of whether the Court has exceeded its proper authority even to review this question; instead, he argues, state legislatures should decide the question. Following this debate, John T. Noonan, Jr. suggests reasons for considering a fetus to be fully human and argues that the fetus deserves the same treatment and protection as every other human. Focusing on this concept, Mary Anne Warren distinguishes between a moral and a genetic sense of "human." By including all *people* as members of the moral community, but not all human beings, she makes an interesting distinction that you may want to extend or challenge. Finally, this chapter ends with a discussion by Jane English of the time when abortion may be permissible and when it may be impermissible. English offers several moral analogies to make her case, admitting that a "conclusive answer to the question whether a fetus is a person is unattainable."

Discrimination and Preferential Treatment

Should a student be passed over in the acceptance process and his or her seat given to a member of a traditionally oppressed group? This is the question before Justice Lewis F. Powell, Jr., who raises the issue of relevant criteria for preferring one person to another. How much should "pragmatic political judgments of a particular time and place" be considered by the Court? Does a university have a right to set a diverse student body as a goal? Powell suggests ways that such a goal can and cannot be legitimately attained. Next, Justice William Brennan represents the majority of the Court in discussing how the Civil Rights Act of 1964 applies to private industry. In the following article, Carl Cohen suggests that equal protection under law does not guarantee equal treatment. Commenting on the *University of California v. Bakke* case, Cohen considers whether or not special considerations should be made based on race. His concern is to determine whether or not merit can be maintained while one group is given preference over another in the selection of students and workers. Robert Fullinwider discusses preferential treatment in the context of past injustices. Can a person rightly be held responsible for injustices that he or she had no part in? Lisa Newton completes our brief dialogue on preferential treatment by arguing against minority quotas. She is concerned about the suspension of the merit system and the reinforcement of racial stereotypes.

Capital Punishment

Is the death sentence ever justified? Under what conditions should a person be put to death? Should cost be a factor in deciding the moral acceptability of the death sentence? Are cases of mistaken identity and judicial error enough to cause us to put aside the death penalty? Recall Socrates, who suffered the death penalty for teaching philosophy to the people of Athens. Many others have been put to death for political rather than criminal acts. In light of this fact, should the death penalty ever be imposed?

This chapter begins with another Supreme Court decision. Justices Potter Stewart, Lewis F. Powell, Jr., and John Paul Stevens assert that capital punishment has two primary purposes, deterrence and retribution. In part, the death penalty serves as a deterrent; in part, it responds to society's "moral outrage" over certain actions. For these two reasons, they support the death penalty for certain crimes. In his dissenting opinion, Justice Thurgood Marshall replies that the death sentence is excessive and its purposes are morally unacceptable. The death penalty robs people of their human dignity and worth, Marshall says, and therefore should not be accepted as punishment in this country. Carrying on the debate is Burton Leiser, who argues for some instances that warrant the death penalty; Ernest Van Den Haag, who promotes deterrence as a justification for capital punishment; and Hugo Bedau, who analyzes and challenges Van Den Haag's main contentions.

Animals and the Environment

Chapter 18 examines the possible rights that animals, the environment, and future generations possess. The idea that the environment must be protected is not a new one, but most arguments for protection of the environment assert human interests. It is prudent for us to respect the environment, because not to respect it will lead to undesirable consequences *for us*. Speaking for the minority of the court, Justice William O. Douglas suggests that the environment be appointed spokespeople to represent it. "The voice of the inanimate object . . . should not be stilled."

Martin Benjamin moves our discussion to the rights of animals by examining three standard responses to questions about ethical restrictions on the way humans treat animals. Benjamin shows that further inquiry into the nature and extent of consciousness in nonhuman animals is necessary.

William Godfrey-Smith analyzes four "intrinsic value" attitudes in order to compare the intrinsic value of natural systems with the economic benefits of using these systems. Godfrey-Smith's position is interesting because he argues not that we benefit by respecting nature, but that nature has an intrinsic worth that must be respected by moral people.

This chapter ends with Joel Feinberg's discussion of whether or not inanimate objects can have rights. Moving beyond rocks and plants, Feinberg examines whether or not we should respect the rights of future generations. He analyzes the conceptual confusions he believes have allowed us to deny rights to animals and to future generations and concludes that we ought to acknowledge the rights of members of endangered species, at the least.

14   Sexual Morality

Hᴏᴡ ꜱʜᴏᴜʟᴅ ᴏᴜʀ ꜱᴏᴄɪᴇᴛʏ ᴛʀᴇᴀᴛ ɢᴀʏꜱ ᴀɴᴅ ʟᴇꜱʙɪᴀɴꜱ? Should these people receive different treatment because of sexual orientation? For example, the military traditionally resists the idea of allowing its gay members to acknowledge their sexual orientation openly and publicly. Is the military's position morally justifiable? More than this question about the possible rights and protections that we may give to a "minority" is the question of privacy. Should any person's work and public life be affected at all because of preference of partners for private, intimate relationships?

One argument claims that homosexuality is immoral because it is unnatural. Is this argument compelling? What if we determine, for example, that charity is not a natural human emotion? Charity might be unnatural. After all, we spend a great deal of time and effort in our society promoting charity. If charity were natural, it would not require such efforts. So if charity is *not* natural to humans, does that mean that it is immoral? The same argument can be made for eating broccoli. Just because a person does not "naturally" like broccoli does not mean that broccoli eating is immoral. (By the way, I love eating broccoli and I am not charitable.)

Finally, there is the question of sexual relations between people. Although the readings in Part Four do not focus on this issue, it is relevant to this discussion. Is sexuality the moral question, or is it the treatment and regard one person has for another? Should we care about the identity of a person's sexual partner or how caring and emphatic people are with each other?

Majority Opinion in *Bowers v. Hardwick*

JUSTICE BYRON WHITE

Reading Questions

1. How does Justice White distinguish between the right to view obscene material in the privacy of one's home (*Stanley v. Georgia*) and the right to homosexual conduct in one's home?

2. What other victimless crimes does White argue do not escape the law, even when they are committed within one's home?

... [R]ESPONDENT WOULD HAVE US AN-NOUNCE, as the Court of Appeals did, a fundamental right to engage in homosexual sodomy. This we are quite unwilling to do. It is true that despite the language of the Due Process Clauses of the Fifth and Fourteenth Amendments, which appears to focus only on the processes by which life, liberty, or property is taken, the cases are legion in which those Clauses have been interpreted to have substantive content, subsuming rights that to a great extent are immune from federal or state regulation or proscription. Among such cases are those recognizing rights that have little or no textual support in the constitutional language. . . .

. . . Sodomy was a criminal offense at common law and was forbidden by the laws of the original thirteen States when they ratified the Bill of Rights. In 1868, when the Fourteenth Amendment was ratified, all but 5 of the 37 States in the Union had criminal sodomy laws. In fact, until 1961, all 50 States outlawed sodomy, and today, 24 States and the District of Columbia continue to provide criminal penalties for sodomy performed in private and between consenting adults. . . . Against this background, to claim that a right to engage in such conduct is "deeply rooted in this Nation's history and tradition" or

"implicit in the concept of ordered liberty" is, at best, facetious.

Nor are we inclined to take a more expansive view of our authority to discover new fundamental rights imbedded in the Due Process Clause. The Court is most vulnerable and comes nearest to illegitimacy when it deals with judge-made constitutional law having little or no cognizable roots in the language or design of the Constitution. . . . There should be, therefore, great resistance to expand the substantive reach of those Clauses, particularly if it requires redefining the category of rights deemed to be fundamental. Otherwise, the Judiciary necessarily takes to itself further authority to govern the country without express constitutional authority. The claimed right pressed on us today falls far short of overcoming this resistance.

Respondent, however, asserts that the result should be different where the homosexual conduct occurs in the privacy of the home. He relies on *Stanley v. Georgia,* . . . where the Court held that the First Amendment prevents conviction for possessing and reading obscene material in the privacy of his home. . . .

Stanley did protect conduct that would not have been protected outside the home, and it partially prevented the enforcement of state ob-

United States Supreme Court, 478 U.S. 92 L Ed 2d 140 (1986).

scenity laws; but the decision was firmly grounded in the First Amendment. The right pressed upon us here has no similar support in the text of the Constitution, and it does not qualify for recognition under the prevailing principles for construing the Fourteenth Amendment. Its limits are also difficult to discern. Plainly enough, otherwise illegal conduct is not always immunized whenever it occurs in the home. Victimless crimes, such as the possession and use of illegal drugs, do not escape the law where they are committed at home. *Stanley* itself recognized that its holding offered no protection for the possession in the home of drugs, firearms, or stolen goods. . . . And if respondent's submission is limited to the voluntary sexual conduct between consenting adults, it would be difficult, except by fiat, to limit the claimed right to homosexual conduct while leaving exposed to prosecution adultery, incest, and other sexual crimes even though they are committed in the home. We are unwilling to start down that road.

Even if the conduct at issue here is not a fundamental right, respondent asserts that there must be a rational basis for the law and that there is none in this case other than the presumed belief of a majority of the electorate in Georgia that homosexual sodomy is immoral and unacceptable. This is said to be an inadequate rationale to support the law. The law, however, is constantly based on notions of morality, and if all laws representing essentially moral choices are to be invalidated under the Due Process Clause, the courts will be very busy indeed. Even respondent makes no such claim, but insists that majority sentiments about the morality of homosexuality should be declared inadequate. We do not agree, and are unpersuaded that the sodomy laws of some 25 States should be invalidated on this basis.

Dissenting Opinion in *Bowers v. Hardwick*

JUSTICE HARRY BLACKMUN

Reading Questions

1. How does Justice Blackmun interpret the right that is called into question?
2. How does Blackmun suggest we define ourselves in our complex, diverse society?
3. How does Blackmun's opinion avoid placing all of us under the constraints of traditional Judeo-Christian values?

THIS CASE IS [NOT] ABOUT "a fundamental right to engage in homosexual sodomy," as the Court purports to declare. . . . Rather, this case is about "the most comprehensive of rights and the right most valued by civilized men," namely, "the right to be let alone." . . .

United States Supreme Court, 478 U.S. 92 L Ed 2d 140 (1986).

Only the most willful blindness could obscure the fact that sexual intimacy is "a sensitive, key relationship of human existence, central to family life, community welfare, and the development of human personality," *Paris Adult Theatre I v Slaton*. . . . The fact that individuals define themselves in a significant way through their intimate sexual relationships with other suggests, in a Nation as diverse as ours, that there may be many "right" ways of conducting those relationships, and that much of the richness of a relationship will come from the freedom an individual has to *choose* the form and nature of these intensely personal bonds. . . .

. . . A way of life that is odd or even erratic but interferes with no rights or interests of others is not to be condemned because it is different." . . . The Court claims that its decision today merely refuses to recognize a fundamental right to engage in homosexual sodomy; what the Court really has refused to recognize is the fundamental interest all individuals have in controlling the nature of their intimate associations with others. . . .

The assertion that "traditional Judeo-Christian values proscribe" the conduct involved, Brief for Petitioner 20, cannot provide an adequate justification for § 16-6-2.* That certain, but by no means all, religious groups condemn the behavior at issue gives the State no license to impose their judgments on the entire citizenry. The legitimacy of secular legislation depends instead on whether the State can advance some justification for its law beyond its conformity to religious doctrine. . . . Thus, far from buttressing his case, petitioner's invocation of Leviticus, Romans, St. Thomas Aquinas, and sodomy's heretical status during the Middle Ages undermines his suggestion that § 16-6-2 represents a legitimate use of secular coercive power. A State can no more punish private behavior because of religious intolerance than it can punish such behavior because of racial animus. "The Constitution cannot control such prejudices, but neither can it tolerate them. Private biases may be outside the reach of the law, but the law cannot, directly or indirectly give them effect." . . . No matter how uncomfortable a certain group may make the majority of this Court, we have held that "[m]ere public intolerance or animosity cannot constitutionally justify the deprivation of a person's physical liberty." . . .

Nor can § 16-6-2 be justified as a "morally neutral" exercise of Georgia's power to "protect the public environment." . . . Certainly, some private behavior can affect the fabric of society as a whole. Reasonable people may differ about whether particular sexual acts are moral or immoral, but "we have ample evidence for believing that people will not abandon morality, will not think any better of murder, cruelty and dishonesty, merely because some private sexual practice which they abominate is not punished by the law." . . . Petitioner and the Court fail to see the difference between laws that protect public sensibilities and those that enforce private morality. Statutes banning public sexual activity are entirely consistent with protecting the individual's liberty interest in decisions concerning sexual relations: the same recognition that those decisions are intensely private which justifies protecting them from governmental interference can justify protecting individuals from unwilling exposure to the sexual activities of others. But the mere fact that intimate behavior may be punished when it takes place in public cannot dictate how States can regulate intimate behavior that occurs in intimate places. . . .

This case involves no real interference with the rights of others, for the mere knowledge that other individuals do not adhere to one's value system cannot be a legally cognizable interest, . . . let alone an interest that can justify invading the houses, hearts, and minds of citizens who choose to live their lives differently.

---

*Editor's note: § 16-6-2 refers to the Georgia state law criminalizing sodomy, which is at issue in *Bowers v. Hardwick*.

Vatican Declaration on Some Questions of Sexual Ethics

Reading Questions

1. How does the Vatican opinion use the concepts of human nature and revealed law to rebuff culturally determined behavior?
2. How does the Vatican invalidate premarital, extramarital, and homosexual relationships? What is missing in these relationships that the Vatican views as essential?
3. What is the Vatican position on "incurable" homosexuality?

ACCORDING TO CONTEMPORARY SCIEN-TIFIC research, the human person is so profoundly affected by sexuality that it must be considered as one of the factors which give to each individual's life the principal traits that distinguish it. In fact it is from sex that the human person receives the characteristics which, on the biological, psychological and spiritual levels, make that person a man or a woman, and thereby largely condition his or her progress towards maturity and insertion into society. Hence sexual matters, as is obvious to everyone, today constitute a theme frequently and openly dealt with in books, reviews, magazines, and other means of social communication.

In the present period, the corruption of morals has increased, and one of the most serious indications of this corruption is the unbridled exaltation of sex. Moreover, through the means of social communication and through public entertainment this corruption has reached the point of invading the field of education and of infecting the general mentality.

In this context certain educators, teachers, and moralists have been able to contribute to a better understanding and integration into life of the values proper to each of the sexes; on the other hand there are those who have put forward concepts and modes of behavior which are contrary to the true moral exigencies of the hu-

Issued in Rome by the Sacred Congregation for the Doctrine of the Faith on December 29, 1975.

man person. Some members of the latter group have even gone so far as to favor a licentious hedonism.

As a result, in the course of a few years, teachings, moral criteria, and modes of living hitherto faithfully preserved have been very much unsettled, even among Christians. There are many people today who, being confronted with so many widespread opinions opposed to the teachings which they received from the Church, have come to wonder what they must still hold as true.

The Church cannot remain indifferent to this confusion of minds and relaxation of morals. It is a question, in fact, of a matter which is of the utmost importance both for the personal lives of Christians and for the social life of our time.

The Bishops are daily led to note the growing difficulties experienced by the faithful in obtaining knowledge of wholesome moral teaching, especially in sexual matters, and of the growing difficulties experienced by pastors in expounding this teaching effectively. The Bishops know that by their pastoral charge they are called upon to meet the needs of their faithful in this very serious matter, and important documents dealing with it have already been published by some of them or by Episcopal Conferences. Nevertheless, since the erroneous opinions and resulting deviations are continuing to spread everywhere, the Sacred Congregation for the Doctrine of the Faith, by virtue of its function in the universal Church and by a mandate of the Supreme Pontiff, has judged it necessary to publish the present Declaration.

The people of our time are more and more convinced that the human person's dignity and vocation demand that they should discover, by the light of their own intelligence, the values innate in their nature, that they should ceaselessly develop these values and realize them in their lives, in order to achieve an ever greater development.

In moral matters man cannot make value judgments according to his personal whim: "In the depths of his conscience, man detects a law which he does not impose on himself, but which holds him to obedience. . . . For man has in his heart a law written by God. To obey it is the very dignity of man; according to it he will be judged."

Moreover, through his revelation God has made known to us Christians his plan of salvation, and he has held up to us Christ, the Savior and Sanctifier, in his teaching and example, as the supreme and immutable law of life: "I am the light of the world; anyone who follows me will not be walking in the dark, he will have the light of life."

Therefore there can be no true promotion of man's dignity unless the essential order of his nature is respected. Of course, in the history of civilization many of the concrete conditions and needs of human life have changed and will continue to change. But all evolution of morals and every type of life must be kept within the limits imposed by the immutable principles based upon every human person's constitutive elements and essential relations—elements and relations which transcend historical contingency.

These fundamental principles, which can be grasped by reason, are contained in "the divine law—eternal, objective, and universal—whereby God orders, directs, and governs the entire universe and all the ways of the human community, by a plan conceived in wisdom and love. Man has been made by God to participate in this law, with the result that, under the gentle disposition of divine Providence, he can come to perceive ever increasingly the unchanging truth." This divine law is accessible to our minds.

Hence, those many people are in error who today assert that one can find neither in human nature nor in the revealed law any absolute and immutable norm to serve for particular actions other than the one which expresses itself in the general law of charity and respect for human dignity. As a proof of their assertion they put forward the view that so-called norms of the natural law or precepts of Sacred Scripture are to be regarded only as given expressions of a form of particular culture at a certain moment of history.

But in fact, divine Revelation and, in its own proper order, philosophical wisdom, emphasize the authentic exigencies of human nature. They thereby necessarily manifest the existence of immutable laws inscribed in the constitutive elements of human nature and which are revealed to be identical in all beings endowed with reason.

Furthermore, Christ instituted his Church as "the pillar and bulwark of truth." With the Holy Spirit's assistance, she ceaselessly preserves and transmits without error the truths of the moral order, and she authentically interprets not only the revealed positive law but "also . . . those principles of the moral order which have their origin in human nature itself" and which concern man's full development and sanctification. Now in fact the Church throughout her history has always considered a certain number of precepts of the natural law as having an absolute and immutable value, and in their transgression she has seen a contradiction of the teaching and spirit of the Gospel.

Since sexual ethics concern certain fundamental values of human and Christian life, this general teaching equally applies to sexual ethics. In this domain there exist principles and norms which the Church has always unhesitatingly transmitted as part of her teaching, however much the opinions and morals of the world may have been opposed to them. These principles and norms in no way owe their origin to a certain type of culture, but rather to knowledge of the divine law and of human nature. They therefore cannot be considered as having become out of date or doubtful under the pretext that a new cultural situation has arisen.

It is these principles which inspired the exhortations and directives given by the Second Vatican Council for an education and an organization of social life taking account of the equal dignity of man and woman while respecting their difference.

Speaking of "the sexual nature of man and the human faculty of procreation," the Council noted that they "wonderfully exceed the dispositions of lower forms of life." It then took particular care to expound the principles and criteria which concern human sexuality in marriage, and which are based upon the finality of the specific function of sexuality.

In this regard the Council declares that the moral goodness of the acts proper to conjugal life, acts which are ordered according to true human dignity, "does not depend solely on sincere intentions or on an evaluation of motives. It must be determined by objective standards. These, based on the nature of the human person and his acts, preserve the full sense of mutual self-giving and human procreation in the context of true love."

These final words briefly sum up the Council's teaching—more fully expounded in an earlier part of the same Constitution—on the finality of the sexual act and on the principal criterion of its morality: it is respect for its finality that ensures the moral goodness of this act.

This same principle, which the Church holds from divine Revelation and from her authentic interpretation of the natural law, is also the basis of her traditional doctrine, which states that the use of the sexual function has its true meaning and moral rectitude only in true marriage.

It is not the purpose of the present declaration to deal with all the abuses of the sexual faculty, nor with all the elements involved in the practice of chastity. Its object is rather to repeat the Church's doctrine on certain particular points, in view of the urgent need to oppose serious errors and widespread aberrant modes of behavior.

Today there are many who vindicate the right to sexual union before marriage, at least in those cases where a firm intention to marry and an affection which is already in some way conjugal in the psychology of the subjects require this completion, which they judge to be connatural. This is especially the case when the celebration of the marriage is impeded by circumstances or when this intimate relationship seems necessary in order for love to be preserved.

This opinion is contrary to Christian doctrine, which states that every genital act must be within the framework of marriage. However firm the intention of those who practice such premature sexual relations may be, the fact remains that these relations cannot ensure, in sincerity and fidelity, the interpersonal relationship between a man and a woman, nor especially can they protect this relationship from whims and caprices. Now it is a stable union that Jesus willed, and he restored its original requirement, beginning with the sexual difference. "Have you not read that the creator from the beginning made them male and female and that he said: This is why a man must leave father and mother, and cling to his wife, and the two become one body? They are no longer two, therefore, but one body. So then, what God has united, man must not divide." Saint Paul will be even more explicit when he shows that if unmarried people or widows cannot live chastely they have no other alternative than the stable union of marriage: ". . . it is better to marry than to be aflame with passion." Through marriage, in fact, the love of married people is taken up into that love which Christ irrevocably has for the Church, while dissolute sexual union defiles the temple of the Holy Spirit which the Christian has become. Sexual union therefore is only legitimate if a definitive community of life has been established between the man and the woman.

This is what the Church has always understood and taught, and she finds a profound agreement with her doctrine in men's reflection and in the lessons of history.

Experience teaches us that love must find its safeguard in the stability of marriage, if sexual intercourse is truly to respond to the requirements of its own finality and to those of human dignity. The requirements call for a conjugal contract sanctioned and guaranteed by society—a contract which establishes a state of life of capital importance both for the exclusive union of the man and the woman and for the good of their family and of the human community. Most often, in fact, premarital relations exclude the possibility of children. What is represented to be conjugal love is not able, as it absolutely should be, to develop into paternal and maternal love. Or, if it does happen to do so, this will be to the detriment of the children, who will be deprived of the stable environment in which they ought to develop in order to find in it the way and the means of their insertion into society as a whole.

The consent given by people who wish to be united in marriage must therefore be manifested externally and in a manner which makes it valid in the eyes of society. As far as the faithful are concerned, their consent to the setting up of a community of conjugal life must be expressed according to the laws of the Church. It is a consent which makes their marriage a Sacrament of Christ.

At the present time there are those who, basing themselves on observations in the psychological order, have begun to judge indulgently, and even to excuse completely, homosexual relations between certain people. This they do in opposition to the constant teaching of the Magisterium and to the moral sense of the Christian people.

A distinction is drawn, and it seems with some reason, between homosexuals whose tendency comes from a false education, from a lack of normal sexual development, from habit, from bad example, or from other similar causes, and is transitory or at least not incurable; and homosexuals who are definitively such because of some kind of innate instinct or a pathological constitution judged to be incurable.

In regard to this second category of subjects, some people conclude that their tendency is so natural that it justifies in their case homosexual relations within a sincere communion of life and love analogous to marriage insofar as such homosexuals feel incapable of enduring a solitary life.

In the pastoral field, these homosexuals must certainly be treated with understanding and sustained in the hope of overcoming their personal difficulties and their inability to fit into society. Their culpability will be judged with prudence. But no pastoral method can be employed which would given moral justification to these acts on the grounds that they would be consonant with the condition of such people. For according to the objective moral order, homosexual relations are acts which lack an essential and indispensable finality. In Sacred Scripture they are condemned as a serious depravity and even presented as the sad consequence of rejecting God. This judgment of Scripture does not of course permit us to conclude that all those who suffer from this anomaly are personally responsible for it, but it does attest to the fact that homosexual acts are intrinsically disordered and can in no case be approved.

The traditional Catholic doctrine that masturbation constitutes a grave moral disorder is often called into doubt or expressly denied today. It is said that psychology and sociology show that it is a normal phenomenon of sexual development, especially among the young. It is stated that there is real and serious fault only in the measure that the subject deliberately indulges in solitary pleasure closed in on self ("ipsation"), because in this case the act would indeed be radically opposed to the loving communion between persons of different sex which some hold is what is principally sought in the use of the sexual faculty.

This opinion is contradictory to the teaching and pastoral practice of the Catholic Church. Whatever the force of certain arguments of a biological and philosophical nature, which have sometimes been used by theologians, in fact both the Magisterium of the Church—in the course of a constant tradition—and the moral sense of the faithful have declared without hesitation that masturbation is an intrinsically and

seriously disordered act. The main reason is that, whatever the motive for acting in this way, the deliberate use of the sexual faculty outside normal conjugal relations essentially contradicts the finality of the faculty. For it lacks the sexual relationship called for by the moral order, namely the relationship which realizes "the full sense of mutual self-giving and human procreation in the context of true love." All deliberate exercise of sexuality must be reserved to this regular relationship. Even if it cannot be proved that Scripture condemns this sin by name, the tradition of the Church has rightly understood it to be condemned in the New Testament when the latter speaks of "impurity," "unchasteness," and other vices contrary to chastity and continence.

Sociological surveys are able to show the frequency of this disorder according to the places, populations, or circumstances studied. In this way facts are discovered, but facts do not constitute a criterion for judging the moral value of human acts. The frequency of the phenomenon in question is certainly to be linked with man's innate weakness following original sin; but it is also to be linked with the loss of a sense of God, with the corruption of morals engendered by the commercialization of vice, with the unrestrained licentiousness of so many public entertainments and publications, as well as with the neglect of modesty, which is the guardian of chastity.

On the subject of masturbation modern psychology provides much valid and useful information for formulating a more equitable judgment on moral responsibility and for orienting pastoral action. Psychology helps one to see how the immaturity of adolescence (which can sometimes persist after that age), psychological imbalance, or habit can influence behavior, diminishing the deliberate character of the act and bringing about a situation whereby subjectively there may not always be serious fault. But in general, the absence of serious responsibility must not be presumed; this would be to misunderstand people's moral capacity.

In the pastoral ministry, in order to form an adequate judgment in concrete cases, the habitual behavior of people will be considered in its totality, not only with regard to the individual's practice of charity and of justice but also with regard to the individual's care in observing the particular precepts of chastity. In particular, one will have to examine whether the individual is using the necessary means, both natural and supernatural, which Christian asceticism from its long experience recommends for overcoming the passions and progressing in virtue. . . .

For Further Thought and Discussion

1. Would society be improved if no one engages in premarital, extramarital, or homosexual relations? How?
2. Do you agree with the Vatican view of human nature?

Homosexuality and the "Unnaturalness Argument"

BURTON M. LEISER

Reading Questions

1. What are the two senses of "natural," or the "law of nature"?
2. Give an example for the descriptive sense and for the prescriptive sense of a law.
3. How does Leiser argue against the "unnaturalness claim" when "unnatural" means artificial?
4. What is the analysis of the "proper function" argument? Do sex organs have a proper function?
5. How does Leiser understand the equation "natural = good?"

[THE ALLEGED "UNNATURALNESS" OF HOMOSEXUALITY] raises the question of the meaning of *nature, natural,* and similar terms. Theologians and other moralists have said that [homosexual acts] violate the "natural law," and that they are therefore immoral and ought to be prohibited by the state.

The word *nature* has a built-in ambiguity that can lead to serious misunderstandings. When something is said to be "natural" or in conformity with "natural law" or the "law of nature," this may mean either (1) that it is in conformity with the descriptive laws of nature, or (2) that it is not artificial, that man has not imposed his will or his devices upon events or conditions as they exist or would have existed without such interference.

The Descriptive Laws of Nature

The laws of nature, as these are understood by the scientist, differ from the laws of man. The former are purely descriptive, whereas the latter are prescriptive. When a scientist says that water boils at 212° Fahrenheit, or that the volume of a gas varies directly with the heat that is applied to it and inversely with the pressure, he means merely that as a matter of recorded and observable fact, pure water under standard conditions always boils at precisely 212° Fahrenheit and that as a matter of observed fact, the volume of a gas rises as it is heated and falls as pressure is applied to it. These "laws" merely *describe* the manner in which physical substances *actually behave.* They differ from municipal and federal laws in that they *do not prescribe behavior.* Unlike manmade laws, natural laws are not passed by any legislator or group of legislators; they are not proclaimed or announced; they impose no obligation upon anyone or anything; their "violation" entails no penalty, and there is no reward for "following" them or "abiding by" them. When a scientist says that the air in a tire "obeys" the laws of nature that "govern" gases, he does *not* mean that the air, having been informed that it *ought* to behave in a certain way, behaves appropriately under the right conditions. He means, rather, that as a matter of fact, the air in a tire *will* behave like all other gases. In saying that Boyle's law "governs" the behavior of gases, he means merely that gases do, as a matter of fact, behave in accordance with Boyle's law, and that Boyle's law enables one to predict accurately what will happen to a given quantity of a gas as its pressure is raised; he does *not* mean to suggest that some heavenly voice has proclaimed that all gases should henceforth behave in accordance with the terms of Boyle's law and that a ghostly policeman patrols the world, ready to mete out punishments to any gases that "violate"

the heavenly decree. In fact, according to the scientist, it does not make sense to speak of a natural law being violated. For if there were a true exception to a so-called law of nature, the exception would require a change in the description of those phenomena, and the "law" would have been shown to be no law at all. The laws of nature are revised as scientists discover new phenomena that require new refinements in their descriptions of the way things actually happen. In this respect they differ fundamentally from human laws, which are revised periodically by legislators who are not so interested in *describing* human behavior as they are in *prescribing* what human behavior *should* be.

The Artificial as a Form of the Unnatural

On occasion when we say that something is not natural, we mean that it is a product of human artifice. My typewriter is not a natural object, in this sense, for the substances of which it is composed have been removed from their natural state—the state in which they existed before men came along—and have been transformed by a series of chemical and physical and mechanical processes into other substances. They have been rearranged into a whole that is quite different from anything found in nature. In short, my typewriter is an artificial object. In this sense, the clothing that I wear as I lecture before my students is not natural, for it has been transformed considerably from the state in which it was found in nature; and my wearing of clothing as I lecture before my students is also not natural, in this sense, for in my natural state, before the application of anything artificial, before any human interference with things as they are, I am quite naked. Human laws, being artificial conventions designed to exercise a degree of control over the natural inclinations and propensities of men, may in this sense be considered to be unnatural.

Now when theologians and moralists speak of homosexuality, contraception, abortion, and other forms of human behavior as being unnatural, and say that for that reason such behavior must be considered to be wrong, in what sense are they using the word *unnatural*? Are they saying that homosexual behavior and the use of contraceptives are contrary to the scientific laws of nature, are they saying that they are artificial forms of behavior, or are they using the terms *natural* and *unnatural* in some third sense?

They cannot mean that homosexual behavior (to stick to the subject presently under discussion) violates the laws of nature in the first sense, for, as we have pointed out, in *that* sense it is impossible to violate the laws of nature. Those laws, being merely descriptive of what actually does happen, would have to *include* homosexual behavior if such behavior does actually take place. Even if the defenders of the theological view that homosexuality is unnatural were to appeal to a statistical analysis by pointing out that such behavior is not normal from a statistical point of view, and therefore not what the laws of nature require, it would be open to their critics to reply that any descriptive law of nature must account for and incorporate all statistical deviations, and that the laws of nature, in this sense, do not *require anything*. These critics might also note that the best statistics available reveal that about half of all American males engage in homosexual activity at some time in their lives, and that a very large percentage of American males have exclusively homosexual relations for a fairly extensive period of time; from which it would follow that such behavior is natural, for them, at any rate, in this sense of the word *natural*.

If those who say that homosexual behavior is unnatural are using the term *unnatural* in the second sense, it is difficult to see why they should be fussing over it. Certainly nothing is intrinsically wrong with going against nature (if that is how it should be put) in this sense. That which is artificial is often far better than what is natural. Artificial homes seem, at any rate, to be more suited to human habitation and more conducive to longer life and better health than caves and other natural shelters. There are distinct ad-

vantages to the use of such unnatural (i.e., artificial) amenities as clothes, furniture, and books. Although we may dream of an idyllic return to nature in our more wistful moments, we would soon discover, as Thoreau did in his attempt to escape from the artificiality of civilization, that needles and thread, knives and matches, ploughs and nails, and countless other products of human artifice are essential to human life. We would discover, as Plato pointed out in the *Republic,* that no man can be truly self-sufficient. Some of the by-products of industry are less than desirable; but neither industry itself, nor the products of industry, are intrinsically evil, even though both are unnatural in this sense of the word.

Interference with nature is not evil in itself. Nature, as some writers have put it, must be tamed. In some respects man must look upon it as an enemy to be conquered. If nature were left to its own devices, without the intervention of human artifice, men would be consumed with disease, they would be plagued by insects, they would be chained to the places where they were born with no means of swift communication or transport, and they would suffer the discomforts and the torments of wind and weather and flood and fire with no practical means of combating any of them. Interfering with nature, doing battle with nature, using human will and reason and skill to thwart what might otherwise follow from the conditions that prevail in the world, is a peculiarly human enterprise, one that can hardly be condemned merely because it does what is not natural.

Homosexual behavior can hardly be considered to be unnatural in this sense. There is nothing "artificial" about such behavior. On the contrary, it is quite natural, in this sense, to those who engage in it. And even if it were not, even if it were quite artificial, this is not in itself a ground for condemning it.

It would seem, then, that those who condemn homosexuality as an unnatural form of behavior must mean something else by the word *unnatural,* something not covered by either of the preceding definitions. A third possibility is this:

Anything Uncommon or Abnormal is Unnatural

If this is what is meant by those who condemn homosexuality on the ground that it is unnatural, it is quite obvious that their condemnation cannot be accepted without further argument. For the fact that a given form of behavior is uncommon provides no justification for condemning it. Playing viola in a string quartet is no doubt an uncommon form of human behavior. I do not know what percentage of the human race engages in such behavior, or what percentage of his life any given violist devotes to such behavior, but I suspect that the number of such people must be very small indeed, and that the total number of man-hours spent in such activity would justify our calling that form of activity uncommon, abnormal (in the sense that it is statistically not the kind of thing that people are ordinarily inclined to do), and therefore unnatural, in this sense of the word. Yet there is no reason to suppose that such uncommon, abnormal behavior is, by virtue of its uncommonness, deserving of condemnation or ethically or morally wrong. On the contrary, many forms of behavior are praised precisely because they are so uncommon. Great artists, poets, musicians, and scientists are "abnormal" in this sense; but clearly the world is better off for having them, and it would be absurd to condemn them or their activities for their failure to be common and normal. If homosexual behavior is wrong, then, it must be for some reason other than its "unnaturalness" in this sense of the word.

Any Use of an Organ of an Instrument that is Contrary to its Principal Purpose or Function is Unnatural

Every organ and every instrument—perhaps even every creature—has a function to perform, one for which it is particularly designed. Any use of those instruments and organs that is consonant with their purposes is natural and proper, but any use that is inconsistent with their principal functions is unnatural and improper, and to that extent, evil or harmful. Human teeth, for example, are admirably designed for their principal functions—biting and chewing the kinds of food suitable for human consumption. But they are not particularly well suited for prying the caps from beer bottles. If they are used for the latter purpose, which is not natural to them, they are liable to crack or break under the strain. The abuse of one's teeth leads to their destruction and to a consequent deterioration in one's overall health. If they are used only for their proper function, however, they may continue to serve well for many years. Similarly, a given drug may have a proper function. If used in the furtherance of that end, it can preserve life and restore health. But if it is abused, and employed for purposes for which it was never intended, it may cause serious harm and even death. The natural uses of things are good and proper, but their unnatural uses are bad and harmful.

What we must do, then, is to find the proper use, or the true purpose, of each organ in our bodies. Once we have discovered that, we will know what constitutes the natural use of each organ, and what constitutes an unnatural, abusive, and potentially harmful employment of the various parts of our bodies. If we are rational, we will be careful to confine our behavior to our proper functions and to refrain from unnatural behavior. According to those philosophers who follow this line of reasoning, the way to discover the "proper" use of any organ is to determine what it is peculiarly suited to do. The eye is suited for seeing, the ear for hearing, the nerves for transmitting impulses from one part of the body to another, and so on.

What are the sex organs peculiarly suited to do? Obviously, they are peculiarly suited to enable men and women to reproduce their own kind. No other organ in the body is capable of fulfilling that function. It follows, according to those who follow the natural-law line, that the "proper" or "natural" function of the sex organs is reproduction, and that strictly speaking, any use of those organs for other purposes is unnatural, abusive, potentially harmful, and therefore wrong. The sex organs have been given to us in order to enable us to maintain the continued existence of mankind on this earth. All perversions—including masturbation, homosexual behavior, and heterosexual intercourse that deliberately frustrates this design of the sexual organs—are unnatural and bad. As Pope Pius XI once said, "Private individuals have no other power over the members of their bodies than that which pertains to their natural ends."

But the problem is not so easily resolved. Is it true that every organ has one and only one proper function? A hammer may have been designed to pound nails, and it may perform that particular job best. But it is not sinful to employ a hammer to crack nuts if I have no other more suitable tool immediately available. The hammer, being a relatively versatile tool, may be employed in a number of ways. It has no one "proper" or "natural" function. A woman's eyes are well adapted to seeing, it is true. But they seem also to be well adapted to flirting. Is a woman's use of her eyes for the latter purpose sinful merely because she is not using them, at that moment, for their "primary" purpose of seeing? Our sexual organs are uniquely adapted for procreation, but that is obviously not the only function for which they are adapted. Human beings may—and do—use those organs for a great many other purposes, and it is difficult to see why any *one* use should be considered to be the only proper one. The sex organs, for one thing, seem to be particularly well adapted to give their owners and others intense sensations of pleasure. Unless one believes that pleasure itself is bad, there seems to be little reason to believe that the use of the sex organs for the production of pleasure in oneself or in others is evil. In view of the peculiar design of these organs, with their great concentration of nerve endings,

it would seem that they were designed (if they *were* designed) with that very goal in mind, and that their use for such purposes would be no more unnatural than their use for the purpose of procreation.

Nor should we overlook the fact that human sex organs may be and are used to express, in the deepest and most intimate way open to man, the love of one person for another. Even the most ardent opponents of "unfruitful" intercourse admit that sex does serve this function. They have accordingly conceded that a man and his wife may have intercourse even though she is pregnant, or past the age of child bearing, or in the infertile period of her menstrual cycle.

Human beings are remarkably complex and adaptable creatures. Neither they nor their organs can properly be compared to hammers or to other tools. The analogy quickly breaks down. The generalization that a given organ or instrument has one and only one proper function does not hold up, even with regard to the simplest manufactured tools, for, as we have seen, a tool may be used for more than one purpose—less effectively than one especially designed for a given task, perhaps, but "properly" and certainly not *sinfully*. A woman may use her eyes not only to see and to flirt, but also to earn money—if she is, for example, an actress or a model. Though neither of the latter functions seems to have been a part of the original "design," if one may speak sensibly of *design* in this context, of the eye, it is difficult to see why such a use of the eyes of a woman should be considered sinful, perverse, or unnatural. Her sex organs have the unique capacity of producing ova and nurturing human embryos, under the right conditions; but why should any other use of those organs, including their use to bring pleasure to their owner or to someone else, or to manifest love to another person, or even, perhaps, to earn money, be regarded as perverse, sinful, or unnatural? Similarly, a man's sexual organs possess the unique capacity of causing the generation of another human being, but if a man chooses to use them for pleasure, or for the expression of love, or for some other purpose—so long as he does not interfere with the rights of some other person—the fact that his sex organs do have their unique capabilities does not constitute a convincing justification for condemning their other uses as being perverse, sinful, unnatural, or criminal. If a man "perverts" himself by wiggling his ears for the entertainment of his neighbors instead of using them exclusively for their "natural" function of hearing, no one things of consigning him to prison. If he abuses his teeth by using them to pull staples from memos—a function for which teeth were clearly not designed—he is not accused of being immoral, degraded, and degenerate. The fact that people *are* condemned for using their sex organs for their own pleasure or profit, or for that of others, may be more revealing about the prejudices and taboos of our society than it is about our perception of the true nature or purpose or "end" (whatever that might be) of our bodies.

To sum up, then, the proposition that any use of an organ that is contrary to its principal purpose or function is unnatural assumes that organs *have* a principal purpose or function, but this may be denied on the ground that the purpose or function of a given organ may vary according to the needs or desires of its owner. It may be denied on the ground that a given organ may have more than one principal purpose or function, and any attempt to call one use or another the only natural one seems to be arbitrary, if not questionbegging. Also, the proposition suggests that what is unnatural is evil or depraved. This goes beyond the pure description of things, and enters into the problem of the evaluation of human behavior, which leads us to the fifth meaning of "natural."

That Which is Natural is Good, and Whatever is Unnatural is Bad

When one condemns homosexuality or masturbation or the use of contraceptives on the ground that it is unnatural, one implies that whatever is unnatural is bad, wrongful, or perverse. But as we have seen, in some sense of the word, the unnatural (i.e., the artificial) is often very good, whereas that which is natural (i.e., that which has not been subjected to human artifice or improvement) may be very bad indeed. Of course, interference with nature may be bad. Ecologists have made us more aware than we have ever been of the dangers of unplanned and uninformed interference with nature. But this is not to say that *all* interference with nature is bad. Every time a man cuts down a tree to make room for a home for himself, or catches a fish to feed himself or his family, he is interfering with nature. If men did not interfere with nature, they would have no homes, they could eat no fish, and in fact, they could not survive. What, then, can be meant by those who say that whatever is natural is good and whatever is unnatural is bad? Clearly, they cannot have intended merely to reduce the word *natural* to a synonym of *good, right*, and *proper*, and *unnatural* to a synonym of *evil, wrong, improper, corrupt*, and *depraved*. If that were all they had intended to do, there would be very little to discuss as to whether a given form of behavior might be proper even though it is not in strict conformity with someone's views of what is natural; for *good* and *natural* being synonyms, it would follow inevitably that whatever is good must be natural, and vice versa, by definition. This is certainly not what the opponents of homosexuality have been saying when they claim that homosexuality, being unnatural, is evil. For if it were, their claim would be quite empty. They would be saying merely that homosexuality, being evil, is evil—a redundancy that could as easily be reduced to the simpler assertion that homosexuality is evil. This assertion, however, is not an argument. Those who oppose homosexuality and other sexual "perversions" on the ground that they are "unnatural" are saying that there is some objectively identifiable quality in such behavior that is unnatural; and that that quality, once it has been identified by some kind of scientific observation, can be seen to be detrimental to those who engage in such behavior, or to those around them; and that *because* of the harm (physical, mental, moral, or spiritual) that results from engaging in any behavior possessing the attribute of unnaturalness, such behavior must be considered to be wrongful, and should be discouraged by society. "Unnaturalness" and "wrongfulness" are not synonyms, then, but different concepts. The problem with which we are wrestling is that we are unable to find a meaning for *unnatural* that enables us to arrive at the con-

clusion that homosexuality is unnatural or that if homosexuality is unnatural, it is therefore wrongful behavior. We have examined four common meanings of *natural* and *unnatural,* and have seen that none of them performs the task that it must perform if the advocates of this argument are to prevail. Without some more satisfactory explanation of the connection between the wrongfulness of homosexuality and its alleged unnaturalness, the argument must be rejected.

For Further Thought and Discussion

1. Is there a sense of "natural" that makes homosexual relations natural?
2. In what sense are "incurable" homosexuals "unnatural"?

Better Sex

SARA L. RUDDICK

Reading Questions

1. How does Ruddick define completeness in sex acts?
2. What are the three ways in which complete sex acts are morally superior to incomplete ones?
3. Explain Sartre's suggestion that "complete sex acts preserve a respect for persons."
4. How might some "traditional sexual vices" be condemned according to the standards argued by Ruddick?
5. In what way does the sense of obligation enhance better sex?

IT MIGHT BE ARGUED that there is no specifically sexual morality. We have, of course, become accustomed to speaking of sexual morality, but

the "morality" of which we speak has a good deal to do with property, the division of labor, and male power, and little to do with our sexual

From Robert Baker and Frederick Elliston, eds., *Philosophy and Sex, revised ed.* (Buffalo, N.Y.: Prometheus Books). Copyright © 1984 by Robert Baker and Frederick Elliston. Reprinted by permission of the publisher.

lives. Sexual experiences, like experiences in driving automobiles, render us liable to specific moral situations. As drivers we must guard against infantile desires for revenge and excitement. As lovers we must guard against cruelty and betrayal, for we know sexual experiences provide special opportunities for each. We drive soberly because, before we get into a car, we believe that it is wrong to be careless of life. We resist temptations to adultery because we believe it wrong to betray trust, whether it be a parent, a sexual partner, or a political colleague who is betrayed. As lovers and drivers we act on principles that are particular applications of general moral principles. Moreover, given the superstitions from which sexual experience has suffered, it is wise to free ourselves, as lovers, from any moral concerns, other than those we have as human beings. There is no specifically sexual morality, and none should be invented. Or so it might be argued.

When we examined our moral "intuitions," however, the analogy with driving fails us. Unburdened of *sexual* morality, we do not find it easy to apply general moral principles to our sexual lives. The "morally average" lover can be cruel, violate trust, and neglect social duties with less opprobrium precisely *because* he is a lover. Only political passions and psychological or physical deprivation serve as well as sexual desire to excuse what would otherwise be seriously and clearly immoral acts. (Occasionally, sexual desire is itself conceived of as a deprivation, an involuntary lust. And there is, of course, a tradition that sees sexual morality as a way of controlling those unable to be sexless: "It is better to marry than to burn.") Often, in our sexual lives, we neither flout nor simply apply general moral principles. Rather, the values of sexual experience themselves figure in the construction of moral dilemmas. The conflict between better sex (more complete, natural, and pleasurable sex acts) and, say, social duty is not seen as a conflict between the immoral and compulsive, on one hand, and the morally good, on the other, but as a conflict between alternative moral acts.

Our intuitions vary but at least they suggest we can use "good" sex as a positive weight on some moral balance. What is that weight? Why do we put it there? How do we, in the first place, evaluate sexual experiences? On reflection, should we endorse these evaluations? These are the questions whose answers should constitute a specifically sexual morality.

In answering them, I will first consider three characteristics that have been used to distinguish some sex acts as better than others—greater pleasure, completeness, and naturalness. Other characteristics may be relevant to evaluating sex acts, but these three are central. If they have *moral* significance, then the sex acts characterized by them will be better than others not so characterized.

After considering those characteristics in virtue of which some sex acts are allegedly better than others, I will ask whether the presence of those characteristics renders the acts *morally* superior. I will not consider here the unclear and overused distinction between the moral and the prudent. I hope it is sufficient to set out dogmatically and schematically the moral notions I will use. I am confident that better sex is morally preferable to other sex, but I am not at all happy with my characterization of its moral significance. Ultimately, sexual morality cannot be considered apart from a "prudential" morality in which it is shown that what is good is good for us and what is good for us makes us good. In such a morality, not only sex, but art, fantasy, love, and a host of other intellectual and emotional enterprises will regain old moral significances and acquire new ones. My remarks here, then, are partial and provisional.

A characteristic renders a sex act morally preferable to one without that characteristic if it gives, increases, or is instrumental in increasing the "benefit" of the act for the person engaging in it. Benefits can be classified as peremptory or optional. Peremptory benefits are experiences, relations, or objects that anyone who is neither irrational nor anhedonic will want so long as s/he wants anything at all. Optional benefits are experiences, relations, or objects that anyone, neither irrational nor anhedonic, will want so long as s/he will not thereby lose a peremptory benefit. There is widespread disagreement about which benefits are peremptory. Self-respect, love, and health are common examples of peremptory benefits. Arms, legs, and hands are probably optional benefits. A person still wanting a great deal might give up limbs, just as s/he would give up life, when mutilation or death is required by self-respect. As adults we are largely responsible for procuring our own benefits and greatly dependent on good fortune for success in doing so. However, the moral significance of benefits is most clearly seen not from the standpoint of the person procuring and enjoying them but from the standpoint of another *caring* person, for example, a lover, parent, or political leader responsible for procuring benefits for specific others. A benefit may then be described as an experience, relation, or object that anyone who properly cares for another is obliged to attempt to secure for him/her. Criteria for the virtue of care and for benefit are reciprocally determined, the virtue consisting in part in recognizing and attempting to secure benefits for the person cared for, the identification of benefit depending on its recognition by those already seen to be properly caring.

In talking of benefits I shall be looking at our sexual lives from the vantage point of hope, not of fear. The principal interlocutor may be considered to be a child asking what s/he should rightly and reasonably hope for in living, rather than a potential criminal questioning conventional restraints. The specific question the child may be imagined to ask can now be put: In what way is better sex beneficial or conducive to experiences or relations or objects that are beneficial?

A characteristic renders a sex act morally preferable to one without that characteristic if either the act is thereby more just or the act is thereby likely to make the person engaging in it more just. Justice includes giving others what is due them, taking no more than what is one's own,

and giving and taking according to prevailing principles of fairness.

A characteristic renders a sex act morally preferable to one without that characteristic if because of the characteristic the act is more virtuous or more likely to lead to virtue. A virtue is a disposition to attempt, and an ability to succeed in, good acts—acts of justice, acts that express or produce excellence, and acts that yield benefits to oneself or others.

Sexual Pleasure

Sensual experiences give rise to sensations and experiences that are paradigms of what is pleasant. Hedonism, in both its psychological and ethical forms, has blinded us to the nature and to the benefits of sensual pleasure by overextending the word "pleasure" to cover anything enjoyable or even agreeable.[1] The paradigmatic type of pleasure is sensual. Pleasure is a temporally extended, more or less intense quality of particular experiences. Pleasure is enjoyable independent of any function pleasurable activity fulfills. The infant who continues to suck well after s/he is nourished, expressing evident pleasure in doing so, gives us a demonstration of the nature of pleasure.[2]

As we learn more about pleasant experiences we not only apply but also extend and attenuate the primary notion of "pleasure." But if pleasure is to have any nonsophistical psychological or moral interest, it must retain its connections with those paradigm instances of sensual pleasure that gives rise to it. We may, for example,

---

[1] This may be a consequence of the tepidness of the English "pleasant." It would be better to speak of lust and its satisfaction if our suspicion of pleasure had not been written into that part of our language.

[2] The example is from Sigmund Freud. *Three Essays on Sexuality,* standard ed., vol. 7 (London: Hogarth, 1963), p. 182. The concept of pleasure I urge here is narrower but also, I think, more useful than the popular one. It is a concept that, to paraphrase Wittgenstein, we (could) learn when we learn the language. The idea of paradigmatic uses and subsequent more-or-less-divergent, more-or-less-"normal" uses also is derived from Wittgenstein.

extend the notion of pleasure so that particular episodes in the care of children give great pleasure; but the long-term caring for children, however intrinsically rewarding, is not an experience of pleasure or unpleasure.

Sexual pleasure is a species of sensual pleasure with its own conditions of arousal and satisfaction. Sexual acts vary considerably in pleasure, the limiting case being a sexual act where no one experiences pleasure even though someone may experience affection or "relief of tension" through orgasm. Sexual pleasure can be considered either in a context of deprivation and its relief or in a context of satisfaction. Psychological theories have tended to emphasize the frustrated state of sexual desire and to construe sexual pleasure as a relief from that state. There are, however, alternative accounts of sexual pleasure that correspond more closely with our experience. Sexual pleasure is "a primary distinctively poignant pleasure experience that manifests itself from early infancy on. . . . Once experienced it continues to be savored. . . ."[3] Sexual desire is not experienced as frustration but as part of sexual pleasure. Normally, sexual desire transforms itself gradually into the pleasure that appears, misleadingly, to be an aim extrinsic to it. The natural structure of desire, not an inherent quality of frustration, accounts for the pain of an aroused but unsatisfied desire.

Sexual pleasure, like addictive pleasure generally, does not, except very temporarily, result in satiety. Rather, it increases the demand for more of the same while sharply limiting the possibility of substitutes. The experience of sensual pleasures, and particularly of sexual pleasures, has a pervasive effect on our perceptions of the world. We find bodies inviting, social encounters alluring, and smells, tastes, and sights resonant because our perception of them includes their sexual significance. Merleau-Ponty has written of a patient for whom "perception had lost its erotic structure, both temporally and physically."[4] As the result of a brain injury the patient's capacity for sexual desire and pleasure (though not his capacity for performing sexual acts) was impaired. He no longer sought sexual intercourse of his own accord, was left indifferent by the sights and smells of available bodies, and if in the midst of sexual intercourse his partner turned away, he showed no signs of displeasure. The capacity for sexual pleasure, upon which the erotic structure of perception depends, can be accidentally damaged. The question that this case raises is whether it would be desirable to interfere with this capacity in a more systematic way than we now do. With greater biochemical and psychiatric knowledge we shall presumably be able to manipulate it at will.[5] And if that becomes possible, toward what end should we interfere? I shall return to this question after describing the other two characteristics of better sex—completeness and naturalness.

Complete Sex Acts

The completeness of a sexual act depends upon the *relation* of the participants to their own and each other's *desire*. A sex act is complete if each partner allows him/herself to be "taken over" by an active desire, which is desire not merely for the other's body but also for her/his active desire. Completeness is hard to characterize, though complete sex acts are at least as natural as any others—especially, it seems, among those people who take them casually and for granted.

---

[3] George Klein, "Freud's Two Theories of Sexuality," in L. Berger, ed., *Clinical-Cognitive Psychology, Models, and Integrations* (Englewood Cliffs, N.J.: Prentice-Hall, 1969), pp. 131–81. This essay gives a clear idea of alternative psychological accounts of sexual pleasure.

[4] Maurice Merleau-Ponty, *Phenomenology of Perception*, trans. Colin Smith (London: Routledge & Kegan Paul, 1962), p. 156.

[5] See Kurt Vonnegut, Jr., "Welcome to the Monkey House," in *Welcome to the Monkey House* (New York: Dell, 1968), which concerns both the manipulation and the benefit of sexual pleasure.

The notion of "completeness" (as I shall call it) has figured under various guises in the work of Sartre, Merleau-Ponty, and more recently Thomas Nagel. "The being which desires is consciousness making itself body."[6] "What we try to possess, then, is not just a body, but a body bought to live by consciousness."[7] "It is important that the partner be aroused, and not merely aroused, but aroused by the awareness of one's desire."[8]

The precondition of complete sex acts is the "embodiment" of the participants. Each participant submits to sexual desires that take over consciousness and direct action. It is sexual desire and not a separable satisfaction of it (for example, orgasm) that is important here. Indeed, Sartre finds pleasure external to the essence of desire, and Nagel gives an example of embodiment in which the partners do not touch each other. Desire is pervasive and "overwhelming," but it does not make its subject its involuntary victim (as it did the Boston Strangler, we are told), nor does it, except at its climax, alter capacities for ordinary perceptions, memories, and inferences. Nagel's embodied partners can presumably get themselves from bar stools to bed while their consciousness is "clogged" with desire. With what, then, is embodiment contrasted?

Philosophers make statements that when intended literally are evidence of pathology: "Human beings are automata"; "I never really see physical objects"; "I can never know what another person is feeling." The clearest statement of disembodiment that I know of is W. T. Stace's claim: "I become aware of my body in the end chiefly because it insists on accompanying me wherever I go."[9] What "just accompanies me" can also stay away. "When my body leaves me/ I'm lonesome for it./ . . . body/goes away I don't know where/and it's lonesome to drift/above the space it/fills when it's here."[10] If "the body is felt more as one object among other objects in the world that as the core of the individual's own being,"[11] then what appears to be bodily can be dissociated from the "real self." Both a generalized separation of "self" from body and particular disembodied experiences have had their advocates. The attempt at disembodiment has also been seen as conceptually confused and psychologically disastrous.

We may often experience ourselves as relatively disembodied, observing or "using" our bodies to fulfill our intentions. On some occasions, however, such as in physical combat, sport, physical suffering, or danger, we "become" our bodies; our consciousness becomes bodily experience of bodily activity.[12] Sexual acts are occasions for such embodiment; they may, however, fail for a variety of reasons, for example, because of pretense or an excessive need for self-control. If someone is embodied by sexual desire, s/he submits to its direction. Spontaneous impulses of desire become her/his movements—some involuntary, like gestures of "courting behavior" or physical expressions of intense pleasure, and some deliberate. Her/his

---

[6] Jean-Paul Sartre, *Being and Nothingness,* trans. Hazel E. Barnes (New York: Philosophical Library, 1956), p. 389.

[7] Merleau-Ponty, *Phenomenology of Perception,* p. 167.

[8] Thomas Nagel, "Sexual Perversion," *The Journal of Philosophy,* 66, no. 1 (January 16, 1969): 13. . . . My original discussion of completeness was both greatly indebted to and confused by Nagel's. I have tried here to dispel some of the confusion.

[9] W. T. Stace, "Solipsism," from *The Theory of Knowledge and Existence;* reprinted in Tillman, Berofsky, and O'Connor, eds. *Introductory Philosophy* (New York: Harper and Row, 1967), p. 113.

[10] Denise Levertov, "Gone Away," in *O Taste and See* (New York: New Directions, 1962), p. 59. Copyright by Denise Levertov Goodman, New Directions Publishing Corporation, New York.

[11] R. D. Laing, *The Divided Self* (Baltimore: Pelican Books, 1965), p. 69.

[12] We need not become our bodies on such occasions. Pains, muscular feelings, and emotions can be reduced to mere "sensations" that may impinge on "me" but that I attempt to keep at a distance. Laing describes the case of a man who when beaten up felt that any damage to his body could not really hurt *him.* See *The Divided Self,* p. 68.

consciousness, or "mind," is taken over by desire and the pursuit of its object, in the way that at other times it may be taken over by an intellectual problem or by obsessive fantasies. But unlike the latter takeovers, this one is bodily. A desiring consciousness is flooded with specifically sexual feelings that eroticize all perception and movement. Consciousness "becomes flesh."

Granted the precondition of embodiment, complete sex acts occur when each partner's embodying desire is active and actively responsive to the other's. This second aspect of complete sex constitutes a "reflexive mutual recognition" of desire by desire.[13]

The partner *actively* desires another person's desire. Active desiring includes more than embodiment, which might be achieved in objectless masturbation. It is more, also, than merely being aroused by and then taken over by desire, though it may come about as a result of deliberate arousal. It commits the actively desiring person to her/his desire and requires her/him to identify with it—that is, to recognize him/herself as a sexual agent as well as respondent. (Active desiring is less encouraged in women, and probably more women than men fell threatened by it.)

The other recognizes and responds to the partner's desire. Merely to recognize the desire as desire, not to reduce it to an inch or to depersonalize it as a "demand," may be threatening. Imperviousness to desire is the deepest defense against it. We have learned from research on families whose members tend to become schizophrenic that such imperviousness, the refusal to recognize a feeling for what it is, can force a vulnerable person to deny or to obscure the real nature of her/his feelings. Imperviousness tends to deprive even a relatively invulnerable person of her/his efficacy. The demand that our feelings elicit a response appropriate to them is part of a general demand that *we* be recognized, that our feelings be allowed to make a difference.

There are many ways in which sexual desire may be recognized, countless forms of submission and resistance. In complete sex, desire is recognized by a responding and active desire that commits the other, as it committed the partner. Given responding desire, both people identify themselves as sexually desiring the other. They are neither seducer nor seduced, neither supplicant nor benefactress, neither sadist nor victim, but sexual agents acting sexually out of their recognized desire. Indeed, in complete sex one not only welcomes and recognizes desire, one desires it. Returned and endorsed desire becomes one of the features of an erotically structured perception. Desiring becomes desirable. (Men are less encouraged to desire the other's active and demanding desire, and such desiring is probably threatening to more men than women.)

In sum, in complete sex two persons embodied by sexual desire actively desire and respond to each other's active desire. Although it is difficult to write of complete sex without suggesting that one of the partners is the initiator, while the other responds, complete sex is reciprocal sex. The partners, whatever the circumstances of their coming together, are equal in activity and responsiveness of desire.

Sexual acts can be partly incomplete. A necrophiliac may be taken over by desire, and one may respond to a partner's desire without being embodied by one's own. Partners whose sexual activities are accompanied by private fantasies engage in an incomplete sex act. Consciousness is used by desire but remains apart from it, providing it with stimulants and controls. Neither partner responds to the other's desire, though each may appear to. Sartre's "dishonest masturbator," for whom masturbation is the sex act of choice, engages in a paradigmatically incomplete sex act: "He asks only to be slightly distanced from his own body, only for there to be a light coating of otherness over his flesh and over his thoughts. His personae are melting sweets. . . . The masturbator is enchanted at never being

---

[13] Nagel, "Sexual Perversion," p. 254.

able to feel himself sufficiently another, and at producing for himself alone the diabolic appearance of a couple that fades away when one touches it. . . . Masturbation is the derealisation of the world and of the masturbator himself."[14]

Completeness is more difficult to describe that incompleteness, for it turns on precise but subtle ways of responding to a particular person's desire with specific expressions of impulse that are both spontaneous and responsive. There are many possible sex acts that are pleasurable but not complete. Sartre, Nagel, and Merleau-Ponty each suggest that the desire for the responsive desire of one's partner is the "central impulse" of sexual desire.[15] The desire for a sleeping woman, for example, is possible only "in so far as this sleep appears on the ground of consciousness."[16] This seems much too strong. Some lovers desire that their partners resist, others like them coolly controlled, others prefer them asleep. We would not say that there was anything abnormal or less fully sexual about desire. Whether or not complete sex is preferable to incomplete sex (the question to which I shall turn shortly), incompleteness does not disqualify a sex act from being fully sexual.

Sexual Perversion

The final characteristic of allegedly better sex acts is that they are "natural" rather than "perverted." The ground for classifying sexual acts as either natural or unnatural is that the former type serve or could serve the evolutionary and biological function of sexuality—namely, reproduction. "Natural" sexual desire has as its "object" living persons of the opposite sex, and in particular their postpuberial genitals. The "aim" of natural sexual desire—that is, the act that

"naturally" completes it—is genital intercourse. Perverse sex acts are deviations from the natural object (for example, homosexuality, fetishism) or from the standard aim (for example, voyeurism, sadism). Among the variety of objects and aims of sexual desire, I can see no other ground for selecting some as natural, except that they are of the type that can lead to reproduction.[17]

The connection of sexual desire with reproduction gives us the criterion but not the motive of the classification. The concept of perversion depends on a disjointedness between our experience of sexual desire from infancy on and the function of sexual desire—reproduction. In our collective experience of sexuality, perverse desires are as natural as nonperverse ones. The sexual desire of the polymorphously perverse child has many objects—for example, breasts, anus, mouth, genitals—and many aims—for example, autoerotic or other-directed looking, smelling, touching, hurting. From the social and developmental point of view, natural sex is an achievement, partly biological, partly conventional, consisting in a dominant organization of sexual desires in which perverted aims or objects are subordinate to natural ones. The concept of perversion reflects the vulnerability as much as the evolutionary warrant of this organization.

The connection of sexual desire with reproduction is not sufficient to yield the concept of perversion, but it is surely necessary. Nagel, however, thinks otherwise. There are, he points out, many sexual acts that do not lead to reproduction but that we are not even inclined to call perverse—for example, sexual acts between partners who are sterile. Perversion, according to him, is a psychological concept while reproduction is (only?) a physiological one. (Incidentally, this view of reproduction seems to me the clearest instance of male bias in Nagel's paper).

Nagel is right about our judgments of partic-

[14] Jean-Paul Sartre, *Saint Genet* (New York: Braziller, 1963), p. 398; cited and translated by R. D. Laing, *Self and Others* (New York: Pantheon, 1969), pp. 39–40.

[15] Ibid., p. 13.

[16] Sartre, *Being and Nothingness,* p. 386.

[17] See, in support of this point, Sigmund Freud, *Introductory Lectures on Psychoanalysis*, standard ed., vol. 26 (London: Hogarth, 1963), chaps. 20, 21.

ular acts, but he draws the wrong conclusions from those judgments. The perversity of sex acts does not depend upon whether they are intended to achieve reproduction. "Natural" sexual desire is for heterosexual genital activity, not for reproduction. The ground for classifying that desire as natural is that it is so organized that it *could* lead to reproduction in normal physiological circumstances. The reproductive organization of sexual desires gives us a *criterion* of naturalness, but the *virtue* of which it is a criterion is the "naturalness" itself, not reproduction. Our vacillating attitude toward the apparently perverse acts of animals reflects our shifting from criterion to virtue. If, when confronted with a perverse act of animals, we withdraw the label "perverted" from our own similar acts rather than extend it to theirs, we are relinquishing the reproductive criterion of naturalness, while retaining the virtue. Animals cannot be "unnatural." If, on the other hand, we "discover" that animals can be perverts too, we are maintaining our criterion, but giving a somewhat altered sense to the "naturalness" of which it is a criterion.

Nagel's alternative attempt to classify acts as natural or perverted on the basis of their completeness fails. "Perverted" and "complete" are evaluations of an entirely different order. The completeness of a sex act depends upon qualities of the participants' experience and upon qualities of their relation—qualities of which they are the best judge. To say a sex act is perverted is to pass a conventional judgment about characteristics of the act, which could be evident to any observer. As one can pretend to be angry but not to shout, one can pretend to a complete, but not to a natural, sex act (though one may, of course, conceal desires for perverse sex acts or shout in order to mask one's feelings). As Nagel himself sees, judgments about particular sex acts clearly differentiate between perversion and completeness. Unadorned heterosexual intercourse where each partner has private fantasies

is clearly "natural" and clearly "incomplete," but there is nothing prima facie incomplete about exclusive oral-genital intercourse or homosexual acts. If many perverse acts are incomplete, as Nagel claims, this is an important fact *about* perversion, but it is not the basis upon which we judge its occurrence.

Is Better Sex Really Better?

Some sex acts are, allegedly, better than others insofar as they are more pleasurable, complete, and natural. What is the moral significance of this evaluation? In answering this question, official sexual morality sometimes appeals to the social consequences of particular types of better sex acts. For example, since dominantly perverse organizations of sexual impulses limit reproduction, the merits of perversion depend upon the need to limit or increase population. Experience of sexual pleasure may be desirable if it promotes relaxation and communication in an acquisitive society, undesirable if it limits the desire to work or, in armies, to kill. The social consequences of complete sex have not received particular attention, because the quality of sexual experience has been of little interest to moralists. It might be found that those who had complete sexual relations were more cooperative, less amenable to political revolt. If so, complete sexual acts would be desirable in just and peaceable societies, undesirable in unjust societies requiring revolution.

The social desirability of types of sexual acts depends on particular social conditions and independent criteria of social desirability. It may be interesting and important to assess particular claims about the social desirability of sex acts, but this is not my concern. What is my concern is the extent to which we will allow our judgments of sexual worth to be influenced by social considerations. But this issue cannot even be raised until we have a better sense of sexual worth.

The Benefit of Sexual Pleasure

To say that an experience is pleasant is to give a self-evident, terminal reason for seeking it. We can sometimes "see" that an experience is pleasant. When, for example, we observe someone's sensual delight in eating, her/his behavior can expressly characterize pleasure. We can only question the benefit of such an experience by referring to other goods with which it might conflict. Though sensual pleasures may not be sufficient to warrant giving birth or to deter suicide, so long as we live they are self-evidently benefits to us.

The most eloquent detractors of sexual experience have admitted that it provides sensual pleasures so poignant that once experienced they are repeatedly, almost addictively, sought. Yet, unlike other appetites, such as hunger, sexual desire can be permanently resisted, and resistance has been advocated. How can the prima facie benefits of sexual pleasure appear deceptive?

There are several grounds for complaint. Sexual pleasure is ineradicably mixed, frustration being part of every sexual life. The capacity for sexual pleasure is unevenly distributed, cannot be voluntarily acquired, and diminishes through no fault of its subject. If such a pleasure were an intrinsic benefit, benefit would in this case be independent of moral effort. Then again, sexual pleasures are not serious. Enjoyment of them is one of life's greatest recreations, but none of its business. And finally, sexual desire has the defects of its strengths. Before satisfaction, it is, at the least, distracting; in satisfaction, it "makes one little roome, an everywhere." Like psychosis, sexual desire turns us from "reality"—whether the real be God, social justice, children, or intellectual endeavor. This turning away is more than a social consequence of desire, though it is that. Lovers themselves feel that their sexual desires are separate from their "real" political, domestic, ambitious, social selves.

If the plaintiff is taken to argue that sensual pleasures are not peremptory benefits, s/he is probably right. We can still want a good deal and forego sexual pleasures. We often forego pleasure just because we want something incompatible with it, for example, a continuing marriage. We must distinguish between giving up some occasions for sexual pleasure and giving up sexual pleasure itself. If all circumstances of sexual pleasure . . . threaten a peremptory benefit, such as self-respect, then the hope and the possibility of sexual pleasure may be relinquished. Since sexual pleasure is such a great, though optional, benefit, its loss is a sad one.

In emphasizing the unsocial, private nature of sexual experiences, the plaintiff is emphasizing a morally important characteristic of them. But her/his case against desire, as I have sketched it, is surely overstated. The mixed, partly frustrated character of any desire is not particularly pronounced for sexual desire, which is in fact especially plastic, or adaptable to changes (provided perverse sex acts have not been ruled out). Inhibition, social deprivation, or disease make our sexual lives unpleasant, but that is because they interfere with sexual desire, not because the desire is by its nature frustrating. More than other well-known desires (for example, desire for knowledge, success, or power), sexual desire is simply and completely satisfied upon attaining its object. Partly for this reason, even if we are overtaken by desire during sexual experience, our sexual experiences do not overtake us. Lovers turn away from the world while loving, but return—sometimes all too easily—when loving is done. The moralist rightly perceives sexual pleasure as a recreation, and those who upon realizing its benefits make a business of its pursuit appear ludicrous. The capacity for recreation, however, is surely a benefit that any human being rightly hopes for who hopes for anything. Indeed, in present social and economic conditions we are more likely to lay waste our powers in work than in play. Thus, though priest, revolutionary, and parent are alike in fearing sexual pleasure, this fear should inspire us to psychological and sociological investigation of the fearing rather than to moral doubt about the benefit of sexual pleasure.

The Moral Significance of Perversion

What is the moral significance of the perversity of a sexual act? Next to none, so far as I can see. Though perverted sex may be "unnatural" both from an evolutionary and developmental perspective, there is no connection, inverse or correlative, between what is natural and what is good. Perverted sex is sometimes said to be less pleasurable than natural sex. We have little reason to believe that this claim is true and no clear idea of the kind of evidence on which it would be based. In any case, to condemn perverse acts for lack of pleasure is to recognize the worth of pleasure, not of naturalness.

There are many other claims about the nature and consequences of perversion. Some merely restate "scientific" facts in morally tinged terminology. Perverse acts are, by definition and according to psychiatric theory, "immature" and "abnormal," since natural sex acts are selected by criteria of "normal" sexual function and "normal" and "mature" psychological development. But there is no greater connection of virtue with maturity and normality than there is of virtue with nature. The elimination of a village by an invading army would be no less evil if it were the expression of controlled, normal, natural, and mature aggression.

Nagel claims that many perverted sex acts are incomplete, and in making his point, gives the most specific arguments that I have read for the inferiority of perverted sex. But as he points out, there is no reason to think an act consisting solely of oral-genital intercourse is incomplete; it is doubtful whether homosexual acts and acts of buggery are especially liable to be incomplete; and the incompleteness of sexual intercourse with animals is a relative matter depending upon their limited consciousness. And again, the alleged inferiority is not a consequence of perversion but of incompleteness, which can afflict natural sex as well.

Perverted acts might be thought to be inferior because they cannot result in children. Whatever the benefits and moral significance of the procreation and care of children (and I believe they are extensive and complicated), the virtue of proper care for children neither requires nor follows from biological parenthood. Even if it did, only a sexual life consisting solely of perverse acts rules out conception.

If perverted sex acts did rule out normal sex acts, if one were *either* perverted *or* natural, then certain kinds of sexual relations would be denied some perverts—relations that are benefits to those who enjoy them. It seems that sexual relations with the living and the human would be of greater benefit than those with the dead or with animals. But there is no reason to think that heterosexual relations are of greater benefit than homosexual ones. It might be thought that children can only be raised by heterosexual couples who perform an abundance of natural sex acts. If true (though truth seems highly unlikely), perverts will be denied the happiness of parenthood. This deprivation would be an *indirect* consequence of perverted sex and might yield a moral dilemma: How is one to choose between the benefits of children and the benefits of more pleasurable, more complex sex acts?

Some perversions are immoral on independent grounds. Sadism is the obvious example, though sadism practiced with a consenting masochist is far less evil than other, more familiar forms of aggression. Voyeurism may seem immoral because, since it must be secret to be satisfying, it violates others' rights to privacy.[18] Various kinds of rape can constitute perversion if rape, rather than genital intercourse, is the aim of desire. Rape is always seriously immoral, a vivid violation of respect for persons. Sometimes doubly perverse rape is doubly evil (the rape of

---

[18] I am indebted to Dr. Leo Goldberger for this example.

a child), but in other cases (the rape of a pig) its evil is halved. In any case, though rape is always *wrong*, it is only perverse when raping becomes the aim and not the means of desire.

Someone can be dissuaded from acting on her/his perverse desires either from moral qualms or from social fears. Although there may be ample basis for the latter, I can find none for the former except the possibile indirect loss of the benefits of child care. I am puzzled about this since reflective people who do not usually attempt to legislate the preferences of others think differently. There is no doubt that beliefs in these matters involve deep emotions that should be respected. But for those who do in fact have perverted desires, the first concern will be to satisfy them, not to divert or to understand them. For sexual pleasure is intrinsically a benefit, and complete sex acts, which depend upon expressing the desires one in fact has, are both beneficial and conducive to virtue. Therefore, barring extrinsic moral or social considerations, perverted sex acts are preferable to natural ones if the latter are less pleasurable or less complete.

The Moral Significance of Completeness

Complete sex consists in mutually embodied, mutually active, responsive desire. Embodiment, activity, and mutual responsiveness are instrumentally beneficial because they are conducive to our psychological well-being, which is an intrinsic benefit. The alleged pathological consequences of disembodiment are more specific and better documented than those of perversity.[19] To dissociate oneself from one's actual body, either by creating a delusory body or by rejecting the bodily, is to court a variety of ill effects, ranging from self-disgust to diseases of the will, to faulty mental development, to the destruction of a recognizable "self," and finally to madness. It is difficult to assess psychiatric claims outside their theoretical contexts, but in this case I believe that they are justified. Relative embodiment is a stable, *normal* condition that is not confined to cases of complete embodiment. But psychiatrists tell us that exceptional physical occasions of embodiment seem to be required in order to balance tendencies to reject or to falsify the body. Sexual acts are not the only such occasions, but they do provide an immersion of consciousness in the bodily, which is pleasurable and especially conducive to correcting experiences of shame and disgust that work toward disembodiment.

The mutual responsiveness of complete sex is also instrumentally beneficial. It satisfies a general desire to be recognized as a particular "real" person and to make a difference to other particular "real" people. The satisfaction of this desire in sexual experience is especially rewarding, its thwarting especially cruel. Vulnerability is increased in complete sex by the active desiring of the partners. When betrayal, or for that matter, tenderness or ecstasy, ensues, one cannot dissociate oneself from the desire with which one identified and out of which one acted. The psychic danger is real, as people who attempt to achieve a distance from their desires could tell us. But the cost of distance is as evident as its gains. Passivity in respect to one's own sexual desire not only limits sexual pleasure but, more seriously, limits the extent to which the experience of sexual pleasure can be included as an experience of a coherent person. With passivity comes a kind of irresponsibility in which one

[19] See, for example, R. D. Laing, *The Divided Self;* D. W. Winnicott, "Transitional Objects and Transitional Phenomena," *International Journal of Psychoanalysis,* 34 (1953), 89–97; Paul Federn, *Ego Psychology and the Psychoses* (New York: Basic Books, 1952); Phyllis Greenacre, *Trauma, Growth, and Personality* (New York: International Universities Press, 1969); Paul Schilder, *The Image and Appearance of the Human Body* (New York: International Universities Press, 1950); Moses Laufer, "Body Image and Masturbation in Adolescence," *The Psychoanalytic Study of the Child,* 23 (1968), 114–46. Laing's work is most specific about both the nature and consequences of disembodiment, but the works cited, and others similar to them, give the clinical evidence upon which much of Laing's work depends.

can hide from one's desire, even from one's pleasure, "playing" seducer or victim, tease or savior. Active sexual desiring in complete sex acts affords an especially threatening but also especially happy occasion to relinquish these and similar roles. To the extent that the roles confuse and confound our intimate relations, the benefit from relinquishing them in our sexual acts, or the loss from adhering to them then, is especially poignant.

In addition to being beneficial, complete sex acts are morally superior for three reasons. They tend to resolve tensions fundamental to moral life; they are conducive to emotions that, if they become stable and dominant, are in turn conducive to the virtue of loving; and they involve a preeminently moral virtue—respect for persons.

In one of its aspects, morality is opposed to the private and untamed. Morality is "civilization," social and regulating; desire is "discontent," resisting the regulation. Obligation, rather than benefit, is the notion central to morality so conceived, and the virtues required of a moral person are directed to preserving right relations and social order. Both the insistence on natural sex and the encouragement of complete sex can be looked upon as attempts to make sexual desire more amenable to regulation. But whereas the regulation of perverted desires is extrinsic to them, those of completeness modify the desires themselves. The desiring sensual body that in our social lives we may laugh away or disown becomes our "self" and enters into a social relation. Narcissism and altruism are satisfied in complete sex acts in which one gives what one receives by receiving it. Social and private "selves" are unified in an act in which impersonal, spontaneous impulses govern an action that is responsive to a particular person. For this to be true we must surmount our social "roles" as well as our sexual "techniques," though we incorporate rather than surmount our social selves. We must also surmount regulations imposed in the name of naturalness if our desires are to be spontaneously expressed. Honestly spontaneous first love gives us back our private desiring selves while allowing us to see the desiring self of another. Mutually responding partners confirm each other's desires and declare them good. Such occasions, when we are "moral" without cost, help reconcile us to our moral being and to the usual mutual exclusion between our social and private lives.

The connection between sex and certain emotions—particularly love, jealousy, fear, and anger—is as evident as it is obscure. Complete sex acts seem more likely than incomplete pleasurable ones to lead toward affection and away from fear and anger, since any guilt and shame will be extrinsic to the act and meliorated by it. It is clear that we need not feel for someone any affection beyond that required (if any is) simply to participate with him/her in a complete sex act. However, it is equally clear that sexual pleasure, especially as experienced in complete sex acts, is conducive to many feelings—gratitude, tenderness, pride, appreciation, dependency, and others. These feelings magnify their object who occasioned them. When these magnifying feelings become stable and habitual they are conducive to love—not universal love, of course, but love of a particular sexual partner. However, even "selfish" love is a virtue, a disposition to care for someone as her/his interests and demands would dictate. Neither the best sex nor the best love require each other, but they go together more often than reason would expect—often enough to count the virtue of loving as one of the rewards of the capacity for sexual pleasure exercised in complete sex acts.

It might be argued that the coincidence of sex acts and several valued emotions is a cultural matter. It is notoriously difficult to make judgments about the emotional and, particularly, the sexual lives of others, especially culturally alien others. There is, however, some anthropological evidence that at first glance relativizes the connection between good sex and valued emotion. For example, among the Manus of New Guinea, it seems that relations of affection and love are encouraged primarily among brother and sister, while easy familiarity, joking, and superficial sexual play is expected only between cross-cousins. Sexual intercourse is, however, forbidden between siblings and cross-cousins but required of married men and women, who are as apt to hate as to care for each other and often seem to consider each other strangers. It seems, however, that the Manus do not value or experience complete or even pleasurable sex. Both men and women are described as puritanical, and the sexual life of women seems blatantly unrewarding. Moreover, their emotional life is generally impoverished. This impoverishment, in conjunction with an unappreciated and unrewarding sexual life dissociated from love or affection, would argue for a *connection* between better sex and valued emotions. If, as Peter Winch suggests, cultures provide their members with particular possibilities of making sense of their lives, and thereby with possibilities of good and evil, the Manus might be said to deny themselves one possibility both of sense and of good—namely the coincidence of good sex and of affection and love. Other cultures, including our own, allow this possibility, whose realization is encouraged in varying degrees by particular groups and members of the culture.[20]

Finally, as Sartre has suggested, complete sex acts preserve a respect for persons. Each person remains conscious and responsible, a "subject" rather than a depersonalized, will-less, or manipulated "object." Each actively desires that the other likewise remain a "subject." Respect for persons is a central virtue when matters of justice and obligation are at issue. Insofar as we can speak of respect for persons in complete sex acts, there are different, often contrary requirements of respect. Respect for persons, typically and in sex acts, requires that *actual present* partners participate, partners whose desires are recognized and endorsed. Respect for persons typically requires taking a distance from both one's own demands and those of others. But in sex acts the demands of desire take over, and equal distance is replaced by mutual responsiveness. Respect typically requires refusing to treat another person merely as a means to fulfilling demands. In sex acts, another person is so clearly a means to satisfaction that s/he is always on the verge of becoming merely a means ("intercourse counterfeits masturbation"). In complete sex acts, instrumentality vanishes only because it is mutual and mutually desired. Respect requires encouraging, or at least protecting, the autonomy of another. In complete sex, autonomy of will is recruited by desire, and freedom from others is replaced by frank dependence on another person's desire. Again the respect consists in the reciprocity of desiring dependence, which bypasses rather than violates autonomy.

Despite the radical differences between respect for persons in the usual moral contexts and respect for persons in sex acts, it is not, I think, a mere play on words to talk of respect in the latter case. When, in any sort of intercourse, persons are respected, their desires are not only, in fair measure, *fulfilled*. In addition, their desires are *active* and determine, in fair measure, the form of intercourse and the *manner* and *condition* of desire's satisfaction. These conditions are not only met in sexual intercourse when it is characterized by completeness; they come close to defining completeness.

Sartre is not alone in believing that just because the condition of completeness involves respect for persons, complete sex is impossible. Completeness is surely threatened by pervasive tendencies to fantasy, to possessiveness, and to varieties of a sadomasochistic desire. But a complete sex act, as I see it, does not involve an heroic restraint on our sexual interpulses. Rather, a complete sex act is a normal mode of sexual activity expressing the natural structure and impulses of sexual desire.

While complete sex is morally superior because it involves respect for persons, incomplete

---

[20]The evidence about the life of the Manus comes from Margaret Mead, *Growing Up in New Guinea* (Harmondsworth, England: Penguin Books, 1942). Peter Winch's discussion can be found in his "Understanding a Primitive Society," *American Philosophical Quarterly*, 1 (1964), 307–34.

sex acts do not necessarily involve immoral disrespect for persons. Depending upon the desires and expectations of the partners, incompleteness may involve neither respect nor disrespect. Masturbation, for example, allows only the limited completeness of embodiment and often fails of that. But masturbation only rarely involves disrespect to anyone. Even the respect of Sartre's allegedly desirable sleeping woman may not be violated if she is unknowingly involved in a sex act. Disrespect, though probable, may in some cases be obviated by her sensibilities and expectations that she had previously expressed and her partners has understood. Sex acts provide one context in which respect for persons can be expressed. That context is important both because our sexual lives are of such importance to us and because they are so liable to injury because of the experience and the fear of the experience of disrespect. But many complete sex acts in which respect is maintained make other casual and incomplete sex acts unthreatening. In this case a goodly number of swallows can make a summer.

In sum, then, complete sex acts are superior to incomplete ones. First, they are, whatever their effects, better than various kinds of incomplete sex acts because they involve a kind of "respect for persons" in acts that are otherwise prone to violation of respect for, and often to violence to, persons. Second, complete sex acts are good because they are good for us. They are conducive to some fairly clearly defined kinds of psychological well-being that are beneficial. They are conducive to moral well-being because they relieve tensions that arise in our attempts to be moral and because they encourage the development of particular virtues.

To say that complete sex acts are preferable to incomplete ones is not to court a new puritanism. There are many kinds and degrees of incompleteness. Incomplete sex acts may not involve a disrespect for persons. Complete sex acts only *tend* to be good for us, and the realization of these tendencies depends upon individual lives and circumstances of sexual activity. The proper object of sexual desire is sexual pleasure.

It would be a foolish ambition indeed to limit one's sexual acts to those in which completeness was likely. Any sexual act that is pleasurable is prima facie good, though the more incomplete it is—the more private, essentially autoerotic, unresponsive, unembodied, passive, or imposed—the more likely it is to be harmful to someone.

On Sexual Morality: Concluding Remarks

There are many questions we have neglected to consider because we have not been sufficiently attentive to the quality of sexual lives. For example, we know little about the ways of achieving better sex. When we must choose between inferior sex and abstinence, how and when will our choice of inferior sex damage our capacity for better sex? Does, for example, the repeated experience of controlled sexual disembodiment ("desire which takes over will take you too far") that we urge (or used to urge) on adolescents damage their capacity for complete sex? The answers to this and similar questions are not obvious, though unfounded opinions are always ready at hand.

Some of the traditional sexual vices might be condemned on the ground that they are inimical to better sex. Obscenity, or repeated public exposure to sexual acts, might impair our capacity for pleasure or for response to desire. Promiscuity might undercut the tendency of complete sex acts to promote emotions that magnify their object. Other of the traditional sexual vices are neither inimical nor conducive to better sex, but are condemned because of conflicting nonsexual benefits and obligations. For example, infidelity qua infidelity neither secures nor prevents better sex. The obligations of fidelity have many sources, one of which may be a past history of shared complete sex acts, a history that included promises of exclusive intimacy. Such past promises are as apt to conflict with as to accord with a current demand for better sex. I have said nothing about how such a conflict would be settled. I hope I have shown that where the possibility of better sex conflicts with obligations and other benefits, we have a *moral dilemma*, not just an occasion for moral self-discipline.

The pursuit of more pleasurable and more complete sex acts is, among many moral activities, distinguished not for its exigencies but for its rewards. Since our sexual lives are so important to us, and since, whatever our history and our hopes, we are sexual beings, this pursuit rightly engages our moral reflection. It should not be relegated to the immoral, nor to the "merely" prudent.

Postscript

I wrote this essay fourteen years ago. Since that time my ideas about thinking and writing, as well as about sexual morality, have been transformed by feminist and anti-militarist politics.

The tone and language of the essay, as well as certain basic presuppositions of its arguments, now ring strangely in my ears. Nonetheless, what has been made public belongs to the public and I am pleased if this early paper still proves useful. In one respect, however, the essay seems seriously insensitive and limited. In 1970 I was largely unaware of the deep and extensive pain suffered by those whose sexuality is labeled "abnormal," "perverted," or "immature." On a more theoretical level, since 1970 we have learned to see the connections between misogyny, homophobia, militarism, and racism. I would like here to acknowledge my debt to the work of the feminist and gay liberation movements, which has made these theoretical connections while fighting ignorant and arrogant sexual politics. As a result many people now lead more complete and pleasurable sexual lives.

For Further Thought and Discussion

1. How does a complete sex act show that one is treating one's partner not merely as a means but also as an end?

2. Can one preserve one's dignity as a human being and still agree to "incomplete" sex acts?

15   Abortion

Abortion is a question that is so frequently and hotly debated that we would think that everyone has a strong and well-considered opinion about it by now. My experience has been that those with the strongest opinions rarely have articulate, well-conceived reasons for their position. That is one part of the problem. Another part of the problem is that people disagree in their basic beliefs about God(s) and moral rules. These readings address the questions surrounding the abortion issue with clarity and precision. Although this chapter is not an exhaustive discussion, it is a start—an opportunity for you to examine your opinion and find more reasons supporting your beliefs.

Like many other moral issues in our society, abortion is interconnected with other beliefs and values. Many people maintain that abortion is morally unacceptable because of God's decree. They cite their religious teachers and sacred texts such as the Bible to justify their claim. This "argument," however, is persuasive only within those religious traditions that accept the truth of the religious books and the moral leadership of their clergy, not to people outside those religions.

Similarly, the debate has been unfruitful because the "pro-choice" advocates have not been sufficiently successful in defining the qualities that guarantee a being's right to protection. If the "pro-choice" advocates could show that a fetus does not satisfy the criteria necessary to be granted the moral status of a person, then the debate might progress. Even that may not be enough, of course. Let's assume that a fetus is a person—that is, that it does have the traits necessary to be treated like a person. Still, that status alone may not be enough to protect it. At least some conditions the pregnant woman faces may override the fetus's right to protection.

Conversely, if we grant full status of "person" to a fetus, other implications follow. We may be obliged to say that cases of rape and incest do not justify abortion. For example, no one would accept as justification for the murder of an adult the argument that the adult was the product of incest or rape.

Majority Opinion in *Roe v. Wade*

JUSTICE HARRY BLACKMUN

Reading Questions

1. How does Justice Blackmun deny the absolute right to privacy in the case of abortion? What legal examples does he call to his defense?

2. Why does the Court "draw the line" regarding the legitimate health of the mother at the end of the first trimester of pregnancy?

3. On what basis does the Court reject the idea that life begins at conception? On what historical and social "evidence" does Blackmun draw?

4. What is the viability of a fetus? Is the choice of fetal viability an arbitrary one, or is Justice Blackmun's concern with the potentiality of a life morally significant and compelling?

... THIS RIGHT OF PRIVACY, whether it be founded in the Fourteenth Amendment's concept of personal liberty and restrictions upon state action, as we feel it is, or, as the District Court determined, in the Ninth Amendment's reservation of rights to the people, is broad enough to encompass a woman's decision whether or not to terminate her pregnancy. . . .

. . . [A]ppellants and some *amici* argue that the woman's right is absolute and that she is entitled to terminate her pregnancy at whatever time, in whatever way, and for whatever reason she alone chooses. With this we do not agree. Appellants' arguments that Texas either has no valid interest at all in regulating the abortion decision, or no interest strong enough to support any limitation upon the woman's sole determination, is unpersuasive. The Court's decisions recognizing a right of privacy also acknowledge that some state regulation in areas protected by that right is appropriate. As noted above, a state may properly assert important interests in safeguarding health, in maintaining medical standards, and in protecting potential life. At some point in pregnancy, these respective interests become sufficiently compelling to sustain regulation of the factors that govern the abortion decision. The privacy right involved, therefore, cannot be said to be absolute. . . .

We therefore conclude that the right of personal privacy includes the abortion decision, but that this right is not unqualified and must be considered against important state interests in regulation.

We note that those federal and state courts that have recently considered abortion law challenges have reached the same conclusion. . . .

Although the results are divided, most of these courts have agreed that the right of privacy, however based, is broad enough to cover the abortion decision; that the right, nonetheless, is not absolute and is subject to some limitations; and that at some point the state interests as to protection of health, medical standards, and prenatal life, become dominant. We agree with this approach. . . .

The appellee and certain *amici* argue that the fetus is a "person" within the language and meaning of the Fourteenth Amendment. In support of this they outline at length and in detail

Excerpts from *Roe v. Wade,* United States Supreme Court. 410 U.S. 113 (1973).

the well-known facts of fetal development. If this suggestion of personhood is established, the appellant's case, of course, collapses, for the fetus' right to life is then guaranteed specifically by the Amendment. The appellant conceded as much on reargument. On the other hand, the appellee conceded on reargument that no case could be cited that holds that a fetus is a person within the meaning of the Fourteenth Amendment. . . .

All this, together with our observation, *supra,* that throughout the major portion of the 19th century prevailing legal abortion practices were far freer than they are today, persuades us that the word "person," as used in the Fourteenth Amendment, does not include the unborn. . . . Indeed, our decision in *United States v. Vuitch* (1971) inferentially is to the same effect, for we there would not have indulged in statutory interpretation favorable to abortion in specified circumstances if the necessary consequence was the termination of life entitled to Fourteenth Amendment protection.

. . . As we have intimated above, it is reasonable and appropriate for a State to decide that at some point in time another interest, that of health of the mother or that of potential human life, becomes significantly involved. The woman's privacy is no longer sole and any right of privacy she possesses must be measured accordingly.

Texas urges that, apart from the Fourteenth Amendment, life begins at conception and is present throughout pregnancy, and that, therefore, the State has a compelling interest in protecting that life from and after conception. We need not resolve the difficult question of when life begins. When those trained in the respective disciplines of medicine, philosophy, and theology are unable to arrive at any consensus, the judiciary, at this point in the development of man's knowledge, is not in a position to speculate as to the answer.

It should be sufficient to note briefly the wide divergence of thinking on this most sensitive and difficult question. There has always been strong support for the view that life does not begin until live birth. This was the belief of the Stoics. It appears to be the predominant, though not the unanimous, attitude of the Jewish faith. It may be taken to represent also the position of a large segment of the Protestant community, insofar as that can be ascertained; organized groups that have taken a formal position on the abortion issue have generally regarded abortion as a matter for the conscience of the individual and her family. As we have noted, the common law found greater significance in quickening. Physicians and their scientific colleagues have regarded that event with less interest and have tended to focus either upon conception or upon live birth or upon the interim point at which the fetus becomes "viable," that is, potentially able to live outside the mother's womb, albeit with artificial aid. Viability is usually placed at about seven months (28 weeks) but may occur earlier, even at 24 weeks. . . .

In areas other than criminal abortion the law has been reluctant to endorse any theory that life, as we recognize it, begins before live birth or to accord legal rights to the unborn except in narrowly defined situations and except when the rights are contingent upon live birth. . . . In short, the unborn have never been recognized in the law as persons in the whole sense.

In view of all this, we do not agree that, by adopting one theory of life, Texas may override the rights of the pregnant woman that are at stake. We repeat, however, that the State does have an important and legitimate interest in preserving and protecting the health of the pregnant woman, whether she be a resident of the State or a nonresident who seeks medical consultation and treatment there, and that it has still *another* important and legitimate interest in protecting the potentiality of human life. These interests are separate and distinct. Each grows in substantiality as the woman approaches term and, at a point during pregnancy, each becomes "compelling."

With respect to the State's important and legitimate interest in the health of the mother, the "compelling" point, in the light of present medical knowledge, is at approximately the end of the first trimester. This is so because of the now established medical fact . . . that until the end of the first trimester mortality in abortion is less than mortality in normal childbirth. It follows that, from and after this point, a State may regulate the abortion procedure to the extent that the regulation reasonably relates to the preservation and protection of maternal health. Examples of permissible state regulation in this area are requirements as to the qualifications of the person who is to perform the abortion; as to the licensure of that person; as to the facility in which the procedure is to be performed, that is, whether it must be a hospital or may be a clinic or some other place of less-than-hospital status; as to the licensing of the facility; and the like.

This means, on the other hand, that, for the period of pregnancy prior to this "compelling" point, the attending physician, in consultation with his patient, is free to determine, without regulation by the State, that in his medical judgment the patient's pregnancy should be terminated. If that decision is reached, the judgment may be effectuated by an abortion free of interference by the State.

With respect to the State's important and legitimate interest in potential life, the "compelling" point is at viability. This is so because the fetus then presumably has the capability of meaningful life outside the mother's womb. State regulation protective of fetal life after viability thus has both logical and biological justifications. If the State is interested in protecting fetal life after viability, it may go so far as to proscribe abortion during that period except when it is necessary to preserve the life or health of the mother. . . .

To summarize and repeat:

1. A state criminal abortion statute of the current Texas type, that excepts from criminality only a *life saving* procedure on behalf of the mother without regard to pregnancy stage and without recognition

of the other interests involved, is violative of the Due Process Clause of the Fourteenth Amendment.

(a) For the stage prior to approximately the end of the first trimester, the abortion decision and its effectuation must be left to the medical judgment of the pregnant woman's attending physician.

(b) For the stage subsequent to approximately the end of the first trimester, the State, in promoting its interest in the health of the mother, may, if it chooses, regulate the abortion procedure in ways that are reasonably related to maternal health.

(c) For the stage subsequent to viability the State, in promoting its interest in the potentiality of human life, may, if it chooses, regulate, and even proscribe, abortion except where it is necessary, in appropriate medical judgment, for the preservation of the life or health of the mother.

2. The State may define the term "physician," as it has been employed [here], to mean only a physician currently licensed by the State, and may proscribe any abortion by a person who is not a physician as so defined.

. . . The decision leaves the State free to place increasing restrictions on abortion as the period of pregnancy lengthens, so long as those restrictions are tailored to the recognized state interests. The decision vindicates the right of the physician to administer medical treatment according to his professional judgment up to the points where important state interests provide compelling justifications for intervention. Up to those points the abortion decision in all its aspects is inherently, and primarily, a medical decision, and basic responsibility for it must rest with the physician. If an individual practitioner abuses the privilege of exercising proper medical judgment, the usual remedies, judicial and intra-professional, are available.

For Further Thought and Discussion

1. Is abortion really a matter of privacy, or is it a question of protecting the religious and moral outlook of some members of society?

2. Can a Supreme Court decision protect the rights of the individual when those rights conflict with a vocal and persistent group within society? Who will be satisfied with any decision?

Dissenting Opinion in *Roe v. Wade*

JUSTICE BYRON WHITE

Reading Questions

1. Justice White objects that the majority opinion is "an improvident and extravagant exercise of the power of judicial review." How does he arrive at this conclusion?

2. Who does Justice White think should make the decisions pertaining to abortion? Why?

3. Which conditions does Justice White envision as justifying abortion?

AT THE HEART OF THE CONTROVERSY in these cases are those recurring pregnancies that pose no danger whatsoever to the life or health of the mother but are nevertheless unwanted for any one or more of a variety of reasons—convenience, family planning, economics, dislike of children, the embarrassment of illegitimacy, etc. The common claim before us is that for any one of such reasons, or for no reason at all, and without asserting or claiming any threat to life or health, any woman is entitled to an abortion at her request if she is able to find a medical adviser willing to undertake the procedure.

The Court for the most part sustains this position: During the period prior to the time the fetus becomes viable, the Constitution of the United States values the convenience, whim or caprice of the putative mother more than the life or potential life of the fetus; the Constitution, therefore, guarantees the right to an abortion as against any state law or policy seeking to protect the fetus from an abortion not prompted by more compelling reasons of the mother.

With all due respect, I dissent. I find nothing in the language or history of the Constitution to support the Court's judgment. The Court simply fashions and announces a new constitutional right for pregnant mothers and, with scarcely any reason or authority for its action, invests that right with sufficient substance to override most existing state abortion statutes. The upshot is that the people and the legislatures

United States Supreme Court. 410 U.S. 113 (1973).

of the 50 States are constitutionally disentitled to weigh the relative importance of the continued existence and development of the fetus on the one hand against a spectrum of possible impacts on the mother on the other hand. As an exercise of raw judicial power, the Court perhaps has authority to do what it does today; but in my view its judgment is an improvident and extravagant exercise of the power of judicial review which the Constitution extends to this Court.

The Court apparently values the convenience of the pregnant mother more than the continued existence and development of the life or potential life which she carries. Whether or not I might agree with that marshalling of values, I can in no event join the Court's judgment because I find no constitutional warrant for imposing such an order of priorities on the people and legislatures of the States. In a sensitive area such as this, involving as it does issues over which reasonable men may easily and heatedly differ, I cannot accept the Court's exercise of its clear power of choice by interposing a constitutional barrier to state efforts to protect human life and by investing mothers and doctors with the constitutionally protected right to exterminate it. This issue, for the most part, should be left with the people and to the political processes the people have devised to govern their affairs.

It is my view, therefore, that the Texas statute is not constitutionally infirm because it denies abortions to those who seek to serve only their convenience rather than to protect their life or health. . . .

For Further Thought and Discussion

1. On what grounds, if any, should abortion be permitted or restricted? How can such grounds be justified?

2. Is there sufficient justification for Justice White's reluctance to allow a decision of abortion to be made by the woman (perhaps with her partner as well) and a competently trained medical person? Why would Justice White prefer to put the decision in the hands of state legislatures?

An Almost Absolute Value in History

JOHN T. NOONAN, JR.

Reading Questions

    1. What is viability and how can it be used as a way of denying recognition of a fetus's humanity?

    2. How does Noonan reply to the distinction that a being who has had experience is more human than one who has not?

    3. Does an appeal to the sentiments of adults provide a sure guide in the case of abortion?

    4. Should social visibility be a relevant consideration in granting moral protections? How does Noonan argue against this requirement?

    5. What obligations follow if a fetus is recognized as fully human?

THE MOST FUNDAMENTAL QUESTION involved in the long history of thought on abortion is: How do you determine the humanity of a being? To phrase the question that way is to put in comprehensive humanistic terms what the theologians either dealt with as an explicitly theological question under the heading of "ensoulment" or dealt with implicitly in their treatment of abortion. The Christian position as it originated did not depend on a narrow theological or philosophical concept. It had no relation to the theories of infant baptism. It appealed to no special theory of instantaneous ensoulment. It took the world's view on ensoulment as that view changed from Aristotle to Zacchia. There was, indeed, theological influence affecting the theory of ensoulment finally adopted, and, of course, ensoulment itself was a theological concept, so that the position was always explained in theological terms. But the theological notion of ensoulment could easily be translated into humanistic language by substituting "human" for "rational soul"; the problem of knowing when a man is a man is common to theology and humanism.

If one steps outside the specific categories used by the theologians, the answer they gave can be analyzed as a refusal to discriminate among human beings on the basis of their varying potentialities. Once conceived, the being was recognized as man because he had man's potential. The criterion for humanity, thus, was simple and all-embracing: if you are conceived by human parents, you are human.

The strength of this position may be tested by a review of some of the other distinctions offered in the contemporary controversy over legalizing abortion. Perhaps the most popular distinction is in terms of viability. Before an age of so many months, the fetus is not viable, that is, it cannot be removed from the mother's womb and live apart from her. To that extent, the life of the fetus is absolutely dependent on the life of the mother. This dependence is made the basis of denying recognition to its humanity.

There are difficulties with this distinction.

One is that the perfection of artificial incubation may make the fetus viable at any time: it may be removed and artificially sustained. Experiments with animals already show that such a procedure is possible. This hypothetical extreme case relates to an actual difficulty: there is considerable elasticity to the idea of viability. Mere length of life is not an exact measure. The viability of the fetus depends on the extent of its anatomical and functional development. The weight and length of the fetus are better guides to the state of its development than age, but weight and length vary. . . . If viability is the norm, the standard would vary with . . . many individual circumstances.

The most important objection to this approach is that dependence is not ended by viability. The fetus is still absolutely dependent on someone's care in order to continue existence; indeed a child of one or three or even five years of age is absolutely dependent on another's care for existence; uncared for, the older fetus or the younger child will die as surely as the early fetus detached from the mother. The unsubstantial lessening in dependence at viability does not seem to signify any special acquisition of humanity.

A second distinction has been attempted in terms of experience. A being who has had experience, has lived and suffered, who possesses memories, is more human than one who has not. Humanity depends on formation by experience. The fetus is thus "unformed" in the most basic human sense.

This distinction is not serviceable for the embryo which is already experiencing and reacting. The embryo is responsive to touch after eight weeks and at least at that point is experiencing. At an earlier stage the zygote is certainly alive and responding to its environment. The distinction may also be challenged by the rare case where aphasia has erased adult memory: has it erased humanity? More fundamentally, this distinction leaves even the older fetus or the younger child to be treated as an unformed inhuman thing. Finally, it is not clear why experience as such confers humanity. It could be argued that certain central experiences such as loving or learning are necessary to make a man human. But then human beings who have failed to love or to learn might be excluded from the class called man.

A third distinction is made by appeal to the sentiments of adults. If a fetus dies, the grief of the parents is not the grief they would have for a living child. The fetus is an unnamed "it" till birth, and is not perceived as personality until at least the fourth month of existence when movements in the womb manifest a vigorous presence demanding joyful recognition by the parents.

Yet feeling is notoriously an unsure guide to the humanity of others. Many groups of humans have had difficulty in feeling that persons of another tongue, color, religion, sex, are as human as they. Apart from reactions to alien groups, we mourn the loss of a ten-year-old boy more than the loss of his one-day-old brother or his 90-year-old grandfather. The difference felt and the grief expressed vary with the potentialities extinguished, or the experience wiped out; they do not seem to point to any substantial difference in the humanity of baby, boy, or grandfather.

Distinctions are also made in terms of sensation by the parents. The embryo is felt within the womb only after about the fourth month. The embryo is seen only at birth. What can be neither seen nor felt is different from what is tangible. If the fetus cannot be seen or touched at all, it cannot be perceived as man.

Yet experience shows that sight is even more untrustworthy than feeling in determining humanity. By sight, color became an appropriate index for saying who was a man, and the evil of racial discrimination was given foundations. Nor can touch provide the test; a being confined by sickness, "out of touch" with others, does not thereby seem to lose his humanity. To the extent that touch still has appeal as a criterion, it appears to be a survival of the old English idea of "quickening"—a possible mistranslation of the Latin *animatus* used in the canon law. To that extent touch as a criterion seems to be dependent on the Aristotelian notion of ensoulment, and to fall when this notion is discarded.

Finally, a distinction is sought in social visibility. The fetus is not socially perceived as human. It cannot communicate with others. Thus, both subjectively and objectively, it is not a member of society. As moral rules are rules for the behavior of members of society to each other, they cannot be made for behavior toward what is not yet a member. Excluded from the society of men, the fetus is excluded from the humanity of men.

By force of the argument from the consequences, this distinction is to be rejected. It is more subtle than that founded on an appeal to physical sensation, but it is equally dangerous in its implications. If humanity depends on social recognition, individuals or whole groups may be dehumanized by being denied any status in their society. Such a fate is fictionally portrayed in *1984* and has actually been the lot of many men in many societies. In the Roman empire, for example, condemnation to slavery meant the practical denial of most human rights; in the Chinese Communist world, landlords have been classified as enemies of the people and so treated as nonpersons by the state. Humanity does not depend on social recognition, though often the failure of society to recognize the prisoner, the alien, the heterodox as human has led to the destruction of human beings. Anyone conceived by a man and a woman is human. Recognition of this condition by society follows a real event in the objective order, however imperfect and halting the recognition. Any attempt to limit humanity to exclude some group runs the risk of furnishing authority and precedent for excluding other groups in the name of the consciousness or perception of the controlling group in the society.

A philosopher may reject the appeal to the humanity of the fetus because he views "humanity" as a secular view of the soul and because he doubts the existence of anything real and objective which can be identified as humanity. One answer to such a philosopher is to ask how he

reasons about moral questions without supposing that there is a sense in which he and the others of whom he speaks are human. Whatever group is taken as the society which determines who may be killed is thereby taken as human. A second answer is to ask if he does not believe that there is a right and a wrong way of deciding moral questions. If there is such a difference, experience may be appealed to: to decide who is human on the basis of the sentiment of a given society has led to consequences which rational men would characterize as monstrous.

The rejection of the attempted distinctions based on viability and visibility, experience and feeling, may be buttressed by the following considerations: Moral judgments often rest on distinctions, but if the distinctions are not to appear arbitrary fiat, they should relate to some real difference in probabilities. There is a kind of continuity in all life, but the earlier stages of the elements of human life possess tiny probabilities of development. Consider, for example, the spermatozoa in any normal ejaculate: There are about 200,000,000 in any single ejaculate, of which one has a chance of developing into a zygote. Consider the oocytes which may become ova: there are 100,000 to 1,000,000 oocytes in a female infant, of which has a maximum of 390 are ovulated. But once spermatozoon and ovum meet and the conceptus is formed, such studies as have been made show that roughly in only 20 percent of the cases will spontaneous abortion occur. In other words, the chances are about 4 out of 5 that this new being will develop. At this stage in the life of the being there is a sharp shift in probabilities, an immense jump in potentialities. To make a distinction between the rights of spermatozoa and the rights of the fertilized ovum is to respond to an enormous shift in possibilities. For about twenty days after conception the egg may split to form twins or combine with another egg to form a chimera, but the probability of either event happening is very small.

It may be asked, What does a change in biological probabilities have to do with establishing humanity? The argument from probabilities is not aimed at establishing humanity but at establishing an objective discontinuity which may be taken into account in moral discourse. As life itself is a matter of probabilities, as most moral reasoning is an estimate of probabilities, so it seems in accord with the structure of reality and the nature of moral thought to found a moral judgment on the change in probabilities at conception. The appeal to probabilities is the most commonsensical of arguments, to a greater or smaller degree all of us base our actions on probabilities, and in morals, as in law, prudence and negligence are often measured by the account one has taken of the probabilities. If the chance is 200,000,000 to 1 that the movement in the bushes into which you shoot is a man's, I doubt if many persons would hold you careless in shooting; but if the chances are 4 out of 5 that the movement is a human being's, few would acquit you of blame. Would the argument be different if only one out of ten children conceived came to term? Of course this argument would be different. This argument is an appeal to probabilities that actually exist, not to any and all states of affairs which may be imagined.

The probabilities as they do exist do not show the humanity of the embryo in the sense of a demonstration in logic any more than the probabilities of the movement in the bush being a man demonstrate beyond all doubt that the being is a man. The appeal is a "buttressing" consideration, showing the plausibility of the standard adopted. The argument focuses on the decisional factor in any moral judgment and assumes that part of the business of a moralist is drawing lines. One evidence of the nonarbitrary character of the line drawn is the difference of probabilities on either side of it. If a spermatozoon is destroyed, one destroys a being which had a chance of far less than 1 in 200 million of developing into a reasoning being, possessed of the genetic code, a heart and other organs, and capable of pain. If a fetus is destroyed, one destroys a being already possessed of the genetic code, organs, and sensitivity to pain, and one

which had an 80 percent chance of developing further into a baby outside the womb who, in time, would reason.

The positive argument for conception as the decisive moment of humanization is that at conception the new being receives the genetic code. It is this genetic information which determines his characteristics, which is the biological carrier of the possibility of human wisdom, which makes him a self-evolving being. A being with a human genetic code is man.

This review of current controversy over the humanity of the fetus emphasizes what a fundamental question the theologians resolved in asserting the inviolability of the fetus. To regard the fetus as possessed of equal rights with other humans was not, however, to decide every case where abortion might be employed. It did decide the case where the argument was that the fetus should be aborted for its own good. To say a being was human was to say it had a destiny to decide for itself which could not be taken from it by another man's decision. But human beings with equal rights often come in conflict with each other, and some decision must be made as whose claims are to prevail. Cases of conflict involving the fetus are different only in two respects: the total inability of the fetus to speak for itself and the fact that the right of the fetus regularly at stake is the right to life itself.

The approach taken by the theologians to these conflicts was articulated in terms of "direct" and "indirect." Again, to look at what they were doing from outside their categories, they may be said to have been drawing lines or "balancing values." "Direct" and "indirect" are spatial metaphors; "line-drawing" is another. "To weigh" or "to balance" values is a metaphor of a more complicated mathematical sort hinting at the process which goes on in moral judgments. All the metaphors suggest that, in the moral judgments made, comparisons were necessary, that no value completely controlled. The principle of double effect was no doctrine fallen from heaven, but a method of analysis appropriate where two relative values were being compared.

In Catholic moral theology, as it developed, life even of the innocent was not taken as an absolute. Judgments on acts affecting life issued from a process of weighing. In the weighing, the fetus was always given a value greater than zero, always a value separate and independent from its parents. This valuation was crucial and fundamental in all Christian thought on the subject and marked it off from any approach which considered that only the parents' interests needed to be considered.

Even with the fetus weighed as human, one interest could be weighed as equal or superior: that of the mother in her own life. The casuists between 1450 and 1895 were willing to weigh this interest as superior. Since 1895, that interest was given decisive weight only in the two special cases of the cancerous uterus and the ectopic pregnancy. In both of these cases the fetus itself had little chance of survival even if the abortion were not performed. As the balance was once struck in favor of the mother whenever her life was endangered, it could be so struck again. The balance reached between 1895 and 1930 attempted prudentially and pastorally to forestall a multitude of exceptions for interests less than life.

The perception of the humanity of the fetus and the weighing of fetal rights against other human rights constituted the work of the moral analysts. But what spirit animated their abstract judgments? For the Christian community it was the injunction of Scripture to love your neighbor as yourself. The fetus as human was a neighbor; his life had parity with one's own. The commandment gave life to what otherwise would have been only rational calculation.

The commandment could be put in humanistic as well as theological terms: Do not injure your fellow man without reason. In these terms, once the humanity of the fetus is perceived, abortion is never right except in self-defense. When life must be taken to save life, reason alone cannot say that a mother must prefer a child's life to her own. With this exception, now of great rarity, abortion violates the rational humanist tenet of the equality of human lives.

For Christians the commandment to love had received a special imprint in that the exemplar proposed of love was the love of the Lord for his disciples. In the light given by this example, self-sacrifice carried to the point of death seemed in the extreme situations not without meaning. In the less extreme cases, preference for one's own interests to the life of another seemed to express cruelty or selfishness irreconcilable with the demands of love.

For Further Thought and Discussion

1. How can we determine the criteria for being a human? What traits should count toward granting human moral standards to a being?

2. For the sake of argument, grant the human status of a fetus. In what sense could self-defense be used to justify abortion? To justify the self-defense argument, must the "aggressor" intend to harm the defender?

On the Moral and Legal Status of Abortion

MARY ANNE WARREN

Reading Questions

1. How does Warren distinguish the *moral* sense of "human" from the *genetic* sense of "human"? How does this distinction affect the argument against killing fetuses?

2. Warren defines the moral community as including all *people* but not all human beings. According to Warren, what traits are central to personhood?

3. Do fetuses in any way satisfy the criteria for personhood?

4. Warren argues that "some human beings are not people, and there may well be people who are not human beings." What examples does she use to make her case?

5. Explain the space explorer analogy. How does Warren use this to protect the right of a woman to have an abortion?

THE QUESTION WHICH WE MUST ANSWER in order to produce a satisfactory solution to the problem of the moral status of abortion is this: How are we to define the moral community, the set of beings with full and equal moral rights, such that we can decide whether a human fetus is a member of this community or not? What sort of entity, exactly, has the inalienable rights to life, liberty, and the pursuit of happiness? Jefferson attributed these rights to all *men,* and it may or may not be fair to suggest that he intended to attribute them *only* to men. Perhaps he ought to have attributed them to all human beings. If so, then we arrive, first, at Noonan's problem of defining what makes a being human, and, second, at the equally vital question which Noonan does not consider, namely, What reason is there for identifying the moral community with the set of all human beings, in whatever way we have chosen to define that term?

On the Definition of "Human"

One reason why this vital second question is so frequently overlooked in the debate over the moral status of abortion is that the term "human" has two distinct, but not often distinguished, senses. This fact results in a slide of meaning, which serves to conceal the fallaciousness of the traditional argument that since (1) it is wrong to kill innocent human beings, and (2) fetuses are innocent human beings, then (3) it is wrong to kill fetuses. For if "human" is used in the same sense in both (1) and (2) then, whichever of the two senses is meant, one of these premises is question-begging. And if it is used in two different senses then of course the conclusion doesn't follow.

Thus, (1) is a self-evident moral truth,[1] and avoids begging the question about abortion, only if "human being" is used to mean some-

From © 1973, *The Monist* 57, 1 (January 1973), LaSalle, IL 61301. Reprinted with permission. "Postscript on Infanticide" from *Today's Moral Problems,* ed. Richard Wasserstrom (New York: Macmillan, 1975). Reprinted by permission of the author and publishers.

thing like "a full-fledged member of the moral community." (It may or may not also be meant to refer exclusively to members of the species *Homo sapiens*.) We may call this the *moral* sense of "human." It is not to be confused with what we call the *genetic* sense, i.e., the sense in which *any* member of the species is a human being, and no member of any other species could be. If (1) is acceptable only if the moral sense is intended, (2) is non-question-begging only if what is intended is the genetic sense.

In "Deciding Who Is Human," Noonan argues for the classification of fetuses with human beings by pointing to the presence of the full genetic code, and the potential capacity for rational thought.[2] It is clear that what he needs to show, for his version of the traditional argument to be valid, is that fetuses are human in the moral sense, the sense in which it is analytically true that all human beings have full moral rights. But, in the absence of any argument showing that whatever is genetically human is also morally human, and he gives none, nothing more than genetic humanity can be demonstrated by the presence of the human genetic code. And, as we will see, the *potential* capacity for rational thought can at most show that an entity has the potential for *becoming* human in the moral sense.

Defining the Moral Community

Can it be established that genetic humanity is sufficient for moral humanity? I think that there are very good reasons for not defining the moral community in this way. I would like to suggest an alternative way of defining the moral community, which I will argue for only to the extent of explaining why it is, or should be, self-evident. The suggestion is simply that the moral community consists of all and only *people,* rather than all and only human beings;[3] and probably the best way of demonstrating its self-evidence is by considering the concept of personhood, to see what sorts of entity are and are not persons, and what the decision that a being is or is not a person implies about its moral rights.

What characteristics entitle an entity to be considered a person? This is obviously not the place to attempt a complete analysis of the concept of personhood, but we do not need such a fully adequate analysis just to determine whether and why a fetus is or isn't a person. All we need is a rough and approximate list of the most basic criteria of personhood, and some idea of which, or how many, of these an entity must satisfy in order to be properly considered a person.

In searching for such criteria, it is useful to look beyond the set of people with whom we are acquainted, and ask how we would decide whether a totally alien being was a person or not. (For we have no right to assume that genetic humanity is necessary for personhood.) Imagine a space traveler who lands on an unknown planet and encounters a race of beings utterly unlike any he has ever seen or heard of. If he wants to be sure of behaving morally toward these beings, he has to somehow decide whether they are people, and hence have full moral rights, or whether they are the sort of thing which he need not feel guilty about treating as, for example, a source of food.

How should he go about making this decision? If he has some anthropological background, he might look for such things as religion, art, and the manufacturing of tools, weapons, or shelters, since these factors have been used to distinguish our human from our prehuman ancestors, in what seems to be closer to the moral than the genetic sense of "human." And no doubt he would be right to consider the presence of such factors as good evidence that the alien beings were people, and morally human. It would, however, be overly anthropocentric of him to take the absence of these things as adequate evidence that they were not, since we can imagine people who have progressed beyond, or evolved without ever developing, these cultural characteristics.

I suggest that the traits which are most central to the concept of personhood, or humanity in the moral sense, are, very roughly, the following:

1. consciousness (of objects and events external and/or internal to the being), and in particular the capacity to feel pain;
2. reasoning (the *developed* capacity to solve new and relatively complex problems);
3. self-motivated activity (activity which is relatively independent of either genetic or direct external control);
4. the capacity to communicate, by whatever means, messages of an indefinite variety of types, that is, not just with an indefinite number of possible contents, but on indefinitely many possible topics;
5. the presence of self-concepts, and self-awareness, either individual or racial, or both.

Admittedly, there are apt to be a great many problems involved in formulating precise definitions of these criteria, let alone in developing universally valid behavioral criteria for deciding when they apply. But I will assume that both we and our explorer know approximately what (1)-(5) mean, and that he is also able to determine whether or not they apply. How, then, should he use his findings to decide whether or not the alien beings are people? We needn't suppose that an entity must have *all* of these attributes to be properly considered a person; (1) and (2) alone may well be sufficient for personhood, and quite probably (1)-(3) are sufficient. Neither do we need to insist that any one of these criteria is *necessary* for personhood, although once again (1) and (2) look like fairly good candidates for necessary conditions, as does (3), if "activity" is construed so as to include the activity of reasoning.

All we need to claim, to demonstrate that a fetus is not a person, is that any being which satisfies *none* of (1)-(5) is certainly not a person. I consider this claim to be so obvious that I think anyone who denied it, and claimed that a being which satisfied none of (1)-(5) was a person all the same, would thereby demonstrate that he had no notion at all of what a person is—perhaps because he had confused the concept of a person with that of genetic humanity. If the opponents of abortion were to deny the appropriateness of these five criteria, I do not know what further arguments would convince them. We would probably have to admit that our conceptual schemes were indeed irreconcilably different, and that our dispute could not be settled objectively.

I do not expect this to happen, however, since I think that the concept of a person is one which is very nearly universal (to people), and that it is common to both proabortionists and antiabortionists, even though neither group has fully realized the relevance of this concept to the resolution of their dispute. Furthermore, I think that on reflection even the antiabortionists ought to agree not only that (1)-(5) are central to the concept of personhood, but also that it is a part of this concept that all and only people have full moral rights. The concept of a person is in part a moral concept; once we have admitted that *x* is a person we have recognized, even if we have not agreed to respect *x*'s right to be treated as a member of the moral community. It is true that the claim that *x* is a *human being* is more commonly voiced as part of an appeal to treat *x* decently than is the claim that *x* is a person, but this is either because "human being" is here used in the sense which implies personhood, or because the genetic and moral senses of "human" have been confused.

Now if (1)-(5) are indeed the primary criteria of personhood, then it is clear that genetic humanity is neither necessary nor sufficient for establishing that an entity is a person. Some human beings are not people, and there may well be people who are not human beings. A man or woman whose consciousness has been permanently obliterated but who remains alive is a human being which is no longer a person; defective human beings, with no appreciable mental capacity, are not and presumably never will be people; and a fetus is a human being which is not yet a person, and which therefore cannot coherently be said to have full moral rights. Citizens of the next century should be prepared to recognize highly advanced, self-aware robots or computers, should such be developed, and intelligent inhabitants of other worlds, should such be found, as people in the fullest sense, and to respect their moral rights. But to ascribe full moral rights to an entity which is not a person is as absurd as to ascribe moral obligations and responsibilities to such an entity.

Fetal Development and the Right to Life

Two problems arise in the application of these suggestions for the definition of the moral community to the determination of the precise moral status of a human fetus. Given that the paradigm example of a person is a normal adult human being, then (1) How like this paradigm, in particular how far advanced since conception, does a human being need to be before it begins to have a right to life by virtue, not of being fully a person as of yet, but of being *like* a person? and (2) To what extent, if any, does the fact that a fetus has the *potential* for becoming a person endow it with some of the same rights? Each of these questions requires some comment.

In answering the first question, we need not attempt a detailed consideration of the moral rights of organisms which are not developed enough, aware enough, intelligent enough, etc., to be considered people, but which resemble people in some respects. It does seem reasonable to suggest that the more like a person, in the relevant respects, a being is, the stronger is the case for regarding it as having a right to life, and indeed the stronger its right to life is. Thus we ought to take seriously the suggestion that, insofar as "the human individual develops biologically in a continuous fashion . . . the rights of a human person might develop in the same way."[4] But we must keep in mind that the attributes which are relevant in determining whether or not an entity is enough like a person to be regarded as having some of the same moral rights are no different from those which are relevant to determining whether or not it is fully a person— i.e., are no different from (1)-(5)—and that

being genetically human, or having recognizably human facial and other physical features, or detectable brain wave activity, or the capacity to survive outside the uterus, are simply not among these relevant attributes.

Thus it is clear that even though a seven- or eight-month fetus has features which make it apt to arouse in us almost the same powerful protective instinct as is commonly aroused by a small infant, nevertheless it is not significantly more personlike than is a very small embryo. It is *somewhat* more personlike; it can apparently feel and respond to pain, and it may even have a rudimentary form of consciousness, insofar as its brain is quite active. Nevertheless, it seems safe to say that it is not fully conscious, in the way that an infant of a few months is, and that it cannot reason, or communicate messages of indefinitely many sorts, does not engage in self-motivated activity, and has no self-awareness. Thus, in the *relevant* respects, a fetus, even a fully developed one, is considerably less personlike than is the average mature mammal, indeed the average fish. And I think that a rational person must conclude that if the right to life of a fetus is to be based upon its resemblance to a person, then it cannot be said to have any more right to life than, let us say, a newborn guppy (which also seems to be capable of feeling pain), and that a right of that magnitude could never override a woman's right to obtain an abortion, at any stage of her pregnancy.

There may, of course, be other arguments in favor of placing legal limits upon the stage of pregnancy in which an abortion may be performed. Given the relative safety of the new techniques of artificially inducing labor during the third trimester, the danger to the woman's life or health is no longer such an argument. Neither is the fact that people tend to respond to the thought of abortion in the later stages of pregnancy with emotional repulsion, since mere emotional responses cannot take the place of moral reasoning in determining what ought to be permitted. Nor, finally, is the frequently heard argument that legalizing abortion, especially late in the pregnancy, may erode the level of respect for human life, leading, perhaps, to an increase in unjustified euthanasia and other crimes. For this threat, if it is a threat, can be better met by educating people to the kinds of moral distinctions which we are making here than by limiting access to abortion (which limitation may, in its disregard for the rights of women, be just as damaging to the level of respect for human rights).

Thus, since the fact that even a fully developed fetus is not personlike enough to have any significant right to life on the basis of its personlikeness shows that no legal restrictions upon the stage of pregnancy in which an abortion may be performed can be justified on the grounds that we should protect the rights of the older fetus, and since there is no other apparent justification for such restrictions, we may conclude that they are entirely unjustified. Whether or not it would be *indecent* (whatever that means) for a woman in her seventh month to obtain an abortion just to avoid having to postpone a trip to Europe, it would not, in itself, be *immoral,* and therefore it ought to be permitted.

Potential Personhood and the Right to Life

We have seen that a fetus does not resemble a person in any way which can support the claim that it has even some of the same rights. But what about its *potential,* the fact that if nurtured and allowed to develop naturally it will very probably become a person? Doesn't that alone give it at least some right to life? It is hard to deny that the fact that an entity is a potential person is a strong prima facie reason for not destroying it; but we need not conclude from this that a potential person has a right to life, by virtue of that potential. It may be that our feeling that it is better, other things being equal, not to destroy a potential person is better explained by the fact that potential people are still (felt to be) an invaluable resource, not to be lightly squandered. Surely, if every speck of dust were a potential person, we would be much less apt to

conclude that every potential person has a right to become actual.

Still, we do not need to insist that a potential person has no right to life whatever. There may well be something immoral, and not just imprudent, about wantonly destroying potential people, when doing so isn't necessary to protect anyone's rights. But even if a potential person does have some prima facie right to life, such a right could not possibly outweigh the right of a woman to obtain an abortion, since the rights of any actual person invariably outweigh those of any potential person, whenever the two conflict. Since this may not be immediately obvious in the case of a human fetus, let us look at another case.

Suppose that our space explorer falls into the hands of an alien culture, whose scientists decide to create a few hundred thousand or more human beings, by breaking his body into component cells, and using these to create fully developed human beings, with, of course, his genetic code. We may imagine that each of these newly created men will have all of the original man's abilities, skills, knowledge, and so on, and also have an individual self-concept, in short that each of them will be a bona fide (though hardly unique) person. Imagine that the whole project will take only seconds, and that its chances of success are extremely high, and that our explorer knows all of this, and also knows that these people will be treated fairly. I maintain that in such a situation he would have every right to escape if he could, and thus to deprive all of these potential people of their potential lives; for his right to life outweighs all of theirs together, in spite of the fact that they are all genetically human, all innocent, and all have a very high probability of becoming people very soon, if only he refrains from acting.

Indeed, I think he would have a right to escape even if it were not his life which the alien scientists planned to take, but only a year of his freedom, or, indeed, only a day. Nor would he be obligated to stay if he had gotten captured (thus bringing all these people-potentials into existence) because of his own carelessness, or even if he had done so deliberately, knowing the consequences. Regardless of how he got captured, he is not morally obligated to remain in captivity for *any* period of time for the sake of permitting any number of potential people to come into actuality, so great is the margin by which one actual person's right to liberty outweighs whatever right to life even a hundred thousand potential people have. And it seems reasonable to conclude that the rights of a woman will outweigh by a similar margin whatever right to life a fetus may have by virtue of its potential personhood.

Thus, neither a fetus's resemblance to a person, nor its potential for becoming a person provides any basis whatever for the claim that it has any significant right to life. Consequently, a woman's right to protect her health, happiness, freedom, and even her life,[5] by terminating an unwanted pregnancy, will always override whatever right to life it may be appropriate to ascribe to a fetus, even a fully developed one. And thus, in the absence of any overwhelming social need for every possible child, the laws which restrict the right to obtain an abortion, or limit the period of pregnancy during which an abortion may be performed, are a wholly unjustified violation of a woman's most basic moral and constitutional rights.[6]

Postscript on Infanticide

Since the publication of this article, many people have written to point out that my argument appears to justify not only abortion, but infanticide as well. For a newborn infant is not significantly more personlike than an advanced fetus, and consequently it would seem that if the destruction of the latter is permissible so too must be that of the former. Inasmuch as most people, regardless of how they feel about the morality of abortion, consider infanticide a form of murder, this might appear to represent a serious flaw in my argument.

Now, if I am right in holding that it is only people who have a full-fledged right to life, and who can be murdered, and if the criteria of personhood are as I have described them, then it obviously follows that killing a newborn infant isn't murder. It does *not* follow, however, that infanticide is permissible, for two reasons. In the first place, it would be wrong, at least in this country and in this period of history and other things being equal, to kill a newborn infant, because even if its parents did not want it and would not suffer from its destruction, there are other people who would like to have it, and would, in all probability, be deprived of a great deal of pleasure by its destruction. Thus, infanticide is wrong for reasons analogous to those which make it wrong to wantonly destroy natural resources, or great works of art.

Secondly, most people, at least in this country, value infants and would much prefer that they be preserved, even if foster parents are not immediately available. Most of us would rather be taxed to support orphanages than allow unwanted infants to be destroyed. So long as there are people who want an infant preserved, and who are willing and able to provide the means of caring for it, under reasonably humane conditions, it is *ceteris paribus,* wrong to destroy it.

But, it might be replied, if this argument shows that infanticide is wrong, at least at this time and in this country, doesn't it also show that abortion is wrong? After all many people value fetuses, are disturbed by their destruction, and would much prefer that they be preserved, even at some cost to themselves. Furthermore, as a potential source of pleasure to some foster family, a fetus is just as valuable as an infant. There is, however, a crucial difference between the two cases: so long as the fetus is unborn, its preservation, contrary to the wishes of the pregnant woman, violates her rights to freedom, happiness, and self-determination. Her rights override the rights of those who would like the fetus preserved, just as if someone's life or limb is threatened by a wild animal, his right to protect himself by destroying the animal overrides the rights of those who would prefer that the animal not be harmed.

The minute the infant is born, however, its preservation no longer violates any of its mother's rights, even if she wants it destroyed, because she is free to put it up for adoption. Consequently, while the moment of birth does not make any sharp discontinuity in the degree to which an infant possesses the right to life, it does mark the end of its mother's right to determine its fate. Indeed, if abortion could be performed without killing the fetus, she would never possess the right to have the fetus destroyed, for the same reasons that she has no right to have an infant destroyed.

On the other hand, it follows from my argument that when an unwanted or defective infant is born into a society which cannot afford and/or is not willing to care for it, then its destruction is permissible. This conclusion will, no doubt, strike many people as heartless and immoral; but remember that the very existence of people who feel this way, and who are willing and able to provide care for unwanted infants, is

reason enough to conclude that they should be preserved.

NOTES

1. Of course, the principle that it is (always) wrong to kill innocent human beings is in need of many other modifications, e.g., that it may be permissible to do so to save a greater number of other innocent human beings, but we may safely ignore these complications here.

2. John Noonan, "Deciding Who Is Human," *Natural Law Forum* 13 (1968): 135.

3. From here on, we will use "human" to mean genetically human, since the moral sense seems closely connected to, and perhaps derived from, the assumption that genetic humanity is sufficient for membership in the moral community.

4. Thomas L. Hayes, "A Biological View," *Commonweal* 85 (March 17, 1967): 677–78; quoted by Daniel Callahan, in *Abortion: Law, Choice and Morality* (London: Macmillan, 1970).

5. That is, insofar as the death rate, for the woman, is higher for childbirth than for early abortion.

6. My thanks to the following people, who were kind enough to read and criticize an earlier version of this paper. Herbert Gold, Gene Glass, Anne Lauterbach, Judith Thomson, Mary Mothersill, and Timothy Binkley.

For Further Thought and Discussion

1. Can we use the space explorer example to discover our intuitions about abortion? Or do our moral intuitions on abortion inform our reply to Warren's example?

2. What is there in our qualities that make us human in the moral sense? Is there anything about these qualities that requires granting rights? Or do we "automatically" grant rights to humans? Could we "automatically" grant rights to fetuses, too?

Abortion and the Concept of a Person

JANE ENGLISH

Reading Questions

1. Why does English think that a "conclusive answer to the question whether a fetus is a person is unattainable"?

2. English likens some cases of abortion to self-defense. She notes that if one's interests are seriously threatened, then abortion may be justified, even acknowledging that the fetus is innocent. What analogies does she employ to reach this judgment?

3. How does English define, or exemplify, a "drastic injury to your life prospects"?

4. What if fetuses are not accorded the moral status of a person? English offers several moral analogies to show that abortion would not always be permissible. What are her examples?

5. Why does English think that the "coherence of attitudes" reflecting the similarity of fetuses and babies is very significant?

THE ABORTION DEBATE RAGES ON. Yet the two most popular positions seem to be clearly mistaken. Conservatives maintain that a human life begins at conception and that therefore abortion must be wrong because it is murder. But not all killings of humans are murders. Most notably, self defense may justify even the killing of an innocent person.

Liberals, on the other hand, are just as mistaken in their argument that since a fetus does not become a person until birth, a woman may do whatever she pleases in and to her own body. First, you cannot do as you please with your own body if it affects other people adversely.[1] Second, if a fetus is not a person, that does not imply that you can do to it anything you wish. Animals, for example, are not persons, yet to kill or torture them for no reason at all is wrong.

At the center of the storm has been the issue of just when it is between ovulation and adulthood that a person appears on the scene. Conservatives draw the line at conception, liberals at birth. In this paper I first examine our concept of a person and conclude that no single criterion can capture the concept of a person and no sharp line can be drawn. Next I argue that if a fetus is a person, abortion is still justifiable in many cases; and if a fetus is not a person, killing it is still wrong in many cases. To a large extent, these two solutions are in agreement. I conclude that our concept of a person cannot and need not bear the weight that the abortion controversy has thrust upon it.

I

The several factions in the abortion argument have drawn battle lines around various proposed criteria for determining what is and what is not a person. For example, Mary Anne Warren[2] lists five features (capacities for reasoning, self-awareness, complex communication, etc.) as her

From the *Canadian Journal of Philosophy* 5, no. 2 (October 1975), pp. 233–43. Reprinted with permission of the publisher.

criteria for personhood and argues for the permissibility of abortion because a fetus falls outside this concept. Baruch Brody[3] uses brain waves. Michael Tooley[4] picks having-a-concept-of-self as his criterion and concludes that infanticide and abortion are justifiable, while the killing of adult animals is not. On the other side, Paul Ramsey[5] claims a certain gene structure is the defining characteristic. John Noonan[6] prefers conceived-of-humans and presents counterexamples to various other candidate criteria. For instance, he argues against viability as the criterion because the newborn and infirm would then be non-persons, since they cannot live without the aid of others. He rejects any criterion that calls upon the sorts of sentiments a being can evoke in adults on the grounds that this would allow us to exclude other races as non-persons if we could just view them sufficiently unsentimentally.

These approaches are typical: foes of abortion propose sufficient conditions for personhood which fetuses satisfy, while friends of abortion counter with necessary conditions for personhood which fetuses lack. But these both presuppose that the concept of a person can be captured in a strait jacket of necessary and/or sufficient conditions.[7] Rather, "person" is a cluster of features, of which rationality, having a self concept and being conceived of humans are only part.

What is typical of persons? Within our concept of a person we include, first, certain biological factors: descended from humans, having a certain genetic makeup, having a head, hands, arms, eyes, capable of locomotion, breathing, eating, sleeping. There are psychological factors: sentience, perception, having a concept of self and of one's own interests and desires, the ability to use tools, the ability to use language or symbol systems, the ability to joke, to be angry, to doubt. There are rationality factors: the ability to reason and draw conclusions, the ability to generalize and to learn from past experience, the ability to sacrifice present interests for greater gains in the future. There are social factors: the ability to work in groups and respond to peer pressures, the ability to recognize and consider as valuable the interests of others, seeing oneself as one among "other minds," the ability to sympathize, encourage, love, the ability to evoke from others the responses of sympathy, encouragement, love, the ability to work with others for mutual advantage. Then there are legal factors: being subject to the law and protected by it, having the ability to sue and enter contracts, being counted in the census, having a name and citizenship, the ability to own property, inherit, and so forth.

Now the point is not that this list is incomplete, or that you can find counterinstances to each of its points. People typically exhibit rationality, for instance, but someone who was irrational would not thereby fail to qualify as a person. On the other hand, something could exhibit the majority of these features and still fail to be a person, as an advanced robot might. There is no single core of necessary and sufficient features which we can draw upon with the assurance that they constitute what really makes a person; there are only features that are more or less typical.

This is not to say that no necessary or sufficient conditions can be given. Being alive is a necessary condition for being a person, and being a U.S. Senator is sufficient. But rather than falling inside a sufficient condition or outside a necessary one, a fetus lies in the penumbra region where our concept of a person is not so simple. For this reason I think a conclusive answer to the question whether a fetus is a person is unattainable.

Here we might note a family of simple fallacies that proceed by stating a necessary condition for personhood and showing that a fetus has that characteristic. This is a form of the fallacy of affirming the consequent. For example, some have mistakenly reasoned from the premise that a fetus is human (after all, it is a human fetus rather than, say, a canine fetus), to the conclusion that it is *a* human. Adding an equivocation on "being," we get the fallacious argument that since a fetus is something both living and human, it is a human being.

Nonetheless, it does seem clear that a fetus has very few of the above family of characteristics, whereas a newborn baby exhibits a much larger proportion of them—and a two-year-old has even more. Note that one traditional anti-abortion argument has centered on pointing out the many ways in which a fetus resembles a baby. They emphasize its development ("It already has ten fingers. . . .") without mentioning its dissimilarities to adults (it still has gills and a tail). They also try to evoke the sort of sympathy on our part that we only feel toward other persons ("Never to laugh . . . or feel the sunshine?"). This all seems to be a relevant way to argue, since its purpose is to persuade us that a fetus satisfies so many of the important features on the list that it ought to be treated as a person. Also note that a fetus near the time of birth satisfies many more of these factors than a fetus in the early months of development. This could provide reason for making distinctions among the different stages of pregnancy, as the U.S. Supreme Court has done.[8]

Historically, the time at which a person has been said to come into existence has varied widely. Muslims date personhood from fourteen days after conception. Some medievals followed Aristotle in placing ensoulment at forty days after conception for a male fetus and eighty days for a female fetus.[9] In European common law since the Seventeenth Century, abortion was considered the killing of a person only after quickening, the time when a pregnant woman first feels the fetus move on its own. Nor is this variety of opinions surprising. Biologically, a human being develops gradually. We shouldn't expect there to be any specific time or sharp dividing point when a person appears on the scene.

For these reasons I believe our concept of a person is not sharp or decisive enough to bear the weight of a solution to the abortion controversy. To use it to solve that problem is to clarify *obscurum per obscurius*.

II

Next let us consider what follows if a fetus is a person after all. Judith Jarvis Thomson's landmark article, "A Defense of Abortion,"[10] correctly points out that some additional argumentation is needed at this point in the conservative argument to bridge the gap between the premise that a fetus is an innocent person and the conclusion that killing it is always wrong. To arrive at this conclusion, we would need the additional premise that killing an innocent person is always wrong. But killing an innocent person is sometimes permissible, most notably in self defense. Some examples may help draw out our intuitions or ordinary judgments about self defense.

Suppose a mad scientist, for instance, hypnotized innocent people to jump out of the bushes and attack innocent passers-by with knives. If you are so attacked, we agree you have a right to kill the attacker in self defense, if killing him is the only way to protect your life or to save yourself from serious injury. It does not seem to matter here that the attacker is not malicious but himself an innocent pawn, for your killing of him is not done in a spirit of retribution but only in self defense.

How severe an injury may you inflict in self defense? In part this depends upon the severity of the injury to be avoided: you may not shoot someone merely to avoid having your clothes torn. This might lead one to the mistaken conclusion that the defense may only equal the threatened injury in severity; that to avoid death you may kill, but to avoid a black eye you may only inflict a black eye or the equivalent. Rather, our laws and customs seem to say that you may create an injury somewhat, but not enormously, greater than the injury to be avoided. To fend off an attack whose outcome would be as serious as rape, a severe beating or the loss of a finger, you may shoot; to avoid having your clothes torn, you may blacken an eye.

Aside from this, the injury you may inflict should only be the minimum necessary to deter or incapacitate the attacker. Even if you know he intends to kill you, you are not justified in shooting him if you could equally well save yourself by the simple expedient of running away. Self defense is for the purpose of avoiding harms rather than equalizing harms.

Some cases of pregnancy present a parallel situation. Though the fetus is itself innocent, it may pose a threat to the pregnant woman's well-being, life prospects or health, mental or physical. If the pregnancy presents a slight threat to her interests, it seems self defense cannot justify abortion. But if the threat is on a par with a serious beating or the loss of a finger, she may kill the fetus that poses such a threat, even if it is an innocent person. If a lesser harm to the fetus could have the same defensive effect, killing it would not be justified. It is unfortunate that the only way to free the woman from the pregnancy entails the death of the fetus (except in very late stages of pregnancy). Thus a self defense model supports Thomson's point that the woman has a right only to be freed from the fetus, not a right to demand its death.[11]

The self defense model is most helpful when we take the pregnant woman's point of view. In the pre-Thomson literature, abortion is often framed as a question for a third party: do you, a doctor, have a right to choose between the life of the woman and that of the fetus? Some have claimed that if you were a passer-by who witnessed a struggle between the innocent hypnotized attacker and his equally innocent victim, you would have no reason to kill either in defense of the other. They have concluded that the self defense model implies that a woman may attempt to abort herself, but that a doctor should not assist her. I think the position of the third party is somewhat more complex. We do feel some inclination to intervene on behalf of the victim rather than the attacker, other things equal. But if both parties are innocent, other factors come into consideration. You would rush to the aid of your husband whether he was attacker or attackee. If a hypnotized famous violinist were attacking a skid row bum, we would try to save the individual who is of more value to so-

ciety. These considerations would tend to support abortion in some cases.

But suppose you are a frail senior citizen who wishes to avoid being knifed by one of these innocent hypnotics, so you have hired a bodyguard to accompany you. If you are attacked, it is clear we believe that the bodyguard, acting as your agent, has a right to kill the attacker to save you from a serious beating. Your rights of self defense are transferred to your agent. I suggest that we should similarly view the doctor as the pregnant woman's agent in carrying out a defense she is physically incapable of accomplishing herself.

Thanks to modern technology, the cases are rare in which pregnancy poses as clear a threat to a woman's bodily health as an attacker brandishing a switchblade. How does self defense fare when more subtle, complex and long-range harms are involved?

To consider a somewhat fanciful example, suppose you are a highly trained surgeon when you are kidnapped by the hypnotic attacker. He says he does not intend to harm you but to take you back to the mad scientist who, it turns out, plans to hypnotize you to have a permanent mental block against all your knowledge of medicine. This would automatically destroy your career which would in turn have a serious adverse impact on your family, your personal relationships and your happiness. It seems to me that if the only way you can avoid this outcome is to shoot the innocent attacker, you are justified in so doing. You are defending yourself from a drastic injury to your life prospects. I think it is no exaggeration to claim that unwanted pregnancies (most obviously among teenagers) often have such adverse life-long consequences as the surgeon's loss of livelihood.

Several parallels arise between various views on abortion and the self defense model. Let's suppose further that these hypnotized attackers only operate at night, so that it is well known that they can be avoided completely by the considerable inconvenience of never leaving your house after dark. One view is that since you could stay home at night, therefore if you go out and are selected by one of these hypnotized people, you have no right to defend yourself. This parallels the view that abstinence is the only acceptable way to avoid pregnancy. Others might hold that you ought to take along some defense such as Mace which will deter the hypnotized person without killing him, but that if this defense fails, you are obliged to submit to the resulting injury, no matter how severe it is. This parallels the view that contraception is all right but abortion is always wrong, even in cases of contraceptive failure.

A third view is that you may kill the hypnotized person if he will actually kill you, but not if he will only injure you. This is like the position that abortion is permissible only if it is required to save a woman's life. Finally we have the view that it is all right to kill the attacker, even if only to avoid a very slight inconvenience to yourself and even if you knowingly walked down the very street where all these incidents have been taking place without taking along any Mace or protective escort. If we assume that a fetus is a person, this is the analogue of the view that abortion is always justifiable, "on demand."

The self defense model allows us to see an important difference that exists between abortion and infanticide, even if a fetus is a person from conception. Many have argued that the only way to justify abortion without justifying infanticide would be to find some characteristic of personhood that is acquired at birth. Michael Tooley, for one, claims infanticide is justifiable because the really significant characteristics of person are acquired some time after birth. But all such approaches look to characteristics of the developing human and ignore the relation between the fetus and the woman. What if, after birth, the presence of an infant or the need to support it posed a grave threat to the woman's sanity or life prospects? She could escape this threat by the simple expedient of running away. So a solution that does not entail the death of the infant is available. Before birth, such solutions are not available because of the biological dependence of the fetus on the woman. Birth is the crucial point not because of any characteristics the fetus gains, but because after birth the woman can defend herself by a means less drastic than killing the infant. Hence self defense can be used to justify abortion without necessarily thereby justifying infanticide.

III

On the other hand, supposing a fetus is not after all a person, would abortion always be morally permissible? Some opponents of abortion seem worried that if a fetus is not a full-fledged person, then we are justified in treating it in any way at all. However, this does not follow. Nonpersons do get some consideration in our moral code, though of course they do not have the same rights as persons have (and in general they do not have moral responsibilities), and though their interests may be overridden by the interests of persons. Still, we cannot just treat them in any way at all.

Treatment of animals is a case in point. It is wrong to torture dogs for fun or to kill wild birds for no reason at all. It is wrong Period, even though dogs and birds do not have the same rights persons do. However, few people think it is wrong to use dogs as experimental animals, causing them considerable suffering in some cases, provided that the resulting research will probably bring discoveries of great benefit to people. And most of us think it all right to kill birds for food or to protect our crops. People's rights are different from the consideration we give to animals, then, for it is wrong to experiment on people, even if others might later benefit a great deal as a result of their suffering. You might volunteer to be a subject, but this would be supererogatory; you certainly have a right to refuse to be a medical guinea pig.

But how do we decide what you may or may not do to non-persons? This is a difficult problem, one for which I believe no adequate account exists. You do not want to say, for instance, that torturing dogs is all right whenever the sum of its effects on people is good—when it doesn't warp the sensibilities of the torturer so much that he mistreats people. If that were the case, it would be all right to torture dogs if you did it in private, or if the torturer lived on a desert island or died soon afterward, so that his actions had no effect on people. This is an inadequate account, because whatever moral consideration animals get, it has to be indefeasible, too. It will have to be a general proscription of certain actions, not merely a weighing of the impact on people on a case-by-case basis.

Rather, we need to distinguish two levels on which consequences of actions can be taken into account in moral reasoning. The traditional objections to Utilitarianism focus on the fact that it operates solely on the first level, taking all the consequences into account in particular cases only. Thus Utilitarianism is open to "desert island" and "lifeboat" counterexamples because these cases are rigged to make the consequences of actions severely limited.

Rawls' theory could be described as a teleological sort of theory, but with teleology operating on a higher level.[12] In choosing the principles to regulate society from the original position, his hypothetical choosers make their decision on the basis of the total consequences of various systems. Furthermore, they are constrained to choose a general set of rules which people can readily learn and apply. An ethical theory must operate by generating a set of sympathies and attitudes toward others which reinforces the functioning of that set of moral principles. Our prohibition against killing people operates by means of certain moral sentiments including sympathy, compassion and guilt. But if these attitudes are to form a coherent set, they carry us further: we tend to perform supererogatory actions, and we tend to feel similar compassion toward person-like non-persons.

It is crucial that psychological facts play a role here. Our psychological constitution makes it the case that for our ethical theory to work, it must prohibit certain treatment of non-persons which are significantly person-like. If our moral rules allowed people to treat some person-like non-persons in ways we do not want people to be treated, this would undermine the system of sympathies and attitudes that makes the ethical system work. For this reason, we would choose in the original position to make mistreatment of some sorts of animals wrong in general (not just wrong in the cases with public impact), even though animals are not themselves parties in the original position. Thus it makes sense that it is those animals whose appearance and behavior are most like those of people that get the most consideration in our moral scheme.

It is because of "coherence of attitudes," I think, that the similarity of a fetus to a baby is very significant. A fetus one week before birth is so much like a newborn baby in our psychological space that we cannot allow any cavalier treatment of the former while expecting full sympathy and nurturative support for the latter. Thus, I think that anti-abortion forces are indeed giving their strongest arguments when they point to the similarities between a fetus and a baby, and when they try to evoke our emotional attachment to and sympathy for the fetus. An early horror story from New York about nurses who were expected to alternate between caring for six-week premature infants and disposing of viable 24-week aborted fetuses is just that—a horror story. These beings are so much alike that no one can be asked to draw a distinction and treat them so very differently.

Remember, however, that in the early weeks after conception, a fetus is very much unlike a person. It is hard to develop these feelings for a set of genes which doesn't yet have a head, hands, beating heart, response to touch or the ability to move by itself. Thus it seems to me that the alleged "slippery slope" between conception and birth is not so very slippery. In the early stages of pregnancy, abortion can hardly be compared to murder for psychological reasons, but in the latest stages it is psychologically akin to murder.

Another source of similarity is the bodily continuity between fetus and adult. Bodies play a surprisingly central role in our attitudes toward persons. One has only to think of the philosophical literature on how far physical identity suffices for personal identity or Wittgenstein's remark that the best picture of the human soul is the human body. Even after death, when all agree the body is no longer a person, we still observe elaborate customs of respect for the human body; like people who torture dogs, necrophiliacs are not to be trusted with people.[13] So it is appropriate that we show respect to a fetus as the body continuous with the body of a person. This is a degree of resemblance to persons that animals cannot rival.

Michael Tooley also utilizes a parallel with animals. He claims that it is always permissible to drown newborn kittens and draws conclusions about infanticide.[14] But it is only permissible to drown kittens when their survival would cause some hardship. Perhaps it would be a burden to feed and house six more cats or to find other homes for them. The alternative of letting them starve produces even more suffering than the drowning. Since the kittens get their rights second-hand, so to speak, *via* the need for coherence in our attitudes, their interests are often overridden by the interests of fullfledged persons. But if their survival would be no inconvenience to people at all, then it is wrong to drown them, *contra* Tooley.

Tooley's conclusions about abortion are wrong for the same reason. Even if a fetus is not a person, abortion is not always permissible, because of the resemblance of a fetus to a person. I agree with Thomson that it would be wrong for a woman who is seven months pregnant to have an abortion just to avoid having to postpone a trip to Europe. In the early months of pregnancy when the fetus hardly resembles a baby at all, then, abortion is permissible whenever it is in the interests of the pregnant woman or her family. The reasons would only need to outweigh the pain and inconvenience of the abortion itself. In the middle months, when the fetus comes to resemble a person, abortion would be justifiable only when the continuation of the pregnancy or the birth of the child would cause harms—physical, psychological, economic or social—to the woman. In the late months of pregnancy, even on our current assumption that a fetus is not a person, abortion seems to be wrong except to save a woman from significant injury or death.

The Supreme Court has recognized similar gradations in the alleged slippery slope stretching between conception and birth. To this point, the present paper has been a discussion of the moral status of abortion only, not its legal status. In view of the great physical, financial and sometimes psychological costs of abortion, perhaps the legal arrangement most compatible with the proposed moral solution would be the absence of restrictions, that is, so-called abortion "on demand."

So I conclude, first, that application of our concept of a person will not suffice to settle the abortion issue. After all, the biological development of a human being is gradual. Second, whether a fetus is a person or not, abortion is justifiable early in pregnancy to avoid modest harms and seldom justifiable late in pregnancy except to avoid significant injury or death.[15]

NOTES

1. We also have paternalistic laws which keep us from harming our own bodies even when no one else is affected. Ironically, antiabortion laws were originally designed to protect pregnant women from a dangerous but tempting procedure.

2. Mary Anne Warren, "On the Moral and Legal Status of Abortion," *Monist* 57 (1973), p. 55.

3. Baruch Brody, "Fetal Humanity and the Theory of Essentialism," in Robert Baker and Frederick Elliston, eds., *Philosophy and Sex* (Buffalo, N.Y., 1975).

4. Michael Tooley, "Abortion and Infanticide," *Philosophy and Public Affairs* 2 (1971).

5. Paul Ramsey, "The Morality of Abortion," in James Rachels, ed., *Moral Problems* (New York, 1971).

6. John Noonan, "Abortion and the Catholic Church: A Summary History," *Natural Law Forum* 12 (1967), pp. 125–131.

7. Wittgenstein has argued against the possibility of so capturing the concept of a game. *Philosophical Investigations* (New York, 1958), $66–71.

8. Not because the fetus is partly a person and so has some of the rights of persons, but rather because of the rights of person-like non-persons.

9. Aristotle himself was concerned, however, with the different question of when the soul takes form. For historical data, see Jimmye Kimmey, "How the Abortion Laws Happened," *Ms.* I (April, 1973), pp. 48ff, and John Noonan, *loc. cit.*

10. J. J. Thomson, "A Defense of Abortion," *Philosophy and Public Affairs* I (1971).

11. *Ibid.,* p. 52.

12. John Rawls, *A Theory of Justice* (Cambridge, Mass., 1971), §3–4.

13. On the other hand, if they can be trusted with people, then our moral customs are mistaken. It all depends on the facts of psychology.

14. *Op cit.,* pp. 40, 60–61.

15. I am deeply indebted to Larry Crocker and Arthur Kuflik for their constructive comments.

For Further Thought and Discussion

1. "If the threat [of pregnancy] is on a par with a serious beating or the loss of a finger, she may kill the fetus that poses such a threat, even if it is innocent person." This is true because "the only way to free the woman from the pregnancy entails the death of the fetus." Would any other situation justify this moral claim? Could a soldier murder his/her commanding officer when ordered to take a similar risk?

2. Would a person be justified in killing an infant even if the parent of the infant seriously harmed (or murdered) that person's family? Would we be morally justified in killing the pet of such an assailant?

16   Discrimination and Preferential Treatment

QUESTIONS OF DISCRIMINATION and preferential treatment cut to the very core of our perception of the society we live in. Many of us believe that hard work, aptitude, and good luck are what it takes to do well in our society. We like to think that people are no longer discriminated against and that everyone has an equal start. Even when we are forced to the realization that some schools are better than others and therefore give better preparation to some students, we tend to blame the families. If your parents cannot afford to live in an affluent suburb, this reasoning goes, then you "deserve" to go to an inferior school.

Alternatively, if we favor groups of people who are not as well off, then we seem to be discriminating against the more advantaged. If we pour extra support into inner-city schools, then suburban schools suffer. If we raise the education budget for special-needs children, then we have to lower the resources spent on intellectually exceptional and average students. No matter what example we use, giving preference to one group appears to discriminate against other groups in society. This issue has been highlighted by policies of preferential treatment for certain minority groups—Native Americans, African Americans, gays, and women—who have a history of discrimination against them and who can show current conditions of inequality.

The readings in this chapter take a look at the issues surrounding discrimination and preferential treatment. As you encounter the principles set forth, see how they might be applied in other contexts of our society. Are they fair? Do they go too far, or not far enough?

Opinion in *University of California v. Bakke*

JUSTICE LEWIS F. POWELL, JR.

Reading Questions

    1. What are Justice Powell's reasons for rejecting the "two-class theory" of the Fourteenth Amendment?

    2. What are Justice Powell's objections to preference in the law? Should court decisions be lifted "above the level of the pragmatic political judgments of a particular time and place"?

    3. What are the petitioner's (University of California) four purposes for giving preference to individual members of groups who have experienced "societal discrimination"?

    4. On what grounds does Justice Powell reject the university's action as part of its goal to attain a diverse student body?

    5. How does Justice Powell justify race or ethnic background as "simply one element in the selection process"?

OVER THE PAST 30 years, this Court has embarked upon the crucial mission of interpreting the Equal Protection Clause with the view of assuring to all persons "the protection of equal laws," in a Nation confronting a legacy of slavery and racial discrimination. Because the landmark decisions in this area arose in the response to the continued exclusion of Negroes from the mainstream of American society, they could be characterized as involving discrimination by the "majority" white race against the Negro minority. But they need not be read as depending upon that characterization for their results. It suffices to say that "[o]ver the years, this Court has consistently repudiated '[d]istinctions between citizens solely because of their ancestry' as being 'odious to a free people whose institutions are founded upon the doctrine of equality.'"

Petitioner urges us to adopt for the first time a more restrictive view of the Equal Protection Clause and hold that discrimination against members of the white "majority" cannot be suspect if its purpose can be characterized as "benign." The clock of our liberties, however, cannot be turned back to 1868. It is far too late to argue that the guarantee of equal protection to *all* persons permits the recognition of special wards entitled to a degree of protection greater than that accorded others. "The Fourteenth Amendment is not directed solely against discrimination due to a 'two-class theory'—that is, based upon differences between 'white' and Negro."

Once the artificial line of a "two-class theory" of the Fourteenth Amendment is put aside, the difficulties entailed in varying the level of judicial review according to a perceived "preferred" status of a particular racial or ethnic minority are intractable. The concepts of "majority" and "minority" necessarily reflect temporary arrangements and political judgments. . . . [T]he white "majority" itself is composed of various minority groups, most of which can lay claim to a history of prior discrimination at the hands of the

United States Supreme Court. 438 U.S. 265 (1978).

State and private individuals. Not all of these groups can receive preferential treatment and corresponding judicial tolerance of distinctions drawn in terms of race and nationality, for then the only "majority" left would be a new minority of white Anglo-Saxon Protestants. There is no principled basis for deciding which groups would merit "heightened judicial solicitude" and which would not. Courts would be asked to evaluate the extent of the prejudice and consequent harm suffered by various minority groups. Those whose societal injury is thought to exceed some arbitrary level of tolerability then would be entitled to preferential classifications at the expense of individuals belonging to other groups. Those classifications would be free from exacting judicial scrutiny. As these preferences began to have their desired effect, and the consequences of past discrimination were undone, new judicial rankings would be necessary. The kind of variable sociological and political analysis necessary to produce such rankings simply does not lie within the judicial competence— even if they otherwise were politically feasible and socially desirable.

Moreover, there are serious problems of justice connected with the idea of preference itself. First, it may not always be clear that a so-called preference is in fact benign. Courts may be asked to validate burdens imposed upon individual members of a particular group in order to advance the group's general interest. Nothing in the Constitution supports the notion that individuals may be asked to suffer otherwise impermissible burdens in order to enhance the societal standing of their ethnic groups. Second, preferential programs may only reinforce common stereotypes holding that certain groups are unable to achieve success without special protection based on a factor having no relationship to individual worth. Third, there is a measure of inequity in forcing innocent persons in respondent's position to bear the burdens of redressing grievances not of their making.

By hitching the meaning of the Equal Protection Clause to these transitory considerations, we would be holding, as a constitutional principle, that judicial scrutiny of classifications touching on racial and ethnic background may vary with the ebb and flow of political forces. Disparate constitutional tolerance of such classifications well may serve to exacerbate racial and ethnic antagonisms rather than alleviate them. Also, the mutability of a constitutional principle, based upon shifting political and social judgments, undermines the chances for consistent application of the Constitution from one generation to the next, a critical feature of its coherent interpretation. In expounding the Constitution, the Court's role is to discern "principles sufficiently absolute to give them roots throughout the community and continuity over significant periods of time, and to lift them above the level of the pragmatic political judgments of a particular time and place."

If it is the individual who is entitled to judicial protection against classifications based upon his racial or ethnic background because such distinctions impinge upon personal rights, rather than the individual only because of his membership in a particular group, then constitutional standards may be applied consistently. Political judgments regarding the necessity for the particular classification may be weighed in the constitutional balance, but the standard of justification will remain constant. This is as it should be, since those political judgments are the product of rough compromise struck by contending groups within the democratic process. When they touch upon an individual's race or ethnic background, he is entitled to a judicial determination that the burden he is asked to bear on that basis is precisely tailored to serve a compelling governmental interest. The Constitution guarantees that right to every person regardless of his background. . . .

We have held that in "order to justify the use of a suspect classification, a State must show that its purpose or interest is both constitutionally permissible and substantial, and that its use of the classification is 'necessary . . . to the accomplishment' of its purpose or the safeguarding of its interest." The special admissions program purports to serve the purposes of: (i) "reducing the historic deficit of traditionally disfavored minorities in medical schools and in the medical profession"; (ii) countering the effects of societal discrimination; (iii) increasing the number of physicians who will practice in communities currently underserved; and (iv) obtaining the educational benefits that flow from an ethnically diverse student body. It is necessary to decide which, if any, of these purposes is substantial enough to support the use of a suspect classification.

If petitioner's purpose is to assure within its student body some specified percentage of a particular group merely because of its race or ethnic origin, such a preferential purpose must be rejected not as insubstantial but as facially invalid. Preferring members of any one group for no reason other than race or ethnic origin is discrimination for its own sake. This the Constitution forbids.

The State certainly has a legitimate and substantial interest in ameliorating, or eliminating where feasible, the disabling effects of identified discrimination. The line of school desegregation cases, commencing with *Brown v. Board of Education* (1954), attests to the importance of this state goal and the commitment of the judiciary to affirm all lawful means toward its attainment. In the school cases, the States were required by court order to redress the wrongs worked by specific instances of racial discrimination. That goal was far more focused than the remedying of the effects of "societal discrimination," an amorphous concept of injury that may be ageless in its reach into the past.

We have never approved a classification that aids persons perceived as members of relatively victimized groups at the expense of other innocent individuals in the absence of judicial, legislative, or administrative findings of constitutional or statutory violations. After such findings have been made, the governmental interest in preferring members of the injured groups at the expense of others is substantial, since the legal rights of the victims must be vindicated. In such a case, the extent of the injury and the consequent remedy will have been judicially, legislatively, or administratively defined. Also, the remedial action usually remains subject to continuing oversight to assure that it will work the least harm possible to other innocent persons competing for the benefit. Without such findings of constitutional or statutory violations, it cannot be said that the government has any greater interest in helping one individual than in refraining from harming another. Thus, the government has no compelling justification for inflicting such harm.

Petitioner does not purport to have made, and is in no position to make, such findings. Its broad mission is education, not the formulation of any legislative policy or the adjudication of particular claims of illegality. . . . [I]solated segments of our vast governmental structures are not competent to make those decisions, at least in the absence of legislative mandates and legislatively determined criteria. Before relying upon these sorts of findings in establishing a racial classification, a governmental body must have the authority and capability to establish, in the record, that the classification is responsive to identified discrimination. Lacking this capability, petitioner has not carried its burden of justification on this issue.

Hence, the purpose of helping certain groups whom the faculty of the Davis Medical School perceived as victims of "societal discrimination" does not justify a classification that imposes disadvantages upon persons like respondent, who bear no responsibility for whatever harm the beneficiaries of the special admissions program are thought to have suffered. To hold otherwise would be to convert a remedy heretofore reserved for violations of legal rights into a privilege that all institutions throughout the Nation could grant at their pleasure to whatever groups are perceived as victims of societal discrimination. That is a step we have never approved.

Petitioner identifies, as another purpose of its program, improving the delivery of health-care services to communities currently underserved. It may be assumed that in some situations a State's interest in facilitating the health care of its citizens is sufficiently compelling to support the use of a suspect classification. But there is virtually no evidence in the record indicating that petitioner's special admissions program is either needed or geared to promote that goal. The court below addressed this failure of proof:

> The University concedes it cannot assure that minority doctors who entered under the program, all of whom expressed an 'interest' in practicing in a disadvantaged community, will actually do so. It may be correct to assume that some of them will carry out this intention, and that it is more likely they will practice in minority communities than the average white doctor. Nevertheless, there are more precise and reliable ways to identify applicants who are genuinely interested in the medical problems of minorities than by race. An applicant of whatever race who has demonstrated his concern for disadvantaged minorities in the past and who declares that practice in such a community is his primary professional goal would be more likely to contribute to alleviation of the medical shortage than one who is chosen entirely on the basis of race and disadvantage. In short, there is no empirical data to demonstrate that any one race is more selflessly socially oriented or by contrast that another is more selfishly acquisitive.

Petitioner simply has not carried its burden of demonstrating that it must prefer members of particular ethnic groups over all other individuals in order to promote better health-care delivery to deprived citizens. Indeed, petitioner has not shown that its preferential classification is

likely to have any significant effect on the problem.

The fourth goal asserted by petitioner is the attainment of a diverse student body. This clearly is a constitutionally permissible goal for an institution of higher education. Academic freedom, though not a specifically enumerated constitutional right, long has been viewed as a special concern of the First Amendment. The freedom of a university to make its own judgments as to education includes the selection of its student body.

Ethnic diversity, however, is only one element in a range of factors a university properly may consider in attaining the goal of a heterogeneous student body. Although a university must have wide discretion in making the sensitive judgments as to who should be admitted, constitutional limitations protecting individual rights may not be disregarded. Respondent urges— and the courts below have held—that petitioner's dual admissions program is a racial classification that impermissibly infringes his rights under the Fourteenth Amendment. As the interest of diversity is compelling in the context of a university's admissions program, the question remains whether the program's racial classification is necessary to promote this interest.

It may be assumed that the reservation of a specified number of seats in each class for individuals from the preferred ethnic groups would contribute to the attainment of considerable ethnic diversity in the student body. But petitioner's argument that this is the only effective means of serving the interest of diversity is seriously flawed. In a most fundamental sense the argument misconceives the nature of the state interest that would justify consideration of race or ethnic background. It is not an interest in simply ethnic diversity, in which a specified percentage of the student body is in effect guaranteed to be members of selected ethnic groups, with the remaining percentage an undifferentiated aggregation of students. The diversity that furthers a compelling state interest encompasses a far broader array of qualifications and characteristics of which racial or ethnic origin is but a single though important element. Petitioner's special admissions program, focused *solely* on ethnic diversity, would hinder rather than further attainment of genuine diversity.

Nor would the state interest in genuine diversity be served by expanding petitioner's two-track system into a multitrack program with a prescribed number of seats set aside for each identifiable category of applicants. Indeed, it is inconceivable that a university would thus pursue the logic of petitioner's two-track program to the illogical end of insulating each category of applicants with certain desired qualifications from competition with all other applicants.

The experience of other university admissions programs, which take race into account in achieving the educational diversity valued by the First Amendment, demonstrates that the assignment of a fixed number of places to a minority group is not a necessary means toward that end. An illuminating example is found in the Harvard College program:

In recent years Harvard College has expanded the concept of diversity to include students from disadvantaged economic, racial and ethnic groups. Harvard College now recruits not only Californians or Louisianians but also blacks and Chicanos and other minority students. . . .

In practice, this new definition of diversity has meant that race has been a factor in some admission decisions. When the Committee on Admissions reviews the large middle group of applicants who are "admissible" and deemed capable of doing good work in their courses, the race of an applicant may tip the balance in his favor just as geographic origin or a life spent on a farm may tip the balance in other candidates' cases. A farm boy from Idaho can bring something to Harvard College that a Bostonian cannot offer. Similarly, a black student can usually bring something that a white person cannot offer. . . .

In Harvard college admissions the Committee has not set target-quotas for the number of blacks, or of musicians, football players, physicists or Californians to be admitted in a given year. . . . But that awareness [of the necessity of including more than a token number of black students] does not mean that the Committee sets a minimum number of blacks or of people from west of the Mississippi who are to be admitted. It means only that in choosing among thousands of applicants who are not only 'admissible' academically but have other strong qualities, the Committee, with a number of criteria in mind, pays some attention to distribution among many types and categories of students.

In such an admissions program, race or ethnic background may be deemed a "plus" in a particular applicant's file, yet it does not insulate the individual from comparison with all other candidates for the available seats. The file of a particular black applicant may be examined for his potential contribution to diversity without the factor of race being decisive when compared, for example, with that of an applicant identified as an Italian-American if the latter is thought to exhibit qualities more likely to promote beneficial educational pluralism. Such qualities could include exceptional personal talents, unique work or service experience, leadership potential, maturity, demonstrated compassion, a history of overcoming disadvantage, ability to communicate with the poor, or other qualifications deemed important. In short, an admissions program operated in this way is flexible enough to consider all pertinent elements of diversity in light of the particular qualifications of each applicant, and to place them on the same footing for consideration, although not necessarily according them the same weight. Indeed, the weight attributed to a particular quality may vary from year to year depending upon the "mix" both of the student body and the applicants for the incoming class.

This kind of program treats each applicant as an individual in the admissions process. The applicant who loses out on the last available seat to another candidate receiving a "plus" on the basis of ethnic background will not have been foreclosed from all consideration for that seat simply because he was not the right color or had the wrong surname. It would mean only that his combined qualifications, which may have included similar non-objective factors, did not outweigh those of the other applicant. His qualifications would have been weighed fairly and competitively, and he would have no basis to complain of unequal treatment under the Fourteenth Amendment.

It has been suggested that an admissions program which considers race only as one factor is simply a subtle and more sophisticated—but no less effective—means of according racial preference than the Davis program. A facial intent to discriminate, however, is evident in petitioner's preference program and not denied in this case. No such facial infirmity exists in an admission program where race or ethnic background is simply one element—to be weighed fairly against other elements—in the selection process. "A boundary line," as Mr. Justice Frankfurter remarked in another connection, "is none the worse for being narrow." And a court would not assume that a university, professing to employ a facially nondiscriminatory admissions policy, would operate it as a cover for the functional equivalent of a quota system. In short, good faith would be presumed in the absence of a showing to the contrary in the manner permitted by our cases.

In summary, it is evident that the Davis special admissions program involves the use of an explicit racial classification never before counte-

nanced by this Court. It tells applicants who are not Negro, Asian, or Chicano that they are totally excluded from a specific percentage of the seats in an entering class. No matter how strong their qualifications, quantitative and extracurricular, including their own potential for contribution to educational diversity, they are never afforded the chance to compete with applicants from the preferred groups for the special admissions seats. At the same time, the preferred applicants have the opportunity to compete for every seat in the class.

The fatal flaw in petitioner's preferential program is its disregard of individual rights as guaranteed by the Fourteenth Amendment. Such rights are not absolute. But when a State's distribution of benefits or imposition of burdens hinges on ancestry or the color of a person's skin or ancestry, that individual is entitled to a demonstration that the challenged classification is necessary to promote a substantial state interest. Petitioner has failed to carry this burden. For this reason, that portion of the California court's judgment holding petitioner's special admissions program invalid under the Fourteenth Amendment must be affirmed.

In enjoining petitioner from ever considering the race of any applicant, however, the courts below failed to recognize that the State has a substantial interest that legitimately may be served by a properly devised admissions program involving the competitive consideration of race and ethnic origin. For this reason, so much of the California court's judgment as enjoins petitioner from any consideration of the race of any applicant must be reversed.

For Further Thought and Discussion

1. In terms of the "two-class theory," can the concept of equal rights be applied equally to groups holding different social advantages?

2. How reasonable is it to divorce the individual from his/her membership in a particular group? Powell argues that the individual is entitled to judicial protection. Should the

court more aggressively expand its protection to include individuals because they are members of a particular ethnic or racial group?

Majority Opinion in *United Steelworkers v. Weber*

JUSTICE WILLIAM BRENNAN

Reading Questions

1. How much weight is placed on the voluntary nature of the affirmative action plan? Does it matter that the union and employer are in the private sector?

2. What were the motivations behind the Civil Rights Act of 1964?

3. What in the legislative history of Title VII allows the Court to justify a union-management agreement "to abolish traditional patterns of racial segregation and hierarchy"?

4. Title VII does not "*require* any employer to grant preferential treatment to any group because of race." How does this condition avoid undue federal regulation?

5. How does the Court's decision in *United Steelworkers v. Weber* protect the interests of white employees as well as "eliminate a manifest racial imbalance"?

C HALLENGED HERE IS THE LEGALITY of an affirmative action plan—collectively bargained by an employer and a union—that reserves for black employees 50% of the openings in an in-plant craft-training program until the percentage of black craftworkers in the plant is commensurate with the percentage of blacks in the local labor force. The question for decision is whether Congress, in Title VII of the Civil Rights Act of 1964, 78 Stat. 253, as amended, 42 U.S.C. § 2000e *et seq.*, left employers and unions in the private sector free to take such race-conscious steps to eliminate manifest racial imbalances in traditionally segregated job cate-gories. We hold that Title VII does not prohibit such race-conscious affirmative action plans. . . .

I

We emphasize at the outset the narrowness of our inquiry. Since the Kaiser-USWA plan does not involve state action, this case does not pre-sent an alleged violation of the Equal Protection Clause of the Fourteenth Amendment. Further, since the Kaiser-USWA plan was adopted vol-untarily, we are not concerned with what Title VII requires or with what a court might order to remedy a past proved violation of the Act.

United States Supreme Court. 443 U.S. 193 (1979).

The only question before us is the narrow statutory issue of whether Title VII *forbids* private employers and unions from voluntarily agreeing upon bona fide affirmative action plans that accord racial preferences in the manner and for the purpose provided in the Kaiser-USWA plan. That question was expressly left open in *McDonald v. Santa Fe Trail Transp. Co.* (1976), which held, in a case not involving affirmative action, that Title VII protects whites as well as blacks from certain forms of racial discrimination.

Respondent argues that Congress intended in Title VII to prohibit all race-conscious affirmative action plans. Respondent's argument rests upon a literal interpretation of §§ 703 (a)[1] and (d)[2] of the Act. Those sections make it unlawful to "discriminate . . . because of . . . race" in hiring and in the selection of apprentices for training programs. Since, the argument runs, *McDonald v. Santa Fe Trail Transp. Co., supra,* settled that Title VII forbids discrimination against whites as well as blacks, and since the Kaiser-USWA affirmative action plan operates to discriminate against white employees solely

[1] Section 703(a), 42 U.S.C., § 2000e-2(a), provides: "(a) It shall be an unlawful employment practice for an employer—"(1) to fail or refuse to hire or to discharge any individual, or otherwise to discriminate against any individual with respect to his compensation, terms, conditions, or privileges of employment, because of such individual's race, color, religion, sex, or national origin; or
"(2) to limit, segregate, or classify his employees or applicants for employment in any way which would deprive or tend to deprive any individual of employment opportunities or otherwise adversely affect his status as an employee, because of such individual's race, color, religion, sex, or national origin."
[2] Section 703(d), 42 U.S.C. § 2000e-2(d), provides: "It shall be an unlawful employment practice for any employer, labor organization, or joint labor-management committee controlling apprenticeship or other training or retraining, including on-the-job training programs to discriminate against any individual because of his race, color, religion, sex, or national origin in admission to, or employment in, any program established to provide apprenticeship or other training."

because they are white, it follows that the Kaiser-USWA plan violates Title VII.

Respondent's argument is not without force. But it overlooks the significance of the fact that the Kaiser-USWA plan is an affirmative action plan voluntarily adopted by private parties to eliminate traditional patterns of racial segregation. In this context respondent's reliance upon a literal construction of §§ 703 (a) and (d) and upon *McDonald* is misplaced. It is a "familiar rule, that a thing may be within the letter of the statute and yet not within the statute, because not within its spirit, nor within the intention of its makers." The prohibition against racial discrimination in §§ 703 (a) and (d) of Title VII must therefore be read against the background of the legislative history of Title VII and the historical context from which the Act arose. Examination of those sources makes clear that an interpretation of the sections that forbade all race-conscious affirmative action would "bring about an end completely at variance with the purpose of the statute" and must be rejected.

Congress' primary concern in enacting the prohibition against racial discrimination in Title VII of the Civil Rights Act of 1964 was with "the plight of the Negro in our economy" (remarks of Sen. Humphrey). Before 1964, blacks were largely relegated to "unskilled and semi-skilled jobs" (remarks of Sen. Humphrey); (remarks of Sen. Clark); (remarks of Sen. Kennedy). Because of automation the number of such jobs was rapidly decreasing (remarks of Sen. Humphrey); (remarks of Sen. Clark). As a consequence, "the relative position of the Negro worker [was] steadily worsening. In 1947 the nonwhite unemployment rate was only 64 percent higher than the white rate; in 1962 it was 124 percent higher" (remarks of Sen. Humphrey). Congress considered this a serious social problem. As Senator Clark told the Senate:

> The rate of Negro unemployment has gone up consistently as compared with white unemployment for the past 15 years. This is a social malaise and a social situation which we should

not tolerate. That is one of the principal reasons why the bill should pass.

Congress feared that the goals of the Civil Rights Act—the integration of blacks into the mainstream of American society—could not be achieved unless this trend were reversed. And Congress recognized that that would not be possible unless blacks were able to secure jobs "which have a future" (remarks of Sen. Clark). As Senator Humphrey explained to the Senate:

> What good does it do a Negro to be able to eat in a fine restaurant if he cannot afford to pay the bill? What good does it do him to be accepted in a hotel that is too expensive for his modest income? How can a Negro child be motivated to take full advantage of integrated educational facilities if he has no hope of getting a job where he can use that education?
> Without a job, one cannot afford public convenience and accommodations. Income from employment may be necessary to further a man's education, or that of his children. If his children have no hope of getting a good job, what will motivate them to take advantage of educational opportunities?

These remarks echoed President Kennedy's original message to Congress upon the introduction of the Civil Rights Act in 1963.

> There is little value in a Negro's obtaining the right to be admitted to hotels and restaurants if he has no cash in his pocket and no job.

Accordingly, it was clear to Congress that "[t]he crux of the problem [was] to open employment opportunities for Negroes in occupations which have been traditionally closed to them" (remarks of Sen. Humphrey), and it was to this problem that Title VII's prohibition against racial discrimination in employment was primarily addressed.

It plainly appears from the House Report accompanying the Civil Rights Act that Congress did not intend wholly to prohibit private and voluntary affirmative action efforts as one method of solving this problem. The Report provides:

> No bill can or should lay claim to eliminating all of the causes and consequences of racial and other types of discrimination against minorities. There is reason to believe, however, that national leadership provided by the enactment of Federal legislation dealing with the most troublesome problems *will create an atmosphere conducive to voluntary or local resolution of other forms of discrimination.*

Given this legislative history, we cannot agree with respondent that Congress intended to prohibit the private sector from taking effective steps to accomplish the goal that Congress designed Title VII to achieve. The very statutory words intended as a spur or catalyst to cause "employers and unions to self-examine and to self-evaluate their employment practices and to endeavor to eliminate, so far as possible, the last vestiges of an unfortunate and ignominious page in this country's history" cannot be interpreted as an absolute prohibition against all private, voluntary, race-conscious affirmative action efforts to hasten the elimination of such vestiges.[3] It would be ironic indeed if a law triggered by a Nation's concern over centuries of racial injustice and intended to improve the lot of those who had "been excluded from the American dream for so long," (remarks of Sen. Humphrey), constituted the first legislative prohibition of all voluntary, private, race-conscious efforts to abolish traditional patterns of racial segregation and hierarchy.

Our conclusion is further reinforced by examination of the language and legislative history of § 703 (j) of Title VII.[4] Opponents of Title VII

---

[3]The problem that Congress addressed in 1964 remains with us. In 1962, the nonwhite unemployment rate was 124% higher than the white rate (remarks of Sen. Humphrey). In 1978, the black unemployment rate was 129% higher. See *Monthly Labor Review,* U.S. Department of Labor, Bureau of Labor Statistics 78 (Mar. 1979).

[4]Section 703 (j) of Title VII, 42 U.S.C. § 2000e-2(j), provides: "Nothing contained in this title shall be interpreted to

raised two related arguments against the bill. First, they argued that the Act would be interpreted to *require* employers with racially imbalanced work forces to grant preferential treatment to racial minorities in order to integrate. Second, they argued that employers with racially imbalanced work forces would grant preferential treatment to racial minorities, even if not required to do so by the Act (remarks of Sen. Sparkman). Had Congress meant to prohibit all race-conscious affirmative action, as respondent urges, it easily could have answered both objections by providing that Title VII would not require or *permit* racially preferential integration efforts. But Congress did not choose such a course. Rather Congress added § 703 (j) which addresses only the first objection. The section provides that nothing contained in Title VII "shall be interpreted to *require* any employer . . . to grant preferential treatment . . . to any group because of the race . . . of such . . . group on account of" a *de facto* racial imbalance in the employer's work force. The section does *not* state that "nothing in Title VII shall be interpreted to *permit*" voluntary affirmative efforts to correct racial imbalances. The natural inference is that Congress chose not to forbid all voluntary race-conscious affirmative action. . . .

Such a prohibition would augment the powers of the Federal Government and diminish tra-

ditional management prerogatives while at the same time impeding attainment of the ultimate statutory goals. In view of this legislative history and in view of Congress's desire to avoid undue federal regulation of private businesses, use of the word "require" rather than the phrase "require or permit" in § 703 (j) fortifies the conclusion that Congress did not intend to limit traditional business freedom to such a degree as to prohibit all voluntary, race-conscious affirmative action.

We therefore hold that Title VII's prohibition in §§ 703 (a) and (d) against racial discrimination does not condemn all private, voluntary, race-conscious affirmative action plans.

II

We need not today define in detail the line of demarcation between permissible and impermissible affirmative action plans. It suffices to hold that the challenged Kaiser-USWA affirmative action plan falls on the permissible side of the line. The purposes of the plan mirror those of the statute. Both were designed to break down old patterns of racial segregation and hierarchy. Both were structured to "open employment opportunities for Negroes in occupations which have been traditionally closed to them" (remarks of Sen. Humphrey).

At the same time, the plan does not unnecessarily trammel the interests of the white employees. The plan does not require the discharge of white workers and their replacement with new black hires. Nor does the plan create an absolute bar to the advancement of white employees; half of those trained in the program will be white. Moreover, the plan is a temporary measure; it is not intended to maintain racial balance, but simply to eliminate a manifest racial imbalance. Preferential selection of craft trainees at the Gramercy plant will end as soon as the percentage of black skilled craftworkers in the Gramercy plant approximates the percentage of blacks in the local labor force.

We conclude, therefore, that the adoption of

---

require any employer, employment agency, labor organization, or joint labor-management committee subject to this title to grant preferential treatment to any individual or to any group because of the race, color, religion, sex, or national origin of such individual or group on account of an imbalance which may exist with respect to the total number or percentage of persons of any race, color, religion, sex, or national origin employed by any employer, referred or classified for employment by any employment agency or labor organization, admitted to membership or classified by any labor organization, or admitted to, or employed in, any apprenticeship or other training program, in comparison with the total number or percentage of persons of such race, color, religion, sex, or national origin in any community, State, section, or other area, or in the available work force in any community, State, section, or other area."

the Kaiser-USWA plan for the Gramercy plant falls within the area of discretion left by Title VII to the private sector voluntarily to adopt affirmative action plans designed to eliminate conspicuous racial imbalance in traditionally segregated job categories. Accordingly, the judgment of the Court of Appeals for the Fifth Circuit is reversed.

For Further Thought and Discussion

1. Should preferential hiring practices be designed to right presently existing inequities such as unequal pay scales, or should preference be determined by the amount of "pain" suffered by earlier member of the designated group?
2. Should the law be used to right past injustices?

Who are Equals?

CARL COHEN

Reading Questions

1. How does Cohen argue that equal protection under the law does not mean equal treatment? What examples does he use to make his point?
2. How does Cohen define an "unfair category"?
3. How are the notions of compensation and integration used to defend preferences for selected minority groups?
4. How does Cohen argue against special consideration based on race? How does he fend off Court decisions that use racial categories to ensure racial integration?
5. What are Cohen's objections to the integration argument made by the University of California?

THE FOURTEENTH AMENDMENT to the U.S. Constitution reads in part: "No State shall . . . deny to any person within its jurisdiction the equal protection of the laws." What is the point of this passage? What would a law be like that did not apply equally to those to whom it applied at all? Imagine the law: "All citizens eighteen years of age and over shall have the right to vote." Under it, the seventeen-year-old and the nineteen-year-old are treated very differently; but all nineteen-year-old citizens are treated in one way (if the law is obeyed) and all seventeen-year-old citizens in another—neither group is denied the equal protection of the law. Suppose,

Reprinted from *National Forum: The Phi Kappa Phi Journal,* Vol. LVIII, Number 1, Winter, 1978.

when I went to register to vote, the county clerk responded to my request with an embarrassed smile, saying: "Ah yes, Mr. Cohen, but, you see, you're Jewish, so—I'm afraid—we can't register you." Well—we'd make short work of him.

Now suppose the law were different. Suppose it read: "All citizens eighteen years of age and over—except Jews—shall have the right to vote." The clerk will not smile when he is handed my application in this case. "I'm sorry, Mr. Cohen," one can hear the mechanical voice of that bureaucrat, "but the law prescribes that Jews may not vote." I am stunned as I read the printed act of Congress he puts before me; but there it is; non-Jews (over eighteen) vote, Jews don't. Suppose the clerk is efficient and incorruptible—all Jews are treated alike with utmost scrupulosity. Then it would appear that all were treated justly under the law, receiving its equal protection.

Surely we never supposed that the equal protection of the law entails identical treatment for everyone. We know that would be absurd. Employers have legal obligations that employees have not. Students have legal rights (and duties) that teachers have not. Rich people must pay taxes that poor people need not. Our legal codes are replete with distinctions—hundreds and thousands of distinctions determining the applicability of the laws. I may be angered by a distinction drawn—yet I will reluctantly agree that if that is the law, and since I am in a specific category, it is fair for me to be obliged under that law, as others are who are in the same class.

We argue about these distinctions—but in three very different ways. We may argue (lawyers are constantly arguing) about who are and who are not in the same class. When you defend a contested deduction on your income tax against the IRS, or I insist that as a college professor I am not a "public official" in the sense that would require public disclosure of my finances, we are disputing over the application of the legal categories drawn, not over the categories themselves.

We may argue—as students of political sci-ence, or as legislators—that it is wise (or unwise) to introduce certain categorical distinctions. For example, should the law distinguish between large and small entrepreneurs in the application of industrial safety regulations? Should the law distinguish between different categories of employment in establishing minimum wage requirements? (And so on.)

We may argue about whether categories of a particular kind should be permitted in the law at all. Some legislation duly enacted, or administrative regulations duly authorized, may distinguish categories of persons we think ought not be distinguished. Some discriminations are worse than unwise; they are unjust.

Return now to the Fourteenth Amendment and its "equal protection clause." The prohibition in that clause bears chiefly on arguments of the third sort. It does not bar legislatures from categorizing, but is interpreted so as to require categories used in laws to have a rational foundation. Some categorical distinctions will by that clause be prohibited altogether. Under Hitler's Nuremberg Laws all Jews were treated alike, but justice in America does not permit that sort of equal protection. The central thrust of the Fourteenth Amendment was, and is, to forbid the use—in law, or by administrators under color of law—of categories intrinsically unfair.

But which categories are unfair? The Amendment itself was clearly designed to insure that blacks, former slaves, were to be as free as whites. The laws were to protect all races equally. Now, more than a century later, seeking to give redress for long-standing racial injustice, we encounter the problem of fairness from the other side. May we, in the honest effort to achieve real equality among the races, distinguish between black and white (and yellow and brown, etc.) given preference to some over others? Does our commitment to the equal protection of the laws permit it?

When the courts, and especially the United States Supreme Court, speak to such questions, they decide not simply what the U.S. Constitution requires, but what (in their view) justice requires. High courts must frame principles to guide the resolution of disputes between real parties, in the case before them and in future cases, Judicial reasoning is often profoundly moral reasoning. Actual cases, faced and decided, are the grist upon which the mill of American justice grinds. We do well to philosophize with the courts, and as they do, in living contexts.

The context now forcing a deeper understanding of "the equal protection of the laws" is that of racially preferential admissions to law schools and medical schools. Some call the problem that of "reverse discrimination," others "benign quotas." Let the name not prejudice the issue. What is *not* before us, or the courts, is the appropriateness of affirmative action. None of the participants in this dispute question the pressing need to take vigorous action, affirmative action, to correct long-standing racial injustice. What is at issue is *what* we may justly do to advance this objective—what categories we may (or must not) use, how we may (or must not) apply them.

The case of *The Regents of the University of California* v. *Allen Bakke,* now before the Supreme Court of the United States, puts this problem in sharp focus. Allan Bakke was twice rejected (in 1973 and 1974) by the medical school of the University of California at Davis. His undergraduate performance was fine, his test scores excellent, his character and interview performance admirable; he ranked very high among the more than 3,000 applicants for 100 seats. But 16 of those seats were reserved for minority-group applicants, who faced admission standards deliberately and markedly lower than did majority-group students like Bakke. The University of California (like many of its sister universities) was determined to enroll a representative proportion of blacks and members of other minority groups in its medical school—however distasteful the double standard believed necessary to accomplish that end.

The Davis medical school established a special committee to fill the reserved slots, and the committee evaluated the minority-group candidates, who competed only against one another. Officially, any disadvantaged person could seek admission under the special program; in fact, all persons admitted under that program from its inception in 1969, were minority-group members. Officially, that committee reported to the admissions committee; in fact, the applicants chosen by the special committee were invariably admitted. In each of the years Bakke was rejected, some minority-group admittees had grade-point averages so low (2.11 in 1973, 2.21 in 1974) that, if they had been white, they would have been summarily rejected.

The University of California does not deny that the overall ranking of many of the minority-group applicants who were accepted—after interviews, and with character, interests, test scores, and averages all considered—was substantially below that of many majority applicants who were rejected. Bakke contends that had his skin been of a darker color he would certainly have been admitted. He argues that, refused admission solely because of his race, he was denied "the equal protection of the laws" guaranteed him by the Fourteenth Amendment to the U.S. Constitution.

All sides in this litigation agree that professional schools may properly use, in screening for admission, a host of factors other than test scores and grade-point averages: dedication or dexterity, compassion or professional aims. All sides agree that persons unfairly injured are entitled to full, appropriate, and timely redress. What remains at issue in this case is one thing only: *preference by race.*

The advocates of racially preferential systems reason as follows: Equal protection of the laws requires different treatment for people in different circumstances. Minority-group members are in very special circumstances. Preference by race is here a reasonable instrument to achieve, for members of minority groups, objectives both just and compelling.

Such preference (not denied by the medical school) is thus defended by two central arguments. The first is grounded in alleged demands of justice: Only by deliberately preferring minority applicants can we give adequate compensation for generations of oppressive maltreatment. The second is grounded in the alleged need of society: If we do not continue to give deliberate racial preference, our medical and law schools will again become what they long were—white enclaves. *Compensation* is the heart of the first argument, *integration* of the second. Both arguments are profoundly mistaken.

Redress is rightly given for injury—not for being black or brown. Members of minority groups have been cruelly damaged, but whatever damage is rightly compensated for (cultural or economic deprivation, inferior schooling, or other), *any* applicant so unfairly damaged is fully entitled to the same special consideration, regardless of his race or ethnic group. The prohibition of special favor by race—any race—is the central thrust of a constitutional guarantee that all will receive the protection of the laws equally. Classification by race for the distribution of goods or opportunities is intrinsically odious, always invidious, and morally impermissible, no matter how laudable the goals in view.

What of the school-desegregation cases in which the U.S. Supreme Court has approved the use of racial categories to insure racial integration? Don't these show that racial preference is permissible if the aim is good? Certainly not. In these cases attention to race was allowed in order to ascertain whether school boards that had been discriminating wrongfully by race had really ceased to do so. Racial identification was there permitted—but only to insure that all students, of whatever race, received absolutely equal treatment. The distinction between that use of racial counting, and the use of racial categories to reintroduce special preference, is sharp and profound.

Can the University of California be defended on the ground that its system of racial preference is not injurious but benign? No. Results, not intentions, determine benignity. All racial quotas have injurious results and therefore cannot be benign. When the goods being distributed are in short supply, and some get more of those goods because of their race, then others get less because of their race. There is no escaping that cold logic. Bakke and others like him are seriously penalized for no other reason than their race. Such a system, as even the Washington State Supreme Court in the *DeFunis* case agreed, "is certainly not benign with respect to nonminority students who are displaced by it."

All this says not an iota against compensation. If redress is due, let us give it, and give it fully. If compensation is to be offered through special favor in professional-school admissions—a questionable mode of payment but a possible one—then let us be certain we look in every case to the injury for which we give redress, and not to the race of the applicant.

If the requirements of justice cannot support racial preference, perhaps the society's interest in integration can. The Supreme Court of California, while upholding Bakke's claim, allowed, *arguendo,* that integration is a compelling interest. "Integration" has different meanings, of course. That ambiguity invites the university's most appealing complaint. "You have told us to integrate," the university has said, in effect, "and when we devise admissions systems designed to do just that, you tell us we may not use racial preference. But the problem is a racial one. We cannot achieve racial balance unless we give special preference to racial minorities. Do not ask the impossible of us. And do not ask us to do in indirect ways what you will not permit us to do directly."

That argument by the University of California is not sound. A considered reply to it (here much compressed) is fourfold.

First, some of the ends in view are important, some are questionable. That the entire package is "compelling" is very doubtful.

(a) Better medical and legal services for minorities is a pressing need, but it is far from obvious that minority professionals reared in city slums will return to practice there. And it is patently unfair to burden them with this restrictive expectation. If the intention to give service to particular segments of the community is to be a consideration in admission to professional school, let that be known, and let all persons, of whatever race, make their case for establishing such intentions, if they claim them.

(b) Some defend preferential admission on the ground that many persons seeking professional help will be "more comfortable" with a lawyer or a doctor of their own race or religion. Possibly true. But the argument based upon this interest, now to serve as a justification of institutionalized racial preference, has long been used to exclude blacks from white hospitals and Jews from gentile law firms. It is an argument in which bigots of every color will take satisfaction.

(c) Diversity of cultural background in the professional schools, and in the professions themselves, will increase the richness of education and of service, and will provide role-models for youngsters from cultural groups long oppressed. These are genuine and worthy interests, but are they compelling in the requisite sense? What *is* compelling is integration in the classical sense: the removal of every obstruction to genuinely equal opportunity, the elimination of every racial qualification. Integration in the now fashionable sense—entailing some *de facto* mix of races approaching proportionality—may be desirable in some contexts and undesirable in others, but is in any case certainly not compelling.

Second, the Supreme Court of California emphasized that no party has shown preference by race in admissions (which all agree is objectionable) to be necessary to achieve appropriate social goals. Even if arbitrary numerical ratios are established as the only acceptable standard of success, that cannot be shown. But from whence comes that standard? The entire history of our nation has been one of ethnic layering, in which different interests and activities tend to be pursued by different cultural and ethnic groups. That is not unwholesome. The effort to homogenize society in spite of this natural tendency is already proving to be divisive, frustrating, and unworkable. Substantial increases of diversity in some professions are reasonably sought. With non-preferential forms of affirmative action pursued vigorously, and admissions criteria enlarged and enriched and applied evenhandedly to all applicants, diversity and *de facto* integration may be much advanced. Still more might be accomplished if various compensatory schemes were introduced, but they must be applied in a racially neutral way. Some majority applicants who deserve compensatory preference will also benefit under such programs, but this is entirely fitting.

There is nothing crafty about this reply. The claim that these are but devious ways to reach the same ends is simply false, and betrays an inclination to introduce racial preference somehow, "through the back door" if necessary. That would be ugly. There is no reason to fear or to be ashamed of an honest admissions program, or of an honest compensatory program, honestly applied. The racial count that results may not be the same as that when racial preference is used, but perhaps it ought not be. Even if the count were the same, the individuals (admitted using principles, not race) would be different, and that makes all the difference. It is certain that substantial progress in diversifying and integrating professional school classes can be achieved without racial preference.

Third, we must see that granting favor on the basis of race alone is a nasty business, however honorable the goal. The moral issue comes in classic form: Terribly pressing objectives (integrated professions, adequate legal and medical service for members of minority groups) appear to require impermissible means. Might we not wink at the Constitution, this once, in view of the importance and decency of our objectives?

Such winking is precisely the hope of every party having aims that are, to that party's profound conviction, of absolutely overriding importance. Constitutional short-cuts have been and will be urged for the sake of national security (e.g., the internment of Japanese-Americans during World War II), for the enforcement of criminal laws (e.g., admission of illegally seized evidence), and in other spheres. But wink we must not! Each party in its turn must abide the restrictions of constitutional process. The single most important feature of a constitution, if it is more than paper, is its preclusion of unjust means. Hence the preciousness and power of the guarantee of equality before the law. When good process and laudable objectives conflict, long experience teaches the priority of process. Means that are corrupt will infect the result and (with societies as with individuals) will corrupt the user in the end. So it is with wire-tapping, with censorship, and with every short-cut taken knowingly at the expense of the rights of individuals. So it is also with racial preference, even when well-intended.

The fourth response to the integration argument is as compelling as the first three, but adds bitter irony. Hating the taste of racial preference in admissions, the advocates of these programs swallow them only because of a conviction that they are so good for us. Bitter but (they think) medicinal. In this, too, they are mistaken. Racial preference is good for nobody, black or white, majority or minority. It will not integrate the races but will *dis*-integrate them, forcing attention to race, creating anxiety and agitation about race in all the wrong contexts, exciting envy, ill-will, and widespread resentment of unfair penalties and undeserved rewards.

It will not serve the minority well if it becomes clear that minority-group students admitted preferentially are less qualified to pursue their studies and to practice their professions. A black psychiatrist at Case Western Reserve University Hospital, Dr. Charles DeLeon, told the *New York Times* in 1974: "I wouldn't hit a dog with some of the minority students I've seen, and I have an idea that you honkies are taking in these dummies so that eight years from now you'll be able to turn around and say, 'Look how bad they all turned out.'"

Above all, racial preference clouds the accomplishments and undermines the reputations of those superbly qualified minority-group professionals who neither need nor get special favor. When, in the minds of everyone, black and white, a physician's dark skin is automatically linked to charity and payoff, who among members of minority groups is served? It is a cruel result.

Racial preference is dynamite. Many who play with such preference are now blinded by honest zeal and hide from themselves the explosions in the sequel. Justice John Marshall Harlan, dissenting in 1896 from the Supreme Court ruling that established the "separate but equal" doctrine, insisted that the U.S. Constitution was and must be color-blind. Some would have the law be color-conscious now so that it can indeed become color-blind in the future. That cannot be. One is reminded of political leaders who "suspend" constitutions to "build a firmer base for democracy." Once established as constitutionally acceptable grounds for discriminatory distribution, racial categories will wax, not wane, in importance. No prescription for racial disharmony can be surer of success.

Official favoritism by race or national origin is poison in society. In American society, built of manifold racial and ethnic layers, it is deadly poison. How gravely mistaken it will be to take new doses of the same stuff, while still suffering the pains of recovery from the old.

For Further Thought and Discussion

1. Can excellence be maintained within a system that gives preference to one group over other groups? Does this apply to the advantages gained by some groups of whites?
2. Is a society better if it "blindly" rewards according to merit or if it uses rewards to prevent racial and ethnic injustice and inequality?

Preferential Hiring and Compensation

ROBERT K. FULLINWIDER

Reading Questions

1. What is the right of equal consideration? How strong is this right?
2. What debt is arguably owed to women because of past discrimination? According to Judith Thomson, who is indebted?
3. What is Thomson's argument? Which premise does Fullinwider challenge? How does he mount the challenge?
4. How is a community's debt to the female applicant justifiably exacted from the white male applicant by setting aside WMA's right to equal consideration for employment? What does Thomson argue? How does Fullinwider reply?
5. What is Thomson's case against this particular WMA? How does Fullinwider reply to the argument that WMA benefited from injustices toward women?

> If a man shall steal an ox, or a sheep, and kill it, or sell it; he shall restore five oxen for an ox, and four sheep for a sheep.
>
> *Exodus 22*

PERSONS HAVE RIGHTS; but sometimes a right may justifiably be overridden. Can we concede to all job applicants a right to equal consideration, and yet support a policy of preferentially hiring female over white male applicants?

Judith Thomson, in her article "Preferential Hiring,"[1] appeals to the principle of compensation as a ground which justifies us in sometimes overriding a person's rights. She applies this principle to a case of preferential hiring of a woman in order to defend the claim that such preferential hiring is not unjust. Her defense rests upon the contention that debt of compensation is owed to women, and that the existence of this debt provides us with a justification of preferential hiring of women in certain cases

[1]Judith Thomson, "Preferential Hiring," *Philosophy and Public Affairs,* 2 (Summer 1973): 364–84.

even though this involves setting aside or overriding certain rights of white male applicants.

Although she is correct in believing that the right to compensation sometimes allows us or requires us to override or limit other rights, I shall argue that Thomson has failed to show that the principle of compensation justifies preferential hiring in the case she constructs. Thus, by implication, I argue that she has failed to show that preferential hiring of women in such cases is not unjust. I proceed by setting out Thomson's argument, by identifying the crucial premise. I then show that Thomson fails to defend the premise, and that, given her statement of the principle of compensation, the premise is implausible.

Thomson's Case

Thomson asks us to imagine the following case. Suppose for some academic job a white male applicant (WMA) and a female applicant (FA) are

From Robert K. Fullinwider, "Preferential Hiring and Compensation," in *Social Theory and Practice,* Vol. 3, No. 3 (Spring 1975), 307–320. Reprinted with the permission of the author and the publisher.

under final consideration.[2] Suppose further that we grant that WMA and FA each have a *right to equal consideration* by the university's hiring officer. This means that each has a right to be evaluated for the job solely in terms of his or her possession of job related qualifications. Suppose, finally, that the hiring officer hires FA because she is a woman. How can the hiring officer's choice avoid being unjust?

Since being a woman is, by hypothesis, not a job related qualification in this instance, the hiring officer's act of choosing FA because she is a woman seems to violate WMA's right to equal consideration. The hiring officer's act would not be unjust only if in this situation there is some sufficient moral ground for setting aside or overriding WMA's right.

Consider, Thomson asks us, ". . . those debts which are incurred by one who wrongs another. *It is here that we find what seems to me the most powerful argument for the conclusion that preferential hiring of women is not unjust*" (emphasis added).[3] We are promised that the basis for justly overriding WMA's acknowledged right is to be found in the principle of compensation. But, at this crucial point in her paper, Thomson stops short of setting out the actual derivation of her conclusion from the application of the principle of compensation to her imagined case. The reader is left to construct the various steps in the argument. From remarks Thomson makes in dealing with some objections to preferential hiring, I offer the following as a fair construction of the argument she intends.

Women, as a group, are owed a debt of compensation. Historically women, because they were women, have been subject to extensive and damaging discrimination, socially approved and legally supported. The discriminatory practices have served to limit the opportunities for fulfillment open to women and have disadvantaged them in the competition for many social benefits. Since women have been the victims of injustice, they have a moral right to be compensated for the wrongs done to them.

The compensation is owed by the community. The community as a whole is responsible, since the discriminatory practices against women have not been limited to isolated, private actions. These practices have been widespread, and public as well as private. Nowhere does Thomson argue that the case for preferring FA over WMA lies in a debt to FA directly incurred by WMA. In fact, Thomson never makes an effort to show any direct connection between FA and WMA. The moral relationship upon which Thomson's argument must rely exists between women and the community. The sacrifice on WMA's part is exacted from him by the community so it may pay its debt to women. This is a crucial feature of Thomson's case, and creates the need for the next premise: The right to compensation on the part of women justifies the community in overriding WMA's right to equal consideration. This premise is necessary to the argument. If the setting aside of WMA's right is to be justified by appeal to the principle of compensation, and the debt of compensation exists between the community and women, then something like the fourth premise is required to gain the application of the principle of compensation to WMA. This premise grounds the justness of WMA's sacrifice in the community's debt.

In short, Thomson's argument contains the following premises:

---

[2]Thomson asks us to imagine two such applicants *tied* in their qualifications. Presumably, preferring a less qualified teacher would violate students' rights to the best available instruction. If the applicants are equally qualified, then the students' rights are satisfied whichever one is picked. In cases where third party rights are not involved, there would seem to be no need to include the tie stipulation, for if the principle of compensation is strong enough to justify preferring a woman over a man, it is strong enough whether the woman is equally qualified or not, so long as she is minimally qualified. (Imagine hiring a librarian instead of a teacher.) Thus, I leave out the requirement that the applicants be tied in their qualifications. Nothing in my argument turns on whether the applicants are equally qualified. The reader may, if he wishes, mentally reinstate this feature of Thomson's example.

[3]Thomson, 380.

1. Women, as a group, are owed a debt of compensation.
2. The compensation is owed to women by the community.
3. The community exacts a sacrifice from WMA (i.e., sets aside his right to equal consideration) in order to pay its debt.[4]
4. The right to compensation on the part of women against the community justifies the community in setting aside WMA's right.

If we assume that the community may legitimately discharge its debt to women by making payments to *individual women,* then from premises 1–4 the conclusion may be drawn that WMA's right to equal consideration may be overridden in order to prefer FA, and, hence, that it is not unjust for the hiring officer to choose FA because she is a woman.

I shall not quarrel with premises 1–3, nor with the assumption that *groups* can be wronged and have rights.[5] My quarrel here is with premise 4. I shall show that Thomson offers no support for 4, and that it does not involve a correct application of the principle of compensation as used by Thomson. I will examine the case for premise 4 in section 4. In the next section I pause to look at Thomson's statement of the principle of compensation.

The Principle of Compensation

In the passage quoted earlier, Thomson speaks of those debts incurred by one who wrongs another. These are the debts of compensation. Using Thomson's own language, we may formulate the principle of compensation as the declaration that *he who wrongs another owes the other.*[6] The principle of compensation tells us that, for

some person B, B's act of wronging some person A creates a special moral relationship between A and B. The relationship is a species of the relationship of *being indebted to.* In the case of compensation, the indebtedness arises as a result of wrongdoing, and involves the wrongdoer owing the wronged. To say that B owes something to A is to say that B's liberty of action with respect to what is owed is limited. B is under an obligation to yield to A what he owes him, and A has a right to it.[7] What B must yield will be a matter of the kind of wrong he has done A, and the optional means of compensation open to him. Thus, it is clearly the case that debts of compensation are grounds for limiting or overriding rights. But our being owed compensation by someone, though giving us some purchase on his liberty, does not give us carte blanche in limiting his rights. The debt is limited to what makes good our loss (restores our right), and is limited to us, his victims.

It might be that, for some reason, WMA directly owes FA compensation. If so, it would immediately follow that FA has a moral claim against WMA which limits WMA's liberty with respect to what he owes her. Furthermore, the nature of WMA's wrong may be such as to require a form of compensation interfering with the particular right we are focusing on—his right to equal consideration. Suppose the wrong done by WMA involved his depriving FA of fair

---

[4]The comments from which propositions 1–3 are distilled occur on pages 381–82.

[5]For a discussion of these issues, see Robert Simon, "Preferential Hiring: A Reply to Judith Jarvis Thomson," *Philosophy and Public Affairs,* 3 (Spring 1974): 312–20.

[6]There are broader notions of compensation, where it means making up for any deficiency or distortion, and where

it means recompense for work. Neither of these notions plays a role in Thomson's argument.

[7]On page 378, Thomson says: "Now it is, I think, widely believed that we may, without injustice, refuse to grant a man what he has a right to only if *either* someone else has a conflicting and more stringent right, *or* there is some very great benefit to be obtained by doing so—perhaps that a disaster of some kind is thereby averted . . . But in fact there are other ways in which a right may be overridden." The "other way" which Thomson mentions derives from the force of debts. A debt consists of rights and obligations, and the force of debts can perhaps be accounted for in terms of superior rights. Then, debts would not be a third ground, independent of the first listed by Thomson, for overriding a right.

opportunities for employment. Such a wrong might be the basis for requiring WMA, in compensation, to forego his right to equal consideration if he and FA were in direct competition for some job. This case would conform precisely to the model of Thomson's stated principle of compensation.

Thomson makes no effort to show that WMA has interfered with FA's chances of employment, or done her any other harm. She claims that it is "wrongheaded" to dwell upon the question of whether WMA has wronged FA or any other woman.[8] As we have already seen, Thomson maintains that the relevant moral relationship exists between *women* and the *community*. Consequently, the full weight of her argument rests on premise 4, and I now turn to it.

Applying the Principle of Compensation to Groups

Thomson asserts that there is a relationship of indebtedness between the community and women. Yet it is the overriding of WMA's right which is purportedly justified by this fact. The sacrifice imposed upon WMA is not due to his directly owing FA. The community owes FA (as a woman), and exacts the sacrifice from WMA in order that *it* may pay its debt. This is supposed to be justified by premise 4.

May the community take *any* act it sees fit in order to pay its debts?[9] This question goes to the heart of Thomson's case: what support is there for her premise 4? What is the connection between the community's liability to women (or FA), and WMA's membership in the community? Can we find in the fact that the community owes something to women a moral justification for overriding WMA's right? In this section I ex-

plore two attempts to provide a positive answer to this last question. These are not Thomson's attempts; I consider her own words in the next section.

First, one might attempt to justify the imposition of a sacrifice on WMA by appeal to distributive liability. It might be urged that since the community owes FA, then every member of the community owes FA and thus WMA owes FA. This defense of premise 4 is unconvincing. While it is true that if the community owes FA then its members collectively owe FA, it does not follow that they distributively owe FA. It is not the case that, as a general rule, distributive liability holds between organized groups and their members.[10] What reason is there to suppose it does in this case?

Though this attempt to defend premise 4 is unsatisfactory, it is easy to see why it would be very appealing. Even though the indebtedness is established, in the first instance, between the community and FA, if distributive liability obtained we could derive a debt WMA owed to FA, a debt that arose as a result of the application of the principle of compensation to the community. In imposing a sacrifice on WMA, the community would be enforcing *his* (derived) obligation to FA.

Second, imagine a 36 hole, 2 round, golf tournament among FA, WMA, and a third party, sanctioned and governed by a tournament organizing committee. In previous years FA switched to a new model club, which improved her game. Before the match the third player surreptitiously substitutes for FA's clubs a set of the old type. This is discovered after 18 holes have been played. If we suppose that the match cannot be restarted or cancelled, then the committee is faced with the problem of compensating FA for the unfair disadvantage caused her by the substitution. By calculating her score averages

---

[8]Thomson, 380–81.

[9]The U.S. Government owes Japanese companies compensation for losses they incurred when the President imposed an illegal import surtax. May the Government justly discharge its debt by taxing only Japanese-Americans in order to pay the Japanese companies?

[10]See Joel Feinberg, "Collective Responsibility," *Journal of Philosophy*, 65 (7 November 1968); and Virginia Held, "Can a Random Collection of Individuals Be Morally Responsible?" *Journal of Philosophy*, 67 (13 July 1970).

over the years, the committee determines that the new clubs have yielded FA an average two-stroke improvement per 18 holes over the old clubs. The committee decides to compensate FA by penalizing the third player by two strokes in the final 18 holes.

But the committee must also penalize WMA two strokes. If FA has been put at a disadvantage by the wrongful substitution, she has been put at a disadvantage with respect to every player in the game. She is in competition with all the players; what the third player's substitution has done is to deprive her of a fair opportunity to defeat all the other players. That opportunity is not restored by penalizing the third player alone. If the committee is to rectify in mid-match the wrong done to FA, it must penalize WMA as well, though WMA had no part in the wrong done to FA.

Now, if it is right for the committee to choose this course of action, then this example seems promising for Thomson's argument. Perhaps in it can be found a basis for defending premise 4. This example seems appropriately similar to Thomson's case: in it an organization penalizes WMA to compensate FA, though WMA is innocent of any wrong against FA. If the two situations are sufficiently alike and in the golfing example it is not unjust for the committee to penalize WMA, then by parity of reasoning it would seem that the community is not injust in setting aside WMA's right.

Are the committee's action and the community's action to be seen in the same light? Does the committee's action involve setting aside any player's rights? The committee constantly monitors the game, and intervenes to balance off losses or gains due to infractions or violations. Unfair gains are nullified by penalties; unfair losses are offset by awards. In the end no player has a complaint because the interventions ensure that the outcome has not been influenced by illegitimate moves or illegal actions. Whatever a player's position at the end of the game, it is solely the result of his own unhindered efforts. In penalizing WMA two strokes (along with the

third player), the committee does him no injustice nor overrides any of his rights.

The community, or its government, is responsible for preserving fair employment practices for its members. It can penalize those who engage in unfair discrimination; it can vigorously enforce fair employment rules; and, if FA has suffered under unfair practices, it may consider some form of compensation for FA. However, compensating FA by imposing a burden on WMA, when he is not culpable, is *not* like penalizing WMA in the golf match. The loss imposed by the community upon WMA is not part of a game-like scheme, carefully regulated and continuously monitored by the community, wherein it intervenes continually to offset unfair losses and gains by distributing penalties and advantages, ensuring that over their lifetimes WMA's and FA's chances at employment have been truly equal. WMA's loss may endure; and there is no reason to believe that his employment position at the end of his career reflects only his unhindered effort. If the community exacts a sacrifice from WMA to pay FA, *it merely redistributes losses and gains without balancing them*.

Even though the golfing example looked promising as a source of clues for a defense of premise 4, on examination it seems not to offer any support for that premise. Indeed, in seeing how the golfing case is different from the hiring case, we may become even more dubious that Thomson's principle of compensation can justify the community in overriding WMA's right to equal consideration in the absence of his culpability.[11] Since Thomson never explicitly ex-

[11]George Sher, in "Justifying Reverse Discrimination in Employment," *Philosophy and Public Affairs,* 4 (Winter 1975), defends reverse discriminations to "neutralize competitive disadvantages caused by past privations" (165). He seems to view the matter along the lines of my golfing example. Thus, my comments here against the sufficiency of that model apply to Sher's argument. Also, see below, section 6, for arguments that bear on Sher's contention that the justification for discriminating against white male applicants is not that they are most responsible for injustice, but benefit the most from it.

presses premise 4 in her paper, she never directly addresses the problem of its defense. In the one place where she seems to take up the problem raised by premise 4, she says:

> Still, the community does impose a burden upon him (WMA): it is able to make amends for its wrongs only by taking something away from him, something which, after all, we are supposing he has a right to. And why should *he* pay the cost of the community's amends-making?
>
> If there were some appropriate way in which the community could make amends to its . . . women, some way which did not require depriving anyone of anything he has a right to, then that would be the best course of action to take. Or if there were anyway some way in which the costs could be shared by everyone, and not imposed entirely on the young white male applicants, then that would be, if not the best, then anyway better than opting for a policy of preferential hiring. But in fact *the nature of the wrongs done is such as to make jobs the best and most suitable form of compensation (emphasis added).*[12]

How does this provide an answer to our question? Is this passage to be read as suggesting, in support of premise 4, the principle that a group may override the rights of its (nonculpable) members in order to pay the "best" form of compensation?[13] If WMA's right to equal consideration stood in the way of the community's paying best compensation to FA, then this principle would entail premise 4. This principle, however, will not withstand scrutiny.

Consider an example: Suppose that you have stolen a rare and elaborately engraved hunting rifle from me. Before you can be made to return it, the gun is destroyed in a fire. By coincidence, however, your brother possesses one of the few other such rifles in existence; perhaps it is the only other model in existence apart from the one you stole from me and which was destroyed. From my point of view, having my gun back, or having one exactly like it, is the best form of compensation I can have from you. No other gun will be a suitable replacement, nor will money serve satisfactorily to compensate me for my loss. I prized the rifle for its rare and unique qualities, not for its monetary value. You can pay me the best form of compensation by giving me your brother's gun. However, this is clearly not a morally justifiable option. I have no moral title to your brother's gun, nor are you (solely in virtue of your debt to me) required or permitted to take your brother's gun to give to me. The gun is not yours to give; and nothing about the fact that you owe me justifies you in taking it.

In this example it is clear that establishing what is the best compensation (best makes up the wrongful loss) does not determine what is the morally appropriate form of compensation. Thus, as a defense of premise 4, telling us that preferential hiring is the best compensation begs the question.

The question of the best form of compensation may properly arise only after we have determined who owes whom, and what are the morally permissible means of payment open to the debtor. The question of the best form of compensation arises, in other words, only after we have settled the moral justifiability of exacting something from someone, and settled the issue of what it is that the debtor has that he can pay.

The case of preferential hiring seems to me more like the case of the stolen rifle than like the case of the golfing match. If WMA has a right to equal consideration, then he, not the community, owns the right. In abridging his right in order to pay FA, the community is paying in stolen coin, just as you would be were you to expropriate your brother's rifle to compensate me. The community is paying with something that does not belong to it. WMA has not been

---

[12]Thomson, 383.

[13]In the passage quoted, Thomson is attempting to morally justify the community's imposing a sacrifice on WMA. Thus, her reference to "best" compensation cannot be construed to mean "morally best," since morally best means morally justified. By best compensation Thomson means that compensation which will best make up the loss suffered by the victim. This is how I understand the idea of best compensation in the succeeding example and argument.

shown by Thomson to owe anybody anything. Nor has Thomson defended or made plausible premise 4, which on its face ill fits her own expression of the principle of compensation. If we reject the premise, then Thomson has not shown what she claimed—that it is not unjust to engage in preferential hiring of women. I fully agree with her that it would be appropriate, if not obligatory, for the community to adopt measures of compensation to women.[14] I cannot agree, on the basis of her argument, that it may do so by adopting a policy of preferential hiring.

Benefit and Innocence

Thomson seems vaguely to recognize that her case is unconvincing without a demonstration of culpability on the part of WMA. At the end of her paper, after having made her argument without assuming WMA's guilt, she assures us that after all WMA is not so innocent, and it is not unfitting that he should bear the sacrifice required in preferring FA.

> . . . it is not entirely inappropriate that those applicants (like WMA) should pay the cost. No doubt few, if any, have themselves, individually, done any wrongs to . . . women. But they have profited from the wrongs the community did. Many may actually have been direct beneficiaries of policies which excluded or downgraded . . . women—perhaps in school admissions, perhaps in access to financial aid, perhaps elsewhere; and even those who did not directly benefit in this way had, at any rate, the advantage in the competition which comes of confidence in one's full membership, and of one's rights being recognized as a matter of course.[15]

[14]And there are many possible modes of compensation open to the community which are free from any moral taint. At the worst, monetary compensation is always an alternative. This may be second- or third-best compensation for the wrongs done, but when the best is not available, second-best has to do. For the loss of my gun, I am going to have to accept cash from you (assuming you have it), and use it to buy a less satisfactory substitute.

[15]Thomson, 383–84.

Does this passage make a plausible case for WMA's diminished "innocence," and the appropriateness of imposing the costs of compensation on him? The principle implied in the passage is, "He who benefits from a wrong shall pay for the wrong." Perhaps Thomson confuses this principle with the principle of compensation itself ("He who wrongs another shall pay for the wrong"). At any rate, the principle, "He who benefits from a wrong shall pay for the wrong," is surely suspect as an acceptable moral principle.

Consider the following example. While I am away on vacation, my neighbor contracts with a construction company to repave his driveway. He instructs the workers to come to his address, where they will find a note describing the driveway to be repaired. An enemy of my neighbor, aware somehow of this arrangement, substitutes for my neighbor's instructions a note describing *my* driveway. The construction crew, having been paid in advance, shows up on the appointed day while my neighbor is at work, finds the letter, and faithfully following its instructions paves my driveway. In this example my neighbor has been wronged and damaged. He is out a sum of money, and his driveway is unimproved. I benefited from the wrong, for my driveway is considerably improved. Yet, am I morally required to compensate my neighbor for the wrong done him? Is it appropriate that the costs of compensating my neighbor fall on me? I cannot see why. My paying the neighbor the cost he incurred in hiring the construction company would be an act of supererogation on my part, not a discharge of an obligation to him. If I could afford it, it would be a decent thing to do; but it is not something I *owe* my neighbor. I am not less than innocent in this affair because I benefited from my neighbor's misfortune; and no one is justified in exacting compensation from me.

The very obvious feature of the situation just described which bears on the fittingness of compensation is the fact of *involuntariness*. Indeed I benefited from the wrong done my neighbor, but the benefit was involuntary and undesired.

If I knowingly and voluntarily benefit from wrongs done to others, though I do not commit the wrongs myself, then perhaps it is true to say that I am less than innocent of these wrongs, and perhaps it is morally fitting that I bear some of the costs of compensation. But it is not like this with involuntary benefits.

Though young white males like WMA have undeniably benefited in many ways from the sexist social arrangements under which they were reared, to a large extent, if not entirely, these benefits are involuntary. From an early age the male's training and education inculcate in him the attitudes and dispositions, the knowledge and skills, which give him an advantage over women in later life. Such benefits are unavoidable (by him) and ineradicable. Most especially is this true of "that advantage . . . which comes of confidence in one's full membership [in the community] and of one's rights being recognized as a matter of course."

The principle, "He who *willingly* benefits from wrong must pay for the wrong," may have merit as a moral principle. To show a person's uncoerced and knowledgeable complicity in wrongdoing is to show him less than innocent, even if his role amounts to no more than ready acceptance of the fruits of wrong. Thomson makes no effort to show such complicity on WMA's part. The principle that she relies upon, "He who benefits from a wrong must pay for the wrong," is without merit. So, too, is her belief that "it is not entirely inappropriate" that WMA (and those like him) should bear the burden of a program of compensation to women. What Thomson ignores is the moral implication of the fact that the benefits of sexism received by WMA may be involuntary and unavoidable. This implication cannot be blinked, and it ruins Thomson's final pitch to gain our approval of a program which violates the rights of some persons.[16]

[16]But, if FA is not given preferential treatment in hiring (the best compensation), are *her* rights violated? In having a right to compensation, FA does not have a right to anything at all that will compensate her. She has a right to the best of the morally available options open to her debtor. Only if the community refuses to pay her this is her right violated. We have seen no reason to believe that setting aside the right of white male applicants to equal consideration is an option morally available to the community.

For Further Thought and Discussion

1. Should we right past wrongs by blinding ourselves to individuals like WMA and preferring individuals who belong to an historically deprived group? Or should each applicant be judged on her or his merits and qualifications? What social implications follow from each reply?

2. Should a present generation carry the debt of its forebears? Do we have any precedent for the case of an earlier generation that creates a moral debt for its descendants?

Bakke and Davis: Justice, American Style

LISA H. NEWTON

Reading Questions

1. What is Newton's argument against "minority quotas"?
2. Why does Newton say that the merit system of America has been suspended by a "quota system" for *some* minority groups?
3. What outcome for racial stereotypes does she envision?
4. How does "procedural injustice produce only substantive harm for all concerned"?

THE USE OF THE SPECIAL MINORITY QUOTA or "goal" to achieve a desirable racial mix in certain professions might appear to be an attractive solution to the problem of justice posed by generations of racial discrimination.[1] Ultimately, however, the quota solution fails. It puts an intolerable burden of injustice on a system strained by too much of that in the past, and prolongs the terrible stereotypes of inferiority into the indefinite future. It is a serious error to urge this course on the American people.

The quota system, as employed by the University of California's medical school at Davis or any similar institution, is unjust, for all the same reasons that the discrimination it attempts to reverse is unjust.[2] It diminishes the opportunities of some candidates for a social purpose that has nothing to do with them, to make "reparation" for acts they never committed. And "they" are no homogeneous "majority": as Swedish-Americans, Irish-Americans, Americans of Polish or Jewish or Italian descent, they can claim a past history of the same irrational discrimina-

tion, poverty and cultural deprivation that now plagues Blacks and Spanish-speaking individuals. In simple justice, all applicants (except, of course, the minority of WASPs!) should have access to a "track" specially constructed for their group, if any do. And none should. The salvation of every minority in America has been strict justice, the merit system strictly applied; the Davis quota system is nothing but a suspension of justice in favor of the most recent minorities, and is flatly unfair to all the others.

The quota system is generally defended by suggesting that a little bit of injustice is far outweighed by the great social good which will follow from it; the argument envisions a fully integrated society where all discrimination will be abolished. Such a result hardly seems likely. Much more likely, if ethnic quotas are legitimated by the Court in the Bakke Case, all the other ethnic minorities will promptly organize to secure special tracks of their own, including minorities which have never previously organized at all. In these days, the advantage of a medical education is sufficiently attractive to make the effort worthwhile. As elsewhere, grave political penalties will be inflicted on legislatures and institutions that attempt to ignore these interest groups. I give Davis, and every other de-

---

[1] See, for example, *The New York Times* editorial, "Reparation, American Style," June 19, 1977.

[2] See my "Reverse Discrimination as Unjustified," *Ethics* 83:308 (July, 1973).

sirable school in the country, one decade from a Supreme Court decision favorable to quotas, to collapse under the sheer administrative weight of the hundreds of special admissions tracks and quotas it will have to maintain.

But the worst effect of the quota system is on the minorities supposedly favored by it. In the past, Blacks were socially stereotyped as less intelligent than whites because disproportionately few Blacks could get into medical school; the stereotype was the result of the very racial discrimination that it attempted to justify. Under any minority quota system, ironically, that stereotype would be tragically reinforced. From the day the Court blesses the two-track system of admissions at Davis, the word is out that Black physicians, or those of Spanish or Asian derivation, are less qualified, just a little less qualified, than their "White-Anglo" counterparts, for they did not have to meet as strict a test for admission to medical school. And that judgment will apply, as the quota applies, on the basis of race alone, for we will have no way of knowing which Blacks, Spanish or Asians were admitted in a medical school's regular competition and which were admitted on the "special minority" track. The opportunity to bury their unfavorable ethnic stereotypes by clean and pub-

lic success in strictly fair competition, an opportunity that our older ethnic groups seized enthusiastically, will be denied to these "special minorities" for yet another century.

In short, there are no gains, for American society or for groups previously disadvantaged by it, in quota systems that attempt reparation by reverse discrimination. The larger moral question of whether we should set aside strict justice for some larger social gain does not have to be taken up in a case like this one, where procedural injustice produces only substantive harm for all concerned. Blacks, Hispanics and other minority groups which are presently economically disadvantaged will see real progress when, and only when, the American economy expands to make room for more higher status employment for all groups. The economy is not improved in the least by special tracks and quotas for special groups; on the contrary, it is burdened by the enormous weight of the nonproductive administrative procedure required to implement them. No social purpose will be served, and no justice done, by the establishment of such procedural monsters; we should hope that the Supreme Court will see its way clear to abolishing them once and for all.

For Further Thought and Discussion

1. If "minority quotas" are not used, how can racial and ethnic abuse be remedied?

2. Is it fair to begin now to treat everyone the same? Imagine a mile race that has progressed until one runner is within yards of the finish line. A judge stops the race and turns to one participant still near the start line. In the name of fairness, the judge orders the removal of the refrigerator strapped to the runner's back, then shouts, "Go!" Is this now a fair race?

17 Capital Punishment

T HE ARGUMENT OVER CAPITAL PUNISHMENT rages on in our society. Each of the two sides contains several approaches. Those who favor capital punishment argue that it prevents certain crimes by prohibiting murderers from murdering again and acting as a deterrent to those considering such a crime. On this side it is also suggested that the death sentence serves as a fitting punishment; if you take a life, you must expect to pay with your own life. Against the death sentence are people with certain religious beliefs and people who see the death sentence as carried out more against some historically oppressed groups than other groups. Some argue that the death sentence sends a mixed message to members of our society: How can we prohibit murder, then use state-condoned murder as a punishment? Let's briefly examine each of these positions.

To the argument that the death penalty deters certain crimes, the rebuttal is that over 90 percent of homicides committed in the United States are crimes of passion, which implies that the murderer has lost rational control of himself or herself. If it is true that the person's passions take control, then there is no reason to think that any deterrent can work. Another answer to this argument is that states exercising the death sentence have about the same, or even higher, instances of the crimes society is trying to deter. If we really want to deter crimes, this argument goes, it would be more sensible and practical to impose capital punishment for deaths resulting from drunk driving; surely most people are in complete control of themselves before they begin to drink alcohol. Still, arguments against the effectiveness of capital punishment as a deterrent do not silence many people in favor of the death sentence, who believe that punishment is appropriate for such heinous crimes as murder, rape, and kidnapping. Perhaps we simply want revenge.

Those who argue against the death penalty point out that a disproportionate number of certain historically disadvantaged groups are sentenced to death. Those favoring capital punishment have two important replies: First, it is not ethnic or racial groups that are singled out for capital punishment, but certain types of crimes. If these crimes are committed more often by one group than another, that alone could explain the apparent discrimination. Second, even if the death sentence is carried out against members of some groups more than members of others, what if a person uses his or her circumstances to justify the crime committed? Should we permit the person to avoid personal responsibility because he or she is poor or a member of an historically oppressed group? No, say the advocates of the death sentence. If circumstances and race were relevant, then all people raised in these circumstances would murder. Yet most people raised in poverty, who are also members of an historically oppressed group, do not commit heinous crimes. Most of these people are responsible, hard working, honest, and conscientious.

What about the argument that a mixed message is sent when the state commits the same "offense" as the murderer? One reply is that people are protected in this society only as long as they obey the rules. By committing this crime, a murderer gives up some of her rights of citizenship and can be put to death.

Majority Opinion in *Gregg v. Georgia*

JUSTICES POTTER STEWART, LEWIS F. POWELL, JR., AND JOHN PAUL STEVENS

Reading Questions

1. What issue makes this case unique for the Court?
2. What two social purposes are served by capital punishment? How seriously does the Court take retribution in the case of grievous offenses?
3. What role does society's moral outrage play on the majority opinion?
4. According to the majority of the Court, what kinds of murderers are likely to be affected by the imposition of the death sentence?
5. How does the Court consider the proportionality of the death sentence to the crimes committed?

THE PETITIONER, TROY GREGG, was charged with committing armed robbery and murder. In accordance with Georgia procedure in capital cases, the trial was in two stages, a guilt stage and a sentencing stage. . . .

. . . The jury found the petitioner guilty of two counts of armed robbery and two counts of murder.

At the penalty stage, which took place before the same jury, . . . the trial judge instructed the jury that it could recommend either a death sentence or a life prison sentence on each count. . . .

United States Supreme Court, 428 U.S. 153 (1976).

The jury returned verdicts of death on each count.

The Supreme Court of Georgia affirmed the convictions and the imposition of the death sentences for murder. . . . The death sentences imposed for armed robbery, however, were vacated on the grounds that the death penalty had rarely been imposed in Georgia for that offense. . . .

We address initially the basic contention that the punishment of death for the crime of murder is, under all circumstances, "cruel and unusual" in violation of the Eighth and Fourteenth Amendments of the Constitution. . . .

The court on a number of occasions has both assumed and asserted the constitutionality of capital punishment. In several cases that assumption provided a necessary foundation for the decision, as the Court was asked to decide whether a particular method of carrying out a capital sentence would be allowed to stand under the Eighth Amendment. But until *Furman v. Georgia* (1972), the Court never confronted squarely the fundamental claim that the punishment of death always, regardless of the enormity of the offense or the procedure followed in imposing the sentence, is cruel and unusual punishment in violation of the Constitution. Although this issue was presented and addressed in *Furman* it was not resolved by the court. . . . We now hold that the punishment of death does not invariably violate the Constitution. . . .

The death penalty is said to serve two principal social purposes: retribution and deterrence of capital crimes by prospective offenders.[1]

In part, capital punishment is an expression of society's moral outrage at particularly offensive conduct. This function may be unappealing to many, but it is essential in an ordered society that asks its citizens to rely on legal processes rather than self-help to vindicate their wrongs.

The instinct of retribution is part of the nature of man, and channeling that instinct in the administration of criminal justice serves an important purpose in promoting the stability of a society governed by law. When people begin to believe that organized society is unwilling or unable to impose upon criminal offenders the punishment they "deserve," then there are sown the seeds of anarchy—of self-help, vigilante justice, and lynch law. *Furman v. Georgia* (Stewart, J., concurring).

"Retribution is no longer the dominant objective of the criminal law," but neither is it a forbidden objective nor one inconsistent with our respect for the dignity of men. Indeed, the decision that capital punishment may be the appropriate sanction in extreme cases is an expression of the community's belief that certain crimes are themselves so grievous an affront to humanity that the only adequate response may be the penalty of death.

Statistical attempts to evaluate the worth of the death penalty as a deterrent to crimes by potential offenders have occasioned a great deal of debate. The results simply have been inconclusive. . . .

Although some of the studies suggest that the death penalty may not function as a significantly greater deterrent than lesser penalties, there is no convincing empirical evidence either supporting or refuting this view. We may nevertheless assume safely that there are murderers, such as those who act in passion, for whom the threat of death has little or no deterrent effect. But for many others, the death penalty undoubtedly is a significant deterrent. There are carefully contemplated murders, such as murder for hire, where the possible penalty of death may well enter into the cold calculus that precedes the decision to act. And there are some categories of murder, such as murder by a life prisoner, where other sanctions may not be adequate.

The value of capital punishment as a deterrent of crime is a complex factual issue the resolution of which properly rests with the legislatures, which can evaluate the results of statistical studies in terms of their own local conditions and with a flexibility of approach that is not available to the courts. Indeed, many of the post-*Furman* statutes reflect just such a responsible effort to define those crimes and those criminals for which capital punishment is most probably an effective deterrent.

In sum, we cannot say that the judgment of the Georgia Legislature that capital punishment may be necessary in some cases is clearly wrong. Considerations of federalism, as well as respect for the ability of a legislature to evaluate, in terms of its particular State, the moral consensus concerning the death penalty and its social utility as a sanction, requires us to conclude, in the absence of more convincing evidence, that the infliction of death as a punishment for murder is not without justification and thus is not unconstitutionally severe.

Finally, we must consider whether the punishment of death is disproportionate in relation to the crime for which it is imposed. There is no question that death as a punishment is unique in its severity and irrevocability. When a defendant's life is at stake, the Court has been particularly sensitive to insure that every safeguard is observed. But we are concerned here only with the imposition of capital punishment for the crime of murder, and when a life has been taken deliberately by the offender,[2] we cannot say that the punishment is invariably disproportionate to the crime. It is an extreme sanction, suitable to the most extreme crimes.

We hold that the death penalty is not a form of punishment that may never be imposed, regardless of the circumstances of the offense, regardless of the character of the offender, and regardless of the procedure followed in reaching the decision to impose it.

NOTES

1. Another purpose that has been discussed is the incapacitation of dangerous criminals and the consequent prevention of crimes that they may otherwise commit in the future.
2. We do not address here the question whether the taking of the criminal's life is a proportionate sanction where no victim has been deprived of life—for example, when capital punishment is imposed for rape, kidnapping, or armed robbery that does not result in the death of any human being.

For Further Thought and Discussion

1. "Although some of the studies suggest that the death penalty may not function as a significantly greater deterrent than lesser penalties, there is no convincing empirical evidence either supporting or refuting this view." How confident can we be that the court decided properly when its reasoning is based at least in part on professed ignorance of outcome?

2. How significant should the irrevocable nature of death be in determining the propriety of capital punishment? What about judicial mistakes and jury error?

Dissenting Opinion in *Gregg v. Georgia*

JUSTICE THURGOOD MARSHALL

Reading Questions

 1. What are Marshall's two reasons for rejecting the death sentence?
 2. Why does Marshall say that the death penalty is "cruel and unusual punishment"?
 3. How does Marshall analyze the Stewart-Powell-Stevens argument for retribution? Why do the utilitarian reasons of the majority of the Court not satisfy Marshall?
 4. What impact on human dignity and worth does Marshall see the death penalty as having?

IN *FURMAN V. GEORGIA* (1972) (concurring opinion), I set forth at some length my views on the basic issue presented to the Court in [this case]. The death penalty, I concluded, is a cruel and unusual punishment prohibited by the Eighth and Fourteenth Amendments. That continues to be my view. . . .

In *Furman* I concluded that the death penalty is constitutionally invalid for two reasons. First, the death penalty is excessive. And second, the American people, fully informed as to the purposes of the death penalty and its liabilities, would in my view reject it as morally unacceptable. . . .

Even assuming, however, that the post-*Furman* enactment of statutes authorizing the death penalty renders the prediction of the views of an informed citizenry an uncertain basis for a constitutional decision, the enactment of those statutes has no bearing whatsoever on the conclusion that the death penalty is unconstitutional because it is excessive. An excessive penalty is invalid under the Cruel and Unusual Punishments Clause "even though popular sentiment may favor" it. The inquiry here, then, is simply whether the death penalty is necessary to accomplish the legitimate legislative purposes in punishment, or whether a less severe penalty—life imprisonment—would do as well.

The two purposes that sustain the death penalty as nonexcessive in the Court's view are general deterrence and retribution. . . . The available evidence, I concluded in *Furman,* was convincing that "capital punishment is not necessary as a deterrent to crime in our society.". . .

. . . The evidence I reviewed in *Furman* remains convincing, in my view, that "capital punishment is not necessary as a deterrent to crime in our society." The justification for the death penalty must be found elsewhere.

The other principal purpose said to be served by the death penalty is retribution. The notion that retribution can serve as a moral justification for the sanction of death finds credence in the opinion of my Brothers Stewart, Powell, and Stevens. . . . It is this notion that I find to be the most disturbing aspect of today's unfortunate [decision].

The concept of retribution is a multifaceted one, and any discussion of its role in the criminal law must be undertaken with caution. . . .

The . . . contentions—that society's expression of moral outrage through the imposition of the death penalty pre-empts the citizenry from

United States Supreme Court, 428 U.S. 153 (1976).

taking the law into its own hands and reinforces moral values—are not retributive in the purest sense. They are essentially utilitarian in that they portray the death penalty as valuable because of its beneficial results. These justifications for the death penalty are inadequate because the penalty is, quite clearly I think, not necessary to the accomplishment of those results.

There remains for consideration, however, what might be termed the purely retributive justification of the death penalty—that the death penalty is appropriate, not because of its beneficial effect on society, but because the taking of the murderer's life is itself morally good. . . .

. . . The mere fact that the community demands the murderer's life in return for the evil he has done cannot sustain the death penalty, for as Justices Stewart, Powell, and Stevens remind us, "the Eighth Amendment demands more than

that a challenged punishment be acceptable to contemporary society." To be sustained under the Eighth Amendment, the death penalty must "compor[t] with the basic concept of human dignity at the core of the Amendment"; the objective in imposing it must be "[consistent] with our respect for the dignity of [other] men." Under these standards, the taking of life "because the wrongdoer deserves it" surely must fail, for such a punishment has as its very basis the total denial of the wrongdoer's dignity and worth.

The death penalty, unnecessary to promote the goal of deterrence or to further any legitimate notion of retribution, is an excessive penalty forbidden by the Eighth and Fourteenth Amendments. I respectfully dissent from the Court's judgment upholding the [sentence] of death imposed upon the [petitioner in this case].

For Further Thought and Discussion

1. Even if the death sentence deterred certain crimes, would we necessarily want it? Would we want to impose death for parking violations?

2. Which crimes should receive the death sentence? Should this sentence be applied to corporate executives who do not aggressively pursue safe working conditions for their employees? What's the difference between a murder that occurs during a robbery and a death that occurs during the pursuit of corporate profit?

Retribution and the Limits of Capital Punishment

BURTON LEISER

Reading Questions

1. Justice Marshall claims that capital punishment denies the wrongdoers worth and dignity. How does Leiser reply to this?

2. How does Leiser morally justify differential treatment for crimes of "passion" and crimes planned in advance?

3. How does Leiser reject torture but not death as punishment for serious crimes?

4. How are crimes against the state defined in this selection? How is capital punishment justified in these cases?

5. What conditions must be met, according to Leiser, before the "proper authorities are justified in carrying it (capital punishment) out"?

Retribution

In his dissent *Gregg v. Georgia,* Justice Marshall said that "it simply defies belief to suggest that the death penalty is necessary to prevent the American people from taking the law into their hands." He went on to assert that Lord Denning's contention that some crimes are so outrageous as to deserve the death penalty, regardless of its deterrent effects, is at odds with the Eighth Amendment. "The mere fact that the community demands the murderer's life for the evil he has done," he said, "cannot sustain the death penalty," for

the Eighth Amendment demands more than that a challenged punishment be acceptable to contemporary society. To be sustained under the Eighth Amendment, the death penalty must [comport] with the basic concept of human dignity at the core of the Amendment; the objective in imposing it must be [consistent] with our respect for the dignity of [other] men.

Under these standards, the taking of life "because the wrongdoer deserves it" surely must fail, for such a punishment has as its very basis the total denial of the wrongdoer's dignity and worth. The death penalty, unnecessary to promote the goal of deterrence or to further any legitimate notion of retribution, is an excessive penalty forbidden by the Eighth and Fourteenth Amendments.

But retributive justice does not deny the wrongdoer's worth and dignity. It assumes it, and makes no sense at all unless the wrongdoer is regarded as a human being capable of making his own decisions, acting upon his own volition, and deserving moral praise or blame for what he does. The death penalty is the ultimate condemnation, morally and legally, of a person who has, through his actions, demonstrated his utter contempt for human worth and dignity and for the most fundamental rules of human society. It is precisely because of a nation's belief in the dignity and worth of those who live under the protection of its laws and because of its adherence to the principle that human life is sacred that it may choose to employ the death penalty against those who have demonstrated their disregard of those principles. . . .

The Limits of Capital Punishment

The death penalty has historically been employed for such diverse offenses as murder, espionage, treason, kidnapping, rape, arson, robbery, burglary, and theft. Except for the most serious crimes, it is now agreed that lesser penalties are sufficient.

The distinction between first- and second-degree murder [does] not permit fine lines to be drawn between (for example) murder for hire and the killing of a husband by his jealous wife. Most murders committed in the United States are of a domestic nature—spouses or other close relatives becoming involved in angry scenes that end in homicide. Such crimes, usually committed in the heat of a momentary passion, seem inappropriate for the supreme penalty. Although they are premeditated in the legal sense (for it takes no more than an instant for a person to form the intent that is necessary for the legal test to be satisfied), there seems to be a great difference between such crimes and those committed out of a desire for personal gain or for political motives, between a crime committed in an instant of overwrought emotion and one carefully charted and planned in advance. It is reasonable, therefore, to suggest that the vast majority of murders not be regarded as capital crimes, because the penalty may be disproportionate to the crime committed and because people caught up in such momentarily overwhelming passions are not likely to be deterred by thoughts of the possible consequences of their actions.

Only the most heinous offenses against the state and against individual persons seem to deserve the ultimate penalty. If the claim that life is sacred has any meaning at all, it must be that no man may deliberately cause another to lose his life without some compelling justification.

Such a justification appears to exist when individuals or groups employ wanton violence against others in order to achieve their ends, whatever those ends might be. However appealing the cause, however noble the motives, the deliberate, systematic destruction of innocent human beings is one of the gravest crimes any person can commit and may justify the imposition of the harshest available penalty, consistent with principles of humanity, decency, and compassion. Some penalties, such as prolonged torture, may in fact be worse than death, but civilized societies reject them as being too barbarous, too brutal, and too dehumanizing to those who must carry them out.

Perpetrators of such crimes as genocide (the deliberate extermination of entire peoples, racial, religious, or ethnic groups) clearly deserve a penalty no less severe than death. Those who perpetrate major war crimes, crimes against peace, or crimes against humanity, deliberately and without justification plunging nations into violent conflicts that entail widespread bloodshed or causing needless suffering on a vast scale, deserve nothing less than the penalty of death.

Because of the reckless manner in which they endanger the lives of innocent citizens and their clear intention to take human lives on a massive scale in order to achieve their ends, terrorists should be subject to the death penalty—particularly because no other penalty is likely to serve as a deterrent to potential terrorists.

Major crimes against the peace, security, and integrity of the state constitute particularly heinous offenses, for they shake the very foundations upon which civilization rests and endanger the lives, the liberties, and the fundamental rights of all the people who depend upon the state for protection. Treason, espionage, and sabotage, particularly during times of great danger (as in time of war), ought to be punishable by death.

Murder for personal gain and murder committed in the course of the commission of a felony that is being committed for personal gain or out of a reckless disregard for the lives or fundamental rights and interests of potential victims ought to be punishable by death.

Murder committed by a person who is serving a life sentence ought to be punishable by death, both because of the enormity of the crime and because no other penalty is likely to deter such crimes.

Any murder that is committed in a particularly vile, wanton, or malicious way ought to be punishable by death.

One of the principal justifications for the state's existence is the protection it offers those who come under its jurisdiction against violations of their fundamental rights. Those who are entrusted with the responsibility for carrying out the duties of administering the state's functions, enforcing its laws, and seeing that justice is done carry an onerous burden and are particularly likely to become the targets of hostile, malicious, or rebellious individuals or groups. Their special vulnerability entitles them to special protection. Hence, any person guilty of murdering a policeman, a fireman, a judge, a governor, a president, a lawmaker, or any other person holding a comparable position while that person is carrying out his official duties or because of the office he holds has struck at the very heart of government and thus at the foundations upon which the state and civilized society depend. The gravity of such a crime warrants imposition of the death penalty.

Because the threat of death is inherent in every act of kidnapping and airplane hijacking—for without such a threat the holding of a hostage would not have the terrorizing effect the perpetrator desires in order to achieve his aim of extorting money or political concessions from those to whom his threats are delivered—those who perpetrate such crimes may appropriately be subject to capital punishment.

But those who commit homicide in a momentary fit of anger or passion, in contrast to those who carefully plan acts as well as those who commit homicide under excusing or mitigating circumstances, may either be fully excused or given some lesser penalty.

From the fact that some persons who bring about the deaths of fellow humans do so under conditions that just and humane men would consider sufficient to justify either complete exculpation or penalties less than death, it does not follow that all of them do. If guilt is clearly established beyond a reasonable doubt under circumstances that guarantee a reasonable opportunity for the defendant to confront his accusers, to cross-examine witnesses, to present his case with the assistance of professional counsel, and in general to enjoy the benefits of due process of law; if in addition he has been given the protection of laws that prevent the use of torture to extract confessions and is provided immunity against self-incrimination; if those who are authorized to pass judgment find there were no excusing or mitigating circumstances; if he is found to have committed a wanton, brutal, callous murder or some other crime that is subversive of the very foundations of an ordered society; and if, finally, the representatives of the people, exercising the people's sovereign authority, have prescribed death as the penalty for that crime; then the judge and jury are fully justified in imposing that penalty, and the proper authorities are justified in carrying it out.

For Further Thought and Discussion

1. The arguments for and against capital punishment appear to come down to one of two concerns. Either we are concerned with the individual person charged with a crime, or we are concerned with the social impact of punishment. Which should we concentrate on, the individual or society?

2. What gives any "authority" the moral right to punish? Keep in mind that the "majority" is often misinformed about oppressed people. Often the desires of oppressed people are not reflected by the "authority."

On Deterrence and the Death Penalty

ERNEST VAN DEN HAAG

Reading Questions

1. What are the two injustices produced by capital punishment? How does Van Den Haag justify to them?
2. How does Van Den Haag argue "that the irrevocable injustice sometimes inflicted by the death penalty would not significantly militate against it"?
3. How does Van Den Haag argue for effectiveness of deterrence?
4. What is the argument against a person's environment causing crime?
5. How does Van Den Haag calculate the net result of the death penalty? What are the gains and the losses?

I

IF REHABILITATION AND THE PROTECTION OF SOCIETY from unrehabilitated offenders were the only purposes of legal punishment, the death penalty could be abolished: It cannot attain the first end, and is not needed for the second. No case for the death penalty can be made unless "doing justice" or "deterring others" is among our penal aims.[1] Each of these purposes can justify capital punishment by itself; opponents, therefore, must show that neither actually does, while proponents can rest their case on either.

Although the argument from justice is intellectually more interesting, and, in my view, decisive enough, utilitarian arguments have more appeal: The claim that capital punishment is useless because it does not deter others is most persuasive. I shall, therefore, focus on this claim. Lest the argument be thought to be unduly narrow, I shall show, nonetheless, that some claims of injustice rest on premises which the claimants reject when arguments for capital punishment are derived therefrom; while other claims of injustice have no independent standing: Their weight depends on the weight given to deterrence.

Reprinted by permission of the *Journal of Criminal Law, Criminology, and Police Science,* © 1969 by Northeastern University School of Law, Vol. 60, No. 2.

II

Capital punishment is regarded as unjust because it may lead to the execution of innocents, or because the guilty poor (or disadvantaged) are more likely to be executed than the guilty rich.

Regardless of merit, these claims are relevant only if "doing justice" is one purpose of punishment. Unless one regards it as good, or, at least, better, that the guilty be punished rather than the innocent, and that the equally guilty be punished equally,[2] unless, that is, one wants penalties to be just, one cannot object to them because they are not. However, if one does include justice among the purposes of punishment, it becomes possible to justify any one punishment— even death—on grounds of justice. Yet, those who object to the death penalty because of its alleged injustice usually deny not only the merits, or the sufficiency, of specific arguments based on justice, but the propriety of justice as an argument: They exclude "doing justice" as a purpose of legal punishment. If justice is not a purpose of penalties, injustice cannot be an objection to the death penalty, or to any other; if it is, justice cannot be ruled out as an argument for any penalty.

Consider the claim of injustice on its merits now. A convicted man may be found to have been innocent; if he was executed, the penalty cannot be reversed. Except for fines, penalties never can be reversed. Time spent in prison cannot be returned. However, a prison sentence may be remitted once the prisoner serving it is found innocent; and he can be compensated for the time served (although compensation ordinarily cannot repair the harm). Thus, though (nearly) all penalties are irreversible, the death penalty, unlike others, is irrevocable as well.

Despite all precautions, errors will occur in judicial proceedings: The innocent may be found guilty,[3] or the guilty rich may more easily escape conviction, or receive lesser penalties than the guilty poor. However, these injustices do not reside in the penalties inflicted but in their maldistribution. It is not the penalty— whether death or prison—which is unjust when inflicted on the innocent, but its imposition on the innocent. Inequity between poor and rich also involves distribution, not the penalty distributed.[4] Thus injustice is not an objection to the death penalty but to the distributive process—the trial. Trials are more likely to be fair when life is at stake—the death penalty is probably less often unjustly inflicted than others. It requires special consideration not because it is more, or more often, unjust than other penalties, but because it is always irrevocable.

Can any amount of deterrence justify the possibility of irrevocable injustice? Surely injustice is unjustifiable in each actual individual case; it must be objected to whenever it occurs. But we are concerned here with the process that may produce injustice, and with the penalty that would make it irrevocable—not with the actual individual cases produced, but with the general rules which may produce them. To consider objections to a general rule (the provision of any penalties by law) we must compare the likely net result of alternative rules and select the rule (or penalty) likely to produce the least injustice. For however one defines justice, to support it cannot mean less than to favor the least injustice. If the death of innocents because of judicial error is unjust, so is the death of innocents by murder. If some murders could be avoided by a penalty conceivably more deterrent than others—such as the death penalty—then the question becomes: Which penalty will minimize the number of innocents killed (by crime and by punishment)? It follows that the irrevocable injustice sometimes inflicted by the death penalty would not significantly militate against it, if capital punishment deters enough murders to reduce the total number of innocents killed so that fewer are lost than would be lost without it.

In general, the possibility of injustice argues against penalization of any kind only if the expected usefulness of penalization is less important than the probable harm (particularly to innocents) and the probable inequities. The possibility of injustice argues against the death penalty only inasmuch as the added usefulness (deterrence) expected from irrevocability is thought less important than the added harm. (Were my argument specifically concerned with justice, I could compare the injustice inflicted by the courts with the injustice—outside the courts—avoided by the judicial process. *I.e.,* "important" here may be used to include everything to which importance is attached.)

We must briefly examine now the general use and effectiveness of deterrence to decide whether the death penalty could add enough deterrence to be warranted.

III

Does any punishment "deter others" at all? Doubts have been thrown on this effect because it is thought to depend on the incorrect rationalistic psychology of some of its 18th- and 19th-century proponents. Actually deterrence does not depend on rational calculation, on rationality or even on capacity for it; nor do arguments for it depend on rationalistic psychology. Deterrence depends on the likelihood and on the regularity—not on the rationality—of human responses to danger; and further on the possibility of reinforcing internal controls by vicarious external experiences.

Responsiveness to danger is generally found in human behavior; the danger can, but need not, come from the law or from society; nor need it be explicitly verbalized. Unless intent on suicide, people do not jump from high mountain cliffs, however tempted to fly through the air; and they take precautions against falling. The mere risk of injury often restrains us from doing what is otherwise attractive; we refrain even when we have no direct experience, and usually without explicit computation of probabilities, let alone conscious weighing of expected pleasure against possible pain. One abstains from dangerous acts because of vague, inchoate, habitual and, above all, preconscious fears. Risks

and rewards are more often felt than calculated; one abstains without accounting to oneself, because "it isn't done," or because one literally does not conceive of the action one refrains from. Animals as well refrain from painful or injurious experiences presumably without calculation; and the threat of punishment can be used to regulate their conduct.

Unlike natural dangers, legal threats are constructed deliberately by legislators to restrain actions which may impair the social order. Thus legislation transforms social into individual dangers. Most people further transform external into internal danger: They acquire a sense of moral obligation, a conscience, which threatens them, should they do what is wrong. Arising originally from the external authority of rulers and rules, conscience is internalized and becomes independent of external forces. However, conscience is constantly reinforced in those whom it controls by the coercive imposition of external authority on recalcitrants and on those who have not acquired it. Most people refrain from offenses because they feel an obligation to behave lawfully. But this obligation would scarcely be felt if those who do not feel or follow it were not to suffer punishment.

Although the legislators may calculate their threats and the responses to be produced, the effectiveness of the threats neither requires nor depends on calculations by those responding. The predictor (or producer) of effects must calculate; those whose responses are predicted (or produced) need not. Hence, although legislation (and legislators) should be rational, subjects, to be deterred as intended, need not be: They need only be responsive.

Punishments deter those who have not violated the law for the same reasons—and in the same degrees (apart from internalization: moral obligation) as do natural dangers. Often natural dangers—all dangers not deliberately created by legislation (*e.g.,* injury of the criminal inflicted by the crime victim) are insufficient. Thus, the fear of injury (natural danger) does not suffice to control city traffic; it must be reinforced by the legal punishment meted out to those who violate the rules. These punishments keep most people observing the regulations. However, where (in the absence of natural danger) the threatened punishment is so light that the advantage of violating rules tends to exceed the disadvantage of being punished (divided by the risk), the rule is violated (*i.e.,* parking fines are too light). In this case the feeling of obligation tends to vanish as well. Elsewhere punishment deters.

To be sure, not everybody responds to threatened punishment. Non-responsive persons may be (a) self-destructive or (b) incapable of responding to threats, or even of grasping them. Increases in the size, or certainty, of penalties would not affect these two groups. A third group (c) might respond to more certain or more severe penalties.[5] If the punishment threatened for burglary, robbery, or rape were a $5 fine in North Carolina, and 5 years in prison in South Carolina, I have no doubt that the North Carolina treasury would become quite opulent until vigilante justice would provide the deterrence not provided by law. Whether to increase penalties (or improve enforcement) depends on the importance of the rule to society, the size and likely reaction of the group that did not respond before, and the acceptance of the added punishment and enforcement required to deter it. Observation would have to locate the points— likely to differ in different times and places—at which diminishing, zero, and negative returns set in. There is no reason to believe that all present and future offenders belong to the *a priori* non-responsive groups, or that all penalties have reached the point of diminishing, let alone zero returns.

IV

Even though its effectiveness seems obvious, punishment as a deterrent has fallen into disrepute. Some ideas which help explain this progressive heedlessness were uttered by Lester Pearson, then Prime Minister of Canada, when, in opposing the death penalty, he proposed that instead "the state seek to eradicate the causes of crime—slums, ghettos, and personality disorders."[6]

"Slums, ghettos, and personality disorders" have not been shown, singly or collectively, to be "the causes" of crime.

(1) The crime rate in the slums is indeed higher than elsewhere; but so is the death rate in hospitals. Slums are no more "causes" of crime than hospitals are of death; they are locations of crime, as hospitals are of death. Slums and hospitals attract people selectively; neither is the "cause" of the condition (disease in hospitals, poverty in slums) that leads to the selective attraction.

As for poverty which draws people into slums, and, sometimes, into crime, any relative disadvantage may lead to ambition, frustration, resentment and, if insufficiently restrained, to crime. Not all relative disadvantages can be eliminated; indeed very few can be, and their elimination increases the resentment generated by the remaining ones; not even relative poverty can be removed altogether. (Absolute poverty—whatever that may be—hardly affects crime.) However, though contributory, relative disadvantages are not a necessary or sufficient cause of crime: Most poor people do not commit crimes, and some rich people do. Hence, "eradication of poverty" would, at most, remove one (doubtful) cause of crime.

In the United States, the decline of poverty has not been associated with a reduction of crime. Poverty measured in dollars of constant purchasing power, according to present government standards and statistics, was the condition of ½ of all our families in 1920; of ⅕ in 1962; and of less than ⅙ in 1966. In 1967, 5.3 million families out of 49.8 million were poor—⅑ of all families in the United States. If crime has been reduced in a similar manner, it is a well-kept secret.

Those who regard poverty as a cause of crime often draw a wrong inference from a true proposition: The rich will not commit certain crimes—Rockefeller never riots; nor does he steal. (He mugs, but only on T.V.) Yet while wealth may be the cause of not committing (certain) crimes, it does not follow that poverty (absence of wealth) is the cause of committing them. Water extinguishes or prevents fire; but its absence is not the cause of fire. Thus, if poverty could be abolished, if everybody had all "necessities" (I don't pretend to know what this would mean), crime would remain, for, in the words of Aristotle, "the greatest crimes are committed not for the sake of basic necessities but for the sake of superfluities." Superfluities cannot be provided by the government; they would be what the government does not provide.

(2) Negro ghettos have a high, Chinese ghettos have a low crime rate. Ethnic separation, voluntary or forced, obviously has little to do with crime; I can think of no reason why it should.[7]

(3) I cannot see how the state could "eradicate" personality disorders even if all causes and cures were known and available. (They are not.) Further, the known incidence of personality disorders within the prison population does not exceed the known incidence outside—though our knowledge of both is tenuous. Nor are personality disorders necessary or sufficient causes for criminal offenses, unless these be identified by means of (moral, not clinical) definition with personality disorders. In this case, Mr. Pearson would have proposed to "eradicate" crime by eradicating crime—certainly a sound, but not a helpful idea.

Mr. Pearson's views are part as well of the mental furniture of the former U.S. Attorney General Ramsey Clark, who told a congressional committee that ". . . only the elimination of the causes of crime can make a significant and lasting difference in the incidence of crime." Uncharitably interpreted, Mr. Clark revealed that only the elimination of causes eliminates effects—a sleazy cliché and wrong to boot. Given the benefit of the doubt, Mr. Clark probably

meant that the causes of crime are social; and that therefore crime can be reduced "only" by non-penal (social) measures.

This view suggests a fireman who declines firefighting apparatus by pointing out that "in the long run only the elimination of the causes" of fire "can make a significant and lasting difference in the incidence" of fire, and that firefighting equipment does not eliminate "the causes"—except that such a fireman would probably not rise to fire chief. Actually, whether fires are checked depends on equipment and on the efforts of the firemen using it no less than on the presence of "the causes": inflammable materials. So with crimes. Laws, courts and police actions are no less important in restraining them than "the causes" are in impelling them. If firemen (or attorneys general) pass the buck and refuse to use the means available, we may all be burned while waiting for "the long run" and "the elimination of the causes."

Whether any activity—be it lawful or unlawful—takes place depends on whether the desire for it, or for whatever is to be secured by it, is stronger than the desire to avoid the costs involved. Accordingly people work, attend college, commit crimes, go to the movies—or refrain from any of these activities. Attendance at a theatre may be high because the show is entertaining and because the price of admission is low. Obviously the attendance depends on both—on the combination of expected gratification and cost. The wish, motive or impulse for doing anything—the experienced, or expected, gratification—is the cause of doing it; the wish to avoid the cost is the cause of not doing it. One is no more and no less "cause" than the other. (Common speech supports this use of "cause" no less than logic: "Why did you go to Jamaica?" "*Because* it is such a beautiful place." "Why didn't you go to Jamaica?" "*Because* it is too expensive."—"Why do you buy this?" "*Because* it is so cheap." "Why don't you buy that?" "*Because* it is too expensive.") Penalties (costs) are causes of lawfulness, or (if too low or uncertain) of unlawfulness, of crime. People do commit crimes because, given their conditions, the desire for the satisfaction sought prevails. They refrain if the desire to avoid the cost prevails. Given the desire, low cost (penalty) causes the action, and high cost restraint. Given the cost, desire becomes the causal variable. Neither is intrinsically more causal than the other. The crime rate increases if the cost is reduced or the desire raised. It can be decreased by raising the cost or by reducing the desire.

The cost of crime is more easily and swiftly changed than the conditions producing the inclination to it. Further, the costs are very largely within the power of the government to change, whereas the conditions producing propensity to crime are often only indirectly affected by government action, and some are altogether beyond the control of the government. Our unilateral emphasis on these conditions and our undue neglect of costs may contribute to an unnecessarily high crime rate.

V

The foregoing suggests the question posed by the death penalty: Is the deterrence added (return) sufficiently above zero to warrant irrevocability (or other, less clear, disadvantages)? The question is not only whether the penalty deters, but whether it deters more than alternatives and whether the difference exceeds the cost of irrevocability. (I shall assume that the alternative is actual life imprisonment so as to exclude the complication produced by the release of the unrehabilitated.)

In some fairly infrequent but important circumstances the death penalty is the only possible deterrent. Thus, in the case of acute *coups d'état*, or of acute substantial attempts to overthrow the government, prospective rebels would altogether discount the threat of any prison sentence. They would not be deterred because they believe the swift victory of the revolution will invalidate a prison sentence and turn it into an advantage. Execution would be the only deterrent because, unlike prison sentences, it cannot

be revoked by victorious rebels. The same reasoning applies to deterring spies or traitors in wartime. Finally, men who, by virtue of past acts, are already serving, or are threatened, by a life sentence could be deterred from further offenses only by the threat of the death penalty.[8]

What about criminals who do not fall into any of these (often ignored) classes? Prof. Thorsten Sellin has made a careful study of the available statistics: He concluded that they do not yield evidence for the deterring effect of the death penalty.[9] Somewhat surprisingly, Prof. Sellin seems to think that this lack of evidence for deterrence is evidence for the lack of deterrence. It is not. It means that deterrence has not been demonstrated statistically—not that nondeterrence has been.

It is entirely possible, indeed likely (as Prof. Sellin appears willing to concede), that the statistics used, though the best available, are nonetheless too slender a reed to rest conclusions on. They indicate that the homicide rate does not vary greatly between similar areas with or without the death penalty, and in the same area before and after abolition. However, the similar areas are not similar enough; the periods are not long enough; many social differences and changes, other than the abolition of the death penalty, may account for the variation (or lack of it) in homicide rates with and without, before and after abolition; some of these social differences and changes are likely to have affected homicide rates. I am unaware of any statistical analysis which adjusts for such changes and differences. And logically, it is quite consistent with the postulated deterrent effect of capital punishment that there be less homicide after abolition: With retention there might have been still less.

Homicide rates do not depend exclusively on penalties any more than do other crime rates. A number of conditions which influence the propensity to crime, demographic, economic or generally social changes or differences—even such matters as changes of the divorce laws or of the cotton price—may influence the homicide rate. Therefore variation or constancy cannot be attributed to variations or constancy of the penalties, unless we know that no other factor influencing the homicide rate has changed. Usually we don't. To believe the death penalty deterrent does not require one to believe that the death penalty, or any other, is the only or the decisive causal variable; this would be as absurd as the converse mistake that "social causes" are the only or always the decisive factor. To favor capital punishment, the efficacy of neither variable need be denied. It is enough to affirm that the severity of the penalty may influence some potential criminals, and that the added severity of the death penalty adds to deterrence, or may do so. It is quite possible that such a deterrent effect may be offset (or intensified) by nonpenal factors which affect propensity; its presence or absence therefore may be hard, and perhaps impossible to demonstrate.

Contrary to what Prof. Sellin *et al.* seem to presume, I doubt that offenders are aware of the absence or presence of the death penalty state by state or period by period. Such unawareness argues against the assumption of a calculating murderer. However, unawareness does not argue against the death penalty if by deterrence we mean a preconscious, general response to a severe, but not necessarily specifically and explicitly apprehended, or calculated threat. A constant homicide rate, despite abolition, may occur because of unawareness and not because of lack of deterrence: People remain deterred for a lengthy interval by the severity of the penalty in the past, or by the severity of penalties used in similar circumstances nearby.

I do not argue for a version of deterrence which would require me to believe that an individual shuns murder while in North Dakota, because of the death penalty, and merrily goes to it in South Dakota since it has been abolished there; or that he will start the murderous career from which he had hitherto refrained, after abolition. I hold that the generalized threat of the death penalty may be a deterrent, and the more so, the more generally applied. Deterrence will not cease in the particular areas of abolition or at the particular times of abolition. Rather, general deterrence will be somewhat weakened, through local (partial) abolition. Even such weakening will be hard to detect owing to changes in many offsetting, or reinforcing, factors.

For all of these reasons, I doubt that the presence or absence of a deterrent effect of the death penalty is likely to be demonstrable by statistical means. The statistics presented by Prof. Sellin *et al.* show only that there is no statistical proof for the deterrent effect of the death penalty. But they do not show that there is no deterrent effect. Not to demonstrate presence of the effect is not the same as to demonstrate its absence; certainly not when there are plausible explanations for the nondemonstrability of the effect.

It is on our uncertainty that the case for deterrence must rest.[10]

VI

If we do not know whether the death penalty will deter others, we are confronted with two uncertainties. If we impose the death penalty, and achieve no deterrent effect thereby, the life of a convicted murderer has been expended in vain (from a deterrent viewpoint). There is a net loss. If we impose the death sentence and thereby deter some future murderers, we spared the lives of some future victims (the prospective murderers gain too; they are spared punishment because they were deterred). In this case, the death penalty has led to a net gain, unless the life of a convicted murderer is valued more highly than that of the unknown victim, or victims (and the non-imprisonment of the deterred non-murderer).

The calculation can be turned around, of course. The absence of the death penalty may harm no one and therefore produce a gain—the life of the convicted murderer. Or it may kill future victims of murderers who could have been deterred, and thus produce a loss—their life.

To be sure, we must risk something certain—the death (or life) of the convicted man, for something uncertain—the death (or life) of the victims of murderers who may be deterred. This is in the nature of uncertainty—when we invest, or gamble, we risk the money we have for an uncertain gain. Many human actions, most commitments—including marriage and crime—share this characteristic with the deterrent purpose of any penalization, and with its rehabilitative purpose (and even with the protective).

More proof is demanded for the deterrent effect of the death penalty than is demanded for the deterrent effect of other penalties. This is not justified by the absence of other utilitarian purposes such as protection and rehabilitation; they involve no less uncertainty than deterrence.[11]

Irrevocability may support a demand for some reason to expect more deterrence than revocable penalties might produce, but not a demand for more proof of deterrence, as has been pointed out above. The reason for expecting more deterrence lies in the greater severity, the terrifying effect inherent in finality. Since it seems more important to spare victims than to spare murderers, the burden of proving that the greater severity inherent in irrevocability adds nothing to deterrence lies on those who oppose capital punishment. Proponents of the death penalty need show only that there is no more uncertainty about it than about greater severity in general.

The demand that the death penalty be proved more deterrent than alternatives can not be satisfied any more than the demand that six years in prison be proved to be more deterrent than three. But the uncertainty which confronts us favors the death penalty as long as by imposing it we might save future victims of murder. This effect is as plausible as the general idea that penalties have deter-effects which increase with their severity. Though we have no proof of the positive deterrence of the penalty, we also have no proof of zero or negative effectiveness. I believe we have no right to risk additional future victims of murder for the sake of sparing convicted murderers; on the contrary, our moral obligation is to risk the possible ineffectiveness of executions.

However [obscured]
pears to be mot [obscured]
cutions are more subje [obscured]
murder. However, this app [obscured]
and does not argue for the abolitio [obscured]

NOTES

1. Social solidarity of "community feeling" (here to be ignored) might be dealt with as a form of deterrence.

2. Certainly a major meaning of *suum cuique tribue*.

3. I am not concerned here with the converse injustice, *which I regard as no less grave*.

4. Such inequity, though likely, has not been demonstrated. Note that, since there are more poor than rich, there are likely to be more guilty poor; and, if poverty contributes to crime, the proportion of the poor who are criminals also should be higher than of the rich.

5. I neglect those motivated by civil disobedience or, generally, moral or political passion. Deterring them depends less on penalties than on the moral support they receive, though penalties play a role. I also neglect those who may belong to all three groups listed, some successively, some even simultaneously, such as drug addicts. Finally, I must altogether omit the far-from-negligible role that problems of apprehension and conviction play in deterrence—beyond saying that, by reducing the government's ability to apprehend and convict, courts are able to reduce the risks of offenders.

6. I quote from the *New York Times* (November 24, 1967, p. 22). The actual psychological and other factors which bear on the disrepute—as distinguished from the rationalizations—cannot be examined here.

7. Mixed areas, incidentally, have higher crime rates than segregated ones (see, e.g., R. Ross and E. Van Den Haag, *The Fabric of Society* (New York: Harcourt, Brace & Co., 1957), pp. 102–4. Because slums are bad (morally) and crime is, many people seem to reason that "slums spawn crime"—which confuses some sort of moral with a causal relation.

8. Cautious revolutionaries, uncertain of final victory, might be impressed by prison sentences—but not in the acute stage, when faith in victory is high. And one can increase even the severity of a life sentence in prison. Finally, harsh punishment of rebels can intensify rebellious impulses. These points, though they qualify it, hardly impair the force of the argument.

9. Sellin considered mainly homicide statistics. His work may be found in his *Capital Punishment* (New

onviction of guilty defendants by juries who do
want to see them executed.

Rehabilitation or protection are of minor importance in our actual penal system (though not in our
theory). We confine many people who do not need
rehabilitation and against whom we do not need protection (e.g., the exasperated husband who killed his
wife); we release many unrehabilitated offenders
against whom protection is needed. Certainly rehabilitation and protection are not, and deterrence is, the
main actual function of legal punishment if we disregard our non-utilitarian ones.

Further Thought and Discussion

1. If some people are capable of responding to the threat of punishment, why would an
effective educational program not achieve the same effect? For those people who cannot be
moved by the threat of punishment, can the threat of death deter their crimes? Is there any
argument left for the deterrence approach of punishment for grievous crimes?

2. Is it ever acceptable for a society to kill an innocent person for the "greater good"?
Would an energetic use of capital punishment be acceptable if it sacrificed a few innocent
people but deterred many homicides?

The Death Penalty as a Deterrent: Argument and Evidence

HUGO ADAM BEDAU

Reading Questions

1. What does Bedau see as Van Den Haag's main contentions? Which of them does
Bedau challenge?

2. How does Bedau define "deterrent"? Why do the definitions not work to resolve
Bedau's central objection to Van Den Haag's claim?

3. What is Bedau's analysis of Van Den Haag's claim that people serving "life"
sentences cannot be deterred except by the death penalty?

From Hugo Adam Bedau, "The Death Penalty as a Deterrent: Argument and Evidence," *Ethics 80*
(1970), 205–217. Copyright © 1970 by The University of Chicago Press. Reprinted by permission of
the publisher and author.

4. How does Bedau argue against the death penalty as a superior deterrent to life sentences?

5. Why does Bedau think that those opposing capital punishment must prove that the most severe punishment adds to deterrence?

PROFESSOR VAN DEN HAAG'S RECENT ARTICLE, "On Deterrence and the Death Penalty,"[1] raises a number of points of that mixed (i.e., empirical-and-conceptual-and-normative) character which typifies most actual reasoning in social and political controversy but which (except when its purely formal aspects are in question) tends to be ignored by philosophers. I pass by any number of tempting points in his critique in order to focus in detail only on those which affect his account of what he says is the major topic, namely, the argument for retaining or abolishing the death penalty as that issue turns on the question of *deterrence*.

On this topic, Van Den Haag's main contentions seem to be these five: (I) Abolitionists of a utilitarian persuasion "claim that capital punishment is useless because it does not deter others." (II) There are some classes of criminals and some circumstances in which "the death penalty is the only possible deterrent." (III) As things currently stand, "deterrence [namely of criminal homicide by the death penalty] has not been demonstrated statistically"; but it is mistaken to think that "non-deterrence" has been demonstrated statistically. (IV) The death penalty is to be favored over imprisonment, because "the added severity of the death penalty adds to deterrence, or may do so." (V) "Since it seems more important to spare victims than to spare murderers, the burden of proving that the greater severity inherent in irrevocability adds nothing to deterrence lies on those who oppose capital punishment."

Succinctly, I shall argue as follows: (I) is not reasonably attributable to abolitionists, and in any case it is false; (II) is misleading and, in the interesting cases, is empirically insignificant; (III), which is the heart of the dispute, is correct in what it affirms but wrong and utterly misleading in what it denies; (IV) is unempirical and one-sided as well; and (V) is a muddle and a dodge.

The reasons for pursuing in some detail what at first might appear to be mere polemical controversy is not that Professor Van Den Haag's essay is so persuasive or likely to be of unusual influence. The reason is that the issues he raises, even though they are familiar, have not been nearly adequately discussed, despite a dozen state, congressional, and foreign government investigations into capital punishment in recent years. In Massachusetts, for example, several persons under sentence of death have been granted stays of execution pending the final report of a special legislative commission to investigate the death penalty. The exclusive mandate of this commission is to study the question of deterrence.[2] Its provisional conclusions, published late in 1968, though not in the vein of Van Den Haag's views, are liable to the kind of criticism he makes. This suggests that his reasoning may be representative of many who have tried to understand the arguments and research studies brought forward by those who would abolish the death penalty, and therefore that his errors are worth exposure and correction once and for all.

I

The claim Van Den Haag professes to find "most persuasive," namely, "capital punishment is useless because it does not deter others," is strange, and it is strange that he finds it so persuasive. Anyone who would make this claim must assume that only deterrent efficacy is relevant to assessing the utility of a punishment. In a footnote, Van Den Haag implicitly concedes that deterrence may not be the only utilitarian consideration, when he asserts that whatever our penal "theory" may tell us, "deterrence is . . . the *main actual* function of legal punishment if we disregard non-utilitarian ones" (italics added). But he does not pursue this qualification. Now we may concede that if by "function" we mean intended or professed function, deterrence is the main function of punishment. But what is deterrence? Not what Van Den Haag says it is, namely, "a preconscious, general response to a severe but not necessarily specifically and explicitly apprehended or calculated threat." How can we count as evidence of deterrence, as we may under this rubric of "general response," the desire of persons to avoid capture and punishment for the crimes they commit? Some criminologists have thought this is precisely what severe punishments tend to accomplish; if so, then they accomplish this effect only if they have failed as a deterrent. Van Den Haag's conception of deterrence is too ill-formulated to be of any serious use, since it does not discriminate between fundamentally different types of "general response" to the threat of punishment.

Let us say (definition 1) that a given punishment (P) is a *deterrent* for a given person (A) with respect to a given crime (C) at a given time (t) if and only if A does not commit C at t because he believes he runs some risk of P if he commits C, and A prefers, *ceteris paribus,* not to suffer P for committing C. This definition does not presuppose that P really is the punishment for C (a person could be deterred through a mistaken belief); it does not presuppose that A runs a high risk of incurring P (the degree of risk could be zero); or that A consciously thinks of P prior to t (it is left open as to the sort of theory needed to account for the operation of A's beliefs and preferences on his conduct). Nor does it presuppose that anyone ever suffers P (P could be a "perfect" deterrent), or that only P could have deterred A from C (some sanction less severe than P might have worked as well); and,

finally, it does not presuppose that because P deters A at t from C, therefore P would deter A at any other time or anyone else at t. The definition insures that we cannot argue from the absence of instances of C to the conclusion that P has succeeded as a deterrent: The definition contains conditions (and, moreover, contains them intentionally) which prevent this. But the definition does allow us to argue from occurrences of C to the conclusion that P has failed on each such occasion as a deterrent.

Definition 1 suggests a general functional analogue appropriate to express scientific measurements of *differential deterrent efficacy* of a given punishment for a given crime with respect to a given population (definition 2). Let us say that a given Punishment, P, deters a given population, H, from a crime, C, to the degree, D, that the members of H do not commit C because they believe that they run some risk of P if they commit C and, *ceteris paribus,* they prefer not to suffer P for committing C. If $D = 0$, then P has completely failed as a deterrent, whereas if $D = 1$, P has proved to be a perfect deterrent. Given this definition and the appropriate empirical results for various values of P, C, and H, it should be possible to establish on inductive grounds the relative effectiveness of a given punishment as a deterrent.

Definition 2 in turn leads to the following corollary for assertions of relative superior deterrent efficacy of one punishment over another. A given Punishment, P_1, is a superior deterrent to another punishment, P_2, with respect to some crime, C, and some population, H, if and only if: If the members of H, believing that they are liable to P_1 upon committing C, commit C to the degree D_1; whereas if the members of H believe that they are liable to P_2 upon committing C, they commit C to the degree D_2, and $D_1 > D_2$. This formulation plainly allows that P_1 may be a more effective deterrent than P_2 for C_1 and yet less effective as a deterrent than P_2 for a different crime C_2 (with H constant), and so forth, for other possibilities. When speaking about deterrence in the sections which follow, I shall presuppose these definitions and this corollary. For the present, it is sufficient to notice that they have, at least, the virtue of eliminating the vagueness in Van Den Haag's definition complained of earlier.

Even if we analyze the notion of deterrence to accommodate the above improvements, we are left with the central objection to Van Den Haag's claim. Neither classic nor contemporary utilitarians have argued for or against the death penalty *solely* on the ground of deterrence, nor would their ethical theory entitle them to do so. One measure of the non-deterrent utility of the death penalty derives from its elimination (through death of a known criminal) of future possible crimes from that source; another arises from the elimination of the criminal's probable adverse influence upon others to emulate his ways; another lies in the generally lower budgetary outlays of tax moneys needed to finance a system of capital punishment as opposed to long-term imprisonment. There are still further consequences apart from deterrence which the scrupulous utilitarian must weigh, along with the three I have mentioned. Therefore, it is incorrect, because insufficient, to think that if it could be demonstrated that the death penalty is not a deterrent then we would be entitled to infer, on utilitarian assumptions, that "the death penalty is useless" and therefore ought to be abolished. The problem for the utilitarian is to make commensurable such diverse social utilities as those measured by deterrent efficacy, administrative costs, etc., and then to determine which penal policy in fact maximizes utility. Finally, inspection of sample arguments actually used by abolitionists[3] will show that Van Den Haag has attacked a straw man: There are few if any contemporary abolitionists (and Van Den Haag names none) who argue solely from professional utilitarian assumptions, and it is doubtful whether there are any nonutilitarians who would abolish the death penalty solely on grounds of its deterrent inefficacy.

II

Governments faced by incipient rebellion or threatened by a coup d'état may well conclude, as Van Den Haag insists they should, that rebels (as well as traitors and spies) can be deterred, if at all, by the threat of death, since "swift victory" of the revolution "will invalidate [the deterrent efficacy] of a prison sentence."[4] This does not yet tell us how important it is that such deterrence be provided, any more than the fact that a threat of expulsion is the severest deterrent available to university authorities tells them whether they ought to insist on expelling campus rebels. Also, such severe penalties might have the opposite effect of inducing martyrdom, or provoking attempts to overthrow the government to secure a kind of political sainthood. This possibility Van Den Haag recognizes, but claims in a footnote that it "hardly impair[s] the force of the argument." Well, from a logical point of view it impairs it considerably; from an empirical point of view, since we are wholly without any reliable facts or hypotheses on politics in such extreme situations, the entire controversy remains quite speculative.

The one important class of criminals deterrable, if at all, by the death penalty consists, according to Van Den Haag, of those already under "life" sentence or guilty of a crime punishable by "life." In a trivial sense, he is correct; a person already suffering a given punishment, P, for a given crime, C_1, could not be expected to be deterred by anticipating the reinfliction of P were he to commit C_2. For if the anticipation of P did not deter him from committing C_1, how could the anticipation of P deter him from committing C_2, given that he is already experiencing P? This generalization seems to apply whenever P = "life" imprisonment. Actually, the truth is a bit more complex, because in practice (as Van Den Haag concedes, again in a footnote) so-called "life" imprisonment always has its aggravations (e.g., solitary confinement) and its mitigations (parole eligibility). These make it logically possible to deter a person already convicted of criminal homicide and serving "life" imprisonment from committing another such crime. I admit that the aggravations available are not in practice likely to provide much added deterrent effect; but exactly how likely or unlikely this effect is remains a matter for empirical investigation, not idle guesswork. Van Den Haag's seeming truism, therefore, relies for its plausibility on the false assumption that "life" imprisonment is a uniform punishment not open to further deterrence-relevant aggravations and mitigations.

Empirically, the objection to his point is that persons already serving a "life" sentence do not in general constitute a source of genuine alarm to custodial personnel. Being already incarcerated and integrated into the reward structure of prison life, they do not seem to need the deterrent controls allegedly necessary for other prisoners and the general public.[5] There are exceptions to this generalization, but there is no known way of identifying them in advance, their number has proved to be not large, and it would be irrational, therefore, to design a penal policy (as several states have)[6] which invokes the death penalty in the professed hope of deterring such convicted offenders from further criminal homicide. Van Den Haag cites no evidence that such policies accomplish their alleged purpose, and I know of none. As for the real question which Van Den Haag's argument raises—is there any class of actual or potential criminals for which the death penalty exerts a marginally superior deterrent effect over every less severe alternative?—we have no evidence at all, one way or the other. Until this proposition, or some corollary, is actually tested and confirmed, there is no reason to indulge Van Den Haag in his speculations.

III

It is not clear why Van Den Haag is so anxious to discuss whether there is evidence that the death penalty is a deterrent, or whether—as he thinks—there is no evidence that it is not a deterrent. For the issue over abolishing the death penalty, as all serious students of the subject have known for decades, is not whether (1) *the death penalty is a deterrent,* but whether (2) *the death penalty is a superior deterrent to "life" imprisonment,* and consequently the evidential dispute is also not over (1) but only over (2). As I have argued elsewhere,[7] abolitionists have reason to contest (1) only if they are against *all* punitive alternatives to the death penalty; since few abolitionists (and none cited by Van Den Haag) take this extreme view, it may be ignored here. We should notice in passing, however, that if it were demonstrated that (1) were false, there would be no need for abolitionists to go on to marshal evidence against (2), since the truth of (1) is a presupposition of the truth of (2). Now it is true that some abolitionists may be faulted for writing as if the falsity of (1) followed from the falsity of (2), but this is not a complaint Van Den Haag makes nor is it an error vital to the abolitionist argument against the death penalty. Similar considerations inveigh against certain pro–death-penalty arguments. Proponents must do more than establish (1), they must also provide evidence in favor of (2); and they cannot infer from evidence which establishes (1) that (2) is true or even probable (unless, of course, that evidence would establish [2] independently). These considerations show us how important it is to distinguish (1) and (2) and the questions of evidence which each raises. Van Den Haag never directly discusses (2), except when he observes in passing that "the question is not only whether the death penalty deters but whether it deters more than alternatives." But since he explicitly argues only over the evidential status of (1), it is unclear whether he wishes to ignore (2) or whether he thinks that his arguments regarding (1) also have consequences for the evidential status of (2). Perhaps Van Den Haag thinks that if there is no evidence disconfirming (1), then there can be no evidence disconfirming (2); or perhaps he thinks that none of the evidence disconfirming (2) also disconfirms (1). (If he thinks either, he is wrong.) Or perhaps he is careless, conceding on the one hand that (2) is important to the issue of abolition of the death penalty, only to slide back into a discussion exclusively about (1).

He writes as if his chief contentions were these two: We must not confuse (*a*) the assertion that there is no evidence that not-(1) (i.e., evidence that [1] is false); and abolitionists have asserted (*b*) whereas all they are entitled to assert is (*a*).[8] I wish to proceed on the assumption that since (1) is not chiefly at issue, neither is (*a*) or (*b*) (though I grant, as anyone must, that the distinction between [*a*] and [*b*] is legitimate and important). What is chiefly at issue, even though Van Den Haag's discussion obscures the point, is whether abolitionists must content themselves with asserting that there is no evidence against (2), or whether they may go further and assert that there is evidence that not-(2) (i.e., evidence that [2] is false). I shall argue that abolitionists may make the stronger (latter) assertion.

In order to see the issue fairly, it is necessary to see how (2) has so far been submitted to empirical tests. First of all, the issue has been confined to the death penalty for criminal homicide; consequently, it is not (2) but a subsidiary proposition which critics of the death penalty have tested, namely, (*2a*) *the death penalty is a superior deterrent to "life" imprisonment for the crime of criminal homicide*. The falsification of (*2a*) does not entail the falsity of (2); the death penalty could still be a superior deterrent to "life" imprisonment for the crime of burglary, etc. However, the disconfirmation of (*2a*) is obviously a partial disconfirmation of (2). Second, (*2a*) has not been tested directly but only indirectly. No one has devised a way to count or estimate directly the number of persons in a given population who have been deterred from criminal homicide by the fear of the penalty. The difficulties in doing so are plain enough. For instance, it would be possible to infer from the countable

numbers who have not been deterred (because they did commit a given crime) that everyone else in the population was deterred, but only on the assumption that the only reason why a person did not commit a given crime is because he was deterred. Unfortunately for this argument (though happily enough otherwise) this assumption is almost certainly false. Other ways in which one might devise to test (*2a*) directly have proved equally unfeasible. Yet it would be absurd to insist that there can be no *evidence* for or against (*2a*) unless it is *direct* evidence for or against it. Because Van Den Haag nowhere indicated what he thinks would count as evidence, direct or indirect, for or against (1), much less (2), his insistence upon the distinction between (*a*) and (*b*) and his rebuke to abolitionists is in danger of implicitly relying upon just this absurdity.

How, then, has the indirect argument over (*2a*) proceeded? During the past generation, at least six different hypotheses have been formulated, as corollaries of (*2a*), as follows:[9]

  i. death-penalty jurisdictions should have a lower annual rate of criminal homicide than abolition jurisdictions;
 ii. jurisdictions which abolished the death penalty should show an increased annual rate of criminal homicide after abolition;
iii. jurisdictions which reintroduced the death penalty should show a decreased annual rate of criminal homicide after reintroduction;
 iv. given two contiguous jurisdictions differing chiefly in that one has the death penalty and the other does not, the latter should show a higher annual rate of criminal homicide;
  v. police officers on duty should suffer a higher annual rate of criminal assault and homicide in abolition jurisdictions than in death-penalty jurisdictions;
 vi. prisoners and prison personnel should suffer a higher annual rate of criminal assault

and homicide from life-term prisoners in abolition jurisdictions than in death-penalty jurisdictions.

It could be objected to these six hypotheses that they are, as a set, insufficient to settle the question posed by (2*a*) no matter what the evidence for them may be (i.e., that falsity of [i]–[vi] does not entail the falsity of [2]). Or it could be argued that each of (i)–(vi) has been inadequately tested or insufficiently (dis)confirmed so as to establish any (dis)confirmation of (2*a*), even though it is conceded that if these hypotheses were highly (dis)confirmed they would (dis)confirm (2*a*). Van Den Haag's line of attack is not entirely clear as between these two alternatives. It looks as if he ought to take the former line of criticism in its most extreme version. How else could he argue his chief point, that the research used by abolitionists has so far failed to produce *any* evidence against (1)—we may take him to mean (2) or (2*a*). Only if (i)–(vi) were *irrelevant* to (2*a*) could it be fairly concluded from the evidential disconfirmation of (i)–(vi) that there is still no disconfirmation of (2*a*). And this is Van Den Haag's central contention. The other ways to construe Van Den Haag's reasoning are simply too preposterous to be considered: He cannot think that the evidence is indifferent to or *confirms* (i)–(vi); nor can he think that there has been no *attempt* at all to disconfirm (2*a*); nor can he think that the evidence which disconfirms (i)–(vi) is not therewith also evidence which confirms the negations of (i)–(vi). If any of these three was true, it would be a good reason for saying that there is "no evidence" against (2*a*); but each is patently false. If one inspects (i)–(vi) and (2*a*), it is difficult to see how one could argue that (dis)confirmation of the former does not constitute (dis)confirmation of the latter, even if it might be argued that verification of the former does not constitute verification of the latter. I think, therefore, that there is nothing to be gained by pursuing further this first line of attack.

Elsewhere, it looks as though Van Den Haag

takes the other alternative of criticism, albeit rather crudely, as when he argues (against [iv], I suppose, since he nowhere formulated [i]–[vi]) that "the similar areas are not similar enough." As to why, for example, the rates of criminal homicide in Michigan and in Illinois from 1920 to 1960 are not relevant because the states aren't "similar enough," he does not try to explain. But his criticism does strictly concede that if the jurisdictions *were* "similar enough," then it would be logically possible to argue from the evidence against (iv) to the disconfirmation of (2*a*). And this seems to be in keeping with the nature of the case; it is this second line of attack which needs closer examination.

Van Den Haag's own position and objections apart, what is likely to strike the neutral observer who studies the ways in which (i)–(vi) have been tested and declared disconfirmed is that their disconfirmation, and, a fortiori, the disconfirmation of (2*a*), is imperfect for two related reasons. First, all the tests rely upon *unproved empirical assumptions;* second, it is not known whether there is any *statistical significance* to the results of the tests. It is important to make these concessions, and abolitonists and other disbelievers in the deterrent efficacy of the death penalty have not always done so.

It is not possible here to review all the evidence and to reach a judgment on the empirical status of (i)–(vi). But it is possible and desirable to illustrate how the two qualifications cited above must be understood, and then to assess their effect on the empirical status of (2*a*). The absence of statistical significance may be illustrated by reference to hypothesis (v). According to the published studies, the annual rate of assaults upon on-duty policemen in abolition jurisdictions is lower than in death-penalty jurisdictions (i.e., a rate of 1.2 attacks per 100,000 population in the former as opposed to 1.3 per 100,000 in the latter). But is this difference statistically significant or not? The studies do not answer this question because the data were not submitted to tests of statistical significance. Nor is there any way, to my knowledge, that these data could be subjected to any such tests. This is, of course, no reason to suppose that the evidence is really not evidence after all, or that though it is evidence against (i) it is not evidence against (2a). Statistical significance is, after all, only a measure of the strength of evidence, not a *sine qua non* of evidential status.

The qualification concerning unproved assumptions is more important, and is worth examining somewhat more fully (though, again, only illustratively). Consider hypothesis (i). Are we entitled to infer that (i) is disconfirmed because in fact a study of the annual homicide rates (as measured by vital statistics showing cause of death) unquestionably indicates that the rate in all abolition states is consistently lower than in all death-penalty states? To make this inference we must assume that (A_1) homicides as measured by vital statistics are in a generally constant ratio to criminal homicides, (A_2) the years for which the evidence has been gathered are representative and not atypical, (A_3) however much fluctuations in the homicide rate owe to other factors, there is a nonnegligible proportion which is a function of the penalty, and (A_4) the deterrent effect of a penalty is not significantly weakened by its infrequent imposition. (There are, of course, other assumptions, but these are central and sufficiently representative here.) Assumption A_1 is effectively unmeasurable because the concept of a criminal homicide is the concept of a homicide which *deserves* to be criminally prosecuted.[10] Nevertheless, A_1 has been accepted by criminologists for over a generation. A_2 is confirmable, on the other hand, and bit by bit, a year at a time, seems to be being confirmed. Assumption A_3 is rather more interesting. To the degree to which it is admitted or insisted that other factors than the severity of the penalty affect the volume of homicide, to that degree A_3 becomes increasingly dubious; but at the same time testing (2a) by (i) becomes increasingly unimportant. The urgency of testing (2a) rests upon the assumption that it is the deterrent efficacy of penalties which is the chief factor in the volume of crimes, and it is absurd to

hold that assumption and at the same time doubt A_3. On the other hand, A_4 is almost certainly false (and has been believed so by Bentham and other social theorists for nearly two hundred years). The falsity of A_4, however, is not of fatal harm to the disconfirmation of (i) because it is not known how frequently or infrequently a severe penalty such as death or life imprisonment needs to be imposed in order to maximize its deterrent efficacy. Such information as we do have on this point leads one to doubt that for the general population the frequency with which the death sentence is imposed makes any significant difference to the volume of criminal homicide.[11]

I suggest that these four assumptions and the way in which they bear upon interpretation and evaluation of the evidence against (i), and therefore the disconfirmation of (2a), are typical of what one finds as one examines the work of criminologists as it relates to the rest of these corollaries of (2a). Is it reasonable, in the light of these considerations, to infer that we have no evidence against (i)–(vi), or that although we do have evidence against (i)–(vi), we have none against (2a)? I do not think so. Short of unidentified and probably unobtainable "crucial experiments," we shall never be able to marshal evidence for (2a) or for (i)–(vi) except by means of certain additional assumptions such as A_1–A_4. To reason otherwise is to rely on nothing more than the fact that it is logically possible to grant the evidence against (i)–(vi) and yet deny that (2a) is false; or it is to insist that the assumptions which the inference relies upon are not plausible assumptions at all (or though plausible are themselves false or disconfirmed) and that no other assumptions can be brought forward which will be both immune to objections and still preserve the linkage between the evidence and the corollaries and (2a). The danger now is that one will repudiate assumptions such as A_1–A_4 in order to guarantee the failure of efforts to disconfirm (2a) via disconfirmation of (i)–(vi); or else that one will place the standards of evidence too high before one accepts the disconfirmation. In either case one has begun to engage in the familiar but discreditable practice of "protecting the hypothesis" by making it, in effect, immune to any kind of disconfirmation.

On my view things stand in this way. An empirical proposition not directly testable, (2), has a significant corollary, (2a), which in turn suggests a number of corollaries, (i)–(vi), each of which is testable with varying degrees of indirectness. Each of (i)–(vi) has been tested. To accept the results as evidence disconfirming (i)–(vi) and as therefore disconfirming (2a), it is necessary to make certain assumptions, of which A_1–A_4 are typical. These assumptions in turn are not all testable, much less directly tested; some of them, in their most plausible formulation, may even be false (but not in that formulation necessary to the inference, however). Since this structure of indirect testing, corollary hypotheses, unproved assumptions, is typical of the circumstances which face us when we wish to consider the evidence for or against any complex empirical hypothesis such as (2), I conclude that while (2) has by no means been disproved (whatever that might mean), it is equally clear that (2) has been disconfirmed, rather than confirmed or left untouched by the inductive arguments we have surveyed.

I have attempted to review and appraise the chief "statistical" arguments (as Van Den Haag calls them) marshaled during the past fifteen years or so in this country by those critical of the death penalty. But in order to assess these arguments more adequately, it is helpful to keep in mind two other considerations. First, most of the criminologists skeptical of (1) are led to this attitude not by the route we have examined— the argument against (2)—but by a general theory of the causation of crimes of personal violence. Given their confidence in that theory, and the evidence for it, they tend not to credit seriously the idea that the death penalty deters (very much), much less the idea that it is a superior deterrent to a severe alternative such as "life" imprisonment (which may not deter very

much, either). The interested reader should consult in particular Professor Marvin Wolfgang's monograph, *Patterns of Criminal Homicide* (1958). Second, very little of the empirical research purporting to establish the presence or absence of deterrent efficacy of a given punishment is entirely reliable because almost no effort has been made to isolate the relevant variables. Surely, it is platitudinously true that *some* persons in *some* situations considering *some* crimes can be deterred from committing them by *some* penalties. To go beyond this, however, and supplant these variables with a series of well-confirmed functional hypotheses about the deterrent effect of current legal sanctions is not possible today.

Even if one cannot argue, as Van Den Haag does, that there is no evidence against the claim that the death penalty is a better deterrent than life imprisonment, this does not yet tell us how good this evidence is, how reliable it is, how extensive, and how probative. Van Den Haag could, after all, give up his extreme initial position and retreat to the concession that although there is evidence against the superior deterrent efficacy of the death penalty, still, the evidence is not very good, indeed, not good enough to make reasonable the policy of abolishing the death penalty. Again, it is not possible to undertake to settle this question short of a close examination of each of the empirical studies which confirm (i)–(vi). The reply, so far as there is one, short of further empirical studies (which undoubtedly are desirable—I should not want to obscure that), is twofold: The evidence, such as it is, for (i)–(vi) is uniformly confirmatory in all cases; and the argument of Section IV which follows.

IV

Van Den Haag's "argument" rests considerable weight on the claims that "the added severity of the death penalty adds to deterrence, or may do so"; and that "the generalized threat of the death penalty may be a deterrent, and the more so, the more generally applied." These claims are open to criticism on at least three grounds.

First, as the modal auxiliaries signal, Van Den Haag has not really committed himself to any affirmative empirical claim, but only to a truism. It is always logically possible, no matter what the evidence, that a given penalty which is *ex hypothesi* more severe than an alternative, may be a better deterrent under some conditions not often realized, and be proven so by evidence not ever detectable. For this reason, there is no possible way to prove that Van Den Haag's claims are false, no possible preponderance of evidence against his conclusions which must, logically, force him to give them up. One would have hoped those who believe in the deterrent superiority of the death penalty could, at this late date, offer their critics something more persuasive than logical possibilities. As it is, Van Den Haag's appeal to possible evidence comes perilously close to an argument from ignorance: The possible evidence we might gather is used to offset the actual evidence we have gathered.

Second, Van Den Haag rightly regards his conclusion above as merely an instance of the general principle that, *ceteris paribus,* "the Greater the Severity the Greater the Deterrence," a "plausible" idea, as he says. Yet the advantage on behalf of the death penalty produced by this principle is a function entirely of the evidence for the principle itself. But we are offered no evidence at all to make this plausible principle into a confirmed hypothesis of contemporary criminological theory of special relevance to crimes of personal violence. Until we see evidence concerning specific crimes, specific penalties, specific criminal populations, which show that in general the Greater the Severity the Greater the Deterrence, we run the risk of stupefying ourselves by the merely plausible. Besides, without any evidence for this principle we will find ourselves at a complete standoff with the abolitionist (who, of course, can play the same game), because he has his own equally plausible

first principle: The Greater the Severity of Punishment the Greater the Brutality Provoked throughout Society. When at last, exhausted and frustrated by mere plausibilities, we once again turn to study the evidence, we will find that the current literature on deterrence in criminology does not encourage us to believe in Van Den Haag's principle.[12]

Third, Van Den Haag has not given any reason why, in the quest for deterrent efficacy, one should fasten (as he does) on the severity of the punishments in question, rather than (as Bentham long ago counseled) on the relevant factors, notably the ease and speed and reliability with which the punishment can be inflicted. Van Den Haag cannot hope to convince anyone who has studied the matter that the death penalty and "life" imprisonment differ only in their severity, and that in all other respects affecting deterrent efficacy they are equivalent; and if he believes this himself it would be interesting to have seen his evidence for it. The only thing to be said in favor of fastening exclusively upon the question of severity in the appraisal of punishments for their relative deterrent efficacy is that augmenting the severity of a punishment in and of itself usually imposes little if any added direct cost to operate the penal system; it even may be cheaper. This is bound to please the harried taxpayer, and at the same time gratify the demand on government to "do something" about crime. Beyond that, emphasizing the severity of punishments as the main (or indeed the sole) variable relevant to deterrent efficacy is unbelievably superficial.

V

Van Den Haag's final point concerning where the burden of proof lies is based, he admits, on playing off a certainty (the death of the persons executed) against a risk (that innocent persons, otherwise the would-be victims of those deterrable only by the death penalty, would be killed).[13] This is not as analogous as he seems to think it is to the general nature of gambling, investment, and other risk-taking enterprises. In none of them do we deliberately cause anything to be killed, as we do, for instance, when we weed out carrot seedlings to enable those remaining to grow larger (a eugenic analogy, by the way, which might be more useful to Van Den Haag's purpose). In none, that is, do we venture a sacrifice in the hope of a future net gain; we only *risk* a present loss in that hope. Moreover, in gambling ventures we recoup what we risked if we win, whereas in executions we must lose something (the lives of persons executed) no matter if we lose or win (the lives of innocents protected). Van Den Haag's attempt to locate the burden of proof by appeal to principles of gambling is a failure.

Far more significantly, Van Den Haag frames the issue in such a way that the abolitionist has no chance of discharging the burden of proof once he accepts it. For what evidence could be marshaled to prove what Van Den Haag wants proved, namely, that "the greater severity inherent in irrevocability [of the death penalty] . . . adds nothing to deterrence"? The evidence alluded to at the end of Section IV does tend to show that this generalization (the negation of Van Den Haag's own principle) is indeed true, but it does not prove it. I conclude, therefore, that either Van Den Haag is wrong in his argument which shows the locus of burden of proof to lie on the abolitionist, or one must accept less than proof in order to discharge this burden (in which case, the very argument Van Den Haag advances shows that the burden of proof now lies on those who would retain the death penalty).

"Burden of proof" in areas outside judicial precincts where evidentiary questions are at stake tends to be a rhetorical phrase and nothing more. Anyone interested in the truth of the matter will not defer gathering evidence pending a determination of where the burden of proof lies. For those who do think there is a question of burden of proof, as Van Den Haag does, they should consider this: Advocacy of the death penalty is advocacy of a rule of penal law which empowers the state to deliberately take human life and in general to threaten the public with the taking of life. *Ceteris paribus,* one would think anyone favoring such a rule would be ready to offer considerable evidence for its necessity and efficacy. Surely, some showing of necessity, some evidentiary proof, is to be expected to satisfy the skeptical. Exactly when and in what circumstances have the apologists for capital punishment offered evidence to support their contentions? Where is that evidence recorded for us to inspect, comparable to the evidence cited in Section III against the superior deterrent efficacy of the death penalty? Van Den Haag conspicuously cited no such evidence and so it is with all other proponents of the death penalty. The insistence that the burden of proof lies on abolitionists, therefore, is nothing but the rhetorical demand of every defender of the status quo who insists upon evidence from those who would effect change, while reserving throughout the right to dictate criteria and standards of proof and refusing to offer evidence for his own view.[14]

I should have thought that the death penalty was a sufficiently momentous matter and of sufficient controversy that the admittedly imperfect evidence assembled over the past generation by those friendly to abolition would have been countered by evidence tending to support the opposite, retentionist, position. It remains a somewhat sad curiosity that nothing of the sort has happened; no one has ever published research tending to show, however inconclusively, that the death penalty after all is a deterrent, and a superior deterrent to "life" imprisonment. Among scholars at least, if not among legislators and other politicians, the perennial appeal to burden of proof really ought to give way to offering of proof by those interested enough to argue the issue.

NOTES

1. *Ethics* 78 (July 1968):280–88. Van Dan Haag later published a "revised version" under the same title in *Journal of Criminal Law, Criminology and Police Science* 60 (1969):141–47. I am grateful to Professor Van Den Haag for providing me with a reprint of each version. I should add that his revisions in the later version were minimal, especially in his Section V which is mainly what I shall criticize. . . .

2. See Massachusetts Laws, chap. 150, Resolves of 1967; "Interim Report of the Special Commission Established to Make an Investigation and Study Relative to the Effectiveness of Capital Punishment as a Deterrent to Crime," mimeographed (Boston: Clerk, Great and General Court, State House, 1968).

3. See the several essays reprinted in Bedau, ed., *The Death Penalty in America,* rev. ed. (New York, 1967), chap. 4 and the articles cited therein at pp. 166–70.

4. The same argument has been advanced earlier by Sidney Hook (see the *New York Law Forum* [1961], pp. 278–83, and the revised version of this argument published in Bedau, pp. 150–51).

5. See, e.g., Thorsten Sellin, "Prison Homicides," in *Capital Punishment,* ed. Sellin (New York, 1967), pp. 154–60.

6. Rhode Island (1852), North Dakota (1915), New York (1965), Vermont (1965), and New Mexico (1969), have all qualified their abolition of the death penalty in this way; for further details, see Bedau, p. 12.

7. Bedau, pp. 260–61.

8. Van Den Haag accuses Professor Thorsten Sellin, a criminologist "who has made a careful study of the available statistics," of seeming to "think that this lack of evidence for deterrence is evidence for the lack of deterrent" (p. 285, col. 1), that is, of thinking that (*a*) is (*b*)! In none of Sellin's writings which I have studied (see, for a partial listing, note 9, below) do I see any evidence that Sellin "thinks" the one "is" the other. What will be found is a certain vacillation in his various published writings, which span the years from 1953 to 1967, between the two ways of putting his conclusions. His most recent statement is unqualifiedly in the (*b*) form (see his *Capital Punishment,* p. 138). Since Van Den Haag also cited my *Death Penalty in America* (though not in this connection), I might add that there I did distinguish between (*a*) and (*b*) but did not insist, as I do now, that the argument entitles abolitionists to assert (*b*) (see Bedau, pp. 264–65). It is perhaps worth noting here some other writers, all criminologists, who have recently stated the same or stronger conclusion. "Capital punishment does not act as an effective deterrent to murder" (William J.

Chambliss, "Types of Deviance and the Effectiveness of Legal Sanctions," *Wisconsin Law Review* [1967], p. 706); "The capital punishment controversy has produced the most reliable information on the general deterrent effect of a criminal sanction. It now seems established and accepted that . . . the death penalty makes no difference to the homicide rate" (Norval Morris and Frank Zimring, "Deterrence and Corrections," *Annals* 381 [January 1969]:143); "the evidence indicates that it [namely, the death penalty for murder] has no discernible effects in the United States" (Walter C. Reckless, "The Use of the Death Penalty," *Crime and Delinquency* 15 [January 1969]:52); "Capital punishment is ineffective in deterring murder" (Eugene Doleschal, "The Deterrent Effect of Legal Punishment," *Information Review on Crime and Delinquency* 1 [June 1969]:7).

9. The relevant research, regarding each of the six hypotheses in the text, is as follows: (i) Karl Schuessler, "The Deterrent Influence of the Death Penalty," *Annals* 284 (November 1952):57; Walter C. Reckless, "The Use of the Death Penalty—A Factual Statement," *Crime and Delinquency* 15 (1969):52, table 9. (ii) Thorsten Sellin, *The Death Penalty* (Philadelphia: American Law Institute, 1959), pp. 19–24, reprinted in Bedau, pp. 274–84; updated in Sellin, *Capital Punishment,* 135–38. (iii) Sellin, *The Death Penalty,* pp. 34–38, reprinted in Bedau, pp. 339–43. (iv) See works cited in (iii), above. (v) Canada, *Minutes and Proceedings of Evidence,* Joint Committee of the Senate and House of Commons on Capital Punishment and Corporal Punishment and Lotteries (1955), appendix F, pt. 1, pp. 718–28; "The Death Penalty and Police Safety," reprinted in Bedau, pp. 284–301, and in Sellin, *Capital Punishment,* pp. 138–54, with postscript (1967); Canada, "The State Police and the Death Penalty," pp. 729–35, reprinted in Bedau, pp. 301–15. (vi) *Massachusetts, Report and Recommendations of the Special Commission . . . [on] the Death Penalty . . .* (1958), pp. 21–22, reprinted in Bedau, p. 400; Thorsten Sellin, "Prison Homicides," in Sellin, *Capital Punishment,* pp. 154–60.

10. See, for discussion surrounding this point, Bedau, pp. 56–74.

11. See Robert H. Dann, *The Deterrent Effect of Capital Punishment* (Philadelphia, 1935); Leonard H. Savitz, "A Study in Capital Punishment," *Journal of Criminal Law, Criminology and Police Science* 49 (1958):338–41, reprinted in Bedau, pp. 315–32; William F. Graves, "A Doctor Looks at Capital Punishment," *Medical Arts and Sciences* 10 (1956):137–41, reprinted in Bedau, pp. 322–32, with addenda (1964).

12. See, for a general review, Eugene Doleschal, "The Deterrent Effect of Legal Punishment: A Review of the Literature," *Information Review on Crime and Delinquency* 1 (June 1969):1–17, and the many research studies cited therein, especially the survey by Norval Morris and Frank Zimring, "Deterrence and Corrections," *Annals* 381 (January 1969):137–46; also Gordon Hawkins, "Punishment and Deterrence," *Wisconsin Law Review* (1969), pp. 550–65.

13. The same objection has been raised earlier by Joel Feinberg (see his review of Bedau in *Ethics* 76 [October 1965]:63).

14. For a general discussion which is not inconsistent with the position I have taken, and which illuminates the logicorhetorical character of the appeal to burden of proof in philosophical argument, see Robert Brown, "The Burden of Proof," *American Philosophical Quarterly* 7 (1970):74–82.

For Further Thought and Discussion

1. In the case of homicide, how should repeat offenders be punished? Would the death sentence be morally appropriate? Would it serve as a deterrent?

2. Should the aim of punishment be to produce desirable consequences in society or to rehabilitate the offender?

18 Animals and the Environment

SHOULD ENVIRONMENTAL CONCERNS BE IMPORTANT TO US? Should the environment and animals have a specially appointed human to defend them against possible abuse?

First, let's look at the reasons for protecting the environment. One often-cited reason is that doing so is in humanity's long-term interests. Destroying the rain forests may prevent us from finding cures to diseases; polluting the air and water may make living considerably more troubled; health hazards diminish the quality of life. These are compelling arguments for the position that we have a vested interest in protecting our environment. Opponents respond that jobs are at stake. For nearly every effort to protect part of the natural environment, jobs are sacrificed; it is insensitive to ignore the welfare of entire industries and the people who work in them.

Another argument favoring the protection of the environment moves us away from our purely "selfish" human viewpoint. The environment is not there for us, goes this argument. It has its own intrinsic value that deserves our protection. We must respect its right to exist whether or not humans benefit from the protection we offer it.

When it comes to arguments for the rights of animals, we are again faced with a reorientation of our traditional view of the human place in the world order. Just like the natural environment, animals have formerly been viewed as ours to do with as we want. Even the Old Testament announces our dominion over the animals of the earth. The moral argument intended to sensitize us is that animals have many more of the qualities that humans possess than we earlier realized. These qualities, it is argued, are what give us our claim to moral protections and other moral rights.

Finally, do we have an obligation to unborn generations? And even if we do owe some consideration to people not yet born, how much do we owe them? It is difficult enough, some might argue, to consider all those living now who are affected by our actions. How much weight should be placed on the well-being of people who do not yet exist? How many generations ahead should we have to consider?

As you read the next several essays, keep your mind set on the practical consequences of your decisions. How much would we have to change our everyday lives
if we find compelling the arguments that the environment, animals, and future generations all have a moral claim on our actions?

Dissenting Opinion in *Sierra Club v. Morton*

JUSTICE WILLIAM O. DOUGLAS

Reading Questions

1. What precedents does Justice Douglas call upon in arguing for the "legal personhood" of inanimate objects, such as natural features of the environment?
2. Why does Justice Douglas have cause for caution in trusting the Congress or federal
agencies in acting favorably toward the environment?
3. According to Justice Douglas, who should have "standing" to argue for the
inanimate objects in the environment?

THE CRITICAL QUESTION of "standing"
would be simplified and also put neatly in focus
if we fashioned a federal rule that allowed environmental issues to be litigated before federal
agencies or federal courts in the name of the inanimate object about to be despoiled, defaced,
or invaded by roads and bulldozers and where
injury is the subject of pubic outrage. Contemporary public concern for protecting nature's
ecological equilibrium should lead to the confer-
ral of standing upon environmental objects to
sue for their own preservation.[1] This suit would
therefore be more properly labeled as *Mineral
King v. Morton*.

Inanimate objects are sometimes parties in litigation. A ship has a legal personality, a fiction
found useful for maritime purposes. The corporation sole—a creature of ecclesiastical law—is
an acceptable adversary and large fortunes ride
on its cases.[2] The ordinary corporation is a "person" for purposes of the adjudicatory processes,

[1] See Stone, Should Trees have Standing? Toward Legal
Rights for Natural Objects, 45 S. Cal. L. Rev. 450 (1972).

[2] At common law, an office holder, such as a priest or the
King, and his successors constituted a corporation sole, a
legal entity distinct from the personality which managed it.
Rights and duties were deemed to adhere to this device
rather than to the office holder in order to provide continuity
after the latter retired. The notion is occasionally revived by
American courts.

United States Supreme Court. 405 U.S. 727 (1972).

whether it represents proprietary, spiritual, aesthetic, or charitable causes.[3]

So it should be as respects valleys, alpine meadows, rivers, lakes, estuaries, beaches, ridges, groves of trees, swampland, or even air that feels the destructive pressures of modern technology and modern life. The river, for example, is the living symbol of all the life it sustains or nourishes—fish, aquatic insects, water ouzels, otter, fisher, deer, elk, bear, and all other animals, including man, who are dependent on it or who enjoy it for its sight, its sound, or its life. The river as plaintiff speaks for the ecological unit of life that is part of it. Those people who have a meaningful relation to that body of water—whether it be a fisherman, a canoeist, a zoologist, or a logger—must be able to speak for the values which the river represents and which are threatened with destruction.

I do not known Mineral King. I have never seen it nor travelled it, though I have seen articles describing its proposed "development." . . . The Sierra Club in its complaint alleges that "One of the principal purposes of the Sierra Club is to protect and conserve the national resources of the Sierra Nevada Mountains." The District Court held that this uncontested allegation made the Sierra Club "sufficiently aggrieved" to have "standing" to sue on behalf of Mineral King.

Mineral King is doubtless like other wonders of the Sierra Nevada such as Tuolumne Meadows and the John Muir Trail. Those who hike it, fish it, hunt it, camp in it, or frequent it, or visit it merely to sit in solitude and wonderment are legitimate spokesmen for it, whether they may be a few or many. Those who have intimate relation with the inanimate object about to be injured, polluted, or otherwise despoiled are its legitimate spokesmen.

The Solicitor General . . . takes a wholly different approach. He considers the problem in terms of "government by the Judiciary." With all respect, the problem is to make certain that the inanimate objects, which are the very core of America's beauty, have spokesmen before they are destroyed. It is, of course, true that most of them are under the control of a federal or state agency. The standards given those agencies are usually expressed in terms of the "public interest." Yet "public interest" has so many differing shades of meaning as to be quite meaningless on the environmental front. Congress accordingly has adopted ecological standards . . . and guidelines for agency action have been provided by the Council on Environmental Quality of which Russell E. Train is Chairman.

Yet the pressures on agencies for favorable action one way or the other are enormous. The suggestion that Congress can stop action which is undesirable is true in theory; yet even Congress is too remote to give meaningful direction and its machinery is too ponderous to use very often. The federal agencies of which I speak are not venal or corrupt. But they are notoriously under the control of powerful interests who manipulate them through advisory committees, or friendly working relations, or who have that natural affinity with the agency which in time develops between the regulator and the regulated. As early as 1894, Attorney General Olney predicted that regulatory agencies might become "industry-minded," as illustrated by his forecast concerning the Interstate Commerce Commission [M. Josephson, The Politicos 526 (1938).]:

> The Commission is or can be made of great use to the railroads. It satisfies the public clamor for supervision of the railroads, at the same time that supervision is almost entirely nominal. Moreover, the older the Commission gets to be, the more likely it is to take a business and railroad view of things.

---

[3] Early jurists considered the conventional corporation to be a highly artificial entity. Lord Coke opined that a corporation's creation "rests only in intendment and consideration of the law." Mr. Chief Justice Marshall added that the device is "an artificial being, invisible, intangible, and existing only in contemplation of law." Today suits in the names of corporations are taken for granted. United States Supreme Court. 405 U.S. 727 (1972).

Years later a court of appeals observed, "the recurring question which has plagued public regulation of industry [is] whether the regulatory agency is unduly oriented toward the interest of the industry it is designed to regulate, rather than the public interest it is supposed to protect."

The Forest Service—one of the federal agencies behind the scheme to despoil Mineral King—has been notorious for its alignment with lumber companies, although its mandate from Congress directs it to consider the various aspects of multiple use in its supervision of the national forests.

The voice of the inanimate object, therefore, should not be stilled. That does not mean that the judiciary takes over the managerial functions from the federal agency. It merely means that before these priceless bits of Americana (such as a valley, an alpine meadow, a river, or a lake) are forever lost or are so transformed as to be reduced to the eventual rubble of our urban environment, the voice of the existing beneficiaries of these environmental wonders should be heard.

Perhaps they will not win. Perhaps the bulldozers of "progress" will plow under all the aesthetic wonders of this beautiful land. That is not the present question. The sole question is, who has standing to be heard?

Those who hike the Appalachian Trail into Sunfish Pond, New Jersey, and camp or sleep there, or run the Allagash in Maine, or climb the Guadalupes in West Texas, or who canoe and portage the Quetico Superior in Minnesota, certainly should have standing to defend those natural wonders before courts or agencies, though they live 3,000 miles away. Those who merely are caught up in environmental news or propaganda and flock to defend these waters or areas may be treated differently. That is why these environmental issues should be tendered by the inanimate object itself. Then there will be assurances that all of the forms of life which it represents will stand before the court—the pileated woodpecker as well as the coyote and bear, the lemmings as well as the trout in the streams. Those inarticulate members of the ecological group cannot speak. But those people who have so frequented the place to know its values and wonders will be able to speak for the entire ecological community.

Ecology reflects the land ethic; and Aldo Leopold wrote in A Sand County Almanac 204 (1949), "The land ethic simply enlarges the boundaries of the community to include soils, waters, plants, and animals, or collectively, the land."

That, as I see it, is the issue of "standing" in the present case and controversy.

For Further Thought and Discussion

1. Do you agree that we should "enlarge the boundaries of the community to include soils, waters, plants, and animals, or collectively, the land"?

2. Can a utilitarian argument be made to protect the "inarticulate members of the ecological group"? Why should we protect them?

Ethics and Animal Consciousness

MARTIN BENJAMIN

Reading Questions

1. In the "indirect obligation" approach, how does Aquinas justify restrictions on at least some cruelty to animals?

2. How effective are Benjamin's objections to Aquinas's "hierarchical world-view" and to Kant's "self-consciousness" condition?

3. How does Benjamin reply to Descartes's definition of humans as language users?

4. How could Bentham's "direct obligation" approach show that at least some animals are sentient? Does their sentience give us a reason not to be cruel to animals?

5. How does Benjamin put together elements of each approach to outline his strategy?

Introduction

Are there any ethical restrictions on the ways in which human beings may use and treat nonhuman animals? If so, what are they and how are they to be justified? In what follows, I will first review three standard responses to these questions and briefly indicate why none of them is entirely satisfactory. Next I will identify what I take to be the kernel of truth in each of the three responses and then I will attempt to blend them into a fourth, more adequate, position. In so doing, I hope to suggest the importance, from an ethical point of view, of further inquiry into the nature and extent of consciousness in nonhuman animals.

Three Standard Positions

Historically, Western philosophers have responded to questions about the nature and extent of ethical restrictions on the human use and treatment of nonhuman animals in three ways. First, those who hold what I label "Indirect Ob-ligation" theories maintain that ethical restrictions on the use and treatment of animals can be justified *only* if they can be derived from direct obligations to human beings. The second type of response, which I label "No Obligation" theories, holds that there are no restrictions whatever on what humans may do to other animals. And the third type of response, which I label "Direct Obligation" theories, maintains that ethical restrictions on the use and treatment of animals can sometimes be justified solely for the sake of animals themselves. I will not elaborate each of these positions.

INDIRECT OBLIGATION

Among the most noted philosophers in the Western tradition, St. Thomas Aquinas (1225–1274) and Immanuel Kant (1724–1804) have acknowledged restrictions on human conduct with regard to the use and treatment of nonhuman animals, but these restrictions are, in their view, ultimately grounded upon obligations to other human beings. Blending views that can be

From Martin Benjamin, "Ethics and Animal Consciousness," in *Social Ethics, Morality and Social Policy*, 2d. ed., (New York: McGraw-Hill, 1982), ed. by Thomas A. Mappes and Jane S. Zembaty. Reprinted by permission of the author.

traced both to the Bible and Aristotle, Aquinas held a hierarchial or means-end view of the relationship between plants, animals, and humans, respectively:

> There is no sin in using a thing for the purpose for which it is. Now the order of things is such that the imperfect are for the perfect . . . things, like plants which merely have life, are all alike for animals, and all animals are for man. Wherefore it is not unlawful if men use plants for the good of animals, and animals for the good of man, as the Philosopher states (*Politics*, i, 3).
>
> Now the most necessary use would seem to consist in the fact that animals use plants, and men use animals, for food, and this cannot be done unless these be deprived of life, wherefore it is lawful both to take life from plants for the use of animals, and from animals for the use of men. In fact this is in keeping with the commandment of God himself (*Genesis* i, 29, 30 and *Genesis* ix, 3).[1]

Nevertheless, it does not follow, for Aquinas, that one can do anything to an animal. For example, one is still prohibited from killing another person's ox: "He that kills another's ox, sins, not through killing the ox, but through injuring another man in his property. Wherefore this is not a species of the sin of murder but of the sin of theft or robbery." And there may even by similarly *indirect* grounds for not harming animals who are no one's property. Thus, Aquinas explains,

> if any passages of Holy Writ seem to forbid us to be cruel to dumb animals, for instance to kill a bird with its young: this is either to remove man's thoughts from being cruel to other men, and lest through being cruel to animals one become cruel to human beings: or because injury

to an animal leads to the temporal hurt of man, either of the doer of the deed, or of another.[2]

Kant, too, held that insofar as humans are obligated to restrain themselves in their dealings with animals, it is due to their obligations to other humans. Thus,

> so far as animals are concerned, we have no direct duties. Animals are not self-conscious and are there merely as a means to an end. That end is man. . . . Our duties towards animals are merely indirect duties towards humanity. Animal nature has analogies to human nature, and by doing our duties to animals in respect of manifestations of human nature, we indirectly do our duty to humanity. . . . If . . . any acts of animals are analogous to human acts and spring from the same principles, we have duties towards the animals because thus we cultivate the same duties towards human beings. If a man shoots his dog because the animal is no longer capable of service, he does not fail in his duty to the dog, for the dog cannot judge, but his act is inhuman and damages in itself that humanity which it is his duty to show towards mankind. If he is not to stifle his human feelings, he must practice kindness towards animals, for he who is cruel to animals becomes hard also in his dealings with men.[3]

Thus Aquinas and Kant both hold what I have labeled "Indirect Obligation" theories with regard to ethical restrictions on the use and treatment of animals. Although they agree that we have obligation *with regard* to animals, these obligations *are not,* at bottom, *owed to* the animals themselves but rather they are owed to other human beings.

There are, nonetheless, significant problems with Aquinas's and Kant's positions, at least in

---

[1] St. Thomas Aquinas, *Summa Theologica,* literally translated by the English Dominican Fathers (Benziger Brothers, 1918), Part II, Question 64, Article 1. Reprinted in Tom Regan and Peter Singer, eds., *Animal Rights and Human Obligations* (Prentice-Hall, 1976), p. 119.

Copyright © 1980 by Martin Benjamin

[2] St. Thomas Aquinas, *Summa Contra Gentiles,* literally translated by the English Dominican Fathers (Benziger Brothers, 1929), Third Book, Part II, Chap, CXII. Reprinted in Regan and Singer, p. 59.

[3] Immanuel Kant, "Duties to Animals and Spirits," in *Lectures on Ethics,* translated by Louis Infield (Harper and Row, 1963). Reprinted in Regan and Singer, p. 122.

their present forms. First, insofar as Aquinas assumes that it is necessary for humans to use animals for food and thus to deprive them of life, his position must be reconsidered in the light of modern knowledge about nutrition. It has been maintained, for example, that a perfectly nutritious diet may require little or no deprivation of animal life and, even if it does, that the average American consumes twice as much animal protein as his or her body can possibly use.[4] Insofar as we continue to consume large quantities of animal foodstuff requiring pain and the deprivation of life, then, we do so, not so much to serve vital nutritional demands, but rather to indulge our acquired tastes. Secondly, insofar as Aquinas's view is based upon a hierarchial world-view and assumes that those lower in the order or less perfect are to serve the good of those higher or more perfect, it is open to a serious theoretical objection. It is, unfortunately, not difficult to imagine a group of beings—perhaps from another part of the universe—who are more rational and more powerful than we. Assuming that such beings are more perfect than we are, it seems to follow, if we adopt the principles underlying Aquinas's view, that we ought to acquiesce in their using us for whichever of their purposes they fancy we would serve. But do we want to agree with the rightness of this? And if we take Aquinas's view, would we have any grounds on which to disagree?

As for Kant's view, the main difficulties have to do first with his emphasis on self-consciousness as a condition for being the object of a direct obligation, and second with his assumption that all and only human beings are self-conscious. I will postpone consideration of the first difficulty until later. For the moment, let me simply develop the second. Even supposing that being self-conscious is a necessary condition for being the object of a direct obligation, it does not follow either that *all* human beings are

the objects of direct obligations or that *no* animal can be the object of such an obligation. First, advances in medical knowledge, techniques, and technology have, among other things, preserved and prolonged the lives of a number of human beings who are severely retarded or otherwise mentally impaired due to illness or accident and the irreversibly comatose (e.g., Karen Ann Quinlan). In our day, then, if not in Kant's, one cannot assume that all human beings are self-conscious. Second, some contemporary researchers have suggested that at least some nonhuman animals have a capacity for becoming self-conscious that has, until recently, been undetected or ignored by humans. Thus, even if we follow Kant and accept self-consciousness as a condition for being the object of direct obligations, it does not follow that *all* and *only* humans satisfy this condition. Some humans, it may turn out, will not be the objects of direct obligations and some animals will.

NO OBLIGATION

If animals are not conscious—that is, if they are not sentient and have no capacity for pleasure, pain, or any other mental states—they may not even be the objects of indirect obligations. Insofar as Aquinas says that it is possible to be "cruel to dumb animals" and Kant says that "he who is cruel to animals becomes hard in his dealings with men," each presupposes that animals, unlike plants and machines, are sentient and are thereby capable of sensation and consciousness. Thus it is surprising to find René Descartes (1596–1650), a renowned philosopher, mathematician, and scientist, comparing animals to machines. Nonetheless, this is just what he did in his influential *Discourse on Method* when he compared machines made by the hand of man with human and nonhuman animal bodies made by the hand of God: "From this aspect the body is regarded as a machine which, having been made by the hands of God, is incomparably better arranged, and possesses in itself movements which are much more admirable than any of

[4] Francis Moore Lappé, "Fantasie of Famine," *Harper's*, 250 (February 1975), p. 53.

those which can be invented by man."[5] Living *human* bodies were, for Descartes, distinguished from living *animal* bodies by the presence of an immortal soul which was a necessary condition for mental experiences. Without a soul, a living biological body was a natural automaton, "much more splendid," but in kind no different from those produced by humans.

For Descartes, the criterion for distinguishing those living bodies which were ensouled from those which were not was the capacity to use language. The former, he believed, included all and only human beings. Among humans, he maintained,

> there are none so depraved and stupid, without even exempting idiots, that they cannot arrange different words together, forming of them a statement by which they make known their thoughts; while on the other hand, there is no other animal, however perfect and fortunately circumstanced it may be, which can do the same.[6]

Insofar as nonhuman animals do appear to do some things better than we do, Descartes added, "it is nature which acts in them according to the disposition of their organs, just as a clock, which is only composed of wheels and weights is able to tell the hours and measure the time more correctly than we can do with all our wisdom."[7] As for the ethical implications of his view, Descartes, in a letter to Henry More, noted that his "opinion is not so much cruel to animals as indulgent to men . . . since it absolves them from the suspicion of crime when they eat or kill animals."[8]

Insofar as Descartes's position presupposes

---

[5] René Descartes, *Discourse on Method,* in *Philosophical Works of Descartes,* translated by E. S. Haldane and G. R. T. Ross (Cambridge University Press), Vol. I. Reprinted in Regan and Singer, p. 61.

[6] *Ibid.*

[7] *Ibid.*, p. 62.

[8] René Descartes, Letter to Henry More, in *Descartes: Philosophical Letters,* translated and edited by Anthony Kenny (Oxford University Press, 1970). Reprinted in Regan and Singer, p. 66.

that all and only human beings have the capacity to use language, it is open to the same sort of criticisms and objections that we raised against Kant. That is, advances in medicine are providing more nonlinguistic humans and advances in science are suggesting that at least some nonhuman animals have more linguistic facility or capacity than we previously supposed. Moreover, even if Descartes were correct in believing that the capacity to use language is uniquely human, why should this, rather than the capacity to feel pain and experience distress, be the principal criterion for determining the nature and extent of ethical restrictions on the use and treatment of animals? It is this objection which sets the stage for positions which hold that humans have direct obligations to at least some animals.

DIRECT OBLIGATION

Jeremy Bentham (1748–1832), the father of modern utilitarianism, held that pain and pleasure were what governed behavior and that any ethical system which was founded on anything but maximizing the net balance of pleasure over pain, dealt in "sounds instead of sense, in caprice instead of reason, in darkness instead of light." Every action, for Bentham was to be assessed in terms of its likelihood of maximizing the net balance of happiness. But, he noted, if the capacity to experience pleasure and pain was what qualified one to be taken into account in estimating the effects of various courses of action, then nonhuman as well as human animals would have to be taken into account insofar as they, too, had the capacity to experience pleasure and pain. Thus, for Bentham, it is sentience, or the capacity for pleasure and pain, that determines whether a being qualifies for moral consideration.

> What else is it that should trace the insuperable line? Is it the faculty of reason, or perhaps the faculty of discourse? But a full-grown horse or dog is beyond comparison a more rational, as well as a more conversable animal than an infant of a day or a week or even a month old. But suppose they were otherwise, what would

it avail? The question is not, Can they *reason* nor Can they *talk?* but, *Can they suffer?*[9]

The question now is, what grounds do we have to believe that animals *can* suffer, can feel pain, or can experience distress? If a being lacks the capacity to convey his suffering, pain, or distress linguistically how do we know that it actually has such experiences and isn't a rather splendid automaton going through the motions?

In response to such skepticism, one holding a utilitarian direct obligation theory must show why he or she believes that nonhuman animals are conscious. There are a number of ways one might go about this. First, one could stress behavioral similarities between human and nonhuman animals in their respective responses to certain standard pain- and pleasure-producing stimuli. Comparing the behavior of nonhuman animals with human infants would be especially forceful here. Second, we could stress relevant neurophysiological similarities between humans and nonhumans. After making these comparisons we may then be inclined to agree with Richard Sergeant when he claims that:

> Every particle of factual evidence supports the contention that the higher mammalian vertebrates experience pain sensations at least as acute as our own. To say that they feel less because they are lower animals in an absurdity; it can easily be shown that many of their senses are far more acute than ours—visual acuity in certain birds, hearing in most wild animals, and touch in others; these animals depend more than we do on the sharpest possible awareness of a hostile environment.[10]

So, if Sergeant is correct in this, at least some animals are conscious and hence, on utilitarian grounds, qualify as the objects of direct obligation.

[9] Jeremy Bentham, *The Principles of Morals and Legislation* (1789), Chapter XVII, Section 1. Reprinted in Regan and Singer, p. 129.
[10] Richard Sergeant, *The Spectrum of Pain* (London, Hart-Davis, 1969), p. 72. Cited by Peter Singer in Tom Regan, ed., *Matters of Life and Death* (Random House, 1980), p. 225.

There are, nonetheless, significant limitations to this view. First, although utilitarianism takes nonhuman animals directly into account in determining ethical obligations, there is no guarantee that animals will, in fact, fare better on this view than they will on an Indirect Obligation view like that of Aquinas or Kant. Contemporary animal welfare advocates who find utilitarianism hospitable to their position have not fully appreciated utilitarianism's indifference to any outcome apart from the maximization of happiness. Thus, for example, on utilitarian grounds, a policy which causes a great amount of pain to animals which also causes an even greater amount of offsetting pleasure to humans, would appear to be ethically justified. Second, one who adopts utilitarianism because it takes direct account of animal suffering, must recognize all of its implications. One of the standard objections of utilitarianism is that it seems, on the face of it, more suited to animals than it is to human beings. Thus Bentham's version was initially caricatured as philosophy for swine because it seemed to imply that it was better to be a satisfied pig than a dissatisfied human; or better to be a fool satisfied than Socrates dissatisfied.

A Fourth Position

Although none of the positions we have examined is entirely satisfactory, each, I believe, has something to recommend it. *Indirect Obligation* theories are correct to stress the difference between what I will call "simple consciousness" and "reflective-consciousness," but they have not adequately characterized the difference nor have they full appreciated its ethical significance. *No Obligation* theories, at least that of Descartes, are correct in emphasizing the relationship between the use of language and the development of reflective-consciousness. And, finally, *Direct Obligation* theories are correct in noting that the possession of simple consciousness (or sentience) in human or nonhuman animals is, by itself, sufficient to give them independent standing in the ethical deliberations of beings who are reflectively-conscious. I will now, very briefly, outline each of these fundamental insights and suggest how they may be integrated into a fourth, more adequate position.

The fundamental insight of *Indirect Obligation* theories is their recognition of a difference between simple and reflective consciousness. Beings having only simple consciousness can experience pain, have desires and make choices. But they are not capable of reflecting upon their experiences, desires, and choices and altering their behavior as a result of such self-conscious evaluation and deliberation. Beings who can do this I will, following John Locke (1632–1704), label "persons." A person, in Locke's view, is "A thinking intelligent being that has reasons and reflection and can consider itself as itself, the same thinking thing, in different times and places."[11] Although they were mistaken in believing that the class of persons fully coincided with the class of human beings, *Indirect Obligation* theorists were correct to emphasize the special status of persons. For only persons are capable of tracing the consequences and implications of various courses of action and then deliberating and deciding to embark on one rather than another on grounds other than self-interest. To do this is part of what it means to have a morality, and it is the capacity for taking the moral point of view (that is, voluntarily restricting one's appetite or desires for the sake of others) that gives the persons their special worth.

The fundamental insight of Descartes's *No Obligation* theory was to recognize the connection between the development and exercise of personhood and the development and exercise of language. As Stuart Hampshire has recently pointed out, although people often associate the use of language primarily with communication, "language's more distinctive and far-reaching power is to bring possibilities before the mind.

Culture has its principal source in the use of the word 'if,' in counterfactual speculation."[12] Only language, then, gives us the power to entertain complex unrealized possibilities. "The other principal gift of language to culture," Hampshire continues, "is the power to date, and hence to make arrangements for tomorrow and to regret yesterday."[13] Thus a being cannot become a person and, in Locke's words, "consider itself as itself, the same thinking thing, in different times and places," without the use of language.

Finally, the fundamental insight of *Direct Obligation* theories was to note that one needn't be a person to be the object of a moral obligation. Simple consciousness or sentience is sufficient to entitle a being to be considered *for its own sake* in the ethical deliberations of persons. If, for example, the capacity to feel pain is sufficient ground for a *prima facie* obligation not to cause gratuitous pain to persons, why is it not also a sufficient ground for a similar obligation not to cause pain to beings having simple consciousness? With regard to the evil of avoidable and unjustifiable pain, the question is, as Bentham emphasized, not "Can they reason nor Can they talk? but, Can they suffer?"

Putting all of this together, we may say that persons, who are characterized as possessing reflective consciousness, may have a higher status than beings having only simple consciousness. Their special worth is a function of the extent to which they use language "to bring possibilities before the mind" and then restrain their more trivial desires for the sake of not harming others whom they recognize, from the moral point of view, as their equals in certain respects. Among the beings whose interests must be taken into account *for their own sake* in the moral deliberations of persons are beings possessing only simple consciousness. To the extent that persons reluctantly cause pain, suffering, and even death

---

[11] John Locke, *Essay Concerning Human Understanding,* ed. by John Yolton (J. M. Dent & Sons, 1961), Vol. One, Book II, Ch. XXVII, p. 281.

[12] Stuart Hampshire, *"Human Nature," New York Review of Books,* XXVI (December 6, 1979), Special Supplement, p. d.

[13] *Ibid.*

to beings possessing simply consciousness in order to meet *important needs,* what they do may be justified by appeal to their higher status or greater worth. But, to the extent that persons inflict avoidable pain and suffering on such beings merely to satisfy certain *trivial tastes or desires,* they pervert their greater capacities. In so doing, they ironically undermine their claim to higher status or worth and thereby weaken any justification they may have had for sacrificing beings having only simple consciousness for important ends.

Whether something is to be classified as an "important need" or a "trivial taste or desire" will frequently be a matter of debate and uncertainty. Yet we should not allow disputes over difficult cases to blind us to the existence of relatively easy cases. There is, for example, little doubt that well-designed, nonduplicative research on animals aimed at preventing or treating disease serves an important need. And it seems just as certain that causing pain to animals in order to test the toxicity of "new and improved" floor polishes or cosmetics serves trivial tastes or desires. And even cases that are not so immediately clear may be resolved by a bit of thoughtful investigation. Thus I suspect that most people who care to learn something about human nutrition and the treatment of animals on modern "factory farms" will be strongly inclined to conclude that factory farming causes pain and suffering to animals for the sake of trivial tastes and desires.[14]

[14] See, for example, Peter Singer, *Animal Liberation* (New York: New York Review, 1975); and Jim Mason and Peter Singer, *Animal Factories* (New York: Crown Publishers, 1980).

Further Inquiry

The foregoing is at best a sketch or outline of a position on the ethical significance of animal awareness. A number of refinements need to be made and a number of questions need to be answered before we can confidently use it to make particular judgments and decisions about the use and treatment of nonhuman animals. First, we must do more in the way of spelling out the crucial distinction between simple consciousness and reflective consciousness. In addition, we must determine the extent to which *various degrees* of both types of consciousness are distributed or realized within members of various classes of human and nonhuman animals. It is important to note here that since there is nothing in the distinction between simple and reflective consciousness that requires it to follow species lines, the investigations in question will involve infants and severely retarded and severely brain-damaged human beings, as well as nonhuman animals.

Among the important questions we must ask is whether, and if so, to what extent, beings who lack reflective consciousness can experience things other than pain and pleasure. For example, can chimps, dogs, pigs, or chickens experience sadness, boredom, loneliness, frustration, apprehensiveness, disappointment, anxiety, and other states that are not as closely identified with determinate behavioral responses as is pain? If so, how would we know? Questions of this kind will, I hope, be soon addressed by philosophers of mind, ethologists, psychologists, neurophysiologists, and others. My principal aim has been to show why, from an ethical point of view, they are important questions.

For Further Thought and Discussion

1. Why does the distinction between simple consciousness and reflective consciousness carry moral significance?

2. Benjamin argues that experiences like "sadness, boredom, loneliness, frustration," and the like are important for determining reflective consciousness. How could we dis-

cover other nonhuman experiences and emotions, and how should they play a role in determining moral standing?

The Value of Wilderness

WILLIAM GODFREY-SMITH

Reading Questions

1. What reasons does Godfrey-Smith give for needing a "new morality"?
2. What are the four "intrinsic value" attitudes delineated by Godfrey-Smith?
3. How does the moral sentiment that natural systems possess intrinsic value conflict with economic cost-benefit analyses?
4. How does the notion of cooperative behavior help Godfrey-Smith conceive of an extended sense of our moral community?
5. Why does Godfrey-Smith want to be able to make an argument that nature has "intrinsic worth"?

THE FRAMEWORK WHICH I EXAMINE is the framework of *Western* attitudes toward our natural environment, and wilderness in particular. The philosophical task to which I shall address myself is an exploration of attitudes toward wilderness, especially the sorts of justification to which we might legitimately appeal for the preservation of wilderness: what grounds can we advance in support of the claim that wilderness is something which we should *value*?

There are two different ways of appraising something as valuable. It may be that the thing in question is good or valuable *for the sake* of something which we hold to be valuable. In this case the thing is not considered to be good in itself; value in this sense is ascribed in virtue of the thing's being a *means* to some valued end, and not as an *end in itself*. Such values are standardly designated *instrumental* values. Not everything which we hold to be good or valuable can be good for the sake of something else: our values must ultimately be *grounded* in something which is held to be good or valuable in itself. Such things are said to be *intrinsically* valuable. As a matter of historical fact, those things which have been held to be intrinsically valuable, within our Western traditions of thought, have nearly always been taken to be states or conditions of *persons*, e.g., happiness, pleasure, knowledge, or self-realization, to name but a few.

It follows from this that a very central assumption of Western moral thought is that value

Reprinted as a shortened version prepared by the author, from "The Value of Wilderness," in *Environmental Ethics*, vol. 1 (Winter 1979), pp. 309–319. Copyright © by William Godfrey-Smith. Used by permission of the author and the publisher.

can be ascribed to the nonhuman world only insofar as it is good for the sake of the well-being of human beings.[1] Our entire attitude toward the natural environment, therefore, has a decidedly anthropocentric bias, and this fact is reflected in the sorts of justification which are standardly provided for the preservation of the natural environment.

A number of thinkers, however, are becoming increasingly persuaded that our anthropocentric morality is in fact inadequate to provide a satisfactory basis for a moral philosophy of ecological obligation. It is for this reason that we hear not infrequently the claim that we need a "new morality." A new moral framework—that is, a network of recognized obligations and duties—is not, however, something that can be casually conjured up in order to satisfy some vaguely felt need. The task of developing a sound biologically based moral philosophy, a philosophy which is not anthropocentrically based, and which provides a satisfactory justification for ecological obligation and concern, is, I think, one of the most urgent tasks confronting moral philosophers at the present. It will entail a radical reworking of accepted attitudes—attitudes which we currently accept as "self-evident"—and this is not something which can emerge suddenly. Indeed, I think the seminal work remains largely to be done.

In the absence of a comprehensive and convincing, ecologically based morality we naturally fall back on *instrumental* justifications for concern for our natural surroundings, and for preserving wilderness areas and animal species. We can, I think, detect at least four main lines of instrumental justification for the preservation of wilderness. By *wilderness* I understand any reasonably large tract of the Earth, together with its plant and animal communities, which is substantially unmodified by humans and in particular by human technology. The natural contrast to *wilderness* and *nature* is an *artificial* or *domesticated* environment. The fact that there are borderline cases which are difficult to classify does not, of course, vitiate this distinction.

The first attitude toward wilderness espoused by conservationists to which I wish to draw attention is what I shall call the "cathedral" view. This is the view that wilderness areas provide a vital opportunity for spiritual revival, moral regeneration, and aesthetic delight. The enjoyment of wilderness if often compared in this respect with religious or mystical experience. Preservation of magnificent wilderness areas for those who subscribe to this view is essential for human well-being, and its destruction is conceived as something akin to an act of vandalism, perhaps comparable to—some may regard it as more serious than[2]—the destruction of a magnificent and moving human edifice, such as the Parthenon, the Taj Mahal, or the Palace of Versailles.

Insofar as the "cathedral" view holds that value derives solely from human satisfactions gained from its contemplation it is clearly an instrumentalist attitude. I does, however, frequently approach an *intrinsic value* attitude, insofar as the feeling arises that there is importance in the fact that it is there to be contemplated, whether or not anyone actually takes advantage of this fact. Suppose for example, that some wilderness was so precariously balanced that *any* human intervention or contact would inevitably bring about its destruction. Those who maintained that the area should, nevertheless, be preserved, unexperienced and unenjoyed, would certainly be ascribing to it an intrinsic value.

The "cathedral" view with respect to wilderness in fact is a fairly recent innovation in Western thought. The predominant Graeco-Christian attitude, which generally speaking was the predominant Western attitude prior to eighteenth- and nineteenth-century romanticism, had been to view wilderness as threatening or alarming, an attitude still reflected in the figurative uses of the expression *wilderness,* clearly connoting a degenerate state to be avoided. Christianity, in general, has enjoined "the transformation of wilderness, those dreaded haunts of demons, the ancient nature-gods, into farm and pasture,"[3] that is, to a domesticated environment.

The second instrumental justification of the value of wilderness is what we might call the "laboratory" argument. This is the argument that wilderness areas provide vital subject matter for scientific inquiry which provides us with an understanding of the intricate interdependencies of biological systems, their modes of change and development, their energy cycles, and the source of their stabilities. If we are to understand our own biological dependencies, we require natural systems as a norm, to inform us of the biological laws which we transgress at our peril.

The third instrumentalist justification is the "silo" argument which points out that one excellent reason for preserving reasonable areas of the natural environment intact is that we thereby preserve a stockpile of genetic diversity, which it is certainly prudent to maintain as a backup in case something should suddenly go wrong with the simplified biological systems which, in general, constitute agriculture. Further, there is the related point that there is no way of anticipating our future needs, or the undiscovered applications of apparently useless plants, which might turn out to be, for example, the source of some pharmacologically valuable drug—a cure, say, for leukemia. This might be called, perhaps, the "rare herb" argument, and it provides another persuasive instrumental justification for the preservation of wilderness.

The final instrumental justification which I think should be mentioned is the "gymnasium" argument, which regards the preservation of wilderness as important for athletic or recreational activities.

An obvious problem which arises from these instrumental arguments is that the various activities which they seek to justify are not always possible to reconcile with one another. The interests of the wilderness lover who subscribes to the "cathedral" view are not always reconcilable with those of the ordinary vacationist. Still more obvious is the conflict between the recreational use of wilderness and the interests of the miner, the farmer, and the timber merchant.

The conflict of interest which we encounter here is one which it is natural to try and settle through the economic calculus of cost-benefit considerations. So long as the worth of natural systems is believed to depend entirely on instrumental values, it is natural to suppose that we can sort out the conflict of interests within an objective frame of reference, by estimating the human satisfactions to be gained from the preservation of wilderness, and by weighing these against the satisfactions which are to be gained from those activities which may lead to its substantial modification, domestication, and possibly even, destruction.

Many thinkers are liable to encounter here a feeling of resistance to the suggestion that we can apply purely economic considerations to settle such conflicts of interest. The assumption behind economic patterns of thought, which underlie policy formulation and planning, is that the values which we attach to natural systems and to productive activities are commensurable; and this is an assumption which may be called into question. It is not simply a question of the difficulty of quantifying what value should be attached to the preservation of the natural environment. The feeling is more that economic considerations are simply out of place. This feeling is one which is often too lightly dismissed by tough-minded economists as being obscurely mystical or superstitious; but it is a view worth examining. What it amounts to, I suggest, is the belief that there is something *morally* objectionable in the destruction of natural systems, or economically "useless" species, do possess an *intrinsic* value. That is, it is an attempt to articulate the rejection of the anthropocentric view that all value, ultimately, resides in *human* interest and concerns.

A feeling persists that cost-benefit analyses tend to overlook important values. One consideration which tends to be discounted from policy deliberations is that which concerns *economically* unimportant species of animals or plants. A familiar subterfuge which we frequently encounter is the attempt to invest such species with spurious economic value, as illustrated in the rare herb argument. A typical example of this, cited by Leopold, is the reaction of ornithologists to the threatened disappearance of certain species of songbirds: they at once came forward with some distinctly shaky evidence that they played an essential role in the control of insects.[4] The dominance of economic modes of thinking is again obvious: the evidence has to be economic in order to be acceptable. This exemplifies the way in which we turn to instrumentalist justifications for the maintenance of biotic diversity.

The alternative to such instrumentalist justifications, the alternative which Leopold advocated with great insight and eloquence, is to widen the boundary of the moral community to include animals, plants, the soil, or collectively *the land*.[5] This involves a radical shift in our conception of nature, so that land is recognized not simply as property, to be dealt with or disposed of as a matter of expediency: land in Leopold's view is not a commodity which belongs to us, but a community to which we belong. This change in conception is far-reaching and profound. It involves a shift in our metaphysical conception of nature—that is, a change in what sort of thing we take our natural surroundings to *be*.

The predominant Western conception of the natural world is largely a legacy of the philosophy of Descartes. This philosophy has alienated man from the natural world through its sharp ontological division between conscious minds and mechanically arranged substances which, for Descartes, constitute the rest of nature. An adequate environmental ethic must, *inter alia*, replace the world-view which emerges from Cartesian metaphysics.

This will involve a shift from the piecemeal reductive conception of natural items, to a *holistic* or systemic view in which we come to appreciate the symbiotic interdependencies of the natural world. On the holistic or total-field view organisms—including man—are conceived as nodes in a biotic web of intrinsically related parts.[6] That is, our understanding of biological organisms requires more than just an understanding of their structure and properties; we also have to attend seriously to their interrelations. Holistic or systemic thinking does not deny that organisms are complex physiochemical systems, but it affirms that the methods employed in establishing the high-level functional relationships expressed by physical laws are often of very limited importance in understanding the nature of biological systems.

The holistic conception of the natural world contains, I think, the possibility of extending the idea of community beyond human society. And in this way biological wisdom does, I think, carry implications for ethics. Just as Copernicus showed us that man does not occupy the physical center of the universe, Darwin and his successors have shown us that man occupies no *biologically* privileged position. We still have to assimilate the implications which this biological knowledge has for morality.

Can we regard man and the natural environment as constituting a community in any morally significant sense? Passmore, in particular, has claimed that this extended sense of community is entirely spurious.[7] Leopold, on the other hand, found the biological extension of community entirely natural.[8] If we regard a community as a collection of individuals who engage in cooperative behavior, Leopold's extension seems to me entirely legitimate. An ethic is no more than a code of conduct designed to ensure cooperative behavior among the members of a community. Such cooperative behavior is required to underpin the health of the community, in this biologically extended sense, *health* being understood as the biological capacity for self-renewal,[9] and *ill-health* as the degeneration or loss of this capacity.

Man, of course, cannot be placed on "all fours" with his biologically fellow creatures in all respects. In particular, man is the only creature who can act as a full-fledged moral agent, i.e., an individual capable of exercising reflective rational choice on the basis of principles. What distinguishes man from his fellow creatures is not the capacity to *act*, but the fact that his actions are, to a great extent, free from programming. This capacity to modify our own behavior is closely bound up with the capacity to acquire knowledge of the natural world, a capacity which has enabled us, to an unprecedented extent, to manipulate the environment, and—especially in the recent past—to alter it rapidly, violently, and globally. Our hope must be that the capacity for knowledge, which has made ecologically hazardous activities possible, will lead to a more profound understanding of the delicate biological interdependencies which some of these actions now threaten, and thereby generate the wisdom for restraint.

To those who are skeptical of the possibility of extending moral principles, in the manner of Leopold, to include items treated heretofore as matters of expediency, it can be pointed out that extensions have, to a limited extent, already taken place. One clear—if partial—instance, is in the treatment of animals. It is now generally accepted, and this is a comparatively recent innovation,[10] that we have at least a *prima facie* obligation not to treat animals cruelly or sadistically. And this certainly constitutes a shift in moral attitudes. If—as seems to be the case—cruelty to animals is accepted as intrinsically wrong, then there *is* at least one instance in which it is *not* a matter of moral indifference how we behave toward the nonhuman world.

More familiar perhaps are the moral revolutions which have occurred within the specific domain of human society—witness the progressive elimination of the "right" to racial, class, and sex exploitation. Each of these shifts involves the acceptance, on the part of some individuals, of new obligations, rights, and values which, to a previous generation, would have been considered unthinkable.[11] The essential step in recognizing an enlarged community involves coming to see, feel, and understand what was previously perceived as alien and apart: it is the evolution of the capacity of *empathy*.

We can, however, provide—and it is important that we can provide—an answer to the question: "What is the *use* of wilderness?" We certainly ought to preserve and protect wilderness areas as gymnasiums, as laboratories, as stockpiles of genetic diversity, and as cathedrals. Each of these reasons provides a powerful and sufficient instrumental justification for their preservation. But note how the very posing of this question about the *utility* of wilderness reflects an anthropocentric system of values. From a genuinely ecocentic point of view the question "What is the *use* of wilderness?" would be as absurd as the question "What is the *use* of happiness?"

The philosophical task is to try to provide adequate justification, or at least clear the way, for a scheme of values according to which concern and sympathy for our environment is immediate and natural, and the desirability of protecting and preserving wilderness self-evident. When once controversial propositions become platitudes, the philosophical task will have been successful.

I will conclude, nevertheless, on a deflationary note. It seems to me (at least much of the time) that the shift in attitudes which I think is required for promoting genuinely harmonious relations with nature is too drastic, too "unthinkable," to be very persuasive for most people. If this is so, then it will be more expedient to justify the preservation of wilderness in terms of instrumentalist considerations; and I have argued that there *are* powerful arguments for preservation which can be derived from the purely anthropocentric considerations of human self-interest. I hope, however, that there will be some who feel that such anthropocentric considerations are not wholly satisfying, i.e., that they do not really do justice to our intuitions. But at a time when *human* rights are being treated in some quarters with a great deal of skepticism it is perhaps unrealistic to expect the rights of nonhumans to receive sympathetic attention. Perhaps, though, we should not be too abashed by this: extensions in ethics have seldom followed the path of political expediency.

NOTES

1. Aldo Leopold, *A Sand County Almanac* (New York: Oxford University Press, 1949), p. 188.

2. Other cultures have certainly included the idea that nature should be valued for its own sake in their moral codes, e.g., the American Indians, the Chinese, and the Australian Aborigines.

Reprinted, as a shortened version prepared by the author, from "The Value of Wilderness," *Environmental Ethics,* vol. 1 (Winter 1979), pp. 309–319. Copyright © by William Godfrey-Smith.

3. We can after all *replace* human artifacts such as buildings with something closely similar, but the destruction of a wilderness or a biological species is irreversible.

4. John Passmore, *Man's Responsibility for Nature* (London: Duckworth, 1974; New York: Charles Scribner's Sons, 1974), p. 17; cf. chap. 5.

5. Aldo Leopold, "The Land Ethic," in *Sand County Almanac,* p. 210.

6. Cf. Aldo Leopold, "The Conservation Ethic," *Journal of Forestry* 31 (1933): 634–43, and "The Land Ethic," *Sand County Almanac.*

7. Cf. Arne Naess, "The Shallow and the Deep, Long-Range Ecology Movement," *Inquiry* 16 (1973):95–100.

8. Passmore, *Man's Responsibility for Nature,* chap. 6; "Attitudes to Nature," p. 262.

9. Leopold, "The Land Ethic."

10. *Ibid.,* p. 221.

11. Cf. Passmore, "The Treatment of Animals," *Journal of the History of Ideas* 36 (1975): 195–218.

12. Cf. Christopher D. Stone, "Should Trees Have Standing? Toward Legal Rights for Natural Objects," *Southern California Law Review* 45 (1972): 450–501.

For Further Thought and Discussion

1. If the economic cost-benefit analysis in the "instrumentalist" approach is sufficient to protect the environment, why go on to formulate an "intrinsic worth" moral perspective?

2. In what sense can wilderness have intrinsic value? Can anything be valuable in its own right and apart from our use and estimation of it?

The Rights of Animals and Unborn Generations

JOEL FEINBERG

Reading Questions

1. How does Feinberg define a right?

2. In Feinberg's definition, rocks and other inanimate objects cannot have rights. Why not?

3. What is the distinction between having duties *regarding* some things and having duties *to* the things?

4. How does Feinberg deny rights to plants? What does he suggest is missing in plants that prevents them from having rights?

5. What case does Feinberg make for respecting the rights of future generations?

EVERY PHILOSOPHICAL PAPER MUST BEGIN with an unproved assumption. Mine is the assumption that there will still be a world five hundred years from now, and that it will contain human beings who are very much like us. We have it within our power now, clearly, to affect the lives of these creatures for better or worse by contributing to the conservation or corruption of the environment in which they must life. I shall assume furthermore that it is psychologically possible for us to care about our remote descendants, that many of us in fact do care, and indeed that we ought to care. My main concern then will be to show that it makes sense to speak of the rights of unborn generations against us, and that given the moral judgment that we ought to conserve our environmental inheritance for them, and its grounds, we might well say that future generations *do* have rights correlative to our present duties toward them. Protecting our environment now is also a matter of elementary prudence, and insofar as we do it for the next generation already here in the persons of our children, it is matter of love. But from the perspective of our remote descendants it is basically a matter of justice, of respect for their rights. My main concern here will be to examine the concept of a right to better understand how that can be.

The Problem

To have a right to have a claim[1] *to* something and *against* someone, the recognition of which is called for by legal rules or, in the case of moral rights, by the principles of an enlightened conscience. In the familiar cases of rights, the claim-

ant is a competent adult human being, and the claimee is an officeholder in an institution or else a private individual, in either case, another competent adult human being. Normal adult human beings, then, are obviously the sorts of beings of whom rights can meaningfully be predicated. Everyone would agree to that, even extreme misanthropes who deny that anyone in fact has rights. On the other hand, it is absurd to say that rocks can have rights, not because rocks are morally inferior things unworthy of rights (that statement makes no sense either), but because rocks belong to a category of entities of whom rights cannot be meaningfully predicated. That is not to say that there are no circumstances in which we ought to treat rocks carefully, but only that the rocks themselves cannot validly claim good treatment from us. In between the clear cases of rocks and normal human beings, however, is a spectrum of less obvious cases, including some bewildering borderline ones. Is it meaningful or conceptually possible to ascribe rights to our dead ancestors? to individual animals? to whole species of animals? to plants? to idiots and madmen? to fetuses? to generations yet unborn? Until we know how to settle these puzzling cases, we cannot claim fully to grasp the concept of a right, or to know the shape of its logical boundaries.

One way to approach these riddles is to turn one's attention first to the most familiar and unproblematic instances of rights, note their most salient characteristics, and then compare the borderline cases with them, measuring as closely as possible the points of similarity and difference. In the end, the way we classify the borderline cases may depend on whether we are more impressed with the similarities or the differences between them and the cases in which we have the most confidence.

It will be useful to consider the problem of individual animals first because their case is the one that has already been debated with the most thoroughness by philosophers so that the dialectic of claim and rejoinder has now unfolded to the point where disputants can get to the end game quickly and isolate the crucial point at issue. When we understand precisely what *is* at issue in the debate over animal rights, I think we will have the key to the solution of all the other riddles about rights.

Individual Animals

Almost all modern writers agree that we ought to be kind to animals, but that is quite another thing from holding that animals can claim kind treatment from us as their due. Statutes making cruelty to animals a crime are now very common, and these, of course, impose legal duties on people not to mistreat animals; but that still leaves open the question whether the animals, as beneficiaries of those duties, possess rights correlative to them. We may very well have duties *regarding* animals that are not at the same time duties *to* animals, just as we may have duties regarding rocks, or buildings, or lawns, that are not duties *to* the rocks, buildings, or lawns. Some legal writers have taken the still more extreme position that animals themselves are not even the directly intended beneficiaries of statutes prohibiting cruelty to animals. During the nineteenth century, for example, it was commonly said that such statues were designed to protect human beings by preventing the growth of cruel habits that could later threaten human beings with harm too. Prof. Louis B. Schwartz finds the rationale of the cruelty-to-animals prohibition in its protection of animal lovers from affronts to their sensibilities. "It is not the mistreated dog who is the ultimate object of concern," he writes. "Our concern is for the feelings of other human beings, a large proportion of whom, although accustomed to the slaughter of animals for food, readily identify themselves with a tortured dog or horse and respond with great sensitivity to its sufferings."[2] This seems to me to be factitious. How much more natural it is to say with John Chipman Gray that the true purpose of cruelty-to-animals statutes is "to preserve the dumb brutes from suffering."[3] The very people whose sensibilities are invoked in the alternative explanation, a group that no doubt now includes most of us, are precisely those who would insist that the protection belongs primarily to the animals themselves, not merely to their own tender feelings. Indeed, it would be difficult even to account for the existence of such feelings in the absence of a belief that the animals deserve the protection in their own right and for their own sakes.

Even if we allow, as I think we must, that animals are the intended direct beneficiaries of legislation forbidding cruelty to animals, it does not follow directly that animals have legal rights, and Gray himself, for one,[4] refused to draw this further inference. Animals cannot have rights, he thought, for the same reason they cannot have duties, namely, that they are not genuine "moral agents." Now, it is relatively easy to see why animals cannot have duties, and this matter is largely beyond controversy. Animals cannot be "reasoned with" or instructed in their responsibilities; they are inflexible and unadaptable to future contingencies; they are subject to fits of instinctive passion which they are incapable of repressing or controlling, postponing or sublimating. Hence, they cannot enter into contractual agreements, or make promises; they cannot be trusted; and they cannot (except within very narrow limits and for purposes of conditioning) be blamed for what would be called "moral failures" in a human being. They are therefore incapable of being moral subjects, of acting rightly or wrongly in the moral sense, of having, discharging, or breaching duties and obligations.

But what is there about the intellectual incompetence of animals (which admittedly disqualifies them for duties) that makes them logically unsuitable for rights? The most common reply to this question is that animals are incapable of *claiming* rights on their own. They cannot make motion, on their own, to courts to have their claims recognized or enforced; they cannot initiate, on their own, any kind of legal proceedings; nor are they capable of even understanding when their rights are being violated, of distinguishing harm from wrongful injury, and responding with indignation and an outraged sense of justice instead of mere anger or fear.

No one can deny any of these allegations, but to the claim that they are the grounds for disqualification of rights of animals, philosophers on the other side of this controversy have made convincing rejoinders. It is simply not true, says W. D. Lamont,[5] that the ability to understand what a right is and the ability to set legal machinery in motion by one's own initiative are necessary for the possession of rights. If that were the case, then neither human idiots nor wee babies would have any legal rights at all. Yet it is manifest that both of these classes of intellectual incompetents have legal rights recognized and easily enforced by the courts. Children and idiots start legal proceedings, not on their own direct initiative, but rather through the actions of proxies or attorneys who are empowered to speak in their names. If there is no conceptual absurdity in this situation, why should there be in the case where a proxy makes a claim on behalf on an animal? People commonly enough make wills leaving money to trustees for the care of animals. It is not natural to speak of the animal's right to his inheritance in cases of this kind? If a trustee embezzles money from the animal's account,[6] a proxy speaking in the dumb brute's behalf presses the animal's claim, can he not be described as asserting the animals *rights*? More exactly, the animal itself claims its rights through the vicarious actions of a human proxy speaking in its name and in its behalf. There appears to be no reason why we should require the animal to understand what is going on (so the

argument concludes) as a condition for regarding it as a possessor of rights.

Some writers protest at this point that the legal relation between a principal and an agent cannot hold between animals and human beings. Between humans, the relation of agency can take two different forms, depending upon the degree of discretion granted to the agent, and there is a continuum of combinations between the extremes. On the one hand, there is the agent who is the mere "mouthpiece" of his principal. He is a "tool" in much the same sense as is a typewriter or telephone; he simply transmits the instructions of his principal. Human beings could hardly be the agents or representatives of animals in this sense, since the dumb brutes could not more use human "tools" than mechanical ones. On the other hand, an agent may be some sort of expert hired to exercise his professional judgment on behalf of, and in the name of, the principal. He may be given, within some limited area of expertise, complete independence to act as he deems best, binding his principal to all the beneficial or detrimental consequences. This is the role played by trustees, lawyers, and ghostwriters. This type of representation requires that the agent have great skill, but makes little or no demand upon the principal, who may leave everything to the judgment of his agent. Hence, there appears, at first, to be no reason why an animal cannot be a totally passive principal in this second kind of agency relationship.

There are still some important dissimilarities, however. In the typical instance of representation by an agent, even of the second, highly discretionary kind, the agent is hired by a principal who enters into an agreement or contract with him; the principal tells his agent that within certain carefully specified boundaries "You may speak for me," subject always to the principal's approval, his right to give new directions, or to cancel the whole arrangement. No dog or cat could possibly do any of those things. Moreover, if it is the assigned task of the agent to defend the principal's rights, the principal may often decide to release his claimee, or to waive his own rights, and instruct his agent accordingly. Again, no mute cow or horse can do that. But although the possibility of hiring, agreeing, contracting, approving, directing, canceling, releasing, waiving, and instructing is present in the typical (all-human) case of agency representation, there appears to be no reason of a logical or conceptual kind why that *must* be so, and indeed that there are some special examples involving human principals where it is not in fact so. I have in mind legal rules, for example, that require that a defendant be represented at his trial by an attorney, and impose a state-appointed attorney upon reluctant defendants, or upon those tried *in absentia,* whether they like it or not. Moreover, small children and mentally deficient and deranged adults are commonly represented by trustees and attorneys, even though they are incapable of granting their own consent to the representation, or of entering into contracts, of giving directions, or waiving their rights. It may be that it is unwise to permit agents to represent principals without the latters' knowledge or consent. If so, then no one should ever be permitted to speak for an animal, at least in a legally binding way. But that is quite another thing than saying that such representation is logically incoherent or conceptually incongruous—the contention that is at issue.

H. J. McCloskey,[7] I believe, accepts the argument up to this point, but he presents a new and different reason for denying that animals can have legal rights. The ability to make claims, whether directly or through a representative, he implies, is essential to the possession of rights. Animals obviously cannot press their claims on their own, and so if they have rights, these rights must be assertable by agents. Animals, however, cannot be represented, McCloskey contends, not for any of the reasons already discussed, but rather because representation, in the requisite sense, is always of interest, and animals (he says) are incapable of having interests.

Now, there is a very important insight expressed in the requirement that a being have interests if he is to be a logically proper subject of rights. This can be appreciated if we consider just why it is that mere things cannot have rights. Consider a very precious "mere thing"— a beautiful natural wilderness, or a complex and ornamental artifact, like the Taj Mahal. Such things ought to be cared for, because they would sink into decay if neglected, depriving some human beings, or perhaps even all human beings, of something of great value. Certain persons may even have as their own special job the care and protection of these valuable objects. But we are not tempted in these cases to speak of "thing-rights" correlative to custodial duties, because, try as we might, we cannot think of mere things as possessing interests of their own. Some people may have a duty to preserve, maintain, or improve the Taj Mahal, but they can hardly have a duty to help or hurt it, benefit or aid it, succor or relieve it. Custodians may protect it for the sake of a nation's pride and art lovers' fancy; but they don't keep it in good repair for "its own sake," or for "its own true welfare," or "well-being." A mere thing, however valuable to others, has no good of its own. The explanation of that fact, I suspect, consists in the fact that mere things have no conative life: no conscious wishes, desires, and hopes; or urges and impulses; or unconscious drives, aims, and goals; or latent tendencies, direction of growth, and natural fulfillments. Interests must be compounded somehow out of conations; hence mere things have no interests. *A fortiori,* they have no interests to be protected by legal or moral rules. Without interests a creature can have no "good" of its own, the achievement of which can be its due. Mere things are not loci of value in their own right, but rather their value consists entirely in their being objects of other beings' interests.

So Far McCloskey is on solid ground, but one can quarrel with his denial that any animals but humans have interests. I should think that the trustee of funds willed to a dog or cat is more than a mere custodian of the animal he protects. Rather his job is to look out for the interests of the animal and make sure no one denies it its due. The animal itself is the beneficiary of his dutiful services. Many of the higher animals at least have appetites, conative urges, and rudimentary purposes, the integrated satisfaction of which constitutes their welfare or good. We can, of course, with consistency treat animals as mere pests and deny that they have any rights; for most animals, especially those of the lower orders, we have no choice but to do so. But it seems to me, nevertheless, that in general, animals *are* among the sorts of beings of whom rights can meaningfully be predicated and denied.

Now, if a person agrees with the conclusion of the argument thus far, that animals are the sorts of beings that *can* have rights, and further, if he accepts the moral judgment that we ought to be kind to animals, only one further premise is needed to yield the conclusion that some animals do in fact have rights. We must now ask ourselves for whose sake ought we to treat (some) animals with consideration and humaneness? If we conceive our duty to be one of obedience to authority, or to one's own conscience merely, or one of consideration for tender human sensibilities only, then we might still deny that animals have rights, even though we admit that they are the kinds of beings that *can* have rights. But if we hold not only that we ought to treat animals humanely, but also that we should do so for the animals' own sake, that such treatment is something we owe animals as their due, something that can be claimed for them, something the withholding of which would be an injustice and a wrong, and not merely a harm, then it follows that we do ascribe rights to animals. I suspect that the moral judgments most of us make about animals do pass these phenomenological tests, so that most of us do believe that animals have rights, but are reluctant to say so because of the conceptual confusions about the notion of a right that I have attempted to dispel above.

Now we can extract from our discussion of animal rights a crucial principle for tentative use in the resolution of the other riddles about the applicability of the concept of a right, namely, that the sorts of beings who *can* have rights are precisely those who have (or can have) interests. I have come to this tentative conclusion for two reasons: (1) because a right holder must be capable of being represented and it is impossible to represent a being that has no interest, and (2) because a right holder must be capable of being a beneficiary in his own person, and a being without interests is a being that is incapable of being harmed or benefitted, having no good or "sake" of its own. Thus, a being without interests has no "behalf" to act in, and no "sake" to act for. My strategy now will be to apply the "interest principle," as we can call it, to the other puzzles about rights, while being prepared to modify it where necessary (but as little as possible), in the hope of separating in a consistent and intuitively satisfactory fashion the beings who can have rights from those which cannot.

Vegetables

It is clear that we ought not to mistreat certain plants, and indeed there are rules and regulations imposing duties on persons not to misbehave in respect to certain members of the vegetable kingdom. It is forbidden, for example, to pick wildflowers in the mountainous tundra areas of national parks, or to endanger trees by starting fires in the dry forest areas. Members of Congress introduce bills designed, as they say, to "protect" rare redwood trees from commercial pillage. Given this background, it is surprising that no one[8] speaks of plants as having rights. Plants, after all, are not "mere things"; they are vital objects with inherited biological propensities determining their natural growth. Moreover, we do say that certain conditions are "good" or "bad" for plants, thereby suggesting that plants, unlike rocks, are capable of having a "good." (This is a case, however, where "what we say" should not be taken seriously: we also say that certain kinds of paint are good and bad for the internal walls of a house, and this does not commit us to a conception of walls as beings possessed of a good or welfare of their own.) Finally, we are capable of feeling a kind of affection for particular plants, though we rarely personalize them, as we do in the case of animals, by giving them proper names.

Still, all are agreed that plants are not the kinds of beings that can have rights. Plants are never plausibly understood to be the direct intended beneficiaries of rules designed to "protect" them. We wish to keep redwood groves in existence for the sake of human beings who can enjoy their serene beauty, and for the sake of generations of human beings yet unborn. Trees are not the sorts of beings who have their "own sakes," despite the fact that they have biological propensities. Having no conscious wants or goals of their own, trees cannot know satisfaction or frustration, pleasure or pain. Hence, three is no possibility of kind or cruel treatment of trees. In these morally crucial respects, trees differ from the higher species of animals.

Yet trees are not mere things like rocks. They grow and develop according to the laws of their own nature. Aristotle and Aquinas both took trees to have their own "natural ends." Why then do I deny them the status of beings with interest of their own? The reason is that an interest, however the concept is finally to be analyzed, presupposes at least rudimentary cognitive equipment. Interests are compounded out of *desires* and *aims,* both of which presuppose something like *belief,* or cognitive awareness. . . .

Whole Species

The topic of whole species, whether of plants or animals, can be treated in much the same way as that of individual plants. A whole collection, as such, cannot have beliefs, expectations, wants, or desires, and can flourish or languish only in the human interest–related sense in which individual plants thrive and decay. Individual elephants can have interests, but the species elephant cannot. Even where individual elephants are not granted rights, human beings may have an interest—economic, scientific or sentimen-

tal—in keeping the species from dying out, and *that* interest may be protected in various ways by law. But that is quite another matter from recognizing a right to survival belonging to the species itself. Still, the preservation of a whole species may quite properly seem to be a morally more important matter than the preservation of an individual animal. Individual animals can have rights but it is implausible to ascribe to them a right to life on the human model. Nor do we normally have duties to keep individual animals alive or even to abstain from killing them provided we do it humanely and nonwantonly in the promotion of legitimate human interests. On the other hand, we do have duties to protect threatened species, not duties to the species themselves as such, but rather duties to future human beings, duties derived from our housekeeping role as temporary inhabitants of this planet. . . .

Future Generations

We have it in our power now to make the world a much less pleasant place for our descendants than the world we inherited from our ancestors. We can continue to proliferate in ever greater numbers, using up fertile soil at an even greater rate, dumping our wastes into rivers, lakes, and oceans, cutting down our forests, and polluting the atmosphere with noxious gases. All thoughtful people agree that we ought not to do these things. Most would say we have a duty not to do these things, meaning not merely that conservation is morally required (as opposed to merely desirable) but also that it is something due our descendants, something to be done for their sakes. Surely we owe it to future generations to pass on a world that is not a used up garbage heap. Our remote descendants are not yet present to claim a livable world as their right, but there are plenty of proxies to speak now in their behalf. These spokesmen, far from being mere custodians, are genuine representatives of future interests.

Why then deny that the human beings of the

future have rights which can be claimed against us now in their behalf? Some are included to deny them present rights out of a fear of falling into obscure metaphysics, by granting rights to remote and unidentifiable beings who are not yet even in existence. Our unborn great-great-grandchildren are in some sense "potential" persons, but they are far more remotely potential, it may seem, than fetuses. This, however, is not the real difficulty. Unborn generations are more remotely potential than fetuses in one sense, but not in another. A much greater period of time with a far greater number of causally necessary and important events must pass before their potentiality can be actualized, it is true; but our collective posterity is just as certain to come into existence "in the normal course of events" as is any given fetus now in its mother's womb. In that sense the existence of the distant human future is no more remotely potential than that of a particular child already on its way.

The real difficulty is not that we doubt whether our descendants will ever be actual, but rather that we don't know who they will be. It is not their temporal remoteness that troubles us so much as their indeterminacy—their present facelessness and namelessness. Five centuries from now men and women will be living where we live now. Any given one of them will have an interest in living space, fertile soil, fresh air, and the like, but that arbitrarily selected one has no other qualities we can presently envision very clearly. We don't even know who his parents, grandparents, or great-grandparents are, or even whether he is related to us. Still, whoever these human beings may turn out to be, and whatever they might reasonably be expected to be like, they will have interests that we can affect, for better or worse, right now. That much we can and do know about them. The identity of the owners of these interests is now necessarily obscure, but the fact of their interest-ownership is crystal clear, and that is all that is necessary to certify the coherence of present talk about their rights. We can tell, sometimes, that shadowy

forms in the spatial distance belong to human beings, though we know not who or how many they are; and this imposes a duty on us not to throw bombs, for example, in their direction. In like manner, the vagueness of the human future does not weaken its claim on us in light of the nearly certain knowledge that it will, after all, be human.

Doubts about the existence of a right to be born transfer neatly to the question of a similar right to come into existence ascribed to future generations. The rights that future generations certainly have against us are contingent rights: the interests they are sure to have when they come into being (assuming of course that they will come into being) cry out for protection from invasions that can take place now. Yet there are no actual interests, presently existent, that future generations, presently nonexistent, have now. Hence, there is no actual interest that they have in simply coming into being, and I am at a loss to think of any other reason for claiming that they have a right to come into existence (though there may well be such a reason). Suppose then that all human beings at a given time voluntarily form a compact never again to produce children, thus leading within a few decades to the end of our species. This of course is a wildly improbable hypothetical example but a rather crucial one for the position I have been tentatively considering. And we can imagine, say, that the whole world is converted to a strange ascetic religion which absolutely requires sexual abstinence for everyone. Would this arrangement violate the rights of anyone? No one can complain on behalf of presently nonexistent future generations that their future interests which give them a contingent right of protection have been violated since they will never come into existence to be wronged. My inclination then is to conclude that the suicide of our species would be deplorable, lamentable, and a deeply moving tragedy, but that it would violate no one's rights. Indeed if, contrary to fact, all human beings could ever agree to such a thing, that very agreement would be a symptom of our species' biological unsuitability for survival anyway.

Conclusion

For several centuries now human beings have run roughshod over the lands of our planet, just as if the animals who do live there and the generations of humans who will live there had no claims on them whatever. Philosophers have not helped matters by arguing that animals and future generations are not the kinds of beings who can have rights now, that they don't presently qualify for membership, even "auxiliary membership," in our moral community. I have tried in this essay to dispel the conceptual confusions that make such conclusions possible. To acknowledge their rights is the very least we can do for members of endangered species (including our own). But that is something.

NOTES

1. I shall leave the concept of a claim unanalyzed here, but for a detailed discussion, see my "The Nature and Value of Rights," *Journal of Value Inquiry* 4 (Winter 1971): 263–277.

Reprinted with permission of the publisher from *Philosophy & Environmental Crisis,* edited by William T. Blackstone, pp. 43–68. Copyright © 1974 by the University of Georgia Press.

2. Louis B. Schwartz, "Morals, Offenses and the Model Penal Code," *Columbia Law Review* 63 (1963):673.

3. John Chipman Gray, *The Nature and Sources of the Law,* 2d ed. (Boston: Beacon Press, 1963), p. 43.

4. And W. D. Ross for another. See *The Right and The Good* (Oxford: Clarendon Press, 1930), app. 1, pp. 48–56.

5. W. D. Lamont, *Principles of Moral Judgment* (Oxford: Clarendon Press, 1946), pp. 83–85.

6. Cf. H. J. McCloskey, "Rights," *Philosophical Quarterly* 15 (1965): 121, 124.

7. Ibid.

8. Outside of Samuel Butler's *Erewhon*.

For Further Thought and Discussion

1. Would sensitivity to future generations have a desirable effect on our present character? Is this sufficient reason to grant moral status to people who do not now, and may never, exist?

2. Even if we grant rights to future generations, how strong would these rights be compared to the rights of people presently alive?

Index